W9-BLO-619

Great Men of American Popular Song

BOOKS BY DAVID EWEN

The Complete Book of Classical Music
The World of Twentieth-Century Music
The Home Book of Musical Knowledge
The World of Great Composers
Panorama of American Popular Music
George Gershwin: His Journey to Greatness
Richard Rodgers
The World of Jerome Kern
Leonard Bernstein
The Encyclopedia of the Opera
The Encyclopedia of Concert Music
Milton Cross' New Encyclopedia of Great Composers and Their Music
      (with Milton Cross)
Music for the Millions
Dictators of the Baton
Music Comes to America
The New Book of Modern Composers
The Story of America's Musical Theatre
The Book of European Light Opera
David Ewen Introduces Modern Music
The Life and Death of Tin Pan Alley
American Popular Songs: From the Revolutionary War to the Present

GREAT MEN OF AMERICAN POPULAR SONG

The history of the American popular song told through the lives, careers, achievements, and personalities of its foremost composers and lyricists—from William Billings of the Revolutionary War to the "folk-rock" of Bob Dylan

David Ewen

PRENTICE-HALL, INC.
Englewood Cliffs, N.J.

Great Men of American Popular Song
by David Ewen

© 1970 by Prentice-Hall, Inc.

Library of Congress Catalog Card Number: 79-110079

Printed in the United States of America · *T*

13-364174-0

Prentice-Hall International, Inc., London
Prentice-Hall of Australia, Pty. Ltd., Sydney
Prentice-Hall of Canada, Ltd., Toronto
Prentice-Hall of India Private Ltd., New Delhi
Prentice-Hall of Japan, Inc., Tokyo

To the memory of Heyman Zimel
1908–1965

forty-three of those years, years of treasurable friendship

Preface

In *Great Men of American Popular Song* the author has attempted to present the most complete biographical, personal, and critical portraits within any collection of the foremost popular-music composers and lyricists of the past and present. The author has also detailed how the composers' and lyricists' most important songs came to be written, how they were first introduced, and how they first became popular.

There was, to be sure, method and calculation in the selection of composers and lyricists treated in detailed chapters. Their biographies were used as the framework in which to portray the evolution and growth of the American popular songs, beginning with national ballads and including sentimental ballads, war songs, songs about the Negro, ragtime songs, "coon shouts" and the blues, show tunes, movie tunes, and the songs of protest of the late 1960's. Within the biographies these and other basic song styles are described, and perhaps for the first time in any volume more than passing notice is given to the changing song lyric and the men who brought about this change.

Yet still more had to go into this book if it were to try to portray a complete picture of the American popular song as seen through the careers of its creators. Neither the writers of songs nor their songs were produced in a vacuum. Both were the products and the voices of their times. And so, woven into the texture of these biographies are the social and political milieus that often inspired the songwriting activity of these composers and lyricists.

Significant, too, are the media for which songs were often written and through which they were so often popularized. Consequently the author felt the necessity of including within the biographies something of the history of the American musical theatre (from the minstrel show to the musical play, vaudeville, burlesque, and revue), of motion pictures, of radio, of recorded music.

The method pursued was to select the one, two—and in rare instances three —creative figures representing each of the changing song styles, or the political and social changes during the period in which they worked, or the media through which their songs were channeled to the public. Thus the first chapter is on William Billings, who represents the songs of the American Revolution, and the last chapter is on Bob Dylan, whose folk rock, in the 1960's, expresses so aptly the younger generation's reasons for rebelling. Dylan's rise to fame and popularity was due to the pivotal force that the recording industry had become in popular music—a force that comes in for discussion in this chapter. Between these two chronological extremes will be found the stories of twenty-eight composers and thirteen lyricists (actually, the number of lyricists is increased if we include composers like Stephen Foster, Irving Berlin, Cole Porter, Harold Rome, and Frank Loesser, who served as their own lyricists).

Contents

Great Men of American Popular Song

GREAT MEN OF AMERICAN POPULAR SONG

From Fuguing Tunes to Martial Tunes

William Billings

America's first popular songs were either religious or political, for religion at first and, after that, politics were of prime concern and interest in the Colonies. William Billings, the first American composer of popular songs, wrote both kinds.

In the beginning there were religious songs. When the Pilgrim Fathers arrived at Plymouth Rock in 1620, their possessions included the *Henry Ainsworth Book of Psalms*. This little volume comprised thirty-nine religious melodies. All were in one voice, all were devoid of bar lines, and all were of English origin. Some were slow and solemn, while others were lively. Many were flexible in meter and rhythm. All had rich embellishments. One of these melodies was the tune now popularly known as "The Old Hundredth," which is still found in modern hymnals as a setting for "Praise God from Whom All Blessings Flow."

1

The Puritans settling the Massachusetts Bay Colony in 1628 brought with them the psalter of Sternhold and Hopkins. But dissatisfaction with the English translations of the religious texts soon led several dissidents to create their own psalm book, "faithfully translated into English metre." This was the *Bay Psalm Book* (as it is now identified), the first book published in the Colonies. The original edition, issued in Cambridge, Massachusetts, in 1640, contained words alone. Not until the ninth edition in 1698 were melodies added.

The Puritans assumed a moralistic attitude toward music—though not the total disdain that legend has long led us to believe. They regarded music that praised God and religion the noblest of all, and this is the music they practiced and popularized. But they practiced it in that highly primitive manner known as the "common way of singing." "Common way" meant that the congregation relied on memory to sing numbers it had learned from its ancestors—each worshiper singing according to his own inclination, taste, and memory. Congregational singing often proved a violent cacophony as each man or woman pursued his own concept of tempo, pitch, and rhythm. In 1700 Reverend Walter Roxbury called this congregational singing "a mere disorderly noise, left to the mercy of every unskillful throat to chop and alter." In 1721 Cotton Mather still described this singing as "an odd noise." A practice known as "deaconing" did not help matters, either. Here the deacon would sing a psalm or hymn line by line, rapping out the proper rhythm with his knuckles on some metal, and the congregation would repeat each line after it had been intoned.

In the early eighteenth century some musical reformers tried to do away with these singing abuses. All of them were clergymen, many having been educated at Harvard. Their goal was to end musical anarchy in church. They violently opposed the "common way of singing" and tried to replace it with "regular singing" or "singing by note." In or about 1714 there was published John Tufts's *A Very Plain and Easy Introduction to the Singing of Psalm Tunes,* followed in 1721 by Thomas Walter's *The Grounds and Rules of Music Explained.* The conservative diehards looked askance on such developments. They enjoyed their own primitive form of religious music-making, and they opposed formal change that necessitated learning new hymns or reading notes. But change is inevitable. By the time William Billings was born in Boston on October 7, 1746, the reform movement had taken root, and Billings became the first significant creative spokesman of this reform.

Fate could hardly have selected a more unattractive-looking candidate to fill so significant a role as reform spokesman. He had one eye, a withered arm, legs of uneven length, and a harsh, grating voice. To physical deformities was added a slovenly appearance and boorish manners. He favored outlandish clothes. He was never meticulous about cleanliness. This, then, was a vulnerable target for abuse and mockery. Billings was such a target, both as man and as musician. Yet his music was heard more widely in its time than that of any other composer in the Colonies. His impact upon the musical culture of his age and his environment was incalculable.

He was a musical pioneer: the first in America to form a church choir; the first in America to organize a singing school; the first in America to use a pitch pipe and to introduce a cello in church services; the first in America to become a professional musician.

Billings's schooling, both academic and musical, ended with his father's death when William was fourteen. The only musical training he had had up to this time came from a local schoolmaster who taught him the elements of singing. At fourteen, William was apprenticed to a tanner, a position hardly calculated to improve his personal appearance or habits of cleanliness. Music fascinated him far more than his trade. He spent hour after hour studying Tans'ur's *Musical Grammar* and committing to memory whatever psalms he could find. But by himself he could progress in music only so far. Throughout his life he remained a musical primitive, with little concept of formal harmony, counterpoint, or composition. What he *did* possess to an uncommon degree was ego, creative drive, and sound instincts.

He was soon writing psalm tunes of his own, scrawling the notes with chalk on animal hides and on the walls. Then he came to the decision to desert tannery for music. He started out as a singing teacher and set up shop near the White Horse Tavern, hanging a sign outside his door that read simply, "Billings: Music." With the dynamic energy and initiative which would characterize him throughout his life, he proceeded to make a vital contribution to the musical society of his times. He formed in Boston the first singing school ever established in the Colonies—a studied attempt to banish forever the horrendous practice of "common way of singing" and replace it with "singing by note." In 1774 he organized a singing class in Stoughton, Massachusetts, which in 1786 became the Stoughton Musical Society, America's first musical organization. One of his students in Stoughton was Lucy Swan, daughter of an army major. Billings married her on July 26, 1774. She was his second wife, the first having been Mary Leonard, whom he had married on December 13, 1764. From his two marriages came six children, five boys and a girl.

Another vital move in Billings's revolt against the unschooled and untrained church-singing practices of his time was the creation of a church choir—once again a first in the New World. He subsequently led the choirs at the Brattle Street Church and at the Old South Church. He was a severe taskmaster, particularly in matters of rhythm and pitch. To establish the proper pitch at the beginning of a number he used a pitch pipe, and to maintain the proper pitch throughout the number, as well as to establish the rhythm, he had a cello play along with the singers.

He was also writing religious music: psalms, hymns, fuguing tunes. The last of these were not formal fugues in the style and technique of Johann Sebastian Bach, but melodies written in the contrapuntal technique of imitation. Billings's music was as slovenly and disreputable as his own appearance. Untrained as he was in the refinements and subtleties of musical science, he broke rules and conventions at will. His voices moved in parallel thirds and sixths. He used consecutive fifths. His doublings were frequently discordant. In short, he perpetrated on paper some of the very things that had characterized the "common way of singing" which he held in such horror.

But, instinctively, he was groping for a more rugged, a more virile, kind of music than the slow and stately hymns that had come from England. The kind of music he was trying to write was more in keeping with the Colonists for whom they were intended—a people hardened by the deprivations and dangers encountered in the making of a new life for themselves in a strange world. His music had a strong rhythmic stride, the bass moving athletically behind a strong, brisk melody in the treble. This music was not afraid of discords. Billings himself described his own writing as "more than twenty times as powerful as the old slow tunes, each part striving for mastery and victory."

Years after Billings's death, Harriet Beecher Stowe vividly remembered Billings's hymn "Majesty" in her book "Poganuc People": "There was a grand, wild freedom, an energy of motion in the old 'fuguing tunes' of that day that well expressed the heart of the people courageous in combat and unshaken in endurance. . . . Whatever the trained musician might say of such a tune as old 'Majesty,' no person of imagination or sensibility could hear it well rendered by a large choir without deep emotion. And when back and forth from every side of the church came different parts . . . there went a stir and thrill through many a stern and hard nature, until the tempest cleared off."

His tough fiber led Billings occasionally to introduce realistic effects into his writing. In one of his hymns the words suggested the clapping of hands; in his music Billings instructed the singers to do just that as they sang. In another hymn, to the words "shall laugh and sing," Billings reproduced a choral effect suggesting laughter.

His first published volume was *The New England Psalm Singer* in 1770. It is here and now that America's first composer of music for the masses emerges with all his ungovernable mannerisms and crudity of speech, qualities that he tried to rationalize in his preface. "Nature," he wrote, "is the best Dictator. All the hard, dry, studied rules that ever were prescribed, will not enable any person to form an air. . . . It must be Nature, Nature must lay the Foundation, Nature must inspire the Thought. . . . For my own part, as I don't think myself confined to any rules for composition, laid down by any that went before me, neither should I think (were I to pretend to lay down rules) that any one who came after me were any way obligated to adhere to them, any further than they should think proper; so in fact I think it is best for every composer to be his own carver."

This is the way Isaac Goldberg once described the music of Billings's first publication: "It is a strange and fearful thing—one of the curiosities of musical literature. It is full of music evolved out of the tanner's inner consciousness. Yet it by no means lacks a certain fascination, sprung from its very uncouthness."

Six years passed before Billings produced a second volume, *The Singing Master's Assistant,* better known as *Billings's Best.* This work comprised some of the hymns he had published in an earlier volume, and several new ones. In his foreword he gave voice to some of the reservations he now held about his first volume: "Kind reader, no doubt you remember that . . . I published a book entitled *The New England Psalm Singer,* and truly a most masterly performance I thought it then to be. How lavish was I of encomiums on this, my infant production! Said I, thou art my Reuben, my first born, the beginning of my strength; but to my great mortification I soon discovered it was Reuben in the sequel all over. I have discovered that many of the pieces were never worth my printing or your inspection."

But it should not be assumed that the technical shortcomings of the first volume had been totally eliminated. The writing is still rough and unschooled. The music still possesses that kind of brusqueness and vitality that simply could not have come out of the Old World.

It is out of this second volume that Billings lifted a hymn called "Chester," which he dressed up with new words to fit a political occasion. In the process he created America's first great war song.

Between the publication of Billings's first two volumes, the political caldron in the Colonies had come to a boil and overflowed with lava-like heat. Passions sought and found outlet in song.

The first American political song was written after the Massachusetts legislature in 1768 upheld the Circular Letter which had been drawn up for distribution throughout the Colonies to denounce new taxes. John Dickinson, a lawyer come to be known as the "Pennsylvania Farmer" and a leading figure in the Pennsylvania legislature, was one of those who stood ready to oppose the taxes vigorously. As an expression of that opposition he wrote a set of stirring verses, "The Liberty Song," to which he joined the melody of a celebrated air, "Hearts of Oak," by William Boyce, the English composer. The chorus of his verses ran as follows:

> *In Freedom we're born and in Freedom we'll live*
> *Our purses are ready*
> *Steady, friends, steady*
> *Not as slaves but as Freemen our money we'll give.*

Words and music of "The Liberty Song" appeared together for the first time in *Bickerstaff's Almanac* in 1769. The song caught on—partly because of Boyce's vivacious melody, which was well known throughout the Colonies, but mainly because Dickinson's words gave voice to the high tensions of the times. The song became the official tune of the Sons of Liberty, the secret order organized to protest actively against unjust taxation. Indeed, "The Liberty Song" became so popular that the Tory opposition was impelled to create parodies in rebuttal. One of them read:

> *In folly you're born, and in folly you'll live*
> *To madness still ready*
> *And stupidly steady*
> *Not as men but as monkeys the token you give.*

The practice of setting timely political lyrics about rapidly developing events to familiar English tunes continued right up to and persisted during the Revolutionary War. Thus a crowning paradox was created: the Colonists used English melodies as propaganda in their war against England. The most notable example of this practice was, to be sure, "Yankee Doodle," which was probably the melody heard in England for the nursery rhyme "Lucy Locket." In or about 1755 Richard Schuckburg used it for a set of nonsense lyrics with which he mocked the disheveled troops of General Braddock in the Colonies. For the next two decades the British troops in the Colonies sang "Yankee Doodle" to taunt the Colonists. During the Revolutionary War the Colonials appropriated it, using it as their battle cry of freedom and singing it lustily when General Cornwall surrendered at Yorktown.

But the most important song to come out of the American Revolution was of exclusively American origin. It was William Billings's "Chester," a religious hymn from *The Singing Master's Assistant,* for whose melody the composer provided in 1778 new martial lyrics:

> *Let tyrants shake their iron rod*
> *And slavery clank her galling chains.*
> *We fear them not; we trust in God.*
> *New England's God forever reigns.*

So widely was "Chester" sung in army camps and in the field of battle, so invigorating a tonic did it prove to be to the spirits of tired soldiers during periods of greatest discouragement and futility, that it has since come to be described as the "Marseillaise" of the American Revolution.

This was not Billings's only war song, though it is his most famous one. Billings's heart was in this war for freedom. Before the Revolution had broken out, he had established intimate contact with some of the leading rebel spirits in the Colonies. He had sung vocal duets with Samuel Adams. Paul Revere was the engraver of his first book of psalms. It was then to be expected that when hostilities erupted Billings should veer from fuguing tunes to martial tunes—his contribution to the war effort. He lifted other melodies from his hymn books to write "Independence," "Columbia," and "Lamentation over Boston," among other war songs, and distributed them to the fighting men. The *Musical Reporter* noted: "Many of the New England soldiers who . . . were encamped in southern states, had his popular tunes by heart and frequently amused themselves by singing them in camp to the delight of all those who heard them."

But he had not altogether abandoned the writing of religious songs. Two volumes appeared in 1779 and 1781 respectively: *Music in Miniature* and *The Psalm Singer's Amusement.* After the Revolution he had two more books of psalms published: *The Suffolk Harmony* in 1786 and *The Continental Harmony* in 1794.

His cacophonies, his awkward musical grammar, and his ungovernable temperament had always inspired severe criticism and mockery from musicians far better schooled than he. One evening, early in Billings's career as a composer, a musician hung two live cats by their tails on the sign outside Billings's house. The point being made was that the screeching of the cats was no different from the sounds produced by Billings's music. To all such critics, Billings gave a worthy response by writing *Jargon,* a composition for four voices, filled with the most outlandish discords.

In the end the last laugh was sounded by Billings. By 1790 his hymns, anthems, psalms, and fuguing tunes were sung throughout the thirteen states. There was hardly a church where a Billings tune was not known and sounded; there was hardly an anthology of religious music published in young America in which one of his melodies was not represented, gems like "Chester" or "When Jesus Wept" or "Be Glad, Then, America" or "The Rose of Sharon" or "Shepherd's Carol." Of all those who wrote songs, religious or political, during Billings's lifetime, those by Billings still remain the most significant.

Billings died in abject poverty in Boston on September 26, 1800. Three days later he was buried in an unmarked grave in the Boston Common.

GREAT MEN OF AMERICAN POPULAR SONG

Songs with Sentiment

Henry Russell

After a nation was born, its people began to sing of things closest to their experiences and to their hearts. Political subjects entered into American popular-song literature, pointing to the way in which most Americans were becoming preoccupied with the manifold problems of building a new state. Songs praised national heroes ("God Save George Washington"). Songs furthered political campaigns ("For Jefferson and Liberty," "Tippecanoe and Tyler Too," "Adams and Liberty"). Songs commented on current events ("The Acquisition of Lousiana," "The Erie Canal Song"). National ballads came into being: "Hail, Columbia," born in the turbulent year of 1798 when America seemed to be drawn into conflict with France; "The Star-Spangled Banner," inspired by the War of 1812.

Songs were written to fight moral battles and promote moral issues—

valuable propaganda to preach against the evils of drink, for example ("Young Man, Shun That Cup," "Father's a Drunkard and Mother's Dead") or to promote woman suffrage ("Let Us All Speak Our Minds If We Dare It").

Generally, the practice initiated before and continued during the Revolution persisted into the early 1800's: that of taking familiar foreign melodies and providing them with new timely lyrics. Gathered into slim little volumes known as "songsters"—the first such being *The American Musical Miscellany* in 1798—these song lyrics, purchased in the street, found their way into the family household.

With public entertainment scarce, catering only to a small minority, singing became a major form of diversion. Songster in hand, a family and their neighbors and friends would gather around the parlor organ or spinet for a song fest. Outside the family parlor, singing was also favored as part of the program in public places—at clubs, quilting bees, political rallies, and so forth.

In the early years following the Revolution not all the songs written and heard were spawned from political, social, or moral issues. After all, a large segment of the singing public were ladies of gentility and refinement who were less concerned with politics and current events than with basic human emotions and sentiments. So many women purchased songsters that many of these song books were slanted with one eye on this feminine market. The editor of *The Parlor Companion,* for example, remarked in his preface that the songs collected and edited in his little volume had "nothing in them to tinge the cheek of modesty with the slightest blush."

America's first sentimental ballad had come during the Revolution. It was "The Banks of the Dee"—words by John Tait, adapted to a famous Irish melody, "Langolee"—a song describing the farewell to his lady by a soldier about to go off to the American colonies to join the British troops.

If "The Banks of the Dee" was America's first sentimental ballad, then "The Minstrel's Return from the War," written in 1825, was the first sentimental ballad to become a hit song. Words and music were the work of John Hill Hewitt, who was editor of *The Republican,* a newspaper he had founded in Greenville, South Carolina, when he wrote his ballad. His brother published the song in 1827, but with so little faith in it he failed to take out a copyright. "The Minstrel's Return from the War" sold thousands of copies in the original edition, but many more thousands in pirated editions. As the composer later wrote: "It was eagerly taken up by the public and established my reputation as a ballad composer. It was sung all over the world—and my brother, not securing the copyright, told me that he missed making at least ten thousand dollars."

Hewitt's next sweepingly successful ballad came during the Civil War, and a dramatic war episode was responsible for its writing. Lamar Fontaine, a member of the Second Virginia Cavalry, was on guard duty one night. Completing his rounds, he turned the post over to his friend John Moore. By stirring the hot coals of a campfire and sending flames leaping into the air, Moore disclosed his position to the enemy to become the fatal target of a bullet. Fontaine found his friend dead. Lying near him was a newspaper headlining a phrase then popular in the press for periods of inactivity during the war: "All Quiet Along the Potomac Tonight." The next day, Fontaine wrote a poem using the head-line as his title and describing the thoughts of his friend as he reminisced about wife and child just before his death. Hewitt was so taken with this poem that he set it to music in 1864, dedicating his song to the "unknown dead of the present revolution." The song proved immensely popular with troops every-where in the North and the South. It was also responsible for commanding officers prohibiting the use of campfires during guard duty.

Other famous ballads by Hewitt included "The Knight of the Raven Black Plume," "Our Native Land," "The Mountain Bugle," and two in which he re-called the Southland nostalgically, "Take Me Home Where the Sweet Magnolia Blooms" and "Carry Me Back to the Sweet Sunny South."

Nostalgia finally brought him back to the South where he taught music and edited a newspaper in Savannah. Then he settled in Baltimore, and it was there that he died on October 7, 1890, having lived through almost the entire century. "When he died at the age of eighty-nine," writes John Tasker Howard, "Balti-more felt that it had lost one of its links with the past. He had seen Fulton's first steamboat on the Hudson, he was present when the first despatch was sent over Morse's telegraph line between Baltimore and Washington, and he was a pas-senger on the first train of cars that pulled out of Baltimore by locomotive."

Symptomatic of the vogue for sentimental ballads in early America was the strong attraction these songs held for concert audiences. To satisfy this demand, English singers began touring America in recitals devoted primarily to ballad literature. One such artist was Joseph Philip Knight. At his recital in New York City on October 9, 1839, he introduced a sea lullaby by which he is still re-membered: "Rocked in the Cradle of the Deep." This ballad, which has retained its popularity with bassos because of its effective low register, immediately be-came the prototype of many similar *basso profundo* numbers.

Another visiting Englishman, named Henry Russell, became Hewitt's most distinguished rival in the writing of sentimental ballads during the first half of the nineteenth century. Since his entire career as a songwriter was confined to the United States, where he lived for eight years, he well deserves to be regarded as an *American* composer of popular ballads, despite his English nationality. Born in Sheerness, England, on December 24, 1812, he began his professional musical career by appearing extensively as a boy singer. He then came to Italy for music study. There one of his teachers was the distinguished opera composer and genius of *bel canto* Vincenzo Bellini. There, too, he came into personal association with the two other celebrated Italian opera masters of that period, Donizetti and Rossini.

Back in England, he had such a difficult time earning a living that he finally decided to try his luck in another part of the world. His first destination was Canada, but that country proved too backward culturally to suit his taste. In 1833 he headed south to the United States, ending his journey at Rochester, New York, where he found employment as organist at the First Presbyterian Church.

What led him to write his first ballad was the hearing of a speech by Henry Clay, the American statesman. Russell asked himself: "Why should it not

be possible for me to make music the vehicle of grand thoughts and noble sentiments, to speak to the world through the power and poetry of song?" With this
aim in mind he wrote "Wind of the Winter Night," a musical setting of a poem
by Charles Mackay.

In 1841 Russell came to New York. There he formed a vocal ensemble
with some of his English friends to give concerts in the East. Russell soon
parted company with his collaborators to set out on his own in solo song recitals
whose main attraction was the presentation of his own ballads. One of these was
"The Old Arm Chair," a tearful mother song which he produced in 1840 (words
as well as music) and which is sometimes singled out as the first "mammy song"
ever written. He also sang such other sentimental numbers of his own creation as
"The Old Family Clock," "The Old Spinning Wheel," "The Old Bell," and
"That Old Gang of Mine."

But the ballad that made the deepest impression on his audiences was
"Woodman, Spare That Tree," which he wrote in 1837 to words by George
P. Morris. The inspiration for it came one day while Russell was taking a drive
into the country with Morris. The latter suddenly recalled that they were near
the very place where, many years earlier, as a boy he had watched his father
plant a tree. Curiosity as to whether the tree was still in existence led both Morris
and Russell to the scene. There they encountered a farmer, ax in hand, about to
cut down the tree for firewood. Summoning all his powers of persuasion, Morris
induced the farmer to spare the tree.

Russell's ballads always made a profound emotional impact on his audiences,
but none stirred them the way "Woodman, Spare That Tree" did. In *Shadows
on the Wall,* John Hill Hewitt described one such reaction: "He had finished the
last verse. . . . The audience was spellbound for a moment, and then poured
out a volume of applause that shook the building to its foundation. In the midst
of this tremendous evidence of their boundless gratification, a snowy-headed
gentleman with great anxiety depicted in his venerable features arose and demanded silence. He asked with tremulous voice: 'Mr. Russell, in the name of
Heaven, tell me, was the tree spared?' 'It was, sir,' replied the vocalist. 'Thank
God! Thank God! I breathe again!,' and he sat down perfectly overcome by
emotion."

Hewitt also provided the following description of Russell on the stage: "He
was rather stout but not tall. His face was prepossessing . . . dark and heavy
whiskers and curly hair. He was an expert at wheedling applause out of audiences
and adding to the effect of his songs by a brilliant piano accompaniment. With
much self-adulation he often used to describe the wonderful influence of his
descriptive songs over audiences."

Russell was not the only one either to introduce or to popularize his ballads.
The Hutchinson Singing Family was an even more powerful agency in circu-
larizing his songs.

Singing families sprouted with fertility all over the country in recitals of
popular songs and ballads in the nineteenth century. There were the Rainers
(Swiss people), the Bakers, the Cheneys, and so forth. By far the most successful
of them all were the Hutchinsons, who came from Milford, New Hampshire.

Sometimes identified as "The Tribe of Jesse," the Singing Hutchinsons were the children of Jesse and Mary Hutchinson, who had sixteen children. Three died in infancy. All the others sang, though only four hit the trail professionally; the others preferred the more sedentary existence of farmers or business people. The four were Aby (a female) and John, Asa, and Judson (males). They made their singing debut in 1839. In 1843 they embarked on their first tour outside their native state. Their programs featured sentimental and dramatic ballads, some often gruesome in their realism. The Hutchinsons were also capable of making news by inflaming audiences with songs of protest. The quartet proved to be powerful propagandists for temperance, woman suffrage, and the abolition of slavery. They also wrote songs of their own—songs like "The Old Granite State" and "Excelsior" (the latter a setting of Longfellow's poem) which met with immense success. In 1845 the Hutchinsons toured England, where Charles Dickens gave them a reception, and Ireland. After that, the Hutchinsons continued touring the United States for many years. In time a second generation of Hutchinsons supplanted the first. The end of the nineteenth century saw singing families passing out of favor (to get replaced by more popular forms of stage and concert entertainment). Aware that their day was over, the Hutchinsons wisely went into retirement.

On their first tour the Singing Hutchinsons were particularly successful with two of Russell's dramatic ballads. "The Maniac" was a particularly lurid portrait of a tormented, insane person. John Hutchinson himself has described how he delivered this ballad: "I sang it alone to the accompaniment of the brothers. Judson and Asa would commence a prelude. Meanwhile I would be in my chair behind them, with the finger of each hand raising the hair on my head, and bringing it in partial dishevelment. Then I would rise, with the expression of vacancy inseparable from mania, and commence." The delivery of the line of the refrain "No, by heaven, I am *not* mad" was always calculated to make the blood of the audience freeze. N. P. Rogers, a friend of the Hutchinsons', reported: "John performed it with appalling power."

The other dramatic ballad by Russell, with which the Singing Hutchinsons enraptured their audiences, was "The Ship on Fire," words by Charles Mackay. John Hutchinson presented it as a solo. This ballad was also a highly realistic portrait in song, this time of a tragedy at sea. An extended piano introduction sketched a tonal picture of a violent storm with sweeping chromatic figures in the bass and piercing chords in the treble. Then the song began, describing a driving gale in which a helpless ship was being tossed and twisted. A mother, a child in her arms, falls on her knees to pray God for mercy. At her side is her husband who dreams of the peace and bliss of a cottage by the shore should they ever survive this danger. Suddenly fire breaks out. The ship is doomed. Mother, father, and child are lowered in a lifeboat, now become "a mere speck on the wave." A cry of joy rises from their lips. From the distance a boat is drifting toward them with help. "Thank God, thank God," they cry out. "We're saved."

It is probably legend that when Hutchinson presented this number in a concert in Canton, Pennsylvania, a member of that audience was so caught by the realism of the song and so overcome by emotion that he fled from the auditorium into the street to ring a fire alarm to summon engines toward the auditorium. Be it as it may, it is fact and not fiction that this ballad was a particular favorite of President Lincoln's.

The Hutchinsons were also responsible for the success of several other Russell ballads. "The Indian Hunter" (words by Eliza Cook) was the first American popular song paying tribute to and pleading for justice for the redskin. "A Life on the Ocean Wave" (words by Epes Sargent) was an early popular-song treatment of the sea; in 1899 it was made the official march of the English Royal Marines. Still another Russell ballad to become a Hutchinson specialty was "The Old Sexton."

Russell wrote over eight hundred ballads, most of them to his own lyrics. Not all were sentimental or dramatic. Some espoused causes: temperance, abolition of slavery, reform of insane asylums, and other similar burning issues of the times. Since Russell sold each of his numbers outright to publishers at an average price of ten shillings each, he never made money from compositions that brought enormous profits to his publishers. His main income came from his concerts. As he explained: "Had it not been that I sang the songs myself . . . the payment for their composition would have meant simple starvation."

He left America in 1841 to return to London. Fourteen years after that he went into retirement. Death came in London on December 8, 1900. He left a song heritage which, with that of Hewitt, marked the beginnings of sentimental balladry in America. He also left two sons destined to make other kinds of contributions to music. Henry Russell became an opera impresario who managed Covent Garden in London, and in the United States, the Henry Russell Opera Company and the Boston Opera Company. Sir Landon Ronald, born Landon Russell, was one of England's most distinguished conductors of symphonic and operatic music.

Songs of the Blackface Minstrel

Dan Emmett

Neither Negro song and dance nor caricatures of Negroes were total strangers to the American stage in the Colonies. Negro dances were sometimes interpolated into performances of plays and operas, though separately as en-tr'actes. After the Revolution, Negro entertainment began to assume increasing importance while attracting ever larger audiences. On December 30, 1799, Gott-lieb Graupner appeared in Boston as a blackface performer singing "The Gay Negro Boy" between the acts of a nonmusical play. (This is the same Gottlieb Graupner who organized a Philharmonic orchestra in Boston early in the nine-teenth century.) The banjo—an instrument inextricably identified with the Negro —achieved prominence for the first time when it was used to accompany the "Bonja Song," which was first published anonymously as an instrumental piece in 1818, and after that dressed up with lyrics by R. C. Dallas. Immediately after the War of 1812, the Negro was often seen on the stage lampooning military uniforms in numbers like "The Guinea Boy" or "The Siege of Plattsburg." In the former, he does a routine in which, against his wishes, he is recruited by the British; in the latter, he is on the American side, though with no greater display of enthusiasm. More ambitious in scope was "Massa George Washington and General La Fayette," a song by Micah Hawkins which James Roberts presented at the Chatham Gardens in New York in 1824. Then, with the War of 1812 over, the Negro discarded military uniforms, reverted to civilian status, and portrayed characters who were simple, forthright, and sometimes naïve and rustic.

In the 1820's and 1830's two performers were particularly successful in blackface routines: George Washington Dixon and Bob Farrell. The songs with which they were identified most often were "The Coal Black Rose," "My Long-Tail Blue," and "Zip Coon." Nobody knows who wrote them. The first two appeared in or about 1827, the third in 1834.

"Zip Coon" is the most celebrated of this trio of songs. Bob Farrell introduced it at the Bowery Theatre in New York on August 11, 1834, after which it became a staple in the repertory of minstrel-show troupes everywhere. The term "Zip Coon" refers to a broadway fop who pretends being a "larned skolar." The lyrics of the song are sheer nonsense, the refrain opening with the line "Possum up a gum tree, coony on a stump." (Today this song is a favorite at square dances where it is identified as "Turkey in the Straw.")

The opening of travel by steamboat on the Mississippi in 1811 accelerated interest in and familiarity with Negro songs and dances. Within a decade or so, hundreds of steamboats were sailing along the banks of this great river. They were floating palaces, then the last word in sumptuous trappings, bringing travelers the kind of good life usually reserved exclusively for the very rich. Mississippi travel, therefore, soon became not merely a convenient mode of transportation from south to north and back again but also as a form of holiday excursion. Elegantly attired ladies and gentlemen rubbed elbows in the brilliant public rooms with traders, cotton planters, professional gamblers, and prostitutes.

Travelers coming north on these steamboats brought back reports of a strange and wonderful music they had heard the colored folk sing in the South: spirituals, and work songs which the black folk improvised as they labored on the docks loading and unloading the cargo. Sometimes Negroes accompanied their singing with eccentric dances: a slouching motion of the body, abrupt rhythmic movements of body and hands, all synchronizing with the rhythm of the song.

Passengers aboard those Mississippi steamboats used to watch these Negroes at work and at play, and listen with fascination to the singing. When these passengers came north, they talked about this music, tried to sing some of it, or to reproduce it on piano or organ. Up North, more and more interest began to be focused on this native song art. In 1838 a New York newspaper expressed pleasure that "composers of this country are turning their attention to the beautiful melodies of the South." It was along the Mississippi that Mark Twain first heard Negro melodies, which delighted him no end. "The music made all other vocal music cheap," he said. And it was from the songs along the Mississippi that Stephen Foster made his acquaintance with Negro folk music, whose impact on him was so decisive.

Out of this growing fascination in the North for Negro song and dance sprang our first native form of musical theatre, one that remained popular for about half a century—the minstrel show.

The North could feel intensely enough about the Negro to respond with highly charged emotion when the Singing Hutchinsons presented their famous abolitionist number, "Get off the Track" (words by Jesse Hutchinson adapted to an old slave melody). The rising abolitionist passions in the North needed outlet in a safety valve, and a valve was provided through songs of protest and sentimental songs about the Negro. Even a more important outlet for seething emotions over the slavery question was found in the minstrel show. As the Negro question assumed ever greater importance, the popularity of the minstrel show developed in equal ratio.

It is possible to pinpoint the place where, the time when, and the performer with whom the first seeds of the minstrel show were planted. The place, Baltimore in Maryland; the time, 1828; the performer, Thomas "Daddy" Rice. "Daddy" Rice was a performer of Negro routines. Behind a theatre in Baltimore, where he was appearing at the time, was a livery stable owned by Jim Crow, attended to by an old Negro slave who (as was then the custom) had taken over his master's name. The slave was deformed. He limped badly, moving his misshapen body with ludicrous contortions. Stumbling along, he chanted to himself a curious ditty with nonsensical lines, accentuating the rhythm of his song with peculiar shuffling motions of the feet.

This old Negro gave "Daddy" Rice the idea for a new impersonation in his act. Rice devised a costume consisting of a broad-rimmed hat worn at a rakish angle; a tattered, patched, ill-fitting suit of clothes; unlaced shoes through one of which the toes had made a passage. Rice then concocted a song with gibberish verses, naming it "Jim Crow" after the character he was portraying. For its refrain he devised a dance inspired by the old Negro's peculiar motions. The opening lines of his nonsense song were:

> *Wheelabout, turn about*
> *Do jis so—*
> *And e'bry time I wheel about*
> *I jump Jim Crow.*

This act created a sensation. Before long, Negro impersonators everywhere were doing "Jim Crow" routines. Parodies of Rice's song, many of them about current events, were heard everywhere. In 1833 "Daddy" Rice's song was given during the intermission of two one-act plays in New York.

"Jim Crow" insured a permanent place for Negro songs in American popular-song literature. It was also the first song to introduce and popularize on the stage a Negroid style of dance to accompany song. The characterization of the Negro in both song and dance now became a favored form of public entertainment. At the same time, the term "Jim Crow" entered permanently into the American language to designate racial discrimination.

Dan Emmett is the acknowledged father of the minstrel show. But he was much more than that. He was also the most successful creator of popular songs (lyrics and music), banjo tunes, and dance tunes. He even wrote plays. As Hans Nathan remarked in his book on Dan Emmett:* "He was a force in nineteenth-century Negro minstrelsy, entertaining urban and rural audiences as banjoist, fiddler, singer, and comedian. His contributions not only include music but lyrics, stump speeches, and plays. It is not that they are merely important in the history of the early-American popular theatre and of early popular music. Their hard-bitten humor, their naïve freshness, and their native flavor lend them an intrinsic value. Like the oils and water colors of itinerant American painters, Emmett's is a folk art. It speaks only to those who, either out of naïveté or sophistication, are capable of delighting in something that is unpolished and of limited means, but sharply defined and direct."

Emmett's father was a blacksmith who had been a pioneer in the settling of the town of Mount Vernon, northeast of Columbus, in Ohio. There, early in 1815, he married Sally Zerick, and on October 29 of the same year their first child was born, named Daniel Decatur.

The boy received some rudimentary instruction in the three r's at the local schoolhouse. After that he learned the printing trade and found a job with a local newspaper. By then he had already learned by himself to play dance tunes on the violin.

When he was eighteen, he left his native city for Cincinnati. There, by falsifying his age, he was able to enlist in the United States Army. In uniform, he specialized in playing the drum and fife. Then, with his real age uncovered, he was unceremoniously mustered out of the army on July 8, 1835.

His career in show business began with a circus in Cincinnati. This was the period during which he wrote his first song, "Bill Crowder," his own lyrics borrowing a tune popular in that day. "The text," says Hans Nathan, "describes the adventures of a Negro who, after having arrived in Cincinnati, picks a fight with a Jewish old-clothesman. . . . The ludicrous figure of Emmett's Jewish old-clothesman, however, was suggested by English stage music; it does not exist in early American Negro minstrel songs."

This song betrays Emmett's interest in Negro songs, an interest that soon led him to learn to play the banjo so that he could accompany himself as a blackface singer. He did such a routine with several circus troupes. Then, joining forces with Frank Brower, a friend who was a popular song-and-dance man, Emmett came to New York in 1842 to advance his career in the theatre. They performed in variety theatres and apparently made a good impression. The newspapers described Emmett as "the great Southern banjoist" and Brower as "the perfect representation of Southern Negro characters."

* *Hans Nathan, Dan Emmett and the Rise of Early Negro Ministrelsy* (Norman, Okla.: University of Oklahoma Press, 1962).

An economic depression in 1842, which struck a body blow at all public entertainments, was directly responsible for the conception of the minstrel show; and Dan Emmett was its parent. Many actors who specialized in blackface routines were thrown out of work as one theatre after another had to close its doors. Bookings became scarce. Necessity was the father of the invention, compelling some of these actors to abandon solo acts and join up in performing groups.

In 1843 Billy Whitlock, an unemployed actor, visited Dan Emmett at his room at a boarding house at 37 Catherine Street. They began practicing some numbers on violin and banjo. As they played, Frank Brower entered. At the spur of the moment, Brower picked up a pair of bones and joined in the performances. Before long a fourth actor, Dick Pelham, came in and used a tambourine to join the concert. When they finished playing, they started to talk about their futures in the theatre, which seemed gloomy, indeed, at the time. Then the idea was born that all four join up in a single act, since individual bookings were impossible to find. This is how the Virginia Minstrels (as the four men decided to call their act) came into being. Working out a formula in which they could fully exploit their respective talents, they gave a benefit performance at the Chatham Theatre on January 31, 1843, after having made a trial run at Bartlett's Billiard Room.

What is now accepted as the official public debut of the Virginia Minstrels took place at the Bowery Amphitheatre on February 6, 1843, as part of a circus show. Here is how the New York *Herald* announced the premiere and described the act: "First night of the novel, grotesque, original, and surprisingly melodious Ethiopian band, entitled the Virginia Minstrels, being an exclusively musical entertainment combining the banjo, violin, bone castanets, and tambourine, and entirely exempt from the vulgarities and other objectionable features which have hitherto characterized Negro extravaganzas."

The program that evening not only marked the official debut of the Virginia Minstrels but also of Dan Emmett as a song composer, for it presented two Dan Emmett all-time favorites, "De Boatman's Dance" and "Old Dan Tucker." The program described the first of these as "a much admired song in imitation of the Ohio boatmen." About "Old Dan Tucker," the program remarked that it was a "Virginian Refrain in which is described the ups and downs of Negro life."

Emmett's prototype for Dan Tucker was one of his acquaintances, a ne'er-do-well who was continually getting into trouble. While "Old Dan Tucker" became a sturdy minstrel-show attraction, not only with the Virginia Minstrels but with competing companies as well, it was destined for fame in areas outside the theatre. At first, its melody was borrowed by the abolitionist movement to denounce slavery. Then the tune was lifted for still other lyrics during the "anti-rent" uprising among the tenant-farmers of New York State. Disguised as Indians and signaling to one another with tin horns, these tenant-farmers expressed their outraged feelings against the feudal conditions imposed upon them by the landowners in a parody of "Old Dan Tucker." The revolt was successful. Leases that had bound the farmers were abrogated, and legislation was finally passed abolishing the feudal system.

The Virginia Minstrels presented a whole evening of their own entertainment for the first time on March 7, 1843, at the Masonic Temple in Boston. It was here and now that the minstrel show can be said to have come fully into its own. Dressed in blue swallow-tailed coats, striped calico shirts, and white pantaloons, the blackface performers danced, exchanged banter, sang numbers like Emmett's own "De Boatman's Dance" and "Old Dan Tucker," did the "Lucy Walk Around" and "The Essence of Old Virginia." The show ended with a parody, or burlesque, written by Emmett.

Emmett continued to write songs for minstrel shows, both during the existence of the Virginia Minstrels and after that, while he appeared with other companies. "My Old Aunt Sally" was published in 1843, the year that also saw the first sheet-music releases of "De Boatman's Dance" and "Old Dan Tucker." "Blue Tail Fly" (more familiar today as "Jim Crack Corn") followed in 1846. "Jordan Is a Hard Road To Travel," in 1853, was a vigorous abolitionist number whose melody was reminiscent of a Negro spiritual. This was sung not only in the minstrel shows but also at the concerts of the Hutchinson Singing Family, whose performances (as reported by Joshua Hutchinson) aroused the "disgust of the American people" at slavery.

In 1858 Emmett became a leading performer with Bryant's Minstrels, one of the most important troupes in the country. His job was to sing, to perform on several instruments including the banjo, to appear in comedy sketches (some of which he wrote), and to create music for walk-arounds and other kinds of finales. It was for a walk-around that Emmett wrote his song classic, "Dixie."

"Dixie" was written one rainy Sunday afternoon in 1859 in Emmett's room at 197 Elm Street in New York. Emmett himself has told how the song was born: "One Saturday night, in 1859, as I was leaving Bryant's theatre where I was playing, Bryant called after me, 'I want a walk-around for Monday, Dan.' The next day it rained and I stayed indoors. At first, when I went at the song, I couldn't get anything. But a line, 'I wish I was in Dixie,' kept repeating itself in my mind, and I finally took it for my start. Suddenly I jumped up and sat down at the table to work. When my wife returned I sang it to her. 'It's all about finished now, except the name. What shall I call it?' 'Why, call it I Wish I Was in Dixie Land,' she said. And so it was." Upon another occasion, Emmett revealed that the idea for "Dixie" came to him during a conversation with his wife when he complained about the miserable weather up North. "I wish I was in Dixie," he remarked to his wife at that time.

Where did the word "Dixie" come from? Is it a contraction of "Mason and Dixon line"? Was it appropriated from the term "dixie" used in the South for a ten-dollar bill circulated by the Citizens of Louisiana (the French word for "ten" being "dix")? Did Emmett come across the word during his travels in the South? Different authorities provide different explanations, leaving the entire question in as much doubt today as it was when Emmett first wrote his song.

A walk-around was a finale in which the entire company participated. In such a routine, the first part of "Dixie" was enacted by several comedians, before the entire company came out and sang the whole number. All this made for a colorful production number intended to portray some of the happier aspects of

Southern slave life. This routine, with the song "Dixie," was introduced by Bryant's Minstrels on April 4, 1859, at Mechanics Hall. (Mechanics Hall was the temple of the minstrel show until it was demolished by a fire a number of years later.) "It made a tremendous hit," Emmett wrote, "and before the end of the week everybody in New York was whistling it."

Everybody—indeed! The lyrics were sold on broadsides in pirated editions. Numerous other pirated editions presented music as well as words. The song was confiscated by minstrel companies everywhere, many performers featuring the melody with their own lyrics. Parodies were concocted. The New York *Commercial Advertiser* commented at the time: " 'Dixie' has become an institution, an irrepressible institution in this section of the country." At last, in 1860, an authorized publication appeared bearing the title "I Wish I Was in Dixie Land," the house of Peters having purchased the rights to the song outright for $500.

But the popularity of "Dixie" was not confined to the North. During the presidential campaign of 1860, the South used it as an anti-Lincoln song, with appropriate lyrics. In its original form, "Dixie" was given by the Rumsey and Newcomb Minstrels in Charleston, South Carolina, in December of 1860. In March of 1861, in New Orleans, "Dixie" created a furor when its melody was used as a march of Zouaves in the spectacle *Pocahontas;* seven encores had to be given. A pirated edition in New Orleans achieved extensive circulation. Finally, dressed up with martial lyrics, the song was adopted by Southern troops as their favorite battle song. This battle hymn made such a strong impression on Southern troops everywhere that just before the charge at Gettysburg, General Pickett asked that it be played to nurture the morale of the soldiers. "It is marvelous with what wildfire rapidity this tune, 'Dixie,' has spread over the whole South," wrote Henry Hotze in *Three Months in the Confederate Army.* One day after General Lee surrendered, President Lincoln was serenaded by a band outside the White House. He made a short improvised speech. "I propose now closing by requesting you to play a certain piece of music or a tune," he said finally. "I thought 'Dixie' one of the best tunes I ever heard. . . . I had heard that our adversaries had attempted to appropriate it. I insisted yesterday that we had fairly captured it."

The South had conveniently forgotten that the melody had been written by a Northerner. Indeed, it even spread a report that the tune had actually originated with a Southern Negro speaking of his sentimental attachment to master and homeland. But in the North, the extraordinary vogue of "Dixie" as a Southern war song caused no end of grief to its author. Some Northern papers even went so far as to condemn Emmett as a renegade, completely forgetting that Emmett had not written it as a war song, let alone a *Southern* war song. To stem the tide of attacks, Emmett prepared some new verses for his melody in which he urged Northern soldiers "to meet those Southern traitors with iron." But the new version never really caught on, and "Dixie" remained the South's leading war song.

Though he made a number of appearances with various minstrel troupes after the Civil War, Emmett's career as a star of minstrelsy and as a creator of minstrel-show songs ended with that conflict. Between 1867 and 1888 he made his home in Chicago. Having lost his talent at singing, he made a number of appearances as a fiddler. For a while he wrote comedy Negro sermons for *The Clipper,* then, between 1872 and 1874, he was the owner and manager of a saloon.

In 1888 Emmett withdrew to the town of his birth, Mount Vernon, Ohio, where he stayed for the rest of life. He made his home in a little cottage where he tended to his garden and raised chickens. From this self-imposed seclusion and retirement, he emerged in 1895 at the invitation of Al G. Field to make a farewell tour as a member of Field's minstrel company. That tour opened in Newark, Ohio, on August 21, and ended the following April 11 in Ireton, Ohio. The big moment of the production came when Emmett, aged eighty, sang "Dixie." "Every time he appeared before the footlights to sing 'Dixie,' the audience went wild," Field has recorded.

Emmett died in Mount Vernon, Ohio, on June 28, 1904, and was buried in Mount View Cemetery. An effort was made to raise funds for the erection of a monument to his memory, but the venture collapsed. In time, the location of his grave could not be found. But in 1927 a memorial tablet was unveiled in Fletcher, North Carolina, and in 1931 a boulder inscribed to his memory was placed on the lawn outside the Knox County Memorial Building in Mount Vernon. Twelve years later, a sentimentalized, fictionalized screen biography was released, named after Emmett's "Dixie," starring Bing Crosby as the composer.

Dan Emmett was the first important performer to come out of the minstrel shows. There were others, though less frequently remembered today: they, too, however, made notable contributions to the American popular-song repertory. There was Billy Emerson who wore a huge sunflower in his lapel to point up the fact that his most famous song routine was "The Big Sunflower," which Bobby Newcomb had written soon after the end of the Civil War. This routine consisted not merely in the presentation of the song but also in the performance of a comical swagger between verses and a clog dance after the chorus. Another song associated with Emerson is a nonsense number of unknown authorship and still popular with glee clubs, "Polly Wolly Doodle."

Cool White (John Hodges), like Dan Emmett, was a minstrel who wrote his own songs, words and music. He and his Serenaders introduced his most famous creation, "Lubly Fan," in 1844, which soon became a highlight of minstrel shows everywhere. An alternate title for this number is "Buffalo Gals," which is the reason it acquired other names based on the cities in which it was sung, such as "Bowery Gals," "Louisiana Gals," and "Pittsburgh Gals."

The most celebrated minstrel of them all was Edwin P. Christy. To him belongs the historic distinction of having once and for all established the pattern followed by all succeeding minstrel shows. It was Christy who was the first to seat his minstrels in a semicircle. It was also Christy who divided an evening's entertainment into three distinct parts. The first, called "olio," placed the interlocuter (a part invariably played by Christy himself in his productions) in the middle of the semicircle. At one end of the circle sat Mr. Tambo (who played the tambourine) and at the other, Mr. Bones (who used clappers or bones).

Mr. Interlocuter asked the questions, and Mr. Tambo and Mr. Bones provided amusing replies. Between such gay exchanges was a variety show made up of solo songs, dances, and choral numbers. The second part of the Christy minstrel show (and all subsequent minstrel productions) was a free fantasia with no set format, but allowing principal performers to exhibit their talent. The third and closing part burlesqued what had transpired earlier.

Edwin P. Christy was born Edwin Harrington in Philadelphia in 1821. Little is known of his early years or about his apprenticeship on the stage. In 1842, with three other performers, he formed the Christy Minstrels, whose debut took place in Buffalo, New York. With enlarged forces, the Christy Minstrels finally appeared in New York City, at Palmer's Opera House, on April 27, 1846. For the next eight years the Christy Minstrels were in their heyday. They gave over 2,500 performances in New York (mainly at Mechanics Hall). Besides, they scored such a triumph in England that they were responsible for creating there a vogue for minstrel shows; English audiences got into the habit of referring to every blackface performer as a "Christy minstrel." Christy retired in 1854, to be replaced as head of his troupe by his adopted son, George Harrington, who also assumed the stage name of Christy. Christy Minstrels continued performing for another fourteen years, passing out of existence with George Harrington's death. As for the founding father, Edwin P. Christy himself, he became a victim to spells of insanity. In 1862 he jumped from a window in New York and died from the fall.

Establishing a permanent format for the minstrel show was one of two major achievements of Edwin P. Christy. The other was providing a showcase for the songs of America's greatest composer in the mid-nineteenth century, for Stephen Foster was a child of minstrelsy. It was for the Christy Minstrels that he wrote his first song; and it was for the Christy Minstrels that he achieved his first masterpieces.

GREAT MEN OF AMERICAN POPULAR SONG

Songs of the Negro–I

Stephen Foster

There is a good reason why Stephen Foster's first song classics were born in the minstrel show. The minstrel show, with its blackface performers, was the stage medium most partial to Negro songs; and the Negro was the source of Foster's highest inspiration.

Stephen Foster was a child of his place and time. The problem of Southern slavery was pressing ever more strongly on Northern consciousness. The growing propaganda for abolition inspired anger in some, dedicated fervor in others, but sentimentality in most—sentimentality toward an oppressed people and toward the environment in which they lived and suffered. This Northern reaction to the subject of the Negro and his slavery, one of the most vital issues of the period, finds a voice in Stephen Foster's songs. That this should be so is not without element of paradox. Foster, the most eloquent spokesman in song for

Negro liberation, was the son of slave owners, all of them Democrats who opposed abolition violently. In addition, he who sang so eloquently about the Southland, knew very little about the territory below the Mason and Dixon line through personal contact; in fact, when he wrote his first classic, he had never even stepped foot there.

Foster was one of the greatest melodists America has produced. Though he was no trained musician, he brought to his best writing the taste, the sound song structure, and at times the inevitability of lyric line that are fruits of trained musicianship. His creative world was a limited one, but within that world he was lord and master. Writing in a popular vein for a popular form of theatrical entertainment, he tapped veins of emotion and beauty the popular song had not known up to that time.

His personal tragedy was that he dissipated his great talent as recklessly as he did his energies and his future. He seemed incapable of capitalizing fully on his great creative powers either artistically or financially. He could write a masterpiece with one hand and a potboiler with the other, often without recognizing the exact value of either. He was even more profligate in his business dealings. He sold some of his songs outright for a pittance, only to have them yield handsome returns to performers and publishers. From most of his masterworks he earned a royalty that brought him an income of approximately $1,000 a year for eight years, not much when we realize how extraordinarily successful some of these songs were. Frequently he permitted one of his songs to appear as the work of somebody else; just as frequently he sold the performance rights to one of his songs for a few dollars.

He was incapable of exploiting his talent the way it deserved. Ingenuous, impractical, maladjusted to his environment, given to dreams and fancies that carried him from reality, he was unable to look after himself. He wasted his life and he wasted his talent. His closing years saw him become a hack and a drunkard, wallowing in poverty, misery, self-pity, and loneliness.

He was born to a family and into an environment hardly calculated to encourage his great gift for music-making or his ambition to devote himself to music professionally. America's economy was expanding in the early nineteenth century. Fortunes were being made in commerce, industry, and through the acquisition of land. Making money was the only barometer of success. Such were the values of Foster's father, Colonel William Barclay Foster, a pioneer in the settling of Pittsburgh. Colonel Foster had acquired social position and financial security through his skill as a trader. He had little sympathy with (or knowledge of) culture. Like most men of his time he regarded preoccupation with music as a hobby for young ladies, and most assuredly not the pursuit of happiness or self-fulfillment for men.

Stephen Foster was born in Lawrenceville, not far from Pittsburgh, on July 4, 1826. He seemed to have been born to make music. He was only an infant when he first tried picking out harmonies on strings of a guitar. When he was seven, he taught himself to play "Hail, Columbia" on a flageolet. From that instrument he progressed to the flute and the piano, both of which he learned to play without formal instruction.

One early influence had profound reverberations on his later musical development: the songs of the Negro. A household slave, Olivia, took him to church services where Stephen drank in the intoxicating brew of Negro shouts and spirituals. (He later quoted some of these tunes in two of his songs.) Negro popular tunes also delighted him no end. He was nine when he became the star performer in a boy's theatrical group when he sang such minstrel-show songs as "Zip Coon," "Jim Crow," and "The Coal Black Rose," in a fashion, says his brother Morrison, "so inimitable and true to nature that, child as he was, he was greeted with uproarious applause, and called back again and again every night the company gave an entertainment, which was three times a week."

In 1839 another of his brothers, William, found an engineering job in Towanda, in eastern Pennsylvania. Stephen joined him there in 1840 and for a brief period attended the Towanda Academy. He soon passed on to the Athens Academy in Tioga Point. It was at this time and place that he wrote the first piece of music he committed to paper, the *Tioga Waltz*. Morrison Foster suggests that Stephen wrote it for the commencement exercises at the academy; others insist that the piece was intended for a school exhibition in the church at Tioga Point on April 1, 1841.

Before the year of 1841 was over, Foster was attending still another school, the Jefferson College at Canonsburg, Pennsylvania. There, as earlier, he was most unhappy in the classroom. A self-contained, moody boy, he found his happiness roaming about the countryside, deep in revery, book and pencil in hand. Indoors he was always making music, usually on the flute. His career at Jefferson College ended after only seven days. With that Foster was through once and for all with formal education (though not with learning through the reading of books). He was determined to direct the lion's share of his energies and efforts on music.

He was writing songs, though not as yet songs about the Negro. The first to be published was "Open Thy Lattice, Love." Issued by George Willig of Philadelphia in December of 1844, its title page identified Foster erroneously as "L. C. Foster." This maiden publishing effort was the setting of a poem by George P. Morris which had appeared in a New York newspaper and which had already been used by another composer (Joseph Philip Knight of "Rocked in the Cradle of the Deep" fame). "It is interesting to compare Knight's music with the song Stephen composed," says John Tasker Howard in his biography of Foster. "Knight's setting is more musicianly, more resourceful in the development of the melodic idea. Stephen's song is far more spontaneous and is often sung today, while Knight's is forgotten."

After that, Foster wrote his own lyrics. "Lou'siana Belle," "Old Uncle Ned," and probably "Oh! Susanna" were written for a young men's club that met twice a week at Foster's home, the singing of popular tunes being a significant part of the agenda. About the premiere of "Lou'siana Belle," Robert Peebles Nevin said in the *Atlantic Monthly* in 1867: "The piece elicited unanimous applause. Its success in the club room opened to it a wider field, each member acting as an agent of dissemination outside, so that in the course of a few nights the song was sung in almost every parlor in Pittsburgh." Nevin then notes that the response to the other two Foster songs was greater still. "Although limited to the one slow process of communication—from mouth to ear—their fame spread far and wide, until from the drawing rooms . . . they were introduced into . . . concert halls, and there became known to Mr. W. C. Peters who at once addressed letters requesting copies for publication. These were cheerfully furnished by the author." Foster received no payment whatsoever from the publishing house of Peters for either "Lou'siana Belle" or "Old Uncle Ned," while "Oh! Susanna" brought the composer an outright payment of one hundred dollars. "The two fifty-dollar bills I received," commented Foster, "had the effect of starting me on my present vocation of songwriter."

All these songs betrayed the influence that the minstrel show had had on Foster's musical thinking. Individual minstrels like Thomas "Daddy" Rice and the leading minstrel companies of the period all appeared in Pittsburgh. Stephen was often found not only in the audience but even backstage trying to peddle his songs. "Daddy" Rice liked and praised some of Foster's numbers but regretted he could not use any, since his act featured only his own compositions. (A number of years later, Rice did purchase a Foster song, "Long Ago Day," but was discouraged from using it because its antislavery sentiment made it unsuitable in the South.) Other minstrels—for example, the Sable Harmonists— found a place for Foster's songs and helped to popularize them. In fact when Peters published Foster's songs he used the heading "Songs of the Sable Harmonists" over the title page of each one.

Both "Old Uncle Ned" and "Oh! Susanna" became minstrel-show favorites. The first song is significant in being Foster's first song about the Negro. It is the lament for an old man who just laid down his shovel and hoe and went to the place "where all good darkies go." We do not know where "Old Uncle Ned" was first heard in public, but we do know that the official premiere of "Oh! Susanna" did *not* take place in a minstrel show. That first performance took place at Andrews' Eagle Ice Cream Saloon in Pittsburgh on September 11, 1847. Only after then did it become popular in minstrel shows, sung by blackface performers to a banjo accompaniment. During the gold-rush days to California in 1849, "Oh! Susanna" (dressed up, of course, with new lyrics) was sung so often by the Forty-niners en route to California that since that time it has been used as a kind of theme song for the gold rush.

"Oh! Susanna," John Tasker Howard has written, "is a glorious bit of nonsense. . . . Here is a love of boisterous fun, of rollicking good humor that . . . shows a wealth of jovial good spirits. . . . The very lilt of the song was catching, so contagious that almost everyone in America was singing it before he realized what he was singing."

Either late in 1846 or early in 1847 Foster came to Cincinnati where, for a while, he worked as bookkeeper in his brother's commission house. In Cincinnati he made a significant move to advance his career as composer by consummating a deal with the powerful New York publishing house of Firth, Pond, and Company. That deal began modestly enough. For the first two Foster songs issued by that firm ("Nelly Was a Lady" and "My Brudder Gum"), Foster's only payment was fifty copies of sheet music. With his third song, "Dolcy Jones," a royalty arrangement was agreed upon: two cents a copy "after the expenses of the publication are paid." For "Dolcy Jones" Foster's total royalties amounted to $21.46. But it was not long before the sheet-music sale of Foster's songs was large enough to insure him a regular income, even if only a modest one.

During the first half of 1850 Foster had eleven songs published, two of which were successful: "De Camptown Races" (originally published on February 19 under the title of " 'Gwine To Run All Night") and "Nelly Bly." Both numbers represented excursions into the world of nonsense Foster had previously invaded with "Oh! Susanna." Both became fixtures in minstrel shows, "De Camptown Races" having been introduced by the Christy Minstrels. In addition to all this, "De Camptown Races" was used by the Forty-niners during the gold-rush days in a parody entitled "Sacramento."

Now that he had hopes of making money through his songs, Foster deserted the business world for good, brushed the dust of Cincinnati off his shoes, and returned to Pittsburgh. His new status as composer also gave him the courage to take a wife. She was Jane Denny McDowell (whom he would immortalize in his love ballad, "Jeanie with the Light Brown Hair" in 1854), daughter of a Pittsburgh physician. They had met a few years before the romance began to flourish. Stephen had a formidable rival for Jane's attentions and affection in Richard Cowan, a handsome and wealthy lawyer. Both happened to visit Jane on the same evening. Foster lingered on, reading a book, while Jane and Richard engaged in polite parlor talk. Then when Cowan left, Foster proposed marriage, insisting that Jane give him her answer then and there. The answer being in the affirmative, they were married on July 22, 1850; on April 18, 1851, their daughter, Marion, was born.

It was not a fortunate marriage. Stephen and Jane were worlds apart—in temperament, outlook, personal ambitions. A practical lady, Jane had little sympathy for Foster's high-handed rejection of material values and his thorough absorption with creative ones. Knowing and caring little about music, she could hardly be expected to accept stoically the sacrifices she had to make continually in terms of security and comfort. These discomforts set in almost as soon as they were married, since the young couple had to move in with the Foster family, in an already well crowded household. When a child was born, Jane became increasingly intolerant to Foster's stout refusal to consider business as a means of livelihood. Nor did Foster make it easy for her to be sympathetic to him. With the exception of his mother, whom he adored, women had never played a very significant part in his life. He was as emotionally detached as he was self-centered and withdrawn, always keeping between himself and his wife and child some impenetrable barrier. His growing appetite for alcohol and his affiliation with stage people aggravated for Jane (a devout Methodist) what had already become a sorry situation. As Jane sulked and nagged and as Stephen withdrew more and more into a shell and grew increasingly moody, communication between them virtually evaporated.

The first year of married life found Stephen creatively productive. It also found him making the personal contact with Ed Christy and the Christy Minstrels that would inspire him to scale heights as a composer. Christy's name as a performer had for some time now been appearing on the title pages of Foster's early songs. On February 23, 1850, Foster communicated directly with Christy for the first time in a letter with which he submitted two songs for Christy's consideration, "De Camptown Races" and "Dolly Day." A year or so later he sold Christy performance rights before publication to "Oh, Boys, Carry Me 'Long" for ten dollars; and in 1852 he once again gave prepublication performing rights to Christy for ten dollars apiece to two of his minor Negro—or, as these songs were then called, "Ethiopian"—classics: "Massa's in de Cold, Cold Ground" and "Old Dog Tray." Both were successfully marketed as sheet music, "Massa's in de Cold, Cold Ground" selling about 75,000 copies during the first two years of publication, and "Old Dog Tray," 48,000.

The union of the Christy Minstrels as performers and Stephen Foster as songwriter brought into existence what is generally regarded as the most famous popular song ever written about a Negro. Sometime in 1851, Christy asked Foster for a new Negro number, and Foster complied with "Old Folks at Home" (or "Swanee River"), which he had then just completed, assigning to Christy not only the performing rights before publication but also the privilege of being listed as its composer. Foster's brother Morrison revealed many years later that the sum Christy paid the composer was $500, but it is extremely likely that his memory had proved false and that Christy had paid probably $15 or at the most $25. The Christy Minstrels introduced "Old Folks at Home" in 1851. Later that year the number was published by Firth, Pond, and Company, its title page describing it as an "Ethiopian melody . . . sung by the Christy Minstrels, written and composed by E. P. Christy."

While planning "Old Folks at Home," Foster asked his brother for a two-syllable name of a river for use in his song. Foster had already considered and rejected "Pedee" as not sufficiently euphonious. Foster's brother came up with "Yazoo," which was hardly better. Upon coming across Suwannee, a river in northern Florida, Foster remarked: "That's it, that's exactly it." But when he finally wrote his lyric, he changed the river's name to "Swanee."

The song became an immediate success after it was introduced by the Christy Minstrels. It was soon heard in minstrel shows all over the country. In less than a year over 40,000 copies of sheet music were sold, an impressive figure at a time when songs usually sold no more than 5,000 or 10,000 copies when successful; by 1854 the sale had reached 130,000. *The World,* on September 11, 1852, described it as "one of the most successful songs that has ever appeared in any country." It added: "The publishers keep two presses running on it, and sometimes three; yet, they cannot supply the demand." The Albany *State Register* noted that the song was "on everybody's tongue, and consequently in everybody's mouth. Pianos and guitars groan with it, night and day; sentimental ladies sing it; sentimental young gentlemen warble it in midnight serenades; volatile young bucks hum it in the midst of their business and pleasures; boatmen roar it out stentoriously at all times; all bands play it; amateur flute players agonize over it every spare moment; the street organs grind it out at every hour; and singing stars carol it on theatrical boards and at concerts."

A success of such dimensions inevitably inspired imitation. Songs sprouted out in luxuriant growth trying to capitalize on the popularity of "Old Folks at Home": "The Old Folks Are Gone," "Young Folks at Home," "The Home Ain't What It Used To Be," and so on. As for Foster's financial return from this giant success (the royalties still being assigned to him, even though Christy's name appeared on the sheet music as composer), it did not go beyond $2,000.

Nevertheless, a solid success it certainly was, and Foster was proud of that. Up to now, he had been condescending toward his Negro (or "Ethiopian") songs, regarding them of less value artistically than his other types of ballads. In fact, his opinion of "Old Folks at Home" was so low that it was he who had suggested that Christy's name appear as its composer. But once "Old Folks at Home" became popular, Foster had serious second thoughts about passing off his own "Ethiopian" songs as the work of others. On May 25, 1852, he wrote to Christy: "As I once intimated to you, I had the intention of omitting my name on my Ethiopian songs, owing to the prejudice against them by some, which might injure my reputation as a writer of another style of music. But I find that by my efforts I have done a great deal to build up a taste for the Ethiopian songs among refined people by making the words suitable to their taste. . . . Therefore I have concluded to reinstate my name on my songs and to pursue the Ethiopian business without fear or shame and lend all my energies to making the business live, at the same time that I will wish to establish my name as the best Ethiopian songwriter." He now proposed that his own name replace that of Christy on all future published copies of "Old Folks at Home." We do not know if Christy replied. In any event, it was a long time before Foster was publicly credited with being the composer of this classic; and even after Foster's death, when the copyright came up for renewal, the question of Christy's authorship presented no end of complications.

But in the songs that Foster wrote for Christy after May of 1852, his own name appeared on the title page, though he still proved highly reluctant to charge Christy more than a pittance for the performing rights before publication. And his best "Ethiopian" endeavors were still being written for and introduced by the Christy Minstrels. These included "Massa's in de Cold, Cold Ground" in 1852 and "My Old Kentucky Home" in 1853.

"My Old Kentucky Home" was Foster's only Negro song inspired by an actual place visited by the composer. This was Federal Home, a stately pillared mansion near Bardstown, the Kentucky home of Judge John Rowan, a member of the United States Senate in 1828 and one of Foster's relatives. Foster visited this place with his wife in 1852, the first time he stepped foot in the South (even though he had already written sentimental ballads about it). In 1922 a subscription was raised to purchase the old house, which was then deeded as a museum to the state of Kentucky. The memorial tablet in the front hall states that Foster actually wrote his ballad at Federal Home, but this is definitely not the case.

An actual person was the inspiration for Foster's last significant ballad about the Negro, and the only one that is not in a Negro dialect—"Old Black Joe." Joe was a slave employed by the McDowell family when Foster used to visit Jane before their marriage. "Some day I am going to put you in a song," Foster told Joe one day. Foster did, but not until 1860 when Joe was dead.

In 1860 the issue of slavery was being grimly decided on the battlefield. There was a sharply decreased interest in sentimental songs about the Negro and nostalgic songs about the Southland. Even if Foster had been able to sustain his former high level of inspiration, he would not have been able to find a wide public any longer for his Negro ballads. Recognizing the grim fact that his market was melting away, Foster turned his creativity into other kinds of ballads. He had, of course, previously written many sentimental ballads that were not about Negroes—for example, his two most famous love songs, "Jeanie with the Light Brown Hair" in 1854 and "Come Where My Love Lies Dreaming" in 1855. But after 1860 he concentrated his creative powers and imagination to subjects far removed from the Negro and the South: to mother, home, love, and the Civil War. "Beautiful Dreamer," which he completed in 1864 only a few days before his death, is one of a meager handful worth remembering.

Late in 1860 Foster went with his wife and daughter to live in New York. He may have made this move because he had recently negotiated a new contract with his publisher and wanted to be closer to his market. Or, as some maintain, he may have become lonely in Pittsburgh, since many members of his immediate family were now either dead or living in other cities. "Whatever the reasons," comments John Tasker Howard, "it was the worst possible move Stephen could have made. New York was not the place for him. Perhaps there was a spot where he could have been happier, or where he might have avoided his sad fate, but certainly the cosmopolitan surroundings of New York, unfriendly to strangers who could not adjust themselves to its environment and withstand its pitfalls, did not offer an atmosphere in which Stephen could either flourish or exist."

He was prolific in New York (there was simply no stemming that creative flood). He produced over one hundred songs. Most, however, were just pot-boilers, hurriedly concocted to produce a quick (though minuscule) financial return, since his earnings from royalties were no longer capable of providing him with even basic necessities. As he lamented in the lyric of his song, "That's What's the Matter," in 1862:

> *We live in hard and stirring times,*
> *Too sad for mirth, too rough for rhymes,*
> *For songs of peace have lost their chimes,*
> *And that's what's the matter.*

A rapidly declining demand for his songs, and with them diminishing financial returns, came hand in hand with physical and moral deterioration. Foster was not well. He was suffering from fevers symptomatic of tuberculosis. He was becoming increasingly morose. More frequently than ever he would now reach to the bottle as an escape from despair and frustrations, an escape that could be effected only after he had drunk himself into a complete stupor. He allowed himself to sink helplessly into the morass of self-pity and squalor. His wife and daughter could finally take these developments no longer. They fled from New York and returned to Pittsburgh, leaving Foster to complete the process of self-destruction without an attending audience, in a miserable room at the American Hotel in the Bowery.

George Cooper tells the rest of the story (as quoted by Harold V. Milligan from a remembered conversation):

"Early one winter morning, I received a message saying that my friend had met with an accident; I dressed hurriedly and went to 15 Bowery, the old lodging house where Stephen lived, and found him lying on the floor in the hall, blood oozing from a cut in his throat and with a bad bruise on his forehead. Stephen never wore any night clothes and he lay there on the floor, naked, and suffering horribly. He had wonderful big brown eyes and they looked up at me with an appeal I can never forget. He whispered, 'I'm done for,' and begged for a drink, but before I could get it for him, the doctor who had been sent for arrived and forbade it. He started to sew up the gash in Stephen's throat, and I was horrified to observe that he was using black thread. 'Haven't you any white thread,' I asked, and he said no, he had picked up the first thing he could find. I decided the doctor was not much good and I went downstairs and got Stephen a big drink of rum, which I gave him and which seemed to help him a lot. We put his clothes on him and took him to the hospital. In addition to the cut on his throat and the bruise on his forehead, he was suffering from a bad burn on his thigh, caused by the overturning of a spirit lamp used to boil water. This had happened several days before, and he had said nothing about it, nor done anything for it. All the time we were caring for him, he seemed terribly weak and his eyelids kept fluttering. I shall never forget it."

Stephen Foster died in Bellevue Hospital in New York on January 13, 1864. His remains were taken to Pittsburgh where funeral services were held on January 21. At the cemetery gate, the funeral cortège was met by a brass band playing "Old Folks at Home" and "Come Where My Love Lies Dreaming." Foster was put to final rest in a grave beside that of his father.

Three pennies and scrip worth thirty-five cents were the extent of his wealth when he died—these and a library of songs that have never been forgotten, and the best of which have never been equaled.

GREAT MEN OF AMERICAN POPULAR SONG

Songs of the Negro–II

James A. Bland

The minstrel show remained popular up until the end of the nineteenth century. Ed Christy's famous troupe was taken over by his adopted son. As the years passed, other minstrel troupes came to prominence: those headed by Primrose and West, Lester and Allen, Billy Emerson, McIntyre and Heath, Al G. Field, Lew Dockstader. The format and the basic routines remained inflexible, but always there were new songs to contribute novelty and freshness.

Before the Civil War the main minstrel-show companies were made up of white performers blackening their faces. Though songs and dances and routines were all Negro in origin, the minstrel show was an avenue of entertainment closed to Negro performers; audiences preferred having their Negro entertainment presented by white people.

After the Civil War, however, all-Negro troupes sprang into being, offering a significant stage medium for gifted Negro entertainers. Some of these Negro companies became highly successful; for example, Callender's Original Georgia Minstrels, Billy Kersand's Minstrels, and the Callender-Haverly Minstrels. These and similar companies provided a highly important avenue through which Negro entertainers and songwriters could travel to popularity and fame.

Out of these Negro minstrel companies there stepped the most significant composer of sentimental Negro songs and songs about the Southland since Stephen Foster's time. He was James A. Bland, a Negro.

Most emancipated Negroes who had musical or theatrical ambitions and who made a beeline for the stage came from backgrounds as humble culturally and socially as they were economically. This had not been the case with Bland. Born in Flushing, New York, on October 22, 1854, he came from a family that had not suffered the terrible scars of slavery. After James A. Bland came into the world, his father went on to get a college education (one of the first Negroes to do so). Diploma in hand, he then became the first Negro ever appointed as examiner in the United States Patent Office.

His post made him bring his family to Washington, D. C., where young James received his early education in the public schools. He was a musical child, always singing to his own banjo accompaniment. In boyhood he worked as a page in the House of Representatives. This work brought him into personal contact with Washington notables, some of whom hired him to perform at their parties or at the exclusive Manhattan Club.

Upon being graduated from high school, James entered Howard University for an education in the liberal arts. His father enrolled with him at the same time to study law. James went through the four-year course with top honors, but his boyhood passion for singing songs and for creating them had not fallen by the wayside. In fact, even as a college student, he became convinced that his future lay in the theatre.

He tried to get a job with a minstrel company as soon as he received his college degree. But minstrel companies did not employ Negroes, and for a while Bland encountered nothing but frustration. But in 1875 an all-Negro troupe directed by Billy Kersand was beginning to find a market, and it was here that Bland got his first job as stage entertainer. Appearances with Billy Kersand's troupe gave Bland a forum in which to present his own songs which he was now creating prolifically, words as well as music. He kept on writing his songs and most often introducing them himself after leaving Billy Kersand to become a member of Callender's Original Georgia Minstrels managed by the Frohman brothers.

Bland's first huge success as a song composer came with a number with which his name will always be affiliated, a number that won him his claim to immortality in popular music. It was "Carry Me Back to Old Virginny," written in 1878, and introduced by George Primrose and his minstrels, after which it became a favorite of minstrel-show troupes, white *and* black. His stimulation to write this classic came at a plantation on the James River in the Tidewater section of Virginia near Williamsburg. Visiting this peaceful setting, Bland was suddenly reminded of a dream described to him by a young lady who was then a fellow student at Howard University. She had told Bland that in her dreams she had seen herself being "carried back to old Virginny," the place "where I was born." The plantation on James River, Bland felt in 1878, must have been just the kind of place the young lady had talked about. He decided to write about Virginia in a ballad, putting the feelings of nostalgia into the heart of an old Negro rather than into that of a young college girl.

The success of "Carry Me Back to Old Virginny" both at its premiere and during its presentations elsewhere marked only the beginning of its history. The last chapters of this story dates closer to our own times than to Bland's. In 1940 the Virginia legislature decreed that Bland's ballad become the official song of its state. When a tombstone was erected on Bland's grave in Merion, Pennsylvania, six years after that, Governor William A. Tuck of Virginia brought further recognition to Bland's song classic by saying: "James Bland put into ever-ringing verse and rhyme an expression of feeling which all Virginians have for their state. 'Carry Me Back to Old Virginny' tells in inspiring song the innate patriotism and love of native heath of all our people, white and Negro alike."

The plantation near Williamsburg which had inspired "Carry Me Back to Old Virginny" was also responsible for the writing of two other unforgettable ballads, both written by Bland in 1879 and both introduced by the composer himself as a member of Callender's Original Georgia Minstrels. They were "In the Morning in the Bright Light" and "In the Evening by the Moonlight." The second is the more famous of the two. Bland wrote it after seeing a group of Negroes sitting before their cabins in the Tidewater section, singing spirituals as they accompanied themselves on the banjo.

Before the year of 1879 ended, Bland contributed one more minstrel-show favorite to the song repertory, "Oh! Dem Golden Slippers." He produced it for the Original Georgia Minstrels as a walk-around. In 1880 Bland wrote and saw introduced two more of his songs that soon took the limelight at minstrel shows everywhere, "Hand Me Down My Walking Cane" and "De Golden Wedding."

When the Callender-Haverly Minstrels began a two-year tour of Europe beginning with 1881, James Bland was one of its star performers as well as contributor to its song repertory. In fact, "Oh! Dem Golden Slippers" was one of the numbers that inspired an ovation when the company made its bow in London at His Majesty's Theatre. When the tour was over, Bland decided to stay in England where in subsequent appearances on the stage he was billed as "The Prince of Negro Songwriters." He even gave command performances for Queen Victoria and the Prince of Wales. He earned a good deal of money but it all dribbled through his fingers. When his popularity was finally on the decline, and bookings became first scarce and then nonexistent, he found himself a pauper.

He came back to the United States in 1901. How he managed to scrape together the price of passage is not known. In America he found a minor desk job in Washington, D. C., which kept him from starvation. But he did not hold this post very long. He left Washington in the early 1900's for Philadelphia where he stayed the rest of his life in the depths of squalor and despair. When he died in Philadelphia, on May 5, 1911, no newspaper took notice of it; and

when he was buried in a Negro cemetery in Merion, Pennsylvania, his grave was
not marked.

More than a quarter of a century passed before posthumous recognition
came his way. In 1939 ASCAP (the American Society of Composers, Authors,
and Publishers) provided the funds to locate and landscape Bland's grave and
to erect a headstone which credited him with having written six hundred songs.
It is probable that Bland wrote that many, since most of what he produced was
not copyrighted, and a good many were lifted by performers who did not hesitate
to claim them as their own. The Library of Congress now lists only fifty-three
songs as definitely Bland's work, and has copies of just thirty-eight of these.
Even if this were the sum total of Bland's achievement, he would still stand as
one of Stephen Foster's most significant successors in the writing of songs for
minstrel shows and songs about the Negro.

GREAT MEN OF AMERICAN POPULAR SONG

Songs of the Civil War–I

George Frederick Root

Many and varied were the passions released by the outbreak of the Civil War: exaltation born of missionary ardor and patriotism; bitterness sprung from hatred and frustrations; heartaches caused by the absence of loved ones. All the varying shades of such feelings, down to the subtlest nuances, found outlet in popular songs. No other American war aroused such an intensity of emotion; and, as an interesting corollary, no other war produced such an eruption of popular-song literature. Over ten thousand songs were inspired by the Civil War. This huge output constitutes a stirring human document, betraying the innermost sentiments on both sides in the struggle. No facet of the war failed to find an echo in song. Indeed, it is altogether possible to re-create the entire history of the conflict through songs.

In the South they sang "Dixie," the work of a Northerner. Almost as if in compensation—or perhaps to complete a paradox—the favorite war song of the North was the work of a Southerner: for "The Battle Hymn of the Republic," with words by Julia Ward Howe, used the melody, "Say, Brothers Will You Meet Us?" the work of William Steffe, a Southern composer of Sunday school songs, and a tune familiar in Southern camp meetings of Negro congregations.

The South, of course, produced war songs of its own, but usually just the lyrics, while the melodies were lifted from various sources. "Maryland, My Maryland," for example, borrowed the famous tune of the German Christmas hymn "O Tannenbaum." "The Bonnie Blue Flag" appropriated the melody of the Irish ditty "The Jaunting Car."

When original melodies were created, they usually came from the North; and some of the best came from George Frederick Root, who is credited with having produced more war songs than any other single person.

Root was a professional musician who, through his contributions to education, had been a powerful force in developing a musical culture in America. He was born in Sheffield, Massachusetts, on August 30, 1820, a descendant of John Roote, one of the first settlers in Farmington, Connecticut. When George Frederick was six, his family moved to North Reading, also in Massachusetts. As a young man, he was sent to Boston in 1838 for intensive musical training. There he found a sympathetic teacher in A. N. Johnson, whose assistant he soon became both as a teacher and as an organist. In Boston, Root met Lowell Mason, one of America's leading music educators. For a while Root assisted Mason in directing the Academy of Music in Boston.

When Root was twenty-four, he came to New York. There he earned his living teaching music in girls' schools and in playing the organ at church. In August of 1845 he married Marie Olive Woodman, a gifted singer. Five years later found him and his wife traveling in Europe where he took lessons in singing from Giulio Alary and Jacques Pothart, besides absorbing whatever musical experiences were available. Upon returning to the United States he followed Mason's example by becoming involved in music education. He helped found a school in New York to train music teachers—the Normal Institute, where Mason was one of the instructors. Like Mason, he helped initiate conventions attracting music teachers from all parts of the East to study and discuss methods of class instruction in singing.

Root's first activity as composer came in 1851 when he wrote the music for a little school play performed by his pupils. His admiration for the songs of Stephen Foster soon led him to write a popular song of his own. Then he turned to sentimental ballads, achieving success with two lugubrious numbers, "The Hazel Dell" in 1853 and "Rosalie, the Prairie Flower" in 1855. He sold the first outright for a small cash settlement. When he offered the second one for $100, the publishing house of Russell and Richardson, expecting a limited sale, preferred a royalty arrangement. This arrangement brought Root several thousands of dollars. For these popular endeavors, Root hid his identity behind the pseudonym of "Wurzel" (the word "Wurzel" being German for "root"). But his mounting success finally convinced him to use his own name for his later songwriting activity.

Root wrote hymns as well as ballads during this period. In 1854 he had published "There's Music in the Air" which many years later became popular as a college song. Between 1853 and 1855 his most celebrated sacred song was released, the evangelical hymn "The Shining Shore."

In 1859 Root settled in Chicago where he found employment as a printer in the publishing establishment his brother had founded one year earlier and in which he himself had a small investment: Root and Cady. Then came the firing on Fort Sumter. Only three days after the attack that set the fuse to the Civil War, Root had his first war song written, printed, and ready for circulation. He called it "The First Gun Is Fired." Typical of the earliest songs of the Civil War, this one was a summons for action, an appeal for courage.

In 1861 he wrote another stirring call to the colors, "Forward, Boys, Forward," and with it his first sentimental war ballad aimed at the home front, "The Vacant Chair." Henry J. Washburn's poem "The Vacant Chair" had been written to commemorate the death of Lieutenant John William Grout of the 15th Massachusetts Volunteer Infantry, who had been killed just as he was about to come home for Thanksgiving on a furlough. The poem then described how his chair at the family dinner had been left empty. By 1861 many a family had a vacant chair at their dinner tables, the reason that Root's ballad affected so many people in both the North and the South.

Root's greatest war song of all, indeed one of the unqualified song classics of the Civil War, appeared in 1862. It was "The Battle Cry of Freedom." Root once revealed that the idea for it came in a flash upon learning that President Lincoln had appealed for forty additional army regiments and more seamen for the navy. Writing "The Battle Cry of Freedom" (or "We'll Rally 'Round the Flag") took a single morning. Hardly was the ink dry on paper when the Lombard Brothers, a popular singing attraction, entered the offices of Root and Cady in search of fresh material for their act. A glance at the manucript of "The Battle Cry of Freedom" convinced them that this was precisely the kind of stuff they were looking for. They introduced the song on July 24, 1862, during a war rally outside the Chicago courthouse. Several days later, the Singing Hutchinsons presented it at a rally at New York's Union Square, where the vociferous audience demanded several repetitions.

The inspirational and morale impact of this song on the fighting men can hardly be accurately estimated. Several unidentified soldiers have left written accounts of the way in which the song had affected their own troops. One such soldier described the depths to which both the spirit and the morale of the Union soldiers had plunged in 1863. Then he added: "By a happy accident, the glee club which came down from Chicago a few days afterwards, brought with them the brand new song, 'We'll Rally 'Round the Flag, Boys,' and it ran through the camp like wildfire. The effect was little short of miraculous. It put as much spirit and cheer into the camp as a splendid victory. Day and night you could hear it by every camp fire and in every tent. Never shall I forget how those men rolled out the line: 'And although he may be poor, he shall never be a slave.' "

To a Confederate major the hearing of this song as sung by some captured Union soldiers was his first strong conviction that the South must lose the war.

"I shall never forget the first time I heard 'Rally 'Round the Flag.' 'Twas a nasty night during the 'Seven Days' Fight,' and if I remember rightly, it was raining. I was on picket when, just before taps, some fellow on the other side struck up the song and others joined in the chorus until it seemed to me that the whole Yankee army was singing. Tom B——, who was with me, sang out 'Good Heavens, cap, what are those fellows made of, anyway? Here we've licked 'em six days running, and now on the eve of the seventh, they're singing 'Rally 'Round the Flag.' I am not naturally superstitious, but I tell you that the song sounded to me like the 'knell of doom' and my heart went down into my boots; and though I've tried to do my duty, it has been an uphill fight with me ever since that night."

"The Battle Cry of Freedom" was sung throughout the country—both at home and on the battlefield. Within two years of publication, 350,000 copies of sheet music had been sold, a figure with few precedents at the time. The immense popularity of the war ballad led Root to mention and quote it in another of his successful war songs, "Just Before the Battle, Mother," in 1863:

> *Hear the "Battle Cry of Freedom,"*
> *How it swells upon the air,*
> *Oh, yes, we'll rally 'round the standard,*
> *Or we'll perish nobly there.*

On April 14, 1865, when Major Anderson helped raise the flag at Fort Sumter to mark the end of the war, the melody of "The Battle Cry of Freedom" floated from across the bay where it was then being performed in the streets of Charleston. President Lincoln told Root: "You have done more than a hundred generals and a thousand orators." Even after the war, this song lost little of its appeal or its power to influence audiences. It was heard at the presidential convention of 1867 and proved a powerful means of creating the proper atmosphere in which General Ulysses S. Grant could be nominated. In 1896, when a monument was erected in Chicago to Root, Jules Lombard temporarily deserted his retirement to sing the ballad he had helped to introduce—before a cheering crowd numbering some ten thousand.

Before the war had ended, Root had written in 1863 the most successful song on the subject of war prisoners: "Tramp! Tramp! Tramp!" By 1863 there had been a good deal of concern among Northern families about the fate of loved ones who had been captured and incarcerated. By depicting the thoughts and emotions of a sad and lonely Union captive, as he dreams of freedom and home, Root once again touched a sensitive nerve that made a whole country throb as if in reflex action. Root wrote "Tramp! Tramp! Tramp!" to fill an empty page in the Christmas issue of the house organ of Root and Cady. When his brother first saw the manuscript, he demonstrated little enthusiasm, remarking: "You've certainly written better numbers before." Nevertheless, "Tramp! Tramp! Tramp!" was Root's greatest song success next to "The Battle Cry of Freedom." He tried to capitalize upon that success by writing a sequel in "On, On, On, the Boys Came Marching." And soon after the end of the war, he tried once again to achieve success with a prisoner's song, "Starved in Prison," in which the captive was doomed to die without ever again seeing home and family.

The end of the war stopped the flow of Root's creativity. He had apparently lost his prime stimulus. He stayed on with the firm of Root and Cady until 1871 when the disastrous Chicago fire destroyed the firm. Its catalogue, plates, and copyright were then acquired by John Church, a Cincinnati firm that opened a branch in Chicago called George F. Root and Sons. For a while, Root was its director, then he resumed his onetime profession of teaching music. In 1872 the University of Chicago conferred on him an honorary doctorate in music.

In 1886 Root paid a belated return visit to England to study its methods in teaching singing. Back in America, he went into retirement. He died on Bailey's Island, off the coast of Maine, on August 6, 1895. Two days after his death, Charles A. Dana, the editor of the New York *Sun*, wrote: "George Root did more to preserve the Union than a great many brigadier generals, and quite as much as some brigades."

GREAT MEN OF AMERICAN POPULAR SONG

Songs of the Civil War–II

Henry Clay Work

Only Henry Clay Work rivaled Root in the production of Civil War song classics. Work, like Root, had been born in New York; like Root, he lived in Chicago where he wrote his war ballads; and like Root, he had these ballads published by the house of Root and Cady.

Henry Clay Work was a descendant of Joseph Work who had come to Connecticut from his native Ireland in 1720. In that state, in the town of Middletown, Henry Clay was born on October 1, 1832. Three years later the family moved to Quincy, Illinois. There the father, a rabid abolitionist, used his home as a way station for the "underground railway" through which Southern slaves fled to Northern freedom. The older Clay became responsible for the liberation of several thousand slaves, an activity that finally sent him to prison. Upon his release, in 1845, the Work family returned to Middletown, where the boy Henry

41

Clay received some schooling. He was then apprenticed to Elihu Greer, a printer. In the attic of Greer's printshop stood a neglected melodeon upon which young Work taught himself the elements of making music. With these at his fingertips, he wrote his first song in the early 1850's, "We Are Coming, Sister Mary," which the publishing house of Firth, Pond issued, and which the Christy Minstrels introduced.

In 1855 Work came to Chicago. He found a job setting music type, a skill in which he soon became such a specialist that he produced some of his own songs directly on type without the preliminaries of working them out on the piano or writing them down on paper.

Work's first success as songwriter came in a Christy minstrel show, even as his debut as composer had previously taken place there. That success came with an antislavery song, "Kingdom Coming," Work's first ballad about the Negro; it was written early in 1862 in Negro dialect. Somewhat timidly, he brought his manuscript to Root and Cady and was conducted into George F. Root's private office. Root described Work as "a quiet and rather solemn looking young man, poorly clad." Root's first reading of the manuscript convinced him that the song was "full of bright, good sense and comical situations in its darky dialect, the words fitting the melody . . . and the whole exactly suited to the times." Root and Cady not only accepted the song for publication, but paid for provocative advertisements to promote curiosity and interest in the number a full week before its release. The Christy Minstrels introduced it on April 23, 1862, to make the song an immediate success. Negro troops then began to favor it, some reputed to have sung it during the closing days of the war while marching into Richmond. Further token of the song's popularity was its use in numerous imitations, parodies, and sequels. One of these was by Work himself, written in 1863 at the request of his publishers: "Babylon Is Fallen!", Work's second Negro song, also in dialect. Its strong abolitionist sentiment was inspired by the announcement that Negro soldiers would be recruited into the Union Army. In a similar vein—with pronounced abolitionist feelings—was "Wake Nicodemus!" in 1864. This song told about a dead Negro, buried in the hollow of a tree, who had pleaded to be awakened on "the day of Jubilo," the day when all Negroes would become freemen.

No more stirringly martial nor passionately patriotic hymn has come out of the Civil War than Work's masterpiece, "Marching Through Georgia." Work wrote it in 1865 as the war was coming to a victorious conclusion for the North. His inspiration had been one of the war's most celebrated campaigns: Sherman's dramatic "march to the sea" late in 1864, which split the Confederate Army into two, cut off some of the main lines of communications, brought the ravages of war to Southern soil, and culminated with the capture of Savannah. This maneuver spelled imminent doom for the Confederacy as the North was quick to realize and as Northern writers stood ready to rhapsodize in poems and songs. All these poems and songs have fallen by the wayside and been forgotten—all except one. The exception, "Marching Through Georgia," has survived, however, only to cause the South no end of displeasure. The South never ceased to regard it with bitterness as a tragic reminder of ignominious defeat, a "hymn of hate." As late as 1916, at the National Convention of the Democratic party, the Southern bloc was on the verge of defecting from the ranks because a poorly informed bandleader had his men strike up the strains of "Marching Through Georgia." Even General Sherman was hostile to the song, feeling as he did that it was responsible for having thrown his other brilliant military campaigns into a shade. "If I had thought when I made that march that it would have inspired anyone to compose a piece," he said at a convention of the G.A.R. in Boston in 1890, "I would have marched *around* the state."

But the popularity of "Marching Through Georgia" has remained unchecked by time. Its thrice-familiar melody was borrowed through the years to promote such causes as woman suffrage and the People's (Populist) party. The melody has also been used for square dances and for a football song at Princeton. It has been performed at probably every meeting, encampment, or parade in which the Grand Army of the Republic was involved. During World War I, British regiments leaving for France marched to its strains, and so did the American army during World War II when it entered Tunis.

One of Work's songs written during the Civil War period but without any war interest or suggestions provides a clue to the direction his creativity would take once that conflict was over. The direction would be toward sentimental balladry, and the clue comes with "Come Home, Father" in 1864. A story by Timothy Shay Arthur, *Ten Nights at a Barroom,* published in 1864, provided Work with the theme for his ballad. This story was often read or summarized at temperance meetings. William W. Pratt's dramatization of the story in 1868 was given many stage presentations and created such an impact upon its audiences that it is said to have been largely responsible for passing many temperance laws. The high dramatic moment in the play came when Mary, the child, appeared at the door of a saloon where she sang Work's "Come Home, Father." With the same intensity and passion he had brought to the problem of abolition, Work here presented the case for temperance. The child is pleading to her father to come home, since her brother, Benny, is sick in his mother's arms and "no one to help her but me." The dramatic ballad progresses to its tragic denouement with Benny's death, whose last words were that he wanted "to kiss Papa good night." The song was a real tear-jerker, no doubt about that. When the National Prohibition party was organized in Oswego, New York, as a political arm of the temperance movement, it adopted "Come Home, Father" as its theme song.

George F. Root's song career had come to a sudden stop with the ending of the Civil War. But this did not prove to be the case with Work, who went on to achieve even greater commercial successes than he had had during the Civil War. Those successes came with sentimental ballads, with "The Lost Letter," with "The Ship That Never Returned," and particularly with "Grandfather's Clock." The last of these was the most successful sentimental ballad of the 1870's; and it was the most successful song, from the point of view of sheet-music sale and financial returns, of Work's entire career. The ballad described a clock which stood ninety years on the floor. It had been purchased on the day Grandfather was born, and it stopped ticking on the day he died. Work wrote the ballad in 1876. It was introduced in the year of its composition in New Haven, Connecticut, by Sam Lucas of the Hyer Sisters Colored Minstrels. A million copies of sheet music were sold, something with few parallels in the song business up to that time.

Tragedy cast gloom over Work's last year. His wife, whom he had married in Chicago during the Civil War, was the victim of a mental disease, and two of his three children died. As a composer he had lost the golden touch, and his personal fortune had been jeopardized through an unfortunate land investment with his brother in Vineland, New Jersey. A broken man in more ways than one, Work died in Hartford, Connecticut, on June 8, 1884.

Songs of the Sentimental Nineties

Paul Dresser

The sentimental ballad—born in the Colonies with "The Banks of the Dee" during the American Revolution and grown to early manhood with Henry Russell, Stephen Foster, and Henry C. Work—dominated the popular-song literature of the 1880's and 1890's. The American people sang, listened, and responded to songs on many a theme to touch the heart: mother, frustrated love, fallen virtue and broken homes, abandoned wives and infants, lovers' quarrels and separations through slight misunderstandings, interrupted wedding ceremonies and brides left at the altar, loneliness and old age, fickleness and constancy, birth and death. The fabric of a complete story would be woven with the threads of a series of verses. Invariably the story preached the moral that virtue was its own reward. After all, the family circle was still the largest market for sheet-music sale, and in the family circle, sound moral standards had to be guarded jealously.

So large was the demand for sentimental ballads that between 1880 and the turn of the new century many publishing houses were built on the cornerstone of just a single hit song. Many a firm—founded with hope, ambition, and a single manuscript, and financed with pennies—bulged suddenly into major powers in the song industry because the singing public had taken a ballad to its heart. This happened, for example, in 1891 to M. Witmark and Sons with Charles Graham's "The Picture That Is Turned Toward the Wall"; to Charles K. Harris's publishing house with Harris's own "After the Ball"; to Joseph W. Stern and Company in 1894 with "The Little Lost Child"—words by Edward B. Marks (a salesman of buttons) and music by Joseph W. Stern (a salesman of neckties); to Leo Feist and Company, in 1894 with Monroe Rosenfeld's "And Her Golden Hair Was Hanging Down Her Back."

One of the first publishers to concentrate its main interest and activity on the sentimental ballad was the house of Willis Woodward. It struck gold with one of its first publications, Banks Winter's "White Wings," a saga of a sailor's return home to his sweetheart after a long absence on the high seas. Banks himself had introduced the song in Boston in 1884 with the Thatcher, Primrose, and West Minstrels, but it did not attract attention until later the same year, at Niblo's Gardens in New York. Pat Howley, then employed by the newly established firm of Willis Woodward, recognized its potential and published it in 1884. This represented Willis Woodward's first big song. By 1887, with the release of Charles Graham's "If the Waters Could Speak As They Flow," Willis Woodward was solidly established as a house of hit sentimental ballads.

In 1887 Willis Woodward helped carve popular-music history by publishing "The Outcast Unknown" not because this ballad had particular significance either in sheet-music sales or in the making of a performing star. The release of "The Outcast Unknown" opens a significant chapter in American popular-song history because its author was soon to become one of the foremost creators of sentimental ballads of his generation.

He was Paul Dresser, born in Terre Haute, Indiana, on April 21, 1857. His name was originally John Paul Dreiser, and he was the older brother (by twelve years) of one of America's most distinguished novelists, Theodore Dreiser.

The Dreiser home was the breeding ground for religious ardor that bordered on fanaticism, superstition, even ignorance, since the father was a man driven by religious mania. Every morning and every evening he had his family kneel in prayer. Each member felt his strong hand of discipline whenever the child wavered, however slightly, from the inflexible line of religious precepts he had been taught. Since Paul, the oldest member of the Dreiser clan, was an unruly, undisciplined boy who was always getting into trouble, he was a perpetual victim of his father's wrath. Convinced, at last, that he could not cope with his boy's seeming incapacity to differentiate between right and wrong, the father placed him in a seminary near Evansville, Indiana, where he hoped Paul would begin his training for the priesthood.

From the beginning, Paul's interest lay in music and the stage. By himself he learned to play the piano and the guitar and managed to acquire a repertoire of minstrel-show tunes which he sang to his own accompaniment. The seminary, then, was an alien world to him. When he was sixteen, he broke ties permanently not only with school but also with home. He appeared as a blackface performer and wrote comedy songs for a traveling medicine show that sold a "wizard oil." He abandoned the troupe in Cincinnati to join a minstrel show that made one-night stands where he was featured as "the sensational comique." In New York, soon afterward, he performed minor roles at Harry Miner's Bowery Theatre before becoming end man for the Thatcher, Primrose, and West Minstrels. Now twenty-three, and comparatively affluent, he changed his name to Paul Dresser (because he felt it would be easier for audiences to remember) and began to put on weight and enjoy the life of a *bon vivant*. He was also beginning to pursue the career of songwriter vigorously. He collected his best numbers into a *Paul Dresser Songster* which he had published and which he sold in the theatre to his audiences.

The partiality of minstrel shows for sentimental ballads led Dresser to produce a number of such songs which became minor successes. One was "I Believe It for My Mother Told Me So," which made Theodore Dreiser weep when Paul sang it for his family for the first time. Another was "The Letter That Never Came," the composer's catharsis upon suffering a frustrated love affair. The latter was performed for the first time by a minstrel troupe in Brooklyn and was published by the firm of T. B. Harms. Pat Howley, the pint-sized hunchback who worked for Willis Woodward, was impressed by it and bought Dresser's "The Outcast Unknown."

"The Outcast Unknown," while bringing Willis Woodward a profit, was no bonanza by any means. Nevertheless, Pat Howley remained convinced that Paul Dresser had uncommon talent as a songwriter and did what he could to persuade the young man to give up acting for good and concentrate on songs. Since this is precisely what Dresser wanted to do anyway, the argument fell on receptive ears. His acting career behind him, Dresser wrote, and Willis Woodward published in 1888, "The Convict and the Bird," which wept copious tears over the plight of a prisoner doomed to spend his life in a cell. A bird, alighting on the windowsill, sang to the convict of sunshine and of freedom. "Come to me each day, come to me, I pray," the convict pleaded to the bird. But, one day, when the bird came to sing his song of hope and cheer, there was no audience to hear him, for the convict was lying dead in his cell. Another Dresser ballad that found its subject matter behind the prison bars was "The Pardon Came Too Late" in 1891.

The 1890's were at hand, a time when the sentimental ballad was in its heyday. His apprenticeship well behind him, his first successes in hand, Paul Dresser entered the decade of the nineties where he would become one of the most successful exponents of the sentimental ballad.

The 1890's have been described as "gay," and to a large degree they were that. This was a prosperous era for the few who had successfully exploited the country's limitless resources for their own profit. Trusts sprang into existence. Uncrowned kings of industry and utility magnates became tycoons. They lived high, wide, and handsome. Elaborately decorated, even flamboyant, establishments like the Imperial Hotel, which now stood in stately grandeur on Broadway and Thirty-second Street, arose to cater to the prevailing appetite for luxury and ornate display among the rich and the powerful. The rich overate, drank too much at places like Delmonico's or Sherry's or Rector's, the last of which was a yellow front building on the square then known as Longacre (now identified as Times). George Rector used to say proudly: "I found Broadway a quiet little lane of ham and eggs and left it a full-blown avenue of lobsters, champagne, and morning-afters." High society flowed toward Rector's and so did stage and opera stars, statesmen and journalists, gamblers and prizefighters, polo players and Wall Street investors. Jim Corbett, the fighter, could be seen here, and so could the journalist Richard Harding Davis, and Charles Dana Gibson, the artist who created the "Gibson girl," symbol of female sophistication as well as pulchritude; also the Vanderbilts, or the portly Diamond Jim Brady, with glamorous Lillian Russell under his arm. Theatres as well as restaurants were enjoying a new prosperity, places like the Casino where lavish musical productions were seen downstairs in the auditorium and upstairs on the roof. Everywhere pleasure reigned as king and glamour as queen.

This was essentially a man's world into which women who rocked the cradle did not intrude. But the women who dwelt on the other side of respectability —the great ladies of the theatre, for example—were deified. They were toasted in champagne and smothered with extravagant gifts, while the wives of the men who paid such lavish tribute remained at home in a world of their own, in which, perhaps, as an inevitable reaction, respectability was made a fetish. For respectability's sake, women swathed themselves in a multiplicity of garments: layers of petticoats, a tightly strapped corset, peekaboo shirtwaists with mutton sleeves. These women, who took such pains to conceal their bodies, regarded their "unfortunate" sisters, whose clothing made no pretense at concealment, with a mingling of contempt and pity, because so few of these would know the warmth, security, and fulfillment of home, husband, and children.

Most of the ballads of the 1890's reflected the pious attitudes of the women at home and the men's concept of how their wives and sisters and daughters should behave. Ballads extolled and sentimentalized over the noblest standards of propriety and behavior while condemning the baser attitudes. The potted palms in restaurants and living room; the lifted skirts in the musical show; the panoply of diamonds worn by a Lillian Russell or a Jim Brady; the champagne drunk from a lady's slipper in a *salle privée*—these tokens of a gay era are not discussed in the songs of the time; not all this, nor the pleasure domes of New York, nor the inebriating life of wine, woman, and song. The songs rather reflected what was acceptable to the "good" society of the time: the woman of the household who wore her virtue like a glittering tiara for all to see and admire; the man whose conscience was hardly ruffled by an assumed double standard of behavior.

Many a composer fed this market with such tear-drenched ballads as "Mother Was a Lady," "She Was Happy Till She Met You," "Two Little Girls in Blue," "She May Have Seen Better Days," "Gold Will Buy 'Most Anything But a True Girl's Heart," "A Bird in a Gilded Cage." Among these songwriters are Stern and Marks, Monroe H. Rosenfeld, Charles K. Harris, Jim Thornton, Harry von Tilzer.

None, however, reflected this period more vividly and more faithfully than Paul Dresser.

When Pat Howley left Willis Woodward to set up a publishing venture of his own in collaboration with F. B. Haviland, he took Paul Dresser with him as staff composer and partner. The first lists of the new firm of F. B. Haviland (which in 1894 changed its name to Howley, Haviland, and Company) included two minor Dresser items: "Once Ev'ry Year" and "Take a Seat, Old Lady." It was not long before Howley and Haviland grew in wealth and power, most of its strength emanating from the sale of Paul Dresser's ballads. The first of their big Dresser releases came in 1895, "Just Tell Them That You Saw Me." Dresser got the idea for this song by reading a newspaper account of how a woman was ruined by a reckless love affair. Dresser's song told how, walking down a street, a man caught sight of a young lady whom he had known in his hometown and who had obviously come upon unhappy times. "Is that you, Madge?" he asks. Then he pleads: "Don't turn away from me." She has only a single message for him to take home. "Just tell them that you saw me. . . . I'm coming home some day. Meanwhile, just tell them that you saw me." This ballad grew so popular that the phrase "just tell them that you saw me" became a favorite greeting throughout America in 1895. "Comedians on the stage," wrote Theodore Dreiser, "newspaper paragraphers, his bank teller or his tailor, even staid business men wishing to appear up to date, used it as a parting salute." A manufacturer capitalized on this vogue by creating and selling lapel buttons carrying the phrase in bold letters.

Dresser was increasingly productive during the next few years. Together with his quota of sentimental ballads came a good stock of war songs during the Spanish-American conflict. But it was with his sentimental ballads that he scored most decisively. Two of these ballads have special significance: his masterpiece, "On the Banks of the Wabash" in 1897, and "The Curse of the Dreamer" in 1899.

No more popular a number about the state of Indiana has ever been written than Dresser's "On the Banks of the Wabash." Theodore Dreiser once wrote that it was he who had suggested to his brother the idea for the song, pointing out how rivers had always been used to good advantage in song literature; Dreiser maintained he even helped Paul write the lyric.

Max Hoffman, a musician employed as orchestrator by the house of Witmark, told Isidore Witmark how and when Dresser wrote his ballad:

"I went to his room at the Auditorium Hotel [Chicago] where, instead of a piano there was a folding camp organ, Paul always carried with him. It was summer. All the windows were open and Paul was mulling over a melody that was practically in finished form. But he did not have the words. So he made me play the full chorus over and over again at least for two or three hours while he was writing down the words, changing a line here and a phrase there, until the lyric suited him. . . . When Paul came to the line, 'through the sycamores the candlelights are gleaming,' I was tremendously impressed. . . . I have always felt that Paul got the idea from glancing out of the window now and again as he wrote, and seeing the lights glimmering on Lake Michigan. . . . The song was published precisely as I arranged it. . . . During the whole evening we spent together, Paul made no mention of anyone's having helped him with the song."

The writing of "The Curse of the Dreamer" was enmeshed in the composer's tragic personal life. In the 1890's Dresser married May Howard, the first of the burlesque queens. May was incapable of constancy. Dresser became fully aware of her extramarital entanglements, but preferred to ignore them. Then May deserted him and their child to go off with another man. This led Dresser to canalize his profound bitterness in a ballad, "The Curse." He regarded the song as such a personal testament that he refused to have it published. Instead, he sought May out and sang his ballad to her. She was apparently touched by its sentiment, and a temporary reconciliation was effected. But it was not long before May became restless and was off hunting again. Once again he was deserted, and this time for good. He now rewrote "The Curse" to provide it with a happy ending. His new ballad was named "The Curse of the Dreamer," with which Dresser realized a resounding success.

By 1901 the importance of Dresser to the economy of his publishing house became officially recognized when it was renamed Howley, Haviland, and Dresser. Dresser was now at the height of his fame and prosperity. Child of the nineties as he was, he lived in the spirit of those times in baronial fashion, either at Gilsey House on Twenty-ninth Street or the Marlborough on Thirty-sixth, maintaining lavishly appointed suites at both. He was a familiar figure at such fashionable restaurants as Delmonico's and Metropole where he frequently entertained not only his friends but often even random acquaintances, in the same kind of regal style to which his own daily life conformed.

He was huge: three hundred pounds spread over six feet of bulk. And every ounce of him oozed with generosity and sentimentality. A needy friend, an actor without a booking, a family incapable of meeting funeral expenses, all found him ready with handsome monetary gifts. He carried a roll of twenty-dollar bills and was quick to remove one for a passing acquaintance obviously come upon hard times. He never passed a beggar by without handing out a dole, nor a horse in the street without feeding it sugar cubes, of which he kept an ample supply at all times. It was said of him that he had as much trouble curbing his beneficence as he did alcohol and women.

His natural sphere was Broadway with its glitter and gloss and its ample opportunities for lavish living. In that setting he contributed a good deal of luster of his own. As long as he enjoyed the sunshine of success, he was expansive, a friend to all, moving about with the air of a born cavalier. The half-million dollars he earned within a few years' time poured like liquid through his thick fingers.

But in the face of adversity he shriveled. And adversity descended with devastating suddenness. The sales of his ballads began showing a perceptible decline in 1902. By 1904 business had become so bad that Pat Howley decided to desert the firm to open a new one of his own, leaving Dresser and Haviland to flounder on what was rapidly resembling a sinking ship. That ship sank in 1905. The firm of Howley-Dresser went into bankruptcy. Dresser now went into business for himself by opening a modest two-room office on the street that has since come to be known as Tin Pan Alley, Twenty-eighth Street.

On that street an unprecedented prosperity was being enjoyed by most of the leading publishers. Million-copy sheet-music sales had become almost weekly occurrences. The new century had opened with the two-million-copy sale of Harry von Tilzer's "A Bird in a Gilded Cage." Before the first decade of the twentieth century was over, not only one but several songs had sold in the neighborhood of five million copies each: "Meet Me Tonight in Dreamland," "Down by the Old Mill Stream," and "Let Me Call You Sweetheart," for example. More than two billion copies of sheet music passed over the counters into customers' hands in those ten years, with a hundred songs achieving or passing the million-mark sale.

Against such a background, Dresser presented a sorry figure. He tried his best to put up an impressive front. He insisted upon coming to his office dressed in frock coat and high silk hat. He maintained (at least outwardly) an air of supreme confidence, insisting to his more fortunate colleagues and competitors that he was on the eve of returning into the groove of success, that the songs he was now writing were better than ever, that he would surely recapture his audiences. But he exuded from his person the subtle smell of failure, which the keen nostrils of his onetime friends and his now formidable competitors readily recognized. They turned away from him—some with derision, and others with pity.

What happened after that could have provided Dresser with the material of one of his lugubrious ballads. Dresser died of a heart attack (or was it a broken heart?) at his sister's home on January 30, 1906. Sick in bed, he continually thought he recognized portents of imminent disaster: now when he espied the number 13; now when he saw a broken horseshoe; now when somebody happened to leave a hat on his bed. "When I arrived," wrote Theodore Dreiser, "he was already cold in death, his soft hands folded over his chest, that indescribable sweetness of expression about his eyes and mouth—the empty shell of the beetle."

He died a man as broken in financial resources and in spirit as in health: he did not leave behind him even the money to pay for his funeral. Death had come to him with the bitter taste of hopeless failure in his mouth.

Yet immediately after his death, the last ballad he had written and published —and which he had been too poor to promote properly—suddenly left the ground and soared. It was "My Gal Sal"—"Sal" being a prostitute with whom he had once been in love and with whom he had lived in her brothel during his early manhood in Evansville, where he was then appearing at the Apollo Theatre. She was, as his song said, "a wild little devil, but dead on the level," and, apparently, he had never forgotten her.

"My Gal Sal" was published in 1905. Later the same year it was introduced in vaudeville by Louise Dresser, one of the meager few who had not deserted him. She was a young entertainer whom Dresser had discovered and whose budding career he had given an important lift. Out of gratitude for all of this, she had assumed Dresser's name. Then, perhaps still out of gratitude, she used Dresser's swan song in her vaudeville act. Before the year of 1906 was ended, the ballad sold several million copies, reaping a harvest for a broken man no longer alive to enjoy the victory. Many years later, in 1942, when Dresser's life story was produced for the screen with Victor Mature playing the composer, it was called *My Gal Sal*.

GREAT MEN OF AMERICAN POPULAR SONG

Songs from Tin Pan Alley

Harry von Tilzer

In or about 1903 a composer-lyricist-newspaperman and man about town by the name of Monroe Rosenfeld was preparing for the New York *Herald* a series of articles on American popular music. Seeking material, he came to 45 West Twenty-eighth Street where the offices of Harry von Tilzer were located. Von Tilzer was already a giant in the production of popular songs—both as a composer and as a publisher. While visiting von Tilzer, Rosenfeld happened to overhear the rasping sounds from a nearby old upright piano. To Rosenfeld those sounds resembled the noises from tin pans. A chain of thoughts led him to identify popular songs as "tin pan music" and the street where those songs were then being created with such fertility as "tin pan alley."

That Rosenfeld should have sought out Harry von Tilzer for material for his articles indicates the high station that this songwriter-publisher already occupied in the industry. That the term "tin pan alley" should have been concocted within von Tilzer's office is more significant still. For years, Harry von Tilzer was identified as "Mr. Tin Pan Alley." His career virtually parallels in time that of Tin Pan Alley. And when Tin Pan Alley died, Harry von Tilzer's career had also ended.

Harry von Tilzer was born in Detroit, Michigan, on July 8, 1872, with the name of Harry Gumm. He was one of five children (one of whom, Albert von Tilzer, also became a songwriter of considerable note). The family moved to Indianapolis when Harry was still a boy. There the father acquired a shoe shop beneath a loft in which a theatrical stock was giving performances. This was Harry's initiation into the theatre, and he fell in love with it at once. When he could muster the price of admission to more formal theatres, he would attend minstrel and burlesque shows, indeed any form of stage entertainment available in Indianapolis. Then he would sit around for hours in the lobby of the city's leading hotel just to catch a glimpse of some of the performers.

He ran away from home when he was fourteen, joining the Cole Brothers Circus with whom he did a tumbling act. One year after that he affiliated himself with a traveling repertory troupe where his varied functions included the playing of the piano (which he learned without any formal instruction), writing songs, and performing juvenile roles. Suspecting that his own name lacked euphony and would therefore be a deficit in a stage career, he now changed it to Harry von Tilzer. Tilzer was his mother's maiden name, to which he affixed a "von" to endow it with additional "class."

As Harry von Tilzer, he now performed with a burlesque company touring the Midwest. When the troupe arrived in Chicago, von Tilzer became acquainted with Lottie Gilson, star of musicals and vaudeville where she was known as "the little magnet" because of her drawing powers at the box office. Lottie liked the young performer, and she liked even better his song, "I Love You Both," which Willis Woodward published in 1892 (von Tilzer's first appearance in sheet music). He had by this time accumulated quite a number of manuscripts, some of which made a further impression on Miss Gilson. She gave him sound advice: He would find far greater rewards in songwriting than in acting, and he could find these rewards more readily in New York than in "the sticks."

Such advice from an established star was not to be dismissed, and von Tilzer did not dismiss it. By working as a groom for a trainload of horses he was able to gain transportation to New York. He arrived there in 1892, with just $1.65 in his pocket. He found a cheap room near the Brooklyn Bridge and a job as a saloon pianist and entertainer that paid him $15 a week.

Slowly his songs were becoming known. A few were presented at Tony Pastor's Music Hall at Union Square, where in 1896 von Tilzer himself was becoming a vaudeville entertainer by joining George Sidney in a German comedy routine. During this period he was writing songs by the carload, completing over a hundred during his first few years in New York. Some he sold outright to entertainers for two dollars apiece. A meager handful got published. One, "De Swellest Gal in Town," had a modest sheet-music sale after being introduced by the minstrel George H. Primrose.

But before the 1890's were over Harry von Tilzer had not a modest but a smash hit song in each of his two hands. First came "My Old New Hampshire Home." He wrote it, with his lyricist Andrew B. Sterling, late one night on the top-floor furnished room they were then sharing on Fifteenth Street. They had to work by the dim illumination provided by the lamplight outside on the street—compelled to keep their room dark for fear that their own light would betray to the landlady that they were home and bring her rushing in on them for past rent. Having put their song down on paper, they made the round of publishers in or near Union Square. There were no buyers. The best they could do was to sell it for fifteen dollars to a small neighborhood printshop owned by William C. Dunn. Even before "My Old New Hampshire Home" could prove itself, Dunn bought a second song from von Tilzer, "I'd Leave My Happy Home for You."

Whereas "My Old New Hampshire Home" had been a nostalgic, sentimental ballad, "I'd Leave My Happy Home for You" was a novelty coon song—one of the first of this species to become successful. True-to-life incidents often provided von Tilzer with song material, and his had happened in 1897 with "I'd Leave My Happy Home for You." At that time von Tilzer was appearing in a show in Hartford, Connecticut. After the performance a young girl came to him backstage, pleading for him to find a place for her in the theatre. Von Tilzer tried to get rid of her by telling her he might be able to do something when the run of his show was over. On closing night he found the girl waiting for him. She was ready to follow him anywhere, she said, even though it meant leaving the palatial home of her wealthy parents. "I'd leave my happy home for you," she told him. Von Tilzer dismissed the girl, but the girl herself and the line she had spoken about leaving her happy home fertilized into a song—a song with a mild Negro dialect. One of the unusual features of this song was that it was the first to use the interpolation of a cooing "oo–oo" in the refrain, something that others would imitate again and again in later years:

> I'd leave my happy home for you, oo–oo, oo–oo,
> You're de nicest man I ever knew, oo–oo, oo–oo,
> If you take me and just break me in de business, too, oo,
> I'd leave my happy home for you, oo–oo, oo–oo.

"My Old New Hampshire Home" was a feature of silver-toned tenors in vaudeville, and "I'd Leave My Happy Home" became such a tour de force for Blanche Ring that it helped to make her a star. The sheet music of both numbers moved in quantities. In time, "My Old New Hampshire Home" accumulated a sale of two million copies, while "I'd Leave My Happy Home" sold a million copies. Dunn suddenly found himself a publisher of influence, instead of a mere printer. And Harry von Tilzer, whose total income from these two solid money-makers was thirty dollars, had become recognized as a songwriter.

Harry von Tilzer had written and had published his first two hit songs in the Union Square section of New York. This was to be expected. At that time Union Square was the Mecca of the song industry.

Before 1890 publishers had been scattered not only in different areas of

New York but even in different parts of the country—in Boston, Chicago, Philadelphia, San Francisco. Just before 1890 Willis Woodward moved its offices to
the Star Building on Thirteenth Street in New York, a stone's throw from Union
Square. M. Witmark and Sons followed suit by coming to 32 East Fourteenth
Street, in the heart of Union Square. Before long, now one, now another, important publishing house found quarters in or near Union Square. Neophytes
among publishers—Stern and Marks, for example—also sought out Union
Square as the base of their operations. By the middle 1890's some of the leading
publishing houses of popular songs were all clustered around Union Square.
This was the first time that they were concentrated in a single restricted geographical area. It is for this reason that it can well be said that it was in Union
Square that Tin Pan Alley was born.

The drift of song publishers to Union Square was analogous to iron filings
moving toward a magnet. The magnet was the amusement and entertainment
places that flourished in that neighborhood. Here in Union Square could be
found Tony Pastor's Music Hall, temple of vaudeville. Here, too, were the
Alhambra and the Union Square Theatre, where lavish musical productions could
be seen. Here were the Academy of Music, home of grand opera and the Dewey
Theatre, a burlesque house. Here, too, were such famous restaurants as Luchow's
and Lienau's and such popular drinking places as Huber's Prospect Garden. Here,
too, was a veritable constellation of beer halls, sporting houses, saloons, penny
arcades.

All these places featured popular music. In doing so they provided a place
where the publishers could "plug" their songs. After all, the only way sheet
music could pass from the counter into the hands of an eager buying public was
by having melodies sung and played in so many different places and so frequently
that they became impregnated into the consciousness of a nationwide audience.

The concept that a song had to be "plugged" to success—in other words,
had to be sold to audiences through promotion and salesmanship the way any
other commodity was—was first crystallized in Union Square. This concept was
evolved by the newcomers in the business. The older publishers, before 1880,
were staid, dignified, standpat businessmen who expected a song hit to be born
and not made. They did little to get one of their songs placed. Frequently (as
had been the case with Stephen Foster) the composer himself had to find the
place where, and the performer with whom, the song got its hearing. These
older publishers sat in their offices and waited for performers to drop in and
pick up some number for their acts; accident or coincidence brought songs to
the notice of entertainers. These publishers did little or nothing to seek out performers and convince them to use specific songs; they would have regarded with
outright disdain or contempt the many devious methods evolved in Union Square
to get a performer to use a song. Such a lackadaisical approach on the part of
the publisher was hardly likely to yield an overabundance of hits. Before 1880
a million-copy sale of sheet music was close to a miracle; a hundred-thousand
copy represented a major success; while sales in the ten thousands were the norm.

But in the 1880's a new breed of publishers began to fertilize. They were
"go-getters" with enough initiative, drive, and imagination to get a song heard

and publicized. Some of these new publishers were printers; others had been salesmen in other fields of endeavor. Many were songwriters, grown weary of disposing of a brainchild for twenty-five dollars or so only to find the publisher reaping all the profits.

Willis Woodward was one of the first to give bribes to performers in minstrel shows and vaudeville to sing numbers published by his firm. Will Rossiter, in Chicago, was one of the first to go out himself into shops to sing his songs and to advertise his songs in trade journals. M. Witmark was one of the first to distribute free copies of sheet music to performing artists. Stern and Marks were the first to use salesmen on the road to market their products.

By the time publishers old and new had been firmly rooted in Union Square, the formula for plugging had been fully established. The song plugger was then usually the head of the publishing firm or the composer himself. Each evening they would visit neighboring restaurants, beer gardens, cafés, theatres, and brothels with pockets stuffed with copies of the latest songs. These would be handed out freely to anybody capable of bringing a song to an audience. Chorus slips, which had the words of the refrain, were distributed to the public so that they could join in the performance. A box of cigars, a free dinner, a modest gift, in some instances cash, proved to be the necessary oil keeping the machinery of song plugging working efficiently. Bribes were distributed freely, and the more freely they were distributed, the more often were the songs performed.

The fertile imagination of the song plugger was soon capable of devising many other ways of getting his songs heard. Singers were planted in the theatre audience. When the stage performer had completed singing a number, the "plant" would rise and sing the refrain several times more. This singing stooge became a fixture in burlesque houses and vaudeville from the time when Gus Edwards, then only fourteen, started the practice from the balcony of Hurtig and Seamon's burlesque house. Singers were also placed with water boys who, in those days, served patrons with drinking water. In 1894 still another method of song plugging was inaugurated: the song slide. First used to exploit "The Little Lost Child," these slides—which dramatized the story of the song by flashing still pictures on the screen, while the performer on the stage would sing the number—became such a favorite that for many years it was an inextricable part of the entertainment in many theatres throughout the country. And song slides proved such a stimulus for the sale of sheet music that De Witt C. Wheeler Company went into high gear in the manufacture of song slides. As many as a thousand sets of a single number were distributed around the country at one time.

Another concept came into being in Union Square: that songs could be manufactured for special events, to meet specialized needs of individual performers, to take advantage of current news, to comment on every passing fashion and fad. In Union Square the song business became a giant factory which manufactured songs from established matrixes. Composers and lyricists became specialists in certain types of song which they produced in wholesale numbers. Some of these writers were best known for sentimental ballads, some for nonsense songs, some for coon songs, some for ragtime songs.

As a songwriter, Harry von Tilzer proved versatile enough to become successful in all such styles. He produced hundreds of numbers as if on an assembly belt. As a publisher, too, he was a legitimate offspring of Union Square by taking advantage of all the new means and methods at a publisher's disposal in marketing a song and plugging it to a million-copy sale.

It did not take von Tilzer long to become his own publisher. On the strength of two publications like "My Old New Hampshire Home" and "I'd Leave My Happy Home for You," W. C. Dunn was able to find buyers for his publishing house. They were Lew Bernstein and Maurice Shapiro, newcomers to the song business. With extraordinary acumen and sound business judgment (which they would demonstrate again and again through the years), Shapiro and Bernstein realized how important von Tilzer could be to their organization. They won over his full support and his friendship by voluntarily paying him $4,000 as an advance on all the future sales of "My Old New Hampshire Home," in spite of the fact that they owned the number outright and were not required to pay its composer any further payments. In addition to this, they soon made von Tilzer a partner in their business, calling the firm Shapiro, Bernstein, and Von Tilzer.

Almost as if in compensation (or gratitude), von Tilzer now went on to write for his own firm one of his most successful ballads, indeed one of the most successful sentimental ballads of the entire era, "A Bird in a Gilded Cage," lyrics by Arthur J. Lamb. The song pointed up a moral so greatly favored by the 1890's, that gold does not buy happiness: The girl had married "for wealth not love" and "though she lived in a mansion grand," she was only "a bird in a gilded cage" whose "beauty was sold for an old man's gold."

It is believed that Lamb originally planned to make the girl in his lyrics the old man's mistress. It was von Tilzer, according to this account, who insisted that their song make it perfectly clear that the two people were married. If this account is accurate, von Tilzer's puritanism did not keep him from trying out his new ballad in a brothel. When he found the girls weeping, he knew he had a hit. The ballad *was* a hit, selling two million copies in only one year following its publication in 1900.

Such a success inspired Harry von Tilzer to break up his partnership with Shapiro and Bernstein and set up shop for himself as Harry von Tilzer Company. In 1902 he left Union Square. Following the lead of so many other music publishers at the time, he came to Twenty-eighth Street, a street soon to become baptized in von Tilzer's own office as Tin Pan Alley. Henceforth the name of Tin Pan Alley and American popular music would become synonymous.

This northward flow of publisher in general, and von Tilzer in particular, followed a direction already taken by opera, theatres, restaurants, beer parlors, and other places of amusement. As an entertainment center of the city, Union Square was rapidly yielding ground to an area farther uptown. The Casino Theatre was on Broadway and Thirty-ninth Street, just a stone's throw from the Metropolitan Opera House. Bustanoby's Restaurant was on Broadway and Thirty-ninth Street, and three streets away was the ultra-fashionable Rector's. Vaudeville had found a new home at the Fifth Avenue Theatre on Broadway and

Twenty-eighth Street, while the queen of vaudeville, Hammerstein's Victoria, would open on Forty-second Street and Broadway in 1904. The Hippodrome, cathedral of spectacles and extravaganzas, opened in 1905 on Sixth Avenue and Forty-third Street. With the destiny of the song industry now tied up so inextricably with the theatre and places of amusement, it had to move closer to the main scene of operations. And this is the reason that the concentration of publishers on Twenty-eighth Street began to take place in the early twentieth century.

And so, Twenty-eighth Street, or Tin Pan Alley, became a street of song. Expansion was the keynote there, for the business had become a high-powered industry yielding fabulous profits. There was a proliferation of publishers, songwriters, and songs each year; also a proliferation of outlets where songs could be exhibited and sold. The sheet-music market had begun to penetrate department and five-and-ten-cent stores. Million-copy sales of a song became almost routine, and a million-copy sale at that time represented a profit of about $100,000 each to publisher and songwriter, what with songwriters now drawing a royalty of 5 percent. When publisher and songwriter were one and the same man, which was often the case, million-copy sale represented a profit of almost a quarter of a million dollars.

Techniques created in Union Square were developed into a science. The machinery for producing songs was operating at maximum capacity and speed—material being created to exploit every possible need, news item, invention, fashion, occurrence. Vogues for song subjects came and went, yielding hits about telephones, airplanes, automobiles, as each of these began to command public attention. When a "good-bye song" hit the jackpot, there followed an efflorescence of "good-bye songs." The same thing was true of songs about Mary, or songs about baseball, or songs about the American Indian, or dialect songs, or songs about Ireland and the Irish. To increase the outflow of songs, large publishers now employed arrangers to write down tunes for illiterate composers and to harmonize them; piano demonstrators exhibited songs for potential clients; staff writers produced songs on order.

Techniques for getting songs performed were also expanded in Tin Pan Alley. The little bribes that had once sufficed to interest performers had now swollen into a giant "payola" (a term that would achieve considerable prominence several decades later, but a practice that had considerable circulation in Tin Pan Alley): expensive jewels, large sums of money, a weekly salary throughout the year, and frequently a share in the song's royalties with the performer's name appearing on the sheet music as one of the writers. Since star performers in vaudeville and in the Broadway theatre had the power to create a song hit almost overnight through the power of their personal appeal and magnetism, and since vaudeville headliners traveling the circuit could carry a song from one end of the country to the other, their significance and potency within the song industry could hardly be overestimated. By 1905, therefore, Tin Pan Alley was distributing about half a million dollars a year to performers.

New areas for plugging songs were uncovered all the time by Tin Pan Alley. Whereas in Union Square most of the pluggers had been the heads of their respective firms, in Tin Pan Alley the song plugger was a professional hired hand whose sole job was to see that songs were played and sung. These employees continually sought out new places into which they could bring their commodities: the six-day bicycle race at Madison Square Garden, baseball games, the Coney Island boardwalk, amateur nights at burlesque houses and vaudeville theatres, local department and five-and-ten-cent stores, river excursion boats, circuses, parades, election campaigns, nickelodeons. Some publishers dispatched their pluggers on trucks to the heart of the city at lunch hour to have them perform on a stage improvised on the back of the vehicle. Some pluggers managed to get songs published in (and promoted by) leading newspapers.

"All day long on Twenty-eighth Street," as this writer said in his book, *The Life and Death of Tin Pan Alley,** "pianos were strummed and thumped inside the converted four-story brownstone houses that lined both sides of the street. The piano demonstrators sat in their cramped cubicles trying out new songs for performers who could bring them to the public. Outside the publishing house loitered the song plugger. Like the 'pullers in' of the cloak-and-suit district farther downtown, the plugger kept his eye alert for possible customers. Espying a vaudevillian, musical-comedy star, restaurant orchestra leader, minstrel, or anybody else capable of bringing a song to an audience, the plugger would use all the powers of his charm and persuasion to convince the performer to enter his establishment and listen to its new tunes. In an effort to keep leading performers from other houses, one publisher after another began to rent out office space as rehearsal rooms. Besides bringing in some additional income, this practice was valuable as an efficacious method by which the firm's songs could be brought, hot off the press, to a performer."

Before his first year in Tin Pan Alley had ended, Harry von Tilzer was one of its kingpins—with four successes whose total sheet-music sale exceeded five million copies. That skein of successes began with his first publication, "The Mansion of Aching Hearts," a sequel to "A Bird in a Gilded Cage." Once again von Tilzer preached the moral that diamonds and gold do not buy happiness. As a boy, roaming the streets of the Bowery, Irving Berlin used to bring tears to the eyes of passersby (and encourage pennies out of their pockets) by singing von Tilzer's "The Mansion of Aching Hearts." And a few years after that, the boy Berlin's affiliation with Harry von Tilzer became closer still when he was employed as a boy stooge, singing von Tilzer songs from the balcony of Tony Pastor's Music Hall.

"The Mansion of Aching Hearts" was followed the same year by three more big numbers by von Tilzer, "On a Sunday Afternoon," "Down Where the Wurzburger Flows," and "Please Go 'Way and Let Me Sleep."

The first of these started out as an idea born on the beach. While enjoying the sand and surf at Brighton Beach, in Brooklyn, von Tilzer came upon this sudden thought: "People work hard on Monday, but Sunday is one fun day." The whole subject appealed to him as much as the consecutive rhyming. He turned his thoughts over to Andrew B. Sterling who fashioned a lyric for him.

---

* David Ewen, *The Life and Death of Tin Pan Alley* (New York: Funk & Wagnalls, 1964).

"Down Where the Wurzburger Flows" was intended as a drinking song for a Broadway musical, *Wild Rose,* but was never used there. Von Tilzer then brought his song to Nora Bayes, then a young performer about to break into vaudeville. She sang it at the Orpheum Theatre in Brooklyn. Midway in her performance she broke down. Von Tilzer, seated in a box, took over for her. The audience went wild and remained unsatisfied until von Tilzer and Miss Bayes had repeated the chorus fourteen times. The management of Orpheum Theatre then prevailed on von Tilzer to continue serving as a stooge for Nora Bayes in the rendition of his song. After that, for another number of weeks, both von Tilzer and Nora Bayes went around to restaurants and other public places plugging the number until it caught fire. For the next few years Nora Bayes, now grown into a star, was identified as "The Wurzburger Girl." This song remained a basic staple in her vaudeville act until it was displaced by another number, this time one written for her by her husband, Jack Norworth, "Shine On, Harvest Moon." (In 1903 von Tilzer produced a sequel to the Wurzburger song in "Under the Anheuser Busch," and that, too, was a success, though certainly not of the proportions of its predecessor.)

The last of the four hit songs von Tilzer wrote and published in 1902 was "Please Go 'Way and Let Me Sleep." This one also owed its initial popularity to the way it was plugged. When the song was introduced in vaudeville by the minstrel Arthur Deming, Harry von Tilzer sat in the audience, seemingly in a deep sleep, snoring. Deming stopped his performance and ordered an usher to wake up the noisy intruder. As von Tilzer was being shaken, he began the refrain in a lazy drawl, "Please go 'way and let me sleep." The novelty of this presentation made for valuable publicity, and valuable publicity made for huge sales of sheet music.

Before producing his next million-copy ballad, which came in 1905 with "Wait 'Til the Sun Shines, Nellie," von Tilzer revealed his versatility by writing a ragtime number ("Good-bye, Eliza Jane") and two coon songs ("Alexander, Don't You Love Your Baby No More?" and "What You Goin' To Do When the Rent Comes 'Round?"). Ragtime and coon shouts as favored song styles in Tin Pan Alley will be commented upon later (see chapter on Irving Berlin). Here we will confine ourselves only to von Tilzer's three classics in these veins, written between 1903 and 1904.

"Alexander, Don't You Love Your Baby No More?" was the prototype of —possibly the motivation for—Irving Berlin's "Alexander's Ragtime Band" a few years later. Von Tilzer wrote this coon song as a result of two personal experiences. One took place at a performance in vaudeville by the minstrels McIntyre and Heath. McIntyre continually inspired guffaws of laughter in the audience by calling Heath "Alexander." This convinced von Tilzer that the name "Alexander" could be used effectively in a song. But he did not write his song until after he had overheard a Negro lady question her boyfriend: "Don't you love your baby no more?"

Still another overheard remark was responsible for von Tilzer's second successful coon song, "What You Goin' To Do When the Rent Comes 'Round?" This time von Tilzer was at a railway station in Miami, Florida. There he heard a Negro woman complain about her man's lazy ways. "What you goin' to do when the rent comes 'round?" the lady inquired. Von Tilzer used this as the theme of a song, while giving the shiftless fellow the name of Rufus Johnson Brown.

Von Tilzer actually reflected the many, varied song fashions in Tin Pan Alley with other hit tunes. He wrote a "mammy song" that is still remembered, "I Want a Girl Just Like the Girl That Married Dear Old Dad." He wrote an Irish ballad, "A Little Bunch of Shamrocks," and he combined the styles of a mammy song with an Irish ballad in "That Old Irish Mother of Mine." He wrote a nostalgic song about the Southland, "Down Where the Cotton Blossoms Grow." Indeed, there was hardly a song style in Tin Pan Alley that von Tilzer did not employ—and employ successfully.

He was even a pioneer at times. He was one of the first in Tin Pan Alley to produce those rural-type songs that proved so popular for many years; he did this in 1902 with "Down on the Farm" and in 1905 with "Where the Morning Glories Twine Around the Door." He was one of the first to write a telephone song, "All Alone," in 1911, or as it is also known, "Hello, Central, Give Me 603." (This was also the first song to employ an actual telephone on the stage when the number was introduced in vaudeville.) He was also one of the first in Tin Pan Alley to write a hit song inspired by a popular social dance: "The Cubanola Glide" in 1909, introduced by Harriet Raymond in the Broadway musical *The Girl from Rector's,* following which it was popularized in vaudeville by Sophie Tucker. Not long after this von Tilzer number grew popular, the mills of Tin Pan Alley began grinding out other dance songs, such as "The Grizzly Bear," "The Bunny Hug," and "The Turkey Trot."

But the sentimental ballad was von Tilzer's forte, and one of his most successful in this vein was "Wait 'Til the Sun Shines, Nellie." Two versions explain how von Tilzer came to write it. One maintains that he overheard a remark while waiting outside a theatre during a downpour. Another insisted that he got the subject for his ballad from a newspaper story about a family, stricken by financial disaster, being consoled by a friend with the words "the sun will shine after the storm." Whatever the origin, we do know that von Tilzer, while detailing the overall idea, had asked Andrew B. Sterling to write the lyrics. Winona Winter (daughter of the songwriter, Banks Winter) introduced it. It was not long before the ballad achieved wide circulation not only in vaudeville but also with barbershop quartets.

Harry von Tilzer was probably the most prolific composer Tin Pan Alley produced. Toward the end of his life he insisted that he had written eight thousand songs and had two thousand of them published. He also insisted that the total sales of his songs went into hundreds of millions. His last hit came in 1925 with "Just Around the Corner." Before he wrote it, he had lost contact with success for a number of years. Then he received a note from Elizabeth Marbury, the Broadway producer, consoling him with the thought that "just around the corner the sun will shine for you." In failure, as in success, von Tilzer could recognize song material when he stumbled across it, so he wrote "Just Around the Corner," and Ted Lewis and his band helped to popularize it (the last time anybody would perform this service for a new song by this venerable songwriter).

Tin Pan Alley changed radically after World War I. The major publishers were no longer concentrated on a single street, but were scattered in different streets on or near Broadway. This was the breakdown of what had long been a monolithic group—and it was only the beginning. In another decade or so most of the leading music publishers would become subsidiaries of motion-picture studios, bringing with this change new methods, new sets of values, a new audience, and new ways of popularizing songs. After that, radio would create still another revolution in the music industry. (These developments will receive more detailed discussion in later chapters.) The old ways of writing and distributing songs, of nursing composers and lyrics from obscurity and inexperience to success, had become obsolete.

Harry von Tilzer represented the old Tin Pan Alley. In the new order that came into being in the music industry in the 1920's and 1930's he was out of place, and he knew it. He went into retirement, spending his last years at the Hotel Woodward in New York, reminiscing about the golden days of Tin Pan Alley to anybody willing to lend an attentive ear. He died in his hotel room on January 10, 1946. A golden age in American popular song died with him.

Songs from Vaudeville

Gus Edwards

The popularity of the minstrel show had begun to wane by the early 1890's. In the spirit of those infectious, frenetic years, audiences (comprising mostly males) were partial to skimpily dressed girls and sex suggestions in song and humor in their stage entertainment. This was the reason box offices flouished in theatres presenting Broadway musicals, burlesque shows, or vaudeville.

The decline of the minstrel show and the rise of vaudeville were practically simultaneous events. When, in the early part of the twentieth century, the last of the great minstrels, Eddie Leonard, became a vaudeville headliner, vaudeville had finally nudged the minstrel show completely out of existence.

Vaudeville was actually born in the minstrel show—in the fantasia section where individual minstrels did their specialties. Lifted out of a minstrel-show context, fantasias became variety shows performed mostly in white face. The word "vaudeville" was first used in the United States to identify variety enter-tainment in Louisville, Kentucky, on February 23, 1871. At that time billboards identified the H. J. Sargent troupe as the "great vaudeville company from Chi-cago." Not long after this, the first theatre describing itself as a vaudeville house opened up in San Antonio, Texas.

A young graduate from the minstrel show became the father of vaudeville. It was he who made variety entertainment a well-paying business. It was he who induced women and children to come into the theatre—the theatre, up to now, catering mainly to males. It was he who created a pattern of procedure which vaudeville would follow for half a century. It was he who was the first to dis-cover new stars for the variety stage.

His name was Tony Pastor. He opened the first theatre ever to devote itself exclusively to variety entertainment in Paterson, New Jersey, on March 21, 1865. This experiment did not do well. One year later Pastor started another such theatre in downtown New York, at 201 Broadway. Here he inaugurated the practice of enticing women and children to see his shows by offering as door prizes dress patterns, kitchenware, toys, and groceries; he also saw to it that only "clean" entertainment was offered. Between 1875 and 1881 Pastor offered his variety shows farther uptown at the Tony Pastor Dramatic and Vaudeville Theatre at 585 Broadway opposite the Metropolitan Hotel. Each bill provided fourteen acts, the last of which combined the entire troupe, with Tony Pastor as star, in an elaborate "specialty."

Finally, on October 24, 1881 (after he had successfully experimented with tours of variety entertainment throughout the United States), he opened the Tony Pastor Music Hall on East Fourteenth Street at Union Square. The advertisement described the place as "the first specialty vaudeville theatre of America, catering to polite tastes, aiming to amuse, and fully up to current times and topics." For his opening program he featured eight acts, including an acrobat, a monologist, a singer of comic songs, and an English music-hall singer. Succeeding bills pre-sented new, young, and still unknown performers who would get their first recognition at Tony Pastor's Music Hall, launching them off on their first flights to blazing success—Lillian Russell, for example (a stage name, which Tony Pastor himself had coined, for Helene Louise Leonard); the Four Cohans, of whom the incomparable George M., though still young, was a significant mem-ber; Harrigan and Hart; Pat Rooney; Emma Carus; May Irwin; Eddie Foy.

Vaudeville caught on. Tony Pastor's Music Hall became one of the city's major show places, and for many years it remained the most important vaudeville theatre in America. But, inevitably, competitors sprang up to threaten Tony Pas-tor's supremacy in this field: Proctor's on Fifth Avenue; Koster and Bial's on West Twenty-third Street; Hyde and Behman's in Brooklyn. Continuous vaude-ville, running uninterruptedly from noon to midnight, was inaugurated in Boston in 1883. Million-dollar vaudeville theatres opened in Chicago (the Majestic) and San Francisco (the Orpheum). Then, in 1904, Oscar Hammerstein opened the Victoria on Forty-second Street to usurp once and for all the tight hold that Tony Pastor had held on his place of first importance in the world of vaudeville.

In the beginning of the twentieth century B. F. Keith entered into partnership with E. F. Albee to open and run a chain of vaudeville houses throughout the country. The Keith-Albee circuit thus came into existence, soon followed by the Proctor circuit, the Klaw and Erlanger circuit, and the Pantages circuit. Each circuit became a well-traveled route for a performing act—a route so extended that performers had no need to change their act more than once every few years. It was also a route by which songs, carried by these performers, could achieve national popularity. Many a hit song was heard for the first time anywhere in a show and was then popularized on the vaudeville circuits. Some of these songs remain forever identified with the one who introduced it: "Throw Him Down, McCloskey" with Maggie Cline; "Kaiser, Don't You Want to Buy a Dog?" with Gus Williams; "The Cakewalk in the Sky" with Ben Harney; "The Little Lost Child" with Della Fox; "Mother Was a Lady" with Lottie Gilson.

Vaudeville developed performers into stars and songs into hits. It also helped bring into existence composers who then became major contributors to Tin Pan Alley. The first song composer to become famous through vaudeville and vaudeville alone (or "variety" as it was still then called) was Tony Pastor himself. Chance rather than calculation made him into a songwriter. He was on his way to the theatre where he was then appearing as performer when he heard the news that Civil War had just broken out. That day he embarked upon an improvisation in his act by making a short patriotic speech and singing the "The Star-Spangled Banner." The furor in the audience that followed sparked an idea which Pastor would henceforth exploit with extraordinary effect as long as he remained an entertainer: commenting on current happenings within the format of a popular song. When some significant event transpired, he would introduce into his act a topical song on that very subject. During the Civil War he invented songs like "The *Monitor* and the *Merrimac*" and "Corcoran's Irish Brigade." After the war he found his song material in kidnappings, elections, fires, new inventions—anything, for that matter, that touched the front page of the local newspaper. In 1886 he introduced in New York a topical song about its mayoralty campaign; it is believed that Abram S. Hewitt's election was brought about largely through the propaganda value of one of the lines in that Tony Pastor topical song, a line that became a catch phrase: "What's the matter with Hewitt? He's all right!"

Gus Edwards was the most important composer whose songwriting career was inextricably bound up with vaudeville. He was born in the German town of Hohensaliza on August 18, 1879, his name having been Gustav Edmond Simon. The Simon family came to America when Gus was eight, finding a home in the Williamsburg section of Brooklyn. Still in his boyhood, Gus began earning his living by working as a tobacco stripper in his uncle's cigar store. The boy soon discovered that Union Square was the center of theatrical activity. From then on he spent his evenings roaming about Union Square trying to devise ways and means of getting in to see the shows without buying a ticket. While thus haunting the various theatres, he was noticed by Lottie Gilson, the vaudeville star, who took an interest in him. Once she discovered that he had a sweet vibrato voice, she hired him as a boy singing stooge in her act. Gus was fourteen when he made his stage debut in this role of stooge—by sitting in the balcony at Hurtig and Seamon's burlesque theatre and rising from his seat to repeat the refrain of ballads like "The Little Lost Child" when Miss Gilson had finished singing it on the stage. This routine became such a favorite with audiences that the boy stooge routine became a fixture. Some maintain that this routine had actually originated with Gus Edwards.

He soon found other jobs as boy stooge with stars such as Emma Carus, Maggie Cline, Imogene Comer, and Helene Mora, featured in the rendition of the popular sentimental ballads of the day. He became so popular as a boy stooge that Tin Pan Alley—ever alert for subject matter for songs—released a number that Gus Edwards had inspired, "A Song in the Gallery."

On and off for a number of years, Gus Edwards worked not only in vaudeville and burlesque houses but also in saloons, club meetings, on ferryboats, even at boxing matches. The house of M. Witmark soon hired him to plug their songs at some of these places. At other times Edwards sold sheet music at the Circle Theatre in New York's Columbus Circle—a theatre which, many years later, he would purchase and rename the Gus Edwards Music Hall.

He was singing in a Brooklyn saloon one day in 1896 when a vaudeville booking agent heard him. Then and there the agent conceived an act in which Edwards and several other boys would appear dressed up in ragged clothes as newsboys, bundles of newspapers under their arms, and sing the current ballads. The agent booked such an act on the vaudeville circuit, calling it the Newsboy Quintet. This marked Edwards's graduation in vaudeville from a seat in the audience as a singing stooge to a place in the spotlight on the stage. The spotlight would be upon him for the next quarter of a century.

On one of the bills on which the Newsboy Quintet was featured, the Four Cohans were the headliners. George M. Cohan, then eighteen, took a liking to Edwards. Although he himself was still pretty much of a neophyte as songwriter, Cohan began giving Edwards pointers on writing songs. Edwards also received an important assist from Paul Dresser, who allowed Edwards to use the piano at the Howley and Haviland office when Edwards embarked on his first experiments in writing songs.

Edwards's first song was "All I Wants Is My Black Baby Back," introduced in the newsboy act in 1898. At that time Edwards was still incapable of putting music notes down on paper and had to enlist the services of a friend.

With the outbreak of the Spanish-American conflict, Edwards enlisted his singing services to the war effort. While entertaining soldiers at Camp Black he met Will D. Cobb, a onetime salesman in a department store, but now a lyricist. A songwriting partnership between Cobb and Edwards was soon established, beginning with "I Couldn't Stand to See My Baby Lose," introduced by May Irwin in 1899. This was followed by a moderate hit published by Howley and Haviland, "I Can't Tell Why I Love You, But I Do."

The collaboration of Cobb and Edwards yielded a modest harvest in the first years of the new century. "I'll Be with You When the Roses Bloom Again" became popular on the vaudeville stage soon after its release in 1901, and then became quite a favorite with hillbilly singers. "In Zanzibar" was interpolated into the Broadway musical *The Medal and the Maid* in 1904. "Good-bye, Little Girl, Good-bye" was written in 1904 to capitalize on the vogue for "good-bye songs" then existing. "If a Girl Like You, Loved a Boy Like Me" followed in 1905.

Though Cobb and Edwards continued working together for the next few years, and with such eminence and distinction that they soon came to be known as "Mr. Words and Mr. Music," Edwards occasionally turned to other lyricists for his words, frequently to Vincent Bryan, for example. It was with Bryan that Edwards realized three hits of major dimension in 1905, all of them published by M. Witmark where Edwards was then employed as staff composer: "He's Me Pal," "Tammany," and "In My Merry Oldsmobile."

"Tammany" had been intended for a party at the National Democratic Club in New York to which Edwards had been invited as toastmaster. Bryan's lyrics made mild sport with some of the political indiscretions of the Democratic party, while both the lyrics and music were also intended to be a takeoff on songs on American-Indian subjects then so popular in Tin Pan Alley. To make sure that this song would hurt nobody's feelings, Edwards sang it to a number of Democratic party leaders before having it heard at the club. The leaders liked it, and so did all those who attended the party. In fact, their enthusiasm was such that the song soon assumed the status of the official theme song of New York's Tammany Hall. Outside Tammany Hall, the song was heard on the stage for the first time when Lee Harrison sang it in the Broadway extravaganza *Fantana*. The performer most credited with making the song popular with the general masses was Jefferson de Angelis.

"In My Merry Oldsmobile" became the first song hit on the subject of automobiles. The front pages of the daily newspaper gave Bryan and Edwards the idea to write it. Two Oldsmobiles had just successfully completed the first trip across most of America ever attempted by automobiles, traversing the distance between Detroit and Portland, Oregon (scene of the Lewis and Clark Expedition) in forty-four days.

The financial bonanza realized by the house of Witmark from numbers like these convinced Edwards that the time had come for him to capitalize on his own hits. Late in 1905 he formed the Gus Edwards Music Publishing Company, offices on Twenty-eighth Street. Two successes of gigantic proportions, both with lyrics by Will Cobb, forthwith placed the new firm on a solid footing. In fact the very first release by the house was "Sunbonnet Sue," which would sell more than a million copies of sheet music. Soon after this came "I Just Can't Make My Eyes Behave," which Anna Held introduced in *A Parisian Model* and with which she henceforth became identified. *A Parisian Model* was one of the leading attractions on Broadway in 1905. Another song by Edwards in this same production was "I'd Like To See a Little More of You," a provocative number sung by girls as they were undressing until, through a trick stage effect, they seemed to appear in the nude. This novel staging was largely responsible for the number's success. Unusual staging helped Lillian Lorraine in 1909 to introduce Edwards's "Up, Up, in My Aeroplane" (one of the earliest songs about aerial navigation) in the *Ziegfeld Follies*. Lorraine sang it in a little flying machine which soared from the stage over the audience's head and back again to the stage.

The most successful song Edwards ever wrote was "School Days," words by Cobb. He wrote it in 1909 for *School Boys and Girls,* a most unusual vaudeville act which he not only devised and wrote but also directed and starred in. He played the part of a schoolmaster in a classroom, the only adult in a cast of children. The children sang, danced, did imitations, performed comedy routines. They brought to the vaudeville stage all the freshness, vitality, charm, and exuberance of childhood. The song "School Days" was the musical high point when the act made its vaudeville bow, and it sold three million copies. From there it went on to become an American song classic.

For almost a quarter of a century, Edwards continued bringing to the vaudeville stage the bright, shining talent of remarkable children—always in some newly conceived schoolroom sketch. He proved so tireless in seeking out new talent that before long the following remark was circulated around Broadway: "Pull your kids in, here comes Gus Edwards!" Edwards brought to the stage many a child whose undeveloped talent eventually flowered into greatness and far-reaching successes in the world of entertainment. For it was in his act that there took place the stage debuts of Eddie Cantor, Georgie Jessel, Lila Lee, Georgie Price, Groucho Marx, Eddie Buzzell, Ray Bolger, Jack Pearl, Eleanor Powell, the Duncan Sisters, to mention just a few. Recognition of Edwards's uncommon flair for sniffing out talent in the raw and in the young was recognized by the motion-picture industry when it screened a musical biography of his life, starring Bing Crosby. This movie, released in 1940, was called *The Star Maker.*

Gus Edwards contributed many a song for these headline school-kid acts of his. "By the Light of the Silvery Moon" was introduced by Georgie Price, then a child, in the Gus Edwards act in 1909. Georgie sang it from a place in the audience where he assumed the role of a singing stooge. During the same year, the success of this love ballad was enhanced when Lillian Lorraine sang it in the *Ziegfeld Follies.* In fact, it was to become *her* song. After 1909 she was often called upon to sing it, the last such occasion taking place in 1933 when the Ziegfeld Theatre reopened with Gus Edwards as one of its attractions. Espying Miss Lorraine in the audience, Edwards called her to the stage and asked her to give a rendition of "By the Light of the Silvery Moon." She graciously complied. But after presenting only the first few measures, she broke down and wept, and was unable to continue.

Two other Edwards songs introduced in his schoolchildren acts in vaudeville between 1910 and 1911 were "If I Was a Millionaire" and "Jimmy Valentine."

In 1928 Edwards went into temporary retirement from the living stage to go to work in Hollywood as performer and director. But in the early 1930's he was back in vaudeville, presenting the last of his schoolchildren acts; some of its young stars included Ray Bolger and the three Lane sisters (Priscilla, Rosemary, Lola). But vaudeville was expiring, and the same infection that was destroying it was also affecting Gus Edwards both as a vaudeville attraction and as a songwriter. He retired in 1938. Six years of poor health followed. He died in Los Angeles on November 7, 1945.

GREAT MEN OF AMERICAN POPULAR SONG

Songs from Operetta

Victor Herbert

Surely it is paradoxical to find that a man who was Irish by birth and German by training should have become America's first significant composer for the popular musical theatre. The paradox continues when we discover that Victor Herbert had little thought of making his fame and fortune in the field that he did. He had every intention of making his mark in serious music as a virtuoso of the cello and as a composer of symphonies and concertos.

There is still one other paradox about Herbert's career. When first he came to the United States—arriving on Sunday, October 24, 1886, aboard the steamship *Saale*—and when he had finally settled his baggage in an apartment on Fourth Avenue and Eighteenth Street, the newspaper reporters who came knocking at his door arrived not to interview *him* but to interview his newly wedded wife. She was the former Theresa Förster, a famous prima donna, whom Herbert had married only six weeks earlier in Vienna. She had been contracted to open the season at the Metropolitan Opera, which is why she was the center of interest. Her husband, completely unknown for the good reason that he had thus far accomplished little, was altogether ignored in the hubbub that followed. All that the reporters had learned about Herbert was that he had been hired as a cellist for the Metropolitan Opera orchestra; and he had been hired only because this was the condition imposed on the Metropolitan Opera by Mme. Förster before she signed her contract.

Mme. Förster—who now called herself Mme. Herbert-Förster—made a spectacular debut at the Metropolitan Opera on November 8, 1886, in the title role of Karl Goldmark's *The Queen of Sheba.* Her striking beauty and majestic carriage made the role and the interpreter one. In addition, she sang and acted in the grand manner. The *Musical Courier* described her performance as a "perfect revelation," while the critic of the *Herald* said that every moment she was on the stage *she* "was the queen."

In 1886, then, the limelight pointed strong and straight on Herbert's wife. As for Herbert, he stood in her shadow, completely obscured by her success. For he was only a humble orchestra player.

But it took less than half a dozen years for the roles to get reversed. By then, Theresa had given up her career as a singer to devote herself to home and husband. Now it was on Victor Herbert that the limelight was focused. By 1886 Herbert had distinguished himself as the conductor of the famous Twenty-second Regiment Band (in succession to the renowned Patrick Gilmore); as a cello virtuoso who had made many appearances with distinguished orchestras and who had introduced his own Second Cello Concerto with the New York Philharmonic; who taught the cello at the National Conservatory in New York. In New York's musical life Herbert had become by 1890 a personality of no small consequence. Wherever great musicians gathered in New York—whether in clubs, concert halls, or in such favored restaurants as Lienau's or Luchow's—Herbert was surrounded by some of the most celebrated musical personalities of that day: the conductors Theodore Thomas and Anton Seidl; the pianists Rafael Joseffy and Moriz Rosenthal; the critic James Gibbons Huneker. All of them were convinced that whether as cellist or as composer—possibly as both—Herbert was destined to scale the heights in serious music.

In time, Herbert *did* scale those heights, but not in serious music. Though he continued making distinguished appearances as cellist and as serious composer, and though he was making his reputation as a conductor of symphonic music, his greatness—indeed, his immortality—was reserved for him in an altogether different world: the world of the popular theatre and popular music. His achievements in serious music are today remembered (if they are remembered at all) by students and music historians. But there is hardly an American who does not remember Victor Herbert for the songs that made him America's first great composer for the musical theatre.

Victor Herbert was born in Dublin on February 1, 1859. Since his father, an artist, died when Victor was only three, the child and his widowed mother went to live with her father. He was Samuel Lover, a famous novelist, poet, and dramatist—the author of the popular *Handy Andy*. Mr. Lover was a dilettante with more than the amateur's competence in both art and music. His cottage, The Vine—situated in Sevenoaks, twenty miles out of London—was the scene for all kinds of cultural activities and social events at which the great of the world of art, literature, theatre, and music gathered. Here and now Herbert's first listening experiences in music took place.

Spending several impressionable years of childhood in such a cultured environment had deep and permanent influence on Herbert. His lifelong passion for the arts, his interests in stimulating conversation on significant subjects, his love and knowledge of what constitutes the good life—all of this had its roots in the soil of The Vine.

His talent for music, which revealed itself early, was not likely to go undetected in a setting like The Vine, nor would it lack encouragement. When Herbert's mother found him attracted to the piano, she began giving him lessons; he was seven at the time. And when his progress betrayed that he was born for music, grandfather Lover insisted that an intensive professional training was now called for. He also insisted that this training take place in Germany, where the best music teachers in Europe could be found.

As it turned out, going to Germany to study music presented no practical problems—and for a simple reason. Victor's mother, during a brief visit to London, had fallen in love with a German physician, Wilhelm Schmid. They married, and in the spring of 1866 they made their home in Stuttgart, where Schmid practiced medicine. Naturally, Victor went to live with them. In Stuttgart Victor attended public and high school, specializing in Latin and Greek, since the stepfather hoped the boy might become a doctor. But Victor was no scholar. Medicine was soon displaced by music—with the blessings of the stepfather and the enthusiastic encouragement of Victor's mother. Herbert deserted high school in 1874 when he was fifteen. For the next two years he studied the cello privately with Bernhard Cossmann. "These lessons," Herbert later revealed, "were no fifteen-minute affairs. I was under the constant eye of my master."

The necessity of earning a living led Herbert to spend four years in various European cities playing his cello in orchestras, some of which were conducted by masters like Brahms, Anton Rubinstein, and Saint-Saëns. For a year, in 1880, he played with Eduard Strauss's orchestra in Vienna—Eduard being the brother of Vienna's renowned waltz king, Johann Strauss II, who carried on the family tradition by performing waltzes, polkas, quadrilles, and other light music in café houses. Working in a Viennese orchestra under Eduard Strauss was an apprenticeship whose importance in Herbert's later development cannot be overestimated: for Herbert, too, would someday write lilting, seductive melodies of his own in three-quarter time and in the infectious spirit of other types of Viennese light music.

These experiences behind him, Herbert was appointed first cellist of the Stuttgart Royal Orchestra conducted by Max Seyfritz. The conductor took a personal interest in young Herbert and began teaching him orchestration and harmony. Spurred on by Seyfritz's warm endorsements, Herbert completed two large works, both of them for cello and orchestra, one a suite and the other a concerto. Both were introduced in Stuttgart with Herbert at the cello and Seyfritz conducting. A Stuttgart critic wrote: "From the talented young musician we have already received many pearls of his exquisite art. We are happy to assert that the work performed yesterday can be counted among the best compositions in the violoncello literature."

Herbert, then, was acquiring quite a reputation in Stuttgart—not only as a musician but also as a dandy and a man of the world. Tall, erect, slim (the later years of indulgence at the dinner table had not yet brought on corpulence), he was striking to look at. His curly brown hair threw a romantic lock over his impressive brow, pointing toward expressive blue eyes. His moustache was always trim. He dressed in the latest style, with tailoring that was elegant without being ostentatious. He was a young man of courtly manners, a man whose conversation was at turns witty and stimulating, continually enriched with anecdotes gathered during his extensive travels. He loved the good things of life, and the good things of life meant not only the refinements of art and culture and music but also gourmet meals, vintage wines, and the company of beautiful women.

Women were attracted to him. One of them was the shapely, beautiful leading soprano of the Stuttgart Opera, Theresa Förster. She hired him as her vocal coach and accompanist. A romance between two such attractive people—with their love of and appreciation of great music a common bond of interest—was a foregone conclusion. They were married in Vienna on August 14, 1886. On October 13 of the same year they boarded the *Saale* at Bremen bound for America, where Theresa had been contracted to open the new season of the Metropolitan Opera in New York.

Despite her success, Theresa Herbert-Förster stayed just a single full season at the Metropolitan. During the second season she made only one appearance. After that, for a few years, she was heard intermittently with various companies in America and Europe. Then she withdrew completely from her career to concentrate on domesticity and her husband.

The stage (figuratively at first, literally much later) now belonged to Victor Herbert and not to his wife. It had not taken him long to outgrow his humble post in the pit of the Metropolitan Opera. On January 8, 1887, he was soloist with the New York Symphony in a performance of his suite for cello and orchestra; four days after that he appeared in a joint recital with a young pianist in Brooklyn. Later the same year he formed his own orchestra which presented concerts of classical and semiclassical music in both New York and Boston. He also founded and played in the New York String Quartet. His appearances as cellist added further luster to his reputation before the decade of the 1880's was over, while his success at the Worcester Music Festival in 1889 drew attention to his talent for conducting the music of the masters. He also distinguished himself as a teacher after joining the faculty of the National Conservatory in New York in 1889 (the same conservatory where Antonín Dvořák would become director a few years later).

The 1890's brought Herbert ever-mounting successes—now in one area, now in another. For the Worcester Festival of 1891 he wrote his most ambitious composition up to that time: *The Captive,* scored for solo voices, chorus, and orchestra. James Gibbons Huneker, then one of the most eminent music critics, said of this music that Herbert had "composed an extremely strong work, picturesque as to coloring and incident and extremely dramatic." More functional, while still revealing another facet of his creative gifts, was the *American Fantasia.* This was an ambitious symphonic medley of patriotic melodies that reached a climax with a Wagnerian-like presentation of "The Star-Spangled Banner," Victor Herbert's musical pledge of allegiance to the country of which he became a citizen in 1902. That fantasia received its world premiere on November 26, 1893, Herbert conducting the Twenty-second Regiment Band of which he had just been made director. This event pointed to another direction in music in which Herbert would soon make notable advances. The Twenty-second Regiment Band had been founded in 1861, and from 1872 until his death twenty years later, Patrick Scarsfield Gilmore, as conductor, elevated it to side with America's most distinguished and highly acclaimed musical organizations. Herbert maintained those high standards during the years in which he held Gilmore's baton. But this experience was just the preface to an even more ambitious conducting assignment. In 1898 Herbert was made the principal conductor of the Pittsburgh Symphony, a post he held with honor for the next five years.

But the swift strides he was making toward success and self-fulfillment as a musician did not completely satisfy him. Melodies kept running helter-skelter through his head all the time—brisk, bright, sunny tunes sometimes; at other times, haunting sentimental tunes. These cried for life on paper, but they were not the kind of melodies usable in a symphony, tone poem, concerto, or opera. Victor Herbert, therefore, was beginning to glance with covetous eyes at the musical theatres where operettas and comic operas (most of them the work of Europeans) were flourishing. Thirty-five European operettas had been mounted in a seven-year period at the Casino Theatre in New York, home of lavish musical productions since its opening in 1882. During the single season of 1894–95, fourteen companies were touring the United States with foreign operettas. Operettas by American composers had also begun to prosper. There was Willard Spencer's *The Little Tycoon,* in 1885, which had a run of five hundred performances in Philadelphia before coming to New York for another extended run. And there was Reginald de Koven's *Robin Hood* in 1890, a score which yielded a song that made a star of Jessie Bartlett Davis and which, from then on, contributed a musical number without which wedding ceremonies in America would seem incomplete—"Oh, Promise Me."

The reigning queen at the Casino Theatre was the glamorous Lillian Russell, the voluptuous singing star with the hourglass figure who was already a sex symbol and the toast of the city. And it was Lillian Russell who was responsible for Victor Herbert's first operetta, *La Vivandière,* written in 1893 at the request of Miss Russell for the Casino Theatre. Nobody seems to know what happened to this operetta. It was never produced—perhaps because, in the end, Lillian Russell lost heart and feared risking her now fabulous reputation on an inexperienced stage composer; or perhaps it was just a bad operetta. In any event, the operetta was never produced and Herbert's score got lost. We have only the testimony of James Gibbons Huneker (as reported by Edward N. Waters in his biography of Herbert) that this music (which the composer had performed for him at the piano) was "light and dainty . . . with humor and enthusiasm."

Herbert's failure to get *La Vivandière* on the stage was frustrating, to say the least. But Herbert had now had his first taste of writing music for the popular musical stage, and it had not been enough to satisfy a now mounting appetite. "I *must* write for the theatre," he told his wife with finality. This conviction led him without too much delay to work on a new operetta score even before knowing what his libretto would be—almost with the grim determination of a man remounting his horse after a fall to prevent future fears about horseback riding.

It was at this juncture in Herbert's life that William MacDonald, director of The Bostonians, a light-opera company, came to Herbert with an invitation to write music for an operetta. The Bostonians had been the company that had mounted De Koven's *Robin Hood*. It was searching for a new work to introduce. The text MacDonald had in mind for Herbert was *Prince Ananias* by Francis Neilson, then a successful librettist and later on an even more successful and eminent writer on political subjects. The setting of the text was France, and the time was the sixteenth century. Its story concerned the efforts of a group of performers to meet the challenge of amusing the king or face death. This challenge was finally met successfully through the efforts of a poet, Ananias. The love interest brought together this poet with the village belle, and an outlaw with a nobleman's daughter.

Prince Ananias was produced in Boston on November 20, 1894. The critics of the *Sun* and the *Post* both maintained that Herbert's score was superior to that generally found in operettas. A reporter for the *Dramatic Mirror* singled out some of the marches and waltzes for special admiration, while complimenting Herbert further on his skill in harmony and orchestration. To Herbert's biographer, Edward N. Waters, one number stood out with particular brilliance: the song "Amaryllis" which opened the second act. Waters called it "one of the gems in all light opera," adding that "the wistful melancholy of Idalia's song, the delicate accompaniment, and the interpolation of a dainty minuet make this a truly extraordinary selection."

That *Prince Ananias* was at least a minor success, then, was due more to the music than to a libretto that was severely attacked; one critic went so far as to suggest that this was one of the worst operetta books ever encountered in the musical theatre of that period. Music, rather than the play, gave the operetta its audience appeal—enough of an appeal to encourage The Bostonians to tour the United States with it, and then retain it in its repertory for two seasons.

Herbert's next operetta was not slow in coming. Harry B. Smith, the notable librettist who had provided De Koven with the text of *Robin Hood,* had been working on a libretto with an Oriental background, fashioned for the tal-

ents of the comedian Frank Daniels. Two producers who jointly had Frank
Daniels under contract, and consequently were interested in Harry B. Smith's
libretto, suggested Herbert as its composer. At first, such a suggestion was
greeted coldly by Smith who considered *Prince Ananias* a total failure. But
when he heard Herbert play for him some of the numbers he was thinking of
putting into the new show, Smith's respect for Herbert mounted. He was now
willing to have Herbert write the rest of the score.

This new Herbert-Smith operetta, *The Wizard of the Nile,* had several out-
of-town tryouts before coming to New York and opening at the Casino Theatre
on November 4, 1895. It stayed there thirteen weeks, then embarked on an
extended tour. During the next decade it was repeatedly revived. *The Wizard
of the Nile,* then, marks the real beginnings of Herbert's success in a musical
theatre which he would dominate with such regal splendor for the next two
decades.

In *The Wizard of the Nile* Frank Daniels played the part of a Persian
magician named Kibosh who was recruited to use his necromantic powers to relieve a drought in ancient Egypt. He gets into trouble, is threatened with death
by royal decree, but ends up as a hero. "Am I a whiz?" is a rhetorical question
that Kibosh asks continually throughout the play (using his famous trick eye-
brows for emphasis). This question became the country's favorite catch phrase
in 1895 and 1896. Just as contagiously did the principal waltz infect the public,
"Star Light, Star Bright," the refrain of a vocal quintet. "Star Light, Star
Bright" is the first jewel in the resplendent necklace of Victor Herbert's song
gems.

If *The Wizard of the Nile* was Herbert's first genuine success, then *The
Fortune Teller* was his first stage masterwork. By the same token, if "Star Light,
Star Bright" is his first song jewel, then "Gypsy Love Song" is his first pure-
white diamond. Three years separate the two productions, a period in which
Herbert had contributed scores for one resounding failure (*The Gold Bug,* in
1896) and one moderate success (*The Serenade,* in 1897). A word about *The
Serenade* might not be out of place before our discussion of *The Fortune Teller,*
because two items bring it special interest. One is a song that courses throughout
The Serenade as a *Leitmotiv:* the serenade "I Love Thee, I Adore Thee," which
assumes many different identities as it courses throughout the operetta. Now it
is heard as a parody of a grand-opera aria, now as a parrot's call, now as a
monk's chant, now as a song of a brigand, and finally as a sentimental ballad
for hero and heroine. This number assumes such prominence within the story
that it has sometimes been described as the operetta's leading character.

The other item that is particularly significant about *The Serenade* was in
the casting of Alice Nielsen as the heroine, Yvonne. Nielsen, then hardly past
her twentieth birthday, was an unknown in the chorus when, one day, Herbert's
wife noticed her and heard her sing. Mme. Herbert persuaded her husband to
star her as Yvonne in *The Serenade.* Herbert himself was more partial to Hilda
Clark, first because she was already an established star, and then because she
had a striking voice. However, acceding to his wife's insistent plea, he decided
to listen to both Miss Nielsen and Miss Clark sing some songs from his new

production before making a final choice. Hilda Clark had the better voice, but Herbert agreed that Alice Nielsen was more infectious and electrifying as a personality. Contractual obligations to Hilda Clark compelled him, however, to alternate the role of Yvonne between the two performers. Since Nielsen proved spectacular—particularly after her rendition of "Cupid and I"—she soon took over the role completely. Thus thrust to stardom, Alice Nielsen went on to sing the principal female roles in two other Herbert operettas, including the triumphant *The Fortune Teller,* which Herbert had written with Nielsen in mind.

The Fortune Teller, whose premiere took place in New York on September 26, 1898, profited no end by casting Alice Nielsen in the dual role of Musette, a Gypsy fortune-teller, and Irma, a Hungarian ballet student. But it was Eugene Cowles as Sandor the Gypsy musician who carried off the operetta's prize song, the "Gypsy Love Song" (also sometimes identified by the first line of its refrain, "Slumber On, My Little Gypsy Sweetheart"). This serenade, in which the verse is quite as distinguished as the chorus, is so true to the Magyar spirit that one is likely to forget that its composer had been an Irishman who had studied in Germany and who by choice had become an American.

An American identity never really emerged in Herbert's songwriting, whose style was now becoming crystallized. Though ragtime, syncopation, and occasionally the blues were beginning to provide composers in Tin Pan Alley with native materials for the manufacture of an indigenous music, Herbert stayed consistently aloof from all such influences. To the end of his days he remained himself: partly Irish and partly German—a rare combination that may be one of the reasons for his unique, permanent success. The touching though seldom cloying sentimentality that clings to his waltzes and love songs and the love of the comic and the infectious spirit of playfulness that brighten his sprightlier melodies come from his Irish heritage. In songs like these one will invariably detect the twinkle that lurks in Irish eyes when they are smiling. On the other hand, his sure technique at harmony and orchestration and his sound feeling for structure—together with his discipline—spring from his German training. That he had a gift of lyricism all his own goes without saying. This was his great strength. But he never allowed this talent to be burdened by, then crushed under, the weight of German academicism and rhetoric. This is perhaps what Deems Taylor meant when he wrote that Herbert's best music represents "pure song at its very best, capable of being sung without accompaniment, if need be, as pure in outline as the melodies of Schubert and Mozart."

Most of Herbert's greatest songs in his more famous operettas were written before World War I: "The March of the Toys" and "Toyland" from *Babes in Toyland;* "Absinthe Frappé" from *It Happened in Nordland;* "Kiss Me Again" from *Mlle. Modiste;* "The Isle of Our Dreams," "Moonbeams," and "The Streets of New York" from *The Red Mill;* "Ah! Sweet Mystery of Life," "I'm Falling in Love with Someone," "Italian Street Song," and " 'Neath the Southern Moon," all from *Naughty Marietta.* Operettas of lesser importance, and far less successful at the box office than those mentioned above, also yielded songs to remember: "Rose of the World" from *The Rose of Algeria* (1908); "To the

Land of My Own Romance" from *The Enchantress* (1911); "Angelus" and the title song from *Sweethearts* (1913); and "When You're Away" from *The Only Girl* (1914).

The lightning speed with which he could write a score—sometimes in a single month, the orchestration included—was made more evident than ever in 1899 when three Herbert operettas were produced within a two-month period: *Cyrano de Bergerac, The Singing Girl,* and *The Ameer.* With *The Viceroy,* Herbert helped launch the new century. Then, as if to catch his second breath, he wrote no more operettas for three years, because during this period he devoted his energies to conducting the Pittsburgh Symphony. But he knew full well where his true destiny lay. In the spring of 1903 he resigned from the Pittsburgh Symphony to reestablish his permanent home in New York City and once again concentrate on writing for the musical theatre. Before that summer came to an end, he had a new score in hand, his first success in the twentieth century. It was *Babes in Toyland.*

Babes in Toyland was an extravaganza rather than an operetta: with emphasis more on spectacle and glamour than on sentiment. This production was an all-too-obvious attempt by its librettist, Glen MacDonough, to take advantage of the success then recently enjoyed on Broadway by *The Wizard of Oz.* Instead of using a fairy garden (Oz) as his setting—or employing such child storybook characters as a witch, a Scarecrow and the Woodman in conjunction with a little girl named Dorothy Dale—MacDonough lifted famous people out of fairy tales and Mother Goose and placed them in such make-believe places as the Garden of Contrary Mary, the Floral Palace of Moth Queen, and Toyland. These places are visited by Little Jane and Little Allen, fleeing from the tyranny of a miserly uncle. The child's world of imagination and fantasy was caught in ballets and production numbers that had greater concern with feasting the eye than in keeping the threads of a complicated plot from unraveling. The show made for a "perfect dream of delight to the children," reported the critic of the *Dramatic Mirror,* "that will recall the happy days of childhood to those who are facing the stern realities of life." Herbert's music was in perfect harmony with the text, as unpretentious, direct, ingenuous, and infectious as childhood itself: "Never Mind, Bo-Peep" and "Toyland," both sung by Tom Tom and a chorus; "I Can't Do the Sum," sung by the children while tapping out the rhythm of the tune with chalk on slates; and the instrumental number, "The March of the Toys," which the music critic of the *Tribune* described as a "capital piece . . . with just a suggestion of the grotesque [which] harmonizes charmingly with the scene."

The next decade saw the production of eighteen Herbert operettas. Four are remembered fondly: *Mlle. Modiste* (1905), *The Red Mill* (1906), *Naughty Marietta* (1910), and *Sweethearts.*

Mlle. Modiste was written for Fritzi Scheff, a prima donna whom Herbert had lured from the Metropolitan Opera in 1903 to play the leading role in an earlier Herbert operetta, *Babette.* In *Mlle. Modiste* Henry Blossom's text traced the career of Fifi from the time she worked as a salesgirl to her success as a prima donna. As Fifi, she had been spurned by the de Bouvrays, the proud, noble family of the man she loves. But as a prima donna with the assumed name of Mme. Bellini, she comes to the de Bouvray estate and wins the family over with her singing. The love interest can now progress to a happy resolution.

To Fritzi Scheff, as Fifi, Victor Herbert assigned one of his most popular waltzes—"Kiss Me Again," which had a curious birth history. It was not intended at first to serve as a love ballad but was planned as a parody of waltz music. As such a parody it was just a segment of a larger number, "If I Were on the Stage," in which several different song and dance styles are parodied, such as a gavotte, a polonaise, and a waltz. Needing some tune to satirize the waltz, Herbert reached into his well-stocked reservoir of never-used song material and found a melody he had written two years earlier. When Herbert played this melody for Mme. Scheff, she did not like it at all. She complained that the register was too low for her voice, that it was not *her* kind of song. Herbert, however, could be persuasive, and in the end Mme. Scheff surrendered. On opening night the audience went into a furor over the waltz section of "If I Were on the Stage." This response led Herbert to lift the piece out of its context, to add a verse to what up to now had consisted merely of a chorus, and to transform a parody into a love ballad. That ballad helped carry Fritzi Scheff to the heights in the world of operetta. Up until her death in 1954, the name of Fritzi Scheff and the title "Kiss Me Again" were virtually synonymous.

The enduring popularity of "Kiss Me Again" sometimes makes it difficult to remember that *Mlle. Modiste* is by no means a one-song score. Two other numbers were also distinctive. "I Want What I Want When I Want It" is one of those tunes with which Herbert helped to give dimension to a character; its vigorous stride and brisk melody helped give an insight into the personality of the old gruff Count Henri de Bouvray, father of the hero. And "The Mascot of the Troop" is a spirited march tune in which the "Marseillaise" is quoted.

The score of *The Red Mill* was more varied and more opulent still. *The Red Mill* had been conceived for two successful comedians—Fred Stone and David Montgomery who, in 1903, had become stars in *The Wizard of Oz* as the Scarecrow and the Woodman. In *The Red Mill* they played the parts of two Americans, stranded in a small town in Holland. As Con Kidder and Kid Conner, they befriend lovely Gretchen and become her allies in breaking up her impending marriage to a man she does not love, the governor of Zeeland. The big scene of this operetta comes during the wedding ceremonies where the two comedians are given ample opportunity to display their versatility as mimics and impersonators. Continually, they burst into the scene and prevent the wedding ceremony from taking place by assuming various disguises, including those of Sherlock Holmes and Dr. Watson, and two Italian organ grinders. They successfully disrupt the marriage proceedings, and after that help Gretchen and the man she loves, Captain Doris van Damm, resolve their disturbed romance.

As the two Italian organ grinders, Fred Stone and David Montgomery present a song called "Good-a-bye, John," the writing of which is still a subject enshrouded in mystery. One year before this number was given in *The Red Mill* and was published by M. Witmark, a song of the same name (by Harry William and Egbert Van Alstyne) was published by Jerome H. Remick and intended for a musical, *The Belle of Avenue A.* But not only were the titles the same! The lyrics and melody of both songs were so much alike that anybody could easily mistake the Van Alstyne number for that of Herbert, and vice versa.

It is ridiculous even to suggest that Herbert was guilty of plagiarism. He could drop from his sleeve more tunes than he could use; his extraordinary inventiveness through the years made it possible for him, almost at a moment's notice, to deliver numbers of any style or mood. There is no other instance in his vast production where he borrowed so much as somebody else's phrase. He had far too much pride in his talent and profession to stoop to borrowing. Besides Herbert's stealing a melody from a song written, published, and become popular only one year earlier would reduce him to a fool.

To add still further to this strange mystery, neither Williams nor Van Alstyne made a move to sue Herbert and Blossom, something they had every right to do and which would surely have brought them a substantial victory in court. In fact, nobody who knew either Williams or Van Alstyne personally ever heard either man comment on the similarity between their song and Herbert's. "Good-a-bye, John" was allowed to stay in *The Red Mill* without interference, and continues to be identified as a Herbert song, though there is good reason to doubt that he wrote it.

But there can be no doubt about the other successful songs in this same production, all of which bear the unmistakable Herbert stamp: the stamp of his winning sentimentality and soft, caressing charm in numbers like "Moonbeams," "The Isle of Our Dreams," and "Because You're You"; the stamp of his light and infectious sense of humor in "Every Day Is Ladies' Day"; the stamp of his gift at producing the proper tone for a big production number in "The Streets of New York," sung by Stone and Montgomery and chorus in the closing scene.

The critical consensus in 1910 was that Herbert had never before created a more consistently appealing nor a more varied score than that for *Naughty Marietta.* The public reaction of Herbert's day was that *Naughty Marietta* was one of the best operettas ever written by an American. And the verdict of later historians and critics is that *Naughty Marietta* is a classic of the American musical theatre.

Rida Johnson Young, author of the text, used eighteenth-century New Orleans as her locale. The core of her plot engages Marietta (a highborn Neapolitan lady come to New Orleans to flee from an undesirable marriage) in a thorny love affair with Captain Dick Warrington, who is on the hunt for a pirate. In a dream, Marietta has heard the fragment of a beautiful melody. She stands ready to marry anybody who can complete that melody for her. Captain Dick does so in time to win Marietta's love and prevent her from entanglements with the pirate who is actually Etienne, son of the lieutenant governor.

The pivot on which the story spins is, then, a song (just as it had been in *The Serenade*). And a good deal of the strength of *Naughty Marietta* springs from the fact that the song is as good as it is—"Ah! Sweet Mystery of Life," one of Herbert's finest song creations. It was introduced by Orville Harrold, a singer of massive stature, whom Herbert had recruited from grand opera to play the part of Captain Dick. The diminutive Emma Trentini (for whom the

part and the music of Marietta were conceived) was also lifted from grand
opera. She brought her rapturous voice to the "Italian Street Song," in which
Marietta nostalgically recalls her native Naples. "I'm Falling in Love with
Someone" (a prime favorite with tenors) and " 'Neath the Southern Moon"
are two love songs, the former, sung by Captain Dick, being a melody unusual
for its chromaticism and intervallic structure; the latter, assigned to a secondary
character, is a romantic effusion which Edward N. Waters described as "a
beautiful poem of tropical warmth . . . a melody of strange nobility set forth
over a starkly bare accompaniment—an exquisite piece of music." More muscular and vigorous than any of the above tunes was "Tramp! Tramp! Tramp!"
(not to be confused with the Civil War ballad of the same name), a choral march
that was destined to be the prototype of all such numbers in later operettas and
musical comedies.

As had been the case with *Mlle. Modiste* and *Naughty Marietta, Sweethearts* was created for a singing star. This time she was Christie MacDonald,
already an established favorite in the popular musical theatre by virtue of her
recent success in *The Spring Maid*. The love story in *Sweethearts* transpires in
ancient Bruges, and its principals are a prince and a girl of seemingly humble
station. The prince has come from the mythical land of Zilania; and the girl
with whom he falls in love is Sylvie, a foundling raised as a daughter by the
proprietress of a laundry. The romance neatly overcomes the insuperable ob-
stacles of the widely separate social positions of the lovers when it is learned
that Sylvie is actually the crown princess of Zilania, who had been abducted
from her land during her childhood.

The title waltz, with its effective two-octave span in the melody, is the
trump card in Herbert's winning hand. Two other numbers are also strong suits:
Sylvie's deeply moving prayer, "Angelus," and the choral episode opening
the second act, "Pretty as a Picture." Of the score as a whole, the music critic
Herbert F. Peyser wrote at that time: "From first to last this music is utterly free
from any suggestion of triviality. The abundant melodic flow is invariably marked
by distinction, individuality, and a quality of superlative charm."

Sweethearts became the instrument with which Herbert (with the collaboration of others) was able to devise a method, or agency, whereby composers,
lyricists, and publishers in America could be protected from the free use of
their songs at public places operating for profit. The idea for this organization
was probably first hatched in 1910 when Giacomo Puccini—then in New York
to attend the world premiere of his opera, *The Girl of the Golden West*—heard
some of his own melodies played in restaurants. Puccini inquired from his publisher's representative how much revenue these performances brought in. When
the representative confessed that no payment was made, Puccini pointed out that
in Europe there existed an organization which saw to it that composers and their
collaborators were compensated through a system of licensing whenever their
music was heard in public places.

The idea to organize a similar society in the United States was discussed
at Luchow's Restaurant on Fourteenth Street in the fall of 1913. Thirty-six men
had been invited; since it rained that day, only eight of them arrived. This poor

attendance was disheartening, and the whole project might have remained still-born then and there but for Herbert's encouragement. One of the men present —Nathan Burkan, an attorney—outlined some of the plans for a society, and a new meeting was set for the Hotel Claridge on Forty-third Street for February 13, 1914.

It was then and there that the American Society of Composers, Authors, and Publishers (ASCAP) was officially born in the presence of a hundred participants. Herbert was offered the presidency, but he declined in favor of George Maxwell and accepted the office of vice-president. Glen MacDonough, Herbert's collaborator, was made secretary; and John Golden, the producer, and Raymond Hubbell, a composer, were elected treasurers. Twenty-two publishers and one hundred and seventy composers and lyricists comprised the initial membership.

A court case was needed to test the legal validity of demanding fees from public places for the use of musical material. An action for infringement of copyright, therefore, was instituted against Shanley's Restaurant in New York, where its orchestra played excerpts from *Sweethearts*. ASCAP suffered setbacks in the lower courts. But on January 22, 1917, the Supreme Court of the United States made a monumental decision favoring ASCAP, which once and for all protected copyrighted songs from unauthorized performances. "If music did not pay, it would be given up," said Oliver Wendell Holmes in his decision. "If it pays, it pays out of the public's pocket. Whether it pays or not, the purpose of employing it is profit, and that is enough."

A battle had been won; but the war was not yet over. Now it was necessary to return to the law courts again and again to make the Supreme Court decision operative. There is no need here to trace the long and arduous road that ASCAP had to take to establish itself. In time, its victory became complete. A system was worked out whereby any institution or medium using songs of ASCAP members had to be licensed in return for an annual fee. By 1922 ASCAP was able to divide a "kitty" of about $200,000 among its almost two hundred members.

The role that Herbert played in this battle was a major one. Raymond Hubbell, who was in the thick of the fight from its very beginnings, put it this way: "Through all the ups and downs of turbulent years, of adverse court decisions and victories, of distracting internal dissensions . . . there stood Victor, 100% American Society, every minute of every day. . . . It never could have been done without him—he just didn't recognize setbacks. The cause, which he knew was just, became the dominating part of him. He just simply forced it through a cloud because he didn't see or feel the cloud."

This was not the first time that Herbert had become entangled in the courts to prove himself a formidable and intransigent fighter. When he was convinced of the cause for which he was battling, he could be a tiger. This had been proved a decade before ASCAP had been first conceived. At that time Herbert had become involved in a personal struggle to vindicate his artistic integrity and, at the same time, to make it impossible for other artists to suffer the humiliation that had been his.

All this had occurred during the early part of the century while Herbert was serving as the conductor of the Pittsburgh Symphony. Marc A. Blumenberg, editor of *Musical Courier,* subjected Herbert to a continuously fierce attack for almost three years. It is possible that Herbert's refusal to advertise in the *Musical Courier* may have drawn out Blumenberg's venom. Whatever the reason, Blumenberg barraged Herbert with accusations that he was no conductor at all, was altogether undeserving of being the head of the Pittsburgh Symphony, and in addition, as a composer of operettas, was a plagiarist. In the issue of July 17, 1901, for example, Blumenberg maintained that "everything Herbert wrote is copied; there is not one original strain in anything he has done, and all his copies are from sources that are comic or serio-comic."

When his patience had reached the breaking point, Herbert decided to fight back, both for the sake of his own honesty and integrity as an artist and for the sake of all other musicians who were being attacked unscrupulously in the *Musical Courier* for a variety of reasons. On October 22, 1902, Herbert instituted a libel suit against the *Musical Courier.* The case lasted six days. Blumenberg and his witnesses failed dismally to prove the existence of basic similarities between Herbert's melodies and those of other composers—particularly under a withering cross-examination by Herbert's attorney, Nathan Burkan, and following the testimony of Herbert's principal witness, Walter Damrosch (then one of the most venerated serious musicians in America). Gilbert Ray Hawkes, the defense attorney, seeing how badly his case was going, tried to make partial amends by insisting that Blumenberg had only the kindest of feelings for Herbert "personally." "We would like him as a friend. But we detest his music and say it is rot. And we earnestly say that the Pittsburgh Art Society disgraced itself when it took him as its musical director." Hawkes then insisted that Blumenberg's published criticisms were "privileged" and that a music journal had every right to publish adverse opinions freely.

In his charge to the jury, the judge maintained that the article was not criticism but libel. "I know of no law that gives the publisher of a paper a right to say an untruthful thing about a private individual or a public individual." The jury was out for two hours, returning with a verdict favoring Herbert and granting him damages of $15,000. An appeal also went against the defendant, though the damages were cut down to a little less than $5,000. Whether the damages were $15,000 or $5,000 meant nothing at all to Herbert who, in either case, had been fully vindicated—a fact recognized by the press and the public. Leading musicians of the city gathered to honor Herbert at a victory dinner. Walter Damrosch, as toastmaster, described Herbert as "the courageous man who with one blow defeated this dragon, this hydra"—referring, of course, to *Musical Courier* and its discredited editor. When Henry E. Krehbiel, the distinguished critic, made his speech, he repeated Blumenberg's accusation against Herbert that Herbert's music was not popular enough even to get played by hand organs. At this point a concealed hand organ suddenly began discharging one beloved Herbert tune after another—to the vociferous joy of all the guests.

Nobody enjoyed this amusing episode more than Herbert, for he was a man who always loved laughter, who had a weakness for perpetrating pranks and tricks and thoroughly enjoyed mischief of all types and varieties. In fact, he

doted on anything that made living more palatable—such as good talk in the
company of his friends; good books, though he always regretted not having
more time for them; the boating and swimming he could indulge in at his
summer place at Lake Placid; good theatre; and most of all, perhaps, good food
and good wines. He was a true gourmet, who always remained faithful to European (and mostly German) dishes and wines. He patronized restaurants in
New York famous for their European cuisines, for example, Luchow's on Fourteenth Street, renowned for its beer and German dishes. Eating was a serious
business with him, and he devoted himself to it with total dedication. He would
regularly plough through an enormous bill of fare, comprising some half a
dozen courses, concentrating on each dish with undivided absorption. He never
allowed serious talk of any kind to intrude while he was eating. Good wines
were so essential a part of his daily life that when Prohibition made them un-
available in America, he seriously planned for the first time to return to Europe
for good. (He dismissed the idea almost as soon as it was born; he knew only
too well that his ties to America had become inextricable.) Vintage wines were
even essential to his work habits, as Isidor Witmark revealed in *From Ragtime
to Swingtime:* "Victor had in his studio a small washtub filled with ice. On this
ice, in true epicurean fashion, he had bottles of beverages to fit each opera. He
had his Rhine wine and Moselle for the German; his clarets and Burgundies
for the French; his Chianti for the Italian."

   Years of overindulgence at the table gave him that huge and portly frame
that once led an artist to describe him as a Frans Hals cavalier. He was large
and round. Like so many big, heavy people, he was usually in jolly spirits. The
twinkle rarely deserted his Irish blue eyes, and his face, which never seemed to
lose its boyish look, rarely reflected anything but a sunny mood. He was, of
course, combustible, as befitting a man with an Irish brogue. But an occasional
outburst of temper—inflamed by injustice, cruelty, or stupidity—would come
suddenly and be dissipated as quickly as summer storms.

   As he grew older—as gray replaced the former dark brown of his curly
hair, and as his boyish face became lined—he might have lost some of his youth-
ful ebullience and vitality. But to the end of his days he remained a warm, generous, fun-loving man, a composer to whom the writing of music was not merely
a way of earning a handsome living but also a way of life.

   His industry was as legendary as his facility and speed; and it remained
that way until the very end. He could work on two, three, or four operettas at
a time, always meeting his deadlines with a score meticulously complete in every
detail. At the same time, in his later years, he would contribute special numbers
and songs for interpolation into other stage productions such as the *Ziegfeld
Follies.* While ploughing through these popular areas, he did not abandon more
serious efforts. Through the years he produced a repertory of symphonic works,
together with two operas: *Natoma,* produced in Philadelphia in 1911, and
Madeleine, seen at the Metropolitan Opera in 1914. He was also a pioneer in
writing an original score for the screen when, in 1916, he wrote music to be
synchronized by a live orchestra with the performance of the motion picture

The Fall of a Nation. He believed implicitly that a composer was no different from other self-respecting workmen who devoted a full day to their jobs.

He could retain a twinkle in his eye, a smile on his lips, and laughter in his heart, in spite of the fact that his later years were not kind to him. World War I had broken out, and the land of Herbert's citizenship was on the battlefield against a country where he had grown up and received his musical training. This ambivalent position—his loyalty to America and his love of all things German—disturbed him no end. He could not honestly direct against the Germans the kind of hate and bitterness that the times were inspiring. He was upset, for example, when as conductor of the New York Orchestra, he had to boycott the works of German composers. "What have Beethoven and Wagner to do with the war?" he asked sadly. At the same time he yielded helplessly to the pressures of a prejudiced public and in doing so, lost some of his self-respect.

The failure of critics and audiences to respond as enthusiastically to his serious music as much as he would have liked was a sore that never healed. Herbert regarded his American-Indian opera, *Natoma,* as his masterwork. Though the world premiere aroused considerable interest and anticipation, the opera itself was annihilated by the critics. They made a shambles of Joseph Redding's libretto, one of them going so far as to say that "it should go down into operatic history as one of the most futile, fatuous, halting, impotent, inane, and puerile ever written." And while critics were more respectful to Herbert's music, nobody looked upon it as an epochal achievement.

Herbert's second and last opera, *Madeleine*—this time with French characters and setting—was received even more harshly a few years later and was dropped from the Metropolitan Opera repertory after six presentations. A projected production in Paris (which led Herbert to make his first return visit to Europe since 1887, and to which he looked forward with excitement) never materialized.

Nor was Herbert prospering in his own backyard—that of the operetta. He was convinced that never had he written a better score than the one for *Eileen.* Its creation had been a labor of love, since the characters and setting were Irish, and into this task he poured his heart. His faith in his music was justified by a later generation, since "Thine Alone" is now fully appreciated as one of his most eloquent ballads—and one of his most successful ones, too. And the waltz "Eileen (Alanna Astore)" is a melody of haunting loveliness. The decidedly Irish flavors in Herbert's musical stew—particularly in a song like "When Shall I Again See Ireland?", a nostalgic tribute to his native land—realized his ambition "to write an Irish operetta" (as he told his audience in a curtain speech) "that would be worthy of the traditions of a great race and its literature."

But *Eileen* was a failure. It lasted only seventy performances; an attempt to revive it—in Cleveland in 1921—repeated the New York failure.

Herbert was never again destined to write an operetta matching the successes he had known before World War I. His work was still much in demand; his operettas kept coming, season after season; and many another musical production called for his services for individual numbers. But though his output remained impressive, he produced little that became popular. The audiences had deserted him, even if producers had remained faithful.

What was happening, of course, was that in the era immediately following World War I, the Victor Herbert operetta was becoming an anachronism. This new age glorified syncopation and jazz, the fox-trot and the Charleston. The gentle, sentimental ballads and waltzes in which lay Herbert's great strength were being pushed into the background by the more virile efforts of an Irving Berlin, a Jerome Kern, a young George Gershwin, a W. C. Handy, and so forth. Victor Herbert did not have to be told that time had passed him by. To a friend he remarked sadly: "My day is over. They are forgetting poor old Herbert."

He died thinking he was a has-been, his death taking place in New York on May 26, 1924, while he was working on a few numbers for the *Ziegfeld Follies*. He had partaken of a modest lunch at the Lambs Club with several friends. Feeling physically uncomfortable after the meal, he went from the Lamb Club to East Seventy-seventh Street to consult his physician, Dr. Emanuel Baruch. As it happened, the physician was not in his office at that moment. Herbert decided to take a walk around the block and return. But before he could reach the street he collapsed, and died instantaneously of a heart attack. Only after his death did his friends discover that Herbert had long suffered from a heart condition, which he had kept a dark secret.

His passing was lamented. There was no question in anybody's mind that he had enriched the American musical theatre and the American popular song prodigiously. "Losing Victor Herbert," said Deems Taylor, "the musical world loses someone it will never quite replace." Another noted music critic, Henry T. Finck, wrote: "On the whole I consider Herbert the greatest musician of all time with Irish blood in his veins." Florenz Ziegfeld described Herbert as "the greatest musician America ever developed." Eddie Cantor said that Herbert "made every aspect of his work so distinctive that the whole world knew that it had one great composer who was able to and did give characteristic expression to the American spirit."

When Herbert died, he belonged to a tradition in the American musical theatre, and in American popular song, that was dying rapidly. He was a voice of the past, not of the future. He was essentially the musical spokesman of Europe and not of America. And yet, almost half a century since his death, his best songs continue to survive. Because of these songs, his screen biography, *The Great Victor Herbert,* proved a treasure house of riches, despite a synthetic story. And also because of these songs, his best operettas—however sadly dated their librettos may be—are continuously revived on stage and screen, for the kind of sentiment and enchantment that Herbert captured so magically in his finest melodies are universal, and can never become obsolete.

GREAT MEN OF AMERICAN POPULAR SONG

Songs from Musical Comedy–I

George M. Cohan

I'm a Yankee Doodle Dandy
A Yankee Doodle do or die,
A real live nephew of my Uncle Sam's
Born on the Fourth of July. . . .

These are the opening lines from the chorus of "The Yankee Doodle Boy," which Johnny Jones, an American jockey come to England to ride in the derby, sings by way of self-introduction in George M. Cohan's first success in the musical-comedy theatre, *Little Johnny Jones.* Cohan himself was playing the role of Johnny Jones. In singing these lines from his own song, Cohan was being autobiographical.

For George M. Cohan *was* a "Yankee Doodle dandy," who for a long time insisted that he had been born on the fourth of July, though his birth certificate implacably places the event one day earlier. Cocky and brash, fully conscious of the many facets of his creativity, he was not only a nephew of Uncle Sam but also a recognizable offspring of a country grown blatant in its pride, a country flexing its muscles with a conscious awareness of its strength.

On the stage—as a performer, writer, stage director, composer—Cohan represented the acceleration of speed and movement which so characterized the turn of the twentieth century in America, with the emergence of the subway and the automobile and the spreading arteries of the railroad. As an early exponent of eccentric dancing, Cohan would throw himself into his movements with a boundless energy that often made him leap over furniture. As a stage director, he would bark at his actors: "Speed! Let's have speed! Lots of it. Let's have perpetual motion!"

Supreme self-confidence and a pride in country that bordered on chauvinism were Cohan's trademarks. With a surpassing sense of creative power, and with an unshakable conviction that there was nothing in the field of entertainment he could not do as well as (if not better than) others, he became a successful actor, dancer, singer, playwright, director, composer of songs, lyricist—and in time also a producer, theatre manager, and theatre owner. Like the America and the country of which he was such an authentic spokesman, he thought in large terms. And like America at the dawn of the twentieth century, he was symbolic of the bulging national ego of that age. His favorite stage routine was to drape an American flag about his person and strut up and down the stage singing praises to his country. The character he most liked to portray, and which he did best, was the egocentric, superpatriotic American with irrepressible energies and dynamism. The songs he liked to write were thoroughly American in spirit, mood, and personality—and often in content as well. "You're a Grand Old Flag," "Any Place the Old Flag Flies," and "My Flag" represented his salute not only to his flag but to his country. "Give My Regards to Broadway," "Hello, Broadway," "The Man Who Owns Broadway," and "Too Long from Longacre Square" were his love songs to his favorite thoroughfares. "Over There," possibly the most famous American war song ever written, was his way of fighting for his country during World War I.

In front of the footlights, Cohan was ever a Yankee Doodle dandy: with his slick, well-tailored American suits; his buttoned shoes topped by gray cloth, and heels built up to give him added height; his hat (whether derby, straw, or top) slightly askew toward one eye. A bamboo cane was held jauntily in hand as he danced about with that kangaroo step so identifiably his. This was the strut of a vain man, a man supremely sure of what he was doing, a man at one with his environment and milieu. Individual, too, was the way he would sing out of the corner of his mouth, with a unique nasal twang; or the way he would deliver to his audience some homespun message, or some greeting, pointing to his public with his forefinger while his eyes drooped slightly. "Here," once said Oscar Hammerstein II, "was the kind of American we all hoped to be when we grew a few years older. Never was a plant more indigenous to a particular part of earth than was George M. Cohan to the United States of his day."

He brought to his musical-comedy texts and to his songs (in both the lyrics and the music) the same kind of strong, unmistakable American personality. He peopled his musicals with American characters. He usually placed them in recognizable American settings. He had them talk in slang the way most Americans did. And he had them sing the kind of simple, somewhat ingenuous, sometimes sentimental songs Americans everywhere were fond of whistling and playing. Because he accomplished what he did in the various areas of the stage— and before anybody else was doing the same thing—Cohan must surely be recognized as the founding father of musical comedy.

Cohan was the third and last child of Jerry (Jeremiah, more formally) and Helen (or Nellie, less formally) Cohan. Their first child died in infancy, and the second, Josephine, came two years before George. Jeremiah Cohan had been performing with various minstrel-show companies when, in 1874, he fell in love with and married Helen Frances Costigan, whose hometown was Providence, Rhode Island. She had never appeared on the stage. Nevertheless, soon after her marriage, she joined her husband in a new vaudeville act billed as "Mr. and Mrs. Jerry Cohan," for which the husband provided all the material, did his own staging, and outside the theatre served as his own manager and advance man. When Helen became pregnant, the Cohans returned to Providence. Then, with infant in arms, the Cohans trouped along the vaudeville circuit. The child would be kept on the move in noisy, dirty trains; would find shelter in shabby boardinghouses and poorly lit, cold hotels; would lie in dismal dressing rooms while the parents were on the stage. Then when the child was old enough to walk and talk, he or she became a part of the Cohan act.

George Michael was born in Providence, Rhode Island, on July 3, 1878. As a child, he received a smattering of schooling in the elementary grades in Providence; also a few violin lessons. He hated both the school and the violin, and he soon abandoned both. From then on, his education came from inside the theatre. As an infant, he made his stage debut by becoming a human prop in "The Two Dans," his father's act. When he was eight, he played the violin in the pit orchestra for another Cohan act, "Daniel Boone"; and when he was nine, he entered a Cohan sketch entitled "The Two Barneys" billed as "Master Georgie." In this official stage debut he was allowed to say a few lines and play the violin. By 1888 the vaudeville act was officially baptized the Four Cohans, with Josephine called upon to perform skirt dances. George expanded his own activities in that act by doing buck-and-wing dances and giving recitations. By the time he was eleven, he was also beginning to contribute some of the material, his first such being a sketch, "Four of a Kind." In his thirteenth year he toured as Peck in *Peck's Bad Boy,* and when he was fifteen, he shared with his sister the act "The Lively Bootblack."

Songwriting for George began when he was sixteen with "Why Did Nellie Leave Home?," the lady in the title named after George's mother. The publishing house of Witmark purchased this number outright for twenty-five dollars and published it—but not before they got somebody to revise Cohan's lyrics. This was both the first and the last time that Cohan ever allowed anybody to tamper with one of his songs. Making no headway as a commercial investment, "Why Did Nellie Leave Home?" became the only Cohan song ever published by Witmark.

Cohan was now becoming a familiar figure around Union Square, where he hounded publishers with his songs and wore down their resistance through the sheer power of his ego and voluble persuasion. "Just goes to show how smart those babies in there are," he commented breezily about the Witmarks when they lost interest in him, "publishing all that bum material written by a lot of hams. Here am I, the best songwriter, walking right by their door with four or five big sure hits under my arm."

Had the Witmarks taken a chance on Cohan's second song, they would have had a mild moneymaker, for "Hot Tamale Alley" was introduced in vaudeville by the headliner May Irwin, and through her efforts aroused a certain amount of interest which in turn stimulated sheet-music sales. A major song success came to Cohan in 1898 with "I Guess I'll Have To Telegraph My Baby," the first popular hit song about wireless telegraphy. Ethel Levey, former star of Weber and Fields extravaganzas, introduced it in vaudeville.

In July of 1899, in Atlantic City, New Jersey, Ethel Levey became Mrs. George M. Cohan. At the same time she also became the fifth principal in the Four Cohans vaudeville act, which by this time was getting top billing all over the country and earning the then-considerable weekly sum of $1,000. George M. Cohan was the mainstay of the act, not only as star performer, but also as author of the sketches, composer and lyricist of the songs, and business manager. (It was about this time that he inaugurated a lifelong habit of making a brief final curtain speech to his audiences with the words "My mother thanks you, my father thanks you, my sister thanks you, and I thank you.") As if to prove that all of this was not enough to sap his seemingly boundless energies, he wrote a considerable amount of material for other performers. In 1901 he wrote a monologue with which Florence Reed made her stage debut to begin her fruitful career in the theatre. Cohan turned out over 150 sketches and monologues, as well as several dozen songs, in a three-year period. In theatrical circles, he was looked upon as "the young genius"—but a genius without the customary aloofness or introversion. In truth, he was regarded as a perfectly wonderful companion, a splendid mixer among men. "He went to ball games, to fights, to bars," says his biographer, Ward Morehouse. "He liked the good fellowship of male companions and enjoyed putting his foot on brass rails . . . and talking of early vaudeville days, now swiftly receding. . . . He was forever in the company of songwriters, actors, musicians, music publishers, agents, vaudeville managers, and, occasionally, Broadway managers and ball players."

A new century was at hand and with it a new age for America and Americans. Cohan was to be its symbol and its spokesman. He knew full well by now that in vaudeville he had soared as high as was possible. His varied talents demanded more space in which to fly, and he realized at once that such space could be found on Broadway. What he was thinking about in particular was musical comedy.

His first experiment in this direction came through the expansion of one of his vaudeville sketches into a three-act play embellished with a dozen songs. *The Governor's Son* came to Broadway on February 25, 1901, starring the five Cohans, with George M. Cohan directing. Broadway rejected it, and it closed after only thirty-two performances. But on the road, for the next two years or so, it did much better. Upon returning to New York *The Governor's Son* more than doubled its initial run in that city. To its author and star performer all this represented success; it also meant, as he firmly told his father, that he had finally been "rescued" from vaudeville.

The expansion of another vaudeville sketch, *Running for Office,* became his second bid for the favor of Broadway, once again with the five Cohans in the cast. The history of *The Governor's Son* was repeated. The box-office returns during its initial New York run left much to be desired, but the road once again responded enthusiastically, and when the show returned to Broadway, the audiences proved more hospitable. Even one of its songs became a lesser hit—a breezy number, "If I Were Only Mr. Morgan," delivered in the now familiar breezy Cohan manner.

A significant development took place in 1904 for Cohan. He formed with Sam H. Harris a producing partnership that lasted many years and for which Cohan would write his greatest stage successes. This relationship between the two men was an ideal one, since each admired the other and himself, each loved baseball passionately, and to each the theatre was the be-all and end-all of existence.

They opened an office on Broadway and Fortieth Street with more hopes and ambitions than ready cash. But they had a good product to sell—of that they were both sure. They planned making their producing bow with the first musical Cohan would write for Broadway, and the first in which he would have a role commensurate with his performing capabilities. The advertisements in the theatrical papers told the story in large type by announcing that sometime in 1904 "the Yankee Doodle comedian" planned to star in "his newest musical comedy—*Little Johnny Jones* (the American jockey)."

When *Little Johnny Jones* opened at the Liberty Theatre in New York on November 7, 1904, the five Cohans had been diminished by one, since Josephine had decided to go off on her own. George M. Cohan played the title role—a character inspired by Tod Sloan, a famous American jockey of that period who had ridden in the English Derby. A character, within a cops-and-robbers plot; songs like "The Yankee Doodle Boy" and "Give My Regards to Broadway"; a recitation with homespun philosophy like "Life's a Funny Proposition"; and an American flag-waving routine—all this represented something fresh, new, and thoroughly American for the musical theatre. However, most critics did not like what they saw and heard. Having been oriented to elegant operettas, they considered this new kind of theatre crude, noisy, and naïve. One of these critics expressed himself as follows: "Mr. Cohan has written a lot of dialogue that has some bright spots, but for the most part is commonplace, to put it kindly; and he has provided a dozen and a half 'musical numbers' whose distinguishing feature is ginger. In fact there is more ginger than music. It is all very Cohanesque."

The critics might send in a negative report; business at the box office might be slack. But Cohan's self-assurance, matched only by his stubbornness, would not allow him to admit that *Little Johnny Jones* was a bad show, that it had no audience appeal. Profiting from two earlier experiences, he decided to close down the New York run after fifty-two performances and go on the road. Once again the road proved receptive to his offering. In city after city and in town after town, *Little Johnny Jones* filled the houses. All this while, Cohan kept on rewriting his show, tightening the action, improving the dialogue. When he brought the musical back to New York on May 8, 1905, it had stronger situations, more effective scenes, and a greater number of laughs. *Little Johnny Jones* now did well enough to stay three months, and to return to New York the following fall for a third engagement.

The show made a good deal of money, putting the producing firm of Cohan and Harris on a firm footing. It also helped make Cohan an important box-office draw—something that the producer A. L. Erlanger realized full well when he asked Cohan to write a musical for Fay Templeton. Fay Templeton, a star in burlesque for many years, was now ready to make her first appearance within a Broadway musical theatre. Erlanger wanted to produce the show for Miss Templeton's debut, suggested that Harris become business manager, and Cohan, the author-composer.

Cohan complied with *Forty-Five Minutes from Broadway,* which opened at the New Amsterdam Theatre on January 1, 1906. As Mary Jane (a housemaid become heiress upon the death of her wealthy employer), Fay Templeton made a triumphant debut within the musical-comedy theatre, especially when she sang "Mary's a Grand Old Name." That production had still another all-important Broadway debut: that of Victor Moore, who had arrived by way of stock companies and vaudeville. His role was that of Kid Burns, onetime professional gambler, but still a hopeless bettor on the horses. Kid Burns is involved in the principal romance of the play, with Mary Jane, and to him the important title song was assigned. A third song hit was "So Long, Mary," which Donald Brian introduced, one year before he became a matinee idol in New York as Prince Danilo in the American premiere of Franz Lehár's *The Merry Widow.*

Forty-Five Minutes from Broadway was a solid success during its out-of-town tryouts. In New York business boomed from opening night on—thanks to some free valuable publicity showered upon it by the chamber of commerce in New Rochelle. New Rochelle was the town "forty-five minutes from Broadway" which provided the setting for the text. The chamber of commerce felt strongly that the show was a slander on its fair community, since the story showed New Rochelle to be a hick town and its inhabitants to be "Rubes." The chamber of commerce even threatened to instigate a citywide boycott of the show. But this boycott never materialized. In fact the chamber of commerce dropped all its charges when it soon came to the realization that the immense success of this music was helping make the town of New Rochelle famous.

Cohan had not written a part for himself in this production. (However, when *Forty-Five Minutes from Broadway* was revived in 1912, he did take over from Victor Moore the role of Kid Burns.) Cohan once again wrote a starring role for himself in the same year of 1906 in *George Washington, Jr.,* where he portrayed a superpatriot who takes over the name of America's first President as an act of defiance against an Anglophile father. A play with such strong patriotic overtones could be expected to send Cohan into the writing of a stirring patriotic song. It did. "You're a Grand Old Flag" allowed Cohan to do one of his beloved flag routines. The idea for the song came to him during a conversation with a Civil War veteran who had been color-bearer during Pickett's charge on Gettysburg. In commenting on the American flag, the veteran remarked proudly: "She's a grand old rag." Cohan originally called his song "You're a Grand Old Rag" and this is the way it was heard on the opening night of his show. But several patriotic societies complained that referring to the American flag as a "rag" was a slur and an insult. Cohan then changed the word "rag" to "flag."

His next few musicals are remembered today primarily because of one or two songs from each. Out of *The Talk of New York,* in 1907 (written to bring Victor Moore back to the stage in the role of Kid Burns), came "When a Fellow's on the Level with a Girl Who's on the Square" and "When We Are M-a-double-r-i-e-d." Out of *Fifty Miles from Boston,* in 1908, emerged one of Cohan's most celebrated songs about the Irish, "Harrigan."

Beginning with 1914, with *Hello, Broadway,* Cohan became interested in the revue as the medium not only for American songs and sketches but also for satire and burlesque. In 1916 and again in 1918 he wrote and produced two revues bearing his name in their titles. He also carried his brand of Americanism and his unique sense of dramatic timing into several nonmusical plays, two of which enjoyed enormous success: *Get Rich Quick, Wallingford* in 1910 and *Seven Keys to Baldpate* in 1913.

There was only one Cohan in the limelight now. The others in his family had fallen by the wayside. His wife, Ethel, deserted the cast of *George Washington, Jr.* after a matinee performance in Cleveland in December of 1906. The Cohans were divorced the following February. (On June 29, 1907, Cohan married Agnes Nolan, a young actress playing minor parts in some of Cohan's productions. She survived him after thirty-five years of devoted marriage.) Josephine had made a brief return to the Cohan fold when all five played together for the last time in *The Yankee Prince.* The father and mother made their last stage appearance in Cohan's *Broadway Jones,* in 1912.

Still under thirty-five, Cohan was one of the most powerful and wealthiest men in the American theatre. In 1911 the firm of Cohan and Harris boasted six hits at one time on Broadway; they also had a controlling interest in seven theatres. Between 1910 and 1917 eleven George M. Cohan plays were mounted on Broadway—five musicals (in three of which he was the star), five nonmusicals, and one revival, once again with himself as star. He had achieved the heights of success in practically every area of the theatre he saw fit to cultivate. He had even invaded the world of silent films by appearing in versions of three of his stage plays released by Artcraft Picture Corporation: *Seven Keys to Baldpate, Broadway Jones,* and *Hit-the-Trail Holiday.*

He worked hard, with an intensity and absorption matched by few. "He talked of slowing down," says Ward Morehouse, "but never did. . . . It has always been popularly supposed that Cohan's writings came easy, but they didn't. He worked fast because of terrific concentration, but he sweated for his best effects; they generally came the hard way. On his so-called vacations he was seldom relaxed. When he was not actually writing or directing or acting, he was thinking, planning, wondering."

He had little time for diversions or hobbies, in fact had little need of them. His passion was baseball, but after his boyhood he never played on a diamond, and later in life he seldom attended a game. He did not play golf, he almost never drove a car or went swimming, and about the only form of physical exertion he favored was walking. Late in life, he developed the reading habit, but before that happened his literary fare had consisted primarily of theatrical trade journals and the daily newspapers.

He was a little man, with so much spring and bounce that it almost seemed as if in place of veins his body had highly charged electric wires. At times he was extremely voluble; at other times he lapsed into long periods of silence. He was a complicated man, a man of many contradictions. One of his friends put it this way: "He was vain and violent tempered, childish at times, sulky and temperamental, but a man with a heart and soul, one who was easily hurt and one who could be a great friend." His generosity was legendary. Through the years he supported armies of theatrical people who had come upon unfortunate days, and he did this unostentatiously and without publicity. He was always entertaining his friends at leading hotels in baronial fashion and was always passing around the most extravagant tips to the help. His word or his handshake were gilt-edge securities. He was soft, sentimental, capable of great affection. Yet when he bore a grudge, it was for keeps; and when he felt a friend had turned against him, he became a most bitter enemy.

By the time the United States became involved in World War I, it seemed there could be no further triumphs for him to enjoy. But there was still one Alpine peak he could scale: the writing of the song with which World War I will always be associated, perhaps the most famous war song ever written in America, and a war song that ultimately won for Cohan the Congressional Medal of Honor—"Over There."

At that time Cohan was living in Great Neck, Long Island, where he had purchased a large, rambling estate in 1914. He woke up on the morning of April 7, 1917, to read in the morning newspaper that Congress had declared war on Germany. "I read those war headlines and I got to thinking and humming to myself," he later revealed to an interviewer, "and for a minute I thought I was going into my dance. I was all finished with both the chorus and the verse, and by the time I got to town I also had a title."

The first time Cohan tried out the song it was received apathetically, and at a place where it might have been expected to make a good showing. This happened at Fort Myers, near Washington, D. C., where Cohan sang it in a show for the troops. Then, in the fall of 1917, Charles King presented it at a Red Cross benefit at the Hippodrome in New York. After that Nora Bayes plugged it in her vaudeville act. Now the song caught fire. Leo Feist paid

$25,000 for publication rights, a shrewd purchase, since within a few months half a million copies of sheet music were sold, with two million copies disposed of by the time the war ended. In addition, the song sold over a million records —including one made by Enrico Caruso, no less. President Wilson called it "a genuine inspiration to all American manhood."

He was at the very zenith of his career when frustration, bitterness, and anger overwhelmed him to the point where he began to lose his zest for the theatre. These emotions were aroused by a strike called on August 7, 1919, by the Actors Equity Association against all theatre managers to compel them to recognize it as the bargaining representative for its members. Another thing that concerned the association was some of the flagrant abuses then victimizing actors, abuses demanding an immediate remedy. The strike closed down twelve Broadway shows overnight. In a month's time twelve more shows were unable to give further performances. Such developments seriously affected the firm of Harris and Cohan.

To George M. Cohan, the closing of his shows—as well as finding his friends standing on the other side of the barricades—represented a personal attack which he took to heart. In the front rank of the Equity forces were many actors whom time and again Cohan had helped with badly needed funds or with jobs, and some actors whom he helped to lift to stardom. Seeing them line up solidly against him in the Equity fight represented to him an act of treachery. That stubborn streak which had always been a part of his makeup, and that combustible Irish temper of his, now made him refuse to recognize the validity of any of the issues raised by Equity in the strike. He argued hotly that the theatre had no place for unionism, that performers had no just cause for grievances. He promised to throw every dollar at his command to defeat Equity. And he swore that should he fail in this fight, he would desert the theatre forever.

Cohan's personal war against Equity did not last long, but as long as it lasted it was filled with bitterness. Cohan regarded many who up to now had been personal friends as enemies. In an attempt to separate himself from them and the others who sided with Equity, he withdrew his membership from both the Friars and the Lambs clubs. He also helped organize, and was president of, the Actors Fidelity League, founded as a rival to Equity, for actors who stood ready to believe as he did.

By the time a new season rolled around, the Actors Equity had won a complete victory. Normalcy returned to the Broadway stage soon after Labor Day. The war on Broadway was over, but Cohan's personal war would recognize no truce. He kept on using his immense influence and popularity to discredit or undermine Equity in every way he could. Again and again he was quoted in the press that he was withdrawing permanently from the American theatre and that he was thinking of setting up shop in London. He was shadowboxing, since he had no opponent facing him in the ring. That opponent had long since been picked as the winner and the champ. The position of Equity in the theatre was now invulnerable.

Though he made a number of trips to Europe, he did not retire from the Broadway theatre. But he did lose much of his former love and excitement and exhilaration for the stage, and for this reason he began curtailing his activities. For one thing, to the astonishment of everybody on Broadway, he dissolved the highly profitable firm of Cohan and Harris in 1920. He ventured into a solo flight as producer with somebody else's play (*The Genius and the Crowd* in September of 1920), but it was unable to get off the ground. Later the same year he brought his play *The Tavern* to Broadway, a nonmusical play which he was always to regard with special pride and affection. The critics were less enthusiastic than he. Cohan fought them back by publishing a series of expensive advertisements refuting their arguments. Then Cohan stepped into the leading role of *The Tavern* (Arnold Daly had created it). But the verdict of the critics of his play had not changed and it rankled in his heart. And his grudge against Equity was still at white heat. Finally, Cohan announced not only that he was closing *The Tavern* but that he was also going into retirement. At the last performance, late in June of 1921, some of the theatre's most distinguished personalities gathered to attend what they believed would be Cohan's last Broadway appearance. They also heard him make a brief, but bitter, speech. "I am going away with great regret. I have done nothing but what I have been forced into doing. If at any time any one can show me how I can return to the theatre and retain my self-respect, I hope it will be pointed out to me. When labor no longer has a stronghold on the profession I may come back."

He did come back, to be sure, even though Equity continued to be a dominant force in the theatre. He came back because theatre blood flowed in his veins, and without the theatre he felt anemic. Two of his own plays were mounted on Broadway in 1922. By the end of 1923 he himself was once again in front of the footlights—the star of a comedy, *The Song and Dance Man*. A year of retirement came after that, devoted mainly to the writing of his autobiography, *Twenty Years on Broadway*. Retirement ended on October 5, 1925, with the production of his comedy, *American Born,* at the Hudson Theatre.

From then on he continued to write and produce musicals and nonmusical plays for a number of years. From time to time he acted in one of them. But the Cohan name had begun to lose its magic. And Cohan the playwright and songwriter was being continually mauled by the critics, most of whom were quite ready to admit that though he had become sadly dated in virtually every area of the theatre, in one he remained with few rivals—that of acting.

A disastrous experience in Hollywood contributed additional gall to a cup overflowing with bitterness. Paramount contracted him to make his talking-picture debut in *The Phantom President*. This was a Rodgers and Hart screen musical starring Jimmy Durante and Claudette Colbert. Cohan was required to play a dual role: as a staid and stuffy banker running for the office of President of the United States and as a charming, ingratiating medicine-show man who bore a striking physical resemblance to the banker. The banker wins the election by having the medicine man do all the campaigning; he even captures the medicine man's sweetheart.

From the very beginning, Cohan's Hollywood experience was a disaster. He resented the fact that he was given billing below Claudette Colbert and Jimmy Durante. He was upset to discover that few of those with whom he had to work were aware of his achievements in the theatre, and that those who were aware of them were not awed. One gatekeeper refused to allow him to park his car on the lot because he was not a "star." One of the executives took him to task for sending in, on yellow paper in pencil, ideas on how the picture should be filmed. In fact, before long, this director made it perfectly clear to Cohan that suggestions were not welcome. The last straw of humiliation came when the director tried to teach Cohan how to do a flag routine with the song "Somebody Ought To Wave a Flag"—he who had originated and popularized flag routines on the stage! Grudgingly, listlessly, in total misery, Cohan somehow managed to complete his assignment. He left Hollywood with a vow never again to appear in motion pictures. "Hereafter I'll get my sunshine at the ball park or in Central Park, or not at all," he remarked. He also confessed that were he given a choice he would have preferred to go to prison in Leavenworth than work in Hollywood.

Cohan returned to Broadway, scene of his former triumphs, once again to star in one of his own plays, *Pigeons and People.* This was in January of 1933. It cannot be said that he received the welcome of a hero. He was on the stage throughout the whole evening in a whimsical escapade about a man who found pigeons more appealing than people, and who liked spending his time in the park feeding the birds. Hardly more than a one-act play extended and distended into three acts, *Pigeons and People* was more of a stunt than a drama, and for a good part of the evening it was just a bore. Richard Watts, Jr., said in the *Herald Tribune:* "After all these years of seeing Cohan, it's the first time I ever realized I could get tired of him."

His stage comedy, *Dear Old Darling,* in 1936, was weaker still; it stayed on the boards just two weeks. Cohan's next play was also a failure. His last play— and his last appearance as a stage performer—took place on May 17, 1940, in *The Return of the Vagabond.* It had the shortest run of any Cohan production— only seven performances in all. "I guess people don't understand me anymore," he told a friend sadly. "And I don't understand them. It's got so that an evening's entertainment won't do. Give an audience an evening of what you call realism and you got a hit. It's getting too much for me, kid. I'll never come back to New York again. They don't want me no more." And this time he kept his word.

On the eve of his sixtieth birthday, Cohan still found himself a millionaire, a man who had made history both on Broadway and in Tin Pan Alley, but also a man whose day as playwright, librettist, and song composer was definitely over. Men far more knowledgeable, far more sophisticated, far more subtle, and far more imaginative than he had come upon the scene to have their brilliance throw his own talents into a permanent shade.

Nevertheless, in one category at least, he was able to maintain his exalted station. As an actor he was still able to show that there were few to equal him. In fact, now more than ever he was able to prove himself one of the most ingratiating, touchingly human and individual performers that the American theatre has known.

In 1933 he was starred in the Theatre Guild production of *Ah, Wilderness!* a comedy that won a Pulitzer Prize for its author, Eugene O'Neill. Four years after that, Cohan assumed the role of President Franklin D. Roosevelt in the Rodgers and Hart musical satire on Washington politics, *I'd Rather Be Right*. "Mr. Cohan presents the Guild with the best performance most of us have ever seen him give," said Gilbert Gabriel in the New York *American* after seeing *Ah, Wilderness!* Brooks Atkinson wrote in *The New York Times* about Cohan's performance in *I'd Rather Be Right*: "Mr. Cohan has never been in better form. The audience was his, and lovingly his, all last evening."

He gathered other honors, too, as the years went on, even if his career as playwright and songwriter had ended. In 1941 he received from President Franklin D. Roosevelt the Congressional Medal of Honor "in belated recognition of the authorship of 'Over There,' " and Cohan's birthday in 1942 was decreed George M. Cohan Day in New York by a proclamation of Mayor La Guardia.

Most significantly, Hollywood—which had treated him so shabbily, having had such little consciousness of his importance—did a sudden turnabout by paying him its ultimate tribute: filming the story of his life. That movie, *Yankee Doodle Dandy*, starred James Cagney as Cohan in a stunning performance that captured an Academy Award. All the great Cohan songs were there; the old flag-waving routine was there; the recognizable stage mannerisms of Cohan were there—all in a stirring account of a vaudeville song-and-dance man who had become an immortal in the theatre. When Cohan saw the production in a private showing, he was visibly moved. Then the film opened in New York on May 30, 1942, to an audience of celebrities who paid almost six million dollars in war bonds to gain admission. A London audience purchased almost a million pounds in war securities to attend the English premiere that fall.

On October 19, 1941, Cohan underwent an abdominal operation from which he made an excellent recovery. He spent the following year quietly— partly at his apartment at 993 Fifth Avenue; partly in West Orange, New Jersey. Then he began growing weaker. He was convinced that he did not have much longer to live. One day he compelled his nurse to take him by taxi to Broadway. He stopped off at the Hollywood Theatre to catch a last glimpse of one of the scenes in *Yankee Doodle Dandy*. It was almost as if he had come to say good-by to his street of streets, Broadway, and to a motion picture which had caught so magnificently the essence of his personality and life's achievements. He never saw Broadway again. He died at his New York apartment on November 5, 1942, his last words being "Look after Agnes."

No, he never saw Broadway again. And yet in a sense he is seeing it all the time—as a statue erected in his honor in the very heart of the Great Stem, at Duffy Square, unveiled in 1959. He stands there immobile, silent, in that section of New York that meant so much to him and to which he had contributed so much. *So much*—and yet most of it has by now been forgotten. Those plays and musical comedy texts of his—however significant they may have been as the beginnings of a genuine American musical theatre—are as obsolete as a horse-drawn trolley car; were it not for biographies of Cohan and histories of the theatre, few people today would even remember what any one of those shows was about. Those magnificent performances of his as actor, first in vaudeville, then in his own shows, and finally in the works of other men will also soon be a dim memory, if even that, for are not an actor's accomplishments writ in water once he has left the scene of his triumphs?

But if Cohan is remembered at all, even to the younger generation, it is because of his songs. They were naïve songs, a conscientious and honest critic must confess. For the most part, they were mawkish in their sentimentality, ingenuous in their humor, cliché-ridden in their philosophy on life. There was very little effort made at a fresh turn of phrase, be it in the words or in the music. But they are, for all that, songs filled with nostalgia, songs that have survived because they give voice to a bygone age, because they are a slice of Americana.

That those songs, corny though they may be, still have the capacity to appeal even to a present-day sophisticated audience was proved as late as 1968, when there came to Broadway a stage musical based on the life of, and studded with songs by, Cohan—*George M.* starring Joel Grey as Cohan. Random episodes from Cohan's life were loosely strung together, sometimes without any seeming rhyme or reason, for the express purpose of providing an excuse for the presentation of Cohan's songs, the unfamiliar ones as well as the famous ones. More than once there was not even an attempt made to fix a song to a biographical incident, but was stuck into the context without any apparent relevance. Except for Joel Grey's performance—remarkable in how it managed to be Cohanesque with very little attempt on his part to look like Cohan or to imitate his mannerisms—there was not much in *George M.* to set the musical theatre afire. But *George M.* drew the crowds into the theatre and inspired a kind response from the critics for one good reason: the show was a veritable cornucopia of Cohanesque song gems. "They are," wrote John S. Wilson in reviewing the original-cast recording, "part of our musical bloodstream. It is virtually impossible not to respond to the vigor and spirit of Cohan's melodies, even those that are tied to his outdated, flag-waving lyrics. His tunes have such a graceful lilt, such a jaunty air, so much sheer enthusiasm . . . that they survive and flourish despite the sentiments and the sentimentality that keep cropping up in the lyrics. Cohan's songs are period pieces. No one is even trying to write songs like that these days and no one is likely to."

And while to Clive Barnes, reviewing *George M.* for *The New York Times,* the show seemed "scrappy, ill-prepared, mediocrely written," its shortcomings were more than compensated for by the omnipresence of Cohan's songs, "which by now have burned their way into the heart and dated into immortality. Before you can say they don't write songs like that anymore, they are singing the next one. . . . It was no accident on the first night that the audience applauded numbers as they came up in the overture. Nor was it an accident when Mr. Grey first throws out 'Give My Regards to Broadway' at the audience, a thrill ran through that was hardly the less real for its being a sign of recognition rather than a gasp of surprise. And all the big numbers are here. . . . And at last the audience went out, for the first time this season, humming the music, even if most of it was more than fifty years old. It has kept well."

GREAT MEN OF AMERICAN POPULAR SONG

Songs with Syncopation

Irving Berlin

Far from Tin Pan Alley, far from the amusement places and madding crowds of Union Square, a new note in popular music was sounding. This was a raucous, strident, uninhibited musical art that would eventually penetrate into Tin Pan Alley and the New York theatre and help to contribute to songwriting a new spirit, new techniques, new textures, a new dynamism. This new music was born in New Orleans, in the red-light district known as Storyville, and it was called "ragtime."

The word "ragtime" probably comes from the clog dancing of the Negroes, which was sometimes described as "ragging." The music itself is also of Negroid origin, tracing its roots back to the spiritual and the religious shout. Even syncopation, one of the basic distinguishing traits of ragtime, sprang from the songs the Negro had imported into the New World from Africa. The strong, sharply marked accents, the placement of a syncopated melody over an even rhythm, were later and more sophisticated developments in America of the hand-clapping and the foot-stamping that accompanied the native songs of the Negro in Africa. "Tiger Rag" was one of the earliest of such American-Negro ragtime classics, believed to be an old French quadrille taken over by the New Orleans jazzmen. Syncopated piano music was the forte of men in New Orleans like Jelly Roll Morton, probably the greatest ragtime pianist in all Storyville and the composer of such early piano rags as "King Porter Stomp."

Syncopation, the conversion of an expected strong beat into a weak one or a weak beat into a strong one, had been used in such early minstrel-show tunes as "Zip Coon" and Dan Emmett's "Old Dan Tucker," which blackface performers presented as examples of authentic Negro song. Syncopation was used even more extensively—and more effectively—in the "coon songs" or "coon shouts" of the 1880's and 1890's. The coon song came into existence in 1883 with Paul Allen's "New Coon in Town." The reprehensible term in this title referring to a Negro is the reason that all such songs were henceforth identified as "coon." And the electrifying performers who delivered those songs came to be known as "coon shouters." One such was May Irwin, a human dynamo who hurled her vocal tones across the footlights the way the ragtime kings of New Orleans produced their instrumental tones with trumpets and clarinets. In 1893 Miss Irwin created a sensation with "The Bully Song," words and music by Charles E. Trevathan, one of the songs from the musical *The Widow Jones*. With this song and her delivery, she established herself as the foremost "coon shouter" of her time and in later years became identified as "the stage mother of ragtime."

One year after the success of "The Bully Song," Ben Harney wrote two important coon songs: "Mister Johnson, Turn Me Loose" and "You've Been a Good Old Wagon But You've Done Broke Down." Harney was a vaudevillian who had received his early training by playing piano rags in saloons in Kansas City and St. Louis. From there he progressed into the minstrel show. These coon songs were published by Frank Harding, but the sheet-music sales were slow. Then May Irwin introduced "Mister Johnson, Turn Me Loose" in the Broadway show *Courted in Court* in 1896 and "You've Been a Good Old Wagon" in vaudeville. Her efforts led M. Witmark and Sons to buy out the publication rights for both numbers and to reissue them. Now, suddenly, a strong market existed for both numbers—a fact leading other publishers to issue coon songs of their own. It can be said that it was with Harney's two coon songs that this genre of Negro popular song came into vogue. As a vaudevillian, starring at Tony Pastor's Music Hall, Ben Harney kept plugging his two numbers. "Mister Johnson, Turn Me Loose" became the highlight of his act, assisted by a Negro named Strap Hill, who sat and sang in the audience as a stooge.

The year of 1896 saw the premiere and publication of two more coon-song classics. One was Barney Fagan's "My Gal is a Highborn Lady," sung by Ernest Haverly of the Haverly Minstrels. The other was Ernest Hogan's "All Coons Look Alike to Me," which the composer himself introduced in vaudeville to his own piano rag accompaniment. In this latter number, a Negro woman consoles herself after being jolted by her man, insisting that all men looked alike to her.

There was nothing in the song to demean the Negro people, beyond the use of the term "coon." But Hogan, a Negro, later in life expressed deep regret at having written a number that, through its immense popularity, did such a disservice to his people by inspiring the writing of other coon songs in which Negroes were ridiculed.

The coon song was a logical outgrowth of the religious shout. It possessed a strong beat and marked syncopations, was in a quick tempo, and demanded a loud, robust delivery. These songs were "shouted," and a number of performers after May Irwin became famous for this kind of delivery. They included Lottie Collins and Imogene Comer and, somewhat later, Emma Carus and Sophie Tucker. These entertainers, and others like them, invigorated their delivery through the interpolation of rubatos, and by singing the melody slightly off key and off rhythm.

Frederick Allen Mills, who had received a training in serious music before he started writing syncopated tunes, was repelled at the direction taken by so many coon songs in casting a slur on the Negro people. He decided to write a coon song of his own which would place the Negro in a more dignified position. To accomplish this, Mills tapped the subject of a Southern religious camp meeting. He called this number "At a Georgia Camp Meeting." It was written as an instrumental two-step in 1897 and as a song with lyrics in 1899. Since no publisher was interested in it, Mills published the number himself, using the name of "F. A. Mills" to identify himself as a publisher and that of "Kerry Mills" as author. Once published, the song made the necessary rounds of amusement places trying to find an interested performer. The song-and-dance team of Genaro and Bailey finally took it for their act. The way they presented it marked the beginnings in show business of the cakewalk, a dance routine that soon found numerous imitators in vaudeville and minstrel shows. The cakewalk had long existed as a dance among Southern Negroes in which they did a strut, or walk— the best strut getting a cake as a prize. But it took Genaro and Bailey to transfer this routine to the stage and make it a routine for blackface song-and-dance men. Upon completing the singing of a verse and chorus of "At a Georgia Camp Meeting," Genaro and Bailey went into an extended cakewalk, bending backward, as they strutted across the stage, tipping a high silk hat off their head, or twirling a cane in hand. This cakewalk and the music that accompanied it made extensive utilization of syncopation.

The ragtime tune that would soon supersede the sentimental ballad as the number-one sales product of Tin Pan Alley's song factory was a logical outgrowth of the coon song and the cakewalk. Its basic element—a syncopated melody over an even, rigid rhythm—was developed by a number of gifted ragtime pianists. One such was Scott Joplin, a pianist who improvised ragtime tunes in the hot spots of Sedalia, Missouri, and in St. Louis. Scott Joplin was encouraged by a Sedalia publisher to write his rags down on paper. The first result was "Original Rag," which appeared in sheet music in 1899, the first time that a piano rag had been published. "Maple Rag," also in 1899, was Joplin's second publication. This is his masterpiece, and today it is a jazz classic.

Piano rags became popular in New York mainly through the efforts of

Ben Harney, by now a top vaudeville headliner. Harney's offerings of piano rags at the Tony Pastor Music Hall were phenomenally popular with vaudeville audiences. He would present not only his own rag tunes but also rag versions of such semiclassics as Mendelssohn's *Spring Song,* Rubinstein's *Melody in F,* and the "Intermezzo" from Mascagni's opera, *Cavalleria Rusticana.* In addition to these efforts, Harney himself wrote some of the earliest ragtime songs to attract interest—"The Cakewalk in the Sky," for example, "I Love My Little Honey," and "My Black Mandy."

The expanding vogue for piano rags aroused controversy in music journals. An editorial writer in the *Musical Courier,* in 1899, wrote: "A wave of vulgar, filthy suggestive music has inundated the country. . . . It is artistically and morally depressing and should be suppressed by press and pulpit. The 'coon song' must go." A reply was made by Rupert Hughes in *The Musical Record:* "If ragtime were called *tempo di raga* . . . it might win honors more speedily. Ragtime will find its way gradually into the works of some great genius and will therefore be canonized." Prophetic words, those!

Beginning with Joe E. Howard's first major song hit, "Hello, Ma Baby," in 1899, ragtime songs began engaging the creative interest and efforts of Tin Pan Alley writers. A success of first importance came out of Tin Pan Alley in 1902 with Hugh Cannon's "Bill Bailey, Won't You Please Come Home?" with which Marie Cahill brought down the house in the musical *Sally in Our Alley.* In our own time it still brings down the house—or holds a television audience fascinated—when revived by a Jimmy Durante, an Eddie Jackson, or an Ella Fitzgerald.

The next few years saw the tide of ragtime songs rising out of Tin Pan Alley like some immense wave to inundate the whole industry. Here are some of the more notable of these ragtime numbers: Chris Smith's "You're in the Right Church, But the Wrong Pew" (1908), interpolated for Bert Williams in the musical *My Landlady,* to become then and afterward one of his most celebrated routines; Bert Williams's own creation, "Let It Alone" (1906), which the sheet music described as "a ragtime philosophical song"; "That Lovin' Rag" by Bernie Adler (1907), introduced by Sophie Tucker in a burlesque show; Albert von Tilzer's "Carrie" (1909), another Sophie Tucker tour de force. By the time Irving Berlin wrote "Alexander's Ragtime Band" (1911) and Lewis F. Muir had become popular with his "Waiting for the Robert E. Lee" (1912)—two of the most famous ragtime songs come out of Tin Pan Alley—the ragtime craze had seized all of America to hold it in an iron grip.

There is no question that it was Irving Berlin who was the most celebrated composer of ragtime songs in Tin Pan Alley, that he well deserved the sobriquet of "ragtime king," which had come to identify him in the early 1910's. "Alexander's Ragtime Band" was by no means Irving Berlin's first essay at ragtime writing. In 1909 he brought syncopation to Mendelssohn's *Spring Song* in "That Mesmerizing Mendelssohn Tune"; in that same year he also wrote two ragtime songs with original melodies, "Stop That Rag" (sung by Stella Mayhew in *The Jolly Bachelors*) and "Yiddle on Your Fiddle, Play Some Ragtime." In 1911, just before he put down on paper the definitive version of "Alexander's Ragtime

Band," he wrote "Ragtime Violin." All of these were good, lively tunes, and many proved profitable. "Alexander's Ragtime Band," however, was the one number that carried him to the very top rank of the songwriting profession. He would continue to hold that top rank with unrivaled brilliance and majesty for the next half century—and in song styles other than ragtime.

Irving Berlin's name was originally Israel Baline, and he was born in the Russian town of Temun, on May 11, 1888, the youngest of eight children. As Jews, the Balines were in perpetual terror of anti-Semitic attacks from Cossacks who would swoop down on the town without warning to create havoc, devastation, and death. One such attack took place when Israel was only four. The family fled into the woods and hid under a blanket until the Cossacks had gone. This grim experience convinced the parents that for the sake of their children, they had to leave Russia and come to America. Once this decision had been arrived at, action followed. The Balines and their possessions crossed the ocean in 1892 to make their first American home in a small, dark, damp basement apartment on Monroe Street in New York's crowded East Side, which swarmed with immigrants. A few weeks later, the Balines moved to a somewhat roomier and better-lit apartment on Cherry Street. The father found employment as a superviser of kosher meats, supplementing his meager income by giving Hebrew lessons to children, and occasionally substituting in the synagogue for an absentee cantor or choirmaster. The Baline children also went to work, four of them in sweatshops.

When Israel was old enough to do so, he helped with the family finances by selling newspapers in the streets. This happened in 1896, when the father's death put a serious drain on the family pocketbook. Meanwhile, the child played ball and tag in the streets, swam in the East River at the foot of Cherry Street, and with his friends formed a gang which engaged rival gangs in fierce battles. He had one other interest, too, an inheritance from his father: singing. But where his father had confined himself to the chants of the synagogue, little Israel doted on the sentimental ballads of the 1890's.

When he was fourteen, Israel ran away from home, terminating his schooling for good. He shifted for himself as best he could. He earned the price of food and shelter by singing ballads in the streets and saloons in or near the Bowery and gathering the pennies with which appreciative onlookers would reward his efforts. His rendition of the day's sentimental ballads in such places as Callahan's in Chinatown and the Chatham on Doyer Street brought him a daily income of about fifty cents. Sometimes he led "Blind Sol," a wandering street singer, through the byways of downtown New York and into its saloons; more than once he assisted Sol in the singing. At one time, Harry von Tilzer hired Israel to become his song plugger at Tony Pastor's Music Hall. One of the acts to which he was assigned was "The Three Keatons," one of whom, Buster, was later to become a star comedian on the silent screen.

In 1906 Israel Baline got a permanent job as a singing waiter at Pelham's Café on Pell Street. His job included not only waiting on the tables and entertaining the clientele with songs but also the writing and singing of parodies on the hit songs of the day. After closing hours he was also required to clean up the place. He was kept busy from dusk to dawn, his salary a dollar a day. One night he sang some of his numbers for Prince Louis Battenberg and his party, which had come to the Bowery for a slumming expedition. The prince was so pleased with Israel's performance that he gave him a five-dollar tip, the equivalent of a week's salary for the young fellow. With a gesture worthy of royalty, the boy turned down the tip. This incident made such an impression on a young newspaperman with the party that he reported the story the next day. In this way, Israel got his first piece of publicity—and, coincidentally, at the hands of a writer later to become one of America's foremost journalists, Herbert Bayard Swope.

Nor far from Pelham's Café was Callahan's. Two of Callahan's employees had written a song, "My Mariuccia Take a Steamboat," introduced in that café in 1906, then published. What Callahan's Café had accomplished, Pelham's Café was determined to emulate. Because of his proven gift at parody, Israel was selected to write the lyrics for a new song, while the saloon pianist, Nick Michaelson, conceived the melody. This song, Israel's first, was called "Marie from Sunny Italy." It was published in 1907 by Joseph W. Stern & Company and earned Israel a royalty of thirty-seven cents. It also brought him a new name, for it was for this publication that Israel concocted for himself the name of Irving Berlin, which we will use from this point on in telling his story.

Irving Berlin's first effort at songwriting came, then, with lyrics and not with music. A year later he did a number in which both the lyrics and the music were his own. By now he had left Pelham's Café to work as a singing waiter at a saloon in Union Square. There a vaudevillian hired him to write a topical number for his act. Since a marathon runner named Dorando was in the news, following his defeat in the 1908 Olympic Games by Johnny Hayes, Berlin wrote a poem about him. The vaudevillian didn't like it and didn't use it. Berlin now tried to market it as a song lyric. He found a taker in Ted Snyder, a young composer-publisher who had just then founded the firm of Seminary Music Company. Snyder offered to pay twenty-five dollars for "Dorando" if Berlin could provide a melody to the words. Berlin, who did not know how to write a note of music, hurriedly dictated a serviceable tune to an arranger in Snyder's office.

"Dorando" accomplished something beyond getting Berlin to write his first melody. It helped established a link between himself and the Seminary Music Company, a link that soon became permanent, with Snyder offering Berlin a permanent job with his company as staff lyricist. For the next two years or so Berlin wrote lyrics to other people's melodies, and proved quite successful in this undertaking—indeed, so successful that by 1910 the New York *Journal* paid him to write several hundred verses for that newspaper. Two of his lyrics (both to music by Ted Snyder) marked Berlin's initiation into the musical theatre: "That Beautiful Rag" and "Sweet Italian Love Song," both heard in 1910 in the revue *Up and Down Broadway*. But Berlin was also writing melodies of his own, the most successful of these being "That Mesmerizing Mendelssohn Tune," "Call Me Up Some Rainy Afternoon," and "Sadie Salome, Go Home," all in 1909. The last of these numbers represented one of the rare occasions when Berlin used somebody else's lyrics (Edgar Leslie's).

"Sadie Salome, Go Home"—a takeoff on opera arias, lyrics in a Yiddish dialect—marked a decisive turning point in the career of one of the greatest comediennes of her generation, Fanny Brice. It was her first attempt to render a Yiddish-type song, a genre that brought her such acclaim in the musical theatre throughout her career. Fanny Brice had been appearing in burlesque in 1910 when she was asked to do a specialty number for a benefit. Having already become a friend of Irving Berlin's, and having come to admire his work, she asked him for material. Here is how she herself has told the rest of the story: "Irving took me in the back room and played 'Sadie Salome' . . . a Jewish comedy song. . . . So, of course, Irving sang 'Sadie Salome' with a Jewish accent. I had never had any idea of doing a song with a Jewish accent. I didn't even understand Jewish, couldn't speak a word of it. But, I thought, if that's the way Irving sings, that's the way I'll sing it. Well, I came out and did 'Sadie Salome' for the first time ever doing a Jewish accent and the audience is loving it. . . . They start to throw roses at me."

When later the same year Fanny Brice made her debut in the *Ziegfeld Follies,* she sang another Jewish-type song by Berlin, "Good-bye, Becky Cohen." It was here and now that she established her reputation as a comedienne whose particular specialty was Yiddish-type songs.

Berlin had already become interested in syncopation and had already produced a number of ragtime tunes when, in 1910 (stimulated by Harry von Tilzer's "Alexander, Don't You Love Your Baby No More?"), he wrote "Alexander and His Clarinet." Berlin was not satisfied with the result and put the song aside. In 1911, when he was made a member of the Friar's Club in New York, he was invited to perform in the *Frolics,* a revue put on annually by that club. For this occasion he was eager to introduce one of his own songs. He returned to "Alexander and His Clarinet," revised its lyrics, and adapted it to a ragtime melody he had produced earlier but had never used. The new song was called "Alexander's Ragtime Band."

For reasons that Berlin himself no longer remembers, he did not introduce "Alexander's Ragtime Band" at the Friar's *Frolics* as he had planned. He tried marketing it for performance, and finally found a place for it at the Columbia Burlesque House on Broadway. The song passed unnoticed. Jesse Lasky, later the famous motion-picture executive, but then producing vaudeville entertainment, thought so little of it he refused to include it in any of his acts. Then, at long last, an electrifying performer of coon songs, Emma Carus, decided that the song was her kind of material and she used it in her vaudeville act in Chicago. The house went into a furor. Other vaudevillians—among them Ethel Levey (former wife of George M. Cohan) and Sophie Tucker—began using the song, too. The spark put a light to a combustible commodity; what followed was conflagration. Before 1911 was over, the whole country was singing, humming, whistling, or dancing to the rhythmic strains of "Alexander's Ragtime Band." The song sold over a million copies of sheet music in the first months of publication.

The ironical part about "Alexander's Ragtime Band" is that when subjected to analysis, this, the most successful ragtime song of all time, is not really ragtime at all. There is only one point in which syncopation can be found—on the word "just" in the chorus. Actually this is more a song *about* ragtime than a song *in* ragtime. Its musical material is derived from a bugle call and a phrase from Stephen Foster's "Swanee River." Basically, "Alexander's Ragtime Band" is a march. Nevertheless, the word "ragtime" in the title, the overall rhythmic vitality of the song as a whole, and the general misconception that the melody was in ragtime, proved a powerful force in making syncopated songs more popular than ever. "Alexander's Ragtime Band" became the most successful song about ragtime ever written. More than any other single number, it helped make such a fad of ragtime songs that for the first time in the history of Tin Pan Alley, sentimental and love ballads had to occupy a secondary place in its scheme of operations.

To this swelling tide of ragtime songs Irving Berlin became a most significant contributor, often with songs now more identifiably ragtime than "Alexander" had been. "Everybody's Doin' It," in 1911, was responsible for making the turkey trot a dance craze. "That Mysterious Rag" and "The Ragtime Jockey Man" were introduced by Berlin himself as one of the star performers in the Broadway revue *The Passing Show of 1912.* In 1913 Irving Berlin was a featured headliner at the Hippodrome in London, billed as "the ragtime king." For this appearance he wrote "The International Rag." Londoners were so convinced that every ragtime tune ever written was the work of Berlin that when, at the conclusion of his act, he invited the audience to suggest which other of his songs they wanted as an encore, they kept shouting at him the title of every ragtime tune they knew, thoroughly convinced that nobody but Berlin could have written it.

In 1914 Berlin's first complete score for a Broadway musical enhanced his career as a writer of ragtime. The musical was *Watch Your Step,* described in the program as a "syncopated musical." One of its numbers was "The Syncopated Walk," written for the stars Vernon and Irene Castle, the dancing idols of the nation. "He is a young master of syncopation," reported one unidentified New York reviewer about Berlin. "This is the first time that the author of 'Alexander's Ragtime Band' and the like has turned his attention to providing the music for an entire evening's entertainment. For it, he has written a score of his mad melodies, nearly all of them of the tickling sort, born to be caught up and whistled at every street corner and warranted to get any roomful a-dancing."

Of course, not all the songs in *Watch Your Step* were syncopated. Some were ballads. One of these was a pioneer in a technique that Berlin would later use again and again with the most extraordinary effect. The ballad was "Play a Simple Melody." This was the first time that Berlin wrote two different melodies and two different sets of lyrics for one and the same chorus—each melody and its lyrics being sung independently the first time, and then both melodies and their lyrics being combined contrapuntally.

By 1912 Irving Berlin's songs were responsible for a good deal of the revenue that kept flowing into the publishing house now named Ted Snyder and Company. Most of this revenue came from Berlin's ragtime songs—but not all.

Already, Berlin was beginning to demonstrate his versatility by producing songs in many styles and scoring sizable hits with them. "Woodman, Woodman, Spare That Tree" was introduced by Bert Williams in the *Ziegfeld Follies of 1911*—one of several songs that helped make Bert Williams such an attraction in the *Follies* for several years. "When the Midnight Choo-Choo Leaves for Alabam'," came in 1912. The first of the immortal Irving Berlin ballads, "When I Lost You," which sold about two million copies, followed in 1913, the year in which, with the collaboration of George Whiting and Ted Snyder, he also wrote the comedy number "My Wife's Gone to the Country," a half-million-copy seller. His uncommon fertility and equally inimitable golden touch finally convinced his publishers to take him into their firm as a partner; after 1912 the publishing house was called Snyder, Waterson, and Berlin. Berlin remained the principal contributor to this firm's success until 1919, when he set out as his own publisher by forming the Irving Berlin, Inc.

The writing of "When I Lost You," Berlin's first successful ballad, came about through a personal tragedy. On February 3, 1913, Berlin married Dorothy Goetz, the attractive sister of Ray Goetz, a Broadway producer. The Berlins spent their honeymoon in Cuba, then returned to New York to set up their first home, on Riverside Drive. Two weeks after they had set up house, on July 17, 1913, Dorothy died of typhoid fever, a disease contracted in Cuba. Berlin was inconsolable. He tried to flee from his sorrow by going on a trip to Europe with his brother-in-law. Then, back again in New York, he had to find some way to voice the intensity of his feelings. He did this in the only way he knew: by writing a song, expressing the thought that he had lost the sunshine and the flowers when he lost Dorothy.

"When I Lost You" was Berlin's first important ballad. From then on, in this medium he would prove himself a master with few rivals. This song was also the first of his autobiographical numbers in which he spoke his inmost feelings. The richest harvest of his autobiographical ballads came during the turbulent period, a decade later, when he fell in love with Ellin Mackay, daughter of the tycoon who headed Postal Telegraph. Almost from their first meeting, in 1924, Irving and Ellin realized that life without each other was unthinkable. A seemingly insurmountable obstacle, however, separated them: the bitter objections of a strong-willed father to a marriage that united his socialite daughter with a Jewish boy who had been raised in the New York City streets and who earned his living writing songs. Mackay did everything at his command to prevent the two lovers from meeting and to discredit Berlin in his daughter's eyes. But in the end the old man was helpless. Ellin and Irving Berlin were secretly married at a ceremony at New York's City Hall on January 4, 1926. They spent their honeymoon in Atlantic City, New Jersey, after which they took a trip to Europe.

The love affair, both its pains and its exaltations, its agonizing frustrations and its rich fulfillment, inspired Berlin's most personal song literature: a repertory of ballads without equal in American popular music for touching sentiment expressed in the simplest and the most affecting melodies and lyrics: "All Alone," "Remember," "Always," "All by Myself," and "What'll I Do?".

His sphere of interests and his significance expanded into several directions beyond that of writing hit ragtime songs and ballads. During World War I, while serving in the American army, he wrote, produced, and acted in an all-soldiers show, *Yip, Yip, Yaphank,* his aim being to raise $35,000 for a badly needed service center at Camp Upton in New York. After opening at the Century Theatre in New York on July 26, 1918, this revue brought in $135,000. It also contributed two more solid hits to Berlin's ever growing repertory: "Mandy" and "Oh, How I Hate To Get Up in the Morning."

After World War I, Berlin reassumed his imperial position among the songwriters of his time by providing the *Ziegfeld Follies of 1919* (one of the most ambitious and expensive productions Ziegfeld had mounted up to this time) with its three most important musical numbers. One was "Mandy" (lifted out of *Yip, Yip, Yaphank*), used for a minstrel-show routine in which Marilyn Miller, the darling of the musical theatre, appeared as George Primrose, the minstrel. The other two Berlin hit songs were: "You'd Be Surprised," a comedy number introduced by Eddie Cantor, with which Cantor realized his only million-copy record sale; and "A Pretty Girl Is Like a Melody," which from then on became the theme song for the *Ziegfeld Follies,* as well as for beauty contests and fashion. Such was Berlin's popularity as a songwriter that he could now command $2,000 a week on the vaudeville circuit singing his hits.

The year of 1919 also found Berlin opening his own publishing company which, henceforth, would issue not only all his own songs but also hits by other writers. To help celebrate the opening of this company, there took place throughout the United States an "Irving Berlin Week," when Berlin songs were heard and played in theatres, nightclubs, dance halls, and other places of entertainment. Hardly had the publishing house had a chance to start the presses rolling when Berlin became a theatre owner, too. In conjunction with Sam H. Harris and Joseph Schenck, he financed the building of the Music Box on Forty-fifth Street west of Broadway, which opened in 1921 with the production of the first *Music Box Revue,* for which Berlin contributed all the material. In that first edition the stars were Wilda Bennett and Paul Frawley, who were heard in the show's big song hit, "Say It with Music"; also the Brox Sisters, heard in an exciting syncopated number, more in the now new jazz style than in the older ragtime manner, "Everybody Step." Three more editions of that revue, all of them written by Berlin, were seen at the Music Box up through 1924—each so brilliantly mounted, so studded with stars, and so filled with invigorating and fresh material that the *Music Box Revue* became a serious rival to the *Ziegfeld Follies.* Out of these three editions stepped a few more Berlin song classics, including "Crinoline Days," "All Alone," "What'll I Do?" and "Pack Up Your Sins." "All Alone" and "What'll I Do?" were interpolated into the *Music Box Revue* in 1923, where they were sung by a young lady up to now a Broadway unknown. Her name—Grace Moore. With these two ballads she reached stardom in the American musical theatre. A few years more and she would become one of America's foremost prima donnas, a star of stars at the Metropolitan Opera and other of the world's leading opera houses.

By the middle 1920's Berlin had risen higher than any popular composer America had known. He was now a one-man trust in music—a major power as composer, lyricist, librettist, publisher, theatre owner, and producer. He was married to the daughter of one of the wealthiest men in the country. The future seemed secure. Then, suddenly and inexplicably, Berlin seemed to have come to a dead end creatively. In or about 1928 he became convinced that the reservoir of his song ideas had run dry. (It was almost in anticipation of such a disaster that in 1927 he wrote "The Song Is Ended"!) Between 1929 and 1932 he wrote little, and nothing he considered of value. By 1932 he said that he was through, that he had nothing more to say within the song form. This also happened to be the period of the great Depression in which a good deal of his accumulated fortune had melted away, piling one misery upon another.

The tide turned in 1932. Two old songs, which he had regarded as inferior and had never published, were discovered. Rudy Vallee sang "Say It Isn't So" on the radio and recorded it for RCA Victor. Then "How Deep Is the Ocean?" began getting heard. For the first time in several years, Berlin's songs were best sellers again, even though in 1932 the sheet-music business was in the doldrums.

The year of 1932 also brought Berlin back to the Broadway musical theatre —this time with a topical musical comedy, text by Moss Hart. *Face the Music* was a musical about the Depression and some of the more humorous effects it had had on American life, customs, and mores. For this musical Berlin produced an eloquent ballad, "Soft Lights and Sweet Music" and a number that became a kind of theme song for the Depression years, "Let's Have Another Cup o' Coffee."

Now back in full stride, Berlin continued to prosper in the Broadway musical theatre with the revue *As Thousands Cheer* in 1933. By 1935 Berlin had traveled from Broadway to Hollywood to help create a long string of screen musical triumphs, some of them starring Fred Astaire. These Irving Berlin screen successes began with *Top Hat* in 1935 (with Fred Astaire and Ginger Rogers) and was followed by the first of several motion pictures serving as a cavalcade of some of Berlin's old song hits—*Alexander's Ragtime Band,* starring Tyrone Power and Alice Faye in 1938.

He was doing better than ever with his songs. In fact, two of his greatest money-makers came during the 1930's. For *As Thousands Cheer* he wrote what has become a classic of the Easter season, "Easter Parade." The melody itself had come from a song called "Smile and Show Your Dimple," which Berlin had written in 1917 and which had been a failure. Requiring a tune for the Easter-parade scene on Fifth Avenue in *As Thousands Cheer,* Berlin fitted the old song with new lyrics. Marilyn Miller and Clifton Webb introduced it in the first-act finale. It then became one of Berlin's hardiest standards, a seasonal favorite; it also contributed the title to another of those screen musicals that served as a frame for Berlin's old song hits, a musical released in 1948, starring Fred Astaire and Judy Garland.

For his first giant success in motion pictures—*Top Hat*—Berlin created a ballad that proved a financial bonanza: "Cheek to Cheek" sung (and danced to) by Fred Astaire and Ginger Rogers. Its initial sheet-music sale brought in royalties in excess of $250,000.

Then, as had been the case with "Easter Parade," Berlin once again lifted one of his old melodies out of his trunk, rehabilitated it with new lyrics, and reaped a new financial harvest (though this time not for himself but for charity). The song was his hymn of allegiance and praise to his country. "God Bless America" had been inspired by a then-recent trip to Europe where Berlin had apprehensively noticed the march of fascism and Nazism, and the gathering war clouds. That trip made him realize more forcefully and dramatically than ever the treasure of American citizenship.

Following his return to America, Kate Smith asked him for a patriotic number for one of her broadcasts. Berlin remembered a melody he had once planned using as a production number for his World War I all-soldiers show, *Yip, Yip, Yaphank,* but which he had discarded at the time. He supplied it with new stirring lyrics in keeping with the spirit of the times in America. Kate Smith sang "God Bless America" for the first time ever over the radio on Armistice Day, November 10, 1938. She then recorded it for Columbia, a best seller. In 1939 the song was heard at the presidential nominating conventions of both parties. As America edged ever closer to the brink of a war that had already exploded in Europe in the fall of 1939, the popularity and the importance of "God Bless America" kept mounting. It was sung and played in public places throughout the country, often in Kate Smith's Columbia recording—at political rallies, presidential birthday balls, athletic events, motion-picture theatres. Nor did its popularity decline to any perceptible degree after the war. In the early 1950's it was chosen in a national poll as the most famous patriotic song in America, second only in importance to the national anthem; there was even a movement set into motion to have "God Bless America" replace "The Star-Spangled Banner" as America's national anthem. In 1955 President Eisenhower was authorized by Congress to present Berlin with a gold medal in recognition of his contributions through his patriotic songs in general and "God Bless America" in particular. Through the years the song gathered royalties in excess of $470,000. Refusing to capitalize on his patriotism, Berlin from the very beginning assigned all the earnings from this song to the Boy and Girl Scouts.

"God Bless America" was one of several songs that Berlin wrote to help the war effort. He wrote numbers for Navy Relief and for the Red Cross, to promote the sale of war bonds, to stimulate arms production. Certainly, his greatest contribution to the war effort, however, came through the writing and production of his second all-soldiers show, *This Is the Army,* which he whipped into shape at Camp Upton, where in the earlier world war he had brought *Yip, Yap, Yaphank* into existence, and where, in 1942, he had been living in a barracks to gather firsthand army experiences.

This Is the Army arrived at Broadway on July 4, 1942. After its New York run, the production toured all of the United States, then was performed for the fighting men and women in all major combat areas, and in the interim was made by Warner Brothers into a screen musical. Its income of about $10 million was assigned to the United States Army Emergency Relief, with an additional $350,000 going to British relief agencies during the London run. Irving Berlin's sole reward for this gigantic enterprise and achievement was the Medal of Merit which General George C. Marshall presented him in Berlin.

Most of the songs in *This Is the Army* were written specifically for that production, among them the title number and "I Left My Heart at the Stage Door Canteen." One, however, was a revival bringing back poignant memories of 1918 and *Yip, Yip, Yaphank:* "Oh, How I Hate To Get Up in the Morning." Dressed in his old World War I uniform, and supported by a male chorus similarly attired (six of whom had appeared with Berlin in *Yip, Yip, Yaphank*), Berlin brought back nostalgically another war and another era by singing his World War I classic in his now thin and broken voice. When a stagehand heard Berlin's performance during a rehearsal, he remarked: "If the composer of that song could hear the way that guy sings it, he'd turn over in his grave."

After the end of World War II, Berlin continued contributing his songs to the American scene—some to the Broadway stage, others to the motion-picture screen in Hollywood. On Broadway he was now destined to achieve the greatest success of his entire theatrical career, artistic as well as financial: with *Annie Get Your Gun,* starring Ethel Merman as Annie Oakley, a lady who was handier with a gun than with men. Rodgers and Hammerstein were the producers of that musical and their plan had been to get Jerome Kern to write the music. But when Kern died suddenly, Rodgers and Hammerstein urged Berlin to consider the assignment. Berlin asked them for a few days' time in which to make a final decision. That weekend Berlin locked himself in a hotel suite and wrote five numbers. When he played them for Rodgers and Hammerstein the following Monday, those two veterans of the musical theatre were stunned into silence, for each of the five numbers was an iridescent gem of its kind, in spite of the haste with which it had been produced, and each remained in the final version of the completed score.

No show by Berlin enjoyed the kind of initial run on Broadway achieved by *Annie Get Your Gun* (over one thousand performances). No Berlin show sold so many original-cast recordings. No Berlin show has been revived more frequently. No Berlin show brought in such fantastic profits to all concerned. And no Berlin show boasted such a proliferation of song hits, ranging from the sentimental and tender to the comic and satirical: "They Say It's Wonderful," "The Girl That I Marry," "You Can't Get a Man with a Gun," "Doin' What Comes Natur'lly," and a number that has since become a kind of theme song for all of show business, "There's No Business Like Show Business." It seemed hardly likely that it would be possible to produce a new number that could deserve a place with such a company of hits. Yet Berlin achieved this seeming impossibility when *Annie Get Your Gun* was so successfully revived at the New York State Theatre in 1966—and he did it with a song, "Old-Fashioned Wedding," that regularly stopped the show.

Musicals following *Annie Get Your Gun* further helped to make valuable additions to the oversized stockpile of Berlin songs: "Let's Take an Old-Fashioned Walk" from *Miss Liberty* in 1949; "You're Just in Love," "It's a Lovely Day Today," and "They Like Ike" from *Call Me Madam* in 1950 (the last a factor, even if a slight one, in lifting General Dwight D. Eisenhower to the Presidency; it was retitled "We Still Like Ike" for a television "special" production of *Call Me Madam* in the fall of 1968); "Empty Pockets Full of

Love" from *Mr. President* in 1962. "You're Just in Love" and "Empty Pockets" make the same kind of contrapuntal use of two different melodies, with two different sets of lyrics, that we first encountered years earlier in "Play a Simple Melody."

There was another peak for Berlin to scale, this time in the movies. There he continued creating scores comprising songs old and new for various mammoth song-and-dance productions. For *Holiday Inn* in 1940 (with Bing Crosby and Fred Astaire) he wrote an all-time classic, while achieving a financial triumph unequaled even by his earlier fabulous hits. That, to be sure, is "White Christmas," now in America second only to "Silent Night," as the best-loved and most frequently heard song about the Yuletide season. It seems to be gathering strength as the years go by, continually gaining momentum in the sales of records and sheet music. Bing Crosby sang it in the motion picture; in time his Decca recording sold about twenty-five million discs. During World War II, "White Christmas" became a favorite of G.I.'s, reminding them nostalgically of home and the holiday season as they ploughed through the mud and waters of distant places fighting a fierce enemy. After the war "White Christmas" became as indispensable to the celebration of the holiday season as the Christmas tree and mistletoe. There seemed to be no end to the new recordings being made year after year, nor, for that matter, no end to the sale of sheet music. In a quarter of a century the song sold about four million copies of sheet music (in 115 different arrangements) while it was recorded over three hundred times selling almost fifty million discs (by far the largest disc sale ever accumulated by a single song). Well over a million copies of instrumental arrangements, octavos, and orchestrations have been disposed of. In 1954 it contributed a title to one of those successful Irving Berlin pictures featuring his old songs as well as new (starring Danny Kaye and Bing Crosby). Since Berlin owned 30 percent of the picture, *White Christmas* became his greatest movie money-maker, over a million and a half dollars; N.B.C. paid $1.5 million for the rights to run it over their television network once each year, for three years, while taking an option on three more yearly telecasts at $700,000 per performance.

There is no parallel to Berlin's career in American popular music. For sixty years he has been in the vanguard of America's most significant and most widely performed song composers—this in spite of ever changing styles and fads and volatile public preferences. Nobody has functioned for so long a time and so fruitfully in the song business as he. Nobody has produced as many standards as he (several hundreds of them), and of such variety and professional skill. "I don't know of five American 'art composers,' " once wrote Virgil Thomson, who distinguished himself both as a serious composer and as a critic of serious music, "who can be compared as songwriters, for either technical skill or artistic responsibility, with Irving Berlin."

Nobody has touched so many bases in the song and entertainment business as he. And nobody has made as much money as he did from songs. What Jerome Kern once said about Berlin holds true today even more solidly than it did yesterday: "Irving Berlin has no place in American music. He *is* American music."

The feeling of inevitability we encounter in a lied is a quality also possessed by a Berlin classic. The melodic line always moves fluidly, gracefully, inevitably. The utter simplicity of his style and structure is most deceiving: it is the simplicity that comes only when perfection has been arrived at.

What is most extraordinary about Berlin's fabulous song career is the fact that Berlin has risen this high with almost no musical equipment to provide him with the fuel for his flight to the highest altitudes of his profession. Today as yesterday he must depend on a musical secretary to get his musical ideas on paper, since he is still much of a musical illiterate. He can still play his piano only by ear, though it is a myth that he uses only two fingers on the keyboard. He can still play only in the key of F-sharp major, using a piano with a special lever under the keyboard capable of transposing any music he is playing into his favored key. He still depends upon his instincts, whether he is producing words or music, for it must be remembered that Berlin is his own lyricist, that his gift for carving a fresh and graceful line of verse is only a few degrees below that of his gift for melody, that in fact he has been one of the foremost lyricists of the twentieth century. (Oscar Hammerstein II once remarked that the most perfect line he ever encountered in a song lyric was "All alone, by the telephone," which, of course, comes from Berlin's "All Alone.") In Berlin's songs, melody and words are of one piece, as if they were conceived together. But with Berlin the lyric usually comes before the melody, the idea behind the lyric dictating the kind of melody Berlin reaches for. Here is how he himself described his way of working: "I usually get a phrase first—words. I keep repeating it over and over, and the first thing I know I begin to get a sort of rhythm, and then a tune. I don't say all my songs are written that way. Sometimes I hear a tune first, and then I start trying to fit words to it. In recent years, I've worked away from the piano. Often a phrase of melody comes to me and I work it out mentally. My keyboard is in my mind."

He always works slowly, the process of creation being filled with anxiety, doubts, continual rejection of material, and perpetual revision. He even suffers actual physical pain while producing a song. Yet, in spite of anguish, he keeps on working because not writing is greater anguish still. "I'm going to keep going just as long as I can knock out a song they like," he told an interviewer when he was in his advanced seventies. "I'm a songwriter like dozens and dozens of others, and as long as I'm able—whether the songs are good or bad—I'll continue to write them because songwriting is no mere business or hobby with me. It's everything. . . . The main thing is to write and keep writing."

His main interest outside his music is his family. He has three daughters: Mary Ellin Barrett, the wife of a magazine editor, and the author of a novel; Elizabeth Fischer, the wife of a London book publisher; and Linda Emmett, the wife of a Parisian banker. They, in turn, have eight children, six girls and two boys. Naturally, one of the boys bears the name of his celebrated grandfather (Irving Berlin Barrett).

Berlin loves having his brood around him, either at his fashionable apartment at Gracie Square in New York City or at the fifty-acre farm he owns in Livingston Manor, in the Catskill Mountains of New York State. Years and years ago, he enjoyed an occasional game of poker, but he has lost his enthusiasm for all forms of gambling. His onetime interest in golf or cooking meals for special friends or painting has also palled. What has remained undiminished is his creative energy—a force that keeps him restless, at times irritable, at times frustrated. New ideas for lyrics and melodies keep spinning in his head, seeking to arrange themselves into a workable pattern like the colors of a kaleidoscope. He may be at the Colony in New York (one of his favorite restaurants), or playing host to friends at his home. Actually his mind is working all the time. "You write in the morning, you write at night," he once explained. "You write in a taxi, in the bathtub, or in an elevator. And after the song is all finished it may turn out to be very bad, but you sharpen your pencil and try again. A professional songwriter has his mind on his job all the time." In any event, Berlin is a songwriter who never stops working. This may very well be the reason that his eyes look with such intensity through his tortoiseshell glasses, and that he is forever so highly charged and so given to nervous gestures and movements. There is no relaxation in creativity.

With his eightieth year only a breath away he was still writing new songs: a new one for the revival of *Annie Get Your Gun,* another new one for the television production of *Call Me Madam* (both of which have already been mentioned). And when on May 5, 1968, his eightieth birthday was celebrated on "The Ed Sullivan Show" (extended for this time alone to an hour and a half) over the C.B.S. network, Berlin was on the stage giving the world premiere to still another new creation, "I Used To Play It by Ear." On that monumental program, which starred Bing Crosby, Ethel Merman, Robert Goulet, and Bob Hope among others, the President of the United States, Lyndon B. Johnson, was seen and heard on tape congratulating Berlin. "America is the richer for his presence," said the President, who then added, "God Bless Berlin." This program, one of many tributes to Berlin both in this country and abroad, was a way of expressing gratitude to a man who has written over eight hundred songs, the scores for nineteen Broadway musicals and eleven Hollywood motion pictures; but (more especially) to a man whose patriotic songs and two all-soldiers shows earn him the honor of being designated as America's musical laureate.

Songs with the Blues–I

W. C. Handy

Like ragtime, the "blues" came into commercial use by way of New Orleans. There the legendary men of jazz—the Buddy Boldens, the Joe "King" Olivers, and others like them—used to improvise the blues just as they would improvise ragtime. Out of New Orleans emerged the first classics in blues literature: "West End Blues," for example, a favorite of Joe "King" Oliver at places like the 101 Ranch or Pete Lala's, or "Livery Stable Blues," popularized by Jack "Papa" Laine's Ragtime Band.

To take one more step farther back in time: The blues of New Orleans was evolved from the sorrow songs which Negroes began improvising soon after Emancipation—on street corners, in brothels, in saloons. This was the music favored by the lower strata of Negro society—gamblers, prisoners, beggars, prostitutes, exploited day laborers: the deep-throated lament of a harassed people bewailing their misfortunes. Where the spiritual represented the Negro's escape into religion from the realities of everyday life (this was the Negro's *Sunday* music), the blues was his music of the rest of the week, describing his manifold trials and woes and frustrations. Spirituals sang of Jesus and Heaven. Blues sang of earthly matters, of the dreary, dismal events and experiences in a cruel everyday world. "De blues ain't nothing! No, de blues ain't nothing, but a good man feelin' blue." This is the refrain of an early blues often heard in honky-tonks. Good men feeling blue, singing intensely of their heartaches and frustrations, gave birth to the rich literature of blues-songs. Singing them provided an emotional outlet. There is a good deal of astuteness in an observation once made by Hugues Panassie when he wrote that "when the Negro sings the blues it is not to give way to his sadness, but to free himself of it."

The Negro often traveled from one town to another, frequently alone, singing laments about his personal misery, often with improvised words. Some of these wandering minstrels had no other occupation but to make music all night; during the day they slept. Others would supplement the scanty income of an occasional job with the pennies and nickels they gathered from an admiring public in public performances.

The earliest blues moaned about many a subject. A villain like Joe Turner was a favorite theme for blues exploitation. Joe Turner was a white officer who would come to Memphis and carry away black men in handcuffs to a Nashville prison. Another theme was the boll weevil which destroyed cotton crops. But most blues were personal lamentations—the hurt inflicted on the singer by a callous society, by impoverished economics, by prison life, by the elements, by racial prejudice, and most of all by the cold, hard-steeled woman or man who no longer returned a love.

Soon the blues acquired a set pattern for both the text and the music. The text was made up of three-line stanzas, often in iambic pentameter, the second line repeating the first. The melody had a slow, lugubrious tune consisting of three four-bar phrases, and distinguished structurally by a flatted third or seventh (often deliberately played or sung out of tune). When the blue note—as these intervals came to be known—was not used, a dissonant harmony took its place. Another technical characteristic of the blues was the way in which a "break" would be interposed to allow the singer to exclaim "Oh, Lawdy!" or "Oh, Baby!" In New Orleans, when the blues received instrumental treatment, these breaks gave a jazz musician the opportunity to embark on spontaneous improvisation.

As popular music—that is, a commercial product distributed in printed sheet music—the blues may be said to have come into the world in the year of 1912, with the first publication of a blues-song: "The Memphis Blues" by W. C. Handy. In the commercial world Handy became one of the most prolific and one of the most successful composers of the blues. One of them, "The St. Louis Blues," is the most famous blues ever created, put down on paper, and published.

Up to the last days of his life, Handy was insistent that he was the inventor of the blues as we know that form today. In his autobiography, *Father of the Blues,* published in 1941, he wrote: "The primitive Southern Negro, as he sang, was sure to bear down on the third and seventh note of the scale, slurring between major and minor. Whether in the cotton field of the Delta or on the levee up St. Louis way, it was always the same. Till then, however, I had never heard this slur used by a more sophisticated Negro, or by any white man. I had tried to convey this effect in 'Memphis Blues' by introducing flat thirds and sevenths (now called blues-notes) into my song, although its prevailing key was major; and I carried this device into my melody as well. I also struck on the idea of using the dominant seventh as the opening chord of the verse of the 'St. Louis Blues.' This was a distinct departure, but, as it turned out, it touched the spot.

"In the folk blues, the singer fills up occasional gaps like 'Oh, Lawdy' or 'Oh, Baby' and the like. This meant that in writing a melody to be sung in the blues manner, one would have to provide gaps or waits. In my composition, I decided to embellish the piano and orchestra score at these points. This kind of business is called a 'break' . . . and 'breaks' became a fertile source of the orchestral improvisation which became the essence of jazz. In the chorus of 'The St. Louis Blues' I used a plagal chord to give 'spiritual' effects in the harmony. Altogether I aimed to use all that is characteristic of the Negro from Africa to Alabama."

A few years before he died, W. C. Handy sent a bitter letter to this writer lamenting the fact that books on jazz and popular music continually maligned him and denigrated his accomplishments by insisting that the blues had existed (including the techniques described by Handy in his autobiography) long before Handy wrote the "Memphis Blues." Regrettably, this writer must also deny Handy the tribute he sought. Handy did not invent the blues. If the blues had not been developed in New Orleans, "The Memphis Blues" and "The St. Louis Blues" would never have been written. But Handy must get his due in being the first to write a blues that was *published,* in being the first to bring the blues out of the Southland and into Tin Pan Alley. These achievements earn him a place of honor in American popular music.

Handy was born in Florence, Alabama, on November 16, 1873, the son of a pastor who considered instrumental music-making and the theatre as the pastimes of the devil. William Christopher Handy was the name the boy grew up with, though in his professional life he much preferred using only the initials of his first two names.

William's grandmother used to point with pride at the child's large ears. She regarded them as proof of his innate musical talent. But the father outlawed all forms of music except singing in his household. Musical activity (for which the boy showed an unusual interest) had to be pursued with the greatest of secrecy. By doing odd jobs William managed to save enough money to buy himself a guitar. When the father discovered the instrument, he ordered the boy to return it to the store and exchange it for an unabridged dictionary. Once at school, William confided to his teacher that his ambition was to be a professional musician. When the teacher, betraying the boy's confidence, revealed this bit of information to William's father, the latter said sternly: "Son, I'd rather see you in a hearse than have you a musician."

Hearing a trumpeter, come from Birmingham to play with the local Baptist choir, filled the boy William with the yearning to learn to play that instrument. At first, unable to purchase a trumpet, he tried to make one for himself from a cow's horn. This effort proved a failure. At last he was able to purchase a trumpet from a visiting local musician by paying him twenty-five cents cash, the rest in installments. On this instrument he learned the elements of playing a wind instrument, becoming sufficiently proficient within a short period of time to be able to play in a band. After that, he joined a touring minstrel-show company. Left stranded on the road when the show went broke, he had to jump freight trains to get home. This experience convinced him to seek out some other way of making a living. His choice finally fell on teaching. In 1892 he was graduated from the Teachers Agricultural and Mechanical College in Alabama. The meager salary he earned as teacher led him to abandon the classroom for a better-paying job as a day laborer. But before long he was back making music. First, as a hand in a steel foundry, he helped organize and direct a brass band there. Then when this foundry closed down during an economic crisis, he depended upon music to make a living. In 1893 he played the cornet at the World's Fair in Chicago. Three years after that, he was hired by Mahara's Minstrels as cornetist, arranger, and performer in the "olio" part of the show. Eventually he was hired to lead the band.

Between 1900 and 1903 Handy taught music at the Teachers Agricultural and Mechanical College. During this period he kept on appearing with Mahara's Minstrels. When he left the minstrel company for good, in 1903, he organized and led the first band with which, for the next quarter of a century, he would give concerts throughout the South: the Negro Knights of Pythias Band, founded in Mississippi.

One day, at a deserted railroad station, he listened fascinated to an old Negro singing a sorrow song to himself. This was apparently the first time he had become conscious of the pathos and beauty of Negro folk laments. This experience was also the earliest of several influences to lead Handy to write his first blues. A second experience came in Cleveland, Mississippi, where he had come to give a concert with his band. A local musical group there performed some ragtime numbers and Negro tunes that made a deep impact on Handy. He was also impressed by the enthusiasm of the audience to each of these numbers, showering the players with coins as well as with vociferous ovations. "This had the stuff people wanted," as he later recalled. "It touched the spot. Their music wanted polishing, but it contained the essence. Folks would pay money for it. . . . That night a composer was born, an *American* composer. Those country black boys had taught me something that could not possibly have been gained from books, something that would, however, cause books to be written."

From this time on, Handy began including on his programs ragtime tunes and Negro folk melodies. The popularity of his band grew in direct proportion to the frequency with which he performed this kind of music. This success stimulated him creatively. Up to now he had written a number of popular songs of the Tin Pan Alley variety—ballads, humorous numbers, and so forth. He now tried to carry over into his writing a Negro identity; he now tried to catch in his melodies something of the spiritual-like melancholy the Negro at the lonely railroad station had brought to his singing. In short, Handy was evolving his own style which, when finally crystallized, would emerge as the blues.

The writing of his first blues came about because of an election. In 1909 E. H. Crump, a reform candidate, was running for the office of mayor in Memphis, Tennessee. Handy favored his candidacy, and, in order to promote it, he wrote "Mr. Crump," a song in a style and idiom to which the Negro population of the city could respond instinctively and favorably. "Mr. Crump" became popular, especially in Memphis's Beale Street; it lured the Negro population to the polls to vote for Crump; and it may very well have spelled the difference between Crump's victory and defeat.

With the campaign over, and with the song having fulfilled the purpose for which it had been written, Handy adapted the melody into a piano piece renamed "The Memphis Blues," publishing it at his own expense in 1912. It had the sixteen-measure length of a typical Tin Pan Alley "pop" tune opening verse, but its use of blue notes put it in a category of its own. "The Memphis Blues" was the first blues to get published. Then, in 1913, a New York publisher bought it for fifty dollars, fitted it out with lyrics by George A. Norton, and reissued it in Tin Pan Alley—the first time a blues-song came out of the New York song factory. "The Memphis Blues" was a hit, and the blues, as a form of popular song, had proved its commercial appeal and value.

Handy was upset to find his firstborn blues bringing in so much money to a publisher and nothing to himself. He decided to write a second blues, which might capitalize on the now national popularity of "The Memphis Blues." He searched the hidden corners of his memory for some idea to translate into a song. As he later revealed in his autobiography, he came up with "a flood of memories. . . . First there was the picture I had of myself, broke, unshaven, wanting even a decent meal, and standing before the lighted saloon in St. Louis without a shirt under my frayed coat. There was also from that same period a curious and dramatic little fragment that till now seemed to have little or no importance. While occupied with my own miseries during the sojourn, I had seen a woman whose pain seemed even greater. She had tried to take the edge off her grief by heavy drinking, but it hadn't worked. Stumbling along the poorly lighted street, she muttered as she walked, 'My man's got a heart like a rock cast in the sea.' . . . By the time I had finished all this heavy thinking and remembering, I figured it was time to get something down on paper, so I wrote 'I hate to see de evenin' sun go down.' If ever you had to sleep on the cobblestones down by the river in St. Louis, you'll understand the complaint."

And so, Handy wrote "The St. Louis Blues," the high-water mark of his career. With Harry Pace, Handy founded a publishing house in 1914 to issue his new blues. The song was not at first successful. Nevertheless, Handy continued writing and publishing blues: "Yellow Dog Blues" in 1914; "Joe Turner Blues" in 1915; "Beale Street Blues" in 1916. The last had originated as "Beale Street." In time, this is the number with which Jack Teagarden, famous jazz trombonist and bandleader, became identified.

And then, suddenly and inexplicably, "The St. Louis Blues" took hold. Sophie Tucker became interested in it and sang it in vaudeville. Gilda Gray caused a sensation when, in 1919, she sang it at the Winter Garden and followed it with a performance of the "shimmy." This marked the beginnings of her stardom. The Victor Company released an instrumental which did so well that other record companies issued versions of their own, vocal as well as instrumental. By the 1930's "The St. Louis Blues" had sold more records than any other popular composition. It was also a best seller as sheet music and in piano-roll recordings. It was arranged for every possible musical instrument or combination of instruments. It appeared in an all-Negro revue (*Change Your Life* in 1930). It was played and sung in numerous motion pictures, beginning in 1929 when Ted Lewis and his band played it in *Is Everybody Happy?;* in fact, this number became such a Ted Lewis specialty that his recording became a best seller, was interpolated into his screen biography, once again named *Is Everybody Happy?* (1943), and was a basic part of his act whenever he made a personal appearance. No single piece of music was looked upon and admired as an indigenous American song classic as this blues was. When Prince George of England married Princess Marina of Greece, they danced to its strains at the wedding ceremony. Queen Elizabeth of England, mother of Elizabeth II, once singled it out as one of her favorite songs. Ethiopia used it as a war song when it was invaded by Italy in the 1930's.

Because of "The St. Louis Blues," Handy won a claim to immortality. The World's Fair in New York in 1939 recognized this fact by choosing him as one of the foremost contributors to American culture. In Memphis a public park was named after him. So were several theatres, schools, swimming pools, and a foundation for the blind. In 1958 Handy's life story was dramatized in motion pictures with Nat King Cole playing the composer; as might have been expected, this movie was called *St. Louis Blues.* In 1969, a six-cent stamp was issued in his honor to celebrate the sesquicentennial of the city of Memphis.

Perhaps the most significant result of Handy's success was the way in which the blues became solidly entrenched as a song form in Tin Pan Alley. One of the numbers published in 1917 took cognizance of the fad for the blues by being named "Everybody's Crazy 'bout the Blues." "Livery Stables Blues" and "Barnyard Blues" were hits in 1918. "Wang, Wang, Blues" and "Wabash Blues" were among the leaders in sheet-music sales in 1921. Jerome Kern wrote "All Alone Again Blues" in 1920; George Gershwin, "The Yankee Doodle Blues" in 1923. In 1926 the George White *Scandals* presented a production number for "The Birth of the Blues," a song by De Sylva, Brown, and Henderson. During this sequence, Handy's "Memphis Blues" and "The St. Louis Blues" were quoted. "Bye, Bye, Blues" became the signature of Bert Lown and his Hotel Biltmore Orchestra in 1930, and in 1932 Harold Arlen wrote a successful blues in genuine blues style called "I Gotta Right To Sing the Blues." (Arlen and his blues will be discussed in detail in a later chapter.) In such an avalanche of blues literature, Handy contributed several classics of his own, notably the "Aunt Hagar's Blues" in 1920 and "East of St. Louis Blues" in 1937, the latter become a Lena Horne specialty.

During his last twenty years, Handy was totally blind. This did not keep him from making public appearances over radio and television or from carrying on the affairs of his prosperous publishing house. During his late years he married his secretary, Irma Louise Logan in 1954. (This was his second marriage, the first having been to Elizabeth V. Price in 1898.) Handy died four years after his second marriage, in New York City on March 28, 1958.

GREAT MEN OF AMERICAN POPULAR SONG

Songs from Musical Comedy–II

Jerome Kern
and P. G. Wodehouse and Otto Harbach

A new vibrant note sounded loud and clear in American popular music with Jerome Kern, and it was sounded almost from the beginning of his long and fruitful career. "Who is this Jerome Kern whose music towers in an Eiffel way above the average primitive hurdy-gurdy accompaniment of the present-day musical comedy?" So inquired Alan Dale, the critic, as far back as 1904. Already some of the enchantment of Kern's lyric line, some of the infectious lightness of his touch, some of the subtlety of his modulations, some of the inexorable logic of his construction, could be detected by the discerning ear. So characteristic of the later mature Kern are these early songs that Kern's lifelong publisher, business associate, and friend, Max Dreyfus, once maintained that Kern's style did not change basically through the years, but just grew increasingly sure-handed in technique and mature in concept.

123

Structurally, Jerome Kern's songs—both the early and the later ones—were not far different from the formulas accepted both on Broadway and in Tin Pan Alley during Kern's time. He adhered to the sixteen-measure verse and the thirty-two-measure chorus which, of course, was the accepted song procedure of the time—the chorus falling in the convenient pattern of A-B-A-B or A-A-B-A (the "A" and the "B" consisting of different eight-measure melodic phrases). Kern's time values are invariably the simple ones encountered in most other popular tunes: 2/4 or 3/4 or 4/4. The sentiments of a Kern song are not far different from those in other song hits of those days. And yet there is a difference between Kern and all those who had preceded him or who were his contemporaries before 1920 that sets him completely apart from the rest of the song business, putting him in a class by himself.

First and foremost, Kern was a master craftsman who made each turn of phrase, each transition, each inflection, each new idea, an inextricable part of the overall structure. "Within the circumscribed boundaries Kern had so often set for himself," this writer has said in *The World of Jerome Kern*,* "he was able to pour a wealth of the most winning sentiment and the most poignant beauty through a lyricism that never lacked spontaneity or originality. He always managed to do something fresh in his melodies to maintain interest, and to do it so gracefully, so spontaneously, and so easily that the melody falls naturally on the ear. Sometimes he achieves a climax through an octave ascent in the recall of the main melody; sometimes, through the interpolation of an unexpected minor ninth interval; sometimes he brings a novel chromatic sequence within a diatonic frame; sometimes he avoids the repetition of his main melodic thought; and sometimes he makes effective use of changes in intervallic sequences. But however he may digress from the norm in his melodic writing, the melody itself always remains fluid and graceful; it is always lovely to listen to."

The utter simplicity and natural flow of each of Kern's songs gives the deceptive appearance of having been written with the greatest of ease, at one sitting, and without catching his breath, so to speak. This, of course, was not the case. Few popular composers worked so painstakingly or experienced such birth pangs of creativity. Oscar Hammerstein II, Kern's lyricist for many years, who probably knew Kern's working habits at first hand better than anybody else, reveals how Kern could spend hours working out a single modulation; how again and again Kern would try "almost frantically to ferret out some attractive and unusual way for creating a bridge from a verse to a refrain." Hammerstein goes on to say: "I have seen him take off his shirt and work in his undershirt, the sweat pouring off him, forgetting completely that I was there and that he was using up my time as well as his own." It is this "unstinting and meticulous work," Hammerstein points out, that was responsible for "the smooth and effortless melodies. . . . Smoothness is achieved only by scraping off roughness. None of these melodies is born smooth. Their themes may have flowed easily

* David Ewen, *The World of Jerome Kern* (New York: Holt, Rinehart and Winston, 1960).

from their talented creator, but their conversion into beautifully rounded refrains was another matter."

The impact that this kind of dedication, mastery, imagination, and freshness had upon those contemporaries alert and intelligent enough to recognize these qualities was, to say the least, overwhelming. To George Gershwin, the first hearing of two Kern songs pointed a destiny that the younger musicians would henceforth follow. George was sixteen, attending his aunt's wedding at a New York hotel. There the band struck up a number so refreshing in its charm and so original in its melodic structure that the boy made a beeline to the bandstand to find out who wrote this song. George discovered that Kern was the composer (a name he was hearing for the first time) and that the song was called "You're Here and I'm Here." Then, when the band played a second Kern tune, "They Didn't Believe Me," Gershwin knew he had found a model and an inspiration. In later years he confessed: "I followed Kern's work and studied each song he composed. I paid him the tribute of frank imitation, and many things I wrote at this period sounded as though Kern had written them himself."

Richard Rodgers was also just a youngster when he got his first hearing of Kern. This happened in 1916, two years after the Gershwin experience. Rodgers, already a passionate theatregoer, attended a performance of the musical *Very Good, Eddie*. Kern's songs made such a profound impress upon the young Rodgers that the boy returned a dozen times to see the same show. From then on Kern was a hero to Rodgers. Rodgers has said: "The influence of the hero on such a hero-worshiper is not easy to calculate, but it was a deep and lasting one. His less successful musical comedies were no less important to a listener of thirteen or fourteen. A large part of one winter most of my allowance was spent for a seat in the balcony listening to *Love o' Mike*."

"Who is this Jerome Kern . . . ?"

He was the youngest of nine boys (only three of whom survived) born to Henry and Fanny Kern. The Kerns were in comfortable financial circumstances. The father earned his living as president of a firm that had the concession to sprinkle the city streets with water; he also dabbled profitably in real-estate investments. Just as he contributed the comforts of a good life to his family, so his wife, Fanny, brought a love of culture, and particularly a passion for music, since she was an excellent pianist.

The youngest son, Jerome David, came into the world in New York City on January 27, 1885. While Jerome was still a child, his father bought a house on East Seventy-fourth Street where the composer's boyhood was lived. At five he started studying the piano with his mother, who proved a severe taskmaster. Intensely musical, he took to his lessons effortlessly, and before long was found continually at the piano, either working on his exercises or improvising. Somewhat later, he made repeated trips to the Episcopal church a mile away to hear the choir practice, even though his family was Jewish, and the visiting of churches was strictly verboten. At the age of ten he saw his first show: Victor Herbert's *The Wizard of the Nile*. When he came home, Jerome played by ear all the tunes he had heard.

In 1895 the Kerns moved to Newark, New Jersey, where the father had acquired a merchandising house. There Jerome attended Barringer High School. His strong musical interests and talent did not pass unnoticed, nor did they lack for admiration. He was always recruited to play the piano or organ at school assemblies and to write the music for the school productions. Teachers referred to him as "the little genius," but in doing so they were thinking of his music-making and not of his achievements in the classroom.

After graduating from high school, in June of 1902, Kern attended Normal College in New York to prepare for a possible career in teaching. At the same time he enrolled in the New York College of Music. This was his first intensive training in music: piano with Alexander Lambert and Paolo Gallico; harmony with Austen Pearce. This study sparked his creativity for the first time. He wrote a piece for the piano, "At the Casino," which was published by the Lyceum Publishing Company in September of 1902.

In 1903 Kern went to Europe, where he stayed about a year. He traveled about a good deal, absorbing musical experiences and doing some study of theory and composition with private teachers in Heidelberg. Finally, he took root in London, where for ten dollars a week he was hired by the Charles Frohman office to contribute musical numbers as filler-in material for Frohman's London productions. One of Kern's numbers was "Mr. Chamberlain," whose main significance comes from the fact that it brought Kern a lyricist with whom he would work so fruitfully in later years, P. G. Wodehouse. Wodehouse, though only twenty-four at the time, had already published stories and verses in various journals and newspapers, and was already a regular columnist for the London *Globe.* Seymour Hicks, a popular actor in London musicals, had brought the young Englishman and the young American together for the express purpose of getting them to write a timely song for him. Their first effort, "Mr. Chamberlain," had political interest, since Mr. Chamberlain was a distinguished English statesman at that time; his son, Neville, became England's prime minister just before World War II. Seymour Hicks sang "Mr. Chamberlain" in *The Beauty and the Bath,* and Kern was the proud parent of his first hit song.

Kern was back in the United States in 1904. He went to work in Tin Pan Alley where he became a song plugger for the firm of Shapiro-Remick. In the same year of 1904 he helped adapt for Broadway the score of an English musical, *Mr. Wix of Wickham,* to which he contributed four numbers of his own. It was this score (Kern's first for Broadway) that made Alan Dale take notice of the young composer.

Somebody else noticed Kern, too: Max Dreyfus, head of Harms, one of the leading publishing houses in Tin Pan Alley. Dreyfus, felt at once that Kern was a composer worth watching, nursing, and promoting. "I decided to take him on," Dreyfus told this writer, "and to start him off by giving him the toughest job I know, selling music." Kern sold Harms's sheet music up Hudson Valley, and plugged Harms's songs in various New York department stores. While performing such menial chores, he kept on writing songs, some of which were published by Dreyfus, starting a composer-publishing affiliation that lasted until Kern's death. One of these songs became Kern's first success in America,

"How'd You Like To Spoon With Me?" The lyrics were by Edward Laska, who had been commissioned by a Broadway producer to write a song for one of his shows. Laska asked Kern to write the melody for his words; it is believed that the melody Kern finally used was something he had written during his high-school days. In any event, "How'd You Like To Spoon with Me?" was turned down by the producer for whom it had been intended, since he did not like the word "spoon" in the title. ("Spoon" was a term then colloquial, the equivalent of "neck" of a later day.) But Kern and Laska apparently did not have much difficulty in interesting the Shuberts, who placed it as a major production number in *The Earl and the Girl,* which opened at the Casino Theatre on November 4, 1905. Georgia Caine and Victor Morley, supported by a female chorus swinging on flower-bedecked swings, sang it and helped make it the musical hit of the whole show.

Interpolation of individual songs by various composers into a musical production whose basic work was the work of somebody else was a general practice in the American theatre in the early 1900's. This practice gave Kern ample opportunity to write for and be presented in American musical comedies during the next few years. Between 1905 and 1912 almost a hundred Kern songs were fitted into about thirty Broadway musicals. This was an apprenticeship for a young composer that helped store up for him a vast knowledge about the musical theatre in general and theatre songs in particular.

On October 10, 1910, Kern married Eva Leale, an English girl, in her hometown of Walton on Thames, seventeen miles from London. He brought his bride back to New York to occupy his bachelor apartment on West Sixty-eighth Street.

In 1912 Kern's career on Broadway expanded into the writing of his first complete stage score—for *The Red Petticoat,* a failure. He did the music for two musicals in 1913, neither of which did any better than *The Red Petticoat.* Then, in 1914, he enjoyed his first Broadway success of solid substance with *The Girl from Utah,* one of whose songs, "They Didn't Believe Me," became his first to sell sheet music in astronomic figures (two million copies). It was also his first classic.

The Girl from Utah was imported from England and had been adapted for American audiences, in the process of which Kern was invited to contribute about half the score. The show opened on August 24, 1914, with Julia Sanderson in the title role. It was with Miss Sanderson in mind that Kern wrote "They Didn't Believe Me" (lyrics by Herbert Reynolds). Its success in the theatre, in Miss Sanderson's poignant rendition, was as formidable as its success away from the stage. This triumph is all the more remarkable when we come to realize how new and revolutionary this song was for its times. A climax is achieved with a magical (and totally unexpected) change of key; a new four-measure thought is suddenly interpolated in the recapitulation section of the chorus, something that was not being done in the songs of that day; the rhythm is changed from consecutive quarter and half notes to triplets without warning. All of this provided continual interest to an exquisite melody, and it continues to catch and hold the ear to this day when well sung.

If Kern opened a new world for the popular song in "They Didn't Believe Me," he was soon to do a similar service for musical comedy. Beginning with 1915 he was associated (in the role of composer) with a series of musicals that came to be known as the "Princess Theatre Shows." The name came from the New York auditorium in which these shows were seen. This theatre was an intimate playhouse accommodating only three hundred. Elizabeth Marbury, who owned it, had to conceive of some kind of production that could make use of such a small place. She hit upon the idea of producing intimate shows, economically budgeted, with each phase conceived along the most modest possible lines. *Nobody Home,* in 1915, was the first of these ventures. It helped strike for the American musical theatre a totally new path, leading away from the splendiferous, expensively produced shows then in vogue toward a new type of entertainment that was smart, witty, sophisticated, and relying more on textual and musical materials than upon scenery, costumes, chorus girls, big scenes, and stars.

Nobody Home had been adapted from an English musical by Guy Bolton, a young Englishman who started out life as an architect, then dropped it for the theatre by writing plays and librettos for musical comedies. *Nobody Home* required just two sets, a small cast, a chorus-girl line numbering only eight females (used sparingly throughout the production), and an orchestra of ten men. This was a bright show involving an Englishman with an American show girl. It was a well-integrated show. And it had a tuneful score, whose high point came with a number called "The Magic Melody." This number attracted the interest of even Carl Engel (one of America's most significant musicologists), a rare instance in those days for a serious musical scholar to find something of value in a popular song. He wrote that "The Magic Melody" marked "a change, a new regime in American popular music. . . . The public not only liked it; they went mad over it. And well they might be, for it was a relief, a liberation."

Nobody Home ran for a few months and brought in a modest profit. This was enough to convince Elizabeth Marbury to put on another production at the Princess Theatre before the end of 1915—similarly modest in intent, design, and material. This time Guy Bolton worked upon a stage farce by Philip Bartholomae, *Very Good, Eddie,* while Schuyler Greene was asked to write the lyrics for Kern's songs. The comedy traced the adventures of two honeymoon couples planning an excursion on the Hudson River Day Line. Somehow the couples get scrambled; one of the young men comes aboard ship with the other man's bride. To preserve appearances, they must maintain the fiction that they are married to each other. This lively escapade placed emphasis on broad comedy as well as on sparkling dialogue and on characterization. So modest was the staging and costuming that one critic described it as a "kitchenette production," while another referred to it as "pleasing parlor entertainment." All in all this was adult fare, derived from a plausible incident and believable misunderstandings. Kern's music proved a most sophisticated collaborator. At one point in his music he interpolated a waltz episode for celesta which parodied Richard Strauss's opera *Der Rosenkavalier* (whose world premiere had taken place only three years earlier, in Germany). More orthodox was the way in which Kern again tapped the rich vein of his wonderful lyricism, in songs like "Nodding Roses" and "Babes in the Wood."

Very Good, Eddie was a major box-office success. It lingered on at the Princess Theatre for over a year to realize a profit of over $100,000. This was all the encouragement Miss Marbury needed to make the Princess Theatre Show a Broadway institution. *Very Good, Eddie* was followed in 1917 by *Oh, Boy!* which had an American college setting. It was even more successful than its immediate predecessor by running for 463 performances, 120 more presentations than *Very Good, Eddie* was able to accumulate.

With *Oh, Boy!* a new writing collaborator was added to the now already successfully established team of Jerome Kern and Guy Bolton. He was P. G. Wodehouse who had not written lyrics to anything by Kern since they had worked together as very young men in London, thirteen years or so earlier. Wodehouse was on an extended visit to the United States in 1917 to write dramatic criticisms for the magazine *Vanity Fair;* in this capacity he attended the first-night performance of *Oh, Boy!* Kern was delighted to see him again. What is more, Kern then and there suggested that Wodehouse team up with him again in writing songs.

P. G. Wodehouse was among the first either on Broadway or in Tin Pan Alley to realize that a song lyric need not necessarily be compounded of clichés, bromides, trite phraseology, mixed metaphors, stilted rhyming, and emotions expressed mawkishly. Actually the writing of song lyrics was not his business at all. His forte as a writer was in novels populated with whimsical characters—books in which humor, satire, fantasy, and farcical situations were ingredients subtly blended into a savory stew. By 1917 he had already invented an odd fellow by the name of Psmith, hero of *Psmith in the City* and *Psmith, Journalist.* A half a dozen years or so after 1917 Wodehouse would become famous for another lovable eccentric character who appeared prominently in several more novels—a butler named Jeeves. An extraordinarily prolific and versatile writer, Wodehouse allowed no area of literary creativity to remain untouched. And in every area—whether he wrote for children or for adults, stories or novels, poems or plays—he drew his material from a seemingly bottomless well of imaginative and fresh ideas. Lyric writing was hardly a medium a self-respecting writer would seriously consider in the early 1900's, but Wodehouse did. He worked hard at it, and produced verses which, without abandoning simple prosody and without overweighting it with literary or sophisticated material that was above the heads of his audiences, were fresh and literate enough to be enjoyed by an adult mentality. This represented a minor revolution in the songwriting business. More than one major lyricist of the 1920's was able to write lyrics in the smart and adult way he did because P. G. Wodehouse had started a trend. Ira Gershwin and Lorenz Hart are just two of many who never hesitated to express their indebtedness and their admiration to "Plum," as Wodehouse is affectionately nicknamed by his friends.

Pelham Greville Wodehouse was born in Guilford, Surrey, England, on

October 15, 1881; received his education at Dulwich College (where he continually neglected schoolwork to write Greek-like farces about his fellow classmates); and started out in the professional world as a banker. Banking soon turned out to be more of an avocation than a vocation, since most of his time was spent writing. In 1903 Wodehouse became a columnist for the London *Globe*. This was also the year in which he first tried his hand at lyric writing by producing the words for "Mr. Chamberlain," to young Jerome Kern's music. Wodehouse stayed with the *Globe* six years, a period in which he also made numerous contributions to other newspapers and magazines. He was beginning to make a good deal of money out of his writing once *Psmith in the City* became a huge success after its publication in 1910. He acquired a country house large enough to accommodate twelve dogs. To make sure they could roam about comfortably indoors as well as outside, Wodehouse had his house practically bare of any but the most essential pieces of furniture. Furniture invaded Wodehouse's house at the same time that a wife entered his life. In 1914 he married Ethel Rowley, a widow who brought with her a daughter, Leonora. The addition of women and the furniture notwithstanding, the dogs remained.

Wodehouse paid the first of numerous visits to the United States in 1904, sometimes staying a few weeks, sometimes (as in 1909) for a full year. Having found a rich market for his literary ware in America, he soon made it a practice to divide his year between New York and London, the years of the Princess Theatre Shows finding him lingering on longer in New York than in London. He continued writing for the American stage after his collaboration with Kern ended. (In fact, his greatest musical-comedy success came in 1934 with *Anything Goes,* for which Cole Porter wrote both the music and the lyrics, while Wodehouse, Bolton, Lindsay, and Crouse were all involved in preparing a suitable text.)

For many years between the two world wars, the Wodehouses made their home in France. Wodehouse was in his villa at Le Touquet on the French Riviera when World War I broke out. For a period, he was arrested and interned by the Nazis. He was released on the condition that he make pro-Nazi broadcasts in English from the Berlin radio. He did so—with tongue in cheek, he now insists, hoping that his whimsy and subtly concealed humor would negate the true purpose of the text he was required to recite. But most of his fellow Englishmen did not seem to recognize either humor or satire in his propaganda. They considered him a traitor to their country, and on several occasions Wodehouse was denounced in Parliament. The taint of Nazidom kept clinging to him for several years, even after the war, and for a while it looked as if his writing career was over as far as his own country was concerned. But in time the whole matter began to lose interest and significance, particularly since Wodehouse kept saying that his attempts at being facetious or whimsical represented stupidity of a high order, and that he deeply regretted ever having been a partner in the whole disagreeable affair. Even those who held high office in England stood ready to forgive and forget. The bloom of Wodehouse's popularity in England returned.

But by then he had decided to live in America permanently. He bought a rambling house and a large plot of wooded ground in a small town in Long Island (Remsenburg), where he pursued the life of an English squire, taking his dogs for long walks on his own grounds; enjoying a spot of afternoon tea, frequently with visitors; and devoting set hours each day for his writing. His enormous literary productivity did not wane with advancing age. Each year saw a new Wodehouse book on the lists. (Wodehouse's publisher once remarked wryly: "I can never seem to remember if 'Plum' is eighty years old and wrote a hundred books, or is a hundred years old and wrote eighty books.") Nor did old age dull the edge of his love of whimsy, fantasy, and gentle English humor. In 1955 he became an American citizen, and in 1956 he expressed his love for his adopted country in a book called *America, I Love You*. The only thing that has changed with Wodehouse is that he has abandoned the writing of song lyrics for good—possibly out of the realization that a new generation of lyric writers, a new breed altogether, had come into existence in the 1920's and 1930's, whose brilliance and virtuosity he could not hope to match. Wodehouse preferred concentrating on fiction and nonfiction, a field in which he remained a leader. But he has not forgotten those old days on Broadway by any means. He likes nothing better than to look back nostalgically to the times when the Princess Theatre Shows were being conceived and to reminisce about those days with Guy Bolton, who is his neighbor at Remsenburg. Bolton and Wodehouse even wrote a delightful book about some of their experiences in the musical-comedy field in general and the Princess Theatre Shows in particular, calling it *Bring On the Girls*.

It is Wodehouse's work in the musical theatre, however, that must concern us here—particularly his contribution in lifting the song lyric from the slums to the respectability, neatness, and cleanliness of a well-tended suburb.

When Kern and Wodehouse were first reunited, early in 1917, it was not for the purpose of creating a Princess Theatre Show but to write the songs for a more formalized and routinized kind of show. *Have a Heart* proved a failure.

Then came the first Princess Theatre Show for which Bolton, Kern, and Wodehouse joined forces—*Oh, Boy!* The addition of Wodehouse as a lyricist —while the writing of the text remained Bolton's exclusive domain, just as the writing of the music was Kern's responsibility—added new strength to the Princess Theatre productions. Wodehouse's skill at versification, his charming turns of phrases, his graceful figures of speech, blended themselves beautifully with Kern's melodies. This was a marriage of true minds, whose offspring in *Oh, Boy!* included the ballad "Till the Clouds Roll By" (a title used years later for the motion-picture story of Kern's life) and a comedy number, "Nesting Time in Flatbush," a delightful takeoff of a ballad popular at that time, "When It's Apple Blossom Time in Normandy."

Oh, Boy! proved a gold mine at the box office; and so did its successor, *Oh, Lady! Lady!* in 1918. In fact, such was the demand for tickets for the latter production that a second company was formed to present the show in the Casino Theatre even while it was enjoying its run at the Princess Theatre. In this production the principal songs were the title number and "Before I Met You." An even more remarkable song written for that show, but dropped from it before opening night because it did not suit the voice of Vivienne Segal, the star of the show, was "Bill." In due time, "Bill" would come into its own as one of the song masterpieces of *Show Boat.*

Oh, Lady! Lady! was the last Princess Theatre Show upon which Bolton, Wodehouse, and Kern collaborated. Actually there was just one more Princess Theatre Show after that, and then this genre of the American musical passed out of existence. It was *Oh, My Dear!* in 1918, whose music was the work not of Kern but Louis Hirsch. By 1918 the novelty of intimate little musical shows had begun to wear off and had become shreds. But if the novelty was over, the influence that this kind of show had upon the theatre continued to be felt for a number of years. Many a writer and producer of musicals had learned from the Princess Theatre Shows the value of sophistication, unconventional approaches, satire, intimate points of view, and a decreasing interest in meretricious display for its own sake. The remarkable musical comedies by Rodgers and Hart in the 1920's would probably never have been written had there been no Princess Theatre Shows.

Not that the more pretentious kind of musical—with big scenes, fabulous costuming, and stars—had gone out of fashion! Far from it! But even in such a production, where the interest lay in superficials, Kern's music proved a powerful asset. One such production was *Sally* in 1920. Since it was produced by Florenz Ziegfeld and boasted the costumes and settings of Joseph Urban, *Sally* could hardly have been anything less than a stunning visual experience and a vehicle for stars. The cast included Leon Errol and Walter Catlett (two of the more notable stage comedians of the time), while its star of stars was the incomparable Marilyn Miller. From her demure personality, overflowing charm, and unique physical appeal flowed a good deal of the glamour and radiance that made *Sally* so enchanting to its audiences. Here she introduced one of the greatest melodies Kern ever wrote, "Look for the Silver Lining." She was also a potent asset in popularizing several delectable tunes, including "Whip-poor-will" and "Wild Rose."

Between *Sally* in 1920 and *Show Boat* in 1927 Kern wrote the scores for nine musicals. The most successful were *Stepping Stones* (1923), its title come from the fact that its stars were Fred Stone, his wife, Allene, and their daughter, Dorothy; *Sunny* (1925), written for Marilyn Miller; and *Criss Cross* (1926), once again featuring the three Stones. From these came three songs well remembered, and deservedly so: "Once in a Blue Moon" and "Raggedy Ann" from *Stepping Stones* and "Who?" from *Sunny.* The last, still a standard, posed a particular problem to its lyricist, Oscar Hammerstein II. The musical refrain opens with a single note sustained for nine beats. A verbal phrase, obviously, could not possibly be stretched over and sustained for nine beats. A single word was needed, but a word with sufficient interest and impact to permit the five repetitions called for by the fact that the nine-beat note was repeated five times in the refrain. By deciding to use the word "who," Hammerstein managed to avoid monotony while sustaining the basic idea of his lyric. Kern always maintained that the reason this ballad became as successful as it did was that Hammerstein had hit upon the word "who" instead of some substitute.

By 1927 Kern was the most successful and the most highly esteemed composer in the American theatre. He was now a wealthy man, who lived in baronial elegance on an estate in Bronxville, New York, with his wife and their only child (a daughter, Betty, born in 1918). Within the house could be found a family of pets, while on the grounds livestock was being raised (including sheep, to remind the Kerns of England). He owned two cars, including a Rolls-Royce, a speedboat on which he would often cruise on Long Island Sound, and a houseboat on which he would sometimes travel to Palm Beach, Florida.

He was the sophisticate who was clothed by expensive tailors, was extremely well read, kept himself informed in many areas outside of music, and literature (including politics, art, international affairs, real estate, architecture, home decorations), and was the *bon vivant* discriminating in the food he ate and the wines he drank.

Occasionally he played golf. Strange to say, he seemed suddenly to have lost all interest in the game when, one fortunate day, he hit a hole in one. He was a devoted member of the Thanatopsis Literary and Inside Straight Club (whose members included George S. Kaufman, Heywood Broun, and Alexander Woollcott). Its activity was confined exclusively to the playing of poker at regular sessions, a pastime to which Kern invariably proved the largest financial contributor. He made bets on horses through a bookmaker, whom he helped to support through his consistent losses. He was also a baseball enthusiast. There was a time when going to the Polo Grounds to see the Giants became a ritual followed every Saturday and Sunday. On one occasion, when both his cars happened to be in use and a taxi was not available, Kern went out and bought a new car so that he could drive to the Polo Grounds and not miss the game.

The Kerns did not entertain lavishly at home since Eva was a quiet, withdrawn, and self-conscious woman who fled from assuming the role of hostess. This did not mean that the Kern house in Bronxville did not swarm with visitors, night after night. Kern loved to surround himself with stimulating people. Sometimes he played his new songs for them. Most often, however, these evenings were consumed by conversations, arguments, and debates, during which Kern smoked continually, argued continually, embarked on lengthy commentaries continually. He liked nothing better than to pluck out of the vast storehouse of facts and figures he had accumulated in a seemingly inexhaustible memory, a forgotten statistic, a recondite allusion, an out-of-the way piece of information. Often he would jump from his seat, in the midst of some discussion, to consult an encyclopedia, dictionary, or other reference book either to prove a point of his own or, preferably, to correct an adversary.

He was a passionate collector of rare books, first editions, manuscripts, and presentation copies, accumulating a library with few equals in private hands including first editions of Shelley or Tennyson, original manuscripts by Swinburne and Samuel Johnson, rare and old editions of Shakespeare, dedication copies of works by Coleridge, Kipling, and so forth—at a total expenditure of about three quarters of a million dollars. When his valuable collection was disposed of in 1929 during a three-day auction in New York, it brought in over two million dollars—evidence of how shrewdly Kern had made his purchases.

In time he also collected stamps, coins, old silver. He grew so fascinated with his possessions of silver goblets, drinking vessels, and other kinds of rare silver items that he set up one of his friends in the silver business at Rockefeller Plaza in New York to create a convenient channel through which he might make his personal purchases.

Some of the things we have thus far said about Kern represent the more or less serious side of his personality. There was a lighter side, too. He had in him a good deal of the schoolboy who never grew up, a good deal of a pixie and prankster. He loved parlor games, such as Twenty Questions, and Guggenheim (also known as Categories), which he invented and which became popular in the 1920's. He enjoyed perpetrating puns, telling funny stories (which he did exceedingly well)—in short, to laugh and to be laughed at. There were few things that brought him such delight as to play practical jokes on his friends or to indulge in ludicrous whimsies. Knowing of Max Gordon's horror of obscenity on the stage, Kern, one day, inserted a lewd episode into the text of *The Cat and the Fiddle,* which was rehearsing in Philadelphia, and conspired with the performers to include it during a rehearsal. Gordon, producer of the show, went into a tantrum until he recognized that he had been the victim of a prank. It did not take much prodding by his mischievous friends for Kern to embark on passionate speeches about temperance or on politics—sometimes in such unlikely places as a balcony from his hotel suite or in a crowded subway car.

He was a man of puzzling contradictions. On the one hand, he was extravagant with his money; on the other hand, particularly in his business dealings, he was as parsimonious as a fishwife. He enjoyed tripping up his friends when he found them making mistakes but could never bring himself to admit that he ever erred. He could be kind, generous, sympathetic, and warm to his friends, but he could also bully them, try to dominate them completely, and grow petulant if they tried to disagree with him. He was a big man in a great many things, but he was also excessively petty in blowing up a small incident out of all proportion.

Perhaps the greatest single paradox about Kern was that though he was precise, methodical, accurate, and systematic in his thinking habits, in his living and working ways he was careless and lackadaisical. He ate at inconsistent hours and never went to sleep or got up at a definite time each day. He worked whenever he felt like it, sometimes in the morning, sometimes in the afternoon, sometimes late at night, sometimes not at all. He worked at the piano, which had a desk attached to the keyboard to allow him to put his melodies down on paper without his leaving the instrument. He would jot down an idea on paper, then turn to the keyboard to try it out. When he liked the result, he would rub his hair with his hands or finish playing the tune with a crashing discord. When dissatisfied, however, he slammed the palms of his hands on the keys.

Melody came before the words. Once his tune was set, he would sometimes play it to his lyricist over the telephone. More often, however, he would have the tune recorded in his own studio and dispatch the disc to his collaborator. Kern was a most meticulous workman. He subjected his material to continual revision, destroyed far more than he preserved. In spite of his seemingly haphazard way of working, he never failed to meet a deadline and never submitted anything he considered below standard. His habit was to produce for a show or movie far more songs than were necessary, often writing alternate numbers for a situation or a scene, and then make a final selection during rehearsals. The songs he discarded were put aside for possible use at another time, in a different play.

Kern's ever keen instinct for sound theatrical values was aroused and stimulated when, in 1928, he read Edna Ferber's novel *Show Boat*. Something deep within him kept insisting that though this story was unorthodox material for a conventional musical comedy, it was material that could carry into the musical theatre a new vitality and freshness. Miss Ferber's novel was a rich chapter from America's recent past, a colorful segment of American life: a time when showboats used to sail up and down the Mississippi bringing the theatre to river towns and hamlets. The characters in Miss Ferber's novel were vivid and picturesque: the gambler, Gaylord Ravenal, and Magnolia, daughter of the owner of the showboat *Cotton Blossom*—the two principals whose lives become inextricably enmeshed and complicated; also Julie, the star of the *Cotton Blossom*, a black-skinned girl married to a half white, who becomes a victim of race prejudice. This was the kind of stuff, Kern felt, that could be fashioned into a new type of musical—a musical concerned with background, atmosphere, and character portrayal; a musical with a logical plot line and strong and believable motivations; a musical with vital social as well as personal problems. Old ideas about musical comedy, Kern realized, would have to be scrapped. Ferber's story made no allowances for chorus girls, contrived routines and production numbers, synthetic humor, elaborate dances. A concept about the musical theatre such as Kern now envisioned was something revolutionary for the 1920's, but it was a concept Kern stood ready to accept because he had vision, courage, and ideals. His first problem was to win Edna Ferber over to his own way of thinking. Once she recovered from the shock of hearing that Kern wanted to make a musical comedy out of her novel, she gave her consent. Kern then used his charm and persuasive logic to interest Oscar Hammerstein II to write text and lyrics; also, he got Florenz Ziegfeld to undertake the production.

For both Kern and Hammerstein the writing of *Show Boat* was a source of bountiful joy and exhilaration—from the moment they had paid their first visit to an old showboat in Maryland and attended one of its performances. Each morning Kern would telephone Hammerstein to play what he had written the day before. Several times a week Hammerstein came to Kern's house to spend fascinated hours of talk—discussing the play, how a certain character should be developed, how a specific song should grow logically from the texture of the play, how a piece of stage business should become an inextricable part of the play. One such conference helped to crystallize the idea that led to the writing of "Ol' Man River." Hammerstein felt the need of a first-act song that reflected the impact of the Mississippi on a Negro dock laborer. Hammerstein told Kern he was thinking about "a song of resignation with a protest implied, sung by a character who is a rugged and untutored philosopher." Kern sensed at once what was needed, and went to work. The result was a song so eloquent in its emotion, so authentic in style, so deeply moving in feeling, that it is often mistaken for a Negro spiritual. In fact, in the Soviet Union, the song has been identified as a spiritual which Kern has borrowed.

Edna Ferber has never forgotten her reaction to "Ol' Man River" when Kern first sang and played it to her. She described the reaction in her autobiography, *A Peculiar Treasure:* "The music mounted, mounted, and I give you my word my hair stood on end, the tears came to my eyes, and I breathed like a heroine in a melodrama. This was great music. This was music that would outlast Jerome Kern's day and mine. I have never heard it since without the emotional surge."

The writing of other numbers was usually accompanied or followed by a similar feeling of either exhilaration or exaltation: the important love duets of Magnolia and Ravenal, "Why Do I Love You?" and "You Are Love"; Julie's plangent commentary on the treachery of love when it is given to one unworthy in "Can't Help Lovin' Dat Man"; the duet "Make Believe." One other main number was lifted by Kern from his own past. It was "Bill," for which P. G. Wodehouse had written the lyrics and which had once been intended for the Princess Theatre Show *Oh, Lady! Lady!* "Bill" seemed an ideal sultry ballad for Julie to sing at the Midway Plaisance in Chicago where she was starred. And "Bill" found the ideal interpreter. She was, to be sure, Helen Morgan: a tousle- and dark-haired girl with dewy eyes and a throbbing voice whom Kern had discovered a year earlier in a revue, *Americana,* where she delivered plangent laments seated atop an upright piano. In *Show Boat* she retained her trademark by singing "Bill" from a seat atop a piano.

Kern was never in better form than when he wrote his music for *Show Boat.* Rising to new heights as a composer, he lifted Hammerstein with him. Hammerstein's text had dramatic truth and power. His lyrics possessed grace and suppleness, with more than one touch of eloquent poetry. His text and lyrics were as important in opening new areas for the American musical stage as was Kern's incomparable score.

Show Boat was a sensational success—financially as well as artistically. Opening in New York on December 27, 1927, in a production typical of Ziegfeld's opulence in costuming and staging, it inspired hymns of praise from the critics who did not desitate to brand it an "American masterpiece," "a triumph," "a complete demonstration of the composer's and lyricist's dependence on their basic ideas." Audiences were hardly less enthusiastic. The show had a run of almost two years, most of that time playing to capacity with a weekly gross of $50,000. Then the show went on a national tour that lasted a full year. In 1929 *Show Boat* reached the screen for the first time (in a silent version except for the music that was synchronized on the sound track). All of this was only the beginning of its prosperity. Twice more *Show Boat* was transferred to the screen, in 1936 and 1951. The number of times the show itself has been revived on the stage, in virtually every city in the country, is now beyond estimate. A 1946 revival on Broadway had a run of more than four hundred performances and grossed over two million dollars. As for Kern's songs, they have become enduring monuments in American popular music. They even invaded the serious concert world, with *Scenario*, a symphonic adaptation which Kern had made at the behest of Artur Rodzinski, the famous conductor, who introduced it with the Cleveland Orchestra in 1941.

Show Boat marked the beginnings of a new age for the American musical theatre. It introduced a new genre: the musical play, in which all the elements of the musical theatre are integrated into a single artistic concept. Kern continued to explore this new world he had helped to discover with two later productions. One was *The Cat and the Fiddle* in 1931, which the program described as "a musical love story." This musical made allowances for musical expansiveness, since one of its two principal characters is a European composer of operas. In line with a plot in which this composer falls in love with an American jazz-crazy girl, Kern could concoct a score that, in a more serious vein than usual, included a charming canzonetta, "The Night Was Made for Love," and a haunting ballad (unfortunately not as popular today as it deserves), "Poor Pierrot," and made it possible for him to interpolate a fugal passage in one of his instrumental episodes. There was a lighter side, too, more in line with the traditions of musical comedy—the hit song "She Didn't Say 'Yes'."

Music in the Air, in 1932, was described as a "musical adventure." The setting of the Bavarian town of Edendorff and a cast of characters that included a village schoolmaster, a theatre producer, and a prima donna might suggest the kind of material to which operettas were so partial. But the way in which every part of the production is coalesced into a consistent whole—the way in which the story line and characters are believable—places it solidly into the camp of the musical play. "At last," remarked Brooks Atkinson after the premiere, "musical drama has been emancipated." With beer-hall tunes and songs that sound like German folk melodies, Kern's score added a good deal of local flavor to this tasty brew. Other numbers—and the more famous ones—are, however, of distinctively American vintage. The two best are "I've Told Ev'ry Little Star" (a melody that Kern derived after listening to the song of a finch) and "The Song Is You."

Kern's last success on Broadway arrived in 1933 with *Roberta*, a musical comedy this time rather than a musical play. Actually, it was basically a Parisian fashion show dressed up with story and songs. The songs proved more important than the story. In fact, one of them, "Smoke Gets in your Eyes," sung by Tamara, the star of the show, in the second act, consistently stopped the show —one of the main reasons *Roberta* became the kind of box-office success it was. After the show closed, "Smoke Gets in Your Eyes" went on to become one of Kern's sturdiest money-makers.

Strange to say, in view of its successful history, "Smoke Gets in Your Eyes" did not make much of an appeal when Kern first played it to his producer, director, and cast. The reason for this is that in its original version the number was in a strict march rhythm. Kern went back home to rewrite it in a slower tempo and in a more sentimental style. This time its general appeal—and its unique suitability for Tamara—could not be mistaken. This song was always a particular favorite with the composer, and with good reason. As this writer has commented in his biography of Kern: "The diatonic skips in the broad upward sweep of the melody and the seductive change of key in the release that follows never seem to lose their capacity to win the ear and heart." Soft, sentimental, and romantic as this song is, it still managed to make an impact in a rock 'n' roll version: revived by The Platters in 1958 in a Mercury recording, the song sold over one million discs.

"Smoke Gets in Your Eyes," remarkable as it was, was not the only song jewel in *Roberta*. For this is the score that includes two other Kern gems: "Yesterdays" and "The Touch of Your Hand."

The last score Kern wrote for Broadway, *Very Warm for May*, was a failure. Oscar Hammerstein's book was judged by Brooks Atkinson to be a "singularly haphazard invention that throws the whole show out of focus and makes an appreciation of Mr. Kern's music almost a challenge." The venture was a sinking ship that had struck an iceberg on its very opening night. The following evening there were only twenty people in the audience, and less than two months after that the show admitted defeat and closed shop. What remained behind, however, was one of Kern's greatest songs, possibly his song of songs: "All the Things You Are." Kern was convinced that it could never become successful because of its unusual intervallic structure and subtle enharmonic changes. He had written it solely to satisfy his creative urge. Nevertheless, he soon saw it rise phoenix-like from the ashes of *Very Warm for May* to become one of the half dozen or so of Kern's greatest commercial successes.

And so, Kern's career on Broadway had come to an end after thirty-five years. For almost ninety musicals he had written either the complete score or parts of the score. The sum total of his songs passes the five-hundred mark, and about fifty of these have become standards. The rest of his biography, the rest of his creative life, are inextricable parts of the history of motion-picture musicals

Kern's affiliation with Hollywood for a time had consisted exclusively in adapting his famous stage musicals for the screen: *Show Boat* and *Sally* in 1929; *Sunny* in 1930; *The Cat and the Fiddle* in 1933; *Music in the Air* in 1934. In 1934 Kern went to Hollywood to write his first original screen score—for *I Dream Too Much*, an RKO production starring the world-famous opera singer, Lily Pons. At first Kern made his home in a suite at the Beverly-Wilshire Hotel. By 1936, however, he had become convinced that most of his work would now be concentrated on the motion-picture industry. He had also fallen in love with California climate, the placidity of its daily life, its scenic beauty. Now convinced that he wanted to live the rest of his life in this setting, he had built for himself and his family a large, beautiful whitewashed brick house on Whittier Drive in Beverly Hills. It came equipped with a studio where Kern could do his work, outfitted not only with his grand piano, radio, and phonograph but also with recording apparatus. Kern, an incorrigible lover of games of chances, also had built a special card room where he could play poker with his favorite cronies.

Between *I Dream Too Much,* released in 1935, and *Centennial Summer* in 1946, the last screen musical for which he prepared an original score, Kern was the contributor of songs to several distinguished screen musicals, out of each could be plucked a batch of song delights: "The Way You Look Tonight," which Fred Astaire introduced in *Swing Time* in 1936 and which captured the Academy Award, and, from this same picture, "A Fine Romance"; "Dearly Beloved" from *You Were Never Lovelier* in 1942, once again introduced by Astaire; "Long Ago and Far Away" from *Cover Girl* in 1942; and "In Love in Vain" and "All Through the Day" from *Centennial Summer.*

During this Hollywood period—though it was not originally intended for any screen production—comes a poignant reminder of World War II in the ballad "The Last Time I Saw Paris." This song, of course, was inspired by the Nazi occupation of Paris in June of 1940, an event that sent Oscar Hammerstein II into the writing of a lyric intended for no other purpose than to sublimate his own emotional responses to this tragedy. Once his lyric was on paper he went seeking a composer; and since he had worked so often and so fruitfully with Kern, Kern was his final choice. Kern's melody was written in a single day. "The Last Time I Saw Paris" holds a singular place among Kern's songs for a number of reasons: it is his only song owing its writing to a historic event rather than to a contractual commitment; it is his only song in which the lyric was written before the melody; it is his only song written with no production—stage or screen—in mind. Kate Smith introduced it on her radio program in 1940. She was just the first of many notable performers to become identified with it and help to sweep it to its deserved popularity—some of the others including Hildegarde, Sophie Tucker, and Noël Coward. Then, in 1941, the song was interpolated into a motion picture, the screen version of the George and Ira Gershwin Broadway musical *Lady, Be Good!* where it was sung by Ann Southern. The only Kern song in an otherwise all Gershwin score, it went on to win the Academy Award, a development which (strange to report) aroused a good deal of anger and opposition from Kern himself. Characteristic of his integrity and high-minded attitude toward his work and his art, Kern felt that this honor should have come to Harold Arlen for "That Old Black Magic." Kern also insisted that since "The Last Time I Saw Paris" had never been written for *Lady, Be Good!* but was just an interpolation, it should not have been considered for an award intended for motion-picture songs. Feeling as he did, Kern launched a campaign that led to a revision of the Academy Award rules: henceforth only songs composed expressly for the screen would be eligible.

A Jerome Kern jubilee was celebrated throughout the United States between December 11 and 17, 1944, in anticipation of his sixtieth birthday. During the same year the National Institute of Arts and Letters elected him a member. Other tributes were also in the making, most notably the production of his motion-picture biography at M-G-M. But Kern, on the eve of his sixtieth birthday, had his eye focused on the future rather than on the past. He was co-producing an important revival of *Show Boat* on Broadway, for which he wrote a new song, "No One But Me" (destined to be his swan song). He was also planning a return to the Broadway stage with a new musical based on the character of Annie Oakley to be produced by the firm of Rodgers and Hammerstein.

Kern left for New York with head swarming with ideas, and with an enthusiasm and a sense of excitement he always felt when an important project was in the planning stage. One small thing caused him concern while he made his journey by train to New York—a superstition. Whenever he left Beverly Hills for New York, habitually his last act was to play a few measures of "Ol' Man River" on the piano. En route to New York he remembered with a start that for the first time he had failed to go through this ritual.

As things turned out, this failure to comply with a superstition proved an omen of tragedy. Kern did not live to see *Show Boat* revived, nor to write a single note of a new Broadway score. At noon, on Monday, November 5, 1945, he collapsed on Fifty-seventh Street and Park Avenue, the victim of cerebral hemorrhage from which he never recovered. He died at Doctors Hospital on Sunday afternoon, November 11, with only Oscar Hammerstein II at his side. Irving Berlin, come to pay a brief call on the sick man, was the first visitor informed that Kern was dead.

The following Monday, funeral services were held in the chapel of Ferncliff Crematory in Hartsdale, New York. Oscar Hammerstein II delivered the eulogy. "We all know in our hearts," he said at the conclusion of a brief and eloquent eulogy, "that these few minutes we devote to him now are small drops in the ocean of our affections. Our real tribute will be paid over many years of remembering, of telling good stories about him, and thinking about him when we are by ourselves. We, in the chapel, will cherish our special knowledge of this world figure. We will remember a jaunty, happy man whose sixty years were crowded with success and fun and love. Let us thank whatever God we believe in, that we shared some part of the good, bright life Jerry led on this earth."

An editorial in the New York *Herald Tribune* remembered him in another way, the way most Americans who never met Kern were to remember him for many years to come: "Genius is surely not too extravagant a word for him. . . . He left us rare treasures."

In spanning Kern's forty years of writing songs for the stage and screen we had the occasion to mention repeatedly the names of two lyricists with whom he achieved so many of his successes. One was P. G. Wodehouse, whose career has already been discussed. The other was Oscar Hammerstein II, about whom we shall have a good deal more to say in a later chapter. But there were other lyricists and lyricist-librettists who shared Kern's triumphs during his productive years. In Hollywood, for example, one of his most significant lyricists was Dorothy Fields with whom he wrote the songs for *When You're in Love, Joy of Living,* and *One Night in the Tropics.* For various other films he also worked with Ira Gershwin (who produced the words for "Long Ago and Far Away" in *Cover Girl*), E. Y. Harburg, and Johnny Mercer. But there is one lyricist above others who deserves our most serious consideration—not only because of his significant affiliation with Kern in writing musical comedies but also because both as a lyricist and as a librettist during half a generation he proved to be a giant in American popular music. I allude, of course, to Otto Harbach.

Harbach was descended from Danish immigrants who, during the Civil War, made their way to Utah by oxcart and foot. His name was originally Otto Hauerbach. Born in Salt Lake City on August 16, 1873, he was the fourth of eight children. He was aimed for the teaching profession. While helping support his family by shining shoes and delivering groceries and newspapers, he attended the Collegiate Institute in Salt Lake (a Presbyterian grade school) in Salt Lake City, and was graduated from Knox College in Galesburg. In 1895, by virtue of winning an interstate prize in oratory, he was given his first teaching job as instructor of English and public speaking at Whitman College in Walla Walla, Washington. Six years later, while on sabbatical leave, he came to New York to take courses for a master's degree in English at Columbia University.

In New York he suddenly changed his ambition and direction. One reason for this change was his rapidly failing eyesight, which he felt would be a serious hindrance to him in his advancement in the teaching profession. But there was still another and stronger motivation. He had attended his first show on Broadway; his love affair with the theatre was at first sight. He now wanted to write for the stage. To earn his living, while trying his hand at writing, he worked as reporter, as insurance agent, then as a copywriter with a leading advertising firm. Evenings and holidays were spent in writing plays. He also wrote a musical-comedy libretto for Karl Hoschna, a young composer also trying to make some headway in the theatre. Together they wrote *The Daughter of the Desert* in 1902, then spent the next six years trying to market it. Nothing came of this venture. Then, at last, luck for both men changed dramatically.

Their operetta *The Three Twins* was produced on Broadway in 1907. It was a solid success. There were some things about this happy turn of events at which Harbach could grumble had he a mind to do so. For one thing, though he had written the lyrics for most of the songs, he had to yield the spotlight entirely to numbers for which other writers had provided the words: "The Yama-Yama Man" (which made Bessie McCoy a star overnight—so much so that she came to be known as the "Yama-Yama Girl") and "Cuddle Up a Little Closer" (which Hoschna had written many years earlier for a vaudeville sketch). Another thing—successful as *The Three Twins* was—Harbach was not making any money out of it. He had sold his libretto outright for one hundred dollars, and the only other income he received was royalty of one cent for each copy of sheet music sold for songs that had little public appeal. But Harbach did not grumble. In fact, he was intoxicated with happiness. He had finally seen one of his plays come to Broadway.

Since he was not making any money, he had to continue to earn his living as an advertising copywriter while working on other musical-comedy and operetta librettos for Hoschna. Then, in 1910, they wrote and had produced *Madame Sherry,* one of the most successful American operettas of the year.

This is the production where "Every Little Movement Has a Meaning of Its Own" was introduced. Harbach was now well on his way toward establishing his reputation as both lyricist and librettist. From this point on, he could well afford to devote himself to lyrics and the writing of librettos on a full-time basis.

When Hoschna died in 1911, Harbach found a new composer to work with in Rudolf Friml, who had just been hired by Arthur Hammerstein, the producer, to write the music for the operetta *The Firefly*. *The Firefly* was not only the first time Harbach worked with Friml; it was also Friml's first attempt ever to write for the musical stage. It was a resounding winner, and it has not been forgotten. Its rich storehouse of song hits made Friml at once a leading operetta composer, and it placed Harbach once and for all as one of the most successful lyricists of his time. These song hits included "The Dawn of Love," "Giannina Mia," "Love Is Like a Firefly," "Sympathy," and "When a Maid Comes Knocking at Your Heart."

Harbach continued working with Friml on and off—until, in 1924, they achieved the greatest success of their career with the operetta *Rose-Marie* (a score that brought to American song literature such classics as "Indian Love Call," the title number, "Totem Tom-Tom," and "The Door of My Dreams"). In *Rose-Marie* Harbach found a helping hand in the writing of lyrics and libretto in the person of Oscar Hammerstein II. Arthur Hammerstein had brought the two young men together in 1920. Young Oscar, too, wanted to write librettos and lyrics, and Arthur Hammerstein felt that he could learn a good deal about this business by working with Harbach, who by 1920 was regarded as an experienced and successful hand. Harbach and Hammerstein teamed together for the first time as librettists and lyricists for *Tickle Me* in 1921. It was a disaster, and so was *Jimmie* which followed it. But in 1923 they wrote the text and lyrics for *Wildflower,* a Broadway musical whose score was also the combined effort of two people—Herbert Stothart, and the then still inexperienced Vincent Youmans. *Wildflower* had a run of 477 performances, a remarkable success for its time, and it boasted two hit songs in "Bambalina" and the title number. On and off, Harbach continued working with Hammerstein. They combined their writing gifts, for example, to create text and lyrics for Sigmund Romberg's music in *The Desert Song,* a classic in American operetta, the place where songs like "One Alone" and "Blue Heaven" were born. And Harbach and Hammerstein also joined forces to work with Jerome Kern—each for the first time with that composer.

It took about a decade between Harbach's first meeting with Kern before they began to become fellow workmen in the theatre. Before their first collaboration was consummated, Harbach and Kern had become good friends. They sometimes spoke of working together, but nothing turned up to help crystallize this plan.

At long last, in 1924, Harbach and Kern were contracted to write a new musical for Marilyn Miller—*Sunny*. Since Harbach had now for a number of years worked so fruitfully with Hammerstein, Harbach suggested that Hammerstein be brought into the writing partnership. Kern agreed, and Harbach and Hammerstein visited Kern at the composer's estate in Bronxville to discuss this project. Here is Hammerstein's own impression of that visit: "I had been told that Kern was a hard man to get along with, a tough guy. He certainly didn't seem so at first meeting. A man . . . with keen eyes and a quick smile, he bounced nimbly from one subject to another giving me the feeling that I would have to be very alert to keep pace with him. He and Otto and I discussed a plot they had already hit upon before my entrance into the collaboration. Jerry stuck to the high spots of the show. He didn't care what came in between. Otto and I would worry about that. He wanted to talk only about the big stuff and his talk developed it and made it bigger. He didn't play any music. It was all story and showmanship that day. But there were interludes when we didn't talk show. We skimmed over other topics and it seemed that Jerry knew something about everything. I felt stimulated and a little dazzled by him as I left his home that afternoon."

After *Sunny* (in which Harbach helped Hammerstein write the words for the song "Who?"), Harbach worked with Kern on four more shows: *Criss Cross* (1926), where he shared the writing of libretto and lyrics with Anne Caldwell; *Lucky* (1927), for which he wrote just the libretto; *The Cat and the Fiddle* (1931), where he wrote both the book and lyrics without an assist from another writer; and *Roberta* (1933), where once again the book and lyrics were exclusively his.

With *The Cat and the Fiddle* Harbach realized his most significant musical comedy with Kern as his collaborator; and with "Smoke Gets in Your Eyes" from *Roberta* Harbach had written his greatest song lyric (as well as probably his biggest money-maker as songwriter). In each instance—*The Cat and the Fiddle* and "Smoke Gets in Your Eyes"—he had proved himself a master in his field, as truly deserving to work with a genius like Kern as Hammerstein was.

Otto Harbach died in New York City on January 24, 1963. In the little less than half a century of his creativity he had produced the text and lyrics (or sometimes just the text) for several hundred productions whose total number of stage performances passed well beyond the twelve-hundred mark.

Songs of the 1920's–I

Vincent Youmans

The end of World War I saw a release from nervous tensions and appre-hensions, and at the same time created an open break with old social concepts. By the time the 1920's were at hand, the new concepts had become hardened and solidified. There followed a decade variously identified as "the roaring twenties" and "the turbulent twenties," of which emancipation from old mores became the keynote. Woman was liberated from the tyranny of the kitchen as well as from those prejudices that for so long had kept her out of a voting booth and from those conventions that had treated her like a sensitive hothouse flower. Women now smoked in public, bobbed their hair, wore their skirts above their knees, drank liquor in speakeasies, and even joined males in an equality of companionship that included the exchange of off-color jokes and profanities.

Sex found a new freedom, indeed even glorification. The tabloid (born in the twenties) emphasized scandals and gave birth to the scandal-mongering columnist. Sex appeal began to dominate the screen marketed by such new idols as Clara Bow, the "It" girl, and Rudolph Valentino, the Latin lover with the drooping bedroom eyes. The bathing beauty was crowned queen in Atlantic City. A renowned judge advocated "companionate marriage" for the young. Many people even tried to shake themselves loose from law and order through the flagrant violation of the Volstead Act, which had made the drinking of alcohol illegal, through corruption and bribery in high places, and through the stoic acceptance by the public of vice, rackets, and gangsters.

This was a hard-boiled period in which cynicism and muck raking flourished and disenchantment with ideals set in; a devil-may-care period in which the philosophy of living for today with no concern for the morrow gained general acceptance; an extravagant period in which people lived high, wide, and handsome, spending big and gambling big, smoking and drinking too much. Excesses became the norm. The songs people now sang reflected what Americans felt and thought: "In the mornin', in the evenin', ain't we got fun?"; I'm runnin' wild, I'm runnin' wild"; "I'm sittin' on top of the world," and so on.

A hyperthyroid era such as this found expression in realistic novels and plays by F. Scott Fitzgerald, Ernest Hemingway, and Elmer Rice which often presented life in the raw; in such frenetic social dances as the Charleston and the Black Bottom; in the needle-edged wit and cynical verses of a Dorothy Parker; in H. L. Mencken's debunking articles; and most of all, perhaps, in a music that had a strong beat, a muscular rhythm, a vigorous stride. The music of jazz, for example . . .

New Orleans went into a decline as a capital of jazz in 1917. Storyville, district of hot trumpets and red lights, was closed by government order soon after World War I broke out. Most of the great men of jazz and most of the distinguished jazz combinations drifted out of New Orleans to find a new home. Some came to Chicago—Freddie Keppard and Sidney Bechet, who found employment at the De Luxe Café; Joe "King" Oliver, heard at the Dreamland Café and Royal Gardens; and the New Orleans Rhythm Kings, a favored attraction at Friar's Inn. Suddenly Chicago emerged as a new Mecca of jazz, not only through the more or less formal presentations at the night spots but also in improvised jam sessions engaging leading jazzmen after their night's work had ended. Before long, younger men appeared in Chicago not only to carry on the Dixieland tradition but also to create a tradition of their own, and sometimes a new style such as boogie-woogie. Louis Armstrong organized the Hot Five for Dreamland Café; and Bix Beiderbecke formed the Wolverines. Other new Chicago combinations included the Blue Friars and the Chicago Rhythm Kings, while new jazz performers embraced Jimmy McPartland, Frank Teschemacher (apostle of white jazz), Earl Hines, Fats Waller, Mezz Mezzrow, and Gene Krupa. New singers of the blues came into vogue—Ma Rainey, for example, and Bessie Smith.

Jazz also invaded New York. As early as 1915 the Louisiana Five was heard at Bustanoby's Restaurant. Two years after that, the Original Dixieland Jazz Band was a hot attraction at Reisenweber's. One of the first new groups appearing in New York to become a basically local product was the one organized by Fletcher Henderson. Henderson differed from the New Orleans and Chicago jazz kings in that he preferred formal orchestrations to improvisations and ad-lib solos. But in color, nuance, technique, his music was rich with the Dixieland spirit. During the next four years his orchestra dominated New York jazz until others came to replace and succeed him—Paul Whiteman, Duke Ellington, Ben Pollack, Cab Calloway.

Another breed of jazz musicians was germinated in New York. These contributed songs for Broadway and compositions for the concert auditorium for which the generic term of "jazz" was used, even though it was essentially a product completely different from that developed in New Orleans and Chicago. These new musicians took from real jazz some serviceable elements—syncopation, the blue note, blues harmonies. Though the music of these creators was carefully written down and orchestrated, it also made effective use of solo passages simulating jazz improvisation.

Most of the leading popular-song composers of the twenties brought to their writing a vigorous and varied rhythmic pulse, strong and changing accentuations, alternating meters, distinct jazz colorations. This was music nervous, high-tensioned, uninhibited. It was the voice of the roaring twenties.

One such composer was Vincent Youmans.

It is just a meager heritage that Youmans bequeathed to popular music— meager certainly when his life work is compared to that of other famous composers. In the dozen or so years that Youmans was creatively active, he published just ninety-three songs. Only three of the twelve musical comedies for which he wrote the music were box-office successes. In Hollywood his total output consisted of songs for merely two motion pictures. There is not much here to sound impressive as the total output of a lifetime—at least if quantity is a guide. But if a creator is to be judged more by quality than quantity, then Vincent Youmans remains today what he was in the 1920's: a composer's composer; an artist of impeccable taste; a workman of extraordinary skill; the evoker of moods and emotions that do not lose their spell.

In the 1920's he was always placed by the musical cognoscenti with the greatest popular composers of that period—with Irving Berlin, Jerome Kern, George Gershwin, and Richard Rodgers. He still belongs to such an august company, however slim and spare is his bundle of songs. As John Chapman once wrote: "He had the bounce of George Gershwin, the feeling for singable, memorable melody of Kern and Richard Rodgers."

Youmans was so discriminating, so self-critical, so determined to give only of his best, that he, above all others, almost never produced a bad song. Indeed, his life work has a higher percentage of standards and hits than that of any of his formidable colleagues and competitors. His publisher, Max Dreyfus—whose healthy respect and admiration for men like Gershwin, Kern, and Rodgers need not be questioned—once said that Youmans was the only composer he knew who could be expected to produce a standard every time he sat down to write a song.

Youmans had the simplicity and the economy of a writer who had reduced his thinking to essentials: not one note that was superfluous can be found in his writing, not a single phrase that had best be omitted, not a single accent that was misplaced. In *A History of Popular Music* Sigmund Spaeth went out of his way to remark on the "amazing economy of musical material" in such Youmans songs as "I Want To Be Happy" and "Tea for Two" and the remarkable way in which their effect spring from "the simplest means." Said Dr. Spaeth: "The former tune has a consistent two-tone pattern, starting with an upside-down cuckoo call and getting its appeal largely from syncopation and inside rhyming. In the latter, the same two tones are again prominent, this time played downwards and followed by a connecting tone, and once more helped by inside rhymes."

Youmans was content to work, for the most part, within the accepted form of the sixteen-measure verse and the thirty-two-measure chorus. But that form for him was all of one piece, and to each part he brought an exalted brand of creativity. He was one of those rare composers with whom the verse of a song is just as distinguished as the chorus—and not just a convenient stepping stone toward a pleasing melody. And he was one of the rare composers of the 1920's whose releases in the chorus represented a new flight of lyricism rather than just stereotyped filler-in material between the first statement of the melody and its recapitulation (as in "I Want To Be with You"). Rhythmically, he was partial to the one-step. Yet as one passes through his songs—the less familiar ones as well as the famous ones—one is never aware of monotony or repetition. He had more strings to his lyre than one. He could write with ritualistic fervor ("Hallelujah," "Great Day," "Rise 'n' Shine"); he could create a lyric line that had the arch and sweep of an art song ("Through the Years" and "Without a Song"); he could present a simple emotion with the most endearing forthrightness ("Tea for Two" and "Sometimes I'm Happy").

He was very much a voice of the 1920's. Songs like "Hallelujah" and "Great Day" echoed the bravado, the heady spirit, the exaltation of a time when prosperity rode high, when there was a "chicken in every pot and a car in every garage." "I Want To Be Happy" reflected a *Weltanschauung* that was part of the spirit of the 1920's, when having fun seemed the ultimate goal of human existence. "Drums in My Heart" was a token of the optimism of the times.

These and other Youmans songs were of their own time, and this is what made Youmans one of that period's most successful composers. But these songs also belong to our own day. They have survived because, as Stanley Green has noted, they have "the rare knack of involving the emotions of their listeners; they are not only remembered, they are experienced. An insinuating phrase here, an intriguing use of syncopation there, give his melodies an adhesive power and also endow them with the quality of deeply personal experiences."

Vincent Millie Youmans, Jr., was born in New York City on September 27, 1898, in a brownstone house on the corner of Sixty-first Street and Central Park West. (The house has since been demolished to make way for a hotel-apartment; the site on which Youmans's birthplace stood is now a restaurant.)

Youmans's father was the owner of a successful men's hat establishment which had been founded in 1862. At the time of Vincent's birth, there were two Youmans hat shops—one at the Albermarle Hotel at 1107 Broadway and the other downtown on Liberty Street. Described as "the hat stylists of the avenue," the establishment was prosperous. And though Youmans's father was far more interested in enjoying life and pursuing the pastimes of a *bon vivant* than in running a thriving business—a weakness that he shared with his brother, his partner—the Youmans hat establishment continued to prosper during Vincent's boyhood. It had expanded into five shops by the time the entire operation was taken over by Knox Hats.

When Vincent was about three, the family moved to a large, sprawling Victorian house in Larchmont, New York, which remained the Youmans home as long as Vincent lived. There, as a child, he was hovered over by an over-solicitous mother, who doted on him because he was not only beautiful but un-usually bright and talented. As a child, Vincent enjoyed making sketches and cartoons, all carefully preserved by the mother. By the time he attained boyhood he had a copiously filled sketchbook. At four he also began revealing his first interest in music which his mother took pains to encourage and develop. Charles André Feller, organist at the First Methodist Episcopal Church in New Rochelle, gave the boy his first piano lessons. The mother saw to it that the boy practiced for several hours every day. Once she came across a newspaper cartoon showing a boy at the piano while children in the streets were playing ball. She turned the cartoon over to Vincent, scrawling the following line under the picture: "Vincent, dear, you cannot go out with the boys until you finish practicing."

Vincent received his academic education in private schools—first at Trinity School in Mamaroneck, New York, then at Heachote Hall, in Rye, New York. He was a good student and a diligent one, but he was also proficient in the school's swimming pool and at the school track meets. Though gregarious, capable of making and holding good friends (including Guy Robertson, who later became a stage star, and Norman Rockwell, become famous as an artist), he was prone to daydreaming. As the boyhood years passed, he showed an in-creasing inclination to cling to his bygone childhood. At an age when most boys would have regarded it as sheer nonsense, Vincent still believed in the existence of fairies. One day, when he was twelve, he was found looking for them in a tree. It seemed as if, like Peter Pan, he refused to grow older.

His father wanted him to become a businessman, but his mother wanted to train him for a profession. For a while it appeared as if the mother—the strong member of the family—won out, since plans were made to send Vincent to Sheffield at Yale for the study of engineering. But Vincent himself put in a vote for business—and without any delays. He never enrolled at Sheffield. In-stead, in 1916, he found a job as a messenger for the Guaranty Trust Company in Wall Street. He held this post just two days. After that he became a runner for another Wall Street bank, this time staying on for three weeks. By then he had become convinced that neither finance nor business were for him. Parental objection notwithstanding—and the objection came mainly from the male side —Youmans now decided to try to make his way in music. He took on a job as piano demonstrator and song plugger at the Tin Pan Alley firm of J. H. Remick & Company, where young George Gershwin (who was Youmans's junior by a single day!) was then employed in a similar capacity. Their paths thus crossed for the first time; it would cross and recross many times in the future.

When America entered World War I, Youmans enlisted in the navy. He was assigned to the Great Lakes Naval Station where for a year and a half he helped produce shows, wrote songs for them, and played the piano in the band. The bandleader, a man named "Red" Carney, was the first to recognize that Youmans showed promise as a composer and was the first to urge him to devote himself to songwriting. One of the songs that Youmans wrote at this time became so popular with Navy bands that it was even featured by the John Philip Sousa band on one of its programs. A few years later, as a successful songwriter, Youmans used this tune for one of his musical comedies and saw it become one of his all-time hits as "Hallelujah."

When Youmans discarded his uniform, he returned to Tin Pan Alley and worked as a song plugger for Harms at a salary of twenty-five dollars a week. With his uncommon gift for detecting talent in the raw, Max Dreyfus, head of Harms, recognized Youmans's creative potential. As he had done for Friml, Kern and more recently for young George Gershwin, Dreyfus stood ready to encourage and direct the young composer. One of the first things Dreyfus did for his new protégé was to get him a job as rehearsal pianist and choral director of Victor Herbert's productions. This experience (Youmans's first in the musical theatre) proved fruitful, as Youmans later confessed by writing: "There are no treatises or instruction books on how to write an opera or musical comedy. Working with a man like Victor Herbert was the luckiest thing that happened to me. No money could have bought the training I received in less than a year."

Youmans's first published song, however, did not carry the Harms imprint. "The Country Cousin" (lyrics by Alfred Bryan) was published on January 16, 1920, by J. H. Remick. The fact that the sheet music featured a photograph of Elaine Hammerstein, a popular actress of that time, came from the fact that Miss Hammerstein had then recently starred in a film called *The Country Cousin,* and the song had been written with the hope of capitalizing on the possible popularity of the movie. This was hope misplaced. The movie, when finally released, was a failure—and so was the song.

At Harms, Youmans renewed his acquaintance with George Gershwin. Both invaded the social world early in 1921 when Dorothy Clark, a pianist working at the New Amsterdam Roof Garden, brought them to a party where Jules Glaenzer, vice-president of the Fifth Avenue jewelry firm Cartier, was host. As they moved among the social elite, Gershwin and Youmans were studies in contrast. Gershwin then was still as "naïve and as lacking in social graces as you are likely to find in anybody," as Glaenzer later recalled to this writer. "Why, I had to take him aside and tell him to get the cigar out of his mouth when I introduced him to a young lady." Gershwin would soon learn the social graces, would soon become as well poised and as much at ease on Park Avenue as he was on Broadway. As for Youmans, in 1921 he was already suave, elegant, sophisticated. He was his father's son. He dressed conservatively—but always in the latest fashion—trim, and neat, his clothes beautifully tailored to sheath the contours of his well-shaped body. His manners were as finely manicured as his fingernails. He had social grace and he had the gift of conversation. He had an eye for beautiful women and a taste for choice liquors.

Gershwin, having become the proud author of a smash hit, "Swanee," and by 1921 having been hired by George White to write the music for the *Scandals,* was further advanced in a musical career than was Youmans. Gershwin, in fact, was a man with influence, and he stood ready to use that influence to further Youmans's fortunes in the theatre. Gershwin urged Alex A. Aarons, the young producer who had been responsible for Gershwin's Broadway debut with *La, La, Lucille,* to use Youmans as a composer for a musical Aarons was then projecting. Aarons, whose admiration for Gershwin was unbounded, consented. However, as insurance, Aarons also hired a veteran show composer, Paul Lannin, to share with Youmans the chore of writing the score. For his lyricist, Youmans chose Ira Gershwin, George's older brother, who, refusing to capitalize on his brother's success, preferred to hide behind the pseudonymn of Arthur Francis.

The musical was *Two Little Girls in Blue.* As it turned out, Aarons did not produce it. By the time the show reached rehearsals, Aarons had sold out his rights to A. L. Erlanger. Ned Wayburn, who was now hired to do the directing, advised both Youmans and Ira Gershwin to keep clear of Erlanger until the show opened. Wayburn feared that were Erlanger to discover that most of the songs had been written by two youngsters, he would have lost heart in the venture.

Two Little Girls in Blue opened on May 3, 1921, with a cast headed by the Fairbanks Twins and Oscar Shaw. As was then the general practice with musicals, it had an inconsequential plot line. A pair of twins en route to India to claim a fortune have the money for only one steamship ticket. One of them goes legitimately, while the other becomes a stowaway. Mistaken identity becomes the warp and woof of what follows after each of the two girls finds a desirable male aboard ship. Ira Gershwin has disclosed how condescendingly, even disdainfully, Wayburn regarded the details of the text. When Gershwin, Lannin, and Youmans were ready to write their songs, Wayburn distributed to each clips of paper on which were scribbled instructions for the types of songs needed for various dance and other routines. Ira Gershwin recalls: "I wish I had kept the memo. All I can recall is that there were eighteen or twenty items, with no mention of possible subject matter or type of melody or mood." What Wayburn had supplied these songwriters were just the time values and one or two general indications such as "opening," "finaletto," and "finale." Ira Gershwin continues: "Obviously, to Wayburn neither the play nor the numbers were the thing—with his dancing-school proprietorship, tempo alone mattered."

Two Little Girls in Blue was no blockbuster. Its run of 135 performances represented a modest return at the box office. What the show did accomplish was to transform two songwriting neophytes—Vincent Youmans and Ira Gershwin —into professionals. The two best songs were "Dolly" and "Oh Me, Oh My, Oh You." The tender lyricism of the first betrayed the influence that Jerome Kern had had upon Youmans at the time. In "Oh Me, Oh My, Oh You," the three-time repetition of a single note—dramatized with subtle accentuation—followed by phrases in which the tones ascended the scale, was the kind of elementary material to which Youmans would henceforth be partial.

In *Lyrics on Several Occasions,* Ira Gershwin discloses that when he first concocted the title of "Oh, Me, Oh, My, Oh, You," he had no intention of sticking to it. He had invented it as a temporary convenience until he could come upon something more suitable. But Youmans was taken with it and insisted that Gershwin retain it, which (as Gershwin confessed freely) "was fine with me because I couldn't think of anything else."

But if *Two Little Girls in Blue* was no blockbuster, *Wildflower* in 1923 most certainly was. Its run of 477 performances was a formidable figure for those days. Its score produced two solid hits in "Bambalina" (describing the eccentricity of a country-fair fiddler who liked to confuse the dancers by suddenly stopping to play in the middle of a phrase) and the title song. For the first time both Youmans and his librettist, Oscar Hammerstein II, acquired status in the musical theatre. However, it must be remembered that both of them had help in their respective departments. The score was shared by Youmans and Herbert Stothart; the libretto by Hammerstein and Harbach.

Like a good many musicals of the early 1920's *Wildflower* depended upon an exotic setting and a picturesque personality for its main textual interest. The setting was Spain; the heroine, a fiery, hot-tempered little peasant girl who can gain an inheritance if she can prove she can control her temper. But in the 1920's the texts mattered little. What did matter a great deal were the songs, and it was the songs that made *Wildflower* as popular as it was. The numbers, said a critic of the New York *World,* "were not only prepared with taste and understanding, but . . . a most essential part in the makeup of the whole. . . . Its music and tempo are extraordinary." As far as Youmans's own contribution was concerned, his writing still showed derivative influences—partly Friml ("Wildflower" reminds one of "Indian Love Call"); mostly, Kern. Kern, in fact, was pretty much on Youmans's mind even after *Wildflower* had been written. When the show had established itself as a solid success, and the first glowing reports of the sheet-music sale of the songs reached Youmans, he rushed home to tell his mother triumphantly: "Imagine—Dreyfus just told me that my songs are now selling more copies than those of Jerome Kern!"

The next musical comedy involving Youmans did not at first appear to be an advance in his career. It was *No, No, Nanette,* which was a dismal failure when it first opened in Detroit in April of 1924. The producer, H. H. Frazee, decided that a major overhauling in all departments was in order. The text (the work of Otto Harbach and Frank Mandel) was completely changed. Five songs were thrown out, displaced by several new ones. Even the principal performers were replaced. By the time this production moved on to Chicago it was basically a different show. With Louise Groody as the vivacious Nanette; with Wellington Cross playing her father, a publisher of Bibles; and with Charles Winninger as their lawyer, *No, No, Nanette* became the frolic of fun-loving, flippant people on a lark getting themselves helplessly enmeshed in amatory difficulties.

Among the new songs written for *No, No, Nanette* after the Detroit fiasco were "Tea for Two" and "I Want To Be Happy," both to lyrics by Irving Caesar. These numbers became standouts in the production, the prime reason that the critic of the *Daily News* in New York called Youmans "about the best musical comedy composer in town." The basic melodic idea of "Tea for Two" was something that had long haunted the composer. He had written it while he was still in the navy; later on he used it as a "vamp" for a song called "Who's Who with You?" which was a part of the score of *Two Little Girls in Blue.* In Chicago, where he was still involved in creating new material for *No, No, Nanette,* Youmans was hunting for a song that the hero could sing to the heroine as an expression of his faith in her fidelity. Working at the piano in his hotel room, he recalled the motive he had concocted some years earlier. He played and re-played it with the hope that further ideas would expand it into a song. But ideas simply would not come. Then somebody in the next room yelled through the wall for him to stop making so much noise at night. Angrily, Youmans banged a discordant chord. Somehow, some way, this discord seemed to release in him a new chain of thoughts. Returning to his motive he found that the entire song of "Tea for Two" came naturally and easily.

Youmans then played his melody for Caesar late one night, insisting that Caesar produce his lyrics then and there. Exhausted by the late hour and eager to get to bed, Caesar hastily concocted a dummy lyric which he hoped would satisfy Youmans temporarily. Caesar had every intention of working on something more desirable the following morning. Youmans, however, went crazy over the dummy lyric, and as Caesar listened to the mating of his words to Youmans's melody, he, too, became convinced that his lyric was just right. The dummy lyric, therefore, became the definitive one.

No, No, Nanette stayed on in Chicago for about a year before coming to Broadway on September 16, 1925. The New York run of 321 performances represented a handsome box-office return, but it hardly indicates how really profitable this production became. For *No, No, Nanette* enjoyed a success that circled the globe. In London it lasted 665 performances. After the Broadway run, three companies toured the United States. Over a dozen other companies made the rounds of Europe, South America, New Zealand, the Philippines, even China. No musical comedy of the 1920's enjoyed such universal acclaim, and few could boast that they drew a profit well in excess of two million dollars, which represented the earnings of this musical.

Youmans was now one of Broadway's most successful composers, as well as one of its most dashing figures. The elegance of dress and manners belonged far more to Park Avenue or Cannes than to the Main Stem. Lean, agile, wiry, he wore his smart clothes well, while the derby on his head gave him an added touch of swank. He exuded charm effortlessly. In the company of friends he revealed a natural wit and gaiety that inevitably made him the focal point of interest in every gathering. He made friends easily—and from many different walks of life: journalists like Ring Lardner; artists like Peter Arno; serious musicians like Rachmaninoff and Fritz Kreisler. His interest, however, belonged more to the social than to the cultural world. He knew a good deal about boating. (Later in life he possessed his own boat which he named after one of his most famous songs, "Carioca.") Fishing remained a favored pastime up to the end of his life. He enjoyed driving his flashy Mercedes convertible at breakneck speed. The *bon vivant* in Youmans, the gay blade, the seeker after the caviar and the champagne of life, represented (consciously or otherwise) the composer's attempt to pattern himself after his father and his uncle Ephraim, both of whom were sybarites. Vincent Youmans was so much a child of his times—those gay, loving, reckless, fun-seeking, feverish 1920's—that he might have stepped out of the pages of a Scott Fitzgerald novel. In fact, he was caught and fixed in one of those Fitzgerald novels, since the character of Abe North in *Tender Is the Night* was patterned after him.

Vincent was also a man in the image of his father in his foot-loose ways. He refused to take root. He kept moving about restlessly from apartment to hotel suite. Larchmont remained home base, to which he returned periodically for brief periods, as if to the womb, for warmth and protection. But in his own bachelor quarters he could not stay put in any one place for any length of time. All of this was not just the consequence of a basic restlessness; it was also the evasion of the responsibilities that a permanent home and valuable possessions would have imposed on him. He could never meet such challenges; and he could never successfully meet the challenge of marriage.

In 1926 he married Ann Varley in Philadelphia. Almost as soon as the honeymoon was over, he knew that he would not adjust to domesticity. While acquiring a house in Westport, Connecticut (where he set up his wife in comfort), he himself preferred staying in a hotel room in New York or else paying visits to his mother in Larchmont. He maintained contact with his wife several times a day by telephone, and he tried buying her forgiveness for his absences with expensive gifts (including a Rolls-Royce). He loved her enough to be fiercely jealous, always vitally concerned where she was or with whom. But he could not harness himself to the restrictions of married life. Soon after he became the father of twins—a son, Vincent, and a daughter, Cecile—he divorced his wife in Reno.

The same incapacity to adjust to a wife marked his relationship with his lyricists. He changed lyricists the way other songwriters changed their ties. He was the only significant popular composer incapable of maintaining a working partnership with a lyricist for a reasonable length of time. His first song had words by Alfred Bryan; Ira Gershwin (going under the name of Arthur Francis) was the lyricist for *Two Little Girls in Blue;* Otto Harbach and Oscar Hammerstein II wrote the words for *Wildflower*. After that, almost with each succeeding production, he went now to one man and now to another for lyrics—to Irving Caesar, Zelda Sears, Walter De Leon, Anne Caldwell, Clifford Grey, Leo Robin, Billy Rose, Edward Eliscu, Gus Kahn, Harold Adamson, Edward Heyman, Buddy De Sylva. Nobody seemed to satisfy him long, even though some of these men were lyricists of great experience and talent. It may be that he never considered the lyric important, convinced that it was the music alone that counted; and so, not having respect for his collaborator, he discarded one when he felt he found somebody better. Or he may have been continually seeking an excellence in words equal to that of his music.

This continual change of lyricists did not impair the quality of his own writing, which remained consistently high. But the same dissatisfaction he revealed for lyricists was repeated in his attitude toward all his other co-workers. This finally led him to try being his own producer, director, publisher, theatre owner—for none of which he was equipped through either ability or experience.

Youmans became his own producer for the first time in *Hit the Deck,* the musical-comedy successor to *No, No, Nanette.* "For the first time," Youmans said at the time, "I am able to select my own singers and my own cast to interpret my music and to play the parts as I would like to have them played. For the past six or seven years, I have been completely at the mercy of the actors." As happens so often, he had beginner's luck. *Hit the Deck* went over big, even though it was not as profitable as *No, No, Nanette.* Its Broadway run lasted over 350 performances. It toured the country in several companies, was produced in several foreign capitals, and was made into a motion picture by RKO in 1930. And two of its songs were best sellers as sheet music before establishing themselves as standards.

Identified as a "nautical musical comedy," *Hit the Deck* had been adapted from a successful Broadway play, *Shore Leave.* The romance of an American sailor for a coffee-shop proprietress in Newport, Rhode Island—a proprietress who becomes an heiress—was transferred to the musical stage by Herbert Fields. It was a better and funnier show than most—made particularly so by Louise Groody's performance as Loulou, the proprietress-heiress. And there was no question that its musical score was one of the best to be heard on Broadway that year.

Strange to say, neither of the two songs that proved so potent in making *Hit the Deck* such a success wherever it was given had been written expressly for that show, being of earlier vintage. One was the rousing sailor's chorus "Hallelujah," which Youmans had composed and had seen become popular when he was still in the navy. The other was "Sometimes I'm Happy." As "Come On and Pet Me," this same melody had been intended for *Mary Jane McKane,* a Youmans musical that had had a brief visit to Broadway in 1923. But this song was not used there, having been dropped when *Mary Jane McKane* tried out of town. The number was now baptized "Sometimes I'm Happy" and was placed in another Youmans musical, this time one that never reached New York—*A Night Out.* Finally, Youmans placed it in *Hit the Deck.* "If 'Sometimes I'm Happy' isn't sung all over the world until you'll be unhappy," commented the critic Alan Dale, "I'll eat my chapeau."

Youmans was visiting Austria when *Hit the Deck,* translated into German, was being produced in Vienna. Not knowing a word of German, he gained admission into the theatre by repeating to the gentleman in the box office, "Youmans, Youmans." He suddenly found himself ushered to the office of the theatre manager who threw his arms around him and embraced him. Four ushers then led Youmans to the royal box. At the end of the first act the orchestra sounded a fanfare. The manager came to the stage to make a brief announcement. Pointing to the royal box, he informed the audience that Youmans was present. The audience rose to its feet and gave the composer a thundering ovation. "You'd think I was Babe Ruth," Youmans remarked with wonder when he described this episode to his friends.

Hit the Deck was the last success Youmans enjoyed on the stage. From then on, he suffered a continual round of failures. *Rainbow* in 1928 ran for twenty-nine performances; *Great Day* in 1929, thirty-six performances; *Smiles* in 1930, sixty-three performances; *Through the Years* in 1932, twenty performances.

Two of these musicals he produced himself (*Great Day* and *Through the Years*), and one of the reasons both were such failures was that Youmans was assuming duties and responsibilities that belonged to professionals. *Great Day* is a good case in point. Youmans conceived the idea for this show, then hired writers to develop it into a text. Meanwhile he not only became his own producer but also purchased the Cosmopolitan Theatre at Columbus Circle in New York to house the show. From the beginning he became enmeshed in all kinds of complications, particularly in disputes with his writers, actors, and costume designer. The gaps created from heated resignations by some of these had to be filled with hurried replacements. There were so many postponements in bringing the production to the stage that it soon came to be known as "The Great Delay." Finally it opened at Youmans's own theatre, the Cosmopolitan, on October 17, 1929, and the thud created by its failure could be heard all the way down to Forty-second Street, a mile away.

Even when he worked with other producers, things hardly went better. Here hard luck, rather than sheer incompetence or temperament, was his worst enemy. *Rainbow*—book by Laurence Stallings and Oscar Hammerstein II and lyrics by Hammerstein—had been conceived as very serious musical theatre. Set during the gold-rush days of 1849, it was projected as a folk musical. It boasted some vivid characterizations, it had sound dramatic interest and believable situations, the dialogue was homespun and rang true, and the songs were basic to the overall artistic pattern. But things big and small went wrong. The decision to delete the love duet ("Who Am I That You Should Care for Me?") left the show without a single ballad. The directorial pace was slow to the point of being just turgid; the first act was so long it lasted until almost eleven o'clock during the evening performance. The wonder of it all is that the critics liked the show as much as they did. To Howard Barnes it was a "prodigal, bright-hued entertainment . . . with absorbing melodramatic overtones which burst through the thin veil of a graceful score and pretty dances." Gilbert Gabriel called it a "stirring treat . . . a lusty, happy, often handsome show." Robert Littell regarded it as "gorgeously different in its high spots." But the audiences did not respond the way the critics did. It is possible that the whole trouble lay in the fact that *Rainbow* was a decade or two ahead of its time.

Working with a producer like Florenz Ziegfeld and in a musical starring Marilyn Miller and Fred and Adele Astaire would tend to suggest the end of Youmans's theatrical misfortunes. But this was most certainly not the case. In writing the songs for *Smiles,* Youmans became upset because Ziegfeld insisted on interpolating into his score songs by Walter Donaldson (including the still popular "You're Driving Me Crazy"). And matters became even worse for Youmans when Marilyn Miller at first refused to sing his "Time on My Hands" because she did not like it; she was supported by Ziegfeld, who also did not like the song. This song, now a classic, had been scribbled one evening on the back of a menu at the Bossert Roof in Brooklyn, while Youmans was waiting for one of his girl friends to return from the powder room. Harold Adamson and Mack Gordon supplied the lyrics. Finally, both Marilyn Miller and Ziegfeld broke down and allowed the song to stay in the show, where it attracted no more interest than the musical-comedy did and was forgotten as soon as the show closed down. It first became successful in England when sung by one of Youmans's friends, Marino Harris. Soon after that, its popularity in America was given its first strong boost through a best-selling recording by Russ Columbo.

Youmans had, then, conflicts and frustrations with his musicals; more times than one he had no respect for the medium or material with which he had to work; he suffered disastrous failures. Yet in spite of all this he never failed to maintain the highest standards he could as a composer. "Time on My Hands" was not the only Youmans classics to come out of a musical that otherwise was a total "dud." From *Great Day* came not one but three gems: "More Than You Know," "Without a Song," and the title number. *Through the Years* brought us the wonderful title number and "Drums in My Heart."

"Through the Years" was the composer's own favorite among his brainchildren. Of all Youmans's songs, this one comes closest to being an art song: in the sensitivity of its feeling, tenderness of its melody, freshness of idiom. The principal melody may be slightly reminiscent of Brahms's famous lied *"Immer leiser wird mein Schlummer,"* but the final product is not pseudo-Brahms, but *echt* Youmans.

Edward Heyman, its lyricist, has sent this writer the story of how he came to write the words for this song masterpiece. "Youmans expressed the importance of this song and told me that of all the melodies he had ever written that this was by far his favorite. He lived in a penthouse apartment in the West Forties, and the night was a rare New York one in which moonlight actually filtered into the room. He turned out all the lights, opened the terrace doors, and sat me in a large chair facing the piano. For a little over one half an hour, he played the melody over and over and over without stopping . . . and then I asked him to stop because the lyric was finished. There was not one word ever changed in that lyric and as it is heard today, it was written then."

Heyman then puts a finger on the reason a song gem like this, with its enormous artistic potential, should have been a failure when first released. "I believe that if *Through the Years* had only been written by Vincent and not produced by him it would have become an American classic like *Show Boat.* It was really the first serious and dramatic musical. In one key scene, for instance, the bride was murdered by a jealous suitor on her wedding day and she dies in the arms of the bridegroom as he sings 'Through the Years' to her . . . and she does come back to him through many years as a ghost. This was a smash hit as a play and as both a silent and talking film. Added to this were some marvelous melodies; the title song has been sung at countless weddings and still is. Why then did *Through the Years* fail? For the same reason that the two other shows which Youmans both wrote and produced failed also. He simply did not know how to be a producer. The shows, *Great Day* and *Rainbow,* live in his melodies although they lasted a scant few days a piece." One brief example of his inability to cope with producer problems follows: "His next-to-favorite song in *Through the Years* was 'Kinda Like You' which he expected to be as popular as 'Tea for Two.' It was sung by Nick Long, Jr., and Ada May Weeks, who was a popular 'soubrette' of the day. The song was a big success in performance, getting encores every night. Five days before opening night, Ada May did something (I can't remember exactly what) which infuriated Vincent and instead of sitting down and weighing the consequences he fired her on the spot! Of course he had a rough time getting a replacement on such short notice and so close to the New York opening. He was forced to take what he could get. She was a young girl who besides not having much talent was understandably frightened. All the lightness went right out of the show and most critics said it was too 'heavy' for a musical and it closed after six weeks."

At that, Youmans did finally enjoy a modest success on Broadway before he called it a day as composer for the theatre. It came with *Take a Chance* in 1932, but, unfortunately, Youmans contributed only part of this score, the rest being the work of Richard A. Whiting and Nacio Herb Brown. What had happened was that a musical named *Humpty Dumpty,* starring Ethel Merman, was suffering excruciating birth pains out of town. To relieve its pains and to allow for an easier delivery, the producer decided on a drastic rewriting job; it was then that Vincent Youmans was called upon to contribute several songs. *Humpty Dumpty* was renamed *Take a Chance,* and was well enough received on Broadway to survive 243 performances. One of the Youmans songs here was a number with a strong revivalist fervor, "Rise 'n' Shine," with which Miss Merman regularly brought down the house.

Take a Chance was the last time Youmans was represented on Broadway. In 1933 he came to Hollywood for his first motion-picture assignment: to write the songs for *Flying Down to Rio.* This was the screen musical in which Fred Astaire and Ginger Rogers made their debut as a song-and-dance team (playing the second leads here, not the starring roles); and this was the production with which musical comedy gained a new lease on life on the Hollywood screen after two years of seeming death. Settled at the Garden of Allah—which was the setting for a good many escapades by motion-picture stars, composers, and writers that contributed some of the color and glamour to Hollywood history—Youmans went to work on his first score with the same kind of condescension he brought to so many of his earlier Broadway assignments. "If I had anything good," he confided to one of his friends at the time, "I wouldn't be putting it into the movie. You can be sure of that!" He had planned to give the producer only some run-of-the-mill stuff, neglecting the fact that he was totally incapable of writing second-rate material. All four songs he wrote for the movie were outstanding. Two of them, "Carioca" and "Orchids in the Moonlight," were master-pieces.

Though Youmans continued putting song ideas down on paper in the ensuing years and accumulated a pile of manuscripts, nothing he wrote was heard again either on Broadway or in Hollywood during his lifetime. *Flying Down to Rio* represented a peak point in his career from which, in 1934, he began to plummet down to personal disaster. First, the Vincent Youmans Company (a publishing house he had founded five years earlier to issue his music) went into bankruptcy, to be bought out by the Miller Music Corporation. Then, in April of the same year (1934) the Cosmopolitan Corporation took a judgment against him for his failure to pay the mortgage interest on the Cosmopolitan Theatre which he had to let go by default. But all this was merely the harbinger of the great disaster awaiting him around the corner.

He was aboard ship traveling to Europe during the summer of 1934, seemingly in good health, when late one night he had a dream that his mother was standing beside him. "Look," she was saying, "Vincent is dying of tuberculosis." He awoke terrified, leaped from bed, and screamed. A half hour later he was stricken with his first hemorrhage.

From then on, though his health might fluctuate, he was victimized by tuberculosis. He paid prolonged visits to Colorado, sometimes staying at a sanatorium, but most of the time living in an apartment-hotel. In the latter place he was attended to in 1935 by an attractive young nurse, Mildred Boots, whom he had first met in 1930 when she was a chorus girl in *Smiles*. Youmans married her in Castle Rock, Colorado, on October 31, 1935, and they set up home at Colorado Springs.

In Colorado Springs Youmans began to study music, though only by fits and starts. During periods when his health was on the upgrade, he would make trips to Hollywood or New Orleans; at the latter city he attended classes in harmony and orchestration at the Music School at Tulane University. With vague ideas in his mind of becoming a serious composer, he began sketching material for a possible symphony. He began copying out orchestral scores to learn what he could about the orchestration methods of the masters. On several occasions he had an opportunity to rehearse the New Orleans Philharmonic. At the same time he kept on writing popular tunes, creating a stockpile he hoped would some day be used in musical shows or the movies. By the time he died, he had over 150 such songs stored away, none of which had ever been heard publicly.

There was a good deal to depress him. Besides his health problems, he was beset by financial troubles. In 1935 he had to file a petition for bankruptcy with liabilities of over half a million dollars and "unknown assets" of negligible value. Yet he was not depressed. On the contrary. Most of the time he was in a kind of euphoric state—a symptom of his disease. He disregarded his physicians by staying up late at night with friends, drinking more than he should, and going out to the late spots. He seemed to have lost little of his capacity to enjoy life. He loved playing his new tunes for his friends, performing them on the piano and (as was characteristic of him) whistling the main melody as he played. He liked nothing better than to hear his friends say that these were the best tunes he had ever written, that he was better than ever.

In 1943 he came back to New York after a prolonged absence. He rented an apartment at Carlton House and began talking of making his long-delayed return to the theatre. But he was no longer thinking in terms of musical comedy. He wanted to introduce a Cuban revue, for which Ernest Lecuona (the composer of the ever popular *Malagueña*) would do the music. Then even before he had had a chance to crystallize his thinking, Youmans changed his mind to become more ambitious still. He was beginning to conceive a giant artistic project: a ballet revue, utilizing the best choreographers and dancers and artists he could hire. Lecuona's music would be used for Cuban dances choreographed by Eugene von Grona. Serious ballet would be represented by Ravel's *Daphnis and Chloë,* for which Leonide Massine would do the choreography. The performers in the revue would include a distinguished guitarist and several world-famous Spanish dancers.

Having found a sponsor in Doris Duke, he went to work to bring his dream to life. The *Vincent Youmans Ballet Revue* opened in Toronto, Canada, on January 20, 1944. The critics annihilated it, calling it a colossal bore. A week later the production limped to Baltimore, where the reviews were just as deadly. After seven presentations in Baltimore the revue died an unlamented death. The financial loss was estimated at $400,000. "I lost much more than that," Youmans remarked sadly. "I lost thirty pounds."

Preparing and working on and worrying over his revue had sapped his strength. Tuberculosis was now beginning to affect his throat: he could only speak in whispers. After a brief period of night life in Hollywood, Youmans returned to Colorado to place himself in the care of his physicians. He rested all day, but at night he went out on the town. His wife, Mildred, finally decided she could live with him no longer. They were divorced in January of 1946.

In 1946 Youmans had to be confined to a sanatorium in Colorado Springs where he stayed a month. He hated hospitals, particularly the limitations they imposed upon his way of life. Against the orders of his doctors, he left the hospital to take a suite at the Park Lane Hotel in Denver. Though he made a pretense of continuing to live the gay social life during evenings, his health was deteriorating all the time. Mrs. Mary Coyle Chase (the playwright who became famous with *Harvey*) was with him a good deal of this time. She left a vivid newspaper account of what Youmans was like in those last weeks: "He would sit in bed and talk for hours to the people who dropped into his room—brokers, bond salesman, hotel maids, waiters—re-creating the past. Until . . . he was unable to get out of bed at all, he would delight Westerners by going to parties, sitting at the piano, playing over his old music, and much of his unpublished music—entrancing his audiences, but straining his own strength cruelly."

Then he lapsed into a coma. "The radio at his bedside," continues Mrs. Chase, "which he always wanted on would give forth now and then with an arrangement of orchestral music. His hand, to the amazement of attendants, would slowly rise and wearily move back and forth in a conductor's motion."

He died in his hotel suite on April 5, 1946. Mrs. Chase, her husband, and

Youmans's nurse and doctor were at his bedside. Before he died he had expressed the wish that his funeral take place in the afternoon. "Show people don't show up until then," he explained. "I don't want to be carried out of half a house." His body was brought back to New York for the funeral, which took place on April 10 at the St. Thomas Protestant Episcopal Church on Fifth Avenue. The house was full, including representatives from ASCAP, such musical celebrities as Fritz Kreisler, Deems Taylor, Lawrence Tibbett, and Gladys Swarthout, among many others, and a legion of his colleagues and friends.

He was cremated. As he had requested in his will, his remains were scattered at Mud Hole, twenty-five minutes from Ambrose Lightship. Two girls and a friend accompanied Youmans's ashes for this final rite. When the ashes were scattered, Youmans's friends threw bouquets of flowers into the water.

Songs of the 1920's–II

De Sylva, Brown, and Henderson

The songwriting team of De Sylva, Brown, and Henderson came into existence as the 1920's were in full stride, and the partnership was dissolved just as the 1920's were drawing to a close. Life does not generally work in such a logical pattern. This time it did. For the songs of De Sylva, Brown, and Henderson—and the musical-comedy contexts in which they were found—were such an inextricable part of the turbulent twenties that it seems only fitting and proper that the 1920's and the collaboration of these three men should have ended at the same time.

De Sylva, Brown, and Henderson is the only successful songwriting combination of three writers working together without interruption for several years. De Sylva and Brown were lyricists. Henderson was a composer. But what made this trio of writers unique—and one of the reasons for its sustained success during the 1920's—was the way in which they functioned with a unanimity of thought, feeling, purpose, and style, as if they were a single person. More times than one, De Sylva and Brown crossed the line from words to music to suggest to Henderson ways and means of developing a melody. Just as often, Henderson refused to stay put in his own backyard by offering ideas for lyrics and contributing valuable suggestions for individual lines or rhymes.

Buddy De Sylva was the dynamo that generated the motor power to operate the activities of his two collaborators. De Sylva was born in New York City on January 27, 1895 (his name originally being George Gard de Sylva). He was the son of a vaudevillian who had toured the circuit until he married; he then entered the profession of law. But it was to the theatre, rather than to the courts, that Buddy gravitated from childhood on. When he was still a child, his stage debut took place with a song-and-dance routine at the Grand Opera House in Los Angeles. This appearance was soon followed by a tour on the Keith vaudeville circuit.

His life in the theatre was nipped in the bud, however, by a practical grandfather who insisted that the boy be raised in the more normal atmosphere of a home and school. Buddy temporarily abandoned the stage to devote himself to schoolwork—first in California's public schools, later at the University of Southern California. He did not, however, cure himself of his stage fever. As a freshman he helped produce college shows, and while attending college he also appeared publicly with a Hawaiian band. In addition to these extracurricular activities, he became interested in writing song lyrics. Al Jolson liked some of them well enough either to sing them or to set them to music. (The first De Sylva song Al Jolson introduced was " 'N Everything.") Several songs—words by De Sylva, music by Jolson—were interpolated into the Winter Garden extravaganza, *Sinbad,* in which Jolson was starring in 1918. They included "Avalon," "By the Honeysuckle Vine," "Chloe," "I Gave Her That," and "They Can't Fool Me." In still another song, "I'll Say She Is," interpolated into *Sinbad* by Jolson, De Sylva profited by collaborating on the words with Gus Kahn; while in "Dixie Rose," where the lyrics represented the joint effort of De Sylva and Irving Caesar, the music was the work, not of Jolson, but of a young, still unknown, still inexperienced boy named George Gershwin. When De Sylva received his first royalty check for his various lyrics (it carried the sweet tune of $16,000!), he knew with finality where his future lay: professionally, in writing lyrics for Tin Pan Alley; geographically, in New York City.

He arrived in New York in 1919 where he found a songwriting job at the publishing house of J. H. Remick. He also signed a contract for a major Broadwas assignment: to collaborate with Arthur Jackson in writing the lyrics for George Gershwin's first musical comedy, *La, La, Lucille.* "Nobody But You," Gershwin's first important song for the stage, came out of this musical comedy, and its lyrics had left the hand of Buddy De Sylva.

Gershwin was the first of many significant, or potentially significant, composers for whom De Sylva provided lyrics. In 1920 the composer with whom he worked was the already formidable Jerome Kern; the musical was the equally formidable *Sally,* starring Marilyn Miller; and their hit songs were the no less formidable "Look for the Silver Lining" and "Whip-poor-will." In the *Ziegfeld Follies of 1921* De Sylva once again served as Kern's partner with the song "You Must Come Over." The same edition, however, also included a song by Rudolf Friml to De Sylva's words, "Four Little Girls in the Future." Still in 1921 came "April Showers" (music by Louis Silvers), an Al Jolson tour de force when he introduced it in *Bombo,* and an Al Jolson favorite ever after. In 1922 De Sylva was Victor Herbert's lyricist in the writing of the operetta *Orange Blossoms,* whose main song was the waltz "A Kiss in the Dark." This was also the year when, collaborating with Ira Gershwin (then still disguising himself as Arthur Francis), De Sylva wrote the words for George Gershwin's "Stairway to Paradise," an elaborate production number in *Scandals.* In 1923 and again in 1924 he worked even more closely with George Gershwin in the *Scandals.* In 1922 he wrote the libretto and lyrics for Gershwin's one-act opera first called *Blue Monday,* then renamed *135th Street,* which enjoyed only a single performance, being removed from the show after opening night. And in 1924, collaborating with Ballard MacDonald, he wrote the words for one of Gershwin's most durable ballads, "Somebody Loves Me." Meanwhile, in 1923, the combination of Al Jolson as both singer and De Sylva's helper in writing the words, and with Joseph Meyer supplying the melody, came one of the greatest hits in De Sylva's career: "California, Here I Come." This song was tried out while *Bombo,* starring Al Jolson, was on the road after its successful Broadway run. The song became a standout at once, and proved such a Jolson trademark that he sang it in no less than three motion pictures (*Rose of Washington Square* in 1939, *The Jolson Story* in 1946, and *Jolson Sings Again* in 1949). Jolson's 1946 Decca recording sold over one million discs.

While Buddy De Sylva was thus becoming one of the most successful lyricists in the Broadway theatre, Lew Brown was also making significant headway as a lyricist. His name was originally Louis Brownstein. He was born in Odessa, Russia, on December 10, 1893. He was five when his family emigrated to the United States. At first they settled in New Haven, Connecticut, and after that in New York City. Brown attended the public schools and De Witt Clinton High School in New York. In his teens, he stole time from his summer job as lifeguard at the beach at Rockaway to jot down verses. Some were original, others were parodies of current song hits. He made his first sale as songwriter when "Don't Take My Lovin' Man Away" was purchased for seven dollars by a publisher. Belle Baker sang it in vaudeville.

He now deserted school to become a professional lyricist by working with the veteran composer Albert von Tilzer. In 1912 they wrote five songs, one of them, "I'm the Lonesomest Gal in Town" being a hit. This partnership lasted a number of years to the mutual advantage of both, since it yielded a harvest. One of their songs was the poignant World War I ballad "I May Be Gone for a Long, Long Time," which Grace La Rue introduced in the revue *Hitchy-Koo* in 1917. Another was a no less effective ballad, "Give Me the Moonlight," also in 1917. A nonsense song with gibberish lyrics, "Oh, By Jingo," was put over by Charlotte Greenwood in the musical *Linger Longer Letty* in 1919. "I Used To

Love You But It's All Over" and "Dapper Dan, the Sheik of Alabam' " were their hit songs of 1920 and 1921 respectively.

In 1922 Louis Bernstein, the song publisher, introduced Brown to Bernstein's protégé: a neophyte in the song business, a young composer with still more promise than fulfillment, named Ray Henderson. Henderson and Brown, at the publisher's urging, started a working arrangement which almost immediately produced a robust product: "Georgette," introduced by Ted Lewis and his band in the *Greenwich Village Follies of 1922*. The firm of Shapiro-Bernstein published "Georgette" the same year, together with another Henderson-Brown number, "Humming."

Ray Henderson, son of a trained musician, was at first directed to serious music. He was born in Buffalo, New York, on December 1, 1896, where his father early taught him the elements of music. How well Ray took to these lessons became apparent when the boy started playing the organ at church services, singing in the church choir, and writing pieces of music. His talent carried him to Chicago where he received a comprehensive training in piano and theory at the conservatory. The necessity of supporting himself brought him to popular music by way of playing the piano in jazz bands, performing popular songs at parties, and serving as accompanist for an Irish tenor.

By the time he left the conservatory, Henderson had decided to make his way in popular rather than in serious music. Coming to New York, he found employment in Tin Pan Alley: first as a song plugger at Leo Feist's; then as arranger and staff pianist at Fred Fisher's; after that as staff pianist and arranger at the firm of Shapiro-Bernstein. Bernstein's personal interest in him brought Henderson a number of assignments as piano accompanist for various vaudevillians, including a dance team, a woman violinist, and the comedian Lew Brice (the brother of Fanny). Bernstein was also the catalytic agent bringing together Henderson with the then already experienced and successful lyricist Lew Brown for the writing of Henderson's first hit song, "Georgette."

Other Henderson songs, during the three years that followed, used lyrics by writers other than Brown. "That Old Gang of Mine" had lyrics by Mort Dixon and Billy Rose (the latter then still earning his living as a court stenographer). Van and Schenck introduced it in the *Ziegfeld Follies of 1923*. Sam M. Lewis and Joe Young provided the words for "Five Foot Two, Eyes of Blue" and "I'm Sitting on Top of the World," both in 1925—the latter popularized by Al Jolson.

Still other lyricists (Bud Green and Buddy De Sylva) were involved with "Alabamy Bound" in 1925, a number that Eddie Cantor and Al Jolson lifted to a million-copy sheet-music sale. "Alabamy Bound" finally made Henderson a big-time composer.

And so, just as the paths of Henderson and Brown had crossed in 1922, so those of Henderson and De Sylva crossed in 1925. The merger of the three men would make a single broad highway leading to success both in Tin Pan Alley and on Broadway. And the first stop on that highway was the George White *Scandals of 1925*.

George Gershwin (who had provided the music for five editions of the *Scandals*) had deserted the *Scandals* in 1924 to advance his career in musical comedy. As Gershwin's replacement, George White chose Ray Henderson. At the same time, Buddy De Sylva (already a veteran as a lyricist for the *Scandals*) and Lew Brown were contracted to provide the words. That 1925 edition had a rather nondescript score, a none too auspicious beginning for this new song-writing trio. But apparently George White was not discouraged, since he re-engaged the three men for his next edition. This time the team hit its full stride.

Their leading love ballad was "The Girl Is You," sung by Harry Richman and Frances Williams. This was a caressing little tune, and so was "Lucky Day," also assigned to Harry Richman. Each of these songs would have attracted attention in many another score, but in the *Scandals of 1926* they had to take second place to two far more exciting numbers: "Black Bottom" and "The Birth of the Blues," each of which is a De Sylva, Brown, and Henderson masterpiece.

With "Black Bottom," De Sylva, Brown, and Henderson appeared, at last, as a spokesman for the turbulent twenties. This was music with a nervous rhythm, restless beat, frenetic accentuation—so apt an expression of those fever-ish times that it inspired one of the most famous social dances of that period. That social dance, the Black Bottom, was developed and patented by Alberta Hunter in 1926; but it owed its inspiration and its basic steps and movements to a routine performed by Ann Pennington in the 1926 *Scandals*. The term "black bottom" was intended to describe the sluggish movement of feet, dragging through the mud in the Suwannee River. Actually, the original idea for this dance was George White's inspiration. When Henderson played for White his dynamic music, White then and there conceived an opening step for the Ann Pennington routine. She used that opening step as the basis of her dance, causing a storm nightly at the Apollo Theatre before the rest of the country began adopting it on the dance floor.

"The Birth of the Blues" was used for a production number dramatizing a battle between the blues and the classics in music. Each of the McCarthy Sisters represented a W. C. Handy blues classic: Margaret, "The Memphis Blues"; Dorothy, "The St. Louis Blues." The Fairbanks Twins then came forward to further the cause of classical music. The resolution of the battle—and the climax of the production number—came with an excerpt from Gershwin's *Rhapsody in Blue*. The De Sylva, Brown, and Henderson song (introduced by Harry Rich-man and danced to by Ann Pennington) was the pivot on which the entire scene rotated; and as Robert Baral noted, the song "swept Broadway like a tornado."

Immediately following their first major success with the *Scandals* in 1926, De Sylva, Brown, and Henderson stepped from revue to musical comedy. In its search for excitement and good times, the 1920's seemed to find college life a happy hunting ground for uninhibited frolic—not in the classroom, to be sure, but in the football stadium, at varsity dances, in fraternity and sorority life, and in the other extracurricular shenanigans of collegians, male and female. Even young men who never went to college liked to wear oversized racoon coats and the rakish hats that the 1920's regarded as collegiate uniform (the ever-present ukulele under the arm, to be sure). The girls wore tight-fitting sweaters (often with the Greek letters of a sorority across the breast), bobby socks, and little beanie hats. The college spirit—and with it, some of the spirit of the 1920's—was carried over into the first of the De Sylva, Brown, and Henderson musicals: *Good News,* opening on September 6, 1927, and running for over five hundred performances. Tait College is the setting, and a football game helps bring the story—the romance of Marlowe, the football hero, and Constance—to a happy resolution. But even before the curtain went up for the first act at the 46th Street Theatre each evening, the audience was put into a proper collegiate frame of mind: ushers, conducting them to their seats, wore college jersey shirts; and just before the overture was played, George Olsen and his band, the pit orchestra, let out three resounding rah-rahs. Another infusion of the college spirit came through songs like "The Girls of Pi Beta Phi," "On the Campus," and, most significantly, "The Varsity Drag." The last (with its exciting misplaced accents and rhythmic energy) helped make Zelma O'Neal a star. The principal love ballad was "The Best Things in Life Are Free." Its importance in the De Sylva, Brown, and Henderson repertory is demonstrated by the way in which it was prominently featured in the motion-picture biography of this songwriting trio (released in 1958) and in the fact that the title of this movie bore the name of the song.

In 1928 De Sylva, Brown, and Henderson planted one foot in the revue and one in musical comedy. Their score for the *Scandals* that year proved a minor effort. But for their musical comedy, *Hold Everything,* they wrote one of their giant successes, "You're the Cream in My Coffee." Shifting its interest from college to professional boxing, this show still remained very much in the spirit of the 1920's, an era that made Jack Dempsey "the No. 1 sports colossus," as one sportswriter described him, and the giant attraction who could lure one million dollars to the gate five times. Bert Lahr, in his first starring role in musical comedy, was cast as a boxer who takes a good deal of punishment in the hapless pursuit of his profession; and Victor Moore played the part of the harassed manager. The honesty of the boxing game and the concept of clean sportsmanship were generously lampooned.

Follow Through, in 1929, directed its comedy on golf and swank golf clubs; *Flying High,* in 1930, was all about air-mail pilots. Both productions ran more than four hundred performances, and both contributed songs to remember. *Follow Through* gave us "Button Up Your Overcoat" (sung by Zelma O'Neal and Jack Haley, and after that given a tap-dance interpretation by Eleanor Powell). *Flying High* contributed "Good for You, Bad for Me," "Thank Your Father," and "Wasn't It Beautiful While It Lasted?"

Still during the 1920's, De Sylva, Brown, and Henderson produced two memorable scores for Hollywood: one was for *The Singing Fool,* starring Al Jolson, and the other for *Sunny Side Up,* with Charles Farrell and Janet Gaynor. Both were released in 1929. *The Singing Fool* was the place where Jolson introduced "Sonny Boy," unquestionably the song highlight of the picture and the routine always calculated to keep the tear ducts of movie patrons flowing freely. "Sonny Boy" was written hurriedly when the shooting of *The Singing Fool* was about to begin; it replaced a song that had been found undesirable. Jolson, in

Hollywood, telephoned De Sylva, Brown, and Henderson in Atlantic City to provide him with a song overnight. "What kind of a song?" inquired Buddy De Sylva. Jolson replied: "A song about a kid—a boy supposed to be my son—a ballad to make people cry." The trio promised to fill the bill. Then, as Eddie Cantor has revealed, "the minute they hung up the songwriters went to work, not on a beautiful ballad, but on the corniest creation they could dream up— just one more practical joke. In no time at all, they called Jolson back, all three singing it into the receiver." Jolson loved it. "It'll be the biggest ballad I've ever sung," he told the songwriters excitedly. "The three songsmiths could hardly keep from laughing, but they solemnly assured Al that they would send him the words and music immediately. When Jolie finally hung up, they started to laugh —and never stopped. What they had written as a joke was the hit of the picture —'Sonny Boy.' " It sold a million and a half copies of sheet music and became a best seller in Jolson's recording. What had started out as a prank ended up as a giant money-maker for the writers.

For *Sunny Side Up*—one of the most charming and highly admired screen musicals in the early history of talking pictures—De Sylva, Brown, and Henderson created a score with three standards: the title number, "Aren't We All?" and "If I Had a Talking Picture of You."

The 1920's turned the corner into 1930, the year that witnessed the last De Sylva, Brown, and Henderson stage musical, *Hold Everything*. Then the partnership broke up. De Sylva went to Hollywood to become a distinguished producer of motion pictures (including several of Shirley Temple's most popular films), and after that to return to Broadway as producer and librettist of such distinguished musicals as *DuBarry Was a Lady* and *Panama Hattie,* for both of which Cole Porter wrote the music; also for Irving Berlin's *Louisiana Purchase.* De Sylva died in Hollywood on July 11, 1950.

With De Sylva's departure for Hollywood, Henderson and Brown continued to work together for a while with still highly fruitful results. They wrote songs for the Broadway musicals *Hot-Cha!* in 1932, *Strike Me Pink* in 1933, and, most important of all, for the *Scandals of 1931,* which boasted one of the most fruitful scores in several years. This is the edition in which no less than five songs soared to the hit class: "Life Is Just a Bowl of Cherries," sung by Ethel Merman; "This Is the Missus," introduced by Rudy Vallee; "My Song," shared by Rudy Vallee and Miss Merman; "The Thrill Is Gone"; and "That's Why Darkies Were Born." This score helped make recording history. Brunswick Records released a twelve-inch platter in which all the hit songs from this revue were recorded by Bing Crosby and the Boswell Sisters, marking the first attempt to reproduce the basic score of a single production in a recording.

Then Lew Brown also went to Hollywood to work for the movies. Henderson now supplied the melodies to other lyricists: to Jack Yellen for the *Scandals of 1935* and the *Ziegfeld Follies of 1943*; to Ted Koehler for *Say When* in 1934; to Jack Yellen and Irving Caesar for the motion-picture musical *George White's Scandals* in 1934; and to Ted Koehler and Irving Caesar for the movie *Curly Top,* starring Shirley Temple in 1935. "Oh, You Nasty Man," from the movie *George White's Scandals,* was responsible for directing the limelight for the first time on the then still unknown Alice Faye who, on the strength of her presentation of this number, was lifted by the producer from a minor role to a starring part. "Animal Crackers in My Soup" from *Curly Top* became a Shirley Temple favorite.

Lew Brown died in New York City on February 5, 1958. By then, Henderson had withdrawn from the songwriting arena to live in retirement in Greenwich, Connecticut, to permit his creativity to take a more serious turn. He was thinking of writing an opera.

But the memories of the golden days of De Sylva, Brown, and Henderson refused to die. They were recalled in 1944 with the song "Together," which the three men had written in 1928 and published as an independent number, suddenly become a huge success when, sixteen years after it had been written, it was interpolated into a nonmusical motion picture, *Since You Went Away,* starring Claudette Colbert and Joseph Cotten. In 1947 came an excellent and highly successful screen adaptation of *Good News* with June Allyson. In 1956 *The Best Things in Life Are Free* brought in a single motion-picture package all the hit songs that had given this trio of songwriters their unique place in popular music, in the Broadway musical theatre, on the Hollywood musical screen, and as song-spokesmen for the decade in which they were at the height of their popularity.

GREAT MEN OF AMERICAN POPULAR SONG

Songs of the 1920's and 1930's–I

George and Ira Gershwin

The "jazz age" is the way some writers have described the 1920's, and the "jazz king" is the way they liked to identify George Gershwin in those years. The 1920's had many a musical voice, but none perhaps that caught so magically and so firmly the spirit and mood of those feverish times and translated them into such durable music.

The aim to use with serious artistic intent some of the tools of jazz (the blues harmonies, the rhythms and accentuations of jazz, jazz colorations, and so forth), together with the infectious appeal of American popular-song melodies, became a concept clear in Gershwin's mind early in his life. On the one hand, he dreamed of bringing to the popular song some of the advanced and sophisticated methods of serious music. On the other hand, he hoped to carry into his serious-music writing much of the irresistible, even inimitable, traits of jazz and popular songs.

169

George was only fourteen when he began articulating his ambition. As Charles Hambitzer's piano pupil, he already had a glimpse of his own promised land: he would be the Moses leading America's popular music out of the bondage of Tin Pan Alley and into the land of milk and honey of great music. During his lessons with Hambitzer, he continually harassed his teacher with arguments on how truly significant American popular music could become in the hands of a creative artist. He insisted that a composer had merely to bring to his popular writing the technical skill of a serious musician to be able to create songs as artistic as those by Schubert and Brahms. At the same time, so argued the young Gershwin, a composer could become thoroughly American in idiom and style if he availed himself of jazz materials.

This, then, was a boy with a mission, carrying upon him the mark of a man of destiny. Gershwin never forgot that mission. He was always studying, experimenting, seeking to equip himself for that fulfillment. When he was sixteen, employed in Tin Pan Alley as a song plugger, he was found late one quiet afternoon in his cubicle practicing Bach's *Well-Tempered Clavier*. A fellow song plugger asked him: "George, are you studying to be a great pianist?" George replied soberly: "No, I'm studying to be a great popular composer." He became a great popular composer, and he became a great serious composer using popular techniques. At the same time he helped create a musical art that sprang naturally from the soil of American backgrounds and experiences, American psychology and culture. And he helped to lift American popular music to artistic significance.

George Gershwin was born in Brooklyn, New York, on September 26, 1898. Originally his name was Jacob Gershvin. The family already included Ira, who was twenty-one months old when George was born. Eight months after George's birth, the family moved to Manhattan's East Side where the two boys grew up. Ira became the student, malleable in and out of the classroom, a boy who doted on reading and sketching and who used his weekly allowance of twenty-five cents to buy admisison into neighborhood theatres. His younger brother, George, avoided books like the plague and the classroom whenever he could manage to do so, preferring the pastime of the city streets with the neighborhood kids.

With nobody in the family being musical, chance rather than calculation made George aware of his own deeply latent musical nature. Once in a while music came into his life, and when it came he was deeply affected. The first time this happened was when he was about six and heard Anton Rubinstein's *Melody in F* on an automatic piano arcade. "The peculiar jumps in the music held me rooted," he later recalled. "To this very day, I can't hear the tune without picturing myself outside that arcade . . . drinking it all in avidly." At another time, during a brief period when the Gershwins lived in Harlem, he happened to overhear some jazz music come floating from Baron Wilkins's nightclub where Jim Europe and his band were performing. He was frozen in his tracks. After that, he often roller-skated to the club to sit on the stone curb outside to listen to the music by the hour.

His most significant musical experience during his boyhood came when he was ten. Playing ball in the school yard, he was struck by the strains of Dvořák's *Humoresque* played on the violin by a fellow student in the nearby auditorium. "To me," Gershwin later said of this music, "it was a flashing revelation of beauty." The performer was an eight-year-old boy named Maxie Rosenzweig. (He subsequently became a violin virtuoso under the name of Max Rosen.) Gershwin sought the boy out and became his friend. From Maxie, George learned for the first time about the world of good music, about the great composers, about the ways in which it was possible to make up original melodies. One day, while visiting Maxie, Gershwin played for him on the piano with one finger a melody he himself had just invented. Maxie told him: "Take my word, George, you haven't got it in you to become a musician."

When George was twelve, an upright piano came into the Gershwin apartment on the East Side. It was acquired for Ira, who had already begun to take piano lessons with his aunt. The extent of Ira's musical education was thirty-two pages in Beyer's. After that Ira left the piano to George, who was now spending all his free hours at it trying to pick out the popular tunes of the day or concocting tunes of his own. Before long, George began taking lessons from local teachers. One proved more inept than the next, until he found Charles Hambitzer.

Throughout this life Gershwin never hesitated to express his profound indebtedness to Hambitzer, and with good reason. Hambitzer represented Gershwin's real musical awakening. A discriminating, sensitive, and well-informed musician, Hambitzer gave his pupil not only a thorough technical training but also an initiation into piano literature. At Hambitzer's instigation Gershwin began going to concerts. So successful was the teacher in arousing his pupil's interest and enthusiasm that the boy bought a large gray ledger into which he pasted the programs of concerts he had attended, together with photographs of composers and performers he cut out of papers and magazines. Gershwin's progress matched his enthusiasm. It did not take Hambitzer long to realize that somebody very special had fallen into his hands. Hambitzer wrote to one of his sisters: "I have a new pupil who will make his mark in music if anybody will. The boy is a genius, without a doubt; he's crazy about music and he can't wait until it's time to take his lessons. No watching the clock for this boy. . . . I believe I can make something of him."

By the time he was fifteen, Gershwin was beginning to play the piano in public: at the school assembly; one summer at a Catskill Mountains resort. He was also beginning to put music down on paper, at first a popular song, "Since I Found You," and after that a piano tango, neither of which was ever published. "He wants to go in for this modern stuff, jazz and what not," Hambitzer revealed to his sister. "But I'm not going to let him for a while. I'll see that he gets a firm foundation in the standard music first."

In writing popular pieces, young Gershwin was already beginning to understand his own direction in music. He loved the music of the masters, but he loved Irving Berlin's "Alexander's Ragtime Band" and the songs of Jerome Kern even more. The realization that his destiny lay with popular music led him to abandon his schooling at the high-school level and to find a job in Tin Pan Alley. In his fifteenth year he was employed by the publishing house of Remick as staff pianist and song plugger. But convinced that a good popular composer must know everything he could about serious music, he continued his piano lessons with Hambitzer and supplemented it with the study of harmony, counterpoint, and orchestration with Edward Kilenyi.

Even as a hack pianist in his cubicle demonstrating Remick's songs for potential clients, Gershwin attracted attention. Irving Caesar, the lyricist, often stopped off at Remick's just to listen to Gershwin play the piano. "His rhythms had the impact of a sledge hammer," Caesar now recalls. "His harmonies were years ahead of their time. I had never heard such playing of our popular music." Harry Ruby, later become a successful song composer in his own right, was also employed in those days as a song plugger. In the performance of his duties he often crossed paths with young Gershwin. He says: "Sometimes when he spoke of the artistic mission of popular music, we thought he was going 'high-falutin.' The height of artistic achievement to us was a 'pop' song that sold lots of copies. We just didn't understand what he was talking about."

Sophie Tucker's interest in Gershwin led to his first publication, the song "When You Want 'Em You Can't Get 'Em," bought by the firm of Harry von Tilzer. Murray Roth, who wrote the lyrics, sold his own rights outright for fifteen dollars. Gershwin preferred a royalty arrangement and accepted an advance of five dollars (which turned out to be his total earnings). Sigmund Romberg also gave a helping hand to the young composer by using "Making of a Girl" in *The Passing Show of 1916,* the first time a Gershwin song was heard in a Broadway musical.

After leaving Remick early in 1917, Gershwin applied to Irving Berlin for a job as his secretary and arranger. He came bringing his own adaptation of a Berlin song. To this day, this manuscript is one of Berlin's proud possessions. Gershwin played his arrangement. "I'll never forget his playing," Berlin told an interviewer. "My song sounded altogether new and different." Berlin informed young Gershwin: "The job is yours at $100 a week if you want it. But I hope you don't take it. You are much too talented to be an arranger for anybody. If you worked for me you might start writing the way I do, and your own original style would be cramped. You are meant for big things." And Gershwin, the boy with a mission, had the courage to turn down a job that would have earned him three times what he could possibly get anywhere else.

Instead of working for Berlin, Gershwin found a job at the publishing house of T. B. Harms under a most unusual arrangement. Impressed by Gershwin's potential, Max Dreyfus, the head of Harms, hired Gershwin for thirty-five dollars a week. Gershwin had no duties or set hours. All that Gershwin was required to do was to write songs and show them to Dreyfus. "He's the kind of boy I like to gamble on," Dreyfus told a friend. The gamble paid off. Dreyfus remained Gershwin's publisher for many years, reaping a financial harvest, not to speak of the personal satisfaction of seeing his discovery become one of the giants of American popular music.

The first Gershwin song published by Dreyfus already had some novel technical approaches. In its changing tonalities and chromatic harmonies, "Some Wonderful Sort of Someone" represented a new sound and a new writing manner for Tin Pan Alley. Other of Gershwin's early songs also revealed fresh, new methods for song structure: the chorus of "Something About Love" ended in a protracted sequence, and the main melody of "I Was So Young, You Were So Beautiful" extended for twenty-four measures instead of the more usual sixteen.

Through Dreyfus's influence, Gershwin found odd jobs playing the piano at rehearsals of stage musicals. Working in this capacity for *Miss 1917* brought Gershwin for the first time into personal contact with a composer whom he admired inordinately—Jerome Kern. When the rehearsal session ended each day, Gershwin would stay at the piano improvising. The first time Kern heard one of those improvisations he became so excited that he rushed home to bring his wife back to the theatre to hear this remarkable young musician.

Dreyfus was also responsible for getting Gershwin to write his first full score for a stage musical. This experience did not turn out well. The musical— a revue, *Half Past Eight*—opened and closed out of town, and Gershwin was never paid for his work. But his very next full-length score brought happier results. The young producer Alex A. Aarons contracted Gershwin to write the music for *La, La, Lucille,* which opened in New York on May 26, 1919. *La, La, Lucille* had a run of over one hundred performances. It produced Gershwin's first song of present-day interest, "Nobody But You," something that he had written while he was still working at Remick's and which he took out of his drawer as the main love ballad for his first Broadway score.

Another Gershwin song in 1919 became his first smash hit—"Swanee," incorporated by Ned Wayburn into his stage show when the Capitol Theatre opened on Broadway on October 24, 1919, as a movie palace. In that production, "Swanee" was given an impressive setting, danced on a darkened stage by sixty chorus girls with electric lights on their slippers. In spite of this elaborate presentation and its handsome trappings, "Swanee" did not make much of an impression. Then Al Jolson became interested in it. He sang it one Sunday evening at the Winter Garden where it caused such a stir that Jolson decided to place it in *Sinbad,* an extravaganza in which he was then starring. The song now soared to success. Within a year it sold over two million records and one million copies of sheet music. In fact, in spite of the heights of greatness to which Gershwin was yet to ascend, he never again achieved a success of such dimensions for one of his songs.

Though superficially "Swanee" was very much like many another song about the Southland, it did have some highly novel approaches. The most revolutionary was the use of the diminished seventh as a cadence, something that was happening to a popular song for the first time. The change in key from verse to chorus and the novel intervallic structure of the chorus were two other examples of Gershwin's adventurous nature, as was the fact that he appended to the chorus a sixteen-measure trio as his first effort to extend the structural boundaries of the popular song.

Between 1920 and 1924 Gershwin wrote the music for the annual *Scandals,* the lavish revue that George White was presenting as competition to the *Ziegfeld*

Follies. In all, Gershwin wrote forty-four songs to the five editions; of these, two have the stamp of Gershwin's coming greatness. In 1922 "Stairway to Paradise" was introduced by Winnie Lightner. This was a number remarkable for its subtle enharmonic changes, daring accentuations, and piquant blue-note writing. Two years later, Winnie Lightner sang "Somebody Loves Me," a gem as remarkable for its fresh and original harmonies as for its rich-blooded lyricism.

But the success that satisfied other popular composers was not enough for Gershwin. He had become a luminary on Broadway, and he was making a good deal of money. His eye, however, remained fixed on a distant horizon. He still felt he had much to learn before he could realize himself creatively the way he wished. He therefore hired orchestral musicians to teach him the different instruments of the orchestra. In 1923 he came to Rubin Goldmark for lessons in harmony.

He also began exploring the possibilities of opening for himself new creative horizons. In 1919 he wrote a *Lullaby* for string quartet whose principal melody was a blues. This was his first attempt to write a serious piece of music in a popular style. (This work was rediscovered many years later by the Budapest String Quartet which introduced it to the world in Washington, D. C., in 1967.) Then, in 1922, he completed a one-act Negro opera, originally entitled *Blue Monday,* but subsequently become known as *135th Street.* Gershwin wrote the little opera for the *Scandals* where it was given only a single performance. George White withdrew it after opening night because he thought the piece too gloomy for a Broadway revue. The drama critics did not like it either, even though it did boast a number of effective blues melodies. In its subsequent revivals as *135th Street,* the opera failed to do much better; but its importance as Gershwin's first step toward his own paradise can hardly be exaggerated.

Despite the failure of *Blue Monday,* Gershwin was beginning to attract a good deal of attention among serious musicians. Beryl Rubinstein, a renowned concert pianist and member of the faculty of the Cleveland Institute of Music, described Gershwin to a newspaper interviewer in 1922 as "a great composer" with "the spark of musical genius which is definite in his serious moods." In *The Dial,* one of the most highly esteemed literary journals of the teens and twenties, Gilbert Seldes wrote in 1923: "Delicacy, even dreaminess, is a quality he [Gershwin] alone brings into jazz music." And on November 1, 1923, an important concert artist, the singer Eva Gauthier, gave a recital of art songs at Aeolian Hall in New York, which included a group devoted to Gershwin's songs (with Gershwin at the piano). "I consider this one of the very most important events in American musical history," reported Carl van Vechten.

Somebody else took notice of Gershwin: Paul Whiteman, now already the acclaimed "king of jazz" who was conductor of the pit orchestra for the *Scandals* when *Blue Monday* was given its solitary performance. From the time he had founded his famous orchestra a few years earlier, Paul Whiteman had been trying to extend the dimensions of popular-music performances: by hiring for his orchestra some of the leading jazz virtuosos of the time; by presenting concerts of popular music in carefully rehearsed performances; by presenting popular songs in fresh, vital orchestrations (mainly the work of Ferde Grofé). Whiteman felt that the time had arrived to give popular music an aura of respectability by bringing it inside a formal concert auditorium. With this in mind he planned an all-American music concert at the Aeolian Hall. He needed a new big work to give the concert a point of climax, and since he had been impressed by *Blue Monday* and by its composer, he asked Gershwin to write the composition for him. What Whiteman was thinking of was a work demonstrating how far American popular music had progressed.

All of this was, of course, completely in line with Gershwin's own ambitions and beliefs. But Gershwin felt he was not yet ready for such an assignment, and this was the reason he refused to promise Whiteman to provide the composition. Nevertheless, ideas for such a composition began percolating in his mind, some while he was at the piano improvising, some while he was on a train bound for Boston.

Reading an announcement in the New York *Herald Tribune* that he was at work on a "symphony" for the now imminent Paul Whiteman concert finally sent Gershwin to the work table. Once he began working, the composition progressed smoothly. In a few weeks' time the *Rhapsody in Blue* was completed in a two-piano version. Time now being of the essence, Ferde Grofé was called in to do the orchestration. But the suggestion, so long believed, that Gershwin did not have the knowledge necessary to perform this orchestration task is sheer nonsense. This was proved in 1926 when Gershwin wrote his own orchestration for the *Rhapsody,* which since then has been the one that symphony orchestras everywhere have used.

Paul Whiteman's "all-American music concert" took place on Lincoln's birthday in 1924. The program was made up of popular songs in symphonic arrangements; symphonic pieces in jazz arrangements; a few original jazz items; and two world premieres, Victor Herbert's *A Suite of Serenades* and Gershwin's *Rhapsody in Blue.* Gershwin's *Rhapsody* was placed in the next-to-the-last slot of what proved to be a long afternoon of dull music-making. There was no question that it stole the whole show. By the time the Gershwin piece was heard, most in the audience had become impatient with ennui and fatigue; the similarity in style and treament of the compositions on the program had induced monumental boredom. But the opening *portamento* in solo clarinet in the *Rhapsody* was an electric shock to magnetize the audience to attention. When completed twenty minutes later, the *Rhapsody* drew an ovation. The next day some leading critics took cognizance of a masterwork (though, it must be confessed, two distinguished representatives, Pitts Sanborn and Lawrence Gilman, found the composition either "meaningless repetition" or "trite and feeble and conventional").

The minority disapproval notwithstanding, the *Rhapsody* proved the highlight of the Whiteman concert, the one work that gave the event meaning and significance. From that afternoon on, the *Rhapsody* went on to become probably the most famous, the best-loved, the most frequently performed, and the most profitable piece of serious music ever written by an American. Whiteman's initial recording for Victor sold a million discs; the celebrated slow section became Whiteman's identifying theme. The *Rhapsody* was adapted for two ballets;

the Roxy Theatre in New York paid Gershwin $10,000 for the rights to present the work in a stage show; Universal purchased performance rights for $50,000, the highest price ever commanded by a musical composition for a movie. The *Rhapsody* was arranged for solo instruments, and for every possible combination of instruments, including a harmonica orchestra and an orchestra of mandolins; it was even transcribed for unaccompanied chorus. The published score was a best seller.

In short, the *Rhapsody* brought Gershwin wealth and fame. But, more significantly, it also marked the first fulfillment of his life's mission. From this point on he would receive consideration as an important *serious* American composer, even though his music was in a jazz style. That consideration grew by leaps and bounds with each succeeding concert work: the Piano Concerto in F in 1925; the Three Preludes, for solo piano, in 1926; the tone poem *An American in Paris* in 1928; the *Second Rhapsody,* for orchestra, in 1931; the *Cuban Overture* in 1932; the *Variations on I Got Rhythm,* for piano and orchestra, in 1934; and the folk opera *Porgy and Bess* in 1935. And it was through many of these serious compositions that Gershwin's posthumous fame grew and spread until he became not only a world figure in music but also a legend and a classic.

From 1924 Gershwin kept one foot in the serious concert auditorium and the other in Tin Pan Alley, Broadway, and Hollywood. He entered a new phase as popular composer in 1924 when he withdrew from the *Scandals* to return to musical comedy. His first such since his maiden effort in 1919 was *Lady, Be Good!* come to the Liberty Theatre on December 1, 1924. After that Gershwin wrote the music for fourteen Broadway musicals. A few were major successes, several were minor ones, a good many were failures. One or two made stage history for one reason or another. None, however, has had either the universality or the durability to survive into our own times, but all of them are either of interest or importance because they had "music by Gershwin."

Lady, Be Good! has particular significance in Gershwin's career, since it is the first musical comedy for which his brother, Ira, wrote all the lyrics. They had collaborated on some songs before this, to be sure. The first time one of their songs was publicly performed was in 1918 when "The Real American Folk Song" was interpolated by Nora Bayes into one of her musicals, *Ladies First.* Ira Gershwin had also been B. G. De Sylva's partner in the writing of the lyrics for "Stairway to Paradise." The brothers, then, had been working together spasmodically and intermittently for a number of years until *Lady, Be Good!* established them into a permanent working arrangement. They remained collaborators as long as George Gershwin lived.

Ira—who was born in New York City on December 6, 1896, almost two years before George—had pursued literary interests from his boyhood days on. While attending Townsend Harris Hall, Ira edited, wrote, illustrated, and distributed a one-page weekly for a period of twenty-six weeks; its reading public consisted of one person, his cousin. From Townsend Harris, Ira passed on to the College of the City of New York. He stayed there two years, in that time writing sketches and verses for the college humor magazine, *Mercury,* and sharing a regular column on the college newspaper *Campus* with E. Y. Harburg, a fellow student.

After leaving college, Ira earned his living for a number of years in various jobs: as cashier at a Turkish bath owned jointly by his father and uncle; as cashier for a traveling circus; as assistant photographer; as a humble employee in a department store. His free time belonged to his writing chores. He reviewed vaudeville shows for *The Clipper*—a job without a salary. In 1918 he sold a sketch for one dollar to the *Smart Set,* edited by H. L. Mencken and George Jean Nathan. Sundry other pieces found their way in places like the New York *Sun* and *Life* (the latter then a humorous weekly). He was also producing song lyrics for which he assumed the pen name of "Arthur Francis" (Arthur being his younger brother, and Frances, his younger sister) so as not to capitalize on George's now burgeoning success. The name of "Arthur Francis" also appears on the sheet music of "Stairway to Paradise" and on all the lyrics Ira wrote for his first Broadway show, *Two Little Girls in Blue,* produced in 1921 with Vincent Youmans's music. He reassumed his own name professionally for the first time in the 1924 musical *Be Yourself,* music by Lewis Gensler and Milton Schwarzwald; he continued using his own name henceforth while working with his brother George.

The partnership of George and Ira Gershwin was a harmonious one, each being in full sympathy with and full understanding of the other's idiosyncrasies, each harboring a healthy admiration and affection for the other, each proving at once a stimulant and an inspiration to the other. Yet in behavior patterns, temperament, outlook, and personality they were worlds apart, as this writer had occasion to note in his biography of George Gershwin:* "Where George was gregarious, a man who flourished at parties and other social affairs, and who thrived on movement, activity, and work, Ira was reticent, shy, mild-mannered, somewhat slow moving. Where women were concerned George was the man of the world whereas Ira always had a disarming naïveté. Ira preferred the sedentary life. He was the kind for whom there's no regrettin' when he's settin' biding his time. It required genuine effort for him to go anywhere or do anything. There were periods . . . when he did not descend from his apartment into the street for days at a time. George had sensitive nerves, and he was given to emotional upheavals and hyperthyroid reactions. Ira was usually even-tempered, placid, soft spoken. George was the idealist, his head in the clouds. Ira was coldly logical and realistic, his feet planted solidly on the ground. George felt he had an artistic mission. Ira regarded himself only as a respectable workman, competent and methodical. George loved work, could work anywhere and anytime, frequently after coming home from a night-long party. To Ira, work was work—certainly less desirable than sprawling on a couch and smoking a series of Montecristo cigars, or spending the day at the races, or the evening at

* David Ewen, *A Journey to Greatness: The Life and Music of George Gershwin* (New York: Holt, Rinehart and Winston, 1956).

poker, or the late and sleepless hours of the night with books and magazines. He once said, 'I have a whole day's work ahead of me. I'm going to change the ribbon on my typewriter.' "

For thirteen years Ira wrote the lyrics for George's music. The influence of words on music was inestimable. The melody usually came before the lyric. Nevertheless, Ira's reservoir of fresh, new ideas for songs, for unusual titles, for intriguing colloquialisms and apt application of everyday phrases and speech, for slow and dry and subtle humor, for exciting rhythmic and rhyming patterns, for verbal euphony—all of this often sparked and inflamed George's creativity. In addition, Ira had a far-sighted, dynamic concept of what the musical theatre should be and could become; on the one or two occasions when he was allowed to try realizing this concept, he became a powerful factor in leading George toward new directions in stage music.

Lady, Be Good! starring Fred and Adele Astaire, inaugurated a skein of successes for the Gershwin brothers. Songs like the title number and "Fascinating Rhythm" are distinguished by rhythmic virtuosity: in the intriguing repeated triplets in cut time in the title song and the exciting changing meters of "Fascinating Rhythm." These—and "The Half of It, Dearie, Blues" with its unusual harmonies and the ballad "So Am I" with its haunting lyricism—were the highlights of the score, but they would have been thrown into a secondary position if still another song had been allowed to remain in the show. That song, "The Man I Love," had been written for the opening scene. But the producer felt it slowed up the action and during out-of-town tryouts it was dropped. It was never again destined to turn up in a stage production, but it did get heard extensively in London, Paris, and New York to become one of Gershwin's biggest hits since "Swanee." It was also one of his most original creations, in the haunting way in which a descending chromatic scale was used as a contrapuntal background to a six-note recurring blues progression.

As for Ira Gershwin's lyrics, they had already begun to prove themselves to be in a class all their own, with few equals or rivals in 1924. As this writer commented in his Gershwin biography: "A line like 'I must win some winsome miss' demonstrates the easy way he now had with a well-turned, well-sounding phrase. A couplet like 'this is tulip weather, so let's put two and two together' pointed to a natural and charming simplicity. The chorus for 'Fascinating Rhythm' showed a verbal virtuosity in following the lead of the music in its intricate rhythmic movements."

With two exceptions, the Gershwin musicals following *Lady, Be Good!* did little to change either the character or the artistic goal of the musical theatre. They adhered to the accepted norm by conceiving the text as a convenient frame for good routines, star performances, skillful stage business. Productions were slick and the overall tone was frequently sophisticated, but the plot invariably remained both stilted and contrived, while characterization was most of the time nonexistent.

Some musicals proved significant because of individual performers. Fred and Adele Astaire starred not only in *Lady, Be Good!* but also in *Funny Face* in 1927. *Oh, Kay!* in 1926, was Gertrude Lawrence's first appearance in an

American musical comedy. Secondary in importance to Miss Lawrence's all-important debut was the comedy of Victor Moore cast as a bootlegger disguised as butler in one of his inimitable Casper Milquetoast characterizations. This little sad-faced man with the broken high-pitched voice achieved what is the high-water mark in his long and rich career as stage comedian with his never-to-be-forgotten delineation of Throttlebottom, the much-neglected vice-president in *Of Thee I Sing* in 1931.

And then, of course, there was Ethel Merman, whose stage debut in *Girl Crazy* in 1930 brought to musical comedy its reigning queen. As Kate Fothergrill, in a dude ranch in Custerville, Arizona, she injected the red blood of a lusty performance. She threw her big, brassy voice across the footlights in "I Got Rhythm," "Sam and Delilah," and "Boy! What Love Has Done to Me!" and brought audience and critics figuratively to their feet. They stayed on their feet for Miss Merman for the next quarter of a century.

Some of the Gershwin shows, even though failures, were important because they yielded song jewels. Out of *Tip-Toes* in 1925 came "Sweet and Low-Down" and "That Certain Feeling," each remarkable for its subtle accentuations and rhythmic patterns; out of the same show also came "Looking for a Boy," in which the distinguished English musicologist, Francis Toye, detected a Brahmsian personality. "How Long Has This Been Going On?" came out of *Rosalie* in 1929. "Liza," written in 1928 for *Show Girl,* was a song that was such a favorite with Gershwin himself that he used to improvise all kinds of variations to it at informal parties. "Liza" had a thoroughly spontaneous presentation when *Show Girl* opened at the Ziegfeld Theatre. Al Jolson's wife, Ruby Keeler, was the star of the show. On opening night, Jolson rose from his place in the audience to sing "Liza" to Ruby Keeler as she danced to its tantalizing rhythm on the stage.

"The Lorelei" was heard in one of the greatest failures the Gershwins sustained on Broadway, *Pardon My English* in 1933. Despite the distinction of the melody, this song is particularly notable in its lyrics for the use of the skat phrase "hey ho-de-ho" which, a year later or so, would become even more popular in the song "It Ain't Necessarily So" in *Porgy and Bess.*

Two Gershwin musicals suggested, and often realized, new horizons for the American musical theatre. *Strike Up the Band* (text by George S. Kaufman and Morrie Ryskind) was a bitter satire against war, big business, secret diplomacy, foreign intrigues. Everything else in the production was subservient to an overall theme in which America goes to war against Switzerland over the issue of chocolate tariffs. The hero of the American victory is Horace J. Fletcher, chocolate manufacturer, who in his dreams sees himself as the commander of the American forces. He falls from this high station, however, when the shocking news is spread that he uses only Grade B milk for his confections.

The book was most unusual for the time in sidestepping many of the accepted practices of musical comedy and reducing deadly serious issues to utter absurdity. Laughter was provoked by every element in the production: in the scintillating text and dialogue; in Ira Gershwin's consistently brilliant lyrics; in Gershwin's continually fresh approaches in his music. The title song and "Entrance of the Swiss Army," both of them takeoffs on pompous military music, the chauvinism of "A Typical Self-Made American," the nimble patter in "If I Became the President," all revealed a new deftness, as well as a new acidity, in Gershwin's musical writing. Gershwin also demonstrated a new expansiveness of thought and structure in his extended finales, in which song, choruses, recitatives, and instrumental episodes were woven into a single multicolored fabric.

Of Thee I Sing in 1931—the first musical ever to win the Pulitzer Prize in drama—was even more skillful in directing the keen-edged dart of satire into the bull's eye. The target here was American politics, specifically a presidential campaign, the Senate, the Supreme Court, and other follies in Washington, D.C., during the years of the Depression. Here, even more than in *Strike Up the Band*, music became a significant, at times even an inextricable, partner to the text in the projection of every situation, comment, and aside. Gershwin always had at his fingertips the right musical idiom or material for every suggestion and nuance of the play. The main songs were "Wintergreen for President," which made a mockery of political parades; the principal love song, the title number, which begins like a patriotic hymn but lapses into Tin Pan Alley sentimentality with the word "baby"; and "Love Is Sweeping the Country." Distinguished though each of these is in its own way, the three songs are hardly more important within the overall context than the choral episodes, orchestral interludes, extended vocal sequences, and quasi-operatic recitatives that go to make up Gershwin's most ambitious score for the popular musical stage. No wonder, then, that the critics found *Of Thee I Sing* "a landmark in American satirical musical comedy," in the words of George Jean Nathan; that the Pulitzer Prize committee broke all precedent by singling it out as the best play of the season; that the firm of Alfred A. Knopf also broke new ground by publishing the text in book form, the first time such a thing ever happened to a musical comedy; and that the production enjoyed the longest Broadway run of any Gershwin musical.

George Gershwin was a human dynamo. He was never happier than when he was in perpetual motion. He crowded into a single day enough exercise, play, work, social and business engagements, and study to fill a more normal man's week. He had more energy when sick than others had when healthy. Harry Ruby, the successful popular composer, perhaps will never forget the time he visited Gershwin in the company of Al Schacht, baseball coach, later baseball's jester. Gershwin was sick in bed with a high fever. Nevertheless, he insisted upon engaging his visitors in lengthy conversation while drawing a pencil sketch of Ruby. When Schacht happened to mention that someday he would like to hear Gershwin play the piano, George jumped out of bed to perform the entire *Rhapsody in Blue*. "Never in all my many years of sojourn on this sphere," comments Ruby, "have I ever seen anything like it. His vitality and purpose were not in the least bit dimmed by his illness."

He was a man of many interests. When he found one, he pursued it with a most extraordinary intensity and drive. At one time his passion was golf; it dominated his thinking, conversation, and play hours. Then he turned to some-thing else, usually one at a time: backgammon, croquet, Ping-Pong, photog-raphy, fishing, swimming, horseback riding, playing roulette, and toward the end of his life, painting. Whatever he did he did consummately well. His golf game was in the 80's. He was one of the best Ping-Pong players among musi-cians. His best photographs were good enough to get exhibited. He enjoyed dancing—the tap variety as well as the social kind—just as he enjoyed all kinds of muscular activity. He became such an adept dancer that he could give Fred Astaire a valuable suggestion for an exit step in *Lady, Be Good!* that brought down the house. (In his autobiography, Astaire gives Gershwin full credit for this.) As for painting, with his first brush strokes Gershwin revealed an un-common talent. The eminent art critic Henry McBride, in reviewing a Gershwin art exhibit, wrote: "He was not actually great as a painter, but that was merely because he had not yet had the time—but he was distinctly on the way to the goal. He had all the aptitudes."

In the last analysis, music was his all-consuming passion. His friends some-times considered him egocentric because he was always talking about his music and always playing his music whenever there was anybody near to hear him. They used to say that "an evening with Gershwin is a Gershwin evening" It was this self-preoccupation that led Oscar Levant to inquire one evening: "Tell me, George, if you had to do it all over again, would you still fall in love with yourself?"

Gershwin had a high regard for what he was doing in music, an unashamed pride in what he was accomplishing, a starry-eyed view of where he hoped to go. He sometimes alluded to George Gershwin in the third person as if Gershwin already belonged to the ages. On one occasion he could describe Manuel de Falla, one of the masters of twentieth-century music, as "a Spanish Gershwin." Upon receiving a complaint from a hotel manager that he was playing the piano too loud and too late in the night, he remarked with undis-guised surprise: "Maybe they didn't know that *Gershwin* is playing?" He used to single out one virtue above all others in discussing his mother: "She is so modest about *me.*"

This supreme self-confidence and self-assurance made it possible for him to accomplish what others, far more experienced and better trained than he, thought impossible or undesirable. Ross Gorman, the clarinetist of the White-man orchestra, insisted that it was impossible to play the opening measures of the *Rhapsody in Blue* the way Gershwin envisioned it. Gershwin insisted that his was the way those opening measures *had* to sound. After many days of pains-taking experimentation with various techniques and reeds, Gorman was finally able to achieve the effect Gershwin had had in mind. On two other occasions some of Gershwin's friends advised him not to open a concerto with a Charles-ton rhythm or to use actual Parisian taxi horns in a tone poem. Gershwin did both, and the Piano Concerto in F and *An American in Paris* are all the better for it.

Then there was the time Gershwin assembled some of his friends in his luxurious apartment on East Seventy-second Street to listen to the first number he had completed for *Porgy and Bess.* He strummed the introductory measures at the piano. Then he thrust his head back, jutted out his lower lip, closed his eyes. His face suddenly began assuming Negroid characteristics. "Summertime, and the livin' is easy," he began singing in a slow, lazy drawl. A beatific expression settled on his face; he had lapsed into euphoria. When he finished the number, his friends expressed their delight. But when Gershwin told them he intended opening his opera with this lullaby, some of the professional musicians in the group had serious doubts. "You can't start a folk opera with a simple song," one of the musicians told him. "You've got to start with a big scene, perhaps a folk dance." Gershwin replied: "It'll all work out just fine, wait and see." It did work out fine; that opening is one of the more memorable moments in twentieth-century American opera. When Gershwin insisted on writing his music in his own way it *always* worked out fine.

He liked women, and they liked him, but he never married. The psychiatrist whom he visited in New York to cure a chronic stomach ailment suspected he had failed to break the silver cord; also that he tended to put woman on a pedestal and became easily disillusioned when the woman did not live up to his ideal. Gershwin contemplated marriage a number of times, but always seemed to find a logical reason for avoiding marriage. The reason he did not marry a chorus girl in one of his musicals—and he was seemingly deeply in love with her—was that he had heard her play some of his songs and he could not live with *that* kind of piano playing for the rest of his life. He rejected one woman because she was older than he; another because she belonged to the social elite of Park Avenue while he "will always have the touch of the tenement in me." Once, on discovering that still another one of his girl friends had become impatient with his procrastinations and had impulsively married another man, he remarked to Ira: "You know, I'd be terribly heartbroken—if I weren't so damned busy."

The loss of a girl left no vacuum in his life because his music did not permit any vacuum to exist. Some of his girl friends insisted that his absorption with his music made it impossible for him to give himself completely to any woman. Women were incapable of penetrating the concrete wall of his creative ego. Gershwin might be attentive, flattering, charming, demonstrative, sentimental, even passionate. Then, suddenly, as if a switch had been turned off, he lapsed into his own thoughts to resolve a musical problem that had suddenly come to mind. An incident at a party is illuminating. He had a beautiful girl on his lap when somebody asked him about a Broadway score upon which he was then at work. Gershwin jumped from his chair to rush to the piano. In his haste and eagerness to play his latest songs he had completely forgotten the girl on his lap and sent her sprawling to the floor.

Gershwin's last work for the stage was also his greatest: the folk opera *Porgy and Bess,* which the Theatre Guild produced with an all-Negro cast in Boston on September 30, 1935, and in New York on October 10. This run, the only one the opera had while Gershwin was still alive, had been more or less of a failure both at the box office and with the critics. But Gershwin knew with finality that he had here reached new heights, and not for a moment did he doubt that his faith would someday be fully justified. When the opera was given its first run-through, he beamed with joy. "It's even more wonderful than I thought it was," he said with a detachment as if he were speaking of somebody else's masterwork. After the unsuccessful New York run of 124 performances, Gershwin easily summoned facts and figures to prove that his opera had really enjoyed an unprecedented triumph. Here is how he figured it out: If a great opera by a Verdi or Puccini received 6 performances a season at the Metropolitan Opera, then the 124 performances enjoyed by *Porgy and Bess* represented a twenty-year run at one of the world's greatest opera houses. But even he, with all his supreme confidence in his masterwork, could not have anticipated the kind of acclaim that his opera would receive not only in America but in virtually every part of the civilized world; and that many of the New York critics who had found fault with the opera when they first heard it would reverse themselves completely by hailing it as a masterwork, and the greatest opera by an American.

After *Porgy and Bess,* Gershwin's music was intended exclusively for motion pictures. He had written his first original score for the screen in 1931 for the Fox production *Delicious,* starring Janet Gaynor and Charles Farrell. In 1935 he went to Beverly Hills and set up residence with Ira and Ira's wife, Lee (Leonore), on North Roxbury Drive to work on *A Damsel in Distress,* an RKO production for Fred Astaire and Joan Fontaine. George lived to write only two more screen scores: *Shall We Dance,* with Fred Astaire and Ginger Rogers, and *The Goldwyn Follies.* For these films he produced songs with the unmistakable Gershwin fingerprints on them: "A Foggy Day," "Nice Work If You Can Get It," "Let's Call the Whole Thing Off," "They Can't Take That Away from Me," "Love Walked In," and "Love Is Here To Stay." Outstanding songs each, yet none capable of capturing an Academy Award.

George Gershwin died on July 11, 1937, from a tumor of the brain. He had been in excruciating physical pain and had been tormented by melancholia for a number of weeks before the real nature of his malady was properly diagnosed. Until this was done, he was believed to be suffering from a nervous breakdown and was being treated by a psychiatrist.

On July 9 he was rushed to the Cedars of Lebanon Hospital for preliminary and exploratory surgery. Then only was it discovered that he was the victim of a cystic degeneration of a tumor on the right temporal lobe of the brain. The major operation took four hours and proved unsuccessful: the tumor was found on that part of the brain that could not be touched. The prognosis was tragic. If he survived, which was doubtful, he would be disabled, blind, or both for life. Mercifully, George Gershwin died the following morning.

Due largely to his influence, the American popular song acquired a new identity, a new methodology, a new artistic status. As a matter of fact, the popular song had once and for all become liberated from the confining limitations previously imposed upon it by generations of composers on Broadway and in

Tin Pan Alley. By virtue of that liberation, other and later writers could continue to endow the American popular song with new dimensions and new importance.

Gershwin may have died leaving many a masterwork unwritten, but not before he had achieved his destiny.

For Ira Gershwin, the death of George meant the loss of a brother, with whom he had been virtually inseparable, and a collaborator. Readjustment to new working habits, to new collaborators, in some ways to a new way of life, would not come easily. But it came. In the ensuing decade or so Ira Gershwin wrote lyrics for Jerome Kern, Harold Arlen, Harry Warren, and Kurt Weill. His lyric writing remained jeweled, as was attested by songs like "The Man That Got Away" and "Long Ago and Far Away" from the motion pictures *A Star Is Born* and *Cover Girl*, or "The Saga of Jenny" and "My Ship" from the Broadway musical *Lady in the Dark*.

The flow of lyrics from his typewriter was reduced to a trickle by the 1960's, and there were more times than one when the well went altogether dry. Writing has always been a slow, painful process for a man who could accept for himself only the most fastidious craftsmanship and meet the most exacting standards of excellence and originality. And his approach to the discipline and routines of creativity had always been, to say the least, lackadaisical. Nevertheless, in 1959 he had published *Lyrics on Several Occasions* which had taken him several years to prepare, since this anthology of his lyrics was accompanied by at times brittle, at times amusing, and at times penetrating commentaries and verbal asides.

Habits of a lifetime have not changed with the passing of years. Ira still spends most of the evening and night with friends, or with that endless stream of visitors from all over the world come to pay their respects. When they leave, the rest of the night is devoted to reading. Today, as yesterday, he is a bookworm. From his voracious reading he has been able to store up a remarkable fund of information on a great variety of subjects. Once when a salesman tried to sell Louis Calhern an encyclopedia, the veteran actor barked: "I don't need an encyclopedia. I know Ira Gershwin!"

Ira is incapable of falling asleep till the early hours of dawn, and so he does not awaken until around noon when he partakes of a leisurely and spare breakfast before the cylinders of his personal mechanism can begin working. Then his day's work begins (with the assistance of his highly efficient secretary, Edgar Carter). There is an impressive pile of mail to go through, and a good deal of it to answer. From all over the world, people write to him for information about George or about Ira's songs and musical shows. Replying to all such queries is a responsibility Ira cannot in all good conscience shirk. If there are Gershwin exhibits anywhere, Ira has to do most of the spade work—tapping the now completed Gershwin archives in the Ira Gershwin home and making a fastidious selection of suitable materials. Ira must attend to the multifarious business details of running the George Gershwin estate and his two publishing companies; make all the necessary decisions and arrangements regarding performances of Gershwin music. All this entails numerous conferences with agents, lawyers, accountants. Beyond and above all this, Ira has his own personal business affairs to watch over: his investments in stocks, bonds and real estate.

If there is still a good deal of mental activity going on with Ira, and a good deal of sustained work, physical movement as such has been reduced to a basic minimum. Ira is more than ever the immovable object against which that irresistible force known as Lee Gershwin, his wife, has more often than not proved ineffectual. Lee always was and still is a dynamo who, bursting into a room, sets off electric sparks that suddenly light up the place. She is still one of the most gracious and hospitable of ladies, whose mere presence would be a source of exhilaration even if she were not the kind of person whose articulate, well-informed and bubbling conversation provides continual stimulation. Where Lee still likes motion—be it in driving the Rolls Royce her husband gave her as a birthday gift, one year, or traveling to New York or abroad—Ira prefers to sit back in a soft chair at home, smoke his cigar, and talk and listen. To get him to leave his house, even to visit a close friend, is an effort; to get him to go with Lee to New York or Europe is a major, and usually frustrating production.

When he first came to Beverly Hills in the 1930's, he used to play tennis and golf. Now he seeks non-mental diversion by occasionally playing pool at home with one of his friends (usually Arthur Freed, the M-G-M producer) or indulge in a game of poker for modest stakes. Except for a Saturday excursion to the race track, or visits twice a year or so to Las Vegas, home is where he likes to hang his hat.

His gambling technique is *sui generis*. He is always taking the long chance, he is a chronic loser, and breaking out even represents for him a personal victory. He is the kind of a poker player who, were he to indulge in the game of stud, goes after the middle straight with three aces facing him. (His friends have baptized the middle straight as an "Ira.") Playing the horses is also based on the Gershwin theory that it is much more fun to come from behind and break out even than to start off winning; that picking horses by chance and intuition is more stimulating than by doping out a racing form.

His gambling habits are just one facet of a personality that delights in the whimsical, the exotic, the unexpected. The stories he most enjoys telling about himself are those in which he became involved in the unusual—such as the fact that he is the only person he knows who has had two appendectomies. He tells these stories about himself with the kind of pan-face Buster Keaton made famous on the silent screen. Those who know Ira only casually never quite know at first whether he is embarking on remembrances of things past (about which his memory is as keen, precise and as well stocked as it ever has been) or whether he is about to embark on some humorous episode. His closest friends, however, *do* know—for he gives himself away with revealing gestures. When he is about to reminisce, he passes his hand wearily across his face, closes his eyes for a moment, then begins to speak in a slow drawl. About to tell a humorous episode, his lips curl into a full circle, and a light gleam leaps into his fully open eyes.

He has a quiet, subdued, highly personalized wit. A few examples should suffice. One evening, Arthur Freed was telling Ira about the motion-picture musical he was producing on Jerome Kern's life. Kern did not like the idea because he insisted that while many people knew his songs, very few knew the name of Jerome Kern. What Kern wanted Freed to do was to use a fictitious name instead of Kern for his screen biography. "A good idea," was Ira's tired comment, between puffs on his cigar. "You can call Kern, J. Fred Coots."

On May 28, 1966, Ira received an honorary doctorate in Fine Arts from the University of Maryland. Awesome in dignity though he appeared dressed in cap and gown, he could not resist the temptation to whisper to the President of the University: "Does this disqualify me from playing the horses?"

In August of the same year, he read in *Variety* that I had been appointed adjunct professor of music at the University of Miami. He wrote to me about it on August 12, the kind of letter I long since have learned to expect from him, and would have been heartbroken had it been in any other vein. It read as follows:

"Dear David:

Now that you're a professor at Miami and I'm a Maryland Doctor of Fine Arts, oughtn't our correspondence henceforth climb the highest mountain (excuse please, songwriter's hyperbole)—I mean reach high intellectual heights? E.g.: Do you agree with Germany's Dr. Max Kaluza's turn-of-the-century decision that Dryden's odes imitated in form the earlier and freer Pindaric odes of Cowley? And what about Beethoven's amateur-composer friend Nikolaus Zmeskall, Baron von Domanovecz—are we to accept forever the Hungarian pronunciation of *Zmeskall* because the Austrians fear to antagonize a Soviet satellite? Matters like these are matters that matter, don't you think? Say, I can do something with that! Let me see. How about:

1. Oh, matters like these are matters that matter:
2. (?) I once weighed one-forty but now am much fatter.
3. (?) Will sugarless Tab make my paunch a bit flatter?
4. (?) I fear me now *these* are the matters that matter.

Well, I tried but it's not very good. I'm afraid that if Pope were alive his couplet about the quatrain above might be:

Yon lyricist strove to reach Academe's summits;
But arsily-varsily downwards he plummets."

Soon after George's death, Ira and his wife, Lee, purchased the house next door on Roxbury Drive in Beverly Hills. Eventually, that house—handsome and spacious though it was—was torn down; from its dust arose a palatial new home, one of the most beautiful on a street famous for elegance. Since both Ira and Lee are passionate art lovers, the walls are covered with famous paintings, most of them of the French Impressionist or post-Impressionist schools. Some of these were inherited from George's collections, while others were later acquisitions. A few paintings in the game room are the work of Ira himself, a hobby which he has long since given up though he showed remarkable aptitude for it.

Ira and Lee were married on September 14, 1926. It had not been a case of love at first sight—they had known each other for several years before going to the altar—but with each it was the first and the last great love of their respective lives.

No portrait of Ira can be complete without quoting his recipe for success in the art of lyric writing. It can be found in *Lyrics on Several Occasions* where he says: "Given a fondness for music, a feeling for rhyme, a sense of whimsy and humor, an eye for the balanced sentence, an ear for the current phrase, and the ability to imagine oneself a performer trying to put over a number in progress—given all this, I still would say it takes four or five years collaborating with knowledgeable composers to become a well-rounded lyricist. I could be wrong about the time element—there no doubt have been lyricists who knew their business from the start—but time and experiment and experience help."

GREAT MEN OF AMERICAN POPULAR SONG

Songs of the 1920's and 1930's–II

Rodgers and Hart

In the early afternoon of June 28, 1967, ninety people gathered for luncheon on the stage of the Alvin Theatre in New York to celebrate Richard Rodgers's sixty-fifth birthday. The guests were handpicked, representing the elite of the worlds of popular music and the musical theatre. The stage of an empty auditorium is surely not the customary place for a luncheon. Rodgers's sixtieth birthday, for example, had been celebrated in the ballroom of the Waldorf-Astoria Hotel. But the hosts—the American Society of Composers, Authors, and Publishers (ASCAP)—had selected this unusual setting for the birthday luncheon in recognition of the significance of the theatre in Rodgers's life, and of the significance of Rodgers's life in the theatre.

Facts and figures—with their cold but unassailable logic—eloquently prove that Rodgers's career has few (if any) parallels. Some of these facts and figures were referred to, now by one speaker, now by another. Rodgers has written the scores for thirty-nine stage productions, nine motions pictures, and four television presentations. He has created some two thousand songs—a hundred or more of which have become standards and are just as likely to grow into classics. Rodgers has captured the Pulitzer Prize twice (one a special award and one a regular one); the Antoinette Perry and Donaldson awards four times; the New York Drama Critics Circle Award and the Emmy (from the Television Academy) twice each; an Oscar from the Motion Picture Academy, a Grammy from the Recording Academy, and several others from different sources. Four of Rodgers's musicals had runs exceeding one thousand performances each, and one of them even passed the two-thousand mark. One of his motion pictures has earned more money at the box office the world over than any other production in cinema history.

However impressive—indeed, however without precedent—such achievements are, they tell only part of the Richard Rodgers story. There was probably not one in the ninety guests at that birthday luncheon who was not aware that single-handedly Rodgers had changed the destiny of the American theatre. When first Rodgers invaded the professional arena, back in 1920, musical comedy was in its early adolescence, with all the defects and shortcomings of immature youth. Musical comedy first arrived at sophistication and adult maturity late in the 1920's and in the 1930's, and this came about largely through the efforts of Rodgers and his lyricist collaborator, Lorenz Hart. When musical comedy was finally transformed into a new art form, which soon came to be known as the musical play, this development became crystallized by Rodgers, working this time with Oscar Hammerstein II as his words partner. In short, the almost forty productions for which Rodgers has contributed the music in half a century have been the steps upon which the American musical theatre ascended to greatness—even to international renown.

Rodgers cannot remember a time when he was not in love with the theatre. Recalling his earliest contacts with the stage, as spectator rather than creator, he has remarked: "Life for me began on Saturdays at 2:30." That love has been a lifetime affair.

Making music, and soon thereafter writing music, came as naturally to him as breathing. Once he had discovered that the piano keyboard was capable of producing pleasant sounds, he and the instrument became inseparable. He was only a child when he made this eventful discovery. At a summer boys' camp in Highmount, New York, when he was eleven, he was found so often at the piano (even though he also enjoyed tennis and swimming and was proficient at both) that the camp newspaper published the following verse:

> Ragtime Dick is full of tune
>   Ragtime bangs the box.
> He's always banging the thing for us
>   That's why he gets no knocks.

Two years later, at still another boys' summer camp, he wrote his first song, words as well as music: "Campfire Days." The words were hardly the speech of an embryo genius ("Campfire days, campfire days, cheery old pals around the blaze," runs the first line), and the melody was not much better. But it was his first creative effort. Hearing it sung by his fellow campers convinced him that what he wanted most of all was to write songs. From then on, and for the next half century, he would keep on writing songs, and in doing so would create one of the richest and most significant epochs in American popular music.

The fates were kind to Rodgers from his birth on, for he was born into a home made gracious and comfortable through ample financial means and through a love of and respect for culture. Rodgers's father, William, was a successful physician who loved books, music, and the theatre, and who, in fact, had always nursed a secret ambition to be a writer. A handsome and dapper man of impeccable manners and engaging wit, he was liked by all, and particularly by his immediate family. Rodgers's mother, Mamie, was a woman more interested in and prouder of cultural achievements than social position. She was an excellent amateur pianist. From his father, Dick learned early in childhood the famous opera arias and the song hits from operettas which the father would sing on many a Sunday evening with his wife accompanying him on the piano. From his mother Dick got his love for the piano.

The town house owned and occupied by the Rodgers family was on Lexington Avenue in New York City. But Dick was not born there. The Rodgers family (which included one other son, Mortimer, four and a half years older than Dick) spent the summers at the sea. They were vacationing at Hammels Station, near Arverne, Long Island, when Dick came into the world on July 28, 1902. The summer ended, and the family returned to their New York house, which they sold when Dick was a year old to acquire more spacious quarters— a four-story brownstone house on 120th Street near Mount Morris Park in uptown New York. This was the setting of Dick's early boyhood and the place where he was first drawn to music.

By the time he was four Dick could pick out on the piano with two fingers several of the Victor Herbert tunes his father had been singing. Two years later, Dick could play with both hands quite an extensive repertory of opera and operetta melodies—all by ear. An aunt was recruited to be his first teacher. Dick was dissatisfied with her. On his own—without the slightest suspicion on the part of his parents—he enrolled in a music school near his house where he continued his piano lessons for two years. He detested formal practice, preferring to spend his time improvising at the piano. But his keen intelligence and even sharper ears made it possible for him to go through his lessons successfully, just by listening to the way his teacher played the piece or exercise assigned for the week, and then imitating her performance without consulting the music.

Something else besides his first piano lessons, and no less significant, happened to Dick Rodgers when he was six. He saw his first show. It was a musical, *Pied Piper,* starring De Wolf Hopper. "The moment the curtain went up," he later recalled, "I was carried into a world of glamour and beauty I had never known existed." From then on he would continue to enter this world of glamour and beauty practically every Saturday matinee. Each new show was an experience to relish and recall. He fell in love with everything connected with each production, including one of the stars, Marguerite Clark, whom he saw in a stage production of *Snow White* when he was nine. Today Dick confesses she was the first female for whom he had a "crush."

A decisive turning point in the boy Rodgers's theatregoing experiences, as well as a turning point in his aspirations as a songwriter, came in 1916 when he saw *Very Good, Eddie,* the Princess Theatre Show with music by Jerome Kern. With the infallible instincts and intuition that always governed him as a man of the theatre, Dick Rodgers—young as he was—knew that something very important was happening on that stage. What he saw was a real *American* musical, with American characters and backgrounds, and most important of all with American popular music that at times was sheer magic. This show made such an impression on him that he went to see it five times more. After that, any show that had Kern's music in it found Rodgers in the auditorium, whether the shows were failures or successes. One winter he spent most of his allowance visiting and revisiting a lesser Kern production called *Love o' Mike.* Kern became Rodgers's musical hero. "The influence of the hero on such a hero-worshiper is not easy to calculate," Rodgers later recalled, "but it was a deep and lasting one."

He was not only listening to popular music. He was also producing it all the time at the piano: at home; at assemblies in the public schools he attended; and even during the exercises when he was graduated from P.S. 166 on January 28, 1916. He was also beginning to concoct tunes of his own, first through improvisations at home, then, in 1914, by writing the words and music of "Campfire Days." After coming home from camp that summer, he produced a second song, "The Auto Show Girl," which his father considered good enough to have multigraphed and distributed to relatives, friends, and neighbors.

Now the songs kept coming thick and fast, and before long they even found a showcase for public exhibition. His brother, Mortimer, belonged to an athletic group called the Akron Club. In 1917 the club decided to put on a show to raise funds to buy cigarettes for American soldiers. Members of the club were recruited to write, direct, and produce the show; but not a single member was a composer. Consequently, Mortimer's kid brother, Dick, was drafted for the job of writing the music. He contributed six new numbers and added "The Auto Show Girl" as a seventh. The production, *One Minute Please,* was given in the grand ballroom of the Hotel Plaza on December 29, 1917. Though this was one of the coldest days in the city's history, the auditorium was crowded. The show brought in three thousand dollars, and a good deal of praise to Rodgers for his songs.

A second amateur show now used his songs. *Up Stage and Down*—mounted (also for charity) in the grand ballroom of the Waldorf-Astoria Hotel on March 8, 1919—had no less than twenty Rodgers numbers. Three became the first by Rodgers to get published: "Twinkling Eyes," "Love Is Not in Vain" and "Love by Parcel Post." Another important first for Rodgers in this show was that he served as the conductor, his first experience with the baton.

In all these song endeavors he had long since stopped the practice of writing his own lyrics. Some were the work of his father, some were by his brother, Mortimer, and some by members of the Akron Club. One of these club members, Philip Leavitt, who recognized Rodgers's uncommon gift for making melodies, was convinced that what the boy needed most now was a permanent lyricist who could stimulate and inspire him and with whom he could work exclusively and permanently. Leavitt knew such a man. His name was Lorenz Hart who had an inborn gift for writing brilliant verses. Hart, as Leavitt informed Rodgers, was a lyricist in search of a composer, just as Rodgers was a composer in search of a lyricist. Rodgers and Hart working together, Leavitt insisted, made sense. Actually it made more than sense. It made theatrical and song history.

Late one Sunday afternoon in 1918, Leavitt brought Rodgers to 119th Street to introduce him to Hart. Dick's first sight of Hart was something of a shock. For one thing, although he and Leavitt had been expected, Hart was in bathrobe and slippers, his hair unkempt, almost as if he had just stepped out of bed. Even as a boy Dick Rodgers had a fetish for meticulousness of appearance and dress; Hart's indifference in this regard caused Rodgers to catch his breath. Besides this, Hart looked like a dwarf. He was only five feet tall, with the smallest body, hands, and feet Rodgers had ever seen in a fully grown person. The fact that Hart had a normal-sized head served only to emphasize by contrast the startling physical undevelopment of the rest of the man. From shock, Dick passed on to embarrassment, nervousness, and self-consciousness. Hart was seven years older than he—a man was being host to a mere boy. By virtue of his added years, Hart was far better educated than Dick, having attended Columbia College where he specialized in journalism. But perhaps what disconcerted Rodgers most, before much time had passed, was to discover the wide range of Hart's interests, experiences, and intellectual resources. Hart was thoroughly schooled in literature, art, and music. He was a man of the world— at least that's the way he appeared to Rodgers—who had already traveled to Europe, drank liquor, and smoked. In his presence, Dick felt like a sixteen-year-old school kid, which is exactly what he was.

Despite Hart's ready tongue with conversation and wit and the easy and fluent way in which his mind leaped from one subject to another, Dick remained tongue-tied for a long while. Then Hart's cat strolled lazily into the room. Hart made a wisecrack about the cat that sent Rodgers into guffaws of laughter. This broke the ice. From that moment on, they were able to exchange ideas, ideals, and experiences volubly. Once they discovered that they both worshiped Jerome Kern and were in love with the Princess Theatre Shows, the gap in their respective ages narrowed and made them contemporaries and equals. Rodgers played some of his tunes for Hart, and Hart read to Rodgers some of his verses. Each was enthusiastic about the other's work. Then they discussed the problem of writing popular songs. Hart could now expand on his pet theories about lyrics. He was in contempt of the sloppy versification, the platitudes and clichés, the maudlin sentiments, and the bad prosody that dominated the lyric writing of the time (the work of P. G. Wodehouse being a rare exception to the rule). Hart insisted that a writer of lyrics should bring to his work the same respect for freshness of thought, originality of phrasing, attention to detail, and skill at versification that any poet does to a serious piece of work. "I heard for the first time," Rodgers later recalled, "of interior rhymes, feminine rhymes, false rhymes. I listened with astonishment as he launched a diatribe against songwriters who had small intellectual equipment and less courage, the boys who failed to take every advantage of every opportunity to inch a little further into territory hitherto unexplored in lyric writing."

Before that afternoon meeting ended, Rodgers and Hart had become partners in the writing of songs. As Rodgers left Hart's house, he kept repeating to himself: "I have a lyricist. I have a lyricist." Actually, as he was soon to discover, he had found much more than a lyricist that day. As he said: "In one afternoon, I acquired a career, a partner, a best friend—and a source of permanent irritation."

They wrote fifteen songs within a period of a few weeks. Hart liked especially something called "Venus" while Rodgers was proud of "Little Girl, Little Boy." But both were happiest with "Any Old Place With You." Lines like "I've got a mania for Pennsylvania" or "I'd go to hell for ya, or Philadelphia" or "I'll call each dude a pest, you like in Budapest" had a dash and a sparkle and a smartness not even encountered in a P. G. Wodehouse lyric. The music also struck new ground. The chorus was sixteen bars and the verse thirty-two, reversing a long-accepted procedure that dictated that verses be sixteen bars and choruses thirty-two. Harmonically, spice—as piquant as a dash of Tabasco sauce —had been introduced through the use of secondary seventh chords. But most important of all this was a *new* kind of love song—romantic at heart yet with an intriguing mischievous glint in its eye.

"Any Old Place With You" marked the real beginnings of the career of Rodgers and Hart, for besides being their first song to get published, it was also their first step into the musical theatre. Eve Lynn and Alan Hale sang it in the Broadway musical *A Lonely Romeo* on August 26, 1919. "What I earned from both the performance and the publication couldn't buy me a suit," Rodgers now says, "but the appearance of one of my songs in a Broadway show was certainly a big moment in my life."

The first musical score upon which Rodgers and Hart collaborated, however, was not for the professional theatre but for an amateur production: the varsity show at Columbia College. Rodgers had entered Columbia in the fall of 1919. He had hardly put a foot into the classroom when he became fired with the ambition to write the music for Columbia's next annual varsity show. With Hart's help, he worked out a musical show which he submitted to the Player's Committee at Columbia. In view of Rodgers's later personal history it is not without significance to point out that the committee included Oscar Hammerstein II, who was then attending Columbia Law School. The committee liked the songs more than the text and suggested that they be used in conjunction with a libretto submitted by another ambitious aspirant, Milton Kroop, a satire on Bolshevism entitled *Fly With Me*. This marriage of script and songs having been successfully consummated, *Fly With Me* was produced at the Hotel Astor on March 24, 1920. Rodgers and Hart had thirteen numbers in the production, all of which were published. In addition, Dick conducted. He did not know it at the time but Dick Rodgers had made history at Columbia: this was the first time that a freshman had contributed the music for a varsity show. That music did not pass unnoticed, for it brought Rodgers his first favorable comment from a reputable newspaperman, S. Jay Kaufman of the *Globe,* who wrote: "Several of the tunes are capital. They have a really finished touch, and will, if transplanted, be whistled. We had not heard of Richard Rodgers before. We have a suspicion we shall hear of him again."

Another who admired the Rodgers score no end was a Broadway veteran, Lew Fields, onetime star of vaudeville and burlesque as a teammate of Joe Weber (Weber and Fields), but since 1915 a producer of Broadway shows. Fields was then planning a new Broadway musical, *Poor Little Ritz Girl.* He wanted Rodgers and Hart to contribute some of its numbers. The other songs would be the work of a hardy veteran of Broadway musical comedies and operettas, Sigmund Romberg. Romberg wrote eight songs; Rodgers and Hart, seven. *Poor Little Ritz Girl* opened on July 28, 1920. It was the Rodgers and Hart contributions, not those of Sigmund Romberg, that drew words of praise from the critics. H. T. Parker said of Rodgers's music: "He writes uniformly with a light hand; now and then with neat modulations or pretty turns of ornament; here and there with a clear sensibility to instrumental voice; and once again with a hint of grace and fancy." Heywood Broun considered the lyrics some of the best he had ever heard in the theatre.

Rodgers and Hart had good reason to be confident that they were on the threshold of success. But, as they were soon to learn much to their distress, that threshold was not so easily crossed. Rodgers and Hart made the rounds of publishers and producers with their songs and reviews only to find little encouragement and no assignments. Amateur groups seemed the only ones willing to use their songs. Rodgers and Hart accepted some of these offers; this, after all, was much better than not getting their songs heard at all. But they did not delude themselves into believing that these amateur shows led anywhere except to a dead end. The songwriters got no cash for their work, and just about the same amount of credit. They tried marketing a new musical comedy, *Winkle Town,* for which Herbert Fields, son of Lew Fields, provided the text. But even parental love and pride could not convince Lew Fields to produce a bad show.

It was the failure of *Winkle Town* to get produced, more than any other single factor, that compelled young Rodgers to take stock of himself. He did not like the result of this investigation. He was still attending Columbia College where subjects like physics and mathematics held no fascination for him. If he was getting nowhere as a songwriter, he felt it was perhaps because he needed more musical instruction. In 1921 he prevailed on his parents to allow him to leave Columbia without a diploma so that he might concentrate on music study. Dick Rodgers spent the next two years at the Institute of Musical Art—a pupil of Percy Goetschius in harmony, George Wedge in ear training, and Henry E. Krehbiel in music history. While still attending the institute he was given a yearly opportunity to write music for shows put on by the school. His writing was gaining in technical security. Intensive music study was transforming an apprentice (working more with instinct and by trial and error than with educated methods) into a trained musician.

He left the institute in June of 1923. Before long he was working again with Lorenz Hart and sometimes with Herbert Fields in writing songs and musical shows for amateur groups. But they did manage to make a brief invasion of the Broadway theatre. The three men (using the pen name of Herbert Richard Lorenz) wrote a satire on Tin Pan Alley called *The Melody Man*. This was basically a nonmusical comedy, since only two songs were used, and these were planned as takeoffs on the kind of synthetic stuff then being dispensed by the music industry. *The Melody Man* came to the Ritz Theatre on May 13, 1924, and left it fifty-five performances later. To Rodgers it seemed more certain than ever that he was having a perpetual rendezvous with failure.

In fact, so convinced had he become that there was no future for him in songwriting that he decided to enter the business world. He was twenty-two years old. His schooling, academic as well as musical, was at an end. Several years of intensive songwriting had not even been able to provide him with pocket money; he was still being supported by his parents. One sleepless night he came to the conclusion that the time had come for him to face reality. He faced it by getting a friend of the family's to give him a job as salesman of children's underwear at a salary of fifty dollars a week. His employer promised him that should he show any aptitude for business, his progress in the firm would be swift.

But Rodgers never stepped foot into the business world. One Sunday evening, the night before he was to begin working for the underwear firm, he received a telephone call from Benjamin Kaye, a friend of the Rodgers family. Kaye had for some months been working with a group of youngsters affiliated with the Theatre Guild (then the most powerful and significant producers of serious theatre in New York). Now meeting at one apartment, now at another, these youngsters were throwing about ideas for an intimate musical revue which they wanted to write, produce, and act in. They had a practical reason for putting on such a show. The Theatre Guild was at that time erecting its own theatre on Fifty-second Street. What the youngsters wanted to do was to raise money to buy handsome tapestries for the auditorium.

The reason Benjamin Kaye called Rodgers that Sunday evening was to ask him and Hart to create the songs for the show. Rodgers was at first indifferent. After all, wasn't he beginning a new life the following morning in business? But Kaye proved persuasive in getting him to come down that very evening to the apartment where the group was discussing the details of their project.

Rodgers went, listened, and was completely won over. The ideas for skits, production numbers, blackouts, comedy routines, dance sequences, were fresh, new, and sparkling. This was the kind of show, he knew, that could use to best advantages the kind of songs Rodgers and Hart were so adept at writing. Besides, Rodgers was shrewd enough to realize that an affiliation with the Theatre Guild (even if only by remote control) was not something that could be lightly dismissed. The directors of the Theatre Guild were after all powers on Broadway, and one strong word from them about Rodgers could open even the tightest of shut doors.

It did not take much argument for Rodgers to convince Hart to join him in the project, for Hart had never given any serious thought to renouncing his ambition to become a successful lyricist. Immediately, all thoughts of being a salesman evaporated into thin air as far as Rodgers was concerned. He was writing songs again for a specific and possibly important project. In two weeks' time Rodgers and Hart completed half a dozen numbers. A seventh they lifted out of their ill-fated, never-produced *Winkle Town*. As it turned out, it was this seventh song that happened to be the making of Rodgers and Hart, for it was "Manhattan," their first hit.

The project planned by the Theatre Guild youngsters was finally named *The Garrick Gaieties,* because it was scheduled for two performances (a matinee and an evening) at the Garrick Theatre—on May 17, 1925. A note in the program helped set the unconventional, slightly impudent tone that dominated the entire production: *"The Garrick Gaieties* is distinguished from all other organizations of the same character . . . in that it has neither principals nor principles. *The Garrick Gaieties* believes not only in abolishing the star system; it believes in abolishing the stars themselves. The members of *The Garrick Gaieties* are recruited, impressed, mobilized, or drafted from the ranks of . . . Theatre Guild productions—a few rank outsiders being permitted to appear; proving we do not intend to become a monopoly."

The second number in this informal and intimate revue was a song called "Gilding the Guild," which explained further that the purpose of the show was to present a "mild dish" of folklore "quaintly childish" or things that were "Oscar Wildish" in pantomime and dance. The amusing, irreverent, satirical, and freshly conceived material that followed was a delectable dish with more spice than sugar: grand opera became the source of not so innocent merriment; Broadway shows and Broadway stars were irreverently burlesqued; an amusing sketch disclosed what would happen if the Theatre Guild ever invaded heaven, and another revealed what transpired at the White House between President and Mrs. Coolidge. Novel routines and unusual choreographic episodes added to the cornucopia of delights. And then, there were the songs of Rodgers and Hart—the best being "Manhattan" and "Sentimental Me"—which, as *Variety* noted, "clicked like a colonel's heels at attention." Other critics liked everything about the show and had no restraint in releasing their storehouse of accolades. Alexander Woollcott regarded the show as "fresh and spirited and engaging . . . bright with the brightness of something new minted." Robert Benchley called it "the most civilized show in town," while to Gilbert Gabriel it was "a witty, boisterous, athletic chowchow."

So favorable a reaction led the Theatre Guild to put on four more performances, all sold out. A regular run was now decided upon. It began on June 8 and continued for twenty-five weeks.

For Rodgers and Hart all this meant not only their first sweet taste of success—which made a god's nectar bitter by comparison, but also their first regular flow of a livable income. Each drew $50 a week in royalties from the show's run. Rodgers was paid an additional $83 a week for conducting. Beyond this, both Rodgers and Hart received sizable royalties from the published sheet music, since both "Manhattan" and "Sentimental Me" were selling exceedingly well. Most important of all, they had found a permanent publisher in Harms, headed by Max Dreyfus, ready to issue what they wrote—an affiliation that continued as long as the Rodgers and Hart era lasted. And Rodgers and Hart were also getting offers from Broadway producers. The story goes that a few years after the opening of *The Garrick Gaieties,* upon visiting the Guild Theatre, Hart pointed to the tapestries and remarked: "Dick, *we* are responsible for them." Rodgers replied softly: "No, Larry, *they* are responsible for us."

Before the year of 1925 ended, Rodgers and Hart saw their new musical comedy, *Dearest Enemy,* come to Broadway. Their weekly income now jumped to several hundred dollars a week each. One year after that Broadway mounted not one but *five* Rodgers and Hart musicals, the royalties from which amounted to more than one thousand dollars a week for each of the two men. Such sudden affluence made Rodgers expansive and extravagant. He rented a terrace apartment at the Hotel Lombardy on East Fifty-sixth Street (leaving his family residence for the first time), sharing an entire floor with an apartment occupied by Edna Ferber. He sported a red La Salle coupe. He dated show girls and frequented nightclubs. There was no doubt about it: his success was intoxicating him and making him lose balance. As his success kept mounting, and his income with it, he quickly adjusted himself to a basic truth. Burning the candle at both ends made a warm light; but it also smoldered creativity and reduced it to ashes. Creativity—the writing of songs, the production of musical comedies—was basic to his happiness. Every other pleasure paled by contrast. He finally arrived at a truth that henceforth would govern his life. Success was important, of course, and so was prosperity. But most important of all—at least to him—was to work, and to work hard and to the best of his abilities.

And he worked hard, perhaps harder than any other Broadway composer. Between *The Garrick Gaieties* in 1925 and *America's Sweetheart* in 1931, he had twelve shows on Broadway and three in London, for which he wrote almost two hundred songs. Hart, of course, was his lyricist, and frequently Herbert Fields served as librettist. With the incandescent fire of their imagination and the courage of their youth, these three young men set themselves the task of writing musical comedies in which innovation would be the keynote: innovation in the kind of subject they chose for their texts; in the way this subject was developed; in the experimental methods and procedures they would use in formulating new techniques for musical comedy. They created a golden age of musical comedy all by themselves, and because of them, musical comedy in the 1920's was well along on its way to adulthood.

Their very first musical, *Dearest Enemy,* already showed their freshness of viewpoint by going to the history book for their plot. Dismissing the warning of veterans of the theatre that musicals based on history were poison to the box office, they took an episode from the American Revolutionary War that had bawdy overtones and, instead of creating a costume play, came up with a stage adventure that sparkled with wit and novelty. *Dearest Enemy* dramatized the efforts of Mrs. Robert Murray to waylay British officers at her home in New York to permit George Washington and his men to make a strategic withdrawal. For the authors, the writing proved a frolic as they spiced the text and the lyrics with discreet suggestions of salaciousness and a generous dose of vivacity. Rodgers maintained a similarly light and gay touch in his music with amusing numbers like "Cheerio" and "Old Enough To Love." But he also created one of his beautiful love ballads in "Here in My Arms." In addition the horizon of musical-comedy writing was extended through his interpolation of duets, trios, choral numbers, and even an instrumental gavotte to evoke the eighteenth century.

In their musical comedies up to 1931 there would be misses as well as hits —in fact, more misses than hits. But the hits were substantial ones, and each represented an unconventional approach to musical-comedy tradition. In *Peggy-Ann,* in 1926, they evoked the strange, disordered, Dadaistic world of dream psychology, as a small-town girl sees herself in dreams experiencing strange adventures in a big city. The authors let their imagination go riot in a fantasy in which the absurd and the impossible become reality, and the most outlandish episodes and characters are accepted as normal. But the text—and the hazy, impressionistic way in which it was developed—was not the sole contribution of *Peggy-Ann.* The show dispensed with an opening chorus—something unheard-of in musical comedy at the time—and there was fifteen minutes of dialogue before a single song was introduced. And the play ended with a slow comedy dance on a darkened stage in place of the expected production-number finale. In his music, Rodgers achieved touches of fantasy through nebulous harmonies and delicate instrumentation, while the background for the dance sequences and the atmospheric backgrounds suggested for the first time, both for him and for musical comedy, an almost symphonic approach.

In *A Connecticut Yankee,* in 1926, they adapted an American classic for musical-comedy treatment, once again stepping on grounds where traditional writers, not to speak of their "angels," would fear to tread. The classic was, of course, the famous story by Mark Twain. Rodgers, Hart, and Fields bring their twentieth-century hero back to Camelot by the simple expedient of having him being hit on the head by a champagne bottle, and having him succumb to dreams in his unconscious state. In sixth-century Camelot he proceeds to bring the refinements of American culture and civilization to King Arthur's court. The anachronism of having twentieth-century mores and technology appear in old Camelot lent itself naturally to sophisticated humor and satire in all departments of musical-comedy writing. More and more nimble now are Hart's verses, keener and sharper grows the edge of his wit and malice, as his lines trip along gaily and easily with the agility of ballet dancer. "Our minds are featherweight, their together weight can't amount to much" is a line from one of his cynical love songs ("I Feel at Home With You"). In another, "On a Desert Island with Thee," he makes the observation: "Let the prudish people quarrel, we'll forget them for the nonce; if they think our love immoral, *Honi soit qui mal y pense.*" Lines like these—and they fell over one another throughout the production—made the lyrics of other writers effete by comparison. And always there was Rodgers's music to keep sprightly pace with melodies filled with unusual rhythmic patterns, deftly conceived melodic lines, and tart harmonizations.

The most important love ballad thus far written by Rodgers and Hart became famous in *A Connecticut Yankee,* though it was not actually written for it. It was "My Heart Stood Still." This number had been done for a London revue, *One Dam Thing After Another,* starring Jessie Matthews and produced by Charles B. Cochran. Just before coming to London, Rodgers and Hart were in a Parisian taxi with two girls. When their taxi almost collided with another car, one of the girls remarked: "My heart stood still." "That would make one helluva good song title," remarked Hart calmly. Rodgers made a note of this idea in a little notebook he always carried with him. They wrote that song on their first evening in London.

Rodgers and Hart, knowing that they had a solid winner in this song, bought out the rights to their own song from Cochran for $5,000 and used it in their very next Broadway production, which was *A Connecticut Yankee.*

Another of their celebrated love ballads of the 1920's was "With a Song in My Heart," used in *Spring Is Here* in 1929. Rodgers had just come back from a weekend in Long Island when this wonderful melody sprang full-grown into his mind. He completed writing the song that evening and then rushed over to try it out on some of his friends, at the home of Jules Glaenzer, the vice president of Cartier, the distinguished jewelry establishment. A month after *Spring Is Here* opened, Rodgers (on a brief visit to Paris) was given a surprise party by Glaenzer at Laurent, the fashionable restaurant on the Champs-Elysées. He had no idea he was to be fêted, believing only that he was having a private dinner engagement with Glaenzer. Then, one by one, his friends began streaming into the restaurant (including Noël Coward and Elsa Maxwell). Suddenly Rodgers heard the orchestra strike up the strains of "With a Song in My Heart." Only then did Rodgers suspect what a glance at the menu confirmed—that he was the evening's guest of honor.

Spring Is Here was not the only one of the lesser musical-comedy successes (artistic as well as financial) from which came Rodgers and Hart song favorites up to 1931. From *The Girl Friend* (1926) we got "The Blue Room"; from *Present Arms* (1928), "You Took Advantage of Me"; from *Heads Up* (1929), "A Ship Without a Sail"; and from *Simple Simon* (1930), "Ten Cents a Dance," made famous by Ruth Etting who introduced it. In these and other songs, Rodgers was always creating surprises for the ear: sometimes by having the melody span an unexpected interval and come to rest on an unexpected note; sometimes by permitting one beautiful thought to be followed immediately by a second thought still more beautiful; sometimes by expanding the structure of his choruses with an extended trio or pattern; sometimes through the interposition of subtle harmonic progressions or unusual modulations.

The melody usually came before the lyrics, Hart having an uncanny gift for molding the supple lines of his verses to the contours of the melody. Hart once gave a clue to the way he operated by explaining how he wrote "Here in My Arms." "I take the most distinctive melodic phrase in the tune and work on that. What I choose is not necessarily the theme or the first line but the phrase which stands out. Next I try to find the meaning of that phrase and to develop a euphonic set of words to fit it. . . . The first line runs like this: 'Here in my arms, it's adorable.' The distinct melodic phrase comes on the word 'adorable,' and the word 'adorable' is the first word that occurred to me, so I used it as my pivotal idea. And as the melodic phrase recurs so often in the chorus it determines my rhyme scheme. Of course, in a song of this sort the melody and euphonics of the words themselves are really more important than the sense." On another occasion he pointed out that in "The Blue Room" the most important note in the melody of the chorus was a half note on which the ascending phrase had come to rest; Hart said he used that half note on which to fix not only the term "blue room" but also all of its varied rhymes, including "new room," "for two room," and so forth.

Young, handsome, dapper, well-mannered, and witty—a famous personality in the most glamorous of all professions and the recipient of an income of several thousand dollars a week—Rodgers was inevitably the cynosure of young girls' eyes everywhere. Girls had always had a strong appeal to him. He confesses he had his first love affair when he was nine years old and from then on the love affairs continued. But when it came time for him to get married, the girl he chose was not from the Broadway or nightclub scene, or a girl whom he had met at a swank social affair, but somebody (so to speak) from his own backyard. He had known her from the time he was seven and she was only a two-month infant ("It wasn't love at first sight," Rodgers insists). Her family knew the Rodgerses well, and Dick was a close friend of her brother's.

She was Dorothy Feiner, an extraordinarily beautiful girl, whom Rodgers saw on and off through the years, since he associated frequently with her brother. After Dick had become famous, he was for Dorothy the man of her dreams. She knew he dated many girls, most of whom were beautiful, glamorous, and sophisticated, and she was convinced that Dick did not give her a single thought —all of which happened to be true. Then one day in 1926 he saw her dressed up for a "date," and it was at that moment that Dick sensed that this was the girl he would someday marry.

He finally did so on March 5, 1930, at the Feiner apartment on Park Avenue, with Rabbi Stephen S. Wise officiating. Dressed in an ivory satin gown cut in medieval style, with long white sleeves made of old lace, and a veil of tulle, she was a vision of loveliness. It is more than husband's pride that has led Rodgers to say: "All brides are beautiful. Mine was the most beautiful of all."

Their first child, Mary, was born on January 11, 1931; their second and last child, Linda, would arrive in 1935. Between his marriage and Mary's birth, Rodgers made a brief visit to Hollywood with Hart to write songs for a movie produced at the First National studios. That movie, *The Hot Heiress,* was a total "bust," and their experiences while they were writing its songs were the kind of unbelievable adventures and episodes that was the norm in Hollywood in those days. Back in New York, Rodgers and Hart used the Hollywood scene, with all its extravagances and absurdities, for a new Broadway musical, *America's Sweetheart,* a satire on the movie industry in general and the star system in particular. Produced in 1931, this was a mild comedy in which, as Gilbert Gabriel took pains to point out, the songs, and the songs alone, were the stand-bys: "Excellent songs, happily phrased, insinuatingly clever and memorable." Brooks Atkinson also went out of his way to praise the songs. "There is a rush about the music and mocking touch in the lyrics that make the score more deftly satirical than the production." The hit number was "I've Got Five Dollars," which became one of the two or so unofficial theme songs of the Depression years of the early 1930's. Other songs had a more amusing turn both in the words and in the music. "I Want a Man" was a malicious takeoff on the sex mania prevailing in the movie capital. "Innocent Chorus Girls of Yesterday" was a lament of has-been stars. "Sweet Geraldine" poked fun at movie magazines in a number in hillbilly style.

America's Sweetheart was the last Rodgers and Hart musical on Broadway for four years. During that period they were back in Hollywood working for Paramount and several other studios. They did the songs for *Love Me Tonight,* one of the most delightful screen musicals of the 1930's, starring Maurice Chevalier and Jeanette MacDonald; and for it they produced one of their best screen scores, including such memorable numbers as "Mimi," "Lover," and "Isn't It Romantic?" Ever concerned with new approaches, they also evolved for this picture a new technique which they called "rhythmic dialogue," in which a musical background was utilized behind spoken dialogue. The songs, the "rhythmic dialogue," and, unquestionably, the performance of Maurice Chevalier were contributing factors in endowing this film with its Gallic personality and charm.

They used their "rhythmic dialogue" and they contributed a number of songs for a picture starring Al Jolson, *Hallelujah, I'm a Bum*—about which the less said the better. They also did the score for *The Phantom President,* in which George M. Cohan made his debut in talking pictures, which, as we had the opportunity to describe in our chapter on Mr. Cohan, was such a personal disaster for him. None of the songs Rodgers and Hart wrote for *The Phantom President* is remembered.

Typical of the way Hollywood used to operate in those years, the most important song Rodgers and Hart wrote while employed in the screen capital was never used in any movie, though it was a pure, shining gem. This song started its existence with the title of "Make Me a Star," and it had been intended for a movie starring Jean Harlow. Both Jean Harlow and the Rodgers and Hart number were dropped from that production. Retitled as "The Bad in Every Man," Rodgers and Hart submitted it to M-G-M for *Manhattan Melodrama,* but when this picture was released the song was not in it. Finally, Hart wrote a completely new lyric for Rodgers's lovely melody. The song, now named "Blue Moon," was published in New York as an independent number without any screen or stage affiliation. As it turned out it had the largest sheet-music sale (well over a million copies) of any song they had thus far created.

All in all, for Rodgers, Hollywood was not a happy adventure. Always a dynamo of ambition and energy, he felt restive because so little of his time was consumed in work, and work, for him, was both a necessity and a passion. A movie assignment for Rodgers could be finished within a few weeks. Then, for the next few months, there was nothing for him to do as far as songwriting was concerned. Since his brain was teeming with all kinds of projects and ideas that could not be released because they had nowhere to go, he was impatient to get back to Broadway to realize himself creatively more fully. In Hollywood he was continually restless or moody.

Hart fared much better, since by nature he was a playboy who far preferred idleness and diversions to working, and who was just as ready to do tomorrow what should be done today. Hollywood society and customs and social habits suited him perfectly. He loved having swarms of friends around him at his swimming pool. He loved going to parties and staying up with people he admired, and who enjoyed his conversation and wit, until the early hours of dawn. The fact that he was required to do so little work while getting paid so handsomely for it was an arrangement which, as far as he was concerned, was heaven-made.

One day, Rodgers read in a newspaper column the question "Whatever became of Rodgers and Hart?" "That really made my head jerk," Rodgers later explained. "I sat right down and wrote him [the columnist] a letter thanking him and telling him we were getting out of Hollywood as fast as we could. The day our contract was up, we climbed aboard the Chief and came back to the United States. I felt as if I had just been given my pardon."

They came back with altogether new concepts of the kind of musical comedies they now wanted to write. By 1934 the musical theatre had made significant artistic progress with productions like Jerome Kern's *Show Boat* and *Music in the Air* and with satires like *Strike Up the Band* and *Of Thee I Sing,* texts by George S. Kaufman and Morrie Ryskind, and words and music by George and Ira Gershwin. These stage masterpieces represented a long forward step in making the play *the* thing, and everything else in the production, even the songs, subservient to the demands of the text. At long last, the horse was pulling the cart, instead of vice versa.

To such a new scheme of things, Rodgers and Hart felt strongly that they could make important contributions. They had a good many unorthodox, exciting ideas of their own to introduce to the stage. What they had in mind particularly was to dispense with the unnecessary appendages which had overburdened musical comedy up to this time, while still choosing fresh new subjects for their librettos and using materials basic to the story line. In short, they were thinking in terms of a "musical play" rather than a "musical comedy": "A new form of musical show," Hart explained, which "will not be musical comedy and it will not be operetta. The songs are going to be part of the progress of the piece, not extraneous interludes without rhyme or reason." Rodgers, too, nursed new ambitions. "I should like to free myself for broader motifs, more extended designs," he explained.

Their first return to Broadway was made with the kind musical they were trying to make obsolete. It was *Jumbo,* a lavish production that was part circus, part musical comedy, part burlesque, and part extravaganza. They accepted this assignment because, having been absent from the Broadway scene for four years, they badly needed an opportunity to remind Broadway producers of their capabilities. Any commission that came their way had to be seized, and when Billy Rose, who was the producer of *Jumbo,* came forward with a proposition, they accepted eagerly. *Jumbo* cannot be said to have advanced the new cause that Rodgers and Hart had hoped to further on Broadway. But *Jumbo* did prove that Rodgers and Hart were tops in their field. For the score of *Jumbo* included three diamonds that could have come only from a Rodgers and Hart jewel case: "The Most Beautiful Girl in the World," "Little Girl Blue," and "My Romance."

With *Jumbo* out of the way and producers once again interested in them, Rodgers and Hart stood ready to battle against crumbling traditions, obsolete methods, and stock procedures and plots that so long had hampered the growth of musical comedy. Frequently, now, they would either write or adapt their own librettos; on other occasions they recruited top writing talent either to assist them or to prepare new texts. Between the years of 1936 and 1942 they were represented on Broadway with nine new musicals. Two can be dismissed as wasted effort. The other seven were box-office successes of the first order, and several of those successes made some kind of historical and artistic contribution which was instrumental in changing the concept of what the theatre should be and suggesting what it could finally become.

In *On Your Toes* (1936) and *I Married an Angel* (1938) they introduced serious ballet into the popular musical theatre for the first time, in both instances with choreography by George Balanchine, then already one of the giant figures in the world of the dance. It was in *On Your Toes* that we find the jazz ballet *Slaughter on Tenth Avenue,* an extended sequence that brings the musical to its climax. *Slaughter on Tenth Avenue*—both as to dance and as to stage music—represented a milestone in the American theatre in 1936. It has remained a treasurable experience. As Richard Watts, Jr., said when *On Your Toes* was revived in 1954: "A sizable number of jazz ballets have passed this way since it first appeared, but it still is something of a classic in its field and the music Mr. Rodgers wrote for it continues to seem one of the major achievements of his career."

In *I'd Rather Be Right* (1937)—book by Moss Hart and George S. Kaufman—Rodgers and Hart achieved a stinging satire on national politics, on people and events that were very much in the news at the time.

In *The Boys from Syracuse* (1938), Rodgers and Hart proved for the first time that you could make a successful musical comedy from a Shakespeare play. In their masterwork, *Pal Joey* (1940), they rejected the long-accepted belief that musical comedy had to be escapist theatre. They chose unsavory characters, involving them in all kinds of disreputable and dishonorable practices, and then ending the show with their main character discredited and ruined and his principal romance shattered. And in their last musical comedy, *By Jupiter* (1942), their plot came out of Greek mythology.

While traveling on these fresh, new paths, Rodgers and Hart did not fail to decorate the passing scenery with the attractions of unforgettable songs. Songs like "There's a Small Hotel" in *On Your Toes;* songs like the title number and "Spring Is Here" in *I Married an Angel;* songs like "Falling in Love with Love" and "This Can't Be Love" in *The Boys from Syracuse;* songs like "I Could Write a Book" and "Bewitched, Bothered, and Bewildered" in *Pal Joey;* songs like "Careless Rhapsody" in *By Jupiter.*

It is, surely, a crowning paradox to discover that this perfect marriage of words and music, of Hart and Rodgers as songwriters, was not the result of a harmonious personal relationship. For all the high esteem that each man held for the other's talent, their collaboration was from the beginning rocked with the storm of dissent and the bitterness of ferment. The truth of the matter was that as personalities Rodgers and Hart were opposites in every way imaginable. When two such opposites rubbed against each other, the abrasive action could not fail to emit hot sparks, and at times to explode into hot flame.

Rodgers was a sober-minded individual who kept regular hours, adhered meticulously to a daily work schedule, and brought to his creativity the same kind of discipline and pragmatism that a successful businessman or banker brings to his own calling. He assigned a definite number of hours each day to composition, permitting nothing or nobody to interrupt him. He was meticulous about meeting deadlines, just as he was fastidious about permitting no song to leave his hand unless he was thoroughly satisfied with it. Rodgers possessed extraordinary creative energy that demanded an outlet. His mind was as keen and precise as his habits were regulated.

He was very much the family man, doting on his wife and two daughters in a ten-room apartment on East Seventy-seventh Street. The frenetic pursuits of his early manhood had long since been discarded, and simpler ones replaced them. He now rarely went to nightclubs. He never smoked or gambled. Drinking was confined to an occasional social cocktail or a Scotch and water before dinner. Even at celebrations he limited himself to no more than a drink or two, insisting that he did not want anything to blur or confuse his pleasure in participating in the occasion. He almost never danced. The only sport that interested him was croquet. What he seemed to enjoy most of all was to be in the company of people he liked, in exchanging stimulating conversations in many areas besides music and the theatre, particularly when he was the host at his own home at small elegant dinner parties.

His friends and acquaintances saw him as a mild-mannered, self-contained man, and rarely given to displays of temperament, indeed, always exuding charm effortlessly. He was a practical man who functioned more through reason than through impulse or emotion, behaving all the time the way he looked: trim and neat. He preferred conservative clothes, was always well groomed, but never suggested the dandy. The assertive jaw and the firm lips revealed strength. But those alive, bright eyes had in them a touch of mockery, betraying that for all his outward dignity and apparent sobriety, he was a man of ready wit and quick tongue—a man thoroughly articulate, able to express himself with neat, and frequently unexpected, turns of phrases or puns. In politics he was a liberal. His ties to the race of his birth were more social and sentimental than strictly religious.

Lorenz Hart (or Larry, as his friends always called him) was a study in contrast. Here was a compact bundle of nerves and neuroses. He was always jumping around, always on the move, always restless, always gesturing. At restaurants or night spots he seemed incapable of staying in one place for any length of time, hopping about from table to table to exchange a bon mot here and a hello there. At theatre, on first nights, he habitually paced the back of the auditorium rather than remain in his seat. His mobile, highly expressive face was a mirror continually reflecting his innermost feelings. His hands were always active; his favorite gesture was to rub his hands together when he was pleased or excited. He usually accentuated a remark with a brief nod of the head.

His bachelor apartment at the Hotel Beresford was in a perpetual state of confusion, because its owner was a man sublimely indifferent to system or regulation. Papers, books, magazines, cigarette butts, were strewn all over the living room. "Big Mary," the maid who kept house for Hart, had long given up any hope of resolving chaos into order, just as she had long since surrendered all hope of getting Hart to lead a normal life. For Hart there were no set hours for eating or sleeping. Parties, frequently all-night affairs, were also improvisations, usually concocted at the last moment. Hart loved parties and hated to see them break up. He enjoyed being surrounded by people, getting the smell of smoke and liquor in his nostrils, and the noise of conversation and laughter in his ears. He loved to laugh, and he loved making others laugh.

Details confused him; he would have none of them. He never knew how much money he was earning or how much he was spending. He kept huge rolls of bills in a pocket which he had to replenish frequently, since he was always the one to pick up the check in restaurants and nightclubs, and since he often yielded to a moment's whim to make an expensive purchase, or use taxicabs even when he had to travel to a different city. When on vacation in Europe, he would take along with him some of his close friends, and he was usually the one who footed all the bills.

He rarely came on time to appointments, and sometimes never even kept them without so much as an apology or an explanation. Commitments did not mean too much, and deadlines were something he preferred not to think about. He detested work with the same passion that he loved social life, and he avoided work whenever he could. Rodgers often waited hours for Larry for their professional sessions; when Larry finally arrived, he proved extraordinarily inventive in concocting excuses as to why he had to leave or why he just could not do any work that day. To somebody like Rodgers who was punctual and efficient, a stickler for getting down to a job without fuss, Hart's lackadaisical ways were a continual source of irritation. Nor could Rodgers ever adjust himself to Hart's mercurial moods and whims.

As long as Hart had the joy of life in his heart, he proved a wonderful companion and a cherishable friend. He was kind, gentle, lovable. His wit and wisdom made talking with him an amusing or exhilarating experience. His unpredictable quixotic ways, his impromptu inventions and pranks, made association with him a perpetual adventure. However much Rodgers found work with Hart a trial, he never stopped being fond of him personally, just as he never stopped admiring Hart's extraordinary talent with words. But being fond of

Hart became increasingly difficult as the years went by. More and more did Hart become lax and careless about his habits, his daily life, his appointments, his rehearsals, his work sessions. More and more was he inclined to procrastinate. More and more did he give way to the temptation of suddenly going off, without warning or explanation, on a long trip, even though there was a show to be written.

He also became increasingly trying as an individual. By the end of the 1930's he had lost the zest that success had once brought him. The mad whirl of endless parties and all-night revels had become a bore. The accumulation of money had never meant anything to him at all, but now he was not even overly enthusiastic about what his money could buy him. He spent it or gave it away, as though he were dealing with Confederate dollars.

The sad truth was that he had become a terribly unhappy man. He was no longer satisfied with his work, which he felt, with ever-growing conviction, did not achieve the lofty standards he had always set for himself. Most intensely of all he suffered because of his pygmy size. The wisecracks that were being concocted along Broadway about him (such as "the shortest distance between two points is Larry Hart") kept pouring salt on an open wound. He felt he was an ugly man and a deformed one. Pathetically, he tried to give the impression of being bigger than he was by wearing elevated shoes, just as he showed his partiality for bigness by smoking large-sized cigars and dating tall girls. In addition to all these problems, he was terribly lonely and terribly envious of Rodgers who had a wife and children within a serene household. Hart could never find a girl to share his life. He was always in the company of beautiful women, whom he was pursuing all the time, and several times he was deeply in love. The girls liked him, liked being with him; but when on several occasions he proposed marriage to one of them, she turned him down.

He took to brooding, sank into melancholia, tried to find relief and escape in alcohol. He sought the company of shabby characters, probably because he was at ease with them, since they were not critical of his behavior, nor worried about his disintegration, nor questioned values that he knew only too well were shoddy. He was often found in an alcoholic stupor—disheveled, his clothing (about which he had once been so fastidious) in a mess. He now almost never kept appointments, often failed to show up for rehearsals, left necessary jobs undone. There were times were Rodgers himself had to make changes in Hart's lyrics, or write new ones, when such revisions were found necessary during rehearsals; Hart could nowhere be found to do the job himself. When *By Jupiter* was being written, Hart was hospitalized for a "rest cure," and some of the work on that production had to be done in his hospital room. Hart did not show up for the out-of-town opening; he seemed to have vanished into thin air.

However nerve-racking it had always been to work with Hart, and however tortured such working sessions had become in later years, Rodgers refused to think of breaking up the partnership. One of the reasons he had decided to revive *A Connecticut Yankee* in 1943 was with the hope that Hart's onetime creative enthusiasm would be revived by this project, that his shattered spirit might somehow be restored to one piece. For a brief while things did work out quite well. Hart went to work with a will (he loved that show!) producing lyrics for four new songs and one with all the brilliant flashes of his old-time wit ("To Keep My Love Alive"). But Hart's spirit soon gave out. Once again he sought solace in drink.

Rodgers had even hoped that Hart could be induced to work with him on an exciting new project offered them by the Theatre Guild in 1942. But Hart had lost the capacity to become stirred by a new assignment, and besides he insisted that the project the Theatre Guild had in mind held no interest for him. He preferred going off to Mexico for an indefinite stay and urged Rodgers to find another man to work with. One day, at Max Dreyfus's office, Hart repeated that he was leaving for Mexico, and once again suggested to Rodgers that he seek out another collaborator. Then he rose suddenly from his seat and left. "A long and wonderful partnership just went out of that door," remarked Rodgers sadly to Dreyfus.

On the night that the revival of *A Connecticut Yankee* tried out in Philadelphia, Hart failed to attend the performance, even though he was in town. He had gone on a binge. Found at last, Hart was rushed to a New York hospital for another "rest cure." When the revival came to New York, Hart was in a state of agitation, mumbling to himself as he paced back and forth in back of the auditorium. Rodgers went looking for him after the final curtain. Hart was nowhere to be found. He was located two days later in a hospital, unconscious, a victim of pneumonia. He died there on November 22, 1943. Rodgers and his wife were outside the hospital room the moment Hart died; they had kept an around-the-clock vigil there.

Alcohol and pneumonia were not the only things that killed Larry Hart. A part of him died a few months earlier when Rodgers told him that he had finally taken Hart's advice and had acquired a new writing partner, Oscar Hammerstein II. Hart was too wise a man not to realize then and there that his own career was now definitely over.

Another part of Hart died the evening that the Theatre Guild production that had been offered to Rodgers and Hart, but which had been written by Rodgers and Hammerstein, opened. That production was, of course, *Oklahoma!* Hart was in the theatre for the opening-night performance. Nobody had to tell him how remarkable, indeed how revolutionary, this musical was. The goal in the musical theatre toward which he had been heading for so many years with Rodgers but which he had never really reached was finally achieved—he saw with brilliant clarity—by Rodgers, but by Rodgers working with another man. Immediately after the premiere, Hart drifted into Sardi's restaurant to congratulate Rodgers. He added lightly: "This thing of yours will run longer than *Blossom Time,*" *Blossom Time* being one of the most successful operettas ever written, music by Sigmund Romberg based on the works of Franz Schubert. Then Hart disappeared into the night.

Hart had come to grips with the terrible realization that creatively speaking his life had just ended. Death came a few months later, but in the time between the opening of *Oklahoma!* and his end he was merely going through the motions of living.

Songs of the 1920's and 1930's–III

Cole Porter

Cole Porter's songs, like the man who wrote them, were always exquisitely groomed, possessed culture, breeding, and social background, and were smart and urbane, often with a touch of cynicism as spice. Porter's songs reflected the attitudes, experiences, and the *Weltanschauung* of one who had been everywhere and had seen everything, whose gamut of experiences extended from the museum and the library to the kitchen and the wine cellar; from the elegance and refinements of Park Avenue, Venice's Lido, and the French Riviera to the exoticism of jungles in Africa and the cultures and mores of other remote places.

Perhaps no other popular composer brought so much of himself and his times into his songs. If we did not know a single fact about Porter, we would know well the kind of man he was from listening to his melodies and lyrics, for he always wrote his own lyrics.

208

What kind of man was he?

He was a man who carried an elfin smile—the smile of a man who indulged in pranks and mischief, who enjoyed laughter, who fed on cynicism. He was a man whose saucer-like eyes were always sparkling to reflect his inner zest and exuberance. He was a man whose conversation was consistently witty, effervescent, sometimes overflowing with enthusiasm, sometimes devastatingly destructive and annihilating.

He was a man with an insatiable appetite for perpetrating pranks on innocent victims. On one occasion he had the bearded Monty Woolley come to one of his fashionable parties accompanied by a beautifully dressed woman—who was also bearded. In the mid-1920's, Porter invented an American couple named Mr. and Mrs. Fitch, who he said came from Muskogee. He filled the newspapers with items about all the swank and exclusive places and parties to which they had been invited. Before long, much to his inordinate delight, he heard some of his acquaintances and friends boasting that they had recently entertained the Fitches. When the thing got out of hand, Porter had one of the columnists report that the Fitches had been killed in an automobile accident.

Porter was a man always tailored with sartorial elegance: conservative dark suits or evening formal wear in New York, but never an overcoat or hat, even if the temperature was zero; brilliantly colored sports jackets and sports shirts in California. But wherever he was, or whatever clothes he wore, he always sported white socks. (For a long time the rumor was circulated that this idiosyncrasy was just a sentimental gesture to his dead grandfather who always wore white socks. But this explanation is nonsense. The truth was that Porter's legs and skin were extraordinarily sensitive. White socks were readily noticed by passersby, thus avoiding accidental kicking. Besides, white socks contained no dyes that might be infectious.) He also never failed to have a carnation in his lapel while fastidiously avoiding any other ostenatious form of decoration, such as jewelry. He was an excessively tidy man in his habits, a man of the utmost precision, a man with a most orderly, disciplined mind. Once he had become accustomed to do something at a certain time, he would continue to do it for years, be it watching a radio "soap opera" (which he followed daily for years, regardless of where he was, or with whom) or going to his California home each year on June 21. He was an extraordinarily gregarious man who loved contact with stimulating people, who was a fabulous host, and who was the most gracious and charming of guests at parties or other social affairs when surrounded by people he liked.

He was a man to whom beauty and luxury were basic necessities. When he had to live in a hotel—and that happened when one of his shows was trying out of town—he would often bring together with his personal belongings several great paintings and his own supply of rare china ashtrays which he distributed throughout the suite. To be confronted daily with the kind of stereotyped art to which hotels are addicted would have caused him physical pain. His own homes, of course, were the final word in elegant appointments. He had three: a spacious apartment on the forty-first floor of the Waldorf-Astoria Towers in New York, formerly known as the "Presidential Suite," since it had once been occupied by President Hoover and by the Duke and Duchess of Windsor; a cottage in

Williamburg, Massachusetts, where he went for weekends; and during summers a mansion at 416 N. Rockingham, in Hollywood, California. In addition to spending some time each year at one of these three places, he was always traveling to remote areas of the world absorbing everything he saw, heard, and learned into the spongelike tissues of his memory. Coming to a new place, he suddenly became the indefatigable tourist determined to touch each point of interest. Once, visiting the island of Jamaica with Moss Hart, for example, Porter became fascinated with its flora and fauna, and as Hart once told us, "He would drive miles to gape at a native shrub or an animal that flourished only in a particularly disagreeable part of . . . [the] country."

Porter was a man who knew how to play as passionately and as intensively as he knew how to work, since play and work were equally indispensable to a full rich life as far as he was concerned. The harder and longer he played, the more he became energized for creativity. Moss Hart had an opportunity to watch at first hand how the playboy in Porter was suddenly transformed into the workman. This happened while they were taking a cruise around the world to write a musical. The first ten days on ship was a time for total relaxation, for good food and champagne, for conversation and deck sports. But when the time came for them to get down to work, Hart reveals, "almost immediately a great change took place. Cole Porter, 'worker,' and Cole Porter, 'playboy,' were two different beings. . . . He worked around the clock. From the time I handed him the outline with the first two or three songs indicated, Cole seemed to withdraw . . . from the human race."

This, finally, was a man with the most extraordinary zest for living life to the full, in the grand manner and large design. He was a legitimate child of the 1920's. In the 1920's Cole Porter and his wife, Linda, established the base of their social operations in Paris in a $250,000 mansion in the Faubourg St. Germain section. The Paris of the 1920's was the cultural haven of the post-World War I American sophisticate, the playground of the social world. This was the Paris of Sergei Diaghilev's Ballet Russe, the Concerts Koussevitzky, George Antheil's *Ballet mécanique,* the music of the "French-Six." This was the Paris of Sylvia Beach and her Shakespeare and Company, of James Joyce's *Ulysses,* which Miss Beach was the first to publish, of Gertrude Stein holding court at Rue de Fleurus assisted by Alice B. Toklas, of Ezra Pound and Ernest Hemingway, of Jean Cocteau holding aloft the banner of the avant-garde movement. This was the Paris of cubism à la Picasso and Braque, where Marc Chagall was bringing the lore and mysticism of eastern European Jewry to his canvases. This was the Paris of Elsa Maxwell and her parties, of Princess de Polignac and her salon, of the international set, and of the splendiferous, extravagant goings-on at the Faubourg St. Germain mansion of Cole and Linda Porter.

The Porter home became the magnet that drew to it the great of Europe's cultural, social, and political life—to entertain and be entertained with the grandeur of a Louis XIV at a modern-day Versailles. Guests were met by two dozen footmen and were entertained now by Maurice Ravel or Igor Stravinsky, playing their own works at the piano; now by the latest rage of Paris's night places; and on one occasion even by the entire company of the Ballet Russe. When the Charleston dance became a fad both in America and in Paris, Charleston parties were held at the Porter home with Bricktop (then an entertainer of American birth whom Porter had discovered in Montmartre) as instructor. When the festivities palled in Paris, the guests would be transported to the Lido in Venice or the French Riviera in motorcades, headed by the Porter Rolls-Royce. Sometimes they traveled by special trains which included nine compartments for the Porters to accommodate their valet and maid, a bar, and sitting rooms, as well as their sleeping quarters.

When the Porters stayed on in Venice for periods longer than a transitory visit, they would rent a palace—the Palazzo Barbaro at the Lido in 1923, and annually between 1925 and 1929 the Palazzo Rezzonico where Robert Browning had died. There, too, the Porters moved about in unparalleled splendor, as their palace became the setting for grandiose balls, and where they initiated (under Elsa Maxwell's guidance) treasure hunts in the canals. Dinner parties were given for 150 guests in a special nightclub built outside the palazzo at the edge of the canal. Fifty gondoliers served as footmen. A Negro jazz band provided the music for dancing, while a string orchestra contributed atmospheric music. French chefs were brought in from Paris for these occasions. The evening's entertainment might include a troupe of tightrope walkers, a world-famous musician, a star of Parisian or London theatres or nightclubs, or Noël Coward or Porter himself singing their own songs, sometimes with lyrics improvised to fit the occasion.

When, in the 1930's, Porter's activities in the Broadway musical theatre demanded a more extended presence in New York, he moved his ménage, parties, escapades, and friends to the Waldorf-Astoria, which remained his principal home up to the time of his death. In time, because his night piano playing disturbed Linda's sleep, because he preferred a cool apartment to a heated one, and because Linda's respiratory ailment troubled him no end, Porter exchanged his one large apartment at the Waldorf for two smaller ones, one directly across the hall from the other, so each could enjoy privacy as well as those living conditions that suited each best. The Porters spent over a quarter of a million dollars appointing and decorating their suites to their own fastidious tastes.

The early 1930's were, of course, a time of social unrest, labor strife, unemployment, and economic upheaval—just as the 1920's had been a time of prosperity, extravagance, abandon. The Depression, however, did not touch the Porters. Besides drawing a huge annual royalty from his songwriting activity and his Broadway musical productions, Porter had inherited a fortune from his grandfather, and his wife, Linda, was a wealthy woman in her own right. The Porters, then, had both the wherewithal and the inclination to continue living in the sober 1930's in the same way they had done in the preceding frenetic decade. As far as they were concerned the calendar had not moved; they were still living in the 1920's, still faithful to its basic philosophy that life must be consumed to the full. This is why Porter's songs catch the essence of the life, spirit, and tempo of the twenties, even though some of them were written in the thirties.

The Porters attended as many as three or four parties a night. When they were the hosts, they continued to entertain in regal manner. Porter's concern over the pleasures of the table remained as discriminating as ever. He was a gourmet of gourmets, and he went to excessive lengths to see to it that his own table represent the culinary art at its finest. Once, in Los Angeles, he was delighted with the taste of chopped steak served at Dick Chasens' restaurant. When his request for the recipe was denied him, Porter sent his butler the next day to order the dish and carry it away carefully folded in a napkin. The chopped steak was then analyzed in a laboratory to enable Porter's chef to prepare it the same way Chasens' restaurant did.

Porter fled from boredom as if it were anathema, finding refuge from it in parties, first nights at the theatre, at nightclubs and other night spots and boîtes, in food and drink, in swimming, hunting, horseback riding, playing with his dogs, parlor games, backgammon, pranks, radio programs, books, art works, talented performers, good conversation, and the music of gifted colleagues. His storehouse of enthusiasms—and, to be quite frank about it, his hates as well—seemed inexhaustible. To an interviewer he revealed that his favorite things included "cats, parties, swimming, scandal, crime news, people, tabloids, movies"; in music, his preferences were Stravinsky, Bach, Mozart, Gershwin, and Rodgers. As for his dislikes, they embraced "baseball, steam-heated rooms, golf, poetry, Belgium, pressed duck, and English railway hotels." He also detested dull people and shopwork conversation. When confronted with them, which happened quite often, he wore an expression of "spectacular boredom" (the phrase is Margaret Case Harriman's), withdrawing completely within himself until he could make a discreet retreat.

"Cole is the most self-indulgent and pleasure-loving man I have ever known," said Moss Hart, "but indulgence and pleasure stop dead the moment songwriting begins." The truth of the matter was that Cole Porter was always working, even when he was playing. Ideas for lyrics and melodies kept spinning in his head all the time, waiting for the various colors and designs to fall into proper place. Ideas came while he was shaving, or in a taxi, or at a railroad station, or even at parties while he was exchanging talk. Such were his powers of concentration that he could work out a song in detail in his mind before getting it down on paper. In fact, Porter rarely went to work at the piano or the table before he had his song clear and precise in mind. Most of his writing was done between eleven and five during the day, and some of his final corrections and changes were made while he sprawled out on a couch and looked blankly at the ceiling.

Here is how Cole Porter himself described his method of working: "First I think of an idea for a song and then I fit it to a title. Then I go to work on a melody, spotting the title at certain moments in the melody. Then I write the lyric—the end first—that way it has a strong finish. It's terribly important for a song to have a strong finish. I do the lyrics the way I'd do a crossword puzzle.

I try to give myself a meter which will make the lyric as easy as possible to write, but without being banal. . . . I try to pick for my rhyme words of which there is a long list with the same ending."

In writing a lyric on some specialized subject he would always precede creativity with intensive research. He began this practice after being severely criticized for having selected flowers that were incompatible growing together. This had happened in "Old-Fashioned Garden." From then on he never used a theme in any of his lyrics without first learning everything he could about it. He made an intensive study of anatomy before writing the song "The Physician," just as he did a good deal of digging into the field of insect and animal life before penning "Let's Do It."

His songs—music as well as words—were, when completed, as exquisitely tailored, as well poised, and as cultured as the man who wrote them. Every phrase—melodic or verbal—was beautifully scultured. Every sentiment was expressed with perfect grooming. Every nuance or shade of emotion was projected in the best possible taste, be the mood light and flippant or sentimental and serious. The melodies and the lyrics both reflect their creator's capacity for sensual responses and for cynical reactions; for reflecting his immense fund of experience in living and traveling; for exposing his seemingly tireless capacity for excitement.

Excitement is one of the distinguishing traits of his gift in composition: the way in which a melody sweeps relentlessly toward a thrilling point of climax, the melody usually sustained by a background of a persistent throbbing rhythm, as in "What Is This Thing Called Love?"; the way in which the melody soars, swells, and expands in the release, as in the *appassionato* section of "In the Still of the Night"; the way in which he is partial to minor-key languor and Slavic-like passions, as in "Night and Day" and "Begin the Beguine."

The songs are also noteworthy for their sophistication—the lyrics, especially. Here Porter reveals a surpassingly masterful use of versification, rhyming (with a special gift for a procession of interior rhymes), fresh figures of speech, spicy suggestions of esoterica and exotica. Only one or two lyricists of his time were his equals in his agile and dexterous phrasing and virtuosity at versification—only a Lorenz Hart or an Ira Gershwin, for example.

The songs, finally, are usually also characteristic for their cynicism. Many Porter love songs are passionate—with a "hunger, yearning, burning inside of me." But just as often they are blasé. Love, then, becomes for him "just one of those things"; he can be "true to you only in my fashion" (combining Porter cynicism with Ernst Dowson sentimentality); love becomes for him something that is mystifying, and love is something that is for sale.

Ideas for his songs came from many different places, people, and personal experiences. A chant heard in Marrakesh in Morocco became the stimulus for "What Is This Thing Called Love?" The rhythms of drumbeats heard from afar in Morocco was the source of "Night and Day." Native music heard on the island of Kalabahi in the Dutch East Indies provided material for "Begin the Beguine." Listening to a native band in Haiti sparked the writing of "Katie Went to Haiti."

His ear was cocked to catch not only tunes and rhythms from far-off places that could prove serviceable but also catch phrases, unusual remarks, bits of byplay that would contribute material for lyrics. In writing "Ain't It Etiquette" he remembered how Peggy Joyce Hopkins continually repeated the question "For instance who?" which he used in that song. When he put "You're the Top" down on paper, it was after he recalled a game played years earlier with Mrs. Alistair Mackintosh in a Paris restaurant when they tried to top each other by presenting in rhymes things that were superlative in their field. "Its De-lovely" was actually born when Cole Porter was taking a world cruise. Watching the sun rise over Rio from the deck, Cole remarked "It's delightful"; his wife, Linda, responded, "It's delicious"; and their friend, Monty Woolley added, "It's de-lovely." Cole Porter used all of that in his song. "Well, did you evah?" was a comment Porter overheard at a party.

Being a workman as well as a creative artist, Porter produced some of his songs to serve a definite function: "My Heart Belongs to Daddy" to allow a change of scene; "Night and Day" to conform to Fred Astaire's limited vocal range; "I Get a Kick out of You" to advance Ethel Merman's best tones (A flat, B flat, C natural); "I Love Paris" to justify Jo Mielziner's stunning Parisian rooftop setting for *Can-Can*.

Other songs reflected Porter's delight in pulling people's legs. His own prank in having invented the characters of Mr. and Mrs. Fitch gave him the idea for "Mr. and Missus Fitch." "Don't Fence Me In" was intended to parody and laugh at those songs popular in the 1930's that imitated cowboy ballads. (Actually, Porter had purchased the title from a Montana cowboy, Bob Fletcher, for $150, and used one or two phrases from the poem Fletcher had written for it.) "Rosalie" was consciously planned to incorporate every kind of verbal and melodic cliché as a rebuke to the motion-picture producer who kept turning down far more original ballads as a title number. (Porter had submitted six different songs which he considered suitable, and when each was rejected, he went into a rage and wrote "Rosalie" as revenge. All his life he considered it the "dreariest" song he had ever written. Yet "Rosalie"—just as "Don't Fence Me In"—became one of Porter's biggest money-makers, the public never recognizing that he had written it with tongue in cheek.) And "Miss Otis Regrets" was first improvised at a party to provide material for Monty Woolley who was putting on an act as a butler.

Cole Porter's early background prepared him well for his later sybaritic life, just as it had trained him well for his later profession. Wealth came to the Porter family from Cole's maternal grandfather, J. O. Cole. His investments in coal and timber in West Virginia had accumulated into a fortune estimated at seven million dollars by the time Cole was born. He was, as most tycoons are, an autocrat who ruled his family with an iron hand and brooked no interference with his decisions or disagreement with his opinions. His daughter, Kate—his favorite—inherited his strength of will and character. His only other child, a son, Louis, was for some reason or another neglected and ignored.

Wealthy, well educated in exclusive Eastern schools, and petite and charming, Kate could, of course, have had her pick of the most desirable men in the town of Peru, Indiana, where the Coles had made their home on a 750-acre fruit ranch. She chose a man of modest circumstances, a druggist by the name of Samuel Fenwick Porter, because he was uncommonly handsome, and because he loved poetry, wrote it, and quoted it by the page. Once married, Samuel and Kate went to live with the domineering J. O. Cole who made no effort to conceal the fact that he had contempt for Samuel for not having been rich and for wasting his time on poetry. Poor Samuel, his was a losing battle from the moment he stepped into the Cole empire. He was thoroughly dominated by his overbearing father-in-law and by his strong-willed wife. Between them they succeeded in fashioning a weak-willed, timid, and at times spirit-broken man—the reason no doubt that his son, Cole, had so little use for him and even less traffic with him.

It was in such a family, in the Indiana town of Peru, that Porter was born on June 9, 1892. He was the third child of Samuel and Kate, the first two of whom had died. As the sole survivor, and as her only child, Kate doted on Cole from his infancy on; he became the be-all and end-all of her existence. She dressed him up in fancy clothes and behaved almost as if she wanted him to be on permanent exhibition. He was never permitted to indulge in games with other children, since she considered all other children rowdies. *She* was intent on raising a gentleman. He began learning to ride a horse during his childhood, and was given a pony of his own when he was only six. And since Kate was intensely musical, a fine pianist, he was given a thorough training in music. He studied both the piano and the violin, the piano in Peru, the violin in Marion, Indiana, thirty miles away. Several hours of each day had to be devoted religiously to practicing on both instruments. He objected violently to those practicing sessions, to be denied playing with children of his own age, to be compelled to travel thirty miles for violin instruction. But there was in him a good deal of his father's meekness and lack of strong fiber: he submitted weakly to his mother's wishes. Had he resisted, he might have found an ally in his father, who instilled in him a love for poetry by reading to him the works of the great poets and discussing them with him. But some of the contempt the rest of the family felt for Samuel Fenwick Porter seeped down from the grandfather through the mother and affected young Cole. He never really became close with his father, but his mother he worshiped, those detested practice sessions at the piano notwithstanding.

When he was ten, he started writing music. His first effort was an operetta comprising a single song, *The Song of the Birds,* which he dedicated to his mother. This was followed by *The Bobolink Waltz,* a piano piece written after he had heard a bobolink singing outside his window. This, too, he dedicated to his mother, who traveled to Chicago where she paid a publisher $100 to publish it.

Cole's childhood pleasures came from solitary pastimes: making up little productions with a toy theatre; cavorting around in a clown's suit. Sometimes he went to the circus, since Peru was the winter home base of the Great Wallace Shows. Of all his childhood experiences, however, the one that made the most indelible impression upon him was a picture on the polychrome curtain of Peru's only theatre, the Emric. It depicted a gondola floating on the Grand Canal in Venice. For some inexplicable reason, this picture aroused the boy's imagination. In all probability, it was the first stimulant in creating a seemingly insatiable appetite for foreign travel all his life—and specifically for visiting Venice.

Since Kate had received her education in fashionable schools in the East, she insisted that her son, Cole, follow suit. And so, when he was thirteen, Cole left his family to attend the Worcester Academy in Massachusetts. He stayed there three years. During all that time, for reasons never adequately explained, he never paid a single visit home, nor did any member of his family visit him. He remained a loner. He made few friends, and to these he never said a word about his father, mother, or grandfather. Most of his spare time was spent at the upright piano which he had brought with him (together with some paintings and some favorite statuary). But after two years he thawed out; once he allowed his fellow students to discover him, they liked him. He was elected president of a mandolin club, editor of the school paper, a performer in the school play, the pianist for the glee club, and an entry in a public-speaking contest. But what his fellow students admired most in him were the songs he was writing all the time, many of them humorous ditties about members of the faculty, some of them, such as "The Bearded Lady" and "The Tattooed Gentleman," delightfully whimsical.

He was graduated from Worcester Academy in early June of 1909 as class valedictorian. Having passed his entrance examinations for Yale, he was rewarded by his grandfather with his first trip to Europe. For a while he lived with a French family to perfect his knowledge of the French language. Then he roamed about Switzerland and Germany. He fell in love with Europe and he fell in love with travel, with neither of which would he ever become blasé until toward the close of his life.

Between 1909 and 1913 Porter attended Yale. His fellow students later remembered him as a young man who drank champagne, gin, and Scotch, who smoked Fatima cigarettes, who was always meticulously groomed and socially poised, and who had a fetish for luxurious living. They also remember that he was crazy about music. Porter was already writing songs all the time, many of them with satirical verses about happenings at Yale. A more commercial item, "Bridget," became his first official publication, released by Remick in 1910. At Yale, Porter also became the leader of the glee club; he helped produce and write the music for college shows; and he concocted football songs, two still a part of Yale's song repertory, "Bingo Eli Yale" and "Bulldog," each published in 1911. In recognition of his contributions to the social and musical activities at Yale, Porter was voted "the most entertaining man" in his class. In the poll for the most "original man" he captured second place. He also appeared on the list of "eccentrics."

From Yale, Porter progressed in 1913 to Harvard Law School, where he roomed with Dean Acheson (later become the Secretary of State under President Franklin D. Roosevelt and President Truman). Porter was a poor law student because his heart was elsewhere. This fact was recognized by Dean Ezra Thayer of the law school, who had seen a school production in which Porter had been a performer and for which he had written the songs. Thayer urged Porter to forget all about law and enter Harvard's school of music. This, of course, was something Cole wanted to do desperately. Knowing full well that his grandfather would veto such a move, he kept the old man completely in the dark about his change of plans. He spent the next three years at the music school studying piano, theory, orchestration, and music history. Though studies like these are calculated to prepare a young man for a career in serious music, Porter knew that his forte was popular-song writing and he had no intention of being deflected from this ambition. In 1915 he had two of his songs placed in Broadway musical productions: "Two Big Eyes" in *Miss Information,* a musical whose basic score was the work of Jerome Kern, and which starred Irene Bordoni; and "Esmeralda" in *Hands Up,* most of whose songs were written by Sigmund Romberg.

His crowning ambition, of course, was to have a Broadway show in which the entire score was his own. He realized this ambition on March 26, 1916, when *See America First* was given at the Maxine Elliott Theatre by Elizabeth Marbury (the same Miss Marbury who produced the Princess Theatre Shows). The text was by T. Lawrason Riggs (whom Porter had befriended at Yale) and was intended as a satire on the kind of patriotic musicals for which George M. Cohan was then famous. The heroine is a girl who dotes on all things British, while her own father is an American superpatriot. While touring the West, the heroine falls in love with an English duke who, in the end, turns out to be a cowhand in disguise.

The reviews were bad, the critics advising their readers to see *See America First* last, and the attendance could be counted nightly on the fingers of a hand or two. *See America First* limped along for fifteen performances, then collapsed. From this wreckage, all that was saved was a single song, "I've a Shooting Box in Scotland," which Porter and Lawrason had actually written for a college show but which they had revised for Broadway. This was Porter's first commercial song in which the world traveler found foreign material as a choice subject for song exploitation: the lyrics mentioned all those exotic places where the author would like to have a villa, a hacienda, a chalet, and so forth. Such sophisticated allusions were certainly foreign to the songwriting material of 1916 and must therefore be considered as the first number in which Porter begins to evolve a song manner and identity of his own. Fred and Adele Astaire, already stars in the theatre, liked the song well enough to use it in their vaudeville act after *See America First* closed. (Fred Astaire revived it on a television "special" over the N.B.C. network on February 7, 1968.)

Concerning the fiasco of *See America First,* Porter said: "I honestly believed I was disgraced for the rest of my life. I sneaked back to the Yale Club, rushed through the lobby, and hid in my room." He spoke of joining the Foreign Legion: "I had to leave town until the smell of my first Broadway show had disappeared." Instead, while occupying an apartment on East Nineteenth Street, he studied composition with Pietro Yon.

Most biographical sketches about Porter speak about his having been a member of the French Foreign Legion in Africa. This belief is the result of a confusion which deserves clarification. During World War I, in 1918, Porter enlisted in the "first foreign regiment" of the 32nd Field Artillery Regiment; less than a year later he was transferred to the Bureau of the Military Attaché of the United States. He was really serving in the French Army as an American citizen, and for this reason was under the direct control of the Foreign Legion. But as for all the stories of how he trudged about Africa as a member of the legion (with a portable piano on his back)—all this is sheer fiction.

He left the uniform in April of 1919 and rented an elegant apartment on 9 rue Gounod, in Paris. His aim was to do some more studying of music, and for this purpose he now enrolled at the renowned Schola Cantorum where he was a pupil of Vincent d'Indy. He was becoming a member of the international set (carefully guided by Elsa Maxwell to go to the right places and meet the right people). One of the places he went to was a fashionable wedding of two of the social elite in Paris—Ethel Harriman and Henry Russell—where he participated in the entertainment by singing some of his songs. They attracted the attention, then the fascinated interest, of one of the most beautiful women, and one of the most distinguished hostesses in Paris, Mrs. Linda Thomas. Then thirty-six years old, she was a Kentucky girl who had been married to, and divorced from, a wealthy newspaper owner.

It did not take Cole Porter and Linda Thomas long to realize they were one of a kind. They began seeing each other more and more frequently until, inevitably, they fell in love. This was the first woman Porter had met whom he wanted to marry. To gain his grandfather's consent for such a match, Porter crossed the ocean in 1919 for a brief visit home. He came back fully frustrated. The grandfather had no sympathy for the kind of life Porter was leading; would not hear of his getting married before he had settled down to a useful career; and gruffly announced that if Porter insisted on staying on in Paris and marrying Linda, the old man would be through with his grandson forever.

With Linda a wealthy woman, and with Porter getting a regular handsome subsidy from his mother, the grandfather's objections could be ignored. Besides, Porter now had good reason to nurse faith in his future as a songwriter. While sailing across the Atlantic homeward, he had met aboard ship Raymond Hitchcock, producer of an annual Broadway revue, *Hitchy-Koo*. Hitchcock was so taken with some of Porter's songs that then and there, during the sailing, he engaged Porter to contribute the entire score for the forthcoming edition of his revue. Porter produced ten numbers for the *Hitchy-Koo of 1919,* which opened on October 6. The only one that proved a hit was "Old-Fashioned Garden," which he had created at the request of the producers who had acquired some beautiful costumes made up for the most part of flowers and needed a musical number for a scene in which these costumes would be used. "Old-Fashioned Garden" sold 100,000 copies of sheet music—not an epic figure, to be sure, but for Porter an indication that he was beginning to reach a public. "Old-Fashioned Garden" remained one of Porter's own favorites all his life, which is why it was revived in the Cole Porter motion-picture biography, *Night and Day.*

And so, back in Paris after "Old-Fashioned Garden" had begun to grow popular, Cole Porter was ready and willing to shrug off his grandfather's objections to his getting married. Cole Porter married Linda quietly in a civil ceremony on December 18, 1919. After spending their honeymoon in southern France, Italy, and Sicily, they lived for a while at Linda's elegant home on Rue de Baum, then for a while at an apartment at the Ritz Hotel. Finally, they bought a mansion at 13 rue Monsieur. Since Linda was an authority on porcelain, French antiques, Chinese paintings, and Egyptology—and since Porter knew so much about art and had such a fetish for exotic treasures—their home became a veritable museum of precious art works and rarities. These found a suitable setting in a house decorated with a maharajah's opulence. The floor coverings, for example, were made of zebra hides, one of the rooms had platinum-colored wallpaper, and some of the chairs were upholstered with red lacquer white kid.

Linda and Cole Porter became the darlings of Parisian society. They threw themselves into that kind of frenetic living that was so rapidly becoming the way of life of what Ernest Hemingway chose to call "the lost generation." The Porters became the living symbols of a decade that lived with laughter and mockery on the lips and a glass of champagne in hand. They and their closest friends (the Baron Nicolas de Gunzsburg, the Duke of Fulco de Verdura, Howard Sturges, Monty Woolley, Noël Coward, Elsa Maxwell, to mention just a few) had their every wish and whim catered to by an entourage of servants.

Porter continued writing songs and, from time to time, getting them heard publicly. For *Hitchy-Koo of 1922* he produced six songs, an unfortunate assignment since that show opened and closed in Boston. Five songs were placed in the *Greenwich Village Follies of 1924*. One of them, "I'm in Love Again" (introduced by the Dolly Sisters), was ignored in that show, but, like several other later Porter classics, it later slowly began to find an audience with sophisticates and finally even the general public. Four years after that, in 1928, a handful of Porter songs turned up in a Parisian revue mounted at the fashionable *Des Ambassadeurs.* Out of this group came a new Porter hit song, though still a minor one, in "Looking at You," which was sung by Clifton Webb. (This song came to Broadway in the musical *Wake Up and Dream* in 1929.)

The Porter songs that had thus far been heard produced some sparks but hardly a flame. What Porter needed most of all to make his creativity fully combustible was the flammable fuel of a stimulating book-musical, rather than a revue. The flammable fuel was finally applied to his creativity by two Broadway book-shows. Both used Paris as the setting—Paris, the city where Porter had been thriving as a playboy of the western world and with whose every alley, byway, and boîte he was so thoroughly familiar.

The first of these book-shows was *Paris,* come to Broadway in 1928, with Irene Bordoni as its star. Here for the first time Porter's personality as a composer and lyricist comes into full focus—with songs like "Let's Do It" (to which Irene Bordoni's French accent contributed such piquant spice), "Two Little Babes in the Wood," and "Let's Misbehave" (though the last of these was dropped from the production before it reached New York). Of Porter's score a critic for *The New Yorker* said: "No one else writing words and music knows so exactly the delicate balance between sense, rhyme, and tune. His rare and satisfactory talent makes other lyricists sound as though they'd written their words for a steam whistle."

The second book-show with a Parisian background was *Fifty Million Frenchmen,* produced on Broadway in 1929, with William Gaxton and Genevieve Tobin as leads. Here we find "You've Got That Thing," "You Do Something to Me," and "Find Me a Primitive Man." So excited was Irving Berlin with these and the other songs in this show that he bought an ad in the newspapers to call *Fifty Million Frenchmen* "the best musical comedy I have seen in years" and "one of the best collection of song numbers I have ever listened to." He added: "It's worth the price of admission to hear Cole Porter's lyrics."

The slick, suave, urbane Cole Porter style was now fully personalized, carrying some of those mannerisms that would henceforth identify and individualize his writing: those leaping rhymes, those cultural allusions, those witty double entendres and those tongue-in-cheek attitudes toward sentimental romance in the lyrics; those swelling, surging melodies, often rising to new heights of expressiveness and sensuality in the release. This Cole Porter song identity was also found in numbers contributed to other stage productions as well: in "What Is This Thing Called Love?" which Frances Shelley introduced in *Wake Up and Dream* in 1929, and for which Walter Winchell conducted a one-man campaign in his widely syndicated column to popularize all over the country; and in "Love for Sale," perhaps the first hit song ever written about love as a profession, a provocative number made all the more prurient and suggestive through Kathryn Crawford's performance in *The New Yorkers* in 1930. Songs like these were as much the voice and the essence of the 1920's as were the verses of Dorothy Parker, the novels of F. Scott Fitzgerald, and the symphonic jazz of George Gershwin.

Cole and Linda Porter deserted Paris in the early 1930's to live permanently in New York. But Paris never really left Cole Porter—just as the 1920's never left him. He continued writing songs about his favorite city for the remainder of his life—love songs to a city, without any of the cynicism and blasé attitudes that characterized his romantic moods about women. He continued, also, writing the type of witty, sophisticated, urbane, and fun-loving songs he had done in the 1920's, almost as if the sober thirties had never brought with it labor struggles, the Depression, social unrest, and an accepted awareness that there was more to life than just having a good time. In New York, as in Paris, the social festivities swirled around the Cole Porters. His way of life did not change, nor did the kind of songs he wrote to express the values of that way of life.

The classics by which Porter will always be remembered and which gave him a place all his own in American popular music came in the first half of the 1930's: "Night and Day" from *Gay Divorce* in 1932; "All Through the Night," "You're the Top," "Blow, Gabriel, Blow," and "I Get a Kick out of You," all from *Anything Goes* in 1934; and "Begin the Beguine" from *Jubilee* in 1935. After Russel Crouse, who collaborated in writing the libretto for *Anything Goes,* had heard Cole Porter play and sing that score for the first time, he remarked: "All I can say is that no doubt Beethoven, Bach, Mozart, Wagner, Brahms, Mendelssohn, Debussy, Chopin, Verdi, Offenbach, Johann Strauss, Haydn, and Francis Scott Key could have marched into the room and I wouldn't have looked up." Walter Winchell, still plugging his favorite composer, wrote in his column: "Cole Porter, to use his own theme, is 'tops.' He is the Kern of the music masters, . . . or the Roosevelt of lyricists." No doubt Winchell's enthusiasm for Porter the lyricist was fired by lines like "flying too high, with some guy, in the sky, is my i-dea of nothing to do"—five rhymes within a single line—in "I Get a Kick Out of You." No doubt, too, Russel Crouse's euphoria upon hearing Porter's songs for the first time was the result of such unusual effects as the hyperthyroid, restless rhythm that surged under the melody of that same song, and the enchanting effect produced by the descending chromatic line in the main melody of "All Through the Night."

"Night and Day" was also unconventional in its musical structure, since the chorus extended for forty-eight measures instead of the traditional thirty-two. Porter wrote this classic for Fred Astaire, who, of course, introduced it in his own inimitable way with song and dance. The idea of using a persistent single note in the verse (B flat) came to Porter during a visit to Morocco where he heard the steady, even beat on a tom-tom from a distance. The source of the exotic melody in the chorus was a religious chant of an Islamic priest also in Morocco. In spite of its completely unorthodox material and technique, "Night and Day" caught on from the very beginning—and to such an extent that it became one of the main reasons the show *Gay Divorce* proved such a box-office attraction. In fact, the song had become popular even before that show opened, having been circulated by big-name bands throughout the country, through repeated performances over the radio, and through several phonograph recordings that had large sales. The success of "Night and Day" kept mounting as later recordings by Paul Whiteman, André Kostelanetz, Benny Goodman, Bing Crosby, and Tommy Dorsey soared to the top of best-seller lists. In the last of these releases, that of Tommy Dorsey, Frank Sinatra was the vocalist, his debut on discs. When Cole Porter's biography was screened, this song achieved still a new status of importance by having the movie named after it.

"Begin the Beguine" had quite a different history. Nobody at first seemed aware that this was something very special—not even Moss Hart who was the first to hear it. Porter and Moss Hart were aboard the *Franconia* on an around-the-world cruise, during which they worked on the musical *Jubilee*. As the ship approached the Fiji Islands, Porter completed writing his song and at once performed it for Hart. Hart later confessed: "I had reservations about the length. . . . Indeed, I am somewhat ashamed to record that I thought it had ended when he was only halfway through playing it." When *Jubilee* came to Broadway, the critics ignored "Begin the Beguine," while the audience showed no visible sign of reaction. Recording and sheet-music sales were negligible. In short, "Begin the Beguine" had the earmarks of having been stillborn. Once *Jubilee* closed, the song passed on to oblivion from which it was rescued more than a year later by Artie Shaw, a then-young jazz-band leader who had just signed his first recording contract. Shaw planned making his record bow on the

Bluebeard label with Friml's "Indian Love Call," arranged with a strong beat and dressed up with jazz rhythms. He needed a number for the "flip" side of his record. Since he was one of a scattered few who had liked "Begin the Beguine," he decided to use it in a lush orchestration. The recording director opposed his choice, insisting the song was dead tissue; but Shaw stood his ground. "Begin the Beguine" and "Indian Love Call" sold over two million discs, the largest sale of any instrumental recording up to that time. This success placed Artie Shaw and his band with the big-name groups, and it carried the song to a place of first importance in our song literature. No Cole Porter song is today more popular or more highly esteemed; and no Cole Porter song is more likely to represent him permanently in the future.

Between "Night and Day" and "Begin the Beguine" came the score for *Anything Goes.* Though the show was a box-office success with 420 performances, when produced in 1934, it was by no means the greatest enjoyed by a Cole Porter musical in the period preceding *Kiss Me, Kate. Panama Hattie,* in 1940, had a run of 501 performances; *Let's Face It,* in 1941, 547 performances; *Something for the Boys,* in 1943, 422 performances; *Mexican Hayride,* in 1944, 481 performances. Nevertheless, even though so many other Porter musicals were far more profitable financially than *Anything Goes,* none before 1945 had a score half so versatile, fresh, and exciting, nor a score so filled with standards. That score is second only to that for *Kiss Me, Kate* for importance and durability; and it showed Cole Porter in some of his most brilliant attitudes, both as a lyricist and as a composer.

That production starred Ethel Merman as a nightclub singer who becomes an evangelist; Victor Moore, as Public Enemy No. 13 disguised as a minister (a public enemy who is as harmless as a cream puff); and William Gaxton as a playboy pursuing a girl he loves, the latter played by Bettina Hall. The best songs were written with Ethel Merman in mind. A song like "Blow, Gabriel, Blow"—a blues, in the style of an evangelist hymn—and "I Get a Kick out of You" were fashioned not only for Miss Merman's vocal range but also for the robust style of her delivery. "You're the Top" (whose lyrics provided Porter with an opportunity to reveal the wide range of his intellectual interests and experiences) was calculated to point up her brassy tones as well as her sophisticated manner. She proved particularly effective in "I Get a Kick out of You" where, by pausing after the syllable "rif" in the chorus, and breaking up the words into syllables while holding on to one syllable longer than indicated, she created a volcanic effect that brought down the house. The main ballad, "All Through the Night," one of Porter's best songs in a purple mood, was assigned to William Gaxton and Bettina Hall.

Porter's talent was no longer being siphoned exclusively through the living theatre. He was now become a significant contributor to screen music. His first original screen score came in 1936, *Born To Dance,* an M-G-M production starring Eleanor Powell and James Stewart; its finest musical number was "I've Got You Under My Skin." One year later Eleanor Powell starred with Nelson Eddy in *Rosalie,* out of which came "In the Still of the Night" and the title number. "I've Got You Under My Skin" and "In the Still of the Night" are *echt* Porter; "Rosalie" is *ersatz,* and (as we already had occasion to remark) consciously planned so by the composer.

Anything Goes was enjoying a healthy existence at the Alvin Theatre, *Born To Dance* and *Rosalie* were attracting capacity crowds to movie theatres the country over, and "Begin the Beguine" had became a two-million-disc seller, all indications that Porter had now reached the peak of his profession. He now seemed that most fortunate of men who did not lack money, nor talent, nor fame, nor the capacity to enjoy life, nor a wife whom he could admire and respect as well as love. He had the world in the palm of his hand when tragedy struck him a crushing blow. As a guest at a house party on the Long Island estate of Countess Edith di Zoppola, Porter went horseback riding on a fractious animal at the Piping Rock Club. Negotiating a hill, the horse was frightened by some bushes, reared and fell, with Cole Porter pinned under the weight of the animal. At the moment Porter did not think he was either seriously hurt or in danger. In fact, he confesses, that while waiting for help he worked on the lyrics of "You Never Know." But when he was extricated from under the animal and rushed to a hospital by ambulance, he became delirious and went into shock.

In the hospital Dr. John J. Moorehead, a bone specialist, found that both of Porter's legs had been shattered; that if there was to be any hope of saving his legs he would have to undergo a series of excruciatingly painful operations. Porter accepted his fate stocially, and willingly consented to begin what was destined to be a protracted and painful ordeal with the hope that he would be able to walk again. Yet even now his sense of humor had not deserted him. "It just goes to show," he told Elsa Maxwell, "that fifty million Frenchmen can't be wrong. They eat horses instead of riding them." He even made a game of his tragedy by baptizing each of his broken legs with a name, calling the left one Josephine and the right one Geraldine.

But the accident and its consequences were no laughing matter. Porter had to suffer one operation after another; by the summer of 1938, his legs were broken and reset seven times, while efforts were also made to repair the damage done to the nerves. He experienced unbearable pain most of the time and remained in total immobility. The legs were saved only after he had been brought back to the operating table more than thirty times within a period of a few years. For about five years Porter was unable to walk and had to use a wheelchair for locomotion; and the harrowing pains continued on and off for a long time after that.

For a while, Porter succumbed to such violent depressions that at times he contemplated suicide. Then, with a Herculean will and an indomitable spirit, he proceeded to lift himself out of the morass of his melancholia and physical agony. He started going to parties and first nights again, even though he could not walk and had to dull his pain with sedatives. He once again tried to fill the role of the gracious host at his apartment. He even resumed foreign travel, though often he had to be carried from one place to the next. And he returned to composing. He had his piano raised on wood blocks so that he might work at the keyboard while seated in his wheelchair. This victory over a tortured body was announced to the world through *Leave It to Me,* a musical for which he not only wrote the songs but which, in spite of harrowing pain, he helped rehearse.

Leave It to Me, in 1938, was the first successful Broadway musical deriving its merriment from the foibles of the Soviet regime; and a good deal of the hilarity circulated around the pathetic character of the American ambassador to the Soviet Union played by Victor Moore—a befuddled little man hopelessly homesick for Topeka, Kansas. The critics raved, but the score was by no means top-drawer Porter, though it was good enough not to interfere with a scintillating text by Bella and Samuel Spewack. Nevertheless one song was a winner, and principally because through it a then still unknown and minor performer became a star of stars—Mary Martin. Wearing ermine wraps at a wayside railroad station in Siberia, she sang "My Heart Belongs to Daddy" with disarming baby-faced and baby-voiced innocence, while going through the motions of a mock striptease. She was, as the critic of the *Mirror* remarked, "an individual triumph."

The ensuing half-dozen years saw a parade of Cole Porter stage musicals that were box-office successes of the first order, and two highly acclaimed motion-picture musicals. Paradoxically, the greatest success enjoyed by a Cole Porter song during this period did not come from any of these productions at all, nor was it something that the creator took seriously. That song was "Don't Fence Me In." It had a curious performance history. It was at first interpolated into a motion picture that was never released *(Adiós, Argentina).* After that Porter discarded the song, but a decade later he resurrected it for Roy Rogers who gave it a thoroughly serious presentation in the motion-picture musical *Hollywood Canteen,* in 1944, even though the composer had written it as a travesty on cowboy ballads. Soon after that Kate Smith sang it over the radio, also in a serious performance. The song ended up as a cowboy ballad, and as such it caught on. Before 1944 was over, a recording by Bing Crosby with the Andrews Sisters sold over a million discs. The number reached the number-one spot on "Hit Parade" where it stayed for several weeks. The song had become so popular by 1945 that a motion picture was built around it. It starred Roy Rogers and it was named *Don't Fence Me In.*

Cole Porter's career went into high gear in the first half of the 1940's with four successive box-office triumphs on Broadway *(Panama Hattie, Let's Face It, Something for the Boys,* and *Mexican Hayride);* with movie adaptations of three of his musicals *(Panama Hattie, DuBarry Was a Lady,* and *Let's Face It);* with original scores for three more movies *(Broadway Melody of 1940, You'll Never Get Rich,* and *Something To Shout About);* and with the projected production of his motion-picture biography starring Cary Grant as Porter, and featuring a cavalcade of Porter's greatest hits (released in 1946 as *Night and Day).*

Then, suddenly and inexplicably, Porter's career went into reverse. After two successive Broadway shows were failures—*Seven Lively Arts* in 1944 and *Around the World* in 1946—Porter found himself an untouchable among Broadway producers. The feeling began to gain momentum on Broadway that

Porter had lost his "touch." Even his resounding Broadway successes of the early 1940's, his severest critics took pains to point out, failed to introduce a single song to rival in quality and originality the achievements of earlier years. Some of his friends were led to suspect that his continual returns to the hospital for operations and his incessant struggle to either ease or ignore his pain had finally taken their toll, weakening Porter beyond repair creatively as well as physically.

It was at this crucial juncture in his career that Porter wrote the music for *Kiss Me, Kate*—the best he had ever done, and one of the best of any composer. And this extraordinary score was written for a production that enjoyed the longest run and netted the largest profits to come from any Porter musical.

The point of departure for *Kiss Me, Kate* was Shakespeare's *The Taming of the Shrew,* parts of which were fitted out with song and dance as the core of the entire production. But *Kiss Me, Kate* did not dwell exclusively in old Padua; nor was it exclusively a musical-comedy adaptation of a Shakespeare comedy the way Rodgers and Hart had done earlier in *The Boys from Syracuse. Kiss Me, Kate* was also vibrantly modern—made so through the device of having a present-day theatrical troupe come to Baltimore to play the Shakespeare comedy. This play-within-a-play technique shifted the center of interest continually from the personal problems besetting the four principals in this company in today's world, to the marital problems of Petruchio and his shrewish wife, Kate, in yesterday's Padua. Within the performance of Shakespeare, the hero and heroine of today's world are able not only to express their own ambivalent feelings for each other but also to resolve those feelings successfully.

Never before or since did Porter have a fresher, more scintillating, and more imaginative text to work with. This was a libretto in which the songs need not be mere ornaments but had to be basic to the story line and to the characters and situations. In short, *Kiss Me, Kate* was a "musical play" as distinguished from "musical comedy." Facing such a challenge for the first time, Porter was able to touch heights he had never before reached as a composer—nor ever again, for that matter. Among his seventeen numbers were romantic and sensual songs, satirical songs, risqué songs, witty songs, nostalgic songs, parodies. Touching every possible base of song style and emotion, Porter proved himself in every style and mood at the top of his creative powers, both as a lyricist and as a composer. There is not a single weak number in a group whose elect include "So in Love," "Were Thine That Special Face," "Wunderbar," "Brush Up Your Shakespeare," "Always True to You in My Fashion," "I Hate Men," "Too Darn Hot," "Where Is the Life That Late I Led?" "I've Come To Wive It Wealthily in Padua."

After opening on December 30, 1948, *Kiss Me, Kate* went on to become the only Porter musical to exceed one thousand performances in New York. But this was only the beginning of its triumphant history. The national company, which opened in Los Angeles in July 1949, toured for three years. The musical was translated into eighteen languages to be performed in capitals around the world. It was the first American musical to be performed in Vienna, Berlin, Jugoslavia, Hungary, Czechoslovakia, Warsaw, and Iceland. It was also seen in Italy, Belgium, Switzerland, Denmark, Sweden, Israel, Japan, Turkey, Spain, and Brazil. It was also the first American musical comedy to be produced by a European opera house—the renowned Volksoper, in Vienna, where it remained in its repertory for over a decade.

Porter's musical-comedy career had begun with two shows about Paris. Fittingly enough, this is the way his career ended, rounding out the circle of his theatrical life neatly. His last two Broadway musicals had Parisian backgrounds: *Can-Can* in 1953 and *Silk Stockings* in 1955. For the first he wrote "I Love Paris" and for the latter "Paris Loves Lovers." To the end he was writing love songs to his favorite city. These last two Porter musicals (like the first two) were box-office successes, thereby ending his thirty-nine years on Broadway on a note of triumph.

Two scores for motion pictures and one for television—and then Porter was through forever. The two films were *High Society* and *Les Girls,* the first of which included his last hit song, "True Love." The television production *Aladdin* was a "special" broadcast over C.B.S. on February 21, 1958.

Porter's will to create was destroyed because for a number of years now he was losing his zest for life. Tragedy followed tragedy in rapid succession. First came the death of his beloved mother, Kate, on August 3, 1952. Learning that she was seriously ill, Porter rushed to Peru. She was unconscious when he arrived and she died without ever learning that her son was at her side. Hardly had Porter recovered from this shock when his wife, Linda, who had been suffering severely from emphysema, passed away, on May 20, 1953, in New York. He had her buried in Peru near his mother's grave, but with a space between them left vacant for himself.

His wife's death plunged him into a chronic loneliness for which he could find no cure. He tried to escape from his smothering melancholia through travel by going to Lisbon and then touring the Greek Islands on a chartered yacht in February of 1956. It did not take him long to realize that he could no longer revive his onetime stimulation and excitement in travel. Back in the United States, he had to undergo two more operations on his legs, his thirty-third operation taking place on February 14, 1958. But nothing could relieve him of the physical torture he was suffering. Then, because a bone tumor was threatening his life, his physicians came to the grim decision that the right leg had to be amputated. The operation, which Porter at first accepted with remarkable stoicism and calm, took place on April 3, 1958.

But the stoicism and the calm evaporated once Porter was faced with the problem of learning to walk with an artificial limb. He tried hard to overcome this problem at first by exercising every day in the gymnasium at the Harkness Pavilion and by getting instructions on the use of an artificial limb. But he soon lost heart in the whole endeavor, rejected the artificial limb for good, and depended upon the services of two valets to carry him around in his apartment.

From this point on, he withdrew more and more into utter isolation. Having completely lost his appetite for all those things that had once been such an inexhaustible source of excitement and exhilaration, he preferred to live as a recluse. He dozed a good deal of the time; he drank alcohol some of the time; occasionally he took a short automobile drive in the city. He discouraged visits from even close friends, but did permit one visitor at a time to share dinner with him. These dinners proved to be funereal affairs for the visitor. Porter would sit frozen at the table, confining his conversation to monosyllables, his face a reflection of utter despair. He picked now on one dish and now on another but actually ate almost nothing at all.

He was totally indifferent to the tributes and honors that were being conferred on him partly out of a genuine appreciation for what he had accomplished, partly with the hope of reviving his interest in his work. A monumental "Salute to Cole Porter" took place at the Metropolitan Opera House on May 15, 1960. Some of the most celebrated stars of stage and screen were on hand to sing his songs. The proceeds (about $65,000) were donated to the Children's Asthma Research Institute and Hospital. Porter refused to attend that affair. He also turned down the invitation to attend the commencement ceremonies at Yale University in June of 1960 when an honorary doctorate of humane letters was conferred on him. For the first time in its history, Yale was willing to confer the degree *in absentia*. A delegation, headed by provost Norman S. Buck, came from the university to Cole's apartment to perform the necessary ceremonies. Dr. Buck delivered a brief tribute in which he said: "You have achieved a reputation as a towering figure in the American musical theatre."

Porter also ignored the party celebrating his seventieth birthday which his friends, colleagues, and admirers celebrated at the Orpheum Theatre in downtown New York. (This place had been selected because it was then presenting a revival of *Anything Goes*.) Cole Porter songs were performed. Then the entire assemblage of several hundred joined in the singing of "Happy Birthday," led by Elsa Maxwell who had served that evening as mistress of ceremonies. But while all this was going on, Cole Porter was home alone, a helpless victim of despair and futility.

In 1964 he seemed to be able to summon enough of his energy and will to continue the practice he had followed for so many years—to go to his California mansion on June 21. In California, as in New York, he remained a recluse; the changed setting was incapable of removing him from his self-imposed isolation. Then, in October of 1964, he was taken to Santa Monica Hospital for the removal of a kidney stone. The operation was routine, and no complications set in. But two days after the operation, on October 15, at 11:05 P.M., he stopped breathing. His physicians insisted that death had come because Porter just did not want to live any longer.

His will had left specific instructions that there be no public funeral or memorial service, and his wish was carried out. His body was brought to Peru, Indiana, where the pastor of the First Baptist Church conducted a simple and brief service for a few relatives and friends. He read the passage "I am the resurrection and the life" from the Bible, and followed it with a quotation from the Lord's Prayer. This was what Porter had asked for. No memorial address was given. Then the body was placed where it belonged, between the two women who had meant the most to him throughout his life—his mother and his wife.

Songs from the Little Revues

Arthur Schwartz and Howard Dietz

During the 1920's, Broadway revues were becoming increasingly splen-diferous in their costuming, scenery, production numbers, and proliferation of stars in the casting. This overindulgence in visual display, ornate window dress-ing, and star-casting had been anticipated in 1919 by Florenz Ziegfeld when he produced the most lavish and the most expensively mounted edition of his *Follies* in its entire history up to that time—its production cost reaching the then all-time high for a revue ($100,000), and an array of stars that brought the weekly payroll to an equally unprecedented sum (over $20,000). That edition offered a caravan of performing talent that included Marilyn Miller, Eddie Dowling, Eddie Cantor, Van and Schenck, the Fairbanks Twins, Bert Williams, Johnny and Ray Dooley, and John Steel. Surely no array in revue history before

1919 could boast such an array of stellar performers! The 1919 *Follies* also provided an incomparably grandiose setting—and a parade of some of the most beautiful girls in America—for two Irving Berlin numbers, "A Pretty Girl Is Like a Melody" and "Mandy."

Ziegfeld was not a man to stand still. The affluent society of the 1920's led him to produce, season after season, ever bigger, ever more opulent editions. And his rivals followed suit: Irving Berlin with his *Music Box Revues;* George White with his *Scandals;* Earl Carroll with his *Vanities;* the Shuberts with the *Greenwich Village Follies.*

But if the 1920's were a period of unprecedented prosperity that were partial to gaudy display and lavish spending, they were also a time when wit, sophistication, iconoclasm, and a rejection of established conventions and mores flourished. It was a time for rebellion. Thus, within the theater, a similar rejection of old values could often be found. The 1920's saw the emergence of a revue far different from the kind being produced by the Ziegfelds and the George Whites of that day, a revue revolting against the meretricious, the expensive, the ornate, through the acceptance of standards more in tune to the spirit of the times.

The intimate, or little, revue—which stood in bold opposition to the methods and the values of the revues like the *Follies* and the *Scandals*—first came to being in 1922 with the *Grand Street Follies.* This production was mounted in a little auditorium called the Neighborhood Playhouse on Grand Street in New York's Lower East Side. The program of the first edition described the show as a "lowbrow show for high-grade morons," but, truthfully, it was slanted toward an intelligence quotient a good deal higher than that reached for by the more prosperous competitors on Broadway. Everybody connected with the *Grand Street Follies* was both young and unknown—two assets that helped encourage boldness, irreverence, and iconoclasm. These people had nothing with which to attract attention or publicity except their talent. But with their talent, together with their irrepressible energies, freshness of viewpoint, wit and mockery, these young people provided a salty commentary on those things that interested them the most. They taunted the Nobel Prize in the sketch "Ignoble Prize," a musical sketch presented in medieval style. They made sport of the Russian Art Theatre in a hillbilly sketch. They impudently mimicked the acting mannerisms and idiosyncrasies of some of the reigning kings and queens of the stage, opera, and ballet, including John Barrymore, Emily Stevens, Fanny Brice, Eva la Gallienne, Feodor Chaliapin, Pavlova, Elsie Janis, and Irene Castle. Current dances were ridiculed; Walt Whitman's poetry was lampooned. The whole adventure proved an escapade which the intelligentsia could relish. And the intelligentsia responded by beating a path down to New York's Lower East Side; the *Grand Street Follies* became the "in show," the show that was talked about so much that it simply had to be seen. Such success, of course, led to further editions of this unusual revue—downtown between 1923 and 1927, and from 1927 to 1929 on Broadway.

The *Grand Street Follies* popularized the concept of the little, or intimate, revue—a species that flourished on or near Broadway in the 1920's with shows like *The Garrick Gaieties,* the *Little Shows, Pins and Needles,* and numerous other similar (though frequently far less successful) productions.

The songs in the *Grand Street Follies* (like the sketches, individual routines, and production numbers) were consistently breezy and impudent in lyrics, and fresh and spontaneous in melodies. All the songs were the work of novices. One of them was Arthur Schwartz. He was then a young lawyer, to whom the writing of popular songs was a hobby. His first published song, "Baltimore, Md., You're the Only Doctor for Me," which had been released in 1923 while Schwartz was still a law student, found a place in the *Grand Street Follies of 1926.* (His total income from this first flight to creativity was a royalty of $8.42.) Four other Schwartz songs were heard in the same edition, including "Little Igloo for Two" and "Polar Bear Strut." Schwartz continued placing songs in intimate revues from then on, and within a few years he emerged as the most significant composer that the intimate revue had nursed from creative infancy.

Schwartz was born in Brooklyn, New York, on November 25, 1900. His father was a successful lawyer who was determined to have his son follow into the same profession. The father, then, had little sympathy or enthusiasm for Arthur's bent for music, which sought to express itself in every way it could. Arthur's first music-making consisted of whistling, blowing into combs, performing on the Jew's harp and the harmonica, and later on learning to play the piano by a hit-and-miss process. Since Arthur's older brother was being given a thorough musical training, the father insisted stoutly that one possible professional musician was one too much for the Schwartz family. Two musicians was unthinkable. Nevertheless, Arthur's musical interests could not be totally suppressed. He soon began inventing tunes, including a number of marches. While attending public school he earned spending money by accompanying silent films on the piano in a Brooklyn movie house.

His academic education took place in the elementary schools, then at Boys High School, all in Brooklyn. In 1916 he was enrolled in New York University. It was there that he received his first formal instruction in music by attending a class in harmony. He continued writing music in college, mostly marches and songs; a football song became a favorite of his fellow undergraduates. But music was not his sole interest at this time. Literature was also a passion. For a time he edited a school weekly, an experience that led him to entertain the ambition of becoming a newspaperman.

Upon receiving his bachelor of arts degree in 1920, he went on to Columbia University for a master's degree in literature. But whatever ambitions Arthur may have harbored at the time to pursue a career in journalism were permanently smothered by an intransigent father who insisted that Arthur study law. Schwartz, therefore, returned to New York University to attend its law school, supporting himself through the three years of law study by teaching English in high schools. In 1924, having become the recipient of a Phi Beta Kappa key at law school, he was admitted to the bar.

He spent that summer—the hiatus between ending his law studies and the beginning of his professional career in law—at a boys' camp in the Adirondack Mountains, Brant Lake Camp. The reason he went there was that a brilliant young (and still unknown) lyricist by the name of Lorenz Hart was a counselor, and Schwartz hoped to get Hart to write lyrics for his music. Some of the songs Schwartz and Hart wrote were used in the camp shows. One, "I Know My Girl by Her Perfume," graduated from the boys' camp into the vaudeville stage. Another, "I Love to Lie Awake in Bed," became successful on Broadway five years later, but under a different title, "I Guess I'll Have To Change My Plan," and with somebody else's lyrics.

That fall, Schwartz was employed by a busy and successful attorney who hated work and therefore preferred turning over his cases to his associates. Still fresh from law school, Schwartz found himself neck deep in a varied practice offering a considerable amount of legal experience. Schwartz was soon able to open a law office of his own and to make what then represented to him a handsome living. But, in spite of his success, his heart was not as much in law as in writing song tunes.

One day, in 1925, he invaded the offices of Harms to play some of his numbers for the composer he admired above all others, George Gershwin. Schwartz described the experience amusingly: "The *Rhapsody in Blue* was over a year old and universally famous. I had collaborated on a song about it in which I openly (and affectionately, I thought) quoted some of its best-known themes." At Harms he played this song for Gershwin. "As he stood behind me patiently, I played a long, aimless introduction and cleared my throat much more than was necessary. Suddenly I wished I had never asked for this preposterous audition, for I began to realize the full extent of my audacity in writing this lily-gilding song. My lyricist's very first lines now seemed to me in questionable taste, and it was difficult to sing them at all. But I finally started:

> O wonderful, wonderful Georgie
> What you've done to me!
> Your classical, jazzical orgy
> Just won't let me be!

"How *dared* I? I could go no further in spite of George's friendly insistence. When I told him I was withdrawing the composition right then and there, he didn't quarrel with my decision. Mercifully changing the subject, he asked me to play some of my other tunes. I found his reactions the warmest, most encouraging I had yet received."

Schwartz's entrance into the musical theatre was a modest one: a single song, "All Lanes Must Have a Turning," which was interpolated in 1924 in *Dear Sir,* a Broadway musical boasting a score by Jerome Kern. The following season was the one in which "Baltimore, Md., You're the Only Doctor for Me" was placed in the *Grand Street Follies,* while in 1926 Schwartz returned to the *Grand Street Follies* with four more numbers. In 1927 he was responsible for half the songs used in an intimate revue, *The New Yorkers,* whose run of about fifty performances spelled failure for both the revue and Schwartz. All these experiences did nothing to convince anybody that Schwartz was better at writing songs than he was in law, but he kept on trying nevertheless, even though Marie Cahill, for whom Schwartz played a song he had written especially for her, told him frankly: "That's terrible."

Nevertheless, *some* encouragement did come Schwartz's way and it proved heartening: to a starving man a slice of bread and butter represents a feast. The encouragement came from Lorenz Hart who urged Schwartz to give up his prosperous law practice and do nothing else but write songs. Hart also advised Schwartz to seek out a lyricist with whom he could establish a permanent partnership. Schwartz had such a lyricist in mind, as Hart spoke. Attending in 1928 a performance of a little revue, *Merry-Go-Round,* Schwartz had been impressed with the skill and smartness of its lyrics, the work of a young advertising man named Howard Dietz. Schwartz had worked briefly with Dietz in the writing of "All Lanes Must Have a Turning," but it was Dietz's work in *Merry-Go-Round* that really convinced Schwartz that this was the lyricist with whom he would like to work regularly and permanently. Schwartz now bombarded Dietz with telegrams and telephone calls to effect some kind of working arrangement, but Dietz remained unapproachable. Then a producer, Tom Weatherly, effected a meeting between the two young men, because he was planning to produce an intimate revue for Broadway and he wanted them to write some of its songs. Schwartz and Dietz did so, the consequence of which was not only the emergence of one of Broadway's formidable words-and-music teams but also the permanent withdrawal of the composer from the practice of law.

Like Schwartz, Howard Dietz was a native New Yorker, born in that city two years before Schwartz, on September 8. He attended the city public schools, and after that Townsend Harris Hall, where one of his fellow students was Ira Gershwin, the latter then planning to prepare himself for a career in teaching. In 1913 Dietz matriculated at Columbia College. During the next few years he became close friends with two fellow students who, in later years, became distinguished lyricists: Lorenz Hart and Oscar Hammerstein II. While attending college, Dietz indulged his bent for writing by contributing humorous pieces and poems to the college journal as well as to various newspaper columns, including the famous one conducted at that time by F. P. A. and Don Marquis. This literary flair brought Dietz not only a prize of $500 for a piece of advertising copy, in a contest sponsored by Fatima cigarettes, but also a job as an agency copywriter.

During World War I, Dietz served in the navy. Shedding his uniform after the war, he did some free-lance work in publicity for various motion-picture companies until he was made director of publicity and advertising of Goldwyn Pictures. When Goldwyn Pictures became M-G-M in 1924, Dietz served in an executive capacity—as director of publicity until 1940, when he was promoted to the office of vice-president of Loew's, Inc. It was Dietz who thought up the idea of using the head of a roaring lion as the symbol for M-G-M and borrowed the Latin aphorism *"Ars gratia artis."* And it was Dietz who was the father of a quip since credited to many others. Late one morning he stumbled across Louis B. Mayer in the elevator at Loew's Building. "Do you always come this late to work?" Mayer inquired sternly. Dietz replied: "Yes, but I always make up for it by going home early."

As a matter of fact, his witty comments have often been borrowed, and more often still quoted. It was Dietz who said that "a day away from Tallulah Bankhead is like a month in the country." It was Dietz who advised a leading M-G-M executive that the only way to reduce audience noise at the then-imminent premiere of *Gone With the Wind* was to dispense with the sale of peanut brittle. After consumption of a gourmet dinner that had made him ill, Dietz despatched, from the lavatory, a butler to his host, Lucius Beebe, to report dutifully that there was no need for concern: the fish had come up with the white wine, and the beef with the red wine. And when Dietz was informed by Arthur Schwartz that Schwartz had a banking account at the Irving Trust, Dietz replied haughtily: "*I* knew it when its name was still Isadore."

For Dietz (as for Schwartz) hours free from the daily routine of earning a living were spent in writing—but in Dietz's case, lyrics instead of music. Dietz's first appearance on the Broadway scene came with "Alibi Baby," for which Arthur Samuel had written the music, and which was sung in *Poppy,* a Broadway musical starring W. C. Fields. It was, however, an anonymous appearance, since Dorothy Donnelly, who was responsible for the text as well as for all the rest of the lyrics, refused to allow Dietz's name to be used either on the program or on the published sheet music of "Alibi Baby." One year later, however, Dietz received full credit for the lyrics of *Dear Sir,* music by Jerome Kern. When he was contracted for this choice assignment, Dietz visited Kern in Bronxville to listen to the music Kern had already completed for that show. Kern then asked Dietz to provide him with some lyrics within the next few days. In the mistaken belief that Kern expected him to have *all* the lyrics ready in that brief period of time, Dietz worked for three straight days with little time off for sleep or food in order to complete the lyrics for twelve songs, all of which he then turned over to the greatly amazed Kern.

Merry-Go-Round, an intimate revue in 1927, was Dietz's next assignment. This was the show that convinced Schwartz that Dietz was the man he needed as his lyricist in order to advance his own career on Broadway.

Having become convinced by Lorenz Hart to exchange law for music, and having finally effected a working arrangement with Dietz, Schwartz stumbled along for a while without making notable progress. Their first joint effort was *The Yankee Doodle Show* produced by Fortuno Gallo. Schwartz's services here consisted of ghostwriting, since he did not get credit for his music on the program. After that he was dispatched to Syracuse, New York, to doctor a musical that opened on Christmas Eve and closed down permanently a few days later— there being more people on the stage each performance than were in the audience.

In 1928 Tom Weatherly and James Pond joined forces to present sophisticated vaudeville shows each Sunday evening at the Selwyn Theatre. This venture sparked in Weatherly the idea to produce a revue for Broadway with similarly bright, shining, fresh materials. In this venture he soon found producing collaborators in Dwight Deere Wiman and William A. Brady, Jr. Finally, *The*

Little Show, as their first production was baptized, jelled and came to the Music Box on April 30, 1929, with a cast headed by Fred Allen, Libby Holman, and Clifton Webb. Most of the songs for this revue were the work of Schwartz and Dietz, and three had particular interest: "I've Made a Habit of You," "Little Old New York," and "I Guess I'll Have To Change My Plan." The last (as we already had occasion to remark in passing) was the same melody Schwartz had used for a Lorenz Hart lyric when they worked in a boys' camp back in 1924. Now given a new lyric, and a suave rendition by Clifton Webb, "I Guess I'll Have To Change My Plan" was well received; but its real success came later on in cabarets in an interpretation by Delyse and Clark. The real song standout in *The Little Show,* however, was "Moanin' Low," not by Schwartz and Dietz, but by Ralph Rainger, the pianist in the pit orchestra. Libby Holman delivered it in her low throbbing tones and Clifton Webb performed to its strains a slow, languorous dance, and the number always stopped the show.

The enthusiastic response of audiences and critics to *The Little Show,* together with its healthy financial returns, put the stamp of success indelibly on the songwriting team of Dietz and Schwartz. They did most of the songs for the second *Little Show* in 1930 (which, regrettably, was no match for its predecessors, either as an overall production or in the quality of the songs). But six weeks after the second *Little Show* had opened, Dietz and Schwartz were once again in full stride, this time with their songs for *Three's a Crowd,* another intimate revue starring Clifton Webb, Libby Holman, and Fred Allen —all doing the kind of dances, songs, and routines that had helped to make them so popular in the first *Little Show.* In *Three's a Crowd,* Libby Holman sang "Something To Remember You By," the best of the Dietz-Schwartz numbers in this score. It had originated as a comedy number entitled "I Have No Words," written for a London musical. Dietz and Schwartz still intended using it for a comic sequence in *Three's a Crowd,* even after new words had been written for it, and it bore a new title. But Miss Holman saw here the makings of a poignant ballad and induced the authors to allow her to sing it in a slow tempo and sultry mood. *Three's a Crowd* was also the place where another song classic was born, though it was not the work of Dietz and Schwartz: "Body and Soul," lyrics by Edward Heyman, Robert Sour, and Frank Eyton, and music by John Green. It had been written as special material for Gertrude Lawrence who had introduced it in London over the B.B.C. before it became a European hit. Max Gordon, the producer of *Three's a Crowd,* heard it in Europe, purchased the American rights, and used it in his revue—sung by Libby Holman and danced to by Clifton Webb and Tamara Geva.

With *The Band Wagon,* in 1931, Dietz and Schwartz became for the first time exclusive contributors of all the songs to a Broadway intimate revue. This development saw them create some of the finest songs of their careers. "I Love Louisa" was used for a Bavarian production number as a first-act finale. "New Sun in the Sky" was introduced by Fred Astaire. And the production's song masterpiece—indeed the most successful song Dietz and Schwartz ever wrote— was "Dancing in the Dark," sung by John Barker and danced to by Tilly Losch. This ballad came into the production while the show was already in rehearsal,

Schwartz suddenly feeling the need in a particular spot in the revue for "a dark song . . . somewhat mystical, yet in slow, even rhythm." The song was written in a single day. One of the two screen musicals inspired by *The Band Wagon* assumed the title of this number.

A good many historians of the musical theatre consider *The Band Wagon* score the best ever written for a revue. Even a serious music critic was impressed. Olin Downes, the music critic of *The New York Times,* wrote: "We have a composer whose melodic vein is not only graceful but characterized at its best by refinement and artistic quality. . . . He is able in many places to deliver a quality of musical workmanship which would command the respect of the most serious composer, and perhaps also the envy."

The Band Wagon was playing at the New Amsterdam Theatre where, in 1931, Jerome Kern was holding auditions for his musical, *Roberta.* One of those who came to try out for a part was a young singer, Kay Carrington, for whom Arthur Schwartz played the piano accompaniments. Though she did not get a job in *Roberta,* Kay Carrington subsequently captured a far more significant assignment outside the theatre. For on July 7, 1934, she married Schwartz, then became the mother of their son, Jonatha In 1954, following Kay's death, Schwartz married again—the former Mary U Hagen Scott.

With *The Band Wagon* Dietz and Schwartz became the most successful songwriting team produced by the intimate revue. They maintained that high station in 1932 with *Flying Colors,* for which they wrote such remarkable songs as "A Shine on Your Shoes," "Louisiana Hayride," and "Alone Together," and in 1935 with *At Home Abroad,* in which "Love Is a Dancing Thing" was introduced.

But in the world of the book-musical Dietz and Schwartz were far less fortunate, though frequently their songwriting efforts were still of a high order. *Revenge with Music,* in 1934, was a courageous attempt to give a musical-comedy treatment to *The Three-Cornered Hat,* the famous Spanish novel by Pedro de Alarcón which served Manuel de Falla for a ballet and Hugo Wolf for an opera. *Revenge with Music,* however, was sluggishly paced, and its high points of interest were too widely separated to avoid boredom. When this musical was revived for television about a quarter of a century later, it once again failed to make much of an impression. But *Revenge with Music* will not be forgotten because Dietz and Schwartz wrote for it two of their unforgettable song gems, "You and the Night and the Music" and "If There Is Someone Lovelier Than You."

Between the Devil, in 1937, was an even greater failure than *Revenge with Music.* After that, Dietz and Schwartz parted company for about a decade. Dietz concentrated his energies on his increasingly demanding duties as publicity and advertising director of M-G-M. Schwartz began working with a new lyricist, Dorothy Fields, with whom he wrote the songs for the musical *Stars in Your Eyes* in 1939. Schwartz also began branching out into a field other than the Broadway stage. (In 1936 he had wandered off temporarily into fresh areas by writing music for *The Gibson Family,* a serial that ran over the radio for thirty-four weeks.) There was a new world for Schwartz to conquer, the movies, and he made his first attack in 1939. Between then and 1946 he worked in Hollywood, writing songs for various motion pictures with such lyricists as Frank Loesser and Leo Robin, among others. He then graduated into the class of motion-picture producers, and was responsible for the Ira Gershwin–Jerome Kern screen musical, *Cover Girl,* and Cole Porter's screen biography, *Night and Day.*

Driving back to New York from California in 1946 gave Schwartz the idea for a revue that drew its material from American backgrounds. Back in New York he reunited with Howard Dietz; enlisted the writing talents of Moss Hart and several others for sketches; and purchased the rights for the title of John Gunther's book, *Inside U.S.A.,* then a best seller. Schwartz then went on to produce a revue with the same title, which opened on April 30, 1948. Dietz and Schwartz, working once again within the format of a revue, were apparently still able to produce a winner, for *Inside U.S.A.* ran for 399 performances. Its best musical numbers were a poignant ballad, "Haunted Heart," and a nimble patter song, "Rhode Island Is Famous for You," detailing the products for which each American state is famous.

And then—at long last!—Schwartz knew the taste of success in musical comedy (even if only modest successes). It came to him not with Dietz but with Dorothy Fields as his lyricist. In 1951 they wrote the songs for *A Tree Grows in Brooklyn,* a musical-comedy adaptation of Betty Smith's best-selling novel, following it in 1954 with their songs for *By the Beautiful Sea.* Both musicals starred Shirley Booth, and both showed a modest profit. Neither production, however, found Schwartz reaching the musical heights he had previously scaled with Dietz. But a gracious, infectious melodic charm is not totally absent from songs like "Love Is the Reason" and "I'll Buy You a Star" from *A Tree Grows in Brooklyn,* or "Alone Too Long" and "More Love Than Your Love" from *By the Beautiful Sea,* though none was successful.

Two later attempts to win success as a composer of musical comedies, with Howard Dietz once again as his lyricist, failed. *The Gay Life,* in 1961, attempted to bring Arthur Schnitzler's Viennese comedy, *Anatol,* to the American musical stage, while *Jennie,* in 1963, starred Mary Martin in a musical-comedy biography of the famous actress Laurette Taylor.

Whatever the reason—possibly their inability to acquire an excellent book —Dietz and Schwartz have proved incapable of repeating in musical comedy the triumphs they had once known in revues. But about this can there be no doubt: While the revue (and particularly the intimate revue) was in its heyday, the songwriting combination of Howard Dietz and Arthur Schwartz had few if any rivals.

Songs with Social Significance

Harold Rome

Just as the then-prospering intimate revue reflected many of the cynical and iconoclastic values of the 1920's, so it sometimes placed a mirror to the more sober, subdued social-conscious world of the 1930's.

The feverish, irresponsible days of the 1920's were over. The age of the collegiate and the flapper, the cynic and the supersophisticate, the free spender and the gay liver, was done with. The new decade—with its social unrest, economic depression, political upheavals—introduced a fresh outlook on life. Business and banks had crumbled under the smashing impact of an unprecedented stock-market crash. Tycoons committed suicide. Jobs became scarce, unemployment a chronic social disease. Apple vendors sprouted along Broadway; breadlines and soup kitchens tried to feed the ever-swelling army of the unemployed; free milk was dispensed by Mrs. William Randolph Hearst at Columbus Circle.

Vacant lots became dotted with shanties. Discontent infected the air: discontent of labor with management, which brought on a rash of strikes, picket lines, and clashes with police; discontent of World War I veterans who marched, like some bedraggled army, to Washington, D. C., only to be dispersed by the militia. Across the ocean, the menace of Nazism, fascism, and communism was throwing an ever-lengthening shadow not only across all of Europe but over America as well. In America splinter groups began peddling foreign ideologies and found takers by the droves.

This was the time when a people had to come face to face with the harsh realities of a decaying society, and assume a healthier and more realistic set of values for themselves. People became interested in social and political problems, in crusades, in the common man. They searched for social cure-alls, and became vitally concerned about the world as a whole. The government in Washington, D. C.—conscious as never before of its obligations to its citizens—embarked on a "new deal" under its recently elected president, Franklin Delano Roosevelt.

The intimate revue became a sounding board for the social and political problems of the times—with songs, production numbers, humor, and satire in which the day's overriding issues found voice. *Shoot the Works,* in 1931, was a Depression-born "cooperative revue": the box-office receipts were shared by the performers, one of whom was the social-conscious columnist Heywood Broun, who lumbered on and off the stage between scenes to make trenchant and flippant social comments. One of the hit numbers in the intimate revue *New Americana,* in 1932, was the song "Brother, Can You Spare a Dime?" (words by E. Y. Harburg, music by Jay Gorney), which outgrew the short-lived production to become something of a theme song for the Depression years. Another song identified with the Depression, "I've Got Five Dollars" by Rodgers and Hart, while introduced in 1931 in the musical comedy *America's Sweetheart,* found another resting place in 1936 in the intimate revue *The Show Is On.* "Let's Put Out the Lights and Go to Bed" (words and music by Herman Hupfeld) advised Depression-oppressed young couples to find solace in the bedroom if they had "no more money in the bank." This number was made popular by Harry Richman, Lili Damita, Bert Lahr, and the ensemble in the George White revue *Music Hall Varieties* in 1932. Even the more lavish revues were sometimes aware of the grim world around them. In the Moss Hart–Irving Berlin revue *As Thousands Cheer,* in 1933, one of the most deeply moving numbers was "Suppertime," in which Ethel Waters sang about a Negro woman preparing supper for her husband without being aware that he had just been lynched. In this same revue President Hoover was mercilessly lampooned, and one of the songs bore the line "We'll all be in heaven when the dollar goes to hell." In *Crazy Quilt,* in 1931, the hit song—by Mort Dixon, Billy Rose, and Harry Warren—was "I Found a Million Dollar Baby," which pointed up a truth for those Depression years that love could be found just as easily in a five-and-ten-cent store as in a more glamorous or grandiose setting.

The first completely social-conscious intimate revue was *Parade,* produced by the Theatre Guild in 1935—a project originally planned for the left-wing Theatre Union. The left-wing point of view lingered on in the Theatre Guild production—with sketches by George Sklar among others, lyrics by Sklar, Paul Peters, and Kyle Crichton, and music by Jerome Moross, all gentlemen with a strong progressive point of view to their thinking. Marc Blitzstein—three years before the production of his proletarian musical *The Cradle Will Rock*—contributed a number called "Send for the Militia." Other material satirized the New Deal and capitalism.

One intimate revue, above and beyond all others, fed on the problems of Depression, political reaction, fascism, governmental bureaucracy, and the greed of capitalism. This was *Pins and Needles,* in 1937, the most successful social-conscious revue ever produced. Its songs were the work of a then-unknown composer-lyricist who forthwith became a leading popular-song spokesman for those troubled years, a major contributor to the best social-conscious intimate revues of the times, Harold Rome.

He was born in Hartford, Connecticut, on May 27, 1908, one of five children to Louis and Ida Rome, the father being the president of the Connecticut Coal and Charcoal Company. Harold attended the public schools in Hartford, and from 1924 to 1926 Trinity College. He early learned to play the piano. While going to school he supported himself by performing in dance bands and playing for dancing classes. From Trinity College he progressed to Yale, where he was a member of the college orchestra with which he made four tours of Europe. Though the idea of becoming professionally involved in music for the rest of his life was remote from his mind, he studied music privately in New Haven. His ambition was to become a lawyer. In 1929, upon graduating from Yale with a bachelor of arts degree, he entered its law school. Within a year he knew that law did not interest him after all, and he transferred to the Yale School of Architecture. He completed his studies there in 1934, gaining a B.F.A. degree, and came to New York to make his way in architecture. But those were the searing years of depression. Opportunities for newcomers were nonexistent. Rome had to accept a job with a Works Projects Agency affiliate at a salary of $23.80 a week, but he supplemented this meager salary by earning a few dollars a week playing the piano. Eventually he found an opening as a draftsman with a well-known New York architect who offered Rome experience in architecture in place of money. The necessity of finding ways and means of supporting himself, while holding down a job that brought him no salary, was the impulse leading him to write his first songs—sometimes the lyrics, sometimes the music, frequently both.

One of his songs was liked so well by Gypsy Rose Lee that she helped him sell it. Another, "Horror Boys of Brooklyn," was used by the Ritz Brothers in a movie, *One in a Million.* There was apparently more money to be made in song-writing than in architecture—a truth that finally convinced Rome to give up architecture for good and devote himself to writing songs and to additional music study (the latter with Arthur Lloyd and Loma Roberts in piano, and Joseph Schillinger, Lehmann Engel, and Meyer Kupferman in composition). For a while, as he put it, he "shunted from pillar to post." Then, during the summer of 1935, he was employed at Green Mansions, an adult camp in the Adirondack Mountains, where his assignment was to write sketches and songs for productions mounted once a week at its little theatre. Rome returned to Green Mansions two summers after that, while spending the winters trying to market his songs with producers and publishers in New York, none of whom showed much interest. One of the criticisms the professions leveled against him most often was that most of his songs reflected too much of a social-conscious view to have commercial appeal. "People may be out of jobs and starving," they told Rome, "but when they listen to or sing songs they still want love songs."

But one person *was* impressed by Rome's social-conscious numbers. He was Louis Schaeffer, head of the International Ladies Garment Workers Union. The union had then recently acquired the Princess Theatre near the Broadway sector (the same Princess Theatre for which Kern, Wodehouse, and Bolton had written their remarkable musical comedies twenty years or so earlier) and had renamed it the Labor Stage. For this auditorium, the union was planning a social-conscious revue which (while recruiting materials from outsiders) would use only members of the union for the cast. Charles Friedman, who had been producing summer shows at Green Mansions, was asked to be director, and Harold Rome was called upon to write the songs.

A good many members of the union wanted to present a serious, realistic social drama—not a revue. In an attempt to get them to change their minds, Schaeffer, some of the writers, and several hired performers offered a preview of a show they had in mind—in a little studio on June 14, 1936. Even the most recalcitrant of the objectors was completely won over. Now came the grueling business of training amateurs to sing, dance, mime, do comedy routines, and so forth. This process consumed more than a year. Even then, the whole production was planned on a most modest scale, with the most humble intentions. Only weekend performances were announced in a three-hundred-seat theatre whose best ticket could be purchased for one dollar. Nothing more was expected from this show than to provide a few hours of entertainment to union members and their friends. For Harold Rome, this unpretentious show was a place where his songs could be heard for the first time within the periphery of Broadway.

Pins and Needles opened on November 27, 1937. It did not close that weekend nor the weekend after that. Word began winging all over the city about the bright, sparkling, witty way in which the current social and political scene was being handled in song, dance, and comedy. As *Variety* later commented: "The very people it mocked and ridiculed—the carriage trade—came in droves." Capitalism and fascism were ridiculed in "Doin' the Reactionary" and "Three Little Angels of Peace Are We." Unionism was glorified in a song like "It's Better with a Union Man." The advertising and promotion of cosmetics were the butt of "Nobody Makes a Pass at Me," the unhappy fate of a girl whose beauty is not enhanced by the products she uses. The reaction of Park Avenue to union tactics was satirized in "It's Not Cricket To Picket." The simple pleasures of the working class were romanticized in "Sunday in the Park" (a song for which Rome received the ASCAP award in 1937). Even love was exhibited from the point of view of a unionist in "One Big Union for Two." The opening chorus of the show, "Sing Me a Song with Social Significance" set the tone for a production described by the New York *Post* as a "Puckish proletarian romp."

Pins and Needles made stage history. No Broadway revue had up to this time boasted so extended a run (1,108 performances). In 1939 the show moved farther uptown to a larger auditorium, the Windsor. The name of the production might alter slightly from time to time: from *Pins and Needles* to *Pins and Needles of 1939* to *New Pins and Needles*. But the basic social and political consciousness prevailed, the material changing with the headlines. The satirical "Four Little Angels of Peace" (Hitler, Mussolini, Eden, and an unidentified Japanese) changed its cast as the years passed to replace Eden with Chamberlain after the Munich pact, and to include Stalin after the Hitler-Stalin nonaggression agreement. Munich, and "peace in our time," inspired the writing of a sketch, "Britannia Waives the Rules" (which was dropped when World War II broke out in 1939). The Nazi-Soviet pact inspired a hilarious takeoff on *The Mikado* in a sketch entitled *The Red Mikado*.

Pins and Needles proved that the social-political-conscious revue was good box office after all. For the next few years similar revues sprang up all along Broadway. Harold Rome became one of the principal contributors of songs to these productions. Max Gordon, the producer, contracted Rome to provide all the songs for *Sing Out the News,* a topical, political-social-slanted revue, in the writing of which George S. Kaufman and Moss Hart had a hand. The best thing in that show was Rome's song, "Franklin D. Roosevelt Jones," which Hazel Scott and a chorus sang in a Harlem christening scene. In 1938 this number received the ASCAP award, and during World War II it was the favorite among the British troops during the evacuation at Dunkirk.

Still with Rome's eyes focused on the daily newspaper, still with a viewpoint that veered sharply to the left, was the revue *Let Freedom Ring,* whose entire life-span consists of just eight performances. This being the period of America's initial involvement in World War II, Rome now directed his songwriting talent to the war effort by producing material for *Lunchtime Follies,* an intimate revue presented in defense plants. But not all of Rome's songs had a political or social ax to grind. Songs in such lavish revues as *The Streets of Paris* in 1940, *Star and Garter* in 1942, and the *Ziegfeld Follies of 1943* were aimed at a market concerned more with entertainment values than political ones.

In 1943 Rome was inducted into the army. Stationed at the New York Port of Embarkation, he worked in the Special Services division, writing material for and organizing army shows, and creating army-oriented songs. One of his productions made the round of army camps in the United States and the combat areas of the Pacific; another was seen in England.

The idea for a revue based mainly on the problems and experiences of the G.I. separated from the army and returned to civilian status once the war was over, began to revolve in Rome's mind while he was still in uniform. He saw it as a kind of peacetime *This Is the Army,* the Irving Berlin all-soldier show. Rome's project was realized only after he had been separated from the service. As *Call Me Mister,* this revue opened at the National Theatre on April 18, 1946, where it stayed for 734 performances before being the source from which a motion picture was made in 1951 with Dan Dailey and Betty Grable.

Much of the material of the stage revue *Call Me Mister* concerned itself with the necessary and often painful readjustment of young people to civilian status in numbers like "Goin' Home Train," "Little Surplus Me," and "Military Life." Some numbers revealed a strong interest in social and political problems, making the revue a legitimate offspring of the little revues to which Rome had been such a significant contributor before the war. "The Senator's Song" was a takeoff on reactionary Southern senators. "The Face on the Dime," introduced by Lawrence Winters, was a poignant tribute to the memory of President Roosevelt. "The Red Ball Express" was a bitter indictment of race prejudice: it told of a Negro G.I., who had distinguished himself in the Transportation Corps in the army, being the only man denied a civilian trucking job because of the color of his skin.

But the big song from *Call Me Mister* had neither political nor military nor social interest. It was a hilarious travesty on the craze for South American songs and dances: "South America, Take It Away." This was something Rome had written some years before *Call Me Mister* had even been a gleam in his eye—a time when the vogue for Latin-American rhythms was at its heights. It could not find a place in any show, and so Rome had put it away. When something special was needed for Betty Garrett in *Call Me Mister,* Rome suggested using "South America, Take It Away"—hesitantly, to be sure, since he felt the song was now dated. The producer, however, liked it; Betty Garrett gave it a stunning presentation; and the song became *the* hit of the whole production.

Rome had another big song hit in 1947, "The Money Song," which had been written for a musical that expired out of town. The reason the song did not die with that show was that the Andrews Sisters recorded it for Decca and it became a best seller.

By the mid-1940's, all varieties of revue were on their way out; a composer and lyricist who specialized in writing material for revues now had to think exclusively in terms of book-shows. Arthur Schwartz and Howard Dietz had been unable to make this transition with the kind of success their great talent deserved. Harold Rome enjoyed a kindlier fate, though not before he, too, had experienced a good deal of fumbling and mishaps.

Rome's first attempt at musical comedy had come while he was still a prime contributor to the social-conscious revue *The Little Dog Laughed,* which expired in Boston after preliminary dismal tryouts in Atlantic City. After that Rome wrote the scores for *Give a Viva* (book by Erskine Caldwell) in 1941; *Calub Catlum's America* in 1942; and *That's the Ticket* in 1948. All proved failures. An attempt to return to success in the medium in which he had proved himself so decisively—the revue—came in 1949 with *Pretty Penny,* which boasted sketches by Jerome Chodorov, was directed by George S. Kaufman, and was choreographed by Michael Kidd. *Pretty Penny* played the summer circuit for twelve weeks without ever reaching Broadway. Contributions to two more revues, Mike Todd's *Peep Show* and *Bless You All,* in 1950 on Broadway did little to remove the taste of failure which Rome had been experiencing ever since *Call Me Mister.*

But beginning with 1950 came four musical comedies which enjoyed varying degrees of success: *Wish You Were Here* in 1952; *Fanny* in 1954; *Destry
Rides Again* in 1959; and *I Can Get It for You Wholesale* in 1962.

Wish You Were Here was a musical version of *Having Wonderful Time*,
Arthur Kober's Broadway comedy about romance in an adult camp in the Berk-
shire Mountains. The title song became Rome's biggest song hit up to that time,
represented on "Hit Parade" for twenty weeks, and selling over a million discs
in Eddie Fisher's recording for RCA-Victor. Second in importance in this score
was "Where Did the Night Go?" Rome had considerable difficulty in devising
a number for the show to follow the evening dance in the social hall. One evening he was entertaining some friends at his home when one of them happened
to murmur the cliché, "Where did the night go?" Rome knew at once he had
found both the title and the idea for the song he needed, and he wrote it the
same night.

Rome also did well with the title song of *Fanny*, another creation that did
not come easily. This was the love song which the hero sang to his girl, even
while he knew he was about to abandon her to go off to the sea. The song, then,
had to be tender while pointing up the fact that the hero was something of a cad.

Fanny, which S. N. Behrman and Joshua Logan adapted from a trilogy of
plays by Marcel Pagnol, starred Ezio Pinza, the onetime star of the Metropolitan
Opera, in his most important Broadway role since *South Pacific*, the Rodgers and
Hammerstein triumph. When *Fanny* was made into a movie, with Charles Boyer
taking over the role created on the stage by Pinza, all the songs were deleted;
but the title number was used as a recurring theme in the background music.
This boycott of Rome's score was to be regretted, for it included several highly
effective numbers (though none became popular), the ballad "To My Wife,"
for example "Love Is a Very Light Thing," and "Be Kind to Your Parents."

Destry Rides Again was a "Western musical" starring Andy Griffith, based
on a story by Max Brand (which had previously been made into the motion
picture starring Marlene Dietrich, where she introduced "See What the Boys in
the Back Room Will Have"). Here the top numbers included "Anyone Would
Love You" and "I Know Your Kind."

I Can Get It for You Wholesale, Jerome Weidman's musical-comedy adaptation of his own racy novel, was the musical in which Barbra Streisand made
her Broadway stage bow, proving herself at once a comedienne of uncommon
talent. Otherwise, a poignant love song of a man to his wife, "Have I Told You
Lately?" and "The Sound of Money" were the main song attractions.

After *I Can Get It for You Wholesale*, came *The Zulu and the Zayda* in
1965, with Menasha Skulnik as its star. This was not a musical comedy, but a
"play with music," for which Rome contributed about a dozen numbers, the
most interesting being "It's Good to Be Alive" and "River of Tears." *The Zulu
and the Zayda* could survive on Broadway for only 179 performances.

Rome, whom friends like to call "Hecky," was married to Florence Miles
on February 3, 1939. For a time they occupied a luxurious penthouse apartment
on Washington Square overlooking Greenwich Village. Subsequently, they

moved to an even more luxurious apartment on upper Fifth Avenue which Rome has overcrowded with valuable paintings and African sculpture, which he has been collecting for many years. He has also done a good deal of painting himself. The painter and the composer in Harold Rome became one in a unique experiment in 1964 at an exhibition at the Marble Arch Gallery in New York. Forty of Rome's paintings were exhibited; but to twelve of these Rome had written songs. This dozen was hung in a separate room where the songs were heard over a loud speaker, the purpose being to look at the paintings and listen to the songs simultaneously. The idea for this kind of an exhibition came to him during a painful two-year period when he was between shows and when he had to deflect his creative energies into painting. "I hate to be not working," he explained, "and I loved the challenge, and also the fact that nobody in the whole world has ever done this before."

GREAT MEN OF AMERICAN POPULAR SONG

Songs with the Blues–II

Harold Arlen
and E. Y. Harburg and Johnny Mercer

The title Edward Jablonski used for his biography of Harold Arlen is *Happy With the Blues*. If Arlen is "happy with the blues," he is justifiably not at all happy being labeled as a composer of the blues. A creator who has produced songs with the variety, technique, style, mood, and structure of, say, "Over the Rainbow," "Last Night When We Were Young," "The Man That Got Away," "I Love a Parade," "I've Got the World on a String," and "It's Only a Paper Moon"—to mention just a few—cannot be conveniently pigeonholed. Few have written more eloquent love ballads in the past quarter of a century or so than Arlen, just as few have rivaled him in writing expressive and dramatic narratives, or songs aflame with evangelistic fervor. Besides, Arlen has written only one song that can be said to be more or less in an authentic blues style: "I Gotta Right To Sing the Blues," and only one in which the twelve-measure scheme of the blues is adhered to, "Blues in the Night." All the other so-called blues by Arlen are in the Arlen manner, rather than in the image of Negro folk songs or New Orleans Jazz even when the word "blues" is found in his titles. Harold Arlen has always been much too original a composer to produce his music from a single matrix.

Arlen's songs are cut to their own measure, rather than adhering strictly to the three-line stanza, and three four-measure musical phrases as dictated by blues tradition. George Gershwin was one of the first, if not *the* first, to recognize how original in structure was "Stormy Weather" by pointing out that in the long arched melody of the chorus there is no repetition of any single phrase from the opening measure right through the words "keep rainin' all the time"—something without precedent either in blues writing or in popular songs. The chorus of "Ill Wind" extends for forty measures instead of the expected thirty-two; while "One for My Baby" has forty-eight measures. "The Man That Got Away" expands to sixty-two measures, "Black Magic" to seventy-two!

Yet for all their apparent avoidance of traditional blues techniques, the blues of Harold Arlen are among the greatest written since the time of W. C. Handy. The essence of the blues, if not the strict formula; the spirit, if not the letter, can be found here. This is music springing from the bosom of New Orlean's Storyville; it seems to rise and soar from the cornet of a Buddy Bolden, the trumpet of Joe "King" Oliver, or the plangent voice of Ma Rainey or Bessie Smith. There is a good deal of the Negro as well as New Orleans in those blues, a good deal of the lamentation of an oppressed people in a cruel world, even if the structure is different from authentic blues.

But Arlen's blues is a music springing from another source, too: from the Hebrew race of which Arlen is a member. These are people who have created sorrow music of their own through the centuries. Listening to Arlen sing his own blues is to recognize how skillfully, how inevitably, he combines the two strains in his creative art: the Negro and the Hebraic. "When he sang," as one of his friends put it, "it was as if he were praying or in a spell." This composer is a man whose father was a cantor in a synagogue and who, in his own boyhood, had participated as a choirboy in synagogal services. There is in Arlen's expansive melodies a good deal of the undulating line of a synagogal chant, a good deal of a cantor's improvisations.

New Orleans had a profound influence on Arlen's boyhood when he started out as a jazz performer and arranger, and this influence never deserted him. As for the Hebrew race and the synagogue—to these he was born. His real name was Hyman Arluck when he came to the world in Buffalo, New York, on February 15, 1905, one of a pair of twins, the first offspring of Samuel and Celia Arluck. (His twin brother died soon after birth.) Since the father was the cantor at the synagogue, synagogal music and Jewish folk songs were influences to which the child Hyman was subjected from his very beginnings, though recordings of opera arias were also strong favorites in the Arluck household.

Hyman was only five when he was recruited for the synagogue choir officiated over by his father. At nine the boy began taking piano lessons with local teachers. It did not take the student long to come to the realization that he detested scales and exercises, nor to recognize that popular music appealed to him much more than the serious variety. By the time he was twelve Hyman deserted Chopin for piano "rags," after having come upon "Indianola," which fascinated him no end, and whose syncopations instantly converted him into a jazz fan. He now began collecting and listening to jazz recordings. "My big interest was in the jazz instrumentation of the day," as he later recalled. "I even ran away from home once to hear the Memphis Five."

Making music had also become a necessity. He played in the public-school orchestra and sang in school productions. Schoolwork was neglected to the point where, in 1921 (in his second year at Hutchinson Central High School), Arlen was dropped from the register. He was now on his own, and could play and sing with Buffalo jazz bands to his heart's content. Except for a brief span at a vocational high school, where he was neither happy nor successful, this marked the end of his academic life.

Cantor Arluck regarded such developments askance. Since he was a total stranger to the world of popular music, he sought out a local young man who had already made his mark in popular music as a lyricist: Jack Yellen. He wanted Yellen to convince Hyman to go back to school and get a college degree. Yellen auditioned the boy. "It was a pretty good indication," Yellen says, "that he was his father's son. He would never be the doctor or lawyer that his father wanted him to be. Afterwards, I called his father and the first thing I said was, 'It's all your fault, he's going to be a musician.' "

Fifteen years old, Hyman Arluck—or Harold Arlen, as we shall henceforth call him—began earning his living playing the piano in Buffalo cafés, in roadhouses, and movie theatres. He formed his own jazz combo called the Snappy Trio which, in spite of the youth of its members, found a number of engagements in the city's red-light district. Before long this group expanded into a five-man ensemble, the Southbound Shufflers, and after that into the Buffalodians, comprising eleven men. Harold Arlen was not only pianist and vocalist but also arranger. "I could always improvise," as Arlen explains, "and I loved to invent unconventional tunes for the men in the band who couldn't do anything but follow the written melody. I wanted them to get off it and sound like somebody from New York." It was Arlen's fresh and novel arrangements that helped bring the Buffalodians to summer resorts, excursion boats, and ballrooms. Then the troupe extended its operations by appearing for extended engagements in Cleveland, Pittsburgh, and in 1925 at the Palace Theatre and the Monte Carlo Night Club in New York City. Meanwhile, the performer-singer-arranger had slowly begun to feel his strength as a composer. Two nondescript songs were written in 1924; two more, in 1925. None was published. Arlen's first piece of published music was a blues fantasy for piano, *Minor Gaff*, which he wrote in collaboration with Dick George, and which appeared in 1926.

He attracted the interest of a bandleader, Arnold Johnson, who hired him as a member of his own group. Arlen made arrangements for and appeared as vocalist with the Johnson band during its appearances at the Central Park Hotel, and in the pit of the George White *Scandals of 1928*. Before 1928 ended, Arlen had separated himself from the Johnson band to appear in vaudeville as vocalist and pianist. Two of his songs now finally got published. The second of these, "The Album of My Dreams," brought Arlen a royalty check of $900, largely due to the fact that Rudy Vallee had recorded it for RCA-Victor.

In 1929 Vincent Youmans took note of Arlen's talent by hiring him as a rehearsal pianist for *Great Day,* a show for which Youmans had written the music and served as producer. At one rehearsal Arlen amused himself while waiting for a routine to begin by improvising a tune of his own on a "vamp" he was soon required to play. Will Marion Cooke, who conducted the Negro chorus in that show, liked what he heard and urged Arlen to shape it into a song. Arlen did so, and Ted Koehler provided the lyrics. That song was "Get Happy," aptly described as a rousing "hallelujah song." It brought Arlen a songwriting contract with a publishing subsidiary of Remick. It also lifted Arlen, the composer, into the Broadway theatre for the first time. "Get Happy" was sung by Ruth Etting in the *9:15 Revue,* which had a brief stay on Broadway. The song was published by Remick, and though the revue in which it had been introduced was a failure, it had quite a substantial sale in sheet music and recordings. Drawing a regular weekly salary from his publishers and accumulating royalties from "Get Happy" made it possible for Arlen to give up performing for composing.

With Ted Koehler now his full-time lyricist, Arlen got an important assignment in 1930: to write songs for shows mounted at Harlem's inimitable night spot, the Cotton Club. This was the club that, since its opening in 1923, had become the Mecca to which streamed all true believers in jazz, come to pay homage to such jazz greats as Duke Ellington, Jimmie Lunceford, and Cab Calloway and their respective bands, and to such immortal interpreters of songs as Aida Ward, Ethel Waters, and Adelaide Hall. The early Cotton Club songs had been produced by Lew Leslie, and its songs had been written expressly for these productions by Jimmy McHugh, composer, and Dorothy Fields, lyricist. Then Dan Healey replaced Leslie as producer, and McHugh and Fields decided to transfer their songwriting activities to Broadway. Mainly on the strength of "Get Happy," Dan Healey called on Arlen and Koehler to replace McHugh and Fields. Their first assignment came in 1930 with two songs. In 1931 Arlen and Koehler had their first Cotton Club hit songs with "Between the Devil and the Deep Blue Sea" (introduced by Aida Ward) and "I Love a Parade" (used as a production number). For the *Cotton Club Parade,* in 1932, Arlen and Koehler wrote "I've Got the World on a String," and, as a specialty for Cab Calloway with obeisance to his celebrated number "Minnie the Moocher," Arlen and Koehler also wrote "Minnie the Moocher's Wedding Day."

The last Cotton Club show in which Arlen was involved saw the birth of his masterpiece, "Stormy Weather," one of the greatest blues ever published. In his biography of Arlen, Edward Jablonski reveals that the song was "all but tossed off . . . at a party." Since this number had been originally planned for Cab Calloway, Arlen kept Calloway's singing style very much in mind in fashioning his melody. As it turned out, Cab Calloway could not appear in that production. Both Arlen and Koehler now agreed that the song really belonged to a female blues singer. Ethel Waters was the one they had in mind, and they used all their powers of persuasion to get Ethel Waters to appear in the Cotton Club production to introduce their number. She did, and her rendition was a sensation. But the song had already become famous even before Miss Waters had sung her first note, having previously been popularized in a best-selling RCA-Victor recording by Leo Reisman and his orchestra with Arlen himself doing the vocal.

In her autobiography Ethel Waters recalls the singing of "Stormy Weather" as the turning point in her life. "When I got out there in the middle of the Cotton Club floor . . . I was singing the story of my misery and confusion . . . the story of the wrongs and outrages done to me by people I had loved and trusted. . . . I sang 'Stormy Weather' from the depths of my private hell in which I was being crushed and suffocated." Other performers would later give unforgettable renditions of "Stormy Weather"—Lena Horne, for example, who in 1933 (though only sixteen years old at the time) was allowed to introduce another Arlen-Koehler blues gem, "Ill Wind," in a Cotton Club production. Nevertheless, whoever else may sing it—and however well—"Stormy Weather" will probably always be remembered as Ethel Water's song.

His successes at the Cotton Club notwithstanding, Harold Arlen did not confine his creativity exclusively to nightclubs. With Jack Yellen as his lyricist he created his first complete score for a Broadway book-show. This was in 1931 with *You Said It* in which Lou Holtz and Lyda Roberti headed the cast. This show went over well enough to survive almost two hundred performances. But what made the most vivid impression was the song "Sweet and Hot," introduced by Lyda Roberti, who subsequently made it her musical signature.

In 1932 Arlen returned to vaudeville to appear as vocalist-pianist in an act starring Ethel Merman. But that year of 1932 was made more significant still for him through the writing of "I Gotta Right To Sing the Blues" interpolated into the Earl Carroll *Vanities* editions of that year. One of the chorus girls in that revue was Anya Taranda, a Powers model. She caught Arlen's eye and heart. The romance thus begun led several years later (on January 8, 1937) to marriage, in Harrison, New York.

In 1933 Arlen was starred in an act called *Stormy Weather* where, supported by a Negro chorus, he presented not only the title number but also other of his blues hits. After opening at the Radio City Music Hall on May 19, this act toured the Loew's vaudeville circuit. This was also the year when Arlen wrote his first songs for Hollywood for the motion picture *Let's Fall in Love*. Three of the five songs Arlen and Koehler wrote for this production were finally used; one was retained merely as material for the background music; and one, the title number sung by Ann Sothern, was a standout.

Now in a high-income bracket, and head over heels in love with Anya, Harold Arlen "settled down to the life of a successful composer," as Jablonski has written. "He dressed well, if conservatively; he began to sport a bachelor button in his lapel (referring to it as a 'blue-ie'). And for a time he even carried a cane. . . . The book cases in his apartment soon filled up. Reading the New York papers opened new vistas to Arlen." In fact, Arlen became a voracious reader. "His tastes ran to philosophical works. . . . He favored aphoristic books. . . . Bob Wachsman described Arlen's reading habits: 'He was a dipper.

He might even be reading eight books at a time, mostly non-fiction.' " Arlen at the same time was also extending his musical horizon by studying harmony with Simon Bucharoff.

But he had very little of the brashness, very little of the loud voice and the egomaniac attitudes, so often accompanying success. Isaac Goldberg (George Gershwin's first biographer) was made forcefully aware of this fact when he interviewed Arlen in 1934 for a newspaper. "In one respect, as even a casual meeting may suggest, the man and his music are one: well-bred, soft, quietly confident, ingratiating. I believe, indeed, that 'ingratiating" is the keyword. About Arlen or his music there seems to be nothing raucous. You feel it in his voice as he sings his pieces; you get it even from his touch on the piano. . . . He is a well-set youth . . . fair, blue-eyed (unless my eyes are none too certain), easy of motion and manner. . . . Arlen is decidedly of the new generation. He is a fine pianist and not at all a bad singer. . . . He plays . . . as unostentatiously as he sings—as unconsciously as most people write, in privacy, a letter."

A single song, placed in an unsuccessful revue (*Americana* in 1932) was to put a finger on Arlen's future as a composer. "Satan's Li'l Lamb" was not a particularly distinguished achievement. ("Satan's Li'l Lamb" was originally called "Satan Had a Little Lamb" but was changed to accommodate the melody.) Its sole importance lies in the two men who collaborated on the lyrics. Each would in the future work individually with Arlen, and each would in time provide Arlen with the word-stimulus he needed to scale the heights in the writing of both the blues and ballads. These two must always be numbered among the six or so of the greatest lyricists America has produced. One was E. Y. Harburg, known as "Yip" ("Yip" is a contraction of "yipsel" or "squirrel"). The other was John H. Mercer, most often referred to as "Johnny."

E. Y. ("Yip") Harburg became Ted Koehler's immediate successor as Arlen's most important lyricist. "Yip" was born in New York City on April 8, 1898. The ghettos of the New York East Side were the setting for a boyhood spent in poverty, at times even in squalor. At P.S. 64, Harburg distinguished himself by writing for the school paper and winning prizes in amateur oratory contests. An excellent student, Harburg had no difficulty gaining admission to Townsend Harris Hall, a school for pupils with outstanding academic ratings. Despite the exacting standards set by this high school, and the backbreaking daily assignments it imposed on its students, Harburg somehow seemed to find the time to help support his family by selling newspapers in the streets and by lighting some of the city streets for Consolidated Edison.

At Townsend Harris, Harburg was coeditor of a literary column in the school paper. His fellow editor was another young man later destined to distinguish himself with song lyrics—none other than Ira Gershwin. Their friendship continued on at the College of the City of New York where Ira stayed just one year while "Yip" remained to get his bachelor of science degree. During his college years, Harburg contributed verses and humorous pieces not only to college publications but also to the renowned newspaper column conducted by

F. P. A. in the New York *World* and to other columns. He also joined Ira Gershwin in providing material for amateur shows put on at the Christadora House Settlement on the East Side.

Upon being graduated from college in 1918, Harburg was sent to South America to represent an American firm. It went out of business almost as soon as Harburg arrived. Left to his own resources, he took one job after another, including one as journalist for a paper in Montevideo, Uruguay. He stayed in South America for about three years, accumulating enough money to form a business of his own, the Consolidated Electrical Appliance Company, which he organized after returning to New York in 1921. He did well enough to be able to support a wife, Marjorie Ernest, whom he married in 1923, and their two children, when they came. In all, he stayed in business eight years. But all that time he kept his fingers and mind nimble writing verses. Then came the stock-market crash and the Depression, which sent Harburg's business toppling in ruins around his ears, leaving him in debt to the discordant tune of a quarter of a million dollars. After that, as he put it, "I had my fill of this dreamy abstract thing called business and I decided to face reality by writing lyrics."

He teamed up with a young but already successful popular composer, Jay Gorney, who had liked Harburg's verses in the newspapers. They placed six songs in Earl Carroll's revue *Sketch Book* in 1929. This, in turn, landed them a contract for Paramount Pictures. There they wrote songs which were interpolated in *Glorifying the American Girl, Roadhouse Nights,* and *Moonlight* and *Pretzels.*

For the Broadway stage (collaborating on his lyrics with Ira Gershwin), Harburg wrote the words for Vernon Duke's first popular song. Only two years later Vernon Duke created his first and probably his most celebrated standard, "April in Paris," with lyrics by Harburg. It did poorly when first introduced by Evelyn Hoey in *Walk a Little Faster.* Some years passed before the song finally caught on, on the impetus of a successful Liberty recording by Marian Chase, a society chanteuse.

There were other assignments for Harburg. In 1931, with Gorney, he wrote some numbers for the intimate revue *Shoot the Works;* and in 1932 his lyrics for still another intimate revue, *Americana,* were set to music by Gorney, Vernon Duke, Burton Lane, and Harold Arlen (the Arlen-Harburg song being "Satan's Li'l Lamb"). It was this *Americana* revue that not only brought Harburg and Arlen together for the first time as co-workers but earned Harburg his first substantial song hit, "Brother, Can You Spare a Dime?" (music by Gorney). Rex Weber and a male chorus introduced it, following which it became a kind of unofficial theme song for the Depression years. This was the first of many lyrics in which Harburg began to betray a strong social consciousness, the roots for which reached far back into the soil of his impoverished boyhood days on the East Side.

The collaboration of Arlen and Harburg—begun inauspiciously with "Satan's Li'l Lamb"—continued in 1932 with "If You Believe in Me," used as a recurrent background theme in the nonmusical Broadway stage production *The Great Magoo.* That show had a life of just eleven performances, but the song

had a much sturdier existence. Retitled "It's Only a Paper Moon," it was interpolated into the movie *Take a Chance,* to become the first of the Arlen-Harburg
standards.

In 1934 Harburg teamed up with Ira Gershwin to write lyrics for a major
Broadway assignment, the successful revue *Life Begins at 8:40.* Arlen wrote the
music for all nineteen songs, a score that included such items as "What Can You
Say in a Love Song?" "Fun To Be Fooled," and "Let's Take a Walk Around the
Block."

One year later, Harburg and Arlen shared Lawrence Tibbett's estate in
Beverly Hills to work for the movies. It was for Tibbett, the distinguished baritone of the Metropolitan Opera before he became a star in the movies, that they
wrote the very memorable ballad "Last Night When We Were Young." Tibbett
wanted to sing it in the motion-picture *Metropolitan,* but it was dropped out of
the final print. Tibbett remained interested in this number, sang it at some of
his concerts, and recorded it for RCA-Victor. One day, Judy Garland (then sixteen) came upon this recording in a pile of old discs. She fell in love with the
song, recorded it for Capitol, and tried (unsuccessfully) to get it interpolated into her own screen musical, *In the Good Old Summertime.* Frank Sinatra was another who was partial to this ballad, but who also failed to get it into one of his
motion-picture musicals (*Take Me out to the Ball Game*). But even without the
benefits of a presentation in motion pictures, "Last Night When We Were
Young" became a Harburg-Arlen favorite with both the general public and its
own creators. Harburg considers this one of the best lyrics he ever wrote, while
Arlen regards it as one of his personal preferences among his own melodies. It is
truly paradoxical that the only song of permanent value that Harburg and Arlen
created during this period in Hollywood should have never reached the screen.

A married man now, Arlen acquired a house on Lookout Mountain Road
in Laurel Canyon. But he could not stay there long. He had to make a hurried
return to Broadway to write songs for a new stage musical, *Hooray for What?* in
1937. Ed Wynn was its star, playing the part of a horticulturist who, in trying
to invent a gas able to destroy insects, comes upon a lethal instrument of war
sought after by the foreign powers. One or two songs had more than passing
interest: "I've Gone Romantic on You" and the blues "Moanin' in the Mornin'."

With *Hooray for What?* entrenched on Broadway, Arlen returned to his
new home in California to work again for the movies. At this time, M-G-M was
planning one of its most ambitious and lavish productions to star the then-rising
star Judy Garland, aged thirteen: a filming of that hardy classic for young people,
L. Frank Baum's *The Wizard of Oz.* As producers of this movie, Mervyn Le Roy
and Arthur Freed had no intention of using the old score from a successful 1903
stage adaptation of this fantasy. On Freed's recommendation, Harburg and Arlen
were contracted to write new songs. They did a dozen numbers, two of them
being top echelon: "We're Off To See the Wizard of Oz" and the song that
made Judy Garland a star of stars and brought Harburg and Arlen an Academy
Award, "Over the Rainbow."

The long, windswept melody of "Over the Rainbow" came suddenly to
Arlen as he was driving in his car from Beverly Hills to Hollywood. He jotted

it down on paper quickly. As he first conceived it, the song was in a slow tempo, with a rich-sounding chordal accompaniment. This did not quite appeal to Harburg who felt that the song seemed more appropriate for a Nelson Eddy than for a thirteen-year-old Judy Garland. Arlen and Harburg decided to ask Ira Gershwin's opinion. Gershwin suggested a quicker tempo and a thinner harmonic treatment. Arlen tried it out that way, and all concerned were delighted with the result. Now that the melody had acquired its true identity, Harburg went to work on the lyrics.

Strange to say, the song was not well liked by the powers at M-G-M. On three different occasions they tried to delete it from the production. Arthur Freed, however, was thoroughly convinced of its value and importance; and it was through his stubborn, intransigent decision to use it that the song was finally allowed to stay in.

As it turned out, "Over the Rainbow" became the crowning song-success of *The Wizard of Oz,* one of the highest altitudes of achievement by Arlen and Harburg, and a number henceforth to become Judy Garland's personal theme song. "It has become a part of my life," Judy told an interviewer. "I have sung it time and again, and it's still the song that's closest to my heart."

From time to time during the next few years, Arlen continued working with Harburg on and off—both in Hollywood and on Broadway. But this did not prevent him from working with other lyricists as well. An association of far-reaching consequence to Arlen as a master of the blues was established in 1941 when Johnny Mercer joined Arlen in writing songs for the motion-picture musical *Blues in the Night.*

Between the time he had worked with Arlen for the first time on "Satan's Li'l Lamb" and almost a decade later when he resumed a writing partnership with Arlen, Johnny Mercer had grown from a novice to full stature as a songwriter with a solid reputation. That reputation was gained in 1933 with "Lazybones," to Hoagy Carmichael's melody—popularized over the radio and on records by Rudy Vallee and Ben Bernie among others. This song—followed immediately by "Goody Goody," a Benny Goodman specialty—was Mercer's admission to Hollywood. It did not take him long to develop his career further in the movie capital. In 1936 Bing Crosby sang "I'm an Old Cowhand" (for which Mercer wrote his own melody) in *Rhythm on the Range.* Soon after that came "Too Marvelous for Words" and "Have You Got Any Castles, Baby?" (both to music by Richard A. Whiting) and "Jeepers, Creepers" and "You Must Have Been a Beautiful Baby" (music by Harry Warren). Good as these screen songs were—and however successful they became—they provided merely a faint clue to Mercer's subsequent importance as a lyricist, particularly when he began working with Arlen.

One need merely to listen to the slow, lazy drawl with which Mercer speaks or sings to know that he is a son of the Southland. He is, as a matter of fact, the descendant of an old, stately family tracing its American genealogy back to the mid-eighteenth century. Mercer was born in Savannah, Georgia, on November 18, 1909. His father was a lawyer who dabbled in real estate. Johnny first showed interest in music when he was six, when he followed a band around the town for a whole day, much to the consternation of his mother who thought he had got lost. "I liked to listen to all the old songs on records," he told an interviewer about his childhood experiences in music. "We had the old cylindrical records then. I remember that one of the songs was 'When It's Apple Blossom Time in Normandy.' A lot of songs made me cry."

Music study and the writing of verses began when he was ten. First he took some lessons on the piano, then on the trumpet. Before long he joined a jazz band, but it survived only a few rehearsals. While attending prep school when he was fifteen, Johnny wrote his first song, "Sister Susie Strut Your Stuff," which he says sounded just like "Red Hot Mama" (a popular tune of that time). The main point of interest in Mercer's song lay in his gift for writing verses in either dialect or the vernacular—a gift he would develop to a remarkable degree in his later years.

He had to leave school in 1927 when his father's business went bankrupt. Coming to New York, and finding a roof over his head in a fourth-floor shabby apartment in Greenwich Village, Mercer tried supporting himself by playing bit parts in plays. But he kept on producing lyrics all the time. A few came to the attention of Eddie Cantor who encouraged him with soothing words of praise, although he did not use anything Mercer wrote.

In 1930 Mercer tried getting a job as performer in *The Garrick Gaieties* edition of that year. He was turned down. But the show used one of his song lyrics, "Out of Breath and Scared to Death of You." A dancer in that revue was Ginger Meehan. She subsequently became Mrs. Johnny Mercer. They took an apartment in Brooklyn.

About this time Mercer won a singing contest sponsored by Paul Whiteman and his orchestra, but it was a year or so before Whiteman got around to hiring Mercer as a replacement for the Rhythm Boys, who had just left the organization. "I was hired," explains Mercer, "not for my voice, I'm sure, but because I could write songs and material generally." For two years or so Mercer was Whiteman's vocalist; he also wrote special material for Whiteman, and at times took over the spotlight as master of ceremonies. Later on, Mercer worked for Benny Goodman's band and for the Bob Crosby orchestra. This extended affiliation with jazz bands and orchestras was the period in which Mercer's career as song lyricist began to flower. He was now signed by a major Hollywood film studio to come to California to work as performer and songwriter. The songwriter soon displaced the performer, as far as the screen was concerned. Occasionally, Mercer reverted to performances by making recordings—particularly for Capitol, a company he had helped to found in 1942 and which was responsible for making him a millionaire.

The motion picture for which Arlen and Mercer were reunited was a Warner Brothers production initially called *Hot Nocturne*. This assignment had strong appeal to both Arlen and Mercer, since it used jazz within a serious-story context, and real jazz was something close to the hearts of both men. One of the important scenes was a prison cell where a Negro prisoner sang a blues. Determined to come up with an authentic product for this episode, Arlen and

Mercer wrote "Blues in the Night." Here Arlen adhered to the traditional blues structure: twelve-bar phrases in the melody with the blue note prominent in the harmony. Mercer, however, avoided the basic blues pattern (three-line stanzas, with the second line repeated); but in mood, feel, and accentuation his verses were also in the genuine spirit of the blues.

Before the picture, *Hot Nocturne,* was released in 1941, "Blues in the Night" became a hit, made so by Jimmie Lunceford's recording in 1940 in which the blues was heard in two different instrumental versions, one on each side of the disc. Within the movie, "Blues in the Night" was sung by William Gillespie. Unquestionably, the scene where this blues was used was the highlight of the whole movie, the rest of the picture leaving a good deal to be desired: for by the time the cameras started turning, the original intent to give a serious, almost documentary, treatment to the subject of jazz and jazzmen had been discarded in favor of a commercial, synthetic story. *Hot Nocturne* was a failure, and in view of the now nationwide popularity of the Arlen-Mercer song, the producers of the motion picture wisely decided to change the name of their production to *Blues in the Night.*

Only one year after "Blues in the Night" came another Arlen-Mercer blues classic, "That Old Black Magic," which Johnny Johnson sang in *Star-Spangled Rhythm.* Unusual though this melody is in its intervallic structure and blues feeling, Arlen insists that the great success the song enjoyed was due more to the lyrics than to the music. "The words sustain your interest," is the way Arlen explains it, "make sense, contain memorable phrases, and tell a story. Without the lyric, the song would be just another song." In time, "That Old Black Magic" became a trademark for Billy Daniels, but Frank Sinatra also recorded it successfully. In the motion picture *Here Come the Waves,* in 1944, the song was interpolated for Bing Crosby to point up in the story the "bobby-socks" craze for Sinatra.

Mercer's unusual gift to spin out a story in his lyrics characterized and distinguished "One for My Baby," written for Fred Astaire for *Sky's the Limit.* Arlen describes this number as a "wandering song," explaining: "Johnny Mercer took it and wrote it exactly as it fell. Not only is it long—forty-eight measures —but it also changes key. Johnny made it work." "One for My Baby" ranks high among Arlen's own favorites, and it ranks high with Fred Astaire. In his autobiography Astaire referred to it as "one of the best pieces of material that was written especially for me." "One for My Baby" was also one of the earliest of Tony Bennett's recording hits.

The number-one hit song of 1945 was a novelty which Arlen and Mercer wrote for Bing Crosby in *Here Comes the Waves.* It was "Ac-cent-chu-ate the Positive." The idea came during an automobile drive. Bandying about possible song ideas for their new picture, Mercer reminded Arlen of a spiritual-like tune Arlen had lately been humming a good deal. Arlen hummed the tune Mercer had mentioned, and as he did so the lyricist, with sublime irrelevance, started quoting a line that had clung to his memory since childhood: "You've got to accentuate the positive." Arlen adapted that line to the tune he was humming. Arlen and Mercer then kept on playing with the words and the music until, by the time they came to the studio, they had the whole number perfectly clear in mind. "It must really have pleased John," Arlen has since remarked wryly. "It was the first time I ever saw him smile."

The unusual way in which "Ac-cent-chu-ate the Positive" came to be written is one of several examples pointing to the unorthodox way in which Mercer and Arlen operate. Arlen explained their rather novel *modus operandi* as follows to his biographer, Jablonski: "After we got a script and the spots for the song were blocked out, we'd get together for an hour or so every day. While Johnny made himself comfortable on the couch, I'd play the tune for him. He had a wonderfully retentive memory. After I would finish playing the songs, he'd just go away without a comment. I wouldn't hear from him for a couple of weeks. Then he'd come around with the completed lyric."

While Mercer was Arlen's principal lyricist in Hollywood during the early 1940's, he was not the only one. Ted Koehler, Arlen's first collaborator, did the words for three songs for *Up in Arms,* starring Danny Kaye. Koehler's major successor as Arlen's lyricist, E. Y. Harburg, worked with Arlen for four numbers in the motion-picture adaptation of Vernon Duke's musical, *Cabin in the Sky;* here one of their songs was the poignant "Happiness Is a Thing Called Joe," sung by Ethel Waters. Arlen and Harburg also wrote two songs for *Kismet* (starring Marlene Dietrich and Ronald Colman), but the less said about this picture and its songs, the better.

It was with Harburg, rather than Mercer, that Arlen finally made a return appearance on the Broadway musical stage. This took place in 1944 with *Bloomer Girl,* whose run of 654 performances represents Arlen's greatest stage success.

Bloomer Girl was a colorful American period piece set in the town of Cicero in or about 1860. Women's rights, personified by Dorothy Bloomer, is a *cause célèbre* of the time and the place, but not the only one. Woven into the texture of the plot were the problems of the Negro and Negro emancipation. The critics were as one in singing the praises of the show, and in particular Agnes de Mille's choreography and the songs of Arlen and Harburg. Ward Morehouse rightly considered this score to be "Harold Arlen's . . . best job for the Broadway stage to date." The overall theme of the text—the cause of freedom and human dignity—was something close to both songwriters. Some of their numbers, then, had a strong social-conscious identity: for example, "The Eagle and Me," a slave song about freedom, and "Man for Sale," with its haunting blues quality. A blues is one of the score's greatest numbers, "I Got a Song," assigned to Richard Huey (onetime redcap, turned actor). He had enormous difficulties mastering its complex rhythmic pattern. As Jablonski reveals: "At one dress rehearsal, the night before opening, Huey simply walked off the stage without finishing the song. Arlen then decided perhaps they should write a new song for the spot, but Harburg refused; they had worked on the song and it must remain. Remain it did." "Right As Rain," "Evelina," and "T'morra', T'morra' " were also important songs.

With *Bloomer Girl* out of the way, the Arlen-Mercer collaboration was resumed: first for the movie *Out of This World* in 1945; then, and more significantly by far, for the Broadway musical *St. Louis Woman* in 1946.

St. Louis Woman aimed high. With book by Arna Bontemps and Countee Cullen, direction by Rouben Mamoulian, and a cast headed by Pearl Bailey, Ruby Hill, and Rex Ingram, *St. Louis Woman* had every intention of being a seriously conceived folk play with music. But this is not the way it ended up. As seen at the Martin Beck Theatre on March 30, 1946, it was basically just one more musical with Negro characters. It was not even good musical comedy, since a heavy gloom hung over a good deal of the production—particularly in the second-act set, in of all places, a funeral parlor.

But the quality of the songwriting was superlative. Johnny Mercer's lyrics were rarely better. In fact they were so good that Jablonski maintains "his work on this one show would have been enough to assure him a niche alongside the few master lyricists." Harold Arlen was also in top form—rarely fresher in his melodic ideas, rarely bolder in his technique. Pearl Bailey sang two of the numbers: "Legalize My Name" and "A Woman's Prerogative." The best song, for both its music and its lyrics, was "Come Rain or Come Shine," unusual in that it had no verse whatsoever, while its thirty-two-measure chorus begins in one key and ends in another.

Arlen did not enjoy a Broadway success rivaling *Bloomer Girl* until 1957 when, with Harburg as lyricist, he contributed the songs for *Jamaica,* in which Lena Horne made her Broadway debut in a starring role. But three years before *Jamaica,* Arlen had been represented on Broadway with another folklike musical, *The House of Flowers,* for which Truman Capote, the distinguished writer, worked within a musical-comedy format for the first time by contributing both the text and the lyrics. Arlen's score was greatly underrated. "A Sleepin' Bee" is a little gem whose exotic personality is realized, as Jablonski explains, through "a sensuous, undulating melody that rises a tenth and drops a fifth in a mere four bars." No less unusual in melodic structure is "I Never Has Seen Snow" while "Two Ladies in de Shade of de Banana Tree" is a tantalizing calypso that has since caught on.

The audience rejected *House of Flowers* in 1957, and they rejected it again a decade later when it returned to New York in an off-Broadway production with a revised text and five new songs. When Clive Barnes wrote in *The New York Times* in 1968 that this musical suffered from "a thin and desultory book," he was undoubtedly pointing to the musical's chief deficit, in both the earlier and the later versions. The main rewards of the revival, was the general consensus among the critics, lay in Arlen's songs.

The setting of *House of Flowers* was the West Indies, to which Arlen returned in *Jamaica.* E. Y. Harburg, who had hatched the idea for this production, wanted a "simple folk tale" to star Harry Belafonte singing calypso numbers. Belafonte was unable to fill this commitment because of a throat ailment. Harburg and Arlen solved the problem of recasting by rewriting the part for an island girl and getting Lena Horne to assume that role. She proved, as Walter Kerr said of her, "an enchantress . . . the most beautiful woman in the world."

Unquestioned highlights were her mocking rendition of the torch song "Take It Slow, Joe" and her spicy presentation of several numbers with a decided social-conscious slant, such as "Push de Button" and "I Don't Think I'll End It All." Other memorable songs in this particularly strong score were the haunting lulla-by "Cocoanut Sweet" and a satirical piece with a political viewpoint, "Leave the Atom Alone."

"A good lyric writer," Arlen once said, "is a composer's best friend." In Mercer and in Harburg, Arlen had found two of the best. But he also worked significantly with a third lyricist who belongs with the elite of his profession— Ira Gershwin. For *A Star Is Born* in 1953 (a remake of an earlier nonmusical movie starring Janet Gaynor), Arlen and Gershwin produced a torch song sweeping across sixty-two measures, "The Man That Got Away"—still one more classic in Arlen's inimitable blues manner. Judy Garland sang it. "Her dark voice sobs, sighs, sulks, and socks [it] out like a cross between Tara's harp and the late Bessie Smith," reported the critic of *Time*. The song became second in importance in Judy Garland's repertory only to "Over the Rainbow."

Anya and Harold Arlen occupy a swank duplex apartment in the East Fifties in New York City. This has been their home base ever since they gave up their home in California. Here Arlen pursues his main diversions of reading, painting, and playing the soft-spoken and gracious host to his many friends. Though there is often a good deal of inner turmoil in Arlen, particularly when he is involved in creation, he always gives the impression of a man at peace with the world and himself, equable in temper and mood, always thoroughly natural and relaxed. He is a gregarious person who enjoys having people around him, encourages guests to drop in on him, and who charms them with his poise and humor and gift at conversation as he puffs on a cigar or pipe. When he is at work, Jablonski reveals, Arlen "will close his eyes, cock his head, furrow his brow in deep concentration while his powerful yet sensitive fingers search among the seven white and black keys for an idea worth keeping." And in performing his songs "he becomes lost . . . as he invests the lyrics with an almost im-passioned delivery."

Among popular composers, Arlen is one of the most serious about his work —painstaking about details, consistently trying to maintain the highest possible integrity, and never giving a second thought as to whether the song he is working on will be a hit or not. There is no hint of condescension in him toward popular music. "I am not one to look down on songwriting," he has said. "Just because it happens to be thirty-two bars—or more, and less than a tone poem—doesn't mean a song doesn't belong to the arts." His attitude toward his own creativity and his immense originality have earned him the singing praises of his most successful rivals. Cole Porter called him "a distinguished personality in music." Richard Rodgers has said: "Harold has a real valid talent, it is his own, and completely original." And Irving Berlin remarked about Arlen: "I don't know anyone who can wrap himself up so much in his work, who is so sincere a writer."

Songs from World War II

Frank Loesser

There is a difference in the impact that the two world wars had upon our song history. While World War I deluged the country with war songs, it failed to produce a single new composer whose first major initiation into songwriting or whose first major successes were the direct result of the war. And while the song production of World War II represented a dribble in comparison to the song deluge of the earlier conflict, it did bring into being a popular composer of the first importance, Frank Loesser. Up to the time of Pearl Harbor, Frank Loesser had been exclusively a lyricist, and a mighty good one; but he had never published a note of music. Pearl Harbor was the motivation and stimulation he needed to write music to his own words for the first time. It was a first try, the aim was flawless, and the bull's eye was hit. Loesser wrote many a war song after that, and when the war ended he went on to grow creatively as a musician to become one of the giant musical figures both on Broadway and in Hollywood.

But it might be wise, momentarily, to retrace our steps by almost a quarter of a century and throw a backward glance at World War I. No American war produced more martial music than this one did; and, with the possible exception of the Civil War, no American war was the inspiration for so many martial songs or sentimental war songs that have since become hardy standards. With its machinery for song production oiled, greased, and working at maximum efficiency, Tin Pan Alley, in 1917, was well geared to supply the public with its seemingly inexhaustible demand for war songs. The boom in the sale of sheet music had never been greater. There is good reason for this. Since many theatres and night spots had to close down for lack of fuel, power, or entertainers (the supply of entertainers sadly depleted by the draft), the American home front was compelled to entertain itself at home by singing the day's tunes around the family piano—much in the same way Americans used to do before the entertainment business had become a flourishing industry. As this author has written in *The Life and Death of Tin Pan Alley:* "There was not a single note in the whole gamut of emotions seizing and holding Americans that was not touched upon by popular songs. Every area of experience was covered; every major war episode was commented upon; anybody and everybody who was directly involved in the war, whatever the capacity, had songs written about them."

The variations on a theme of the Kaiser were apparently limitless. Hundreds upon hundreds of songs commented upon the dire fate awaiting him once "Uncle Sam is through," as one of the songs noted in its title. The Kaiser would hang under the linden tree; he would be whipped; he would be killed; he would hang from a sour apple tree; he would be found with a lily in his hand. Still other songs heaped opprobrium upon insult: "The Crazy Kaiser" or "Hunting the Hun" or "The Kaiser Is a Devil."

Similarly inexhaustible in its variations were songs about the pain of separation of loved ones, and the loneliness of both the doughboy on the field of battle and those he left behind: "I May Be Gone for a Long, Long Time" or "Bring Back My Daddy to Me" or "Send Me Away With a Smile."

There were songs in praise of the Allies ("Belgian Rose," "Lorraine, My Beautiful Alsace Lorraine," "Joan of Arc," "Lafayette, We Hear You Calling"); songs about various branches of the services ("Rose of No Man's Land" for the Red Cross, "On the Seas There Are Others Heroes, Too," "Tell It to the Marines"); songs to stir and arouse the fighting spirit of men in uniform ("We're Going Over," "We'll Knock the Heligo-into Heligo-out of Heligoland," "We Don't Want the Bacon, What We Want Is a Piece of the Rhine"); and there were songs either to sustain morale at home or to support the war through civilian means ("We'll Do Our Share, While You're Over There," "Keep Cool, the Country's Saving Fuel"); there were even humorous war songs ("K-K-K-Katy," which came to be known as the stammering song, "If He Can Fight As He Can Love, Good Night Germany," "Oui, Oui, Marie," "When Yankee Doodle Learns to Parlez-Vouz Français").

Everybody who was writing songs was writing about the war, and some of these songs will always identify World War I: George M. Cohan's "Over There"; Irving Berlin's "Oh, How I Hate To Get Up in the Morning"; "Goodbye, Broadway, Hello, France" by C. Francis Reisner, Benny Davis, and Billy Baskette, which started out as a production number for the *Passing Show of 1917* and ended up selling four million copies of sheet music; and two ballads, each of which sold two to three million copies, George Whiting's "Till We Meet Again" and "There's a Long, Long Trail" by Zo Elliott and Stoddard King.

People sang not only at home but also at community sings, at songfests in theaters, at bond rallies. Tin Pan Alley inaugurated competitions for war songs in motion-picture houses, providing half a dozen or so of its latest products, hot off the press, and contributing the performers to sing them; the audience was then asked to select its favorite. This is how "Till We Meet Again" was heard for the first time, in a Detroit movie-house competition, where it received first prize. Singing songs about the war was accepted as the patriotic thing for folks at home to do; beyond this, it proved the safety valve allowing for a release for pent-up emotions. Indeed, to George Creel's Committee on Public Information, singing represented so important a facet of the war effort that the government released song books for distribution in theatres and sent out performers to lead audiences in singing the war songs. Another proof of how highly the government esteemed song in the war effort was the fact that despite shortages in just about everything, Tin Pan Alley was provided with its full quota of paper for the printing of sheet music.

World War II was also the source of and inspiration for many a distinguished song that has since become an inextricable part of our permanent literature: Jerome Kern's "The Last Time I Saw Paris"; "I'll Walk Alone" by Sammy Cahn and Jule Styne; "The White Cliffs of Dover" by Nat Burton and Walter Kent; Irving Berlin's "White Christmas"; "Comin' in on a Wing and a Prayer" by Harold Adamson and Jimmy McHugh; "I'll Be Seeing You," which Irving Kahal and Sammy Fain had written before the war but which needed the war to spiral it to the heights of success; and Irving Berlin's "God Bless America," also a prewar product, but become during the war the country's second national anthem.

The overall quality of the war songs of World War II was for the most part as high as, and probably higher than, those of the world war that had preceded it; but there is no doubt that in comparison to the mountainous song output between 1917 and 1919, that between 1942 and 1946 represents a mere molehill. For this sharp decline in volume one can provide a sound explanation. The song business had undergone a major revolution between the two world wars. Tin Pan Alley—at least as it had functioned since the beginning of the century—no longer existed. No longer was the publishing house the nursery in which composers could be developed, where songs could be manufactured by the carload to meet every changing mood, or interest, of the public; where songs could be promoted to success through song pluggers; where the publisher himself was the dominant force in discovering new creative talent, in seeking out the right performer to introduce and popularize a song, in evolving new methods of promotion, and in running a business in which, as in all successful businesses, the supply could meet the demand.

After 1930 most of the major publishing houses in New York were acquired by the motion-picture studios. The birth of talking pictures demanded a ready-made supply of songs at hand for the numerous "all-talking, all-singing" productions being projected. The publishing house now became an off-shoot of the motion-picture industry. No longer did the publisher seek out new composers, determine what songs to publish and on what subjects, and how best to promote them. He had become more or less of a figurehead, "clipping coupons like bankers," as one publisher put it, "where once we were makers of song hits and great composers." The motion-picture executive was the man in power now. He ordered the songs that were needed for his productions, and was not in the least interested in issuing independent numbers that had no place in a specific film assignment. To write a song just for its own sake, or because it was on some timely theme, was a luxury few composers and lyricists could afford to indulge in, since there were few powerful publishers now left that did not have direct screen affiliations. The onetime assembly belt that had manufactured songs by the thousands had broken down. The movie industry was seeing to it that the new songs that were being written were handpicked, most of them written on commission, by lyricists and composers under contract to the studio. Under such an operation, the mass output of songs during World War I could not help being drastically reduced.

In spite of the radical reduction in the number of war songs being written, promoted, and popularized, good songs were being produced, as we have previously commented. And in spite of the fact that the publishing house could no longer be the nursery where a neophyte composer or lyricist could develop to greatness through the experience of writing and having published hundreds of songs—encouraged and directed by the almost parental solicitude of his publisher—some fresh, new musical voices did manage to emerge during those war years. None proved more significant than Frank Loesser.

Frank Loesser was born within a household supercharged with intellectualism in New York City on June 29, 1910. His father was a piano teacher, a native of northern Germany, who combined his love for and knowledge of great music with veneration for all things cultural. He instilled into his family a respect for books, art, and philosophy, as well as music. The oldest son, Arthur, became a distinguished concert pianist and critic. A sister, who came next in age, became a scholar with university degrees. Frank was born after his sister. He alone, of the entire family, seemed immune to anything that had the slightest suspicion of things intellectual. He resisted formal education as if it were some contagious disease, preferring to go his own way haphazardly in whatever interested him. He did show signs of interest in music, in improvising at the piano when he was only six, and even writing a song, "The May Party," the same year. But the academic way of learning music, which his father and older brother had favored, was just not for him. He preferred to pick up whatever bits of musical knowledge he could without formal direction and to use that knowledge in whatever way his instincts dicated. The only reason his father did not interfere was that Frank's interest lay mainly in popular music, in which the boy was dabbling all the time. And, like all Germanic-trained serious musicians, father Loesser had nothing but contempt for this kind of music.

Most of Loesser's music-making was done not on the piano but on the harmonica, on which he became sufficiently adept to win third prize in a harmonica-playing contest held in New York.

Meanwhile, there was his academic schooling, about which his father would tolerate no nonsense. Loesser was graduated from the Speyer School in New York from which he progressed to Townsend Harris Hall. Even though Frank Loesser had to prove himself a good student at Speyer School, since Townsend Harris Hall accepted only the cream of the student crop, the quality of his work once he had entered high school was never equal to his capabilities. His heart was not in Latin or the sciences or mathematics, upon which Townsend Harris Hall played so great a stress. Where Loesser's heart belonged was to writing tunes—also to creating verses and drawing sketches. Nevertheless, he was graduated from Townsend Harris and passed on to the College of the City of New York, of which the high school was an adjunct.

His entire college career lasted a single year. Then he deserted the school-room for good, to make his way in the business world. First he became an office boy in a wholesale jewelry concern. Then, convinced that he preferred a job in journalism, he became a reporter for a small paper in New Rochelle, New York. While holding this job he was called upon to write couplets for each guest attending a Lions Club Dinner. One of the couplets he still remembers betrays rather grimly how much he had yet to learn about writing verses. It read:

> *Secretary Albert Vincent,*
> *Read these minutes, right this instant!*

Loesser did not stay long in journalism; in fact, he did not remain long enough in any one job to learn its basic routines. He worked as a process server for a lawyer, and he was an inspector for a chain of restaurants. He sold ads for the New York *Herald Tribune*. He worked as a pianist in a mountain resort, and he appeared in vaudeville in an act requiring him to draw caricatures. He served as press representative for a small movie company. He even filled the post of knit-goods editor for *Women's Wear*. He was drifting along with the tide (to borrow a cliché from a popular song *not* by Loesser) and was arriving nowhere. But of one thing he was confident during all those years of drifting: He would never surrender the joy of writing verses and prose. One verse, "Armful of You," was sold to a vaudevillian for fifteen dollars. In prose and verse he sold special material to various stage performers and radio programs.

Finally he got his first song as a songwriter, employed by the Tin Pan Alley firm of Leo Feist to write lyrics for Joseph Brandfon's melodies. His salary was forty dollars a week. None of these songs was either published or used, and so at the end of the year Loesser was fired.

In 1931 he published one of his songs: "In Love with the Memory of

You," bought by the same firm of Leo Feist which had recently dismissed him from its employ. The words were by Loesser. The music was the work of another novice, but one whose stature would eventually loom to giant proportions in serious music: William Schuman, subsequently become not only one of America's most significant composers of serious music, but also one of its leading educators (as president of the Juilliard School of Music) and after that one of its foremost administrators (as president of the Lincoln Center for the Performing Arts).

Nothing much happened to "In Love with the Memory of You," just as nothing much happened to the lyrics Loesser kept on writing for the next three years. In 1934 "I Wish I Were Twins" (music by Joseph Meyer and Eddie de Lange) attracted some notice while, in 1936, Loesser contributed most of the lyrics for a Broadway revue that survived only five performances. During this period, when his total earnings from his lyric writing could not have paid the price for a single full-course dinner, he supported himself by playing the piano and singing songs at the Back Drop, a night spot on Fifty-second Street. This place attracted a theatrical clientele, one of whom was a blonde, attractive radio singer, Lynn Garland. And this is where Loesser met the young lady who would soon become his wife.

Lynn Garland and Frank Loesser were married in Hollywood in 1936, Loesser having come to California to write songs for Universal Pictures. Nothing distinguished came from this assignment, though several of his songs were used in various pictures; Universal allowed Loesser's contract to expire.

Loesser went from Universal to Paramount, and it was there—beginning with the song "Man of Manakoora" (music by Alfred Newman), introduced by Dorothy Lamour in *The Hurricane*—that Loesser climbed out of the ignominious depths in which he had been languishing so many years to become one of the most productive and successful lyricists in Hollywood. Within a few years he wrote lyrics to over fifty songs—music by various composers, including several famous ones—and they were heard in more than thirty motion pictures. A good many of these songs were formidable successes: "Small Fry" and "Two Sleepy People," both to music by Hoagy Carmichael; "See What the Boys in the Back Room Will Have," music by Frederick Hollander, made famous by Marlene Dietrich; "I Don't Want To Want To Walk Without You, Baby," music by Jule Styne; "Jingle, Jangle, Jingle," music by Joseph Lilley. Songs like these brought Loesser a yearly income in five figures, and made it possible for him to live in the style befitting a Hollywood great, even to the point of hiring a chauffeur to drive his expensive car. But the main reason for a chauffeur was not that he wanted to impress his colleagues but that he got some of his best song ideas in the mornings while riding in his limousine—and in Los Angeles traffic (even in those years) the simultaneous effort of driving a car and concentrating on a song lyric was hardly calculated to insure a very long or healthy existence.

By 1941 Loesser was recognized as one of the top-flight lyricists in the movie industry. The idea of becoming a composer as well was furthest from his mind. Then at Pearl Harbor the treachery of the Japanese pushed America into

World War II. Like every other American, Loesser was stirred to the depths of his being by this tragedy. Being a creative person he had to find an outlet by writing a song lyric. Suddenly there sprang to his mind the words Chaplain William Maguire of the United States Navy was reputed to have said during the height of the attack on Pearl Harbor: "Praise the Lord and Pass the Ammunition." Here, Loesser knew, he had the makings of a stirring war song.

Habitually, whenever Loesser completed a lyric, he would concoct a dummy tune for the purpose of studying the ebb and flow of his lines. He followed this practice for "Praise the Lord and Pass the Ammunition," and when he demonstrated his lyrics for his friends, he used his dummy tune as a functional showcase for his words. His friends liked the lyrics, but they liked the tune even more; and what they liked best of all was the way in which words and music suited each other, and how together they had the personality and flavor of folk music. It was on their counsel that Frank Loesser finally decided to publish his own melody with his lyrics. Kay Kyser recorded it, to achieve a million-disc sale. The song was broadcast so often over the radio, often in Kyser's recording and sometimes in other instrumental and vocal renditions, that the Office of War Information suggested to all radio stations that the song be broadcast no more than once every few hours to avoid familiarity breeding contempt. In short, the then recently declared war by America had already produced its first great war song. More than that, it had given birth to a new composer.

As long as the war lasted, Loesser continued to produce war songs (music as well as words), most of them while he served in uniform. He wrote songs about the WACs ("The WAC Hymn" and "First Class Private Mary Brown"); songs about the various other branches of the service ("Sad Bombardier," "Salute to the Army Air Force," and "What Do You Do in the Infantry?"). The last of these, following a successful recording by Bing Crosby, became the theme song for the infantry throughout the war (this in spite of the fact that some high-ranking officers frowned upon its sardonic allusion to the fact that all that the infantry seems to be doing is march, march, march).

It was at the request of the infantry that Loesser produced the second of his two war classics, "The Ballad of Rodger Young." The infantry was looking for some musical number glorifying its branch of the service. Loesser, after some research, found an ideal subject for his ballad in a newspaper account about the heroism of Private Rodger Young. He was a short, slight-of-build soldier of twenty-five who wore glasses and was hard of hearing. Despite his physical limitations, he single-handedly attacked a hidden Japanese machine-gun nest on a hill at Munda, New Georgia, an island in the South Pacific. He died in this action and was posthumously awarded the Congressional Medal of Honor. His citation read: "Private Young's bold action in closing with this Japanese pillbox and thus diverting its fire, permitted the platoon to disengage itself without loss, and was responsible for several enemy casualties."

Loesser's ballad was heard first on Meredith Willson's coast-to-coast radio program in 1945. The original plan of this program was to give the song the grand treatment, with a large orchestra and chorus, and a good deal of patriotic hoopla. During the first rehearsal, a studio usher remarked to Willson that the song would sound far better if it were presented simply, preferably by a folk singer accompanying himself on the guitar. Willson mulled over this suggestion, finally recognized its wisdom, and accepted it. A single voice (that of Earl Wrightson), accompanied by guitar, introduced it on the program. Some time later, a single voice, once again with guitar accompaniment, was heard on the sound track when a newsreel depicted the return to America of Rodger Young for burial. The impression made by the ballad on the Meredith Willson broadcast was profound and immediate. In the ensuing months it became one of the most frequently sung war tunes, particularly following recordings by Burl Ives, John Charles Thomas, Nelson Eddy, and many others.

Having been transformed by the war from a lyricist into a lyricist-composer, Frank Loesser continued writing melodies to his own words when the conflict was over. Back in Hollywood, he had two winners in "Tallahassee" and "I Wish I Didn't Love You So," the latter made popular by Dinah Shore. By 1949 he captured an Oscar for "Baby, It's Cold Outside," introduced in *Neptune's Daughter* where Esther Williams and Ricardo Montalban first sang it seriously, after which Red Skelton and Betty Garrett gave it a comedy treatment. It is surely of more than passing interest to remark that this song—the only one to win an Oscar for Loesser—had never been intended for *Neptune's Daughter,* nor for any commercial use whatever, for that matter. He had written it for his own amusement long before *Neptune's Daughter* was being planned, and he often entertained his friends at parties with it. He had every intention at the time of keeping this song out of the marketplace.

In 1948 Loesser made his first contribution to the Broadway musical theatre with songs for *Where's Charley?* This was a musical-comedy adaptation of an old stage favorite, *Charley's Aunt,* which had been amusing audiences in England and America since 1892 by having a man disguise himself as a woman, cavorting about in woman's clothes while assuming female mannerisms and attitudes. George Abbott was recruited to make the textual adaptation and to direct the production. *Where's Charley?* starring Ray Bolger, had a run of 792 performances.

One of its two hit songs was "Once in Love with Amy," in the singing of which Ray Bolger called upon his audience to join him in the refrain. This routine (which regularly brought down the house and became one of the specialties by which Bolger will probably always be remembered) came about not through calculation but through accident. When *Where's Charley?* had its first matinee, the seven-year-old son of one of the show's producers (Cy Feuer) was seated in the front row. During the singing of "Once in Love with Amy," Bolger either forgot some of his lines or (splendid showman that he was) pretended he did. In any case, he stopped the music, looked helplessly at the audience, and muttered, "What are the words, I've forgotten them." The boy (who had heard Bolger sing this number both at his home and at rehearsals dozens of times and therefore knew it well) rose from his seat and sang the lines Bolger had forgotten. Bolger then invited the boy to join him in singing a reprise of the refrain. After that, Bolger asked the audience to join him in a community song by repeating each line of the refrain after him. The whole episode created so much enthusiasm that Bolger kept the routine in the show. Of course, having somebody in the audience participate with a performer in singing a number was nothing new in show business. It had been a practice long popular in vaudeville and burlesque houses where a singing stooge would be planted in the audience and where audiences often joined the performer in singing the refrain of a popular song again and again. But the practice had so long been discarded that in 1949 it proved a refreshing novelty; and Bolger's ability to inject a feeling of spontaneity and improvisation into his performance made the whole affair decidedly appealing.

"Once in Love with Amy" was one of two major song hits from *Where's Charley?* the other being "My Darling, My Darling," which for several weeks' running occupied the top position on radio's "Hit Parade." During this period, another Frank Loesser song—but one that had never been intended for either stage or screen but had been published as an independent number—also appeared on "Hit Parade," and for a while the two songs took turns in usurping the first and second places. The song was "On a Slow Boat to China," which Kay Kyser helped make successful through his recording.

With Loesser's first Broadway musical a box-office triumph, he went on to achieve not only a musical-comedy masterpiece but one of those stage phenomena that enjoy over a thousand performances. For the successor to *Where's Charley?* was the formidable *Guys and Dolls* in 1950, which brought to the Broadway box office over twelve million dollars. Many more millions were gathered through the various touring companies, through a Samuel Goldwyn superspecial motion picture starring Frank Sinatra, Marlon Brando, and Jean Simmons, and through the sale of the original-cast recording albums of both the stage and the screen productions.

Guys and Dolls was a saga of Broadway and the screwball characters that make Broadway the colorful thoroughfare it is—all derived from stories by Damon Runyon, adapted by Jo Swerling and Abe Burrows. Gambling is the meat and drink of its main characters, most of whom are picturesquely identified as Angie the Ox or Harry the Horse or Nicely-Nicely Johnson. The production —its tempo kept moving at a breathless pace through George S. Kaufman's skillful direction—opens with a trio of gamblers selecting their horses for the day's races in a number to which Loesser ingeniously gave a canonic three-voice treatment. But the main plot concerns the efforts of several Broadway gamblers to find a safe haven for a crap game (which they ultimately find in a sewer). Nathan Detroit is forced to delay his ever-imminent marriage to the night club singer Adelaide for fourteen years; some gambling temptation always interferes with his going through with the ceremony. The main romance, however, entangles Sky Masterson, a Broadwayite as flamboyant in his personality as he is in his dress, with a demure and innocent Salvation Army lass, Sarah Brown. Innocence proves stronger than corruption, for it is through Sky Masterson's efforts that the Salvation Army Mission is saved.

Both as a lyricist and as a composer, Loesser was here in his element; and when he was in his element, he was one of the elect. Wide, indeed, was his gamut.

His gift with comedy numbers has few rivals in musical comedy: "Fugue for Tinhorns" (or "I've Got the Horse Right Here"); "Adelaide's Lament," about her psychosomatic colds (which Moss Hart once maintained was the best single musical-comedy number he had ever seen); "A Bushel and a Peck"; "Take Back Your Mink"; and the title number. But Loesser was no less impressive in producing an emotional ballad where the emphasis is more on a soaring melody full of expressive and deeply felt emotions as in "I'll Know," "I've Never Been in Love Before," and "If I Were a Bell." (No less poignant a ballad is "A Woman in Love," which Loesser wrote for the motion-picture adaptation of the musical.)

Guys and Dolls was as good as it was (and there are few musicals in the history of our theatre that are better) not only because of the lofty standards set by Loesser in his lyrics and music. Every element of the production was on an equally high plane: the sprightly text, much of it in Broadway vernacular; George S. Kaufman's direction; the remarkable choreography of Michael Kidd, especially in the "crap game" ballet set in a sewer. Indeed, there is no segment in the production that is superfluous; no part that serves merely as window dressing. Everything fits, as Abe Burrows has said: "Nothing is in there that doesn't belong. There are no love ballads which are written in a different language from the dialogue. When a mugg sings a love song, its a mugg-type love song. The dances are strictly in character. There's a crap-game ballet which looks like a crap game. A real Runyon crap game. In this show we didn't care about how a single number or scene would go. We didn't concern ourselves with reprising songs for no reason at all. We cared about the whole show and nothing went in until it fit. . . . We each had to tailor our contributions to the basic needs of the show. Cutting, adding, and giving up dearly beloved things because they didn't belong. It was the same when we were casting. We chose our cast for believability, and authenticity. We didn't worry about so-called names. We wanted people who fit, people who looked like Runyon's people should look, and talked like them."

Loesser returned briefly to Hollywood, after Guys and Dolls, to write another felicitous and highly varied score, this time for the films. The motion picture was Hans Christian Andersen, a Samuel Goldwyn production starring Danny Kaye in the title role, released in 1953. A rich harvest of song hits was eloquent testimony that the Loesser who wrote the score for Guys and Dolls had not lowered his standards in working for the screen. The motion picture was studded with gems: "Anywhere I Wander," "The Inch Worm," "No Two People," "Thumbelina," and "Wonderful Copenhagen." Few if any motion-picture musicals of the 1950's could boast a score as opulent as this one.

Back again on Broadway, after his temporary hiatus in Hollywood, Loesser created not only the score but also the text for Most Happy Fella, a production whose dramatic values, characterizations, and authenticity of dialogue lifted it several rungs higher above the status of musical comedy.

Samuel Taylor, a distinguished playwright, was the one responsible for getting Loesser to write this show. He called to Loesser's attention a stage play

by Sidney Howard, *They Knew What They Wanted,* which had earned the
Pulitzer Prize in 1924, insisting that it could become effective musical theatre
in the right hands. Loesser was skeptical. "I didn't like the play," he explained.
"I thought it was a tragedy about a lot of sad people having a terrible time of
things. It was about as musical as a land mine." But Taylor could not be swayed.
Being a persuasive talker, reinforced by a thoroughly logical and practical approach to the theatre, Taylor finally extracted from Loesser a promise that he
would reread the play, keeping in mind its possible potential for musical treatment. Loesser complied and, as he confessed, "was astonished to find that it
wasn't tragic at all. It was funny. All about wonderfully funny people to whom
all sorts of things happened, some hilarious, some sad. I read the play six more
times just to nail down my opinion. I nailed. . . . Take out all the political
talk, the labor talk, the religious talk. Get rid of all that stuff and you've got
a good love story."

It was not only a good love story but an unusual one. Tony is a simple-
minded, warmhearted middle-aged California winegrower. He carries on a correspondence with Rosabella, a waitress who had served him in a San Francisco
restaurant. He finally proposes marriage in one of his letters, and to make sure
that her answer is in the affirmative he sends her a photograph of his foreman,
a handsome young man, Joe, in place of one of his own. Since Rosabella does
not remember Tony she is readily fooled. She comes to Tony's farm to marry
him. She is not only shocked to discover that her future husband is no longer
young and far from physically appealing but that at the very moment of her
arrival he is confined to a wheelchair, having recently been involved in an automobile accident. She controls her first instinct to run away. But before long she
falls in love with Joe, the foreman. Nevertheless, Tony's overflowing love, his
tenderness and softness of nature, are irresistible. Rosabella marries him, but
this does not keep her from having an affair with Joe as a result of which she
becomes pregnant. Tony drives Rosabella out of his house, while showering her
with venomous hate and anger. But he soon realizes how much she has come to
mean to him and that he cannot live without her. He follows her to the bus
station to tell her he is ready to accept her coming child as his own bambino, if
Rosabella is ready and willing to forget Joe.

This was far from being just a convenient pretext for songs and musical
comedy routines. This was a taut, tense drama with many warmhearted and
even humorous episodes, and as such it called for ambitious musical treatment.
Music plays such a vital role in the projection of the story and in the presentation and delineation of character that *Most Happy Fella* is almost an opera:
three quarters of the text uses some form of music. Sprinkled throughout the
play are all kinds of arias, folk songs, dances, instrumental passages, choral
pieces, speech accompanied by orchestra. A few of the numbers were popular
enough to become hits: "Standin' on the Corner," a hillbilly type of tune; "Big
D," a song imitating the style of some of the songs of the 1920's; the ballad,
"Joey, Joey." But most of the other musical episodes and excerpts intensified
the dramatic action, threw new light on character, heightened the atmosphere

and background to such an extent that Brooks Atkinson described *Most Happy Fella* as a "musical drama [with] such an abundant and virtuoso score in it that it has to be taken on the level of theatre."

For Loesser, *Most Happy Fella* represented an artistic victory of the first importance, since it proved him to be much more than just a composer of successful musical-comedy scores. This, after all, was the largest canvas upon which he had thus far worked and the fact that a genuine work of stage art emerged from his efforts caused him no small satisfaction. *Most Happy Fella* stayed on Broadway for about two years (after opening in 1956) and received the Drama Critics Award as the year's best musical. *Most Happy Fella* brought Loesser another blessing as well. The star who played the part of Rosabella was Jo Sullivan. Loesser (having divorced his wife a few years earlier) married Jo Sullivan in 1959.

With *Greenwillow*, in 1960, Loesser once again served as his own librettist (with the assistance of Lesser Samuels) and once again sought to create a musical with serious overtones and aspirations. There was much loveliness in *Greenwillow*, in both the play and the music, as it told the story of a man in an imaginary town victimized by *Wanderlust*. Though married and with a family, he is continually off on solitary wanderings for indefinite periods. His son is afraid to marry the girl he loves for fear of having inherited his father's weakness, but eventually reassures himself of his own strength of will. This drama, spoken almost in a whisper, and maintaining a consistently subdued mood—combined with music that for the most part was pastoral—lacked popular appeal. *Greenwillow* was a failure—but a failure of which its creator could well be proud.

It may even very well be that Loesser was prouder of *Greenwillow* than he was of *How To Succeed in Business Without Really Trying*, though he had never said so. But *How To Succeed in Business*, which opened in 1961, is one of the most successful musicals ever produced. None of those involved in this collaboration, I am sure, had any ambition to create a work of art—Loesser least of all. They wanted a show that had solid entertainment value. A satirical novel by Shepherd Mead was adapted by Abe Burrows, Jack Weinstock, and Willie Gilbert into a surefire musical-comedy text—one almost as brilliant and freshly conceived as that for *Guys and Dolls*. A go-getter young fellow, Finch, starts out as a window cleaner. Through guile, opportunism, ruthlessness, perseverance, and the determination to succeed he goes from one job to a higher one at World Wide Wickets, a giant organization, and ends up as chairman of the board of directors. With Robert Morse as the youngster hell-bent for the heights of success, and Rudy Vallee as president of World Wide Wickets, *How To Succeed in Business* profited from ideal casting, as well as from expert stage direction. And with musical numbers like "I Believe in You," "Grand Old Ivy," "Brotherhood of Man"—numbers upon which was sprinkled a gentle dose of spice—the show had songs to remember.

And so, the composer-lyricist of *Guys and Dolls* and *Most Happy Fella* was back again on top, where he belonged. *How To Succeed in Business Without Really Trying* had a run of 1,417 performances; received the Pulitzer Prize in drama (the fourth musical in stage history to do so) and the Antoinette Perry and the Drama Critics Circle awards. Road companies sold out auditoriums everywhere, and the motion-picture adaptation proved a box-office gold mine. As it turned out, *How To Succeed in Business Without Really Trying,* was Loesser's last stage musical. He had ended his career on Broadway on a note of triumph.

The writing of songs, and at times texts, for the stage, was only one of the activities that had tapped Loesser's seemingly inexhaustible fund of energy. Another was the direction of his prosperous publishing firm, the Frank Music Corporation on West Fifty-seventh Street in New York City. A human dynamo, Loesser was a man who required little sleep (often no more than five hours) and who, during his waking hours, was virtually always in perpetual motion. He got up regularly about 7 A.M. and began a sixteen-hour day of frenetic activity. Work exhilarated him; idleness was a bore. The day after *Most Happy Fella* opened he said he was taking a vacation. "I'm tired," he complained. "I'm going to Las Vegas for a long, long holiday—and this time I mean it. I'll be back in three days."

He was volatile of mood, often fluctuating between enormous exuberance, optimism, and enthusiasm to the depths of despair. As he talked, his nervous energy made him fidget about a good deal. He used slang freely and tried to maintain the impression that he was, after all, an uncouth fellow without a touch of culture to blemish this image. "I haven't cracked a book since *Beau Geste,*" he might tell you. He might also insist that what he did not know about music could fill a multivolume encyclopedia. But all this was a façade. Penetrate beyond it and you encountered a penetrating intelligence, a thorough knowledge of the theatre, a command of musical and verbal techique that may have come from experience rather than textbooks and the classroom, but which nonetheless was comprehensive. He was one of the few composers for the popular musical theatre who were not satisfied to produce just the basic melodies for their shows. He insisted upon writing out the full harmonies for an entire number himself, to prepare his own overtures, to develop his own transitional material and all the other episodes and interludes called for by the production—chores usually left to the hands of professional orchestrators.

Just as he had worked too hard, so he had smoked too much (almost four packs a day). In the end, cigarettes killed him. He died of cancer at the Mount Sinai Hospital in New York on March 28, 1969. He was only fifty-nine.

GREAT MEN OF AMERICAN POPULAR SONG

Songs from Musical Plays–I

Rodgers and Hammerstein

One glorious era in Richard Rodgers's career closed when, after almost two decades, his partnership with Lorenz Hart ended. A still more glorious one opened up for Rodgers when Oscar Hammerstein II stepped into Hart's shoes.

He stepped into those shoes reluctantly. When Rodgers was compelled to face the disagreeable truth that working with Hart had rapidly been progressing from the difficult to the impossible, he visited Hammerstein at Hammerstein's farm in Doylestown, Pennsylvania, to discuss with him his problems with Hart. At that time, there were plans afoot for Rodgers and Hart to do a musical based on an original text by Ludwig Bemelmans (this musical never materialized). Rodgers had found Hart elusive and unapproachable—so much so that Rodgers was considering the possibility of calling in another lyricist-librettist to work with him. Would Hammerstein be interested? Hammerstein was interested, to be sure, since Rodgers was even then one of the most successful composers for the American theatre. But he turned down the offer because he did not wish to do anything to harm Hart, who was now so vulnerable to hurt. Then Hammerstein made a suggestion, typical of that man, but of a generosity not often encountered in a profession where selfishness and personal gain are the rule. "Get Hart to work with you on this Bemelmans thing," Hammerstein said, "and if he falls by the wayside, I'll gladly step in and finish the job for him, without anybody being the wiser."

As it turned out, the Bemelmans venture never progressed beyond the talking stage. As time passed, it became increasingly obvious that Hart had lost his interest and capacity for work and that if Rodgers were to continue in the theatre he would have to seek out a new writing partner. And once again, Hammerstein was the man he wanted.

It represented an act of faith in Hammerstein's talent and Rodgers's own courage in defying practicality to seek Hammerstein out as a collaborator at that time. For Hammerstein was then at the lowest plateau of his career. He had previously known the heights, both creatively and commercially, but suddenly success became elusive, as one failure followed another in a distressing procession that seemed to have no end. The theatre world was quite certain that Hammerstein had "written himself out," that his career was over. But Rodgers knew that a man of Hammerstein's creative imagination, literary powers, artistic daring, and consummate knowledge of the theatre could not possibly be "through," but must inevitably—given the proper conditions and the right time —return to the altitudes he had once occupied. Rodgers was convinced that the right time was "now"—that is, in 1943, when the Theatre Guild had offered Rodgers and Hart a commission to make a musical out of the American folk play *Green Grow the Lilacs,* a commission that Lorenz Hart turned down in no uncertain terms. And Rodgers felt instinctively that the proper conditions for Hammerstein might be realized the moment Rodgers began to work with him.

And so, while Hart was still alive—and had again and again insisted he did not want to do any work for a long time to come—Rodgers invited Hammerstein for lunch at the Barberry Room on Madison Avenue in New York. Would Hammerstein be interested in joining him in adapting *Green Grow the Lilacs* into a musical? Hammerstein replied that he knew the play well, had long been conscious of its potential as an American folk musical, and that his fingers were itching to get to work on this project. In fact, Hammerstein had once suggested to Jerome Kern that they make the musical adaptation, but Kern lacked enthusiasm. Still interested in *Green Grow the Lilacs,* Hammerstein tried acquiring the rights from the Theatre Guild. It was then that he heard for the first time that the Guild had already discussed the venture with Rodgers and Hart and therefore could not release the rights.

But now Hart was out of the picture completely, and Rodgers had come to him with the very play that had so long been so close to his heart. It did not take Hammerstein long to give his enthusiastic consent. Before lunch was over they had come to a meeting of minds on some of the ways in which the adaptation could be made. Or as Rodgers himself put it: "What happened between

Oscar and me was almost chemical. Put the right components together and an explosion takes place. Oscar and I hit it off from the day we began discussing the show."

Like Hart, Hammerstein was seven years older than Rodgers, but here the similarity between the two lyricists ends. Hammerstein was tall and gangling where Hart had been a miniature, with graceful movements. Hart's hyperthyroid nervousness and restlessness found their opposites in Hammerstein's inner serenity, in his composure under pressure, in his almost lethargic ways and the slow pace of his bodily motions. Where Hart was volatile and quixotic, Hammerstein was always predictable. Hammerstein could always be counted upon to see a job through on time, to keep appointments, to be present whenever needed, and never to forget a promise. He was, in short, Hart's counterpart in the very same way that Hart had been Rodgers's counterpart—even to the way Hammerstein regimented his daily life. He rose early each day, and was already at his desk hard at work by 9:30. After dinner, he liked spending the evening quietly with his family and one or two friends rather than go out to elaborate dinners or parties. By midnight he was asleep. In one significant way, however, Rodgers and Hammerstein were different—in their work. Rodgers could produce melodies spontaneously, easily, and swiftly; sometimes a finished product, requiring no further revision, was completed in the time others take to write a letter. Hammerstein's lyrics came slowly and with pain. It was not unusual for Hammerstein to spend weeks on one lyric as he devoted the most fastidious effort and extensive time on a single phrase. The final result of this hard labor was a simplicity and a grace that had the earmarks of utter spontaneity. Rodgers used to say that Hammerstein's lyrics lend themselves so naturally to music that all Rodgers had to do with a Hammerstein lyric was to put it on the piano and the melody would write itself.

Hammerstein came from a family that had distinguished itself in the theatre. His grandfather, Oscar Hammerstein I, was a world-famous opera impresario, whose Manhattan Opera had proved a formidable competitor to the Metropolitan Opera early in the twentieth century. He also built and operated the Victoria Theatre, New York's palace of vaudeville during the same period. This theatre was managed by William Hammerstein, the lyricist's father. Arthur Hammerstein, a highly successful producer of Broadway plays and musicals, was the lyricist's uncle.

The second Oscar, however, was being directed to law rather than the stage, though he had loved the theatre from his boyhood days on. After attending three years at Columbia College, he passed on to its law school in the fall of 1915. At college, he contributed lyrics and sketches for the varsity shows, in some of which he was also a performer. Some time during the period of his law study —and while working as a process server for five dollars a week—he decided that he wanted to gamble his future on the theatre rather than on law. He also wanted to marry Myra Finn, and needed a job to support her. In 1917 he deserted law study once and for all, and induced his uncle Arthur to hire him as stage manager and general utility man for one of Rudolf Friml's operettas, *You're in Love;* and during the summer of the same year he got married.

He progressed quickly in the theatre from assistant to full manager. He also began to do more writing: first, a song lyric that was placed in a show produced by his uncle; then, a four-act tragedy without music whose entire performing history consisted of four performances in New Haven.

His first musical comedy came soon after that. It was *Always You* (music by Herbert Stothart), produced early in 1920 by Arthur Hammerstein. It was for this production that Oscar's lyric writing received its first favorable critical comment. A reporter for *The New York Times* found that Hammerstein's verses "are more clever than those of the average musical comedy." *Always You* was a failure. His next musical, *Tickle Me* (music once again by Stothart, while the lyrics represented a collaborative effort with Otto Harbach) was a minor success. But in 1923, with *Wildflower,* Hammerstein shared a giant success with three writing partners, the lyrics being the joint effort of Harbach and Hammerstein, and the music being the work of Stothart and young Vincent Youmans. *Wildflower* stayed on Broadway over a year. Two of its songs represented Hammerstein's official entry into the arena of success: "Bambalina" and the title number.

During the next fifteen years or so, Hammerstein became one of the most prolific and successful and venerated librettists and lyricists on Broadway. With Jerome Kern he wrote *Show Boat,* which made stage history, as well as *Music in the Air* and the song that won an Academy Award, "The Last Time I Saw Paris." With Rudolf Friml, he wrote *Rose-Marie* and with Sigmund Romberg, *The Desert Song* and *The New Moon*—all three belonging with the greatest and most successful American operettas ever written.

Then lean years suddenly and inexplicably followed the fat ones. Both on Broadway and in London Hammerstein encountered one failure after another. Not one of eight consecutive productions had a run exceeding seven weeks, and one of these lasted only one week. His luck in Hollywood was no better. After several screen failures, a Hollywood producer paid him $100,000 to scrap a contract calling for four pictures. "He can't write his hat," that producer maintained.

The meeting of the talents of Hammerstein and Rodgers in the writing of their first musical, therefore, represented a crucial juncture in the careers of both men.

In a most curious way—so much so that coincidence practically has the appearance of some predetermined destiny—the activities, associations, and biographical events of Hammerstein and Rodgers were interrelated time and again. For example, both men had fathers named William. Both young men had spent their summers at the same boys' camp and had attended the same college (though at different periods). Both had wives by the name of Dorothy (Dorothy being Hammerstein's second wife), and both met these wives aboard a transatlantic liner. Hammerstein's first wife had been a distant relative of Rodgers's.

And Rodgers's father had been the physician who had delivered Hammerstein's first two children.

Rodgers and Hammerstein had met for the first time in 1915 at Columbia University. Hammerstein was appearing in a varsity show, for which he had written some of the material; Dick Rodgers was a member of the audience. After the show, Dick's brother, Oscar Hammerstein's classmate, took him backstage to introduce him to Oscar, an event that the young Dick regarded with no little awe.

Four years later, Hammerstein and Rodgers wrote some songs for an amateur production, and a year after that they wrote another one for a Columbia varsity show. This marked the end of their efforts at collaboration for a twenty-year period. However, they never lost sight of each other in those years, since they met frequently at various opening nights and social events, and were completely aware of each other's achievements and ever-mounting success.

Then came the time for them to join forces again—in the musical adaptation of *Green Grow the Lilacs* for the Theatre Guild. They were destined to remain creative partners for the next two decades and in the process to change the course and destiny of the American musical theatre.

From their initial discussions on how best to make a musical out of *Green Grow the Lilacs,* both Rodgers and Hammerstein realized that they would have to strike out boldly in altogether new directions. All the old values, formats, and conventions of musical comedy would have to be jettisoned once and for all. Some approaches, in fact, would have to be so revolutionary as to depart completely from anything the musical theatre had thus far attempted. What they had to do was to create an altogether new genre—a "musical play" as distinguished from "musical comedy": a production in which the play *was* the thing, and every other element was to be subservient to the play; where the plot line and the character delineation had to dictate the kind of material that would be used, instead of vice versa. Efforts in the direction of the musical play had already been previously attempted in productions like the Jerome Kern–Oscar Hammerstein musical *Show Boat,* and in the Pulitzer Prize winning *Of Thee I Sing* with score by the Gershwin brothers. But compared to what Rodgers and Hammerstein were now planning—and reducing their planning to details— these earlier efforts at musical-play writing had been tentative and elementary. The adaptation of *Green Grow the Lilacs* called for much sharper deviations from the norm both in the overall concept and in each of its components; once they had set their course, Rodgers and Hammerstein did not for a moment hesitate to follow it without deviation.

Green Grow the Lilacs had been a folk play, a love story told simply, unaffectedly in the tradition of true folklore. The setting was the Midwestern Indian country at the turn of the present century; the protagonists, Laurey and Curly. Curly's shyness provides the obstacle to the consummation of this romance and leads both lovers to assume a false attitude of hostility to each other; another obstacle is the presence of a despicable character, Jud Fry, who is also interested in Laurey. Jud Fry invades the wedding ceremony of Laurey and Curly (once the lovers have solved their personal relationship). Drunk, he menaces Curly with a knife only to become the fatal victim of his own blade in the scuffle that follows. An improvised court then and there exonerates Curly, allowing the wedded pair to go off on their honeymoon to the territory eventually to become known as Oklahoma.

Rodgers and Hammerstein were convinced that the homespun folk character of the play, with its overall subdued and relaxed atmosphere, had to be retained in the musical: not only in the kind of text and songs they would write but also in the kind of choreography that would be required. No formal dance routines would suffice here; indeed, nothing less than American folk ballet of the highest caliber. One of America's leading ballet dancers and choreographers, Agnes de Mille, was engaged to prepare the dance routines worthy of the repertory of any major American ballet company.

The play had no humorous episodes to speak of, and so the kind of comedy that inspires loud guffaws was not to be considered. Instead, there would be an infusion of a mild and subtle brand of humor that was basic to the characters: Ado Annie, a girl who simply could not say "no" to men, for whom Rodgers and Hammerstein wrote the two amusing numbers "All er Nothin' " and "I Cain't Say No"; and a sardonic narrative, "Pore Jud," in which this disagreeable and thoroughly disliked individual tries to imagine the reaction of his neighbors to his death.

In other unconventional ways, too, this musical would have to be different from that usually encountered in Broadway productions: in the character delineation of Jud Fry and in the inclusion of a murder scene, two jarring discords for a theatre that was always partial to consonant harmonies. Flimsily attired chorus girls to arouse the sexual appetite of male audiences would be excess baggage and had to be eliminated. And, perhaps most significantly, the characterizations had to be such a strong element in a thoroughly well-balanced production that there would be no place in the production for stars to steal the limelight.

"You can do everything in the theatre you want," Rodgers has always maintained, "just so long as you do it *right*." Rodgers and Hammerstein were determined to do their job "right" by meeting the play on its own terms, even if it meant a digression from those practices to which audiences had long been accustomed in their musicals. And so, in writing *Oklahoma!*—as their musical finally came to be called—they conceived a production representing a brave new world for the theatre, and from its opening moments: a male voice offstage chanting a simple folklike tune, "Oh, What a Beautiful Mornin'," while the only person on the stage was a woman churning butter. Rare, indeed, was there a musical that did not open with a fanfare of shouting chorus girls in an elaborate production number!

The Rodgers and Hammerstein score boasted at least one song that had popular appeal to join the top echelon on "Hit Parade": "People Will Say We're in Love." This is the only song in the production where the melody was written before the lyrics (Rodgers and Hammerstein having early come to the decision that since the lyrics, like the dialogue, were an inextricable part of the text, it was wiser to get the lyrics for a specific situation or scene done before Rodgers planned his music). The writing of "People Will Say We're in Love" posed a particular problem to its authors. This is the love duet of Laurey and Curly, but because of Curly's shyness and Laurey's resentment at his diffidence, the lovers put on an outward show of antagonism to each other. The song had to suggest this and yet remain romantic. Once Rodgers recognized the problem, he put down on paper a melody he felt would strike the proper mood, melody coming to him spontaneously. Rodgers's melody spurred Hammerstein on to create lyrics in which Curly and Laurey caution each other against showing any outward demonstrations of tenderness lest neighbors misunderstand their attitude to one another; at the same time the words also suggested, more through innuendo than outright statement, the true feelings of the young people for each other.

If "People Will Say We're in Love" was of "Hit Parade" variety, most of the other thirteen songs in *Oklahoma!* had the flavor and the personality of authentic Western folk music, particularly numbers like "The Surrey with the Fringe on Top," "Kansas City," "The Farmer and the Cowman," and the title number with which the production ends. No less remarkable than Rodgers's gift of catching the personality of American folk songs in his melodies was Hammerstein's gift of using the vernacular in endowing the songs with their strong American identity. Other numbers—of interest for their exquisite tenderness rather than for their American folk character—were no less inextricably bound up with characters and story: "Many a New Day," for example, or "Out of My Dreams" or "Laurey Makes Up Her Mind."

The history of *Oklahoma!* is by now such a thrice-familiar tale that it is necessary here merely to review a few basic facts: how everybody directly or remotely connected with the production (with the single exception of Rodgers), and many who were not, were convinced that *Oklahoma!* had all the makings of a box-office disaster. When the motion-picture executive Harry Cohn learned that a good deal of this production would be devoted to serious American ballet, he asked with amazement: "You mean—one of *those* things?" He proceeded to pirouet while placing the tip of his forefinger on his head. Others maintained that when people wanted culture or art they went to the Metropolitan Opera or to the ballet but on Broadway people wanted to be entertained. And how could a musical prove entertaining that boasted no stars, no chorus girls, no laughs, no big production numbers, no popular dance routines? "No Girls, No Gags, No Chance" was the message relayed back to Broadway when *Oklahoma!* tried out in New Haven.

Then *Oklahoma!* opened in New York on March 31, 1943. The first-night audience stood up and cheered at the final curtain, and the critics the following morning could not summon sufficient superlatives to express their delight and enthusiasm. The rest is familiar history. The phrase "No Girls, No Gags, No Chance" was changed to "No Girls, No Gags, No Tickets." *Oklahoma!* had the longest run in the history of the Broadway theatre up to that time—five years and nine weeks for a total of 2,212 performances. A national company toured for ten years, while the original company, once it left Broadway, had a tour of its own covering seventy cities in fifty-one weeks. In addition, companies were formed in Europe to present the show in Berlin, London, South Africa, Sweden, Denmark, Australia, and other distant places. A special troupe toured the Pacific to entertain the American armed forces (this being the time of World War II). It would be impossible to estimate the millions who saw the show live. And those who did not could hear the entire infectious scores on Decca records which exceeded the selling mark of one million albums, *Oklahoma!* being the first Broadway musical to offer an original-cast recording of an entire score, since that time become standard procedure in the recording business. And many millions more could see the production on the screen when it was filmed in the then-new Todd-O-A process, starring Shirley Jones and Gordon MacRae, released in 1955.

The original investment of $83,000—which had proved such a long and heartbreaking process to collect, much of it coming from theatre-loving people as an act of charity to the Theatre Guild—brought in a profit of over $5 million. Each investor owning 1 percent (then valued at $1,500) earned well over $50,000. The Threatre Guild drew in a profit of $4 million. Rodgers and Hammerstein each earned over $1 million.

On the strength of such unprecedented triumph, Rodgers and Hammerstein began expanding their operations. They founded their own publishing company, calling it Williamson because both their fathers were named William. They created their own theatre-producing unit. In time they not only produced all their own shows but also took on a similar chore for shows by other writers, frequently with fabulous financial returns, as was the case with Irving Berlin's *Annie Get Your Gun.* In short, they built up a theatrical empire that soon grossed many millions a year and extended far beyond the boundaries of the United States.

Also on the strength of the early phenomenal response to *Oklahoma!* Rodgers and Hammerstein were contracted to write a score for the movies. Their assignment was *State Fair* in 1944, starring Dick Haymes and Jeanne Crain. Two song classics came from this venture: "It's a Grand Night for Singing" and "It Might As Well Be Spring," the latter winning the Academy Award.

In creating the Academy Award winning number, Hammerstein encountered no end of difficulty in conceiving his lyrics. The song was planned for the heroine, a young girl suffering despondency even though she is soon to go on a spree to the state fair. Not until it occurred to Hammerstein that her mood resembled spring fever did the dawn of an idea begin to break. But state fairs are held not in the spring but in the fall. Hammerstein solved this by pointing out in his lyrics that the time the girl is singing might be autumn, but the way she was feeling made it seem like spring. Once the matter was thoroughly clarified in his mind—and enthusiastically accepted by Rodgers—Hammerstein could complete his lyric in a week's time, which for Hammerstein represented lightning speed. When Hammerstein turned his lyric over to Rodgers in their office, he left for about an hour to meet Max Dreyfus. Returning to his own office, Hammerstein found that Rodgers had completed the song, and that not a single note ever required change. To this day "It Might As Well Be Spring" has remained one of the supreme song creations by Rodgers and Hammerstein.

It remained the musical highlight of the picture when in 1962 Paramount made a new version (with Pat Boone and Ann-Margret among others), for which Richard Rodgers wrote five new numbers (words as well as music).

What do you do for an encore after *Oklahoma!*? How can you write anything for the Broadway stage that would not be anticlimactic after a triumph of such magnitude? Rodgers and Hammerstein answered these questions eloquently, with three musical plays, each since become a classic, each with an initial Broadway run exceeding one thousand performances: *South Pacific* in 1949 (1,925 performances); *The King and I* in 1951 (1,246 performances); and *The Sound of Music* in 1959 (1,443 performances). *Carousel* in 1945, another landmark, came close to the thousand mark with 890 performances (it represented the American musical theatre at the Brussels Exposition in 1958), while *Flower Drum Song,* in 1958, had a healthy Broadway existence with 601 performances. All these, in time, were successfully transferred to the screen, while *The Sound of Music* was destined to make motion-picture history with the largest gross at the box office throughout the world. All these, in their original-cast recordings, were resounding best sellers, topped by *The Sound of Music* which sold about eight million copies of the film sound track recording and about five million copies of the original-cast Broadway recording.

To emphasize the artistic as well as the financial importance of the above-named productions is the fact that through them Rodgers and Hammerstein became the recipients of the Pulitzer Prize in drama (for *South Pacific*), two New York Drama Critics Circle Awards for the best musicals of the year (for *Carousel* and *South Pacific*), together with twenty-five Donaldson Awards and seventeen Antoinette Perry Awards.

For Hammerstein the long road back to success that had started with *Oklahoma!* and ended with *The Sound of Music* meant complete self-fulfillment as a writer of texts and lyrics. The promises he had shown so forcefully in *Show Boat* in 1927 were now fully realized. Here was no longer a librettist creating synthetic books for the convenience of performers or composers or routines (as had been the case when he had worked with Friml or Romberg) but a dramatist who frequently introduced into his fresh dialogue, into his inventive development of a story line or delineation of a character, humanity, compassion, and tenderness, as well as a seemingly infallible instinct for theatrical values. As a lyricist, for all the disarming simplicity of his style and lack of pretense in his choice of words, he was again and again capable of achieving not just functional lines on which a composer can hang his melodies, but a true poet whose subtlety and nuances of expression brought artistic distinction of a high order to lyric writing.

Hammerstein proved his unique powers in the handling of words on one occasion without the benefit of Rodgers's collaboration. This happened just before Rodgers and Hammerstein had gone out to Hollywood to do the score for *State Fair*. On December 2, 1943 (just about eight months after *Oklahoma!* had opened), Oscar Hammerstein brought to Broadway one of the most unique experiments the American theatre has known—*Carmen Jones*.

This was a musical play which modernized Bizet's opera *Carmen*. Put into an American-Negro setting, *Carmen Jones* translated both the action and the characters of the opera into modern terms. The bullfighter, Escamillo, became a prizefighter, Husky Miller; Don José is transformed into Joe, a corporal in the army. Seville changes into a Southern town in America during World War II. The heroine of the opera is transformed into Carmen Jones, an employee in a parachute factory. As in the opera, the dramatic peak comes at the end of the play when Carmen Jones is killed by Joe, whom she has discarded in favor of the prizefighter, outside the fighting arena in which Husky is engaged in a championship bout. What was particularly novel about this modern American treatment of a classic French opera, beyond the use of an all-Negro cast, was the fact that Bizet's music was used to Hammerstein's new and appropriate lyrics with little change, the melody almost in each case being heard exactly as it is in the Bizet opera: in songs like "Dat's Love" (in the opera, the famous "Habanera"); "Dere's a Café on de Corner" ("Seguidille"); "Dis Flower" ("The Flower Song"); "My Joe" ("Micaëla's Air"); and "Stan' Up and Fight" ("Toreador Song").

By the time 1944 rolled around, with *Oklahoma!* fully established as an artistic and financial triumph and *Carmen Jones* selling out the house for a run that would extend over a year, Hammerstein's return to victory after a long and extended period of defeat became an accepted fact along Broadway. He himself reacted to this sudden change of fortune with a quiet charm, humor, and modesty which characterized all the things he said and did. In a full-page advertisement in *Variety,* he announced in a big, bold headline: "I've Done It Before and I Can Do It Again." There then followed underneath it a listing of all the failures he had suffered in New York and London in the few years preceding *Oklahoma!*

But far greater victories were yet in store for Hammerstein during the years that followed, and all of them came about because of the inimitable relationship that existed between him and Rodgers.

They were as one—both as creative artists and as friends. Both were family men whose satisfaction in raising their children and catering to their wives (together with their mutual interest in books, art, and the theatre) made them completely disinterested in seeking out more exciting pursuits. Neither man drank liquor to excess, was interested in sports, gambled, was a chain smoker, or was an habitué of all-night parties. The Rodgerses raised their two daughters at their duplex apartment on East Seventy-first Street in the winter and in the summer at their country house in Rockmeadow, in Southport, Connecticut. Hammerstein's family also occupied two homes: a five-floor brick house on East Sixty-third Street for the winter and a functioning farm, Highland, at Doylestown in the Bucks County region of Pennsylvania for out-of-town living. Together, Rodgers and Hammerstein conducted their business affairs at a ten-room suite at 488 Madison Avenue in New York, which Rodgers visited regularly to keep his fingers on the pulse of all their activities, but which Hammerstein generally avoided, preferring to confine his business dealings and decisions to telephone conversations with his partner from his own little private office on the ground floor of his New York house. Both families got along so extraordinarily well that a fast friendship was developed and made permanent. And so, it was not difficult for Rodgers and Hammerstein to be as close in their friendship as they were in work. Holding similar liberal views about politics and religion and being equally passionate about participating in humanitarian and charitable endeavors further helped to cement their personal relationship. They were in fact so much alike that each could practically predict the other's reactions to any given situation; and most of the time each would come up with almost identical solutions to any given problem. This unanimity of soul, spirit, interests, and personality was combined with a most profound respect of the one for the other's talent and judgment, which seemed to make it impossible for either one to do anything without first discussing it with the other. As a mutual friend once remarked: "I can't show one of them a window card for a Chinese laundry without his calling the other for an opinion."

As collaborators, as well as friends, they were also ideal mates. Both loved the theater and *knew* the theatre and were determined to give it their very best without concessions to expediency or compromises with ideals. To do less than that would have represented to each man a disreputable abuse placed on him by his talent and his integrity. Both were driven by the same artistic impulse to extend the artistic horizons of the musical theatre far beyond the existing boundary lines; both possessed the same brand of adventure and courage—to do the new and the unconventional, and at times the provocative, without concern for public, critical, or box-office reaction. Both men were sticklers for the most minute details without ever losing sight of the larger design. And both men demanded from everyone who worked with them everything he or she could give.

Rodgers and Hammerstein evolved a working arrangement which, for them at any rate, proved ideal. Before a line was put down on paper, they spent countless hours, which often stretched to weeks and months, discussing every phase of the play, every piece of stage business, the types of song that were required and where best they would fit, the kind of performers they would need, and so forth. Hammerstein might be the man in charge of writing the words, and Rodgers might be the musician. Nevertheless, neither hesitated to give the other helpful suggestions in the other man's field. More than once Hammerstein revised his lyrics at Rodgers's request because he knew that the lyrics were being improved. And Hammerstein never hesitated to suggest to Rodgers the kind of music he felt was needed for a certain situation: perhaps some background music for spoken dialogue; perhaps a musical episode to tie together some stage action; perhaps some musical phrases interpolated to help project an emotional or atmospheric effect Hammerstein was trying to achieve.

Once every detail was clear in mind, they separated—each to perform his own job. Hammerstein always wrote the lyrics before Rodgers did the music, although long before the lyrics reached Rodgers he had done a good deal of thinking about, and gathering of, various ideas that could be used. Hammerstein liked working on his farm in Doylestown, walking up and down nervously in his second-floor studio (which had a balcony) as he pieced together phrases and lines. When he arrived at something that satisfied him, he would write it down, using an old-fashioned upright bookkeeper's desk which Jerome Kern once presented him because he knew Hammerstein liked to do his writing standing rather than seated. When a lyric was finished, Hammerstein invented a dummy tune to try out the words—"melodies so terrible," his wife once confessed, "that they want to make you cry." The lyric completed, Hammerstein dispatched it at once to Rodgers for the musical setting, which more often than not would be completed before Hammerstein had an opportunity to catch his breath.

Dialogue was done in a different way, by means of a dictating machine (Hammerstein liked to hear the sound of his lines) and a secretary who transcribed the dictation on paper. Then came an intensive period of revision when Hammerstein worked painstakingly on every word and phrase. Once a scene was completed, he would act out all the parts.

The problem of casting, meanwhile, was being solved all the while that the play was being written. Sometimes an established star like Mary Martin or Gertrude Lawrence was an inevitable choice. More often, however, Rodgers and Hammerstein stood ready to gamble on unknowns, or on performers from fields alien to the musical theatre, to fill principal roles. Ezio Pinza and Helen Traubel, both of them stars of opera, had never appeared in Broadway musicals till Rodgers and Hammerstein picked them out for the major roles in two of their own. Yul Brynner was a complete unknown when, after a single audition, both Rodgers and Hammerstein seized him for the all-important part of the king in *The King and I*. Similarly many a novice, many a performer then languishing in obscurity, were the choices for various Rodgers and Hammerstein productions —to be developed as stars of the first rank: performers like Celeste Holm, Howard Keel, John Raitt, Shirley Jones, to mention just a few.

Once the play was written, the casting completed, and the various other collaborators (scenic and costume designers, director, choreographer, and so forth) had been chosen, the work *really* began: the grueling period of rehearsal. Rehearsals consumed twelve hours a day, seven days a week, with Rodgers and Hammerstein always at hand to make necessary changes, to give valuable suggestions to various departments, and to keep an ever-vigilant eye and ear that details were not being neglected. Hammerstein usually remained seated in the auditorium—to all outward appearances thoroughly calm and detached—making numerous notes which he then transmitted to the proper authorities. Rodgers, on the other hand, was seemingly all over the theatre, a bundle of released nervous energy. Now he made sure to test the acoustics, now he checked on the lighting, now he meticulously followed the staging. Confronted with carelessness or sloppiness, Rodgers would be scathing in his criticisms; and he was even more merciless in his attack if a singer or the orchestra tried to change the tempo, or the slightest nuance, of what he had put down on paper. Then suddenly and without warning, this man who had been shouting from all parts of the theatre would lapse into complete silence, withdrawing into himself as if to isolate himself completely from the goings-on on the the stage. He was now trying to be the audience and get objective impressions.

Out-of-town tryouts were more hectic still, for now Rodgers and Hammerstein had audience reactions to guide them. Intensive rewriting would often have to take place and had to be done in white-heat haste. The new material had to be learned by the cast just as quickly. Those rehearsals of rewritten material had to be done in the mornings if there was a matinee that day, or all day long if there was only an evening performance to do; the working day now stretched out to eighteen hours for everybody concerned.

On opening nights, Rodgers and Hammerstein suddenly reversed the personalities they had revealed at rehearsals and tryouts. Now it was Hammerstein's turn to be high-strung and jittery. He would mutter curses under his breath each time something went wrong, however trifling. All the time he was in constant dread that the whole production would collapse. By the time the premiere ended he was a physical and mental wreck. Rodgers, on the other hand, would sit imperturbably in his seat, confident that the job had been done well and that everything would progress smoothly, which was usually the case.

The opening-night performance over, their many friends and relatives would swarm around Rodgers and Hammerstein to congratulate them and exclaim that this was their *chef d'oeuvre*. Each man is enough of a realist not to take any of this reaction seriously, since the admirers and well-wishers on first nights are hardly representative of the audiences who pay a good price to see a show and do not know the authors personally. The reviews are the first things that count. These would be awaited usually at Sardi's restaurant, to be read aloud if they were raves, or *sotto voce* if the critics found the play wanting. If the play had met with accolades, there would be a party somewhere, which Rodgers and Hammerstein rarely attended. They preferred going home to rest from the harrowing ordeal of the preceding weeks. After all, a new ordeal would soon have to be suffered: the writing of their next musical.

One thing was certain: the next show they wrote would be completely different from the one that had preceded it. Neither Rodgers nor Hammerstein had any appetite for reheating and eating again yesterday's meal. One other thing was also certain: whatever demands their new project would make upon them for its full realization, Rodgers and Hammerstein would be ready to meet those demands, however impractical or controversial or revolutionary those demands might be. It took imagination of a high order and an indomitable will and courage to try the impossible or to do something that was never done before by selecting for musical-play treatment the subject matter of *Oklahoma! Carousel, South Pacific, The King and I,* and *The Sound of Music.* And it took artistic intransigence to deal with these unorthodox subjects the way they required.

Take, for example, *Carousel,* which was the immediate successor to *Oklahoma!* being produced in 1945. *Carousel* was based on Ferenc Molnar's play *Liliom,* which the Theatre Guild had produced successfully—but with the setting changed from Budapest to a coastal town in America's New England. Its characters consequently were no longer Hungarians but New England sailors, fishermen, and mill hands. And the time was set back from the early twentieth century to 1873. As a stage play *Liliom* was a source of stage enchantment. But as a musical it posed one imponderable problem after another. Changing the characters to Americans and the setting to New England represented a solution to one of those problems since, in 1945, America was at war with the Nazis and Fascists, and Hungary was an ally of Nazi Germany—making both Budapest and Hungarians highly disagreeable for consumption by American audiences at the time. But there were more difficult problems still. Half of the play was realistic. This was the romance, marriage, and marital complications of a happy-go-lucky and irresponsible operator of a carousel in an amusement park (to whom Rodgers and Hammerstein gave the name of Billy Bigelow) and a demure, unsophisticated mill girl the writers called Julie Jordan. Billy's imminent fatherhood fills him with inordinate pride and ambition. He now must get money, and lots of it, to meet the needs of his coming child. Being the kind of person he was, he tried to get the money in a holdup, in which he becomes a fatal victim. From this point on, the play passes to fantasy: first to Purgatory where Billy is doomed to spend fifteen years; then back to earth where he returns for a single day to redeem his soul by bringing to his now grownup daughter, on her graduation day, the hope and courage she needs to face life.

A play that was half fantasy and half realistic, a play in which the hero is killed midway in the story, a play in which tragedy stalks throughout the play even though in the end there is a happy resolution—this is not the stuff of which Broadway musicals are made. But Rodgers and Hammerstein were not trying to write a typical Broadway musical. They were now thinking expansively in terms almost of musical drama rather than a musical play. And for such a drama Rodgers had to conceive a score far more ambitious than the one he had done for *Oklahoma!*—a score of such depth, dimension, and scope that at times it touches the boundary line of opera.

Once and for all Rodgers broke through the structural limitations of the sixteen-bar introduction and the thirty-two-bar chorus of the usual musical-comedy song. He produced, in one place, a seven-minute musical narrative, 'Soliloquy," in which Billy Bigelow reveals his changing reactions to the thought of becoming a father, a narrative made up of eight different important musical ideas which progress in the style of a *durchkomponiert Lied*. This was the first musical number that Rodgers and Hammerstein completed for *Carousel*. Once they had that song on paper, they heaved a sigh of relief not only because the number was dramatically so potent but because it proved to their satisfaction that, as they put it, they had "the play licked."

Other unusual musical procedures could now be undertaken with complete faith in their practicality: the set of symphonic waltzes, played under the opening scene—set in an amusement park and dominated by a carousel. All kinds and types of musical episodes could be interpolated throughout the play to help project atmosphere, heighten tensions, intensify emotions: now heard as background to spoken dialogue; now used as a catalytic agent between one episode in the play and the next; now becoming a kind of commentator on what was going on in the story. Extended musical sequences could be introduced combining song, dialogue, recitatives, and orchestral interludes. But songs were by no means neglected—songs so exalted in their melodic content and so surpassingly touching in their emotion that popular appeal is combined with artistic purpose: the principal love song, "If I Loved You," and also "When the Children Are Asleep," "What's the Use of Wond'rin'?," and a song (one of several Rodgers and Hammerstein would produce in the next few years) which had such a feeling of the spiritual and the sublime that Cole Porter said there was a kind of holiness about it—"You'll Never Walk Alone." There were gay, ebullient numbers, too, the most famous being "June Is Bustin' Out All Over" (as invigorating as the fresh breezes of the vernal season) and numbers thoroughly New England in character and personality, such as "Blow High, Blow Low," "This Was a Real Nice Clambake," and "Geraniums in the Winder." "Composer Rodgers has swathed it [*Carousel*] with one of the warmest and most velvety scores," reported *Time*. "More than a succession of tunes, the music helps to interpret the story. . . . Hammerstein has caught the spirit with his lyrics." And Lewis Nichols wrote in *The New York Times* that in *Carousel* could be found "one of the most beautiful Rodgers score, and some of Hammerstein's best rhymes."

There is a poignant anecdote connected with the tender "What's the Use of Wond'rin'?" In 1954 *Carousel* was being revived, and one day late in 1953 Rodgers brought Jan Clayton to the Majestic Theatre to listen to some auditions for the principal roles. They arrived early, and the theatre was still deserted. Neither said a word, but both suddenly remembered that the Majestic Theatre was the place where *Carousel* had originally played, and that Jan Clayton was the one who had created the role of Julie. Rodgers recalls: "The idea occurred to us simultaneously. Jan stood on the same spot on the stage where she'd stood nine years before, and I went to the piano. She sang 'What's the Use of Wond'rin'?' to the empty seats. I don't mind saying we were both a little teary."

If *Allegro,* in 1947, represented for Rodgers and Hammerstein a temporary setback (it had a run of just 315 performances), it was nevertheless a failure with moments of grandeur and nobility, as well as extraordinary originality. The idea Rodgers and Hammerstein tried to project, in a text original with Hammerstein, was the victory of idealism over materialism, a victory personified in a doctor who at first prefers financial rewards and social position to the practice of sound medicine to the best of his abilities. In the end he returns to his humble hometown to reject the glitter and gloss of his former life to devote himself to the serious business of curing sick neighbors. With two such triumphs as *Oklahoma!* and *Carousel* behind them, Rodgers and Hammerstein had no hesitancy in embarking upon even more radical departures in accepted stage procedures than heretofore. Most of the time they dispensed with scenery and costumes and had the action take place on an empty or half-empty stage. Colors were flashed on a background screen from time to time to accentuate moods. Rodgers and Hammerstein also lifted the chorus out of Greek drama to comment on what was happening in the play, sometimes in song, sometimes in speech. Some of the critics were delighted with these experiments, and one or two were even rhapsodic in their praises. But where the audiences were concerned, Rodgers and Hammerstein were perhaps moving too fast away from tradition and the *status quo. Allegro* was not an audience show, and audiences stayed away. But *Allegro* was a far better musical than its failure in 1947 would suggest. Both Rodgers and Hammerstein were proud of it, in spite of the fact that the show incurred a large financial deficit. Hammerstein often spoke of reviving it with some basic changes. Regrettably, he never lived to do so. About all that most theatregoers remember about *Allegro* are two significant musical numbers: "A Fellow Needs a Girl" and "The Gentleman Is a Dope."

But if there was any suspicion in anybody's mind that Rodgers and Hammerstein had exhausted their artistic and box-office potential, it was put to permanent rest with *South Pacific* in 1949. Here was a production that one veteran showman (Arthur Hammerstein) would call "the perfect musical" while another (Michael Todd) would describe it as "the greatest musical ever written." Here was a production that arrived at the Majestic Theatre with the then-unprecedented advance sale of over one million dollars. Here was a production that, from its first evening of out-of-town tryouts, was an obvious blockbuster. And a blockbuster it most assuredly was: with a Broadway run of 1,925 performances (only 323 less than the epoch-making record established by *Oklahoma!*); with its Broadway box-office draw of nine million dollars, a sum without equal in Broadway history; with a national company touring for several years breaking every known box-office record wherever it came, and grossing in the very first year of its tour over three and a half million dollars; with its capture of every possible prize, including the Pulitzer Prize for drama (only the second musical to do so, and the first since *Of Thee I Sing*), the New York Drama Critics Award as the season's best musical, nine Donaldson and seven Antoinette Perry awards; with its sale of over two million copies of sheet music and over one million copies of the original-cast recording; and with its motion-picture adaptation becoming one of the highest income getters in the history of talking pictures up to that time not only in America but in Europe as well.

Unlike *Oklahoma! Carousel*, and *Allegro*, *South Pacific* did not seem at first sight to be a subject alien to the conformist musical theatre. On the surface it seemed the kind of material that would always have been welcomed by traditional musical-comedy and even operetta writers. The source was *Tales of the South Pacific* by James Michener (a collection of stories about American men and women in the armed forces during World War II serving on a South Pacific Island), a book that received the Pulitzer Prize in literature following its publication in 1947. From these stories, Hammerstein (with Joshua Logan as his collaborator in preparing the text) selected two for the stage adaptation, "Our Heroine" and "Fo' Dolla." Out of these the collaborators picked the love story of Emile de Becque—a middle-aged French widower who had become a wealthy planter on the South Pacific island—and the American nurse in the armed forces, Ensign Nellie Forbush. The problems that loomed as insurmountable to their romance—principally the fact that he had lived with a Polynesian girl with whom he had had two children and the dramatic episode attending a major maneuver in the war involving the French planter—were ideal for musical-comedy treatment; nothing here, surely, to upset even the most staunch traditionalist. But difficulties there were, nevertheless, each calling for the kind of integrity and independence of thought and the determination to stick to their high standards for which Rodgers and Hammerstein had already distinguished themselves.

For one thing, the script called for a hero who was a middle-aged widower —not a handsome, dashing young fellow. To make an older man the other half of the central romantic theme was something no musical before would have considered. But Rodgers and Hammerstein accepted the necessary, and with such success that Ezio Pinza—who was lifted from the Metropolitan Opera to play de Becque, in his Broadway musical debut—became a new matinee idol overnight.

More iconoclastic still was the subsidiary love plot between an American marine, Cable, and Liat, the young Tonkinese daughter of Bloody Mary. It is quite true that miscegenation had been dealt with in *Show Boat* two decades earlier. But Rodgers and Hammerstein not only stood ready to deal with the subject again but were determined to use that subject as propaganda for racial tolerance by writing a song called "Carefully Taught," preaching the moral that "you've got to be taught to be afraid" of people with different-colored skins or people with eyes "oddly made." However much their friends, advisers, and colleagues tried to dissuade Rodgers and Hammerstein from injecting propaganda into a musical, Rodgers and Hammerstein remained unshakable. Let the South boycott the musical if they resented the song, and let the bigots raise a hue and cry. The Cable-Liat romance would stay in their play, would receive prominent attention. And the song would *not* be deleted. "This number," Michener explained, "represented why they [Rodgers and Hammerstein] had wanted to do the play, and that even if it meant failure of the production it was going to stay in. . . . Courage and determination such as this counts for something in art."

Just as "Carefully Taught" was essential to the play as it was conceived and developed by its authors, so many of the other songs in the score were basic to the characters who presented them, throwing a new light on their personalities and giving them a new dimension. Rodgers himself made this point clear when he wrote: "I tried to weave de Becque's character into his songs—romantic, rather powerful, but not too involved—and so I wrote for him 'Some Enchanted Evening' and 'This Nearly Was Mine.' Nellie Forbush is a Navy nurse out of Arkansas, a kid whose musical background probably had been limited to the movies, radio, and maybe a touring musical comedy. She talks in the vernacular, so her songs had to be in the vernacular. It gave me a chance for a change of pace, and the music I wrote for her is light, contemporary, rhythmic: 'A Cockeyed Optimist,' 'I'm Gonna Wash That Man Right Outa My Hair,' 'I'm in Love with a Wonderful Guy.' Cable's songs—'Younger Than Springtime' and 'Carefully Taught'—are like the man, deeply sincere, while Bloody Mary's songs, 'Bali Ha'i' and 'Happy Talk,' try to convey some of the languor and mystery of her race."

Some of the melodies came with facility and speed. It took Rodgers five minutes to write "Bali Ha'i." He was drinking his coffee while dining with some friends when Hammerstein turned the lyrics over to him. Rodgers started writing before he had even finished drinking his coffee, and in a matter of minutes the song was written. "Happy Talk" took Rodgers twenty minutes. Rodgers was sick in bed when the lyrics arrived by messenger. Twenty minutes later Hammerstein called to inquire if the messenger had arrived. "I've already written the melody," Rodgers informed him.

"Some Enchanted Evening"—the love song shared by de Becque and Nellie Forbush—became the hit-parade number of the production. It had a magical tenderness that is still irresistible. But another love song, this one belonging exclusively to Nellie, proved appealing for the feeling of excitement, exuberance, and ebullience it helped to engender—"I'm in Love with a Wonderful Guy." A good deal of this heady-wine spirit came from Rodgers's lusty melody—but not all. The repetition of the phrase "I'm in love" five times, in the closing line of the chorus, creates a powerful momentum that helps to sweep the song to a most exciting conclusion. It might be added that it was Rodgers who suggested this repetition, an idea Hammerstein seized upon. When Mary Martin (who created the role of Nellie Forbush) first tried out "I'm in Love with a Wonderful Guy," it was late at night at Joshua Logan's apartment. "I almost passed out," she confessed. "I was so excited. After the repeats I fell off the piano bench and I remember that the management had to call up to complain of the noise."

In writing Bloody Mary's songs Rodgers had to try to achieve an exoticism in line with the racial background of this character. An Oriental exoticism was a strain Rodgers had to reach for and realize even more frequently and consistently in the Rodgers and Hammerstein musical that succeeded *South Pacific*— *The King and I* in 1951. For *The King and I* was set in Siam in the early 1860's; and all the characters (except four) were Orientals. Dialogue, song, choreography, therefore, had to have a definite Oriental identity—but without lapsing into caricature and the clichés which the Western world has come to associate with Orientals. As Hammerstein said: "What was required was the Eastern sense of dignity and pageantry and none of this business of girls dressed in Oriental costumes and dancing out onto the stage and singing 'ching-aling-aling' with their fingers in the air." As for the music, it had to have an Eastern character without being authentically Oriental, since Rodgers knew nothing of authentic Oriental music, with its esoteric scales, instruments, and structures. "I couldn't write an authentic Far-Eastern melody if my life depended upon it," as Rodgers himself confessed. "If I could, I wouldn't. A too-accurate re-creation of Siamese music would have jarred the ears of an American audience and sent it out of the theatre into the streets shrieking with pain." What he tried to do, as he explained, "was to say what the Far East suggests to me musically, to write a score that would be analogous in sound to the look of a series of Siamese paintings by Grant Wood. I myself remained a Broadway character, not somebody disguised in Oriental get-up." His melodies remained basically American, but in some of them he sprinkled the kind of intervallic structure encountered in Far-Eastern music, while in his instrumentation he was often partial to the flute, cymbals, the gong, and the harp, the better to suggest Far-Eastern tone colors.

We shall soon have more to say about Rodgers's music and the altogether new dimensions it revealed in his writing. But, first, a word about *The King and I* itself. Today, when it has become common practice to adapt successful motion pictures into stage musicals it hardly seems like an innovation of any great moment to do so. But in 1951 this had never before been done, and so from its very beginnings *The King and I* compelled Rodgers and Hammerstein to venture into ground upon which nobody else had thus far tread. The movie had been *Anna and the King of Siam,* starring Rex Harrison and Irene Dunne, which in turn had been taken from a novel by Margaret Landon. Gertrude Lawrence had seen the movie, saw herself as Anna, and convinced Rodgers and Hammerstein to write the stage musical for her. Rodgers and Hammerstein accepted the idea eagerly because, as Rodgers explained, "we are allergic to formulae."

Anna, of course, is the prim English schoolmistress brought to Siam by its despotic and swaggering king to teach his children, and to introduce to his people some of the ways of the Western world. She is at first repelled by the king's despotic behavior, but eventually she finds that beneath his rough exterior there is softness and warmth. She begins to look upon the king kindly just as she becomes endeared to his children. But the king has broken his word to her, something she refuses to tolerate, and for this reason announces her determination to return to England. However, before she can do this, she is instrumental in averting a diplomatic disaster for the Siamese court with the arrival of a high diplomatic mission from England. Then, with the king's sudden death, she finds it impossible to separate herself from the royal children.

With no love interest to involve the two principal characters, even though they are singularly attracted to each other; with a story ending with the death of the principal male character, the king; with virtually all the principal characters (with the exception of Anna) Orientals, compelling Rodgers and Hammerstein to maintain a consistent Oriental atmosphere without becoming too esoteric— all these were difficulties that were eventually surmounted with the ease and grace of a trained athlete doing the hurdles. Every element of the production jelled: the incomparable performances of Gertrude Lawrence (the last of her career, since she died of cancer in 1952 while the play was still running) and Yul Brynner in the two leading roles; the stunning Oriental sets designed by Jo Mielziner and the equally stunning costumes devised by Irene Sharaff from rare silks imported from Thailand; Jerome Robbins's fabulous choreography (his first such assignment in the Broadway theatre); and Hammerstein's text and lyrics and Rodgers's music. Out of this perfect synchronization of all the elements of the theatre what emerged was a picture of the Orient and its people which, as Danton Walker said in his review, proved to be "a flowering of the arts of the theatre with moments . . . that are pure genius."

In his role as composer, Rodgers went one step beyond *Carousel* and *South Pacific* in his development as a musical dramatist. As he said: "I've tried to tell the story through music. *The King and I* is truly a musical drama with every song advancing the plot. We ask the audience to believe that the people on the stage, who face many serious problems of life, will suddenly stop talking and burst into song. We tried to avoid the reality by the singing, and the singing by the reality." And so, music and words and dramatic action become inextricably one.

More and more here than before the significance of Rodgers's score does

not depend exclusively on the eloquence or effectiveness of individual numbers
—although the score of *The King and I* literally overflows with them. Other
musical methods also had to be extensively employed. For example, instruments
are used with telling effect at the beginning of the play to take the place of
spoken dialogue. Anna has just arrived in Siam and cannot speak a word of that
country's language; she is met by the king's minister who cannot speak English.
And so, a clarinet and a bassoon in the orchestra exchange thematic phrases to
speak for them. (As the play progresses, however, the audience becomes accustomed to the incongruity of having Siamese speak English perfectly—and so,
this device can soon be discarded.)

Musical bits continually tie scenes together, flow like an undercurrent to
important stage action, punctuate or accentuate passages of dialogue, assist
characters to make their entrances and exits. Fragments of a melody in flute,
viola, and cello help Anna to prove that her own shapely figure refuses to conform to the ample circumference of a hoop skirt. A saucy little march, with
Oriental skips in the melody, helps bring to the stage the princes and princesses
—the dynamics increasing in direct proportion to the size of the children. Highly
descriptive background music helps to make vivid the frenetic plans evolved by
Anna and the king for the party for the visiting diplomats. Etcetera, etcetera.

Nowhere, however, did Rodgers's background music prove more effective
—and achieve its aim in suggesting rather than imitating Oriental music—than
in his background effects for the principal ballet conceived by Robbins. "The
Small House of Uncle Thomas" tried to retell the story of *Uncle Tom's Cabin*
within the techniques and gestures of the Siamese dance. "Its subtleties are
many," said a critic for the New York *Herald Tribune,* "its humor so fleet that
one is hard put to select the key moments of a dance pattern so wholly absorbing." Instead of creating a formal choreographic score, with an Oriental identity,
Rodgers employed for this dance only percussive effects, produced by wood
blocks and ancient cymbals, xylophone, and gongs, to punctuate the commentary
of the spoken chorus. The various choreographic episodes, then, are accompanied
by rhythm and percussive sounds which re-create the same kind of naïve and
childish realism found in the dance.

Since so many of the songs from *The King and I* have become classics, it
is superfluous to add that this Rodgers score is studded with melodic gems. Again
the composer reveals his extraordinary gift for word-setting—for projecting an
emotion, for enlarging the canvas on which he is painting, for achieving an incomparable poignancy by amplifying a germinal melodic idea into a soaring and
expansive lyrical outburst. There was "Hello, Young Lovers," perhaps one of
the greatest songs to come out of a Rodgers and Hammerstein production. This is
no longer a popular song; this is an art song in the best traditions of the great
German composers of lieder. Notice how the delicate staccato notes introduce
the song and instantly create tonal magic. Notice, too, the freshness and individuality of the harmonic background to the haunting melody. Notice further
how the eloquence of the melody of the chorus is heightened because the preceding introduction had been unaccompanied. Other numbers, too, have the
same brand of haunting, expressiveness, and individuality: "We Kiss in a

Shadow," "I Have Dreamed," and the king's extended narrative, "A Puzzle-ment." More formal, however, and more traditional in concept—though by no means any less effective as an element in the play—are songs like "I Whistle a Happy Tune," "Getting to Know You," and "Shall We Dance?"

The King and I was able to achieve theatrical art of the highest order with-out alienating audiences. On the contrary—the audiences were spellbound, and helped make the show one of the giant successes of the Rodgers and Hammer-stein epoch. The Broadway run lasted 1,246 performances; an immensely lucra-tive national tour that began in Hershey, Pennsylvania, on March 22, 1954, ended in Philadelphia on November 7, 1955; revivals sprang up in all parts of the country year after year—and continue to do so still—to endow it the status of a permanent stage classic; and finally, a brilliantly produced motion picture captured six Academy Awards and was selected by the Film Daily Poll as the best motion picture of the year (1956).

Rodgers and Hammerstein returned to an Oriental subject and Oriental characters in their next box-office triumph, *Flower Drum Song* in 1958. But be-fore this happened there had been much to disturb and rock the smooth sailing of their lives. For one thing, they had suffered on Broadway two successive failures—actually one outright failure, and another which made such a small profit on its return and had such a limited run (358 performances) that by the now well-established Rodgers and Hammerstein standards it was considered a failure. The latter was *Me and Juliet* in 1953, a musical comedy this time—*not* a musical play—describing what happens in the theatre to the performers and the play during the run of a successful musical. Parts of this musical were better than the sum, songs like the tango "No Other Love" and an excellent narrative, in the style of "Soliloquy" in *Carousel* and "A Puzzlement" in *The King and I*, "The Big Black Giant," a vivid description of what the audience looks like to the performer on the stage. As for the failure—*Pipe Dream* in 1955—this, too, was planned as a musical comedy, based on John Steinbeck's *Sweet Thursday*. The setting was Cannery Row, a shabby neighborhood in Monterey, California, and its characters comprised misfits, failures, and plain bums. Brooks Atkinson regarded this production as Rodgers and Hammerstein "in a minor key" (which was phrasing it mildly and with good manners), while Richard Watts, Jr., maintained that it "hardly reveals the Masters at the peak of their distinguished form." These and other critics were right, and so were the audience who stayed away. This was not a good musical, and it was made worse by some unbelievable production mistakes, the most glaring of which was the casting of Helen Traubel, the distinguished Wagnerian soprano of the Metropolitan Opera, as the madam of a bordello. The best songs in this Rodgers score have been forgotten, a fate they do not deserve: "Ev'rbody's Got a Home But Me" and "All At Once You Love Her."

But the temporary loss of their magic touch in the theatre was the least of the worries of the two collaborators. Before *Pipe Dream* could open, Rodgers became victimized by a cancer of the gum posterior of the last tooth. He had to undergo a serious operation of neck and jaw in which both the left jawbone and the glands in the neck had to be removed. The operation was a total success; the cancer had been arrested. But for months Rodgers suffered intense pain and discomfort, and this was the time *Pipe Dream* was being rehearsed. For months after that, he went through mental agonies until he became fully assured that the cancer was no longer a threat. His painful physical disabilities, his speech difficulties for a while, and the continual necessity of keeping a handkerchief to his mouth to arrest the flow of saliva did not keep him from attending rehearsals, the out-of-town tryouts, and finally the New York opening.

Then, during the writing of the *Flower Drum Song,* Hammerstein began suffering from a stomach ailment. This, too, required surgery—and once again, as with Rodgers, it proved so successful that Hammerstein could complete work on text and lyrics after a period of postoperative recuperation.

But the years separating *The King and I* from *Flower Drum Song* was not altogether without compensations. It was during this time that Rodgers completed a remarkable score, this time not for the stage, but for television. It was for a documentary series, *Victory at Sea,* describing American and Allied naval operations during World War II. Televised by N.B.C. in 1952–53, this production received the George Foster Peabody citation and the Sylvania Award, the two highest honors that a television production could capture. Nobody doubted that however remarkable was the work of Henry Salomon and Richard Hansser in gathering and editing the films, Richard Rodgers's contribution to the success of this venture was no negligible one. *Variety* described his score as "the finest original work of its kind produced by an American composer," and the United States Navy conferred on Rodgers the Distinguished Public Service Award in 1953. The whole score was recorded, and parts of it were assembled by Robert Russell Bennett into a symphonic suite that has become a part of the semiclassical repertory. (The tango "No Other Love" from *Me and Juliet* took its melody from one of the sections of this television score, "Beneath the Southern Cross.")

Another television project proved almost as triumphant: *Cinderella,* this time the combined effort of Rodgers and Hammerstein. It had been commissioned by the Columbia Broadcasting System, and was televised on March 31, 1957, with Julie Andrews in the title role. It has been estimated that somewhere between seventy-five and a hundred million people watched this spectacle over the 245 station network Columbia had gathered for this gala event. *Cinderella* made no pretense at being anything but pure, unsophisticated delight for old and young. And its score lent enchantment with vocal numbers like "Ten Minutes Ago," "In My Own Little Corner," "Do I Love You?" and instrumental episodes like the orchestral gavotte and waltz. *Cinderella* has since been staged in several American cities and (in a pantomime version) in London; in 1965 it was completely redone for television with a new cast and a new production, once again televised over the C.B.S. television network.

The stage success of *Flower Drum Song,* in 1958, removed some of the sour taste left behind among theatregoers by the two previous productions of Rodgers and Hammerstein. This, too, was a musical comedy, but one in which some of the well-established routines and formulas of musical comedy were combined with a fresh, novel subject. The main problem stressed in this text (adapted by Hammerstein and Joseph Fields from a novel by C. Y. Lee) is that of the generation gap—but the one that exists between the older generation of Chinese in San Francisco, true to their Oriental traditions and heritage, and the younger one that has discarded many of the Oriental trappings to be assimilated into American society. There was a kind of generation gap in the Rodgers score, too. The old world to which the Chinese elders clung was represented by songs like "A Hundred Million Miracles," "Grant Avenue," and the music to the second-act ballet and the wedding march just before the final curtain. The new world of Chinese-become-American is found in "You Are Beautiful," "I Enjoy Being a Girl" (fetchingly presented by Pat Suzuki in her stage debut), and "Don't Marry Me" which led into the kind of buck-and-wing dance for which vaudeville and the older brand of musical comedy had so long been famous. That *Flower Drum Song* was entertainment *in excelsis* was proved by its six-hundred-performance run on Broadway, and by the success of its year and a half tour; it remained entertainment of a high order when it was made into a motion picture starring Nancy Kwan, released in 1961.

If *Flower Drum Song* cast a backward glance at musical comedy, *The Sound of Music,* in 1959, was also a reminder of things past in the American musical theatre—in this instance, the operetta. It retained much of the sentimentality, sweetness, and old-world grace and charm of operetta, but of course it did not neglect to sidestep many of the absurdities to which the old-time operetta had been addicted, nor did it fail to face some pretty serious issues within its pleasing context. *The Sound of Music* started out to tell the story of the Trapp Family Singers—a singing family from Salzburg, Austria, which, when the Nazis came to power, achieved success in the concert world as a choral group headed by the father and mother. Maria Augusta Trapp had told the story in an autobiography which provided Howard Lindsay and Russel Crouse with the bare essentials of a text which they proceeded to fill in generously with their own brand of varied materials—something to please everybody. The production catered to those who doted on adorable children, who had religious leanings, who were fascinated by glamorous geographical settings and who were concerned with international problems and the recent tragic history in Europe. There was saccharine in this brew, it is true; but (as the authors had intended) the saccharine diluted the cloying sweetness with a taste of bitterness. For although Maria Rainer, a postulant at the Nonnberg Abbey in Austria, first becomes the governess of seven delectable youngsters (the offspring of the widower, Captain Georg von Trapp of the Austrian Navy), and then succeeds in becoming von Trapp's wife, the story—thus far bathed with the radiance and warmth of summer sunshine—turned to autumnal and winter gloom with the Nazi invasion of Austria. Captain von Trapp refuses to serve the Nazis. All the Trapps must then flee the country, making their escape on foot over the mountains after performing at a music festival.

There is sweetness in abundance in the Rodgers score, particularly in those songs intended for the children, such as "Do, Re, Mi" (a melody using the ascending notes of the diatonic scale with which Maria, played by Mary Martin, gives the children their first lesson in singing), "You Are Sixteen," and "So

Long, Farewell," as well as in one or two numbers that Miss Martin performs without the collaboration of the children, such as "My Favorite Things" and the title song. Nostalgia for Austria, and a good deal of local color could be found in "The Lonely Goatherd" and "Edelweiss." Religion makes its musical presence felt in the very opening—an orchestral overture but an *a cappella* religious chorale, "Preludium." And while a song like "Climb Every Mountain" is not essentially religious, it has much of the spirituality and inspirational force of religious music.

There was rapture in some of the criticisms. John Chapman called it "stunning and exciting." Frank Aston described the score as "the loveliest music imaginable." Robert Coleman prophesied that the show would be a "titanic hit." But there were a good many other critics who were far less enthusiastic. "It is disappointing to see the American musical stage succumbing to the clichés of operettas," said Brooks Atkinson. Walter Kerr remarked that the show becomes "not only too sweet for words but almost too sweet for music."

But the public gave the final answer and gave it in no uncertain terms. The answer came with the 1,443 performances *The Sound of Music* enjoyed on Broadway and the almost 1,000 more performances given by the national company on a tour that started in February of 1961 and ended in November of 1963. Then came the film version, starring Julie Andrews. It will take a long time yet before the final total is added up as to just how much this picture has earned around the world. Already, it has exceeded by far the box-office receipts of any picture yet produced, and it has a long life still stretching before it; it is likely to establish a box-office record of between a quarter of a billion and half a billion dollars which will stand as an all-time record for years and years to come. And finally there are the recordings of the original Broadway cast album and the motion-picture sound track combining to sell over ten million copies—once again something without precedent, once again something that is not likely to be equaled for a long time to come.

The Sound of Music may not be the greatest of the Rodgers and Hammerstein creations, but it is certainly financially the most successful. And so, the age of Rodgers and Hammerstein (about which Cole Porter once said caused "the most profound change in forty years of musical comedy") ended as it had begun, on an unprecedented note of triumph.

During the writing of *The Sound of Music,* Hammerstein once again was being troubled by intense pains in his stomach. This time the sickness was far more serious than it had been a few years earlier. By the time *The Sound of Music* was produced, only three people were informed by Hammerstein's physician that Hammerstein was nursing a malignant cancer—the three people being Dorothy Hammerstein, and Dick and Dorothy Rodgers. But Hammerstein was not fooled for long. He knew the seriousness of his condition, and he knew that the days of his life were now numbered—although for a long time he gave no clue to anybody of his suspicions. When he finally did speak out, it was when he knew with finality that the end was not too far off. And he spoke out to express the wish of dying at home in Doylestown near those he loved, and not in a hospital. His wish was carried out. He died in his bed in Doylestown on August 23, 1960, and was given a simple, dignified funeral attended by only forty people, those who had been closest to him. The lyrics of "Climb Every Mountain" were recited at the service by Howard Lindsay who added a eulogy which said in part: "We shall not grieve for him. That would be to mourn him and he would not want that. On the occasion of Gertrude Lawrence's services he said so in so many words: 'Mourning does not become the theatre. Mourning is a surrender to an illusion that death is final.' " But there was mourning, nevertheless—deep, intense mourning by all those who loved him and by the hundreds upon hundreds of thousands who never knew him but who came to love him through his writings. "One of the great creative talents of this era was lost to the American theatre," remarked one New York newspaper in an editorial. It was in recognition of this indisputable fact that both in New York and in London all theatre lights were extinguished for a few minutes as a tribute to the passing of a theatrical giant.

Rodgers was inconsolable. "I am permanently grieved" is all he said, but this simple line reflected a hurt which would never heal. Hammerstein had not only been a valuable collaborator who helped Rodgers attain the peaks of musical achievement in the American theatre; Hammerstein had not only been a business partner who helped bring enormous wealth to Rodgers; Hammerstein had also been Rodgers's closest friend, almost his alter ego. Rodgers would continue living and continue working, for his is the kind of personality that would never allow himself to be conquered by tragedy or suffering. But with Hammerstein gone, he knew, he would never be quite the same again—either as a man or as a creative artist.

He did not withdraw from the theatre, for the theatre was as integral a part of his being as his heart and lungs. For *No Strings,* produced in 1962, text by Samuel Taylor, he served as his own lyricist, and proved that he had a highly skillful, professional hand with words as well as with music. There were several songs of outstanding interest in this score (for grief does not destroy genius): the title number, "The Sweetest Sounds," and "Nobody Told Me," each a Richard Rodgers jewel. And the text and staging had a number of exceptional deviations from the norm and some unusual innovations. Reduced to its bare essentials, the plot told the love story in France of a Negro Parisian fashion model, with a Pulitzer Prize winning novelist who is white. But no effort was made to introduce interracial themes or problems until the end of the play, treating the love affair as it would that of any two beautiful people. Only in the final scene are we suddenly reminded that the two lovers are of different races, for the novelist has come to the conclusion that the time has arrived for him to desert the playgrounds of France and return home to America and begin working again on a book. Since he knows full well that this sweetheart can suffer only the slings and arrows of outraged discrimination in America, he parts from her forever.

The musical was called *No Strings,* and there were no strings in the orchestra Rodgers used here. But this is only a minor digression from general practices. For a long time convinced that keeping an orchestra in the pit created an artificial barrier between music and the stage action, Rodgers here placed his instrumentalists in the wings of the stage. At certain points in the story, one, two, or three instrumentalists would stroll casually on the stage (even though they played no roles in the play), stand behind or between the performers, and provide an instrumental obbligato as musical commentary to what was being said. These musicians, as Walter Kerr explained in his review, were "invited to insulate themselves into the story-telling onstage. The man with the flute is apt to slip between two lovers. . . . In short, the composer's hirelings are used to support rather than to intercept the principals and . . . Mr. Rodgers' impudent resettlement works."

Another novelty was Rodgers's attempt "to push the walls of the theatre out," to use his own words. He accomplished this by requiring a minimum amount of scenery which, like most of the stage props, were easily movable. Very often the performers themselves moved scenery and props about as part of the action.

No Strings was received well enough by the critics, and did well enough at the box office (580 performances) to convince Rodgers that he could henceforth be his own lyricist if he wished. But this arrangement did not satisfy him. He felt the need of the stimulation, the inspiration, that a gifted lyricist-collaborator like Lorenz Hart and Oscar Hammerstein II could bring a composer. For a while he tried to effect a permanent working arrangement with Alan Jay Lerner, one of the theatre's most gifted lyricists and librettists. But a clash of temperament, points of view, concepts on what represented good and original theatre, disrupted the partnership by the time the first draft of their projected musical was completed. Rodgers bowed out of the picture gracefully without comment or explanation, giving Lerner full freedom to use his libretto in any way he wished (even though the basic idea for this play had originated with Rodgers). When that production finally reached Broadway, its score was the work of Burton Lane (composer of *Finian's Rainbow*), and the musical was called *On a Clear Day You Can See Forever*.

Rodgers then worked with Stephen Sondheim as his lyricist in *Do I Hear a Waltz?* produced in 1965. Just before he died Hammerstein had advised Rodgers to seek out a young and up-and-coming lyricist as his future collaborator rather than one with an established reputation to his credit. Sondheim was young and up-and-coming, but he had already established his reputation with nothing less than *West Side Story,* for which he had provided the lyrics to Leonard Bernstein's music. Rodgers felt that working with youth might prove an invigorating tonic and he had every hope that *Do I Hear a Waltz?* might mark the beginning of a new long-lived collaboration.

Do I Hear a Waltz? was a gentle love story set in Venice between an American girl and an Italian shopkeeper which ended in frustration. The musical-comedy text was by Arthur Laurents, adapted from his own successful Broadway stage play, *The Time of the Cuckoo.* But in the musical the story developed so slowly as to become sluggish, was spoken with such a controlled emotion as to lack feeling, let alone excitement. What had been planned by Laurents, Rodgers, and Sondheim as a quiet and tender idyll turned out to be a thoroughly dull affair. *Do I Hear a Waltz?* was a failure, and that was the end of the Rodgers-Sondheim partnership.

One or two other ideas were then tried out by Rodgers and dropped long before they were completely put down on paper—now for one reason, now for another, but always because Rodgers was dissatisfied with his material. But the same creative restlessness, irresistible drive, complete dedication to his art, and all-pervading love for the theatre that had kept him productive in the theatre for almost half a century cannot fail to keep him thinking, planning, and working on new projects filled with new methods and ideas. "If there ever comes a time," Rodgers has said, "when there are only five legitimate theatres in New York, I'd love to have one of them. And if we ever get down to only one, I'd want that one to be mine." And just as certainly, Rodgers wants to be the man —and Rodgers will be the man—to write the show and its songs for that one theatre.

GREAT MEN OF AMERICAN POPULAR SONG

Songs from Musical Plays–II

Lerner and Loewe

More times than once in earlier chapters—and perhaps most noticeably in the one preceding this—impressive figures and facts were marshaled to underscore the success of now this musical, and now that one. Facts and figures will once again have to be assembled here and now, for we are about to discuss the careers of two writers—a composer and a lyricist—who created one of the most successful productions in the history of our living musical theatre, and possibly one of the most successful musicals the world has known, with the possible exception of *The Sound of Music, My Fair Lady*. Not even the greatest triumphs of Rodgers and Hammerstein, towering though these were, surpassed the historic achievements of *My Fair Lady* in income, public and critical responses, and durability. The facts and figures stagger the imagination; merely running through them statistically can make for exciting reading.

Its Broadway run broke all existing records with 2,717 performances. Three and three-quarter million theatregoers paid over twenty million dollars (more than the combined gross of the New York runs of both *Oklahoma!* and *South Pacific*) at the Broadway box office. A touring company brought in another nineteen million dollars over a five-year period, while twenty-one foreign productions in eleven languages (from places as far apart geographically as Iceland and Japan) earned another thirty million dollars. In England, its run of 2,281 performances established a record for that country, while in Stockholm the musical had a two-year run. The American national company brought the show to the Soviet Union in 1960 where it was accorded a reception described by a cabled report to *The New York Times* as "nothing short of fabulous." The report added: "This is perhaps one of the warmest responses ever to have appeared in the Soviet press. And it is a rare thing indeed to read Soviet comments on American art containing not a single 'but.' " A production in Hebrew, in Israel, in 1964, had a run "more successful than anyone had dreamed," according to still another news item, all of its 327 performances playing to capacity houses. Motion-picture rights sold for an all-time high of five and a half million dollars' advance and a percentage of the gross. Fifty recordings of the score were pressed not only in English but also in Hebrew, Spanish, and Italian. The original-cast recording of the Broadway production sold more than five million albums, released by Columbia Records. "It's the biggest thing we've seen since we've been in business, and that's three hundred years," said a representative of the publishing house of Chappell, which issued the music to realize still another rich lode through the sale of individual songs, song albums, and various arrangements and transcriptions.

So mountainous has been the success of *My Fair Lady* that people tend to forget that two other treasurable contributions to the musical theatre were made by the team of Lerner and Loewe: *Brigadoon,* for example, a masterpiece in its own right, which had preceded *My Fair Lady; Camelot,* an awesome spectacle though hardly a masterpiece, which followed it.

In fact, the partnership of Lerner and Loewe lasted seventeen years, and in that time it proved one of the most distinguished words-and-music combination Broadway has known. Yet, as had been the case with Rodgers and Hart, this ideal artistic mating of two creative minds had brought together people who were worlds apart—in nationality, background, upbringing, ideals, and *Weltanschauung.* In the end, those differences had to lead to a permanent creative divorce.

In the things that counted least, the two men were alike. Both were of the same height (five-foot-seven); both had the same kind of male attractiveness, though Lerner was slighter of build, and Loewe was bulkier. Both were *bon vivants,* gourmets, in certain instances even hedonists. Both smoked continually. (When Loewe had to give up smoking for good, following his heart attack, he maintained contact with tobacco by chewing on unlighted cigarettes!) Both had once been boxers—with Lerner (then in college) losing his left eye in a bout.

But in the things that counted—in their creative life and outlook—they were opposites. Lerner was precise and analytical; exact in his facts; given to calm evaluations and understatements. Loewe was effusive, exuberant, partial to excessive exaggerations. Lerner was an artist who had to revise, rewrite, and change and delete continually before he was satisfied with what he had written. Loewe detested revising once he had put a melody down on paper; abhorred the necessity of having to rework an idea, a chore that nauseated him the same way as would eating over again some food he had just spit out. And he was in horror of deadlines.

To Lerner, to live meant to create. As a man of considerable wealth long before he started making a living out of writing—much of it inherited from his father in 1954, some of it came from the income of the successful chain of women's wear stores called Lerner Shops—he could well afford to remain idle all his life. But that for him would be existing, not living. Loewe, however, has never had any particular will to create. Writing had been the means by which he could, initially, support himself; and after that, by which he could buy the kind of life and luxury that meant so much to him—a beautiful estate in Palm Springs, California, and another one in southern France; a yacht; playing games of chance at high stakes whether in Cannes or in Las Vegas (though of recent years he vows he has given up gambling for good); enjoying the finest foods and the choicest wines that could be purchased; being in the company of the most beautiful women he could find.

They had an unusual way of working. Once the idea for a musical became clarified in Lerner's mind he talked it out, thought it out, and finally produced an outline: "Not a precise outline," he will tell you, "but a detailed one. That's because I don't want to confine the story too much. I want the people to come alive. Then Fritz and I write three quarters of the score. After that I can't wait to write the play proper, and I generally write it in a rush, in three weeks, day and night. My main tack is book writing, and in the songs to dramatize the key conflicts and character traits. Once you provide the outline, write three quarters of the score, and do the book, it becomes clear what other songs you need for balance and variety."

Once Lerner and Loewe agree on the place for a song, and on the kind of song it should be, they concoct its title. Lerner then takes a week or so to work out his lyrics. With words in hand, Loewe works on his melody at the piano. Usually, the tune comes easily, and that is when it comes best. Loewe is not the kind of composer who enjoys hunting tunes, running after them, trying to capture them. Tunes have to come to *him*.

Brigadoon, first, and after that *My Fair Lady* represented for Loewe the climactic point of a highly picaresque career in many different places. He was born in Vienna on June 10, 1904, the son of one of Vienna's most distinguished performers in operettas (he had sung in the world premieres of Oskar Straus's *The Chocolate Soldier* and Franz Lehár's *The Merry Widow*). Thus the boy Frederick, from childhood on, was nursed musically on Austria's popular music, and it was not long before he began writing some of his own. Having begun piano lessons at five, and having started to pick out his own tunes on the piano when he was seven, he soon learned how to put down his melodies on paper.

Some of the songs he wrote as a child were actually sung by his father in various European operetta theatres; and one of them, "Katrina," written when Loewe was only fifteen, was not only performed and published, but sold two million copies of sheet music throughout Europe.

Such success notwithstanding, Loewe's ambition in music lay not in composition but in playing the piano. He received an intensive piano training at the Stern Conservatory in Berlin, following which he studied with two of the foremost virtuosos and teachers in Europe at the time, Ferruccio Busoni and Eugène d'Albert. Meanwhile, when he was thirteen, he had become the youngest virtuoso to appear as soloist with the Berlin Symphony. His piano study culminated in 1922 with the winning of the Hollander Medal in Germany. After that, for a while, he studied composition with Nikolaus von Reznicek, but not with any intention of deserting the concert stage.

Convinced that America offered the greatest opportunities for a budding concert pianist, he crossed the Atlantic in 1924 and gave a recital at Town Hall, New York. Nobody took much enthusiastic notice of him, neither the listeners scattered in the auditorium nor the second- and third-string critics who devoted only a few lines to him. The necessity of earning a living compelled him to accept whatever jobs as pianist he could find, including one at the Rivoli Theatre in New York (a motion-picture house) and another in a Greenwich Village nightclub. But even such humble assignments were not too easy to get. And so, Loewe abandoned music to become a busboy in a cafeteria, and after that to teach horseback riding in a mountain resort, and to earn five dollars a bout as a prizefighter in Brooklyn. All this was not only a sharp departure from his lifelong ambition in music but worse still was proving a shortcut to poverty. This led him to desert New York and try his luck in the West, where he did hardly better financially in such varied occupations as cowpuncher, gold prospector, and a mailman on horseback. Back East again, he played popular tunes on the piano on ships making regular sailings from Miami to Havana and back, mainly for passengers whose throats had become parched by the Volstead Act then still in force and for whom Havana offered (among other pleasures) the delights of the bottle. From Miami, Loewe returned to New York where, in the early thirties, he found steady work playing the piano in a German beer hall. The wide range of Loewe's experiences in these years of *Wanderlust* and *Wanderjahre* once led Ira Gershwin to describe him as "the reincarnation of Ignace Jan Paderewski, Casanova de Seingalt, Tom Mix, Brillat-Savarin, Bet-a-Million Gates and Terry McGovern. Not to mention Baron Munchausen."

In 1931 Loewe married Ernestine Zwerline, an Austrian girl employed as the New York manager of the Hattie Carnegie enterprises. By this time Loewe had begun writing popular songs again—American songs, but fried in Austrian *"schmaltz."* One was "Love Tiptoed Through My Heart," sung by Dennis King in *Petticoat Fever,* a Broadway stage play in which this was the only musical number. Another Loewe piece of music, "A Waltz Was Born in Vienna"—he was still incapable of freeing himself from his Austrian background—was used as background music for a dance by Gomez and Winona in the *Illustrators Show,* produced on Broadway in 1936 where it lasted all of five days. More ambitious, however, was his first complete score for a stage production. Called *Salute to Spring,* text by Earl Crooker, it was produced in St. Louis during the summer of 1937. This production, in turn, brought Loewe and Crooker an assignment from Dwight Deere Wiman, the eminent Broadway producer, for a Broadway musical. *Great Lady,* in 1937, hardly survived a month. Having thus far failed to earn enough from his songwriting to pay his bills, Loewe returned to the piano: at first to play in restaurants where he earned a regular weekly salary; then to reappear in a recital (this time in Carnegie Hall) in 1942. His reemergence as a concert pianist proved no more successful than his American debut had been eighteen years earlier. Loewe admitted defeat, and once and for all dismissed from mind and heart all thought of ever becoming a virtuoso.

He would, instead, make another try to get a hearing in the Broadway theatre as composer—stimulated by an opportunity that came unexpectedly at the Lambs Club, of which he was a member, and whose clientele consisted exclusively of people from the theatre. A producer approached him with an offer to write the music for a Detroit-produced musical, but only on two conditions: one, that he could complete his score in two weeks (something Loewe was certain he could do); two, that he could immediately find a lyricist-librettist to work with (a much more difficult task for Loewe). Pondering this problem, and determined not to allow an assignment to slip through his fingers for lack of a collaborator, he happened to see nearby a young man who had contributed material to the *Lambs Gambol,* a satirical revue put on by the club for its members. Loewe introduced himself to Lerner, explained his problem, and bluntly inquired if Lerner wanted to work with him. To Loewe's amazement, Lerner consented—for what Loewe did not know was that Lerner, too, was a man with high hopes and dreams about his place in the theatre without having heard a single call from Broadway. They shook hands and sealed the partnership of Lerner and Loewe that was destined to make stage history.

The problem of having to earn a living—a problem that so haunted Loewe all his life—did not exist for Lerner. He was born to wealth, in New York City on August 31, 1918. His father owned a successful chain of stores featuring women's clothes and accessories. That operation enabled the father to raise his son in style and elegance, with more than enough funds available for training in whatever profession the boy might select.

Lerner's talent lay in writing. By eleven he had become convinced he would someday work for the theatre, and his father did nothing to discourage his ambitions and dreams. Lerner's boyhood pastime was to write melodies for various poems, and then concoct a new set of verses for those same melodies. His schooling took place in exclusive private schools in England and America: the Bedales School in Hampshire, England; then at Choate School in Connecticut. At the latter school he was coeditor of the school yearbook—his fellow editor being John F. Kennedy, later the President of the United States. Lerner also wrote a school football song.

In 1936 Lerner entered Harvard, where in 1938 and 1939 he wrote sketches and lyrics for two Hasty Pudding Shows. A song from each of these two productions were published commercially: "Chance To Dream" and "From Me to You." As an undergraduate, he also wrote college songs with Bobby Parks (the bandleader at the Stork Club in New York) and, with Stanley Miller, an intimate revue, *The Little Dog Laughed*. During the summers of 1936 and 1937 he attended the Juilliard School of Music in New York to learn something about music.

He was graduated from Harvard in 1940 with a bachelor of science degree. He found employment in a successful advertising firm (Lord and Thomas) writing radio scripts. (His refusal to enter the family business had long since been accepted by his father stoically. "I don't find the dress business very interesting," his father remarked, "so why should he?") During the next two years, Lerner ground out some five hundred radio scripts, including some of the "Philco Hall of Fame" shows and for the Chamber Music Society of Lower Basin Street programs. Upon leaving the advertising agency, in 1942, Lerner became a free-lance radio script writer. But though he had plenty of work to do, he was not progressing one inch closer to Broadway where his heart lay.

His meeting with Loewe at the Lambs Club, in 1942, was just as providential for him as it was for Loewe, for it represented Lerner's first commission to write for the stage.

They finished their assignment in the specified time of two weeks. Called *Life of the Party,* it was produced in Detroit in October of 1942. Some liked it; many didn't. But in spite of unfavorable reactions, Lerner and Loewe were undismayed. They had liked working together and somehow they sensed that if they continued collaborating Broadway would be just around the bend.

It was—and with their very next effort, *What's Up?* which opened in November of 1943. It starred Jimmy Savo as a potentate from East India come to America with his advisers for an international conference. They get stranded in a girls' college where they must be quarantined due to an outbreak of measles. East Indian characters chasing American college girls with both singing songs that more often than not had the lilt and the *Gemütlichkeit* of Viennese operetta music (a style from which Loewe had difficulty freeing himself) carried incongruity almost to the border line of the ridiculous. Lerner did not hesitate to call *What's Up?* "a disaster."

Their next show was far better, and it did better: *The Day Before Spring,* in 1945, boasting a deftly written text about a college reunion where lovers of many years past find that the ashes of their supposedly dead romance still slightly aglow, enough to think of (but at a last moment renege in) running off together. At least two songs showed that Loewe was finally beginning to forget Vienna and to think more in terms of Broadway: "God's Green World" and "My Love Is a Married Man" hinted strongly that in writing music for Broadway Loewe had finally found his true metier.

And he proved this decisively in 1947 in one of the most delectable musicals come out of Broadway, *Brigadoon,* "a whimsical fantasy" that never fails to spellbind audiences however many times it is revived and in whatever medium it is shown (whether on the screen in 1954 with Gene Kelly and Cyd Charisse or as a stunning television "special" produced about a decade after that).

The idea originated with Lerner. All his life Lerner had nursed a secret ambition to write a fantasy in the vein of James M. Barrie, one of Lerner's favorite authors. A chance remark by Loewe that faith can move mountains sparked a sudden thought in Lerner that perhaps it can move towns as well. And so he invented a Scottish town, Brigadoon, which disappeared in 1747, but returned to life one day every century. With two young present-day Americans happening to stumble upon this magic place on the one day of its existence in this century, a romance soon develops between one of them, Tommy, with a Scottish lass, Fiona. But to Tommy's distress, he soon learns the secret of Brigadoon, and that his experiences are just fantasies soon to evaporate into nothingness when the day is over. Back in America, Tommy cannot forget Brigadoon. Though he knows it cannot reappear for another hundred years, he must go back to Scotland to look for it. Faith is his ally, and the force that enables Tommy to step into the Highland mists and find Brigadoon.

Faith in such an imaginative text had the power to lead Loewe completely out of Vienna and into, of all places, Scotland—just as Tommy was finally led into Brigadoon. Loewe suddenly discovered a gift for capturing a Scottish feeling and taste in songs like "The Heather on the Hill," "Waitin' for My Dearie," and "Come to Me, Bend to Me." But though other of his songs were more American in their identity than Scottish, they did not lack the felicitous touch—the nostalgic charm and the grace—of his Scottish-type songs. In fact, one of these, "Almost Like Being in Love," became the first major song hit by Lerner and Loewe, one of the leaders in the sale of sheet music and recordings and in number of presentations over radio and television all through 1947 and well into 1948.

"A vibrant work of art," as Brooks Atkinson described it, *Brigadoon* contributed a footnote to stage history by becoming the first musical selected by the New York Drama Critics Circle as the best play of the year.

Having finally purged his subconscious creativity of Vienna, Loewe could now proceed to write another outstanding score, but this time for a thoroughly American text. *Paint Your Wagon,* in 1951, told of the boom and then disintegration of a mining camp in the American West during and after the gold-rush days of the mid-1800's. The influence of *Oklahoma!* the Rodgers and Hammerstein musical play, could be sensed not only in many of the serious overtones of the Lerner text but also in Agnes de Mille's American folk-ballet sequences, and in Oliver Smith's realistic designs and costumes. Perhaps, too, the influence of Rodgers seeped into the texture of Loewe's writing far more than he suspected, since some of his songs boasted an American folk authenticity, such as Rodgers had created in *Oklahoma!* together with at times a dramatic strength and vitality which Loewe had not previously disclosed. Three songs have special importance, and have survived, even though the musical itself was a failure. I am alluding to "They Call the Wind Maria" (with which, a decade later, Robert Goulet auditioned for his role in *Camelot,* and which achieved popularity for the first time due to Goulet's renditions on television and records and in night clubs); also ballads like "I Talk to the Trees" and "Wand'rin' Star." The songs retained their effectiveness in the motion-picture adaptation of *Paint Your Wagon* released in 1969.

The Lerner and Loewe musical that followed *Paint Your Wagon* five years later carried them to the pinnacle of their careers; for the musical was *My Fair Lady*.

Making Bernard Shaw's *Pygmalion* into a musical was not a project that sprang from the minds of Lerner and Loewe. The venture was first conceived by the motion-picture producer Gabriel Pascal, after he had filmed *Pygmalion* in England (the first Shaw play to reach the screen). Pascal tried convincing Shaw that *Pygmalion* could be made into an impressive stage musical. Shaw turned him down in no uncertain terms, never having forgotten the indiscretions that had been perpetrated on his play *Arms and the Man* when it became the Oscar Straus operetta *The Chocolate Soldier*. Shaw was not the man to make the same mistake twice.

But soon after Shaw's death, Pascal was able to get an option on *Pygmalion* from the Shaw estate for possible musical adaptation. Unfortunately, none of the famous composers, lyricists, and librettists on Broadway shared his enthusiasm. They were convinced that *Pygmalion,* with music, would be a colossal bore. After all, the climax of Shaw's play came when the cockney girl had finally learned to speak English with the correct diction, and the play ended with the separation of hero and heroine. Two such ingredients—the *cognoscenti* of Broadway insisted—could produce only a lethal concoction that would prove poison at the box office.

When Pascal died in 1954, the plan to make *Pygmalion* into a musical seemed a dead issue. But Lerner and Loewe apparently inherited both Pascal's enthusiasm and vision. It was now their turn to try to get the rights and the necessary backing for a production that had been summarily turned down by the who's-who on Broadway. That Lerner and Loewe had the perseverance to go through all the complex legal maneuvers necessary to get the rights from the Shaw estate—negotiations that consumed almost a year—was the proof of the faith they had in this venture. Once this knotty problem was unraveled, Lerner and Loewe did a strong-sell on Rex Harrison to appear in the leading male role (a daring piece of casting, for though Harrison had all the poise, charm, and sophistication for the role, he could not sing, and his role required him to sing several important numbers) and acquired a then comparative newcomer and unknown for the female lead, Julie Andrews (another piece of courageous casting). By this time their enthusiasm had been able to muster all the arguments Lerner and Loewe needed to convince Goddard Lieberson, the brilliant and far-sighted president of Columbia Records, to get the Columbia Broadcasting Company to provide the production cost of $400,000. This accomplished, it was not difficult now to buy the top talent available for every department of the production: Moss Hart, as director; Cecil Beaton to design the costumes; Oliver Smith to do the sets; Hanya Holm to prepare the choreography.

Perhaps the wisest decision Lerner made, in wrestling with the problems posed by Shaw's play, was to let Shaw and his play speak for themselves, and to tamper with them as little as possible. Except for a number of minor interpolations explaining what Shaw had indicated had taken place offstage, the Shaw play was left intact. Songs, dances, and handsome production numbers—together with some remarkable bits of stage business, most of which were devised by Moss Hart while the play was in rehearsal—would change *Pygmalion* from the classic it had been on the dramatic stage to the classic it might become in the musical theatre. Of this, Lerner was thoroughly convinced.

And so story and dialogue remained basically Shaw—which, as it turned out, was not a bad way to begin. An ignorant, gauche cockney girl is transformed by Henry Higgins, a phonetician, into a grand lady who at the grand Embassy Ball is successfully palmed off as a grand duchess. Once this has been accomplished, Higgins tries to convince himself he is through with the girl, but he has become accustomed to her face, and the thought that she might marry a rich young man, Freddy, disturbs his emotional equilibrium no end. The most significant alteration Lerner made in the Shaw play was to provide it with a happy ending, with Liza's return to Higgins. But even here Lerner was remaining true to Shaw, for in his preface the author had indicated that the ultimate union of Liza and Higgins, in spite of the way his play had ended, was not altogether impossible.

The talents of all those involved in *My Fair Lady* fused and blended into a masterwork of musical theatre with few rivals. Lerner's infrequent interpolations were so much in the Shavian style and spirit that it was difficult to know where Shaw ended and Lerner began, and vice versa—a higher compliment than which it is difficult to endow to a librettist. Never before had Lerner produced one lyric after another which glistened like pure diamonds. Loewe emerged with a score that magically fused the Continental charm and genteel manners which he brought to so much of his writing (particularly in a number like "The Ascot Gavotte"), with a seemingly unending reservoir of infectious melodies, some of them as impishly Shavian as were Lerner's lyrics. Whatever he did, Loewe accomplished with impeccable taste and a sure hand: be it cockney songs (Liza's "Wouldn't It Be Loverly?" or the two numbers of her father, Doolittle, "Get Me to the Church on Time" and "With a Little Bit of Luck"); be it songs pointing up Higgins's urbanity ("Why Can't the English?" "I'm an Ordinary Man," and "A Hymn to Him"); or be it songs that had all the hallmarks of Broadway hit show tunes ("On the Street Where You Live," "I Could Have Danced All Night," and "I've Grown Accustomed to Her Face").

The zenith of the production was "The Rain in Spain," which through the genius of the director, songwriters, and performers transformed a highly undramatic situation—Liza's ability at last to pronounce "Spain" and "rain" correctly instead of "Spine" and "rine"—into theater magic. For this episode, Loewe created a tune in a pseudo-Spanish melody in a tango rhythm which helped Moss Hart, as director, concoct a scene combining song and pantomime mocking a bullfighter swinging his cape at the face of a bull, with a fandango dance, into a sequence that lit up the entire theatre and filled the hearts of the audience with an incandescent glow.

A motion-picture production of *My Fair Lady* was a number of years off by contractual agreement (it was finally produced in 1964 to receive eight Academy Awards, including one for the best picture of the year). Arthur Freed, producer at M-G-M, shrewdly hit upon the plan of anticipating the screening of *My Fair Lady* by creating a motion picture with some of the ingredients that had made the musical play a classic from its opening-night performance on. Lerner and Loewe, of course, would write the songs. Cecil Beaton would design the sets and costumes, and the story would concern itself once again with the magical change in a clumsy, gawky, unrefined young girl into a radiant young woman of beauty, charm, and refinement. Colette had told that story in *Gigi,* and this was the property that Arthur Freed used as a vehicle for his own *My Fair Lady.* With Paris of the 1890's as a setting, including a scene in the famous Maxim's, and with Leslie Caron as Gigi supplemented by Louis Jourdain, Maurice Chevalier, and Hermione Gingold, the Continental allure of *My Fair Lady* was not too difficult to recapture. And with Lerner and Loewe producing songs which were not obliterated by the tremendous shadow cast by their wonderful score for *My Fair Lady, Gigi* could not fail to be a winner. A winner it was, of giant proportions—a major box-office attraction, for one thing, and, for another, winner of nine Academy Awards (the first time this ever happened in motion-picture history), including one for the title song and another for the picture itself.

But as good as the title song was—and its long arched melodic line is one of the most original Loewe ever wrote—it had strong competition in several lighter numbers that quickly betrayed the nimble fingers of Lerner as lyricist and Loewe as composer: "The Night They Invented Champagne," "I'm Glad I'm Not Young Anymore," "I Remember It Well," and "Thank Heaven for Little Girls."

Camelot was the last of the Lerner and Loewe collaborations—produced on Broadway in 1960. Based on T. H. White's novel, *The Once and Future King, Camelot* retold the familiar story of King Arthur, his wife, Guinevere, and Sir Launcelot, and the members of the Round Table, and the love that arose between Guinevere and Sir Launcelot. To glance at some of the names affiliated with this stage production is to make obvious that here in their new Broadway musical—as formerly in their motion-picture *Gigi*—its creators were consciously trying to concoct another *My Fair Lady.* Called upon for their services were many of those who had previously worked on *My Fair Lady:* Lerner and Loewe; Moss Hart as director; Julie Andrews as leading female performer; Robert Coote to play a subsidiary role; Franz Allers to serve as musical director; Robert Russell Bennett to do the orchestrations. Unfortunately, a musical production is not a food preparation which by utilizing the same ingredients in specified proportions you can inevitably create the gourmet dish enjoyed at an earlier meal. *Camelot* was by no stretch of the imagination another *My Fair Lady.*

Surely what was most lacking was a text to equal Bernard Shaw's *Pygmalion,* though this was not the sole deficit in *Camelot. Camelot* was a helpless victim of a continuous, seemingly endless, round of mishaps. Lerner and Loewe were no longer working harmoniously together—as more and more Loewe succumbed to his lackadaisical ways of writing his music and more and more yielding to the temptation of running away from necessary revisions. In addition, Loewe was a sick man. He had suffered a heart attack in 1958, and during the writing and rehearsing of *Camelot* he could not command those physical resources that the preparation of a major production demanded. While *Camelot* was being rehearsed Loewe was physically indisposed from time to time. But that was not all that struck this unfortunate musical. Moss Hart suffered a heart attack, and Alan Jay Lerner had to be hospitalized with bleeding ulcers. A good deal of *Camelot* then had to be brought into being either with major collaborators absent or under harrowing stresses, tensions, and conflicts.

When one comes to think of it now, it is amazing that *Camelot* turned out as well as it did, even if it was no *My Fair Lady*. As enacted by Richard Burton as King Arthur (in the pre-Elizabeth Taylor period of his life), Robert Goulet (in a highly impressive Broadway debut), and Julie Andrews; with a few delectable tunes like the title song and "If Ever I Would Leave You" (both became huge hits), and with the sumptuous settings and costumes that spared no expense, *Camelot* was attractive to look at and listen to, was agreeable if not earthshaking entertainment. Despite the negative reports submitted by most of the critics, *Camelot* gave a sound financial return to its investors both as a stage play and as a lavishly mounted motion picture.

But the success of *Camelot* could not heal the wounds that had been festering in both Lerner and Loewe as they were working on it. Once the curtain went up on the production, an invisible but temporary one descended upon the partnership that had created the songs. This break meant that Lerner would have to seek new composers to work with, say, Burton Lane for *On a Clear Day You Can See Forever* and André Previn for *Coco*. As for Frederick Loewe, for a long time he found retirement preferable to adjusting himself and his personal work habits to some other librettist-lyricist. But for the project to make a stage musical out of the motion picture *Gigi*, Loewe's retirement and silence might have remained permanent. As it stands—it's Lerner and Loewe once again; and with it, some more magical nights in the musical theater, and some more delectable songs to remember them by.

Songs from the Movies–I

Harry Warren and Al Dubin

Like the Broadway theatre and Tin Pan Alley, motion pictures have proved through the years a nursery where important new song composers and lyricists can be nurtured and developed. This, of course, became true only after the screen had erupted into sound. But actually the history of motion-picture music does not begin with sound films. The silent movies have a popular-song history of their own. They created their own tradition on which later sound-screen music could continually feed and grow to healthy maturity, producing a new breed of composers and lyricists.

Songs and motion pictures became united (even if at first just illicitly) from the time the motion-picture industry was in its infancy: in the nickelodeon. Song slides, circulated within the motion-picture house early in the twentieth century, helped to popularize songs. These slides even became a basic part of

310

motion-picture entertainment at that time. In addition to slides, song pluggers would invade nickelodeons to provide live entertainment by singing the tunes published by the houses they represented. Amateur nights and songfests (the latter particularly popular during World War I) were two more ways of plugging songs and bringing live entertainment inside the nickelodeon. Then, most significantly, there was the pianist in the pit to provide a continuous flow of appropriate background music for the movie. It was with this last practice that the union of music and the movies was first legitimatized.

Some of the early movies inspired the writing of popular songs. One of the first such was "Poor Pauline" (words by Charles McCarron, music by Raymond Walker), written in 1914 about the escapades of the heroine in the Pearl White serial *The Perils of Pauline*. (This song was resurrected in 1947 for a motion picture entitled *The Perils of Pauline,* where it was sung by Betty Hutton.) The two-reelers in which Charlie Chaplin became the screen's first distinguished comedian were the subject for "Oh, Those Charlie Chaplin Feet," while the silver screen's first sweetheart was the heroine of the song "Sweet Little Mary Pickford."

These, and similar songs in the 1910's, were not intended to be performed in conjunction with the movies from which they drew their subject. But it did not take long for music to get written explicitly for the movie—either to exploit a special production or to provide it with musical background.

The first original musical score for the screen came in 1916 with Victor Herbert's background music for *The Fall of a Nation.* As Victor Herbert explained at that time: "For the first time in the history of American pictorial drama, a complete accompanying score will be played that has never been heard anywhere else. . . . In brief, the musical program will not be a mosaic or a patchwork of bits of Wagner, Grieg, Beethoven . . . and other writers. It will be strictly new. . . . This must seem to many people as a revolutionary departure from the older fields of musicianship."

The Fall of a Nation opened at the Liberty Theatre in New York on June 6, 1916. Victor Herbert's music was not played by a pit pianist (as was then the custom) but by an orchestra. *The Fall of a Nation* was not a very good motion picture, even in 1916. It was badly received, and proved a dismal failure. But having been the first motion picture to engage the services of a composer of stature for an original score entitles *The Fall of a Nation* to an important paragraph in screen history. "Without a doubt," wrote a critic for *Musical America,* "the most important and valuable element in *Fall of a Nation* is the music. . . . The incredibility of many of the scenes is considerably lessened by the effect that Mr. Herbert's score has provided. . . . His score is interesting and worthwhile from a purely musical standpoint. . . . [It] is not only synchronized with the picture, but its rhythms are in absolute accord with the tempo of the action. Mr. Herbert's stimulating score clearly indicates the marked advance that music is making in the domain of the photoplay and should prove encouraging to composers who have not yet tried their hand at this type of work."

Two years later came the first theme song ever written for a movie: "Mickey," or "Pretty Mickey," by Neil Williams, intended at first to exploit a motion picture starring Mabel Normand, but then used as a recurrent theme in many theaters either by the pit pianist or by the pit orchestra.

It was through the theme song that leading popular-song composers and lyricists began invading the motion-picture industry. Theme songs became the heart and spine of the musical background for the silent movies for which they had been created. These songs also served to promote and publicize the movie throughout the country. Finally, these theme songs became the first to get written for and about the movies and some were to become giant sheet-music successes in Tin Pan Alley.

Erno Rapee was the first successful composer of theme songs. He was the diminutive-sized Hungarian-born musician, then serving as principal conductor at the Roxy, the movie palace in New York named after and directed by S. L. Rothafel, who was known to all his friends as "Roxy." To Rapee goes the credit of producing the first theme song to become a nationwide hit: "Charmaine," words by Lew Pollack, written in 1926 to exploit the motion picture *What Price Glory?* of which Charmaine was the heroine. By virtue of the monumental financial success of this number, theme songs began getting a wide distribution in the late 1920's. Rapee was responsible for writing some of them, such as "Diane" for *Seventh Heaven* in 1927 (where Janet Gaynor received an Academy Award for her performance) and, in 1928, "Angela Mia" for *Street Angel.*

One of the most formidable hit songs of the 1920's was a motion-picture theme song. This was "Ramona," words by L. Wolfe Gilbert and music by Mabel Wayne. "Ramona" was commissioned for a motion picture of the same name starring Dolores del Rio. However, long before the picture was released, the song was catapulted to nationwide success mainly through performances by Paul Whiteman and his orchestra, and by Gene Austin. More than two million copies of sheet music were sold, together with many millions of records (a recording by Gene Austin alone accounting for the sale of over two million discs). This song also provided a line or two to the history of radio broadcasting. Paul Whiteman and his orchestra performed it on a coast-to-coast broadcast from a New York studio. The vocal was sung by Dolores del Rio at Joseph M. Schenck's home in Hollywood. This was the first time that the technique of broadcasting a performance from both ends of the country simultaneously had been tried—a major technological advance for those days.

By the end of the 1920's, when the screen acquired sound, there was hardly a movie that did not boast a theme song. Realizing as they did that a song performed throughout the country bearing the name of a picture could prove a powerful and inexpensive way of movie promotion, producers commissioned songwriters to create a theme song for practically every movie being produced. *Varsity Girl* had "Varsity Girl, I'll Cling to You"; *The Pagan* had "Pagan Love Song" (a hit); *Woman Disputed* had "Woman Disputed, I Love You"; *Madonna of Avenue A* had "My Madonna." This practice soon grew so outlandish and the abuses of titles so preposterous that Dorothy Parker tried destroying the theme-song vogue once and for all by writing lyrics for *Dynamite Man* entitled "Dynamite Man, I Love You."

But the theme song could not be killed. It had a new lease on life with the coming of the all-talking, all-singing motion picture.

Talking-singing motion pictures sprang into existence on October 6, 1927, with the release of the Warner Brothers production *The Jazz Singer,* starring Al Jolson. This was basically a silent movie. But at intermittent moments in the picture the silence was broken to allow Jolson to sing some of his favorites, including "Toot, Toot, Tootsie," "Blue Skies," and "Mammy." The interpolation of a few moments of speech was an improvisation. During the filming of a scene in which Jolson, as the cantor's son, sang for his mother some popular tunes, Jolson abandoned his script to ad-lib the following lines: "Wait till ya hear this, mama. . . . When I'm a hit I'm gonna take ya to Coney Island and I'm gonna buy ya the prettiest black silk dress that'll make a noise when ya walk. Will ya like that mama?" The ad-lib remarks were recorded and made such an impression on the producers that they decided to let them stay in the film. Thus speech as well as song was first used in a major motion picture. The impact of *The Jazz Singer* on audiences throughout the country was the force that obliterated the silent movie from existence.

The Jazz Singer grossed over three million dollars, a box-office record for that time. Success inspires imitation. Motion-picture theatres began wiring for sound. Major studios changed their plans and equipment to embrace talking-singing pictures.

Out of M-G-M- there came in 1929 a backstage yarn about chorus girls and their boyfriends, *The Broadway Melody.* This was the first screen revue (a revue, in spite of the slight plot used to thread together the various singing and dancing attractions). This was the first screen musical all of whose songs were written specifically for that production. And (possibly as a logical sequence) this was the first screen musical to win the Academy Award as the best motion picture of the year. Nacio Herb Brown (a real-estate operator turned composer) wrote all the music to Arthur Freed's words. Two of their songs from this production yielded rich dividends in their own right through publication and recordings: the title number and "The Wedding of the Painted Doll."

Musicals of all types and varying quality began to burst out of the major studios to flood the motion-picture market. Nacio Herb Brown and Arthur Freed kept on writing hit numbers for some of them: "You Were Meant for Me" and "Singin' in the Rain," both sung by Charles King in the *Hollywood Revue* in 1929; "The Chant of the Jungle" introduced in 1929 by Joan Crawford in *Untamed;* the already-mentioned "Pagan Love Song," the theme music for *The Pagan* starring Ramon Novarro who introduced it, also in 1929.

In 1930 Nacio Herb Brown and Arthur Freed wrote "Should I?" and "The Woman in the Shoe" for *Lord Byron of Broadway* and "The Moon Is Low" for *Montana Moon.* Then, following a brief hiatus, the screen musical achieved a new and even greater vogue than it had done in 1929 and 1930, to allow Brown and Freed to continue their successful collaboration with songs like "All I Do Is Dream of You," "Love Songs of the Nile," "My Lucky Star," "After Sundown," and "Good Morning."

Hollywood's now voracious appetite for songs made it swallow up music publishing firms (which led to the disintegration of Tin Pan Alley) and significant composers and lyricists. In order to put its hands on a rich backlog of songs from which it could draw for the production of screen revues and musicals,

Warner Brothers paid ten million dollars for the acquisition of three major Tin Pan Alley outfits (Harms, Witmark, and Remick, assembled into a single unit renamed Music Publishers Holding Corporation). M-G-M followed suit by buying out Leo Feist, Robbins, and one or two lesser firms. In rapid succession, other publishers were absorbed by the leading Hollywood studios.

Then, through the persuasive powers of fabulous contracts, Hollywood enticed the leading popular songwriters of Broadway and Tin Pan Alley to come West and write for the movies. This great new "gold rush" began in 1929 with Irving Berlin; continued in 1930 with Jerome Kern, Walter Donaldson, and Sigmund Romberg; went into high gear in 1931 with George and Ira Gershwin and Rodgers and Hart.

But the acquisition of songs and songwriters was coupled with another all-important development in the history of motion-picture music: the building up in Hollywood of creative talent of its own. Some of the most important music written for the screen in the first decade of sound pictures was the work of such men—some of whom had been novices, while others had been comparative unknowns, when they started working for the movies. In Hollywood they soared to greatness and to the accumulation of phenomenal financial successes as composers and lyricists of motion-picture songs.

The market having been flooded with screen musicals between 1929 and 1931, movie audiences were become sated of films with synthetic plots where song and dance had become routinized within stereotypes. One movie palace in New York went so far as to advertise: "No musicals." What had alienated the public was not the genre itself half so much as the dull pattern to which Hollywood was clinging in the making of screen musicals. The genre could continue to delight audiences whenever fresh new materials and approaches were being introduced. How true this was was certainly proved in 1933 with *Flying Down to Rio,* for which Vincent Youmans wrote his first original screen score and in which Fred Astaire and Ginger Rogers became song-and-dance stars of the first magnitude (on the heels of their previous success in *The Gay Divorcee*). With songs like "Carioca," "Flying Down to Rio," and "Orchids in the Moonlight"; with a story that was handled with a light touch and in good humor; and with the magic of the dance steps and song renditions of Fred Astaire and Ginger Rogers, *Flying Down to Rio* recaptured audiences lost to screen musicals.

There was still one other motion-picture musical that helped revive audience interest in this kind of motion picture. It was *Forty-Second Street,* in 1932, in which Ruby Keeler and Dick Powell became stars; in which spectacular new ideas, with novel angle shots, were introduced by Busby Berkeley; and in which an all-important pair of songwriters, Harry Warren and Al Dubin, first became musical kingpins in Hollywood.

Harry Warren had begun his songwriting career as composer on Broadway and in Tin Pan Alley. But it was with the movies that he achieved the heights of his success.

He was of Italian background, his father having emigrated from Calabria.

After coming to America, the family, comprising eleven children, changed its name from Guaragna to Warren. The father made an excellent living by making and selling custom-made riding boots and was able to provide well for even a large family. When Harry Warren was born on Christmas Eve of 1893, it was in a comfortable apartment in the Columbia Heights section of Brooklyn, a neighborhood populated by the middle class.

Warren received his first academic schooling in a Catholic school which he attended between his seventh and eighth years. Innately musical, he found an outlet for his instincts and interests in music by going to church and listening to the organ and the choir. Before long he became a member of that choir. Then, one day, he came upon his father's accordion, which he proceeded to learn to play without any formal guidance. Later on he got a set of drums from the neighborhood barber which in short order he mastered sufficiently to get jobs in local bands.

He pursued these musical activities while attending P.S. 155 in Brooklyn. From there he went on to Commercial High School. He did not stay there long. When he was fifteen, he impulsively left high school determined to forget once and for all this business of acquiring an academic education. He joined a carnival show, and with his first savings he purchased a battered secondhand piano for seventy dollars which he learned to play by ear.

During the next few years he supported himself as best he could. For a while he played the piano in a restaurant in Sheepshead Bay near Coney Island. Then he found employment as a stagehand at Loew's Liberty Theatre in the Brownsville section of Brooklyn. Finally, he was hired as a jack-of-all-trades by the old Vitagraph studios then filming silent movies in New York; he served as an "extra," played mood music on the piano, helped stagehands carry and manipulate props. Eventually he rose to the post of assistant director. During this period, on December 18, 1917, he married Josephine Wensler and set up home in a Brooklyn apartment where, in 1918, a son was born to them (who died when he was only twenty). Later on, in 1924, came their second and last child, a daughter.

After America declared war on Germany, Warren enlisted in the navy. He was stationed in Long Island, where he was put in charge of all the entertainment. He started a band that gave regular concerts. He put on stage and movie shows. He was doing something else, too, though this was not part of his military duties: he was writing songs. One of his earliest was "How'd You Like To Be a Sailor?"

The war over, Warren supported his family by playing the piano in various beer gardens, nickelodeons, and dance halls. He was writing more and more songs. One was "I Learned to Love You When I Learned My A, B, C's." While it failed to find a home with a publisher, it did manage to arouse the interest of Stark and Cowan in Tin Pan Alley, which hired him in 1920 as song plugger and piano demonstrator. Warren hastily proceeded to justify the confidence his firm had in him by writing "Rose of Rio Grande" which, in 1922, became his first publication. It was a minor success, but more so as an instrumental than as a song with lyrics by Edgar Leslie. In 1923 Warren's "I Love My Baby and My

Baby Loves Me" and "Back Home in Pasadena" did so well in sheet-music sale that Warren was hired by Shapiro-Bernstein as staff composer.

His star was rising as he produced hit songs like "Nagasaki," "Where the Shy Little Violets Grow," and "Way Down South in Heaven." Billy Rose, then planning to produce Broadway revues, took notice of Warren and accepted two of his songs for *Sweet and Low* in 1930, both of them successful: "Cheerful Little Earful" (lyrics by Ira Gershwin) and "Would You Like To Take a Walk?" For Billy Rose's *Crazy Quilt* in 1931, Warren wrote "I Found a Million Dollar Baby in a Five and Ten Cent Store." In addition to working on Broadway for Billy Rose, Warren wrote in 1931 the complete score for the Broadway musical *The Laugh Parade,* starring Ed Wynn, whose best numbers were "Ooh That Kiss" and "You're My Everything." But his biggest money-maker was a song published independently in 1931, "By the River Sainte Marie." The curious thing about this last number is that it had been written a decade earlier, in 1921, but no publishers were interested in it, convinced as they were that a religious song did not have a chance to sell ten copies. Reinald Werrenrath, the distinguished concert baritone, and Lennie Haydon (then a member of Charles Previn's orchestra) featured it over the air—and still Tin Pan Alley showed no interest in the number. At last, one of Warren's close friends, Jack Bergman, did a strong-sell on the publisher Robbins, who—more out of friendship for Bergman than out of admiration for the song—brought it out in 1931. It took hold immediately—popularized by Kate Smith—and stayed on the top of the best-seller lists for many months.

Already in 1929, Warren had begun to place songs in the movies with "Cryin' for the Carolines" and "Have a Little Faith in Me," both interpolated into *Spring Is Here.* Then, in 1932, when Hollywood was getting its second wind in the production of screen musicals, the Warrens—convinced that Hollywood was the place a songwriter could ply his trade most successfully—rented a large house in Beverly Hills in anticipation of his coming success. He was proved right before many weeks had passed. In 1932 Darryl F. Zanuck (at that time a producer at Warner Brothers) was projecting *Forty-Second Street* at his studio's most lavish and ambitious musical. Al Dubin, a lyricist then employed by Warners, was Zanuck's natural choice for the writing of the lyrics. Almost as obvious was his selection of Warren as composer. For the publishing house of Remick had by now become a Warner Brothers subsidiary; and since Warren had enjoyed a long and successful career as staff composer at Remick's, he was in Zanuck's direct line of vision during the planning of *Forty-Second Street.*

Thus one of the most successful screen musicals of the early 1930's was the catalyzing agent bringing Warren and Dubin together. From then on, throughout the 1930's, they would create some of the screen's most impressive songs.

Al Dubin had been one of the first lyricists to get a studio contract in Hollywood after motion pictures began talking and singing. He was born in Zurich, Switzerland, on June 10, 1891, the son of a physician. As an infant of two, he was brought by his family to the United States, where it made its home in Pennsburg, Pennsylvania. There Al Dubin attended public schools and the Perkiomen Seminary; he also made his first attempts at writing song lyrics. In the years just before World War I in Europe, Dubin made his home in New York, where he found employment as staff lyricist in Tin Pan Alley. He also wrote special material for vaudevillians. In 1916 he had a taste of success with " 'Twas Only an Irishman's Dream" for which Rennie Carmack wrote the music. But luck ran out, and the songs he peddled after that failed to find a buyer among publishers, let alone a successful public market. Dubin had to support himself as a singing waiter in a Philadelphia bar. Discouragement, as well as patriotism, led him to enlist in the army when America entered World War I. He was attached to the entertainment unit of the 77th Division, with which he went overseas and for which he wrote a number of songs.

After the war, back in harness in Tin Pan Alley, Dubin was able to make considerable headway in the song business. With Joseph Meyer as composer (and Billy Rose as fellow lyricist) he wrote "A Cup of Coffee, a Sandwich, and You" in 1925, which was interpolated for Gertrude Lawrence and Jack Buchanan in *Charlot's Revue of 1926* (a musical importation from London). Also in 1925 came "Nobody Knows What a Red-Headed Mama Can Do" (music by Sammy Fain), and between 1925 and 1926, "The Lonesomest Gal in Town" and "My Dream of the Big Parade" (music by Jimmy McHugh).

A Warner Brothers contract brought him to Hollywood in 1929. There he established a working arrangement with the composer Joe Burke, whose fame had already been solidly grounded with songs like "Oh, How I Miss You To-night," "Carolina Moon," and "Yearning Just For You." The first assignment Zanuck gave Burke and Dubin was to write songs for the expensively mounted screen musical *Gold Diggers of Broadway*. Burke and Dubin had only one week to do the job. They delivered their goods on schedule, and as if to prove that in their case haste did not make waste, the delivery included "Tip Toe Through the Tulips" and "Painting the Clouds with Sunshine."

Dubin continued working with Joe Burke for the next three years. In 1930 their songs were heard in five screen musicals, including *Big Boy,* which starred Al Jolson. They also wrote and had published several numbers that had no screen affiliations. Then, after 1932, Joe Burke went to work with other lyricists (no less fruitfully, it might be added). And Al Dubin joined Harry Warren to write the songs for *Forty-Second Street*.

Forty-Second Street set a pattern many a later screen musical would follow slavishly. This had a backstage story. A girl from the chorus line gets a chance to prove herself when she suddenly steps into the shoes of a star who had suffered an accident. In the process, the girl meets the boy, and the boy gets the girl (though innumerable complications have to be overcome in the process). The story did not matter much, just so long as it allowed the cameras to focus their lenses from every possible angle on stunning, ingeniously contrived dance patterns employing large forces; also, just so long as Ginger Rogers (at the head of a bevy of chorines) could present songs like "We're in the Money" and could join Glenda Farrell and Ruby Keeler in a splendiferous production number while presenting "Shuffle Off to Buffalo" and the title number; and just so long as stars like Dick Powell and Bebe Daniels could be heard singing "Young and Healthy" and "You're Getting To Be a Habit With Me."

Such songs by Warren and Dubin in *Forty-Second Street* represented one of the richest and most varied crops the young talking screen had thus far fertilized. Since this movie proved a box-office bonanza (with an assist from the publicity derived by having a "Forty-Second Street Special" carrying the stars across the country by train), Warren and Dubin could expect to be kept busy. For Eddie Cantor, in *Roman Scandals,* they wrote in 1933 "Keep Young and Beautiful." The year of 1934 was a banner one for them, bringing "The Boulevard of Broken Dreams" in *Moulin Rouge,* "I'll String Along With You" in *Twenty Million Sweethearts,* and "I Only Have Eyes for You" in *Dames.*

Warren and Dubin now needed that final stamp of approval to confirm their reigning position in screen music—an Oscar. Though the Academy of Motion Pictures Art and Sciences had established an annual award for distinguished contributions to the screen in 1928, not until four years later did it include a category for songs. In 1934 "The Continental" by Con Conrad (words by Herb Magidson) became the first song capturing an Oscar (after being introduced by Fred Astaire and Ginger Rogers in *The Gay Divorcee*).

Warren and Dubin did not have long to wait for their own Oscar. They got it in 1935 with "Lullaby of Broadway," the big number in *Gold Diggers of Broadway,* sung by Wini Shaw (supported by about a hundred chorines and chorus boys) in an immense set resembling the interior of Taj Mahal. The writing of "Lullaby of Broadway" had been to Warren an emotional release, for truth to tell he detested Hollywood at the time and he was pining for Broadway, Lindy's, and his colleagues in the song-publishing business. The melody expressed his nostalgia for New York, and since Dubin knew all about Warren's feelings he produced lyrics that would put to words what Warren felt. The motion-picture producers did not like the song when they heard it and turned it down. But when they got wind of the rumor that Al Jolson wanted it they suddenly changed their mind and used it.

The Warren and Dubin hit songs kept coming as long as screen musicals remained in demand. "About a Quarter to Nine" became an Al Jolson specialty after he introduced it in *Get into Your Dance;* "I'll Sing You a Thousand Love Songs" was heard in *Cain and Mabel,* and "With Plenty of Money and You" in *Gold Diggers of 1937*—all three songs written in 1936. "Remember Me?" was found in *Mr. Dodd Takes the Air* and "September in the Rain" in *Stars Over Broadway* in 1937.

By 1939 Warren and Dubin were going their separate ways. Dubin (who died in New York City on February 11, 1945) never again captured an Academy Award. But he did write lyrics for several resounding hit songs including "South American Way" with Jimmy McHugh and "Feudin' and Fightin' " with Burton Lane.

Separation from Dubin—and seeking out other lyricists with whom to work—did not break Warren's phenomenal string of screen-song successes. In time he got two more Oscars: in 1943, for "You'll Never Know" (lyrics by

Mack Gordon), which Alice Faye sang in *Hello, Frisco, Hello,* and which sold over a million copies of sheet music; in 1946, with "On the Atchison, Topeka, and the Santa Fe" (words by Johnny Mercer), a Judy Garland triumph in *The Harvey Girls.*

By the time the screen musical went into its second great decline, as far as public reaction was concerned, soon after World War II, Warren had added quite a number of songs to his now formidable library of standards. Most of them were in collaboration with Mack Gordon as his lyricist (Gordon, whose earlier partnership with Harry Revel had also enriched screen music). In the closing 1930's and early 1940's Warren and Gordon produced the following: "Chattanooga Choo Choo," a Glenn Miller offering in *Sun Valley;* "I Had the Craziest Dream" performed by Harry James and his orchestra in *Springtime in the Rockies;* "There'll Never Be Another" in *Iceland;* "My Heart Tells Me," sung by Betty Grable in *Sweet Rosie O'Grady;* and "The More I See You" and "I Wish I Knew" in *Diamond Horseshoe.*

Warren also collaborated successfully with Johnny Mercer in writing "Jeepers Creepers," "You Must Have Been a Beautiful Baby," and the already mentioned "On the Atchison, Topeka, and the Santa Fe"—each a triumphant sheet-music and record seller. And with Ira Gershwin he created what he now believes to be the best score of his entire career, the songs for *The Barkleys of Broadway* (1948), a starring vehicle for Fred Astaire and Ginger Rogers.

Even after the public began rejecting screen musical in the mid-1940's—and the studios stopped making them in quantity—Warren kept on creating significant songs. A retiring, modest man who holds publicity gimmicks and attention-getting devices in horror, Warren has never perhaps quite seized the limelight of attention in the same way many other songwriters have done (in some instances songwriters far less gifted and successful than he). Warren is, for example, the only songwriter who, nominated for an Oscar, had to learn from a broadcast, while driving with Harold Arlen, that he was the winner. When the announcement was made, Warren said nothing. Finally, they came to their destination. Warren now made an oblique mention to the then-unprecedented achievement of having just received this third Oscar. He ordered Arlen to "walk two Oscars behind me."

Arlen (Warren's neighbor in Beverly Hills when Arlen had a home in California) is one of the many famous songwriters who hold Warren in the highest esteem. So did Jerome Kern, and so does Ira Gershwin. All three shared Warren's enthusiasm for golf which they played almost daily at the Hillcrest Country Club in the 1940's. "The three of us may be fine songwriters," once commented Ira Gershwin to a friend, "but we were certainly lousy golfers."

Golf is still a passion with Warren. He permits nothing and no one to interfere with his daily round at the golf club. But other interests of earlier years have long since been discarded. He used to drink alcohol a good deal, but is now a moderate imbiber of a drink or two, usually at a party. He also used to do considerable gambling and was a chronic loser. He is probably the only person who ever made fifteen straight passes at the Las Vegas dice table only to break out even. "Even when I had a phenomenal streak of luck in poker, I just couldn't win," he remarks. "If I broke out even after a game it represented a major victory."

His present-day pleasures besides golf include "fooling around at the piano," as he puts it, "kibitzing with friends," playing a game of pool from time to time, once in a while going out for dinner—and, of course, his family, which now includes not only his wife and daughter but also four grandchildren and one great-grandchild (all living in Beverly Hills). He is a wealthy man, not through his ASCAP rating (which remains high), but through the purchase and sale of various houses in which he has lived in Beverly Hills since he built his first one in 1937. His present home, on Sunset Drive, which he has occupied since 1956, cost him a little over $100,000 to build; he has already been offered over $350,000 for it. But in addition to the profits he has accumulated through the sale of his houses, he has also amassed a comfortable fortune in the stock market, thanks to the shrewdness and perspicacity of his wife. He himself, he confesses, knows absolutely nothing about stocks.

He still writes songs but, as he will tell you without bitterness, "there just isn't a market for the kind of old-fashioned numbers I used to do and which I still love to create." He adds: "When rock 'n' roll first became popular I was convinced that it was a passing fad and that another age of ballads would return as an inevitable reaction. But I was wrong. Rock music is bigger than ever —just look at those best-selling lists of current records—and only occasionally does the old-fashioned type of love ballad make an impression on the public."

But it has been a good life and a productive one, and Warren is not the kind of man to harbor deep-rooted regrets, or to allow frustrations and disappointments to embitter his pleasant way of life. Another hit or two now, however, would make his life just about perfect.

Songs from the Movies–II

James Van Heusen and Sammy Cahn

After the end of World War II, public apathy toward screen musicals brought about another serious setback in this kind of production, even though on occasion a profitable market existed for such special presentations as *An American in Paris* (which won the Academy Award as the best picture of the year), *The Band Wagon, Funny Face,* or *South Pacific.* But the run-of-the-mill musicals that had flourished in the 1930's and early 1940's had small chance of survival beyond their initial presentations, and so this kind of musical was being scrupulously avoided by the studios. But motion-picture history repeated itself in the 1960's. As had happened when talking pictures first came into existence, the screen musical suddenly became big business not only in the United States but throughout the world. All this came about in the heels of the fabulous success enjoyed by productions like *The Sound of Music, My Fair Lady, Mary*

Poppins, Thoroughly Modern Millie, Camelot, among many others. By the end of 1969 no less than six multimillion-dollar productions were released (not to count the many on a lesser budget): *Funny Girl, Hello, Dolly!, Finian's Rainbow, Oliver, Sweet Charity,* and *Paint Your Wagon. Funny Girl* and *Hello, Dolly!* (each starring Barbra Streisand) were budgeted at thirty million dollars. And even before waiting to see how this huge investment in musical-comedy productions turned out, the studios were already going into high gear in the preparation, filming, or completion of many more musicals, among them *On a Clear Day You Can See Forever* (with Barbra Streisand), *Goodbye, Mr. Chips, Cabaret, Fiddler on the Roof,* and *Man of La Mancha,* among many, many others.

Even when screen musicals came few and far between—between the middle 1940's and the 1960's—when the few superspecials that were being projected before the cameras more often than not called only for fully established and topflight songwriters, even then there was no serious downgrading in the quality of music being written for the movies, nor was there a marked lessening in the number of talented composers and lyricists the screen helped to incubate. For in spite of the lack of screen musicals, songs continued to be written for and receive a hearing on the screen, in nonmusical productions. Sometimes these served as numbers played or sung under the opening credits, or immediately following the closing scene (but frequently never even heard within the picture itself). In the 1950's, as in the late 1920's, producers were aware of the potency of a successful song (particularly an Academy Award winning song) in promoting the movie for which it had been written. A successful song like this often spelled the difference of several million dollars at the box office, especially when the song bore the same title as the movie, and even more especially if the song received an Oscar.

Only one team of songwriters managed to capture four Oscars each—James Van Heusen, composer, and Sammy Cahn, lyricist. Working together, they received Academy Awards between 1957 and 1963 with "All the Way," "High Hopes," and "Call Me Irresponsible." In addition, with Johnny Burke as his lyricist, Van Heusen received his first Academy Award in 1944 for "Swinging on a Star," while Sammy Cahn's first Oscar had come in 1954 with the title number for "Three Coins in a Fountain," music by Jule Styne.

The writing of title songs for important films and less important ones has been a particularly strong suit for Cahn and Van Heusen. They are probably the songwriters major studios come to first when title numbers are needed. Cahn and Van Heusen get between $20,000 and $25,000 for a single title song—a solid investment for any studio since many a Cahn–Van Heusen song has hit the jackpot as far as public acceptance is concerned. Among the successful movies profiting from their songs have been: *The Tender Trap* with Frank Sinatra and Debbie Reynolds; or *Pocketful of Miracles* with Bette Davis; or *Where Love Has Gone* with Susan Hayward and Bette Davis; or *Thoroughly Modern Millie* with Julie Andrews. Some of these title songs were nominated for Academy Awards. More times than once a picture started out with one title and ended up with another, because the song Cahn and Van Heusen had written was so good and so commercial that it seemed practical for the picture to borrow its title from the song. This happened with *Be My Love, It's Magic,* and *All the Way.*

Writing title songs presents no problem when the picture is called, say, *Indiscreet,* or *Where Love Has Gone,* for they provide Sammy Cahn with lyric ideas that practically write themselves. But, unfortunately, for Cahn, too many movies boast titles which are either so specific or so unsuitable for song ideas that Cahn is compelled to turn many a mental somersault to concoct a subject inspired by the title that makes sense. Somehow, some way, he invariably manages to do so, even when he is compelled to write numbers with titles like "The World of Suzie Wong" or "The Man with the Golden Arm" or "They Came to Cordura" or "Come Blow Your Horn." And it is this particular talent for taking outlandish titles and making them into intelligible, logical song matter that has put Cahn in a class by himself.

He always succeeds in finding some serviceable subject—frequently one that has no relationship whatsoever to the movie for which the song is intended. And once having hit upon his subject, the rest is easy going. The neat phrase, the freshly conceived line, the glib rhyming and rhythm come leaping into his mind with such abundance that his main problem is selection and rejection rather than invention. These are the kind of lyrics (to quote what Richard Rodgers once said about Hammerstein's words) that you can put on your piano, and the melody comes by itself. At least that's the way it seems when a lyricist and his composer are responsive to each other's talent, and when the composer has the same kind of facility in concocting fresh, spontaneously conceived, soaring melodies with the same fertility that his lyricist creates the words. And in James Van Heusen, Sammy Cahn has found such a composer.

When he was born in Syracuse, New York, on January 26, 1913, James Van Heusen's name was Edward Chester Babcock. Long after he changed his name, he has been called "Chester" by his mother, Frank Sinatra, and others.

His grandmother insists that on his mother's side James Van Heusen is a direct descendant of Stephen Foster. Whether this is so or not—incontrovertible evidence to that effect has never been made public—it is nevertheless true that, like his distinguished predecessor in songwriting, James was a musical boy. He began studying the piano early, and before long was writing songs. His father, a builder (who played the cornet), was determined that the boy get a sound academic education rather than specialize in music. But the father became disenchanted when James was expelled from high school in his early teens for having perpetrated a prank. What happened was that at a school assembly at Central High School, James was called upon to sing something to demonstrate a Speak-o-Phone recording apparatus. He made this demonstration with a facetious number, "My Canary Has Rings Under His Eyes," which he had heard a few nights earlier over the radio. The students went into an uproar, pandemonium was let loose in the auditorium, and Van Heusen was expelled.

When he was fifteen, he found a part-time job as a radio announcer for WSYR, in Syracuse, for fifteen dollars a week. This was the time he changed his name. The manager of the radio station insisted that there was a profane sound to "Edward C. Babcock," when at the end of every program the words "Your announcer has been Edward C. Babcock" were used to sign off. "I tried to explain as best a fifteen-year-old boy could," Van Heusen explains, "that Babcock was an old English name as was Hancock, Glasscock, or just plain Cock, and that the original meaning of Babcock was old English, Badcock, meaning 'fighting rooster.' The manager's judgment prevailed and the name James Van Heusen was invented by my boyhood buddy who occasionally sang on my radio program with me—Ralph Harris (subsequently become Lena Horne's manager). He looked out of the window, and saw an ad for Van Heusen's collars (they did not make shirts in those days, if I remember correctly) and simply said, 'That's a good name, Van Heusen,' and I said, 'What goes with it?' 'James,' was Ralph Harris's instantaneous response, 'I've always liked the name.' The manager was delighted with the name change and I kept my job. I liked it for the reason that my parents did not know I was skipping school. Legally, the name has never been changed, and to this day my pilot's license, passport, and other papers still read 'Edward Chester Babcock, also known as James Van Heusen.'"

In those days, orchestra leaders over the radio took pride in introducing new songs over the air, and tried to do so on every program. While attending Central High School, Van Heusen made it a practice to listen to every radio orchestra he could, and particularly to the new songs. He took down the lyrics in Gregg shorthand (having learned to do about 120 words a minute one summer) and marked down on paper at least the main eight-bar strain of the music (which in most songs was repeated three times). Thus with his lyrics intact and correct, and with the core of the music noted down (the parts of the song he had been unable to catch he would compose himself), he was able to sing on his radio programs brand-new songs by top songwriters long before the sheet music had become available. Because these songs were so new, many of his listeners came to the hasty conclusion that Van Heusen had written them. The "Canary" song that got him expelled from high school had been introduced by Guy Lombardo and his orchestra.

Having been ousted out of Central High School, Van Heusen continued his schooling at Cazenovia Seminary, now a junior college exclusively for girls, but then a coeducational boarding school, founded by the Methodist Church and headed by a minister. There he devoted himself far more assiduously to writing pop tunes and ballads than to learning religious hymns or completing homework for his classes. Once when he was expelled from the seminary for his songwriting activity, the minister drove him home, twenty miles away, handed him over to James's father, and exclaimed: "Don't bring him back!" James was reinstated but soon found himself thrown out once again, this time for having been found hanging around poolrooms. (Cazenovia conveniently forgot Van Heusen's disreputable scholastic past when, in 1961, it presented him with its first Distinguished Alumnus Award.) Between 1930 and 1932 Van Heusen attended Syracuse University where he received instruction in piano and voice.

One of his friends—and coincidentally on several occasions his lyricist—

was Jerry Arlen, the younger brother of Harold Arlen, the song composer. Through Jerry, some of Van Heusen's songs were brought to Harold Arlen's attention. At that time, Harold Arlen was the staff composer for the Cotton Club in New York's Harlem. Since he had just been contracted to go to Hollywood and write songs for the screen, Harold Arlen needed a temporary replacement at the Cotton Club. He thought well enough of Van Heusen's manuscripts to invite him to come to New York. Van Heusen did so in 1933, but did not fare too well (even though one of his numbers, "Harlem Hospitality," became his first published song). As he put it: "The show was a 'flop' and the song was terrible." The inevitable now took place: Van Heusen was without a job. Too proud to come home defeated, he stayed on in New York, writing song after song. He had over five hundred numbers to market, but while trudging from one publisher to the next found no takers for any of them. To support himself while waiting for luck to change, he took on a job operating a freight elevator at the Park Central Hotel, doing a good deal of his songwriting in that elevator. The hotel orchestra played one of his tunes, "There's a House in Harlem for Sale," which the Santly Brothers Music Publishing Company not only bought but also went on from there to hire Van Heusen as one of its staff pianists.

He did not hold this post long. In 1934 Van Heusen found employment in various other publishing establishments in Tin Pan Alley, going from one company to another, and usually dismissed because he insisted on plugging his own songs to potential clients rather than the numbers his company wanted him to plug.

In 1938, while employed as staff pianist at Remick's (then already a subsidiary of Music Publishers Holding Corporation, owned by Warner Brothers) Van Heusen met Jimmy Dorsey, the celebrated bandleader. To Dorsey's lyrics, Van Heusen wrote the melody for "It's the Dreamer in Me." Remick's turned it down, but Leo Feist bought it and built it up into a 90,000-copy sale—a very modest success, but Van Heusen's biggest one up to then. Eddie De Lange now became his principal lyricist. Working with De Lange was not easy for the simple reason that Van Heusen had a permanent problem in catching up with him and getting him to work. At that time Eddie De Lange was a bandleader of the then-popular group the Hudson–De Lange Orchestra. Eddie wrote songs with Hudson (including "Moonglow"), besides waving the stick for the band's performances and singing the vocals. In short, he was quite a busy fellow. There were times when the only occasion Van Heusen was able to catch De Lange to get him to write lyrics for him was after 2 A.M., when the band had completed playing for the evening.

Nevertheless, Eddie De Lange (who died in 1949) did manage to do a number of lyrics for Van Heusen. Some of these melodies Van Heusen had written as a boy, two of which did quite well: "So Help Me" and "Can I Help It?" Then, in 1938, came "Deep in a Dream," which sold almost 200,000 copies of sheet music. This was followed in 1939 by "All This and Heaven Too" and "Heaven Can Wait." Van Heusen was on his way to a career.

Still with Eddie De Lange as his lyricist, Van Heusen made his debut as

Broadway composer with songs for *Swingin' the Dream* in 1939. This was a musical-comedy "swing" version of Shakespeare's *A Midsummer Night's Dream,* but with New Orleans as its setting. "Darn that Dream" was this show's big number, introduced by Benny Goodman and his orchestra, who subsequently popularized it on records and over the radio.

Meeting up and getting to work with Eddie De Lange was only one of several important developments in Van Heusen's career while he was employed at Remick's. Another was his friendship with Frank Sinatra to whom he was introduced by Henry Sanicola, then a counter boy at Witmark's (another subsidiary of the Music Publishers Holding Corporation). Sinatra's later passionate espousal of Van Heusen's songs was no small factor in the composer's mounting successes. A third development came with the acquisition of a new lyricist—Johnny Burke.

Here is how Van Heusen remembers his first meeting with Burke: "He just came into the office [Remick's] to shoot the breeze. He said to me, 'Got any tunes?' I said, 'Sure!' So we went and wrote 'Oh, You Crazy Moon.' The next time he was in, we did 'Polka Dots and Moonbeams.' Soon after that came 'Imagination.' "

The first of these, "Oh, You Crazy Moon," was introduced and made popular by Tommy Dorsey and his orchestra. "Polka Dots and Moonbeams" was recorded by Tommy Dorsey and his orchestra with Frank Sinatra doing the vocal (the first time Sinatra sang a Van Heusen song). "Imagination," though introduced by Fred Waring and his Pennsylvanians, became a favorite of Glenn Miller and his orchestra. One additional fact about "Polka Dots and Moonbeams" is worth noting: It became one of three Van Heusen songs to reach radio's "Hit Parade" in a single week, the other two being "All This and Heaven Too" and "Shake Down the Stars." This may very well have been the only time a composer had three songs on one program on "Hit Parade."

"Imagination" was the song responsible for bringing Van Heusen to Hollywood. Mark Sandrich, producer of the Astaire–Ginger Rogers screen musicals, heard the song, fell in love with it, and yelled out to one of his assistants, "Get me *that* guy!" "I was unknown to him except for having written 'Imagination,' " reveals Van Heusen. "He was shooting tests at Paramount in New York and I was dragged there to meet him, having been on an extended drunk. He, or rather Paramount, signed me to do two pictures. After Sandrich examined my list of songs and collaborators, he asked me if I would work with Frank Loesser, as my lyricist, since Loesser was under contract to Paramount. Naturally I agreed. But eventually, Johnny Burke—who had long since become a top lyricist for many of Bing Crosby's movies—took a large reduction in his usual Bing Crosby salary in order to do *Love Thy Neighbor* for Sandrich. I became his composer again—and we became a Hollywood songwriting team after that picture, when Bing personally asked me to write the songs for *Road to Zanzibar,* one of which became a hit, 'It's Always You.' "

After that, for the next few years, came other "Road" pictures starring Crosby, Bob Hope, and Dorothy Lamour. Crosby, of course, sang the best of these Van Heusen songs in these various films, recorded them, and, most assuredly, was more than passingly influential in making some of them national favorites—numbers like the title song and "Moonlight Becomes You" from *Road to Morocco;* "Personality" and "Put It There" from *Road to Utopia;* and "But Beautiful" and "You Don't Have To Know the Language" from *Road to Rio.* In all, Van Heusen wrote songs for almost twenty movies in which Bing Crosby starred, though some of Van Heusen's later numbers were done with Sammy Cahn as his lyricist rather than Johnny Burke.

During World War II, and even before America had become involved, James Van Heusen pursued two professions not one. While writing his hit songs for the screen under the name of James Van Heusen, he worked at Lockheed Aircraft as test pilot under his real name, Babcock. Not one of the 120 other employees at the Lockheed plant had the slightest idea that this fellow Babcock who worked with them was the same one who was writing the songs they heard, sang, and loved—including "Sunday, Monday or Always" which achieved the top spot on "Hit Parade." "I was just 'one of the guys,' " Van Heusen says. "The fact that I was a test pilot at Lockheed was kept a secret from Paramount Pictures in the early days of my employment there because, as Johnny Burke warned me at the time—if they knew I was test-flying airplanes at Lockheed they would not assign me to a picture, in the middle of which I might be killed in a crash. Some months later, when the United States declared war, I was a hero when it became known that I had been doing the test-flying job on the sly. The schedule at Lockheed was: four days running I would get up at 4 A.M. to start flying at 5 A.M., and I would be back home, or at the studio, by noon. Then after two and a half days off, I would fly three days beginning at 1 P.M., and I could go to the studio in the morning. Being young and able to survive without too much sleep I juggled both occupations."

Before the partnership of Van Heusen and Burke ended, there were still some triumphs in store for them. The most important, of course, came in 1944 with the winning of an Oscar (Van Heusen's first) for "Swinging on a Star." This was the number Bing Crosby, in the role of a parish priest, sang with a boy's choir in that glowing picture *Going My Way,* which received an Academy Award in its own right as the best picture of the year. "Swinging on a Star" was a difficult number for Burke to conceive. Leo McCarey, producer-director of *Going My Way,* had given him definite instructions to write a song for Bing which would expound the Ten Commandments and which he would sing to a group of "dead-end kids." "What I want," McCarey told them, "is the Ten Commandments in a rhythm song." Burke puzzled over this problem for a long time without coming up with a single idea. Then one evening he was dining at Bing Crosby's house. When one of Bing's sons misbehaved at the table, Bing upbraided him for behaving like a "mule." To Burke—who at that very moment was still pondering on the kind of lyrics he should write for McCarey—the remark provided a useful theme: a kid refusing to better himself because he was as stubborn as a mule. One thought led to the next in a delightful chain of absurd images: what a kid would be like if he behaved like a fish, or like a pig, and so forth. The following morning Burke had all his lyrics on paper and before day was done Van Heusen had written his melody. The song was not exactly the Ten Commandments in a rhythm song, but both Burke and Van Heusen felt that it might fill the bill obliquely. It did. Neither Burke nor Van Heusen ever denied that they were well paid for their labor pains in conceiving "Swinging on a Star." Once the picture was released, the song was recorded in over two hundred versions (that of Crosby, of course, being the leader with its more than one-million-disc sale); and the figures of the sheet-music distribution were hardly less impressive.

One year later, Van Heusen and Burke were twice nominated for Academy Awards: for "Aren't You Glad You're You?", sung by Bing Crosby in *The Bells of St. Mary's,* and "Sleighride in July," introduced by Dinah Shore in *Belle of Yukon.* They did not get that much-coveted award again, but they did manage to achieve further impressive sales both for the recordings and the sheet music of each of these numbers, as well as for "Mr. Music" and "Sunshine Cake," two more screen songs that owe their introduction and success to Bing Crosby.

A serious illness that stretched through 1954 and 1955 made it impossible for Johnny Burke to do any writing, creating a serious problem for Van Heusen: Van Heusen was under contract to write exclusively with Burke and for the publishing house they had founded, Burke and Van Heusen, Inc. This situation compelled Van Heusen to write songs with other lyricists, under assumed names. I will let him tell the story himself, in what surely must have been the most curious and frustrating period of his career: "I wrote 'I Could Have Told You' for Frank Sinatra, and used the name Arthur Williams, which was my father's first name and my mother's maiden name, and when Frank Sinatra asked me to write themes for the pictures *Not as a Stranger* and *Young at Heart,* he and I and Henry Sanicola formed the music company, Maraville Music, which was to publish almost all our songs during the next thirteen years. I turned in the melodies 'You, My Love' for *Young at Heart* and 'Not as a Stranger' for the picture of the same name, and left it to Sinatra to obtain the lyrics. They were eventually written by Mack Gordon and Buddy Kaye respectively. I wrote 'Somewhere Along the Way' with Sammy Gallup, and put the name of Ada Kurtz (who was a girl friend of mine at the time) on it, and manufactured the name Kurt Adams out of the letters of her name for the music credit. I put the name Arthur Williams on the song 'Funny Thing,' which was recorded by Tony Bennett, and I put phony names on dozens of other songs—some that you would know, and some that you would not. Eventually the exclusive contract was revised. Hit songs of mine were appearing without my name on them. Since then, some have been republished with my name."

But once the exclusive contract was changed and James Van Heusen could begin issuing his songs under his own name, he acquired a new writing partner. At that very time, Sammy Cahn was deserting Jule Styne (or vice versa)—Styne being the composer with whom Cahn had soared to the highest mountains of success (to use a lyricist's cliché) in the movies. Bing Crosby, who was being starred in a movie-remake of the Cole Porter musical *Anything Goes,* was the one who suggested that Van Heusen and Cahn pair up, since four new numbers were needed for that production and Crosby wanted Van Heusen to write them. And so, with a composer deprived of his lyricist by a serious illness, and a lyricist deprived of his composer through personal disagreements and incompatibility, Bing Crosby became the matchmaker to bring about the words-and-music marriage of what was to become a sustained idyllic creative romance.

Sammy Cahn was a New York boy, who had been born as Sammy Cohen in a drab tenement on Cannon Street in New York's Lower East Side on June 18, 1913. ("It took me almost half a lifetime and three thousand miles to take me from Cannon Street on the East Side to Canon Drive in Beverly Hills," Cahn remarks wryly.) He was the only boy in a family of girls, four of whom studied the piano. Sammy's parents, immigrants from Galicia, had the dream that made tolerable the drab poverty of virtually every Jewish parent in those days: They hoped Sammy would someday become a professional man, preferably a doctor, and they stood ready to make every sacrifice necessary to help to bring this about. But Sammy's inclinations lay far from the schoolroom. By the time he reached his early adolescence those interests had begun to focus themselves more and more on music.

At his Bar Mitzvah Sammy discovered for the first time that music had commercial possibilities when he saw his mother paying the musicians for their services. It had never occurred to him that anybody could make money by playing music. A year later, having by this time done some studying on the violin, he played the instrument in the Catskill Mountains resorts during the summers (the so-called Borscht Belt). Winter evenings were spent in an orchestra playing for various parties and other social functions. It was at this time that Cahn started to find pleasure in handling words as well as music, by concocting parodies on popular song hits. As for school, he was continually a truant from Seward Park High School so that he could earn enough money (by racking up balls in the nearby poolroom) to pay the price of admission for the movies.

He soon left school for good. For a while he worked as a violinist in the pit orchestra of burlesque houses. Then he began shifting from one job to another in a desperate attempt to find a place for himself in the commercial world. Sometimes for a few days, sometimes for a couple of weeks, he was employed at various menial occupations: as a "candle boy" in a meat-packing plant; as an usher in a movie house; as a tinsmith; as an operator of a freight elevator; as a cashier in a restaurant; and as a porter in a loose-leaf bindery plant.

One day, when he was sixteen, he attended a vaudeville show where Jack Osterman, a headliner, got a magnificent hand for singing one of his own songs. This performance, and the enthusiastic response of the audience, brought home to Cahn the fact that perhaps there might be a future in songwriting. On his way home from the theatre he wrote his first song lyric, "Like Niagara Falls, I'm Falling for You." One day after that, he produced thirty songs—words *and* music. Since he felt more at ease in writing words than music, he soon enlisted the musical collaboration of Saul Chaplin, a young man who played the piano in the orchestra where Cahn was one of the violinists. Chaplin's name at that time was Kaplan, but the moment Cahn and Kaplan began working together Cahn insisted he change his name explaining: "Cahn and Kaplan—that sounds like a dress firm!" And so, Kaplan became Chaplin, and Chaplin became Cahn's composer. They produced a whole library of popular songs which they methodically submitted to one publisher after another, all of whom were singularly disinterested. Cahn recalls that they visited one publisher (Al Piantadosi) one hundred times and were thrown out a hundred times. "Why do you keep going back all the time?" Chaplin asked Cahn. Cahn replied: "Because they always let me in first."

Cahn's parents had long since surrendered their dreams and hopes of making Sammy into a doctor. They kept nudging him now to try to find for himself a place in the business world. Partly due to their nagging, and partly because after all he had to earn a living, Cahn worked for three years at the United Dressed Beef Company (on the same site on which the United Nations stands today). But all his spare time was devoted to songwriting. The publishers remained totally indifferent, but another market opened up for him and Chaplin: writing special material for various singers, band acts, and comedians. To put on himself the stamp of professionalism once and for all, Cahn rented space in the West Forty-sixth Street office of Beckman and Pransky, booking agents known as the William Morris Agency of the Borsht Belt. This space did double duty, for besides being Sammy's office by day, it became his bedroom at night. He was not making much money from producing all that special material, but he did get to meet a good many famous performers, including Milton Berle, Danny Kaye, Phil Silvers, Betty Hutton, Bob Hope, and Frank Sinatra. Some of them even used some of his material.

His first publication was a song called "Shake Your Head from Side to Side," for which he wrote both the words and the music. Since he was only sixteen at the time, he had to bring along his father (who at that time owned a little restaurant) to sign the contract for him. But his real beginnings as a successful lyricist came some years after that, in 1935. Through the promotion of his good friend, Lou Levy (at that time a dancer with Jimmie Lunceford's band and subsequently a successful publisher), Cahn and Chaplin were commissioned to write a special number for the Lunceford band. They wrote "Rhythm Is Our Business," and it was enough of a hit for Lunceford to use it henceforth as his signature. "Rhythm in My Nursery Rhymes," also in 1935, was another number written for and introduced by Jimmie Lunceford and his band. Cahn and Chaplin then wrote "The Glen Gray Casa Loma Corporation" for the Glen Gray Casa Loma Orchestra for its first appearance at the Paramount Theatre in New York. Before long, the two songwriters were being sought after by one band after another to write special songs and material for them. He and Chaplin were also hired by Jack Kapp (a pioneer in getting songs written especially for recordings) to write numbers for Ella Fitzgerald, Andy Kirk, and others. In fact, it was "Until the Real Thing Comes Along," by Cahn and Chaplin, that was largely responsible for bringing Andy Kirk's band to the attention of the music world through a Decca recording.

Bigger still, from the point of view of income, was "Shoe Shine Boy" which he and Chaplin wrote for the Cotton Club revue in Harlem where it was introduced by Louis Armstrong. When Cahn wrote his lyrics for this number, he was (in spite of the fact that his songs were now getting played so extensively) in serious danger of being locked out of his office, since he had defaulted on his rent for several weeks. To raise rent money, Cahn sold one-third interest of his share in "Shoe Shine Boy" to a performer for $15. That $15 investment had a yield of about $15,000.

And now Cahn could afford to rent an apartment on Fifty-seventh Street and Sixth Avenue. There, one day, Chaplin and Lou Levy came calling to describe an unusual experience they had just had at the Apollo Theatre in Harlem. One of the performers sang a Yiddish number, "Bei mir bist du schoen," and, although there were very few Jews in the audience, the song seemed to have made an enormous impression. It was Lou Levy's thought for Cahn to write English lyrics for this melody which would be adapted for Cahn by Chaplin. Without too much interest in the whole idea, and certainly with a good deal less enthusiasm, Cahn went downtown to Second Avenue to acquire a copy of the song. He played it through a number of times and then dismissed the project from his mind. But during the next few weeks Lou Levy kept insisting that the song had possibilities with English lyrics, and Cahn kept insisting that you just can't make a hit with a Yiddish song. But apparently Levy's persuasion was stronger than Cahn's resistance. Cahn decided to make a try at producing some suitable words. The first two lines popped into his head at once: "Bei mir bist du schoen, Now let me explain, Bei mir bist du schoen means that you're grand." After that, other lines practically wrote themselves with a slight assist of a word or two from two different popular tunes then in circulation: "Tutta bella, tutta bella, Umbrella Man" and "Wunderbar." The words "bella bella" and "wunderbar" fell neatly into place in Cahn's lyrics, and in fifteen minutes the lyric was completed.

Acquiring the rights to the song possessed no problem. The Yiddish original was the work of Sholom Secunda, who had published the song himself (a practice common to Yiddish songwriters on Second Avenue), who then disposed of the rights for a pittance to J. and J. Kamen. For $150 Cahn and Chaplin were able to buy out all the rights not only for "Bei mir bist du schoen" but for four other Yiddish songs. But marketing the new Anglicized "Bei mir bist du schoen" was quite another matter. Most everybody was convinced the way Cahn had been that there just was no market for Yiddish-type songs. And so the manuscript lay on Cahn's piano, seemingly destined for permanent neglect.

One evening, Lou Levy brought to Cahn's apartment the Andrews Sisters —a three-girl singing combination that thus far had been incapable of attracting the interest of booking agents or recording companies. They picked up the manuscript of "Bei mir bist du schoen" and asked Cahn to play it for them. Something about the number caught their fancy. They grouped themselves behind Cahn and began singing it to Cahn's jazzed-up accompaniment. The Andrews Sisters were immediately sold on the song, but convincing Jack Kapp, the head of Decca, to record it was no minor obstacle. Eventually, Kapp gave in. "Bei mir bist du schoen" became the biggest novelty number of 1938, earning somewhere in the neighborhood of three million dollars. The Decca recording by the Andrew Sisters sold over a million discs and instantly put them in the class of recording stars; Priscilla Lane sang it in a movie, *Love, Honor, and Behave*. (The only one who failed to profit from this rich gold strike was the man who had written the song in the first place—Sholom Secunda; he had sold out his rights for pennies. But in the early 1960's Secunda managed to reacquire the rights to his melody and to renegotiate a new deal with the publishers—a belated victory which proved more satisfying to Secunda's ego than to his bank balance.)

Cahn and Chaplin followed "Bei mir bist du schoen" with a second Yiddish-type number adapted for American audiences—"Joseph, Joseph," which once again the Andrews Sisters recorded for Decca. This, too, was a big novelty number, though of course not of the proportions of its predecessor.

By this time, Cahn and Chaplin were beginning to make regular appearances on "Hit Parade," sometimes even in the number-one position. Warner Brothers took cognizance of this fact and hired them to work at their Vitaphone studios in Brooklyn. When these studios closed down, Warner brought the songwriters to Hollywood where, for some inexplicable reason, they kept on collecting their weekly checks without getting a single assignment. "We couldn't even get on the lot," Cahn recalls. When this contract was terminated, Cahn and Chaplin transferred to the Republic studios where they sold a story that was filmed—and it was through this story that they finally managed to get some of their songs used in a Hollywood-made production.

They were not progressing very far nor very rapidly—this much was obvious. Before long, Cahn and Chaplin decided to end their collaboration. A movie producer now introduced Cahn to another composer—Jule Styne who at that time was a vocal coach at 20th-Century and had already produced a number of impressive hit tunes including "I Don't Want To Walk Without You," which both Bing Crosby and Harry James promoted to success.

The first number coming from this new union of Cahn and Styne was an ace—"I've Heard That Song Before." Its writing came about in a curious way. Styne was demonstrating some of his melodies for Cahn. One sounded like borrowed material, and with his none-too-rare lack of tact which he regards as integrity, Cahn mentioned: "I've heard that song before." The belligerent fire in Styne's eyes at this comment, and the way in which Styne's facial muscles tightened, revealed at once that Cahn was probably losing a collaborator before he had acquired him. Cahn tried to recover his lost ground by adding: "I mean that this would make a wonderful title for your melody—'I've Heard That Song Before.'" Styne was mollified to a point where he agreed wholeheartedly that the title was a good one, but that it needed a different kind of melody, which he proceeded to write. Bob Crosby and his orchestra performed it in the movie *Youth on Parade,* and Harry James and his orchestra sold a million discs of their recording.

The soaring fortunes of Frank Sinatra, both on records and in the movies (this was in the days before he hit the skids and had to make his dramatic comeback in a nonsinging role in *From Here to Eternity*), lifted many an early Cahn-Styne song to the peaks of commercial success. In the single year of 1944, Sinatra either introduced or popularized (or both) "Saturday Night Is the Loneliest Night in the Week," "As Long As There's Music," "Come Out, Come Out," "I Fall in Love Too Easily," and "I'll Walk Alone"—the last, one of the most poignant ballads come out of World War II. During the next few years Sinatra helped boost to the hit class still other Cahn-Styne inventions, including "Five Minutes More" and "The Things We Did Last Summer." But Sinatra was by no means the only person promoting the Cahn-Styne combination, now one of the hottest songwriting teams in the movie business. Doris Day became identified with "It's Magic" and "It's a Great Feeling"; Dinah Shore, with "I'll Walk Alone," which she introduced in the movie *Follow the Boys* in 1944 before Sinatra made his own highly successful Capitol recording; Kay Kyser and his orchestra with "There Goes That Song Again"; and Vaughn Monroe with "Let It Snow."

Jule Styne, chafing to get back to Broadway, was becoming restless in Hollywood, while Sammy Cahn preferred remaining put in Beverly Hills with his family. And so by September of 1948, they split up—but only for the time being. When they became reunited to write some more song for the movies, they were able to cap their past successes with the crown of an Academy Award, the writing of which is a story Cahn will tell you at the slightest hint in your eye of interest or curiosity. Twentieth Century-Fox was planning a superspecial musical in their first Cinemascope production, *Pink Tights,* starring Marilyn Monroe, Frank Sinatra, and Dan Dailey, with choreography by Robert Alton, and the whole to be produced by Sol C. Siegel. Frank Sinatra was determined that nobody but Cahn and Styne be called upon to write the songs and it was because of Sinatra, and his refusal to accept rejection, that the two songwriters at long last resumed their collaboration (an arrangement which, it might be added, made neither Styne or Cahn happy).

For *Pink Tights,* Cahn and Styne produced a score that Cahn is convinced is the best they had ever done. Everything, then, seemed to be falling nicely into place into the making of what was expected to be the greatest screen musical ever produced. But a day before shooting began, Marilyn Monroe left for Japan with Joe Di Maggio, leaving this spectacle of spectacles without its star of stars. The production came to its dead end then and there and never materialized.

Cahn and Styne were hanging around their office at 20th Century-Fox with no work to keep them busy when Sol C. Siegel dropped in to inquire if they could write a song called "Three Coins in a Fountain." "We could write you a song called 'Eh,' if you want us to," was Cahn's quick response. Siegel then explained that 20th Century-Fox had just completed filming a picture in Italy which the New York office wanted to call *We Believe in Love.* Siegel, Zanuck, and many others thought *Three Coins in a Fountain* a far more salable title. "We feel," Siegel explained, "that if you could write a song called 'Three Coins in a Fountain' that's a knockout we can convince New York to call the picture by the same name." Unfortunately, Siegel went on to explain, Cahn and Styne could not see the picture—since all the prints were then in the hands of those responsible for the dubbing, the scoring, and the other necessary final chores. Nor was a single script available in California, every copy still in Italy. "Well," Cahn pleaded, "could you at least tell me what the picture is about?" Siegel's pithy summary was hardly helpful: "It's about three American girls in Italy who throw coins in a fountain." And with that Siegel left.

Cahn went over to his typewriter and in a few minutes had four lines of the chorus on paper. Styne, no less a professional, had a suitable melody for those lines ready less than a half hour later. Both agreed that what they had just written had the Italian flavor and the nostalgia the title song needed. Writing the rest of the song now became a matter of mere routine.

Two hours later Siegel was back in their office to inquire if Cahn and Styne had given some thought to the song he had suggested. "We not only gave it some thought," Cahn replied, "but we wrote it." Siegel loved it when Cahn demonstrated it for him and dragged the songwriters to Zanuck's office who proved even more enthusiastic. "The thing to do," Siegel suggested to Cahn, "is for you to make a demonstration record and send it on to New York." Cahn countered with a suggestion of his own: Sinatra was then working for 20th Century-Fox. Why not have him make the "demo"? Sinatra proved agreeable, his "demo" was dispatched by air to New York, and all resistance was finally broken down to calling the picture *Three Coins in a Fountain*. (Incidentally the "demo" was used in the movie as the soundtrack background.)

"Three Coins in a Fountain" became the most important of all the Cahn-Styne copyrights. Frank Sinatra sang it on the sound track under the titles, and then went on to make his best-selling recording for Capitol. The song won the Academy Award. So potent was the publicity and propaganda value of the title number that the motion picture went on to become one of the highest box-office grosses in 1954; even the producers stood ready to admit that without that song the movie would not have done half so well. Coincidental with this development came the fact that from 1954 on the Fountain of Trevi in Rome, which had inspired the song, became a major tourist attraction for American visitors to the Holy City.

By the time Styne and Cahn had temporarily ended their partnership in 1948, they had made an important bow in the Broadway musical theatre with an excellent score for *High Button Shoes,* a show with a run of over seven hundred performances in 1947–48. A mixture of vaudeville, burlesque, and musical comedy, *High Button Shoes* starred Phil Silvers and Joey Faye as a couple of swindlers in New Brunswick, New Jersey, in 1913, and Nanette Fabray. One of the best numbers was a ballet conceived by Jerome Robbins in which the Keystone Kops and the bathing beauties of the old Mack Sennett silent-film farces were used with uninhibited slapstick humor. The score produced four standards: "I Still Get Jealous," "On a Sunday by the Sea," "Papa, Won't You Dance With Me?" and "You're My Girl."

Nobody could deny that Cahn and Styne had proved themselves ideal songwriting partners. In fact, *Time,* in a cover story, placed them second only to Rodgers and Hammerstein as the most important words-and-music team in the business. But away from their work, they did not harmonize quite so well; in fact they had little empathy for each other. And so, in spite of their successes, there came the time when their emotions were stronger than their creative impulses. They decided to go their separate ways. Styne went toward ever bigger and better achievements both in Hollywood and on Broadway, including a score for what is surely one of the most successful musicals ever produced, *Funny Girl,* starring Barbra Streisand first on the Broadway stage and after that on the screen. Sammy Cahn, having found a working partner whom he could like personally as much as he could admire professionally, did just as well, and from the very beginning. For one of the earliest assignments to come to Cahn and Van Heusen was from Frank Sinatra to write the title number for the motion picture *The Tender Trap.* This was followed by "Love and Marriage," one of several songs for the TV musical adaptation of Thornton Wilder's play *Our Town,* starring Sinatra. "The Tender Trap" was a big money-maker. "Love and Marriage" became one of the best songs born on the television screen and recognized as such by being the recipient of an Emmy (the first song ever to get this honor) and a Christopher Award.

Two of the three songs with which Cahn and Van Heusen subsequently received Oscars were written for and introduced by Sinatra. The first, in 1957, was "All the Way," from the screen biography of the nightclub comedian Joe E. Lewis—*The Joker Is Wild.* (So popular did this song become in England that when the motion picture was released there it changed its title to that of the song.) James Van Heusen says that the melody had been written to dramatize Joe E. Lewis's loss of voice—one of the dramatic episodes in the picture, after Lewis had been methodically and surgically operated upon by gangsters. "The big jump musically at the end of the second bar, to the middle of the third bar," explains Van Heusen, "was specifically designed to be difficult for him to sing, and he was supposed to break down dramatically."

Two years later, Cahn and Van Heusen wrote "High Hopes" for the non-musical picture *A Hole in the Head,* once again with Sinatra as star. This number was written hurriedly—indeed, virtually at the zero hour—to meet the sudden decision of the producer to use a song in order to intensify an emotional situation that had arisen in the story between father and son. Because of the haste with which the decision had been reached to use a song, and the greater speed with which it was written, it had to be recorded and shot in the picture simultaneously on the very last day of the shooting. Van Heusen played the accompaniment on the piano as quietly as possible, so that it could later be removed and replaced by an orchestra. This is one of the rare instances, if not the only one, that side-stepped the practice of recording the songs on the sound track first, in a recording studio, and then complete the lip synchronization during the photography.

Cahn bears a sentimental attachment for "High Hopes" in a way he does to none other of his songs—and with good reason. At Peter Lawford's house, Senator John F. Kennedy, then running for President, asked Cahn to write him a campaign song. Cahn decided to prepare a parody of "High Hopes," which began "K–E–Double-N–E–D–Y, He's Got High Hopes." It was used with strong impact throughout the campaign.

"High Hopes" brought their authors their second Oscar. The third came for "Call Me Irresponsible," which Jackie Gleason, performing as a drunkard, sang to his wife's clothes dummy in *Papa's Delicate Condition* in 1963. Actually Cahn and Van Heusen had been written this song eight years earlier, when this same picture had first been planned for Fred Astaire. Cahn had always harbored a burning ambition to write a song for Astaire, and when Cahn was asked to do one for *Papa's Delicate Condition* he replied: "I'll pay the studio anything they ask for this privilege." He and Van Heusen wrote the song and Astaire thought it wonderful. But the picture, for some reason or other, was shelved—and Astaire never had the opportunity to introduce it. When, finally, the script was taken off the shelf and Jackie Gleason was chosen to replace Fred Astaire, the producer planned no songs for it. Nevertheless, once again a last-minute decision was responsible for the interpolation of "Call Me Irresponsible" to fill an important spot in the story. The picture turned out to be such a dud that the song probably would have been relegated to oblivion had not Frank Sinatra recorded it. In fact, were it not for the fact that Sammy Cahn was an intimate friend of Martin Rackin's, the production head at the studio, the song would not have remained in the picture, having been cut out by the writer-producer. Sammy stormed into the front office, had his strong say, and won the battle. "Call Me Irresponsible" stayed in the picture—and, having won an Academy Award, is the only reason that *Papa's Delicate Condition* is remembered, if it is remembered at all.

Sinatra's efforts on behalf of Cahn and Van Heusen remained indefatigable —so much so that Cahn and Van Heusen have almost come to be regarded as Sinatra's personal songwriters. (In Hollywood they say that "Cahn put more words in Sinatra's mouth than anybody else—which is not the easiest thing to do.") In 1958 Sinatra popularized three Cahn–Van Heusen songs: "Come Fly with Me," "Indiscreet," and "To Love and Be Loved." The first was the title number of a Frank Sinatra recording album for Capitol. (Later on it was also used as the title of an M-G-M motion picture where it was sung on the sound track by Frankie Avalon.) "To Love and Be Loved" was introduced in the non-musical picture *Some Came Running,* in which Sinatra was costarred with Dean Martin and Shirley MacLaine. "Indiscreet" came from a motion picture starring Cary Grant and Ingrid Bergman.

Some of the later songs with which Sinatra is undoubtedly identified are "Pocketful of Miracles" in 1961, "My Kind of Town" in 1964, and "September of My Years" in 1965. The last of these was the title song of a Frank Sinatra album for Reprise which received two Grammy Awards from the National Academy of Arts and Sciences.

In 1968 Cahn and Van Heusen wrote the title song for *Star,* the screen biography of Gertrude Lawrence starring Julie Andrews. Saul Chaplin was the producer of this picture—the same Saul Chaplin with whom Sammy Cahn had written his first songs.

That Cahn and Van Heusen are both in temperament and in working habits poles apart is par for the course, since this has been true of many other highly successful collaborators. Van Heusen is the more solemn, the more dignified, and the more serious member of the team, though he does not hesitate to reveal that his "favorite things," in the order of their importance, are "chicks, booze, music, and Sinatra." He has no trouble getting any of these because (1) he is a man of wealth, (2) his well-stocked bar is the least of his expense, (3) music is his lifework, and (4) his many years of friendship with Sinatra has kept them together as if with cement.

Van Heusen has other passions as well, of which flying his own plane is undoubtedly the most significant. With his first royalty checks from his initial song hit, "It's the Dreamer in Me," he paid for flying instruction. With his income from "Deep in a Dream" he bought his first plane—a Luscombe Silvaire, which he flew from coast to coast five times. Since then he has acquired a number of different planes (his latest being a Hughes 300 helicopter) and accumulated various ratings including the top one in the field (Airline Transport), a commercial rating, and an instructor's rating in helicopters and rotor aircraft. He has, however, never given a single lesson to anybody. "It's too much of a responsibility," he explains. Sammy Cahn does not share this enthusiasm with Van Heusen. "Sammy has flown in the 'chopper' with me on occasion," says Van Heusen, "but he really doesn't like being off the ground. He says, 'Birds don't try to write songs so what am I trying to fly for?' "

Other Van Heusen interests include his camera; the collecting of manuscripts of famous composers which decorate the walls of his master bedroom, hallway, and parts of the living room (a collection including items by Brahms, Tchaikovsky, Wagner, Vaughn Williams, Puccini, Stravinsky, and Gershwin, to mention just a few); and the owning of several different living establishments. He bought his first house in 1940 in Palm Springs; then replaced it with another one there, in the Thunderbird Heights, next door to one owned by Bing Crosby; and after that he acquired ten acres of land in Palm Desert. As of now, he has four places he can call home: an apartment in New York on West Fifty-seventh Street; an apartment in North Hollywood at Cahuenga Boulevard; and a large ranch in Yucca Valley in California's Mojave Desert; and a place at Brant Lake, in upstate New York.

Sammy Cahn is the impish, puckish alter ego of this songwriting combination. James Van Heusen has confessed that the one reason he gets along so well with Sammy—both as a fellow workman and as a friend—is because Sammy is a born wit, and you can never possibly anticipate the kind of humorous reaction he will give to any situation. "He has a brain for humor," says Van Heusen. "He is like a comic who deals with punch lines, no feed lines, just gags. He keeps me laughing all the time."

Sammy was for a long time a teetotaler, while Van Heusen and a martini glass try their best to be inseparable. The main reason Cahn avoided alcoholic beverages so long was that ever since he was thirteen he suffered severely from peptic ulcers. This condition was cured at last by an operation when Cahn was forty-nine. During all those ulcerous years Cahn never touched a drop of anything stronger than seltzer. One time, early in their career as songwriters for 20th Century-Fox, and before Van Heusen had a chance to move his music and pencils into the office-bungalow, picturesquely named "The Purple Cow," he fitted it out with a case of gin, vermouth, a refrigerator, an ice machine, lemons, and glasses. Let Van Heusen tell the rest of the story. "Sammy, after observing me and the rest of the music department, who would meet us in our bungalow at 5:00 or 5:30, drinking martinis, finally condescended to have *one* martini with us. He went home to Gloria—stoned—insisting that he had had only *one* martini. What she did not know until some time later is that it was one of *my* martinis, which was the equivalent of five made in an oversized old-fashioned glass."

Sammy is the talker, Van Heusen, the listener, and both are happy in their respective roles. "Bottle-bald, twinkle-eyed," wrote C. Robert Jennings in *Show,* "Van Heusen looks like a Prussian Junker gone soft." Cahn, in appearance, is a study in contrast. Jennings describes him as "thin-haired, bespectacled, and moustached [looking] more like a tailor or a taxi driver—or a chipmunk that has just poked its head blinkingly out of a dark nest." To Barbra Streisand he "looks like a Jewish dentist."

Cahn is a day worker, Van Heusen works best at night. But both are professionals to the tips of their fingers—in their capacity to work hard, quickly, fill any demand made on them, and always meeting deadlines. Cahn once remarked that he might not be the greatest lyricist in the world but he is certainly one of the most dependable. "If I tell a fellow he'll have a song Friday morning, comes Friday morning he gets his song." The same is true of Van Heusen. Cahn is the more facile and prolific of the two, often capable of producing as many as half a dozen lyrics in a single morning. He concocted for Van Heusen all the lyrics for the television "special" *Our Town,* in a single day; the following morning he was able to complete several more lyrics for another composer.

During the many years in which they hammered out their formidable repertory of hit songs, most of them for the movies, both Cahn and Van Heusen operated out of their Beverly Hills or North Hollywood places—either at Van Heusen's Cahuenga Boulevard apartment or at Sammy Cahn's elegant home in Holmby Hills which he owned at that time. "The fun begins when Sammy comes bouncing into Jimmy's . . . apartment," explains C. Robert Jennings, "or Jimmy into Sammy's house at noon, though Jimmy's idea of an early start is still 8 P.M. Resplendent in his alpaca sweater, yellow slacks, and uncommon eagerness, Sammy has, as someone remarked, the air of a troubled horseplayer looking for a lost ticket. Jimmy has just awakened, is slightly foggy."

Describing their *modus operandi,* Jennings adds: "Sammy thinks of the titles, Jimmy of the tunes. Sammy gropes for a neat turn of phrase, brings it out on the typewriter, giving utmost consideration to its singability. . . . Then long, discursive discussions. Jimmy might interrupt for a midafternoon snack and a cup of coffee. Sammy charges ahead, 'embarrassed because lyric writing comes so easily for me.' Sammy thinks of something and miraculously it molds into Jimmy's musical something. Sammy sings continually, hums, *te-dums,* flays the air with a jab of finger or a sweeping arm gesture. . . . After only eight bars, Sammy cracks: 'You know something? I think the song is finished. . . . Or Jimmy might ask, 'And how are you gonna conclude this song?' And Sammy will answer, 'I will let you know the conclusion whenever we come to the finish.' When they do, Jimmy mixes the king-sized Tanqueray martinis and 'we stagger away from each other very happy.' "

What Sammy Cahn refers to as "the moment of truth" is when he tries out his new song for friends, and especially when he is demonstrating it for a prominent singer who wants to introduce it. Sammy has a little voice, somewhat rasping and unusually unpleasant. He insists on accompanying himself on the piano, even though he can handle only a single key (F major). Yet, strange to say, he is one of the best "demonstrators" in the business—a born singing salesman for his products. His capacity to "put a song over" is one of the reasons he has been able to convince so many distinguished stars to grab his song at first hearing— not only Sinatra and Crosby, but also Tony Martin, Perry Como, Dean Martin, Paul Anka, Vic Damone, Tony Bennett, Peggy Lee, and dozens of others. In some strange way—despite his bad singing and worse piano playing—he can project a mood or build up an emotional climate in a song the way it deserves, and the way it can be heard to its best advantage.

Despite the fact that Sammy Cahn's income is astronomic, 90 percent of all the songs he writes are done free of charge. This is because he is daily—sometimes hourly—called upon "as a very special favor" to write material for parties, benefits, Bar Mitzvahs, birthdays, and other ceremonies, appearances of his friends in nightclubs, charitable institutions, and so forth. "People always ask me why I do so much work without getting paid for it. The answer is simple. It's because I like to write. Doodling with words at a typewriter is one of my greatest pleasures. If the studios didn't pay me for my work, I'd work for them gratis, too."

Cahn married Gloria Delson on September 5, 1945, and they raised their two children—a son, Steven, and a daughter, Laurie—in their rambling, white, ivy-covered house on South Mapleton Drive. Since getting divorced from Gloria in 1964, Sammy Cahn divides his time between his luxurious bachelor house on North Canon Drive in Beverly Hills and his apartment on East Fifty-fifth Street in New York. Separated by only a few streets from each other in New York, Van Heusen and Sammy Cahn managed to write the music for two Broadway musicals, neither one proving successful: *Skyscraper,* based on Elmer Rice's play *Dream Girl* in 1965; and *Walking Happy* (derived from the play *Hobson's Choice*) in 1966. (The title song of *Walking Happy* became a hit, while *Skyscraper* yielded two fine songs in "Everybody Has the Right to Be Wrong" and "I'll Only Miss Her When I Think of Her.")

Sammy Cahn has revived his partnership with Jule Styne for a Broadway musical, leaving Van Heusen with the problem of (temporarily at least) finding a new lyricist. This is not the only recent change in Van Heusen's life. For one thing he ended his longtime bachelorhood by marrying the former Mrs. William Perlberg, who had once been a member of the Brox Sisters of Broadway revue fame. For another, he has decided to spend most of his marital life at Brant Lake rather than at Yucca Valley which had so long been his favorite retreat.

Songs from the Movies–III

Henry Mancini

Between 1952 and 1958, while working on the Universal-International lot, Henry Mancini contributed background music for over one hundred pictures. One was *The Glenn Miller Story* in 1954, with which he received an Academy Award nomination for the first time. No less a distinguished achievement for him, this time without the benefit of any academy recognition, was his score for *The Benny Goodman Story* in 1956.

Despite his fertility and some of the recognition it brought him, this period in the 1950's was apparently just the time of apprenticeship. Full mastery of his formidable creative resources in writing music for the movies came in the 1960's. Since 1960, few composers have had more important assignments than Mancini, few could command higher fees and more exacting rights and terms.

And with good reason. Mancini has proved himself one of the most important and most original composers produced by the motion-picture industry in the 1960's. In that decade he captured three Academy Awards: one in 1961 for his background music for *Breakfast at Tiffany's;* two for songs, "Moon River" in 1961 (also from *Breakfast at Tiffany's*) and "Days of Wine and Roses" in 1963. He was nominated for Academy Awards several times more, notably for "Bachelor in Paradise," "Charade," "Sweetheart Tree," and "Dear Heart." He was also responsible for some of the most highly esteemed (as well as some of the most freshly conceived and orchestrated) musical sound tracks of the period, particularly with scores for *Breakfast at Tiffany's, Days of Wine and Roses, Charade, Hatari,* and *The Pink Panther.* Recordings of his screen music brought him an armful of Grammy Awards from the National Academy of Recording Arts and Sciences, besides placing his own orchestral and choral performances of his music in the top rank of best-selling discs.

Such mounting success, which placed Mancini with the elect of Hollywood composers, would be expected to inspire supreme self-confidence. Self-confidence Mancini possesses, and with it a composure and serenity which are qualities not often encountered in the motion-picture industry. This man Mancini, one realizes at once, is somebody who knows what he is doing, where he is going, and is fully aware of his capabilities to meet any assignment, however demanding or significant. This is also a man who is not afraid of experiment or innovation, things from which the usual successful Hollywood composers flee.

Not that there is any suggestion of superegotism about him. He is, therefore, something of a *rara avis,* that "rare bird" among his fellow workmen, most of whom are hyperthyroid, of excessive nervous energy, in perpetual fear of losing their grip on both their talent and their success, yet hiding their inner doubts and questionings and fears behind a façade of arrogance.

Basically, Mancini is a simple man. He does not dress ostentatiously, though of course he is always well groomed. He does not try to overwhelm you with overdoses of charm, though his manners are polished and refined. He is not ashamed to tell you that he is a family man, excessively devoted to his wife, and inordinately proud of his two daughters, twins born in 1952, and his son, who preceded them by two years.

He is tall and slim, and wears his hair closely cropped to conceal the fact that its growth has become thin of late. He makes a dignified impression, but he has the capacity of always putting his visitor at ease and continually he enlivens the conversation with his infectious laughter. He likes best to be in the company of musicians and to talk shop, possibly because his extra-musical interests are minimal. He loves sailing. Taking even a short trip aboard his own thirty-foot cruiser with his wife and family is his idea of a perfect holiday. Skiing and swimming are other physical activities he enjoys, while away from athletics his main interest (and that of his wife as well) is the collection of great art (they own thirteen Rodins). He is no party or afternoon-cocktail man. He enjoys the solitude of his home in Holmby Hills. Never driven by social ambitions, nor by passion for accumulating wealth, he is thoroughly content with the life he leads today, working to the best of his capacities and thoroughly satisfied with the kind of kudos the industry and the public have given him. Frankly, he could ask for nothing more—except perhaps always to be writing still better music.

Henry Mancini came to success by way of a thorough musical background, come from comprehensive study at such institutions as the School of Music at the Carnegie Institute of Technology and the Juilliard School of Music in New York. Mancini was born in Cleveland, Ohio, on April 16, 1924. He is the son of a steelworker whose favorite pastime was to play the flute. When Henry was an infant, the family moved to the little town of Aliquippa, Pennsylvania, where the father found employment in the local steel mill and diversion by playing his flute in the local Sons of Italy Band. When Henry was eight, he got his first music lessons—on the piccolo and flute. Study of the piano came five years after that. Meanwhile he had mastered the piccolo and flute well enough to join his father as a member of the Sons of Italy Band. It must be confessed, however, that at first Mancini was not overenthusiastic about music, and certainly not about spending hours practicing. He preferred by far to play football. But a strict parent compelled him to continue with his music study, for which he has ever since been grateful.

Henry's interest in music took on life when he began listening to the big bands of the 1940's in recordings. Artie Shaw was his first passion. For hours at an end he would write out Artie Shaw arrangements from listening to Shaw's recordings. He even worked upon those arrangements in his classes in high school. "I learned some music by doing this," he now recalls, "but it did not do my academic standing much good."

His fascination for Artie Shaw soon palled, however. It was then that he came upon Glenn Miller and his orchestra. "I became a Glenn Miller 'nut' after hearing one of his recordings for the first time and have stayed that way ever since." This preoccupation with big bands in general and Glenn Miller's orchestrations in particular led him to become a member of local dance bands where he played the flute, now his prime instrument. In 1937, as a member of the Pennsylvania All-State Band, he won first prize in flute-playing. Meanwhile he had begun taking lessons in compositions and theory from Max Adkin, conductor and arranger for the Stanley Theatre Orchestra in Pittsburgh, who he now looks upon as the man who exerted the greatest influence in his own musical career and was responsible for the direction his career would take. By the time Mancini was graduated from high school in 1942, his class yearbook could describe him as follows: "A true music lover, collects records, plays in the band, and has even composed several beautiful selections. He hopes someday to have his own orchestra."

Dreaming of a career in jazz, Mancini sent some of his own arrangements to Benny Goodman. Benny Goodman bought one of them, then encouraged Mancini to come to New York and work for him. "It didn't take long for both Benny and me to find out I wasn't ready for such an ambitious assignment." What Goodman knew and what Mancini suspected was that more study was necessary, even though while attending high school Mancini had attended the School of Music at the Carnegie Institute of Technology in Pittsburgh. Mancini, therefore, enrolled at the Juilliard School of Music in New York with the intention of getting a thorough musical education, particularly in composition and theory. But such plans were frustrated by World War II. Mancini was called to uniform. He saw overseas duty with both the infantry and the air corps.

When the war ended and Mancini had shed his uniform, he joined the Glenn Miller band which had been reorganized and directed by Tex Beneke—Glenn Miller having come to his untimely death in a transport plane over the English Channel in 1944. Mancini's duties consisted of playing the piano and making arrangements, a job he held for three years between 1945 and 1948. During this period he fell in love with Virginia O'Connor, the young and attractive singer who worked with the orchestra. They were married on September 13, 1947; and in 1950 their first child, a son, was born.

The years between 1948 and 1952 were difficult one for the Mancinis. He did odd jobs making arrangements for nightclub singers and small jazz groups. Most of the time, Mancini confesses, he spent "starving." Then in 1952 he was given a two-week assignment to write music for pictures made on the Universal-International lot. He stayed six years. With eloquent appropriateness, in view of Mancini's almost lifelong adoration of Glenn Miller and his affiliation with the Glenn Miller band, one of his most important assignments was to write the score for *The Glenn Miller Story,* starring James Stewart as the bandleader, the score, of course, made up mostly of Glenn Miller standards. "Having followed the band so closely when I was younger, and having played in the band when I was older, I could have written out most of the arrangements from memory." Another excellent Mancini score was used in *Touch of Evil,* in 1957, a motion picture directed by Orson Welles, which is still being exhibited from time to time in colleges and universities as an important example of the film art.

While Mancini was thus employed at Universal-International writing music for its productions, he became a friend of Blake Edwards, a young writer also employed at the studio. When Edwards was promoted to director, he had Mancini work for him on one of his films. Blake liked Mancini's music, liked the way Mancini worked, and most of all liked the fresh ideas Mancini was already beginning to introduce into his writing. When Edwards was given the assignment to direct a series of television productions entitled *Peter Gunn,* he asked Mancini to provide the necessary music. And so, in 1958, Mancini found a new area to fertilize—television.

Economy dictated that the television series use a small ensemble. The musical style most effective for the limited personnel available to him, Mancini felt, would be one that used jazz idioms. Besides he was convinced that jazz was the proper kind of music for a mystery series, which *Peter Gunn* was—not *real* jazz (for Mancini does not profess to be an expert on the subject) but music that is influenced by jazz and is jazz-oriented; music with a strong jazz beat; melodies in the traditional blues style and structure. Mancini put it this way: "Blake Edwards is a 'hip' guy who knows what's going on in all fields. He even told the barber how to cut Craig Stevens' hair for the part of Peter Gunn. Before that, Craig had hair with a sort of marcel wave in it. Blake Edwards had it cut short. You might say that if Blake didn't want a marcel wave in Craig's hair, he didn't want it in the music either." *Peter Gunn,* in short, was not the place for long-hair stuff.

Unlike other composers for television, Mancini did not work from any script or outline. He insisted upon seeing the final product on the screen before he would begin thinking of the kind of music that would be needed. "That way," he explained, "I could capture the true mood. . . . I wrote between ten and fifteen minutes of music per show. We didn't have rehearsals, and that ought to tell you something about the quality of musicians we used. It usually took about three hours to record a show, and before long we had an open house scene going at every session. As a matter of fact, so many people came we finally had to ban visitors."

Blake Edwards would be one of the first to confess that much of the extraordinary success of the *Peter Gunn* series was due to Mancini's extraordinary background music—a powerful factor in each episode to project mood, build suspense, underline emotional nuances, suggest atmosphere. The *Peter Gunn* score was nominated for an Emmy Award by the Academy of Television of Arts and Sciences, besides achieving wide distribution through best-selling records. An album conducted by Mancini for RCA-Victor was voted in 1959 as the "best jazz record of the year" by the country's foremost disc jockeys in the annual poll conducted by *Down Beat* magazine; this recording also captured two Grammies, one for the "best album of the year" and the other for the "best arrangement of the year." About a million copies of this release were sold. The theme from *Peter Gunn* also became a best-seller in Ray Anthony's recording for Capitol.

Writing the music for *Peter Gunn* represented a significant turning point in Mancini's career. He did not hesitate to say so to an interviewer for the *Daily News* in New York: "It was the . . . big break for me. The use of the jazz idiom, applied dramatically to the story, put music on everybody's mind as far as TV is concerned." Mancini was called upon by Edwards to write the music for another television series, *Mr. Lucky. Mr. Lucky* was certainly no *Peter Gunn* and the public (and the ratings) rejected it. Nevertheless, recordings of Mancini's music from this series brought him two more Grammy Awards besides carrying Mancini's own performance for RCA-Victor once again to the best-selling lists.

While working for television, Mancini had deserted motion pictures, but only temporarily. He returned to Hollywood in 1960 on a free-lance basis. He found ample, significant assignments awaiting him in the major studios. In 1960 he wrote the background music for *High Time;* in 1961, for *The Great Impostor, Bachelor in Paradise,* and most significantly, *Breakfast at Tiffany's,* for the last of which he got his first two Academy Awards.

Breakfast at Tiffany's was the screen adaptation of Truman Capote's story. It starred Audrey Hepburn, and it was with her limited vocal range in mind that Mancini wrote "Moon River." The song recurred throughout the picture, sometimes in the background music in an effective rendition by an amplified harmonica, and on one occasion moodily chanted by Audrey Hepburn. Andy Williams issued a Columbia album entitled *Moon River,* a release that sold two

million copies; from that time on Williams's rendition of "Moon River" became
so celebrated that he adopted it as his signature for his television programs.
Besides winning the Academy Award as the best screen song of the year, "Moon
River" collected a number of Grammies: as the best song of the year; the best
record of the year; the best arrangement; and the best recording (that of Henry
Mancini and his orchestra). This was the first Mancini song for which Johnny
Mercer wrote the lyrics (Mercer still regards these lyrics as the best of his
career). This was the first Mancini song to become a hit. And this was the first
Mancini song to graduate into a standard. To date almost five hundred different
recordings have been made of it, and over a million copies of sheet music have
been sold. It is believed to have earned in excess of a million dollars, with
Mancini and Mercer each receiving royalties of about $250,000.

Mancini and Mercer captured a second Oscar for the screen's best song—
and only one year later. They got it with the title number of *Days of Wine and
Roses* in which Jack Lemmon and Lee Remick starred as chronic alcoholics. Once
again Andy Williams released an album using for its title that of the song; once
again he achieved a best seller (over one million albums); and once again the
song gathered a handful of Grammies, including one as the best song of the
year.

If Mancini failed to get the screen's highest award for a song after that,
it was not because he was not nominated. "Charade" (lyrics by Mercer), "Dear
Heart" (lyrics by Jay Livingston and Ray Evans), and "Sweetheart Tree" (lyrics
by Mercer) were in the running in their respective years. In addition, Mancini
was nominated for his background music to *The Pink Panther* in 1964.

The hit songs that Mancini has produced for motion pictures represent only
one facet of his far-reaching contribution to motion-picture music. No less significant is the high quality of his musical background, much of it overstocked
with treasurable melodic thoughts which will someday acquire lyrics, be revived,
and emerge as prime public favorites. (*The Pink Panther,* for example, had
seven such wordless melodic gems, interpolated almost unobtrusively into the
overall score; *Hatari* and *Soldier in the Rain* possess short instrumental gems
whose value is not diminished when divorced from the motion picture.) The
relevance of his music to the incident, episode, or background for which it was
intended must also be noted (most background music for films could easily be
used for any number of motion pictures, in the same way Rossini used to borrow
an overture from one opera and use it for several others). Mancini's writing is
vividly programmatic as he seeks out the precise music that does full justice to,
or enhances, the scene projected on the screen. In his search for the musical *mot
juste,* in his insistence on musical realism, Mancini is not afraid to employ the
most unusual effects and instruments, and he often does so with remarkable
results. He used a calliope for a most descriptive amusing little tune, to a boogie-
woogie rhythm, as background music for the scene in *Hatari* in which a girl is
being followed by a baby elephant, while for the recurring theme in the same
movie he required an untuned piano. He brought a kind of homespun small-town
fascination to "Moon River" when it was played by an amplified harmonica. In
Experiment in Terror he employed a leitmotif for the villain strummed on (of

all things!) an autoharp, contributing thereby not a little to the atmosphere of terror being projected. In *Wait Until Dark* he introduced into the orchestra an ancient Chinese instrument of the flute family, a Sho, whose haunting, exotic sounds were just what one of the episodes called for.

He is one of the few composers in Hollywood who refuse to discuss or even think of the kind of music or songs a picture requires, while it is in its working stages. There are never any conferences between him and the producer or director either when the script is completed or even when the shooting begins. His creative juices just cannot begin to flow until he sees the final product, the completed picture, and then he sees the picture through again and again until the ideas begin to come to him thick and fast.

"Each picture is different," he told an interviewer. "Sometimes there'll be just a basic theme like in *The Pink Panther*. It'll run all the way through in different settings. In other cases you'll have various individual songs. Some of these we call source music because they're actually made by a band or a singer, in other words, a source that you can see in the picture. In *Breakfast at Tiffany's* there are four or five of these in the party scene alone. . . . When I approach a film I always think cinematically. I want to do my job for the picture honestly. I always approach a score as to what is best for the picture—not what's best for a record album, or the shortest cut to a hit song. That's the reason why so many of my scores—however effective they might be as part of a film—are unsuitable for recordings, since they consist of a series of fragments." His scores for *Wait Until Dark, Shot in the Dark,* and *Days of Wine and Roses* were never recorded in albums.

His strong feelings of obligation to pass on his own experiences, as well as ideas, to a younger generation of composers for the screen has led him into the field of musical pedagogy. He has written a practical guide to professional orchestration, *Sounds and Scores.* He has also endowed a chair at the University of California at Los Angeles for screen composition, so that potential new composers of motion-picture music might get their basic training at the craft in the classroom. "This is a very delicate craft," he has explained. "It takes great sensitivity, time, effort, and experience." Having become one of the top men in his field, Mancini is determined to give a helping hand to others, the newcomers.

GREAT MEN OF AMERICAN POPULAR SONG

Songs of Protest

Bob Dylan

Even while the Broadway stage and the Hollywood screen were disgorging important songs and developing important new composers and lyricists, another medium was becoming increasingly prominent not only to do a similar service to American popular music, but to go one step further: to create an altogether new brand of American popular song. The new medium was phonograph reproduction, and the new American popular song it helped to circularize to a point where all other types of songs had to take second place to it was "rock 'n' roll." In time, recorded music would usurp the place of first importance previously occupied by Tin Pan Alley, the stage, and the screen as an agency for the creation and dissemination of popular music, and as the prime force in the making of hit songs. In time, too, the new music would completely throw into a shade the kind of love songs with sentiment and other types of soft-voiced ballads for which the stage and screen were famous.

347

Recorded music has gone through an undulating career of peaks and depths. Time and again, through the years, it appeared that recorded music had become obsolescent, to be replaced first by talking pictures, then by radio, and after that by television. Yet each time the knell of doom was sounded, the record business confounded the prophets of gloom by arising phoenix-like from its ashes of defeat to become even more powerful and vigorous than it had been previously. Today, of course, records completely dominate the music business, so much so that at any given period nine out of ten hit songs—perhaps even nineteen out of twenty—have become popular through records rather than through a stage or screen production; and more often than not most of these hits are in the "rock" idiom.

Recorded music was born on December 15, 1877, for that was the date when Thomas A. Edison filed a patent application for a machine capable of reproducing recorded sound. Within thirteen years, the Edison phonograph, and the cylinder disc, which was the earliest form of recording, were on the market. At least one publishing house in Tin Pan Alley sensed the importance of recorded music as a means of disseminating popular songs. That publisher was Joseph W. Stern & Company, which in 1897 founded the Universal Phonograph Company on East Twentieth Street where recordings of coon songs (sung by May Irwin) and popular tunes (sung by Lottie Gilson and Meyer Cohen) were transferred to cylinders. However, the time was still too premature for recorded music to become a profit-making business. The Universal Phonograph Company soon closed its doors. But the phonograph and the cylinder survived—not only in some homes, but particularly as an attraction in penny arcades.

The first recording that can be regarded as a best seller came in 1905, the Victor release of "The Preacher and the Bear," written by Arthur Longbrake, a publisher assuming the pen name of Joe Arzonia, and sung by Arthur Collins. Actually, this recording had a sustained success, maintaining such a healthy sale for two decades that it accumulated a larger total sale than any other single record released before 1919.

Prosperity came to recorded music during and immediately after World War I. Such superstars as Eddie Cantor and Al Jolson were making records, some of which were best sellers; sales figures for records rose for the first time to as high as one million discs for a single release. Eddie Cantor's first big sellers were "That's the Kind of a Baby for Me" in 1917 and "You'd Be Surprised" in 1919. These and similar successes brought him the first long-term exclusive contract given an artist—a five-year agreement from Brunswick guaranteeing him a quarter of a million dollars in royalties. Al Jolson's recording of "Swanee" in 1919 sold a million discs. The first popular orchestra to become a recording favorite was Ben Selvin and his band, whose version of "Dardanella" was one of the biggest recording hits in 1919. Ben Selvin and his orchestra is believed to have made more recordings than any other organization—almost ten thousand, some historians maintain, during an extended career in which he used nine different names and performed for nine different companies. No single recording by Ben Selvin, however, entered the elite class of a million-disc sale. That honor went first to Paul Whiteman and his orchestra for "Whispering" (coupled with "Japanese Sandman") in 1920, and "Three O'Clock in the Morning" in 1922.

All songs mentioned above were introduced and popularized on the stage before achieving recording success. The first instance of a song become a success exclusively through the medium of recording is a number by George Stoddard called "Mary" (which, of course, is not the "Mary" George M. Cohan had written years earlier). Stoddard's "Mary" had neither been published nor had it been publicly performed when Victor recorded it. Its sale of 300,000 discs within three months (bringing its author a royalty of about $15,000) was the first hint that the new medium of recording was now capable of making unknown songs into hits.

The 1920's were boom years for records, with a long procession of best sellers by such stellar performers as Jolson, Cantor, Sophie Tucker, Frank Crumit, Frank Munn, and the most successful of them all, Gene Austin, whose "That Silver Haired Daddy of Mine" and "My Blue Heaven" in 1927 and "Ramona" in 1928 made him the highest paid recording star in the business. "My Blue Heaven" (which he, more than any other performer, helped to make one of the leading hit songs of the 1920's) is believed to have sold five million discs; "Ramona," between one and two million.

Perhaps nothing proves so decisively the growing power of the record companies than their capacity to make hits of songs that previously had never been heard of or had been total failures. Today, songs like Hoagy Carmichael's "Star Dust" or Vernon Duke's "April in Paris" or Cole Porter's "Begin the Beguine" are deservedly placed with the all-time classics in American popular music. When these was first introduced, they were ignored to a point where it seemed almost certain that they were destined for permanent obscurity. Then "Star Dust" was recorded by Artie Shaw and his orchestra to sell two and a half million discs and to become instantly a solid favorite with the music public. "Star Dust" was subsequently recorded almost five hundred times in almost as many arrangements; and it became the only record that was reproduced on both sides of the same disc, in two different performances, one by Tommy Dorsey and his orchestra and the other by Benny Goodman and his band. Artie Shaw's recording of "Begin the Beguine" was also the starting point from which this masterpiece went on to innumerable recordings and performances. And Vernon Duke's "April in Paris"—a total "flop" when introduced in the revue *Walk a Little Faster*—suddenly acquired a new life, and has remained vigorous ever since, following a successful recording by Marian Chase for Liberty.

The recording boom in the 1920's collapsed even as did the overall economy. The Depression of the early 1930's made the purchase of records a luxury few could afford. But another factor had entered into the precipitous decline of the record business: the emergence to general popularity of a dangerous rival, in the form of radio. Now, with the flip of a dial, the American public could hear all the popular songs it could possibly consume (besides a good deal of other entertainment and reports of current events). The ears of America were pinned first to earphones, then to the loudspeaker, for an evening's diversion from the greatest stars of stage and the concert world, without paying anything for the privilege (except, of course, for the cost of the radio). The phonograph in the living room and the stack of records piled nearby became untouchables. The phonograph industry tried to use extensive promotion to combat this alarming development ("music you want *when* you want it" became one of its pet slogans); it also improved the quality of reproduction through the development of orthophonic means. After all, about forty million records had been sold each year in the 1920's, a sizable business to say the least. By the early 1930's this figure had been cut to about one fourth, and the figures were dipping further with each passing month. But the record industry had no intention of dying without a struggle.

A curious development soon began to take place which had nothing to do with promotion, and very little with the rapidly developing quality of reproduction through electrical processes. Once radio had ceased to be a toy, and the novelty had worn off, it not only failed to deal a lethal blow to records but, on the contrary, brought to it an altogether new and greater prosperity. The reason was simple. Radio was creating new singing stars whose names and personalities had become household fixtures: people like the Happiness Boys, Frank Munn, Arthur Tracy ("the street singer"), Rudy Vallee, Morton Downey, the Mills Brothers, Kate Smith, Jane Froman, to mention just a few of the leaders. The numbers they sang over the radio—many of which were being heard for the first time anywhere—became nationwide hits literally overnight, as each of these singers began commanding an audience of millions at a single performance. And the slogan which the recording industry had invented had proved to be far more than a catch phrase. It carried a basic truth. People *did* like hearing the songs of their preference (and by the performers they favored) when they felt like listening to them. To satisfy this need, they had to buy records. In the 1940's the sale of records soared to 100 million discs; in the 1950's to 150 million; in the 1960's to between 200 and 350 million.

A highly significant reason for these soaring figures is that the radio had become not an enemy but an ally in more ways than one. And in no way was the radio more potent in advancing the cause of records than through the emergence of the disc jockey. But before this happened, an all-important decision had to be handed down by the courts. As radio was becoming popular all over the country, numerous little stations dotted the map to cater to a limited geographical area. These stations were not affiliated with a large network to receive its programs, and they could not afford to pay for live entertainment. Consequently, these little stations made up their programs through recorded music. This practice led the major record companies to institute suit maintaining that the broadcast of recorded music without payment represented an infringement of copyright. The action went all the way to the Supreme Court which upheld the right of any radio station to use records for its programs without paying the record companies. (Of course, these stations were required to pay a license fee to ASCAP which controlled the music, but this was a negligible expense.)

What this decision meant was that recorded music now literally flooded the air waves. And so the disc jockey (a term coined by *Variety*) was born not only to select and play the records but also to make frequently spontaneous comments about the music or the performer, or anything else relevant that came to his mind. The first such disc jockeys were Al Jarvis in Hollywood and Martin Block in New York, each presiding over a program entitled "Make Believe Ballroom." Four months after Martin Block had broadcast his first program, he had four million dedicated listeners every single day. So popular did the disc jockey become that—except for news bulletins—little else was being heard over the radio, particularly in the smaller cities and towns. By 1960 three thousand disc jockeys were employed by 3,500 stations—the most celebrated being Jarvis, Block, Bob Clayton, and Dick Clark. By their selection of records, by their favorable comments, and most important of all by the frequency with which they played any one record, these jockeys suddenly acquired the power to dispatch an army of buyers to the stores to buy the record that had thus been promoted.

It was a disc jockey in Memphis (Dewey Phillips) who inaugurated Elvis Presley's career by playing and replaying his first recording, "That's All Mama" coupled with "Blue Moon Kentucky," each side seven times consecutively. This disc began selling not only in Memphis but elsewhere, too—and Presley was on his way. Another disc jockey (Bill Randle) took an old and long-forgotten motion-picture theme song, "Charmaine," which had just been revived in a recording by an orchestral outfit led by an unknown conductor, Mantovani. Not only did this record become a best seller, but at the same time Mantovani's career was launched. A North Carolina disc jockey was even capable of reviving an old and dated recording of "Heartaches," which Ted Weems and his orchestra had made in 1937. He played it so often, by popular request, that a reissue of this old Ted Weems release sold three million discs.

And so, stimulated by disc jockeys, the public was buying more records than ever, and the record companies were achieving an unprecedented prosperity whose highest peak is not yet in sight. But who was this buying public? By the mid-1950's, almost half of the country's population was under twenty-five years of age. This was an affluent society in which youngsters at any given time had more spending money in their pocket than many of their parents had earned in a week years earlier. The bulk of the recording market consisted of youngsters. They were paying the piper, and they were calling the tune. And the tune, or tunes, they were calling for was rock 'n' roll. This was *their* music. Youngsters with an altogether emancipated concept of morality could no longer be expected to sigh over the possibility of holding hands and looking at the moon. Youngsters, with little of a past to look back on, could hardly respond to nostalgia. And youngsters—with their irrepressible vigor, physical and emotional dynamism, hyperthyroid energies, and explosive emotions—could hardly relate to the slow, stately, and haunting melodies their parents cherished.

These youngsters were a new breed that had to have its own music, a music that could make it "jump." It found that music in rock 'n' roll. This is the first time in our song history that music written by youngsters, sung and played by youngsters, and catering to youngsters spoke of the things youngsters were most interested in and concerned about—and in their own language. Rock 'n' roll is "the medium in which some of our best poets have chosen to express themselves," a writer in the *Village Voice* was saying, while no less a musical author-

ity than Leonard Bernstein could remark over television: "Don't try to escape
rock 'n' roll. Try to understand it. It has something to tell adults."

The term "rock 'n' roll is believed to have been the concoction of a disc
jockey in Cleveland, Alan Freed, in the 1950's. He was a dynamic personality
who was not content to sit back while a record was being played. Sometimes he
sang along with it; sometimes he would beat out the rhythm of a song by bang-
ing his hand on a telephone book. His preference was songs with a strong beat
to them, which he soon began referring to as "rock 'n' roll," a phrase he had
lifted from the lyrics of one of the numbers he used to play.

But rock 'n' roll was not born in the 1950's. It dated back two decades before then, to the so-called rhythm and blues songs which came out of the fields
and shanties of the south. This was a vigorous, swinging music with strong
accentuations which the Negroes used to play and sing, into which they would
interpolate wails, groans, and exclamations, and which they would render with
emphasis on a regular, heavy beat. Some of these numbers were recorded and
released under the category of "race records." This is how they first became
familiar in the North after the end of World War II, where pioneers of rock
'n' roll music—men like Muddy Waters, for example, or Chuck Berry—made
recordings of songs in a similar style. They would back themselves with an intimate ensemble of instruments capable of emphasizing the beat—electric guitars, various types of drums, the double bass. Then came intimate singing groups,
comprising three or four musicians, providing their own percussive accompaniments. One such was Bill Haley and his Comets whose Decca release of "Rock
Around the Clock" sold over a million discs in 1953, and two years later was
used on the sound track of the background music for the motion picture *The
Blackboard Jungle,* once again performed by Haley and his Comets. In 1954
another singing group called the Crew Cuts had a best-selling rock 'n' roll
record in 'Sh-Boom" which they made for Mercury and which the Chords released with equal success for Cat Records.

In 1956 a young rock 'n' roll singer, accompanying himself on the guitar,
was a guest performer on the Jackie Gleason "Stage Show" program over television. His name was Elvis Presley. With his wildly waving hair and extended
sideburns, his suggestively undulating hips, and his moans and groans, he sang
"Heartbreak Hotel." What happened after this is a by no means insignificant
development for both the song and the social history of our times. Only a few
weeks after this appearance, Presley's RCA-Victor recording of "Heartbreak
Hotel" had passed the million mark in sales. The young had found their idol;
and now, more than ever, rock 'n' roll songs with their lamentations and exclamations, with their often nonsensical lyrics, with their piercing sounds and
vigorous beat became the music of the young. Rock 'n' roll—with Elvis Presley
now as its high priest—might horrify the adult world, and it did. Frank Sinatra
described it as "rancid-smelling aphrodisiac" and Pablo Casals might speak of
it as "poison put to music." But to the youngsters, Elvis Presley was *their* representative, and his songs were the kind of music to which they could give vent
to their sexual urges, pent-up emotions, their tendency to soar to the heights of

ecstasy and plunge to the depths of despair within minutes, their yearnings and inner torment. They stood ready to put their money where their enthusiasm lay. In less than two years after "Heartbreak Hotel" a dozen of Presley's recordings had sold from one to two million discs each—"Hound Dog," "Blue Suede Shoes," "All Shook Up," "Hard Headed Woman," and so forth. And it was not only American youth but the youth of practically the entire world that had found its spokesman in Presley. Virtually every popularity poll conducted anywhere found him holding first place, just as virtually every list of best-selling records invariably found an Elvis Presley number on top.

As the years passed, the Presley fad—for this is all that it was considered in the late 1950's—refused to die; nor did the enthusiasm for rock 'n' roll abate. On the contrary rock 'n' roll was gaining ground all the time. New performers seized the center of the stage as proponents of this new kind of popular music, and readily found a waiting army of adulating admirers. And then, early in the 1960's, a group from England, the Beatles, not only equaled Presley's popularity but even surpassed it, mostly with numbers written by two of their members. First Europe went wild over them, beginning with their first million-copy-disc sale, "She Loves You" in 1963, and continuing with equally fabulous sales of such other numbers as "P.S. I Love You," "I'll Get You," "I Want to Hold Your Hand," "All My Loving," and "I Wanna Be Your Man." Then young America became thoroughly victimized. When the Beatles made their television debut on "The Ed Sullivan Show" in February of 1964, they performed before an audience numbering close to seventy million.

The Beatles brought with them not only a new sophisticated sound in their own rock 'n' roll numbers but also an unorthodox visual image. They wore flowing feminine locks of hair, suits several sizes too tight, and high-heeled boots—an appearance that the more rebellious youth throughout the world soon began to emulate. The frenetic renditions by the Beatles, as well as their unusual getup, represented a total break with the handsome, neatly groomed, sexually appealing young men with whom the popular song had so long been identified: the Perry Comos, Bing Crosbys, Vic Damones, Dean Martins, and Frank Sinatras—even as their songs were a far cry (literally as well as figuratively) from the soft, sweet, wooing sounds which the Comos, Sinatras, and others had made into a popular singing art.

The limelight now shone brilliantly not only on the Beatles but on other small singing groups—Herman's Hermits, the Rolling Stones, the Righteous Brothers, the Supremes, the Four Seasons, the Monkees, the Beach Boys. Some of these and many other singing combos seemed bent on appearing to the eye as odd as possible as they went through the most extravagant vocal and physical gyrations. There was room for each one of these groups in the hearts of the young. Sociologists were becoming fully aware that in all this something new and possibly significant was taking place, though they could hardly have guessed at the time that this was the beginning of youth's revolt against the establishment, which would achieve such excessive and frightening proportions as the 1960's were drawing to a close.

For all its oddities and eccentricities, rock 'n' roll music was becoming in-

creasingly original and sophisticated—so much that even some of the older intelligentsia were beginning to take note and at times to admire. Some of these
newer rock 'n' roll songs achieved exotic effects through the use of old modes,
through a simulation of English renaissance music, through a return to the
baroque era with sometimes Bach-like accompaniments, or through the borrowing of formulas from the Hindus, such as ragas. Others began using some of
the techniques of avant-garde serious composers: polytonal combinations, changing tonalities without the benefit of modulations, polymeters, cross rhythms, and
even strange sounds produced through electronic means, and through such unusual instruments as the harpsichord, the sitar, the calliope, baroque trumpets,
and so forth. The words, too, advanced from the often guttural, unrecognizable
diction of the older days to lyrics that had poetic overtones, giving point and
meaning to what the young people were thinking, feeling, and rebelling against.

And so, today, rock is far different from what it was when it first came to
popularity in the mid-1940's. It is no longer merely music with a strong, regular
beat, accentuations, dynamic force, blues colorations. It is a polyglot language
combining many different elements, some borrowed from country-and-western
music as well as from jazz, some lifting materials from the folk song of bal-
ladeers as well as from Tin Pan Alley (whose clichés it satirizes), and combining them with the beat and force and the blues of old-time rock 'n' roll.

Possibly the most significant development in present-day rock is the way
in which the revolt of youth against society is openly expressed, or symbolized,
or concealed within Dadaistic verses. The young people found themselves in a
chaotic world not of their making. The mushroom cloud lifted by experimental
atomic and hydrogen bomb tests spread an ominous shadow to darken the
future of the young generation, and even threatened to obliterate that future
completely. These young people said they could not understand euphemisms
that referred to minor wars as "police action" and the wiping out of Vietnamese
towns and villages and peoples as a "pacification program"; euphemisms that
designated lies from places on high as a "credibility gap." These young people
insisted they could not comprehend why the richest nation in the world, in its
most affluent period, could allow one third of a nation to suffer from malnu-
trition. They saw themselves surrounded by racial strife, bigotry, assassinations,
a swelling tide of crime with none of which their elders seemed able to cope.
And so the young rebelled. The more active ones instigated riots, burned draft
cards, inspired protest marches, created love-ins, and seized college campuses,
in one or two instances even stopping an entire university from functioning at
all. Nonconformism became the new conformity. Young rebels negated whatever their elders had held in esteem—morality, cleanliness, attractive appearance,
good manners and breeding, patriotism, social position, the earning of money.
For a while, during the 1968 presidential primaries, some of the more passive
rebels found an outlet in political action with Eugene McCarthy as their hero;
but when McCarthy failed to capture the nomination, these rebels reverted, for
the time being at any rate, to their former passivity, but this did not mean that
they had found peace with themselves or were satisfied with the *status quo*. The
least active, the most timid, or those who felt that any struggle with an estab-

lishment too strong to be shaken was futile, sought to flee from reality through psychedelic drugs.

In the past, protests against injustice, inequality, poverty, prejudice, were the material out of which folk singers fashioned their songs. The popular song simply did not have the "green thumb" with which to fertilize successfully such arid areas as these. Folk singers like Joan Baez are still potent voices of protest. But protest—because it has become such a basic part of today's young movement —has also penetrated rock music. And it has done so in the songs of Bob Dylan, who started out as a folk singer in his own right with his own songs of protest before turning to the creation of "folk rock," in which folk music and rock music became one.

Of those composers who first came to fame through recordings, and of those composers who have used the popular idiom of rock as a medium of protest, none has enjoyed a more dramatic and more influential career than Bob Dylan.

The first musical impression that would later influence Dylan's career came when he was still a boy. He heard an old Negro street singer perform a rhythm and blues song while accompanying himself on a guitar. Dylan listened spellbound. Then, feeling the need for an outlet for his seething emotions, he took two spoons out of his pocket (which he carried around since he liked to use them in beating out rhythms in the manner of a pair of castanets) and began punctuating this performance with his clicking spoons. He followed the street singer wherever he went; then found others to follow. One of them presented him with an old badly mutilated guitar, upon which the boy Dylan learned to play without instruction.

His second important influence was meeting and listening to the blues singing of Big Joe Williams; Dylan was eleven at the time. "The way I think about the blues tunes," Dylan later conceded, "comes from what I learned from Big Joe Williams. . . . But what makes the real blues singers so great is that they are able to state all the problems they had; but at the same time, they were standing outside of them and could look at them."

The third and greatest influence of all was the folk singer Woody Guthrie. Through records, Dylan had come to know some of Guthrie's songs of protest against poverty, degraded immigrant camps, the plight of the Okies, the Dustbowl, the abuse of migrant works, the plight of refugees. On one occasion, in Carmel, California, Dylan heard Woody Guthrie in a concert; it proved a revelation. Guthrie was now his idol. When Dylan finally met Guthrie for the first time, the folk singer was in the hospital, wasting away with a rare hereditary disease which attacks and destroys the nervous system. Seeing his idol withered, bedridden, a mere shell of a human being, did not in any way reduce in Dylan's eyes the giant stature of the creative person. On the contrary, this meeting with Guthrie, far from bringing horror or disenchantment, seemed to give Dylan strength and the moral courage to proceed on his own, on a path which Guthrie's songs had lit up for him with such fluorescent lighting that following it to its final destination was merely to pursue a simple, well-illuminated road. Henceforth, Dylan's dream was to perform folk songs that would protest against the abuses of man by men and society, abuses that Dylan had himself witnessed time again during his boyhood and youth.

His name was originally not Bob Dylan when he was born on May 21, 1941, in Duluth, Minnesota; it was Robert Zimmerman. "Bob Dylan" was a name he concocted at the dawn of his singing career, in 1962, adopting half the name of his favorite modern poet, Dylan Thomas. Since the father of the Zimmerman family was a humble appliance dealer, the household (which numbered just two boys besides the parents) was not a very prosperous one. In search of better opportunities for himself, the father took his family to live in nearby Hibbing. But Hibbing was a town that was slowly being dessicated economically. "I was raised," says Dylan, "in a town that was dying." The family made another move, this time to South Hibbing where the economic conditions were somewhat healthier and the family could at least enjoy a modestly comfortable life.

Dylan attended the public schools in Hibbing and was graduated from Hibbing High School, no mean achievement for a boy who was more often away from Hibbing than in it. Between his tenth and eighteenth years he ran away from home seven times, traveling by any means of locomotion available—by foot, in boxcars, by hitching rides—and covering a wide area from the Dakotas to California. He was learning at first hand the meaning of personal suffering and want, as well as inequality and injustice. He was running away from the domination of his parents and the constrictions of a small town, but actually he was being helplessly driven by a nervous restlessness, an inability to stay put anywhere for any length of time—a trait to which he was addicted all his life. But these years of *Wanderjahre* were not without their blessings. As has already been described, it enabled him, when he was ten, to get his first guitar. (Later on he learned to make music also on an autoharp, harmonica, and piano.) A year later it made it possible for him to meet Big Joe Williams, and recognize the importance of the blues. And when he was thirteen, it brought him a job with a traveling carnival, an experience during which he met all sorts of people —from roustabouts and day laborers to gamblers and prostitutes—and to sing songs for them to his own guitar accompaniments.

He left home and South Hibbing again after having graduated from high school and after having already written his first ballad, a song to Brigitte Bardot. This was the time he got his first job as entertainer, singing folk songs in a striptease joint in Central City, Colorado, during brief intervals when the girls were offstage. The clientele, more interested in sex than in folk music, froze up during his performance; he was fired after a week and a half. Discouragement led him to enter the University of Minnesota on a scholarship in the spring of 1960, with the hope of training himself for some profession more profitable than folk singing. But there, too, he proved a total flop. As he later explained in one of his free-verse poems ("My Life in a Stolen Moment"), "I sat in science class an' flunked out for refusin' to watch a rabbit die. I got expelled from English class for using four-letter words in a paper describing the English teacher." His entire university career lasted six months, the only compensation from which was an opportunity to sing with a folk-song ensemble at a coffeehouse near the campus.

It was at this point in his life that Woody Guthrie became an influence that shook him the way a typhoon might a twenty-foot schooner. Eigheen years old now, Dylan decided he would make his last flight from home. His destination was New York, and he landed in Greenwich Village. For a while, until he found a roof over his head in the Lower East Side at the home of some acquaintances, he slept in subways. During the day he tried earning a living by singing folk songs in the small cafés and coffeehouses in Greenwich Village with the nickels and dimes that some of the more appreciative and generous listeners would drop into the basket that he circulated among the clientele. He was always hungry, always cold (this being wintertime), always footsore and physically depleted. But he kept on nevertheless—driven as much by Guthrie's inspiration as by personal ambition. These were hard times—no doubt about that —but these were the days when slowly Dylan was acquiring his own manner, both in the kind of songs he was beginning to write and in the way he was presenting them to the public—singing in a raw, harsh, imprecise voice that, for all its gruffness, throbbed with genuine emotion and sometimes even with genuine tenderness. He accompanied himself now on the guitar, and now on the harmonica, which was attached to his neck by wire. He would stop his singing either to perform on both the guitar and the harmonica simultaneously or to deliver personal commentaries on various subjects in a slow drawl filled with vernacular and unbelievable syntax—seemingly the words of a gross illiterate until you took the trouble to understand what he was trying to say. There was beginning to enter a haunting quality to his act, heightened and intensified by the dreamy, faraway look in his eyes (caused by his myopia) and his sensitive, mobile, expressive face. In what he wrote and whatever he did, he was himself—a fact symbolized by the fact that, while performing, he wore the same threadbare, often dirty clothes that were his entire wardrobe off the stage, his hair resembling an overused mop, his face and neck often betraying the fact that a bath and they had long been total strangers.

He was appearing in places like the Gaslight Café on MacDougal Street and Gerde's Folk City on West Fourth Street. It was in the latter that he was finally discovered—by Robert Shelton, folk-music critic of *The New York Times*. After hearing Bob Dylan for the first time, Robert Shelton wrote in *The New York Times* on September 29, 1961: "A bright new face in folk music is appearing at Gerde's Folk City. Although only twenty years old, Bob Dylan is one of the most distinctive stylists to play in a Manhattan cabaret in months. Resembling a cross between a choir boy and a beatnik, Mr. Dylan has a cherubic look and a mop of tousled hair he partly covers with a Huck Finn black corduroy cap. His clothes may need a bit of tailoring, but when he works his guitar, harmonica, or piano and composes new songs faster than he can remember them, there is no doubt that he is bursting at the seam with talent."

Only one month after this notice appeared, of which only an extract had been quoted above, Bob Dylan was recording his first album for Columbia, entitled simply *Bob Dylan*—the only recording made by Dylan in which not a single of his own songs was used. (His second album, *The Freewheelin' Bob Dylan,* included only two of his numbers; but after that his recording albums were devoted exclusively to his own creations; and in some of them the jackets were graced with his poety.) Less than two months after Shelton's article appeared, Dylan was giving his first concert, on November 4, 1961, at the Carnegie Chapter Hall. That he was making headway was soon proved to him in the tangible form of earnings of well over a thousand dollars by February of 1962, representing record royalties and small fees for public appearances. He felt he could now afford to rent an eighty-dollar-a-month apartment at West Fourth Street where he could have the peace and quiet he needed for creativity. His songs and poems came thick and fast—faster even than he could put them down on paper. Always there was a message for him to propound, a seamy side of present-day living to uncover, or a current event that called for social or political comment. Inevitably he filled his songs with compassion for the underdog, and at times he brought to his writing an engaging and fresh sense of humor.

His second album for Columbia, *The Freewheelin' Bob Dylan,* included the song that suddenly made him a favorite not only with devotees of protest songs and folk ballads, but also with the rock generation: "Blowin' in the Wind." In lyrics that were partly symbolic, filled with imagery, but never specific in detailing the shameful acts of prejudice, injustice, and bigotry, and in a melody that moved simply and freely, gaining its effect through repetitious phrases, "Blowin' in the Wind" was the kind of song the young of the 1960's could respond to. Whoever was a victim of, or deplored, what was happening in this country found an emotional release by singing "Blowin' in the Wind." Apparently there were many such. A Warner Brothers release by Peter, Paul, and Mary sold almost two million discs besides receiving a Grammy as the best folk recording of the year. The integration movement adopted it as one of its favorite protest songs, second in importance only to "We Shall Overcome."

Bob Dylan had been stimulated by racial problems before he had written "Blowin' in the Wind": in "The Ballad of Emmett Till," in 1962, about the Negro lad who was lynched in Mississippi for having whistled at a white woman. Dylan would be affected in his writing about the integration movement many times after "Blowin' in the Wind." But the civil-rights movement was not the only problem he had to sing about. There was the horror of war and those who would use God as an ally in mass murder ("With God on Our Side"). There was the stalking danger of world annihilation by the hydrogen bomb ("A Hard Rain's Gonna Fall" and "It's All Right with Me"). There was the murder of innocent people ("The Lonesome Death of Hattie Carroll," "The Ballad of Hollis Brown," and "Who Killed Davey Moore?"). There were the evils perpetrated by munition makers for the sake of profit ("Masters of War") and the fears and frustrated hopes for the world of tomorrow ("When the Ships Come In"). And there were problems closer home: the generation gap ("The Times They Are A-Changing"), of sex relations ("Don't Think Twice, It's All Right" and "All I Really Want To Do"). Some of his performances were unique, some left a good deal to criticize. In the quality of his voice and in the poverty of his rhythmic or harmonic background he betrayed the education gap in his development. He frequently played the guitar badly. Similarly, in many of his poems and lyrics naïve thoughts are expressed in a childish manner, while many of his melodies were synthetic, concocted of successive repetitious phrases, and progressing along familiar patterns. And yet, when he is good, he is very good. Some songs are vitalized by their unusual intervallic structure, by his use of discords, by their energy and vitality. Some of his poems and lyrics are so beautifully fashioned that Daniel Kramer has remarked that he "may well be the man that established this medium [recordings] as a place for the poet." And his delivery is as emotionally compelling as it is personal. The English critic George Harrison put it this way in talking about Dylan's uniqueness as a composer, lyricist, poet, and performer: "I like his whole attitude. The way he dresses, the way he doesn't give a damn, the way he sings discords and plays discords. The way he sends up everything." And Ralph Gleason made a comment in the San Francisco *Chronicle* with which all Dylan fans will readily concur: "To judge him by the standards of others is a total mistake."

He was the articulate voice of the youth of the 1960's, a point strongly emphasized by Burt Korall in *The Saturday Review* in a penetrating article, "The Music of Protest": "Dylan caught the tenor of the times. Innocence was a thing of the past. . . . He realized that isolation from true reality was as unbearable as the reality itself. Yet this did not prohibit him from immersing himself in surrealistic pessimism. After clearly indicting the world in his 'Blowin' in the Wind,' he turned to an inverted mode of writing, couching his point of view within a rush of words and images, oblique and abstract, often approaching hallucination: dreams more frightening than reality. This is the subterranean Dylan, living in song in a demimonde of 'haunted, frightened trees'; dwarfs; clowns who seem blind; intransigent policemen. On occasion he surfaced to sing of love relationships (often unfulfilling) and to express youth's alienation from the older, reactionary generation who simply won't understand what it's all about, as on 'It's Alright, Ma, I'm Only Bleeding.' Dylan, the observer, would make things right if he could, but the governing forces block renewal of effort."

He continued to make record albums, and they sold extraordinarily well. Other groups recorded his ballads and found an enormous market. Dylan was making extensive concert appearances—in concert halls, colleges, folk festivals, over television. He was becoming a rich man—and a family man, too, for he had married Sarah Lownds with whom he raised a son and a daughter. He was something of a cult in folk-song circles. But through it all he remained unchanged—a solitary, restless man who always had to be on the move (now living at the home of his manager or at one of his friend's, and now at a hotel) who had no interest in possessions and avoided them (except for his motorcycle), and who continued to have a sublime indifference to his personal appearance whether at home, on the stage, or in public places. He favored denim jeans, a turtleneck shirt, a worn-out jacket, or just plain corduroy work clothes and boots. His hair was perpetually disheveled. His worshipers did not mind— in fact, they even tried to dress and look like him.

That he clung tenaciously to his passion for freedom, the truth as he saw it, and independence was proved on May 12, 1963, on "The Ed Sullivan Show." He planned a protest number in a comic vein for that occasion, "Talking John Birch Society Blues," a plan with which both Mr. Sullivan and his producer, Bob Precht, were in accord. But the program editor of the Columbia Broadcasting System insisted that the number was too controversial to be used. In spite of Ed Sullivan's objections, the number was deleted, and Bob Dylan refused to appear on the program.

The fierceness of his determination to be free to write as he felt eventually lost him most of the passionate devotees of folk ballads and protest songs who had idolized him up to now. The time had come, felt Dylan, when he had said all he had to say about what was wrong with the world around him. He felt the need to become more personal, to delve deeper into his inner self, to write protest songs not against society but against his own place in it: about his utter loneliness, his hunger for personal freedom, his futility in trying to find a Utopia for mankind. "I want to write from inside me," he explained. He put the same thought into a song, "My Back Pages," in which he confessed that he once thought he knew everything about the world's problems but that since that time he has grown "younger." And so, he recorded *Another Side of Bob Dylan, Bringing It All Back Home,* and *Highway 61 Revisited,* albums that shocked the protest-song and folk-ballad cliques, particularly with a number called "It Ain't Me Babe" that for the most part was rock. At the Newport Folk Festival on July 25, 1965, he sent these former admirers into a panic when, in the second half of the program, he abandoned his acoustical guitar for an electrified one, and then proceeded to sing folk songs in a rock idiom. What these disenchanted Dylanites failed to recognize was that rock 'n' roll passages had appeared in his older protest songs they had admired so much and that Dylan's thumping guitar accompaniments to those ballads carried a strong rock beat.

What his onetime passionate advocates failed most to comprehend was that in creating "folk rock," Dylan was not selling and despoiling his art for a pot of gold, but that he was being true to himself and his artistic instincts. This was the direction he simply had to go *now,* come what may. "I got bored with my old songs," is the way he put it. "I can't sing 'With God on Our Side' for fifteen years. I was doing fine, you know, singing and playing my guitar. It was a sure thing, don't you understand, it was a sure thing. I was getting very bored with that. I couldn't go out and play like that, I was thinking of quitting." He did not quit. What he did do was to allow himself to be driven by new creative impulses and new themes in his lyrics and music, and thus cater to a new audience —the vast army of youngsters who were crazy about rock. By being true to himself, rather than any segment of his public for the sake of expediency, Bob Dylan was able to achieve an even greater following than he had had known previously. His ballad "Mr. Tambourine" made stars of the Byrds, and was one of the best-selling recordings in seven countries. In view of this vastly increased prosperity, Dylan can easily be accused that he was running after success by entering the popular field more boldly than he had done before. But those who know him know better. They know he speaks from the depths of his being when he says: "All I'm doing is saying what's on my mind the best way I know how. And whatever else you may say about me, everything I do and write comes out of me."

This magnificent career, which was continually spiraling, almost collapsed permanently in August of 1966 when Dylan broke his neck in a motorcycle accident. For a time it seemed he would never again be able to sing and play again. But on January 5, 1968, Dylan released his first new album in seventeen months, and the first since his accident, *John Wesley Harding,* which he recorded in Nashville with an unamplified guitar, harmonica, piano, bass, and drums. It was a runaway best seller. The gem here is a song called "Dear Landlord," which (as Dan Sullivan noted in a review in *The New York Times*) "has an attractive offbeat melodic line—the kind of tune that goes where you don't expect it to, but sounds right once it gets there." Significant, too, though more for its rhythmic ingenuity than for its melody, was "I'll Be Your Baby Tonight."

And so, Dylan returned to recording. And late in November of 1968 he announced he was resuming his concert work at a fee of $50,000 an appearance against a percentage. If it is a new Bob Dylan, a popular Bob Dylan, that is now capturing an ever-larger audience, it is also a Bob Dylan who has evolved from, and not negated, the old one. As Mike John wrote in *High Fidelity* in reviewing the *John Wesley Harding* album: "He hammers in several themes: I am simple; I am kind; I am lonely; I have been misunderstood; I am not my image." Dylan is still protesting. "A real person," continues Mike John, "sweats and scratches under the pop superstructure. *John Wesley Harding* is neither an apology nor a new direction. It is a very personal note from an old friend."

"A new Dylan?" inquires Burt Korall about Dylan's new rock idiom. "Hardly," Korall answers immediately. "He's just a bit more direct, relaxed, open. His means and manners may change but he retains a unity of image. He is the questioning and needling voice of the 1960's."

Index

Index

365